Pilgrim flanked by Devotion and Curiosity (Conrad Hietling, *Peregrinus affectuose per terram sanctam et Jerusalem a Devotione et Curiositate conductus*, Augsburg, 1713, frontispiece). By permission of the British Library (10025.cc.4).

The Uses of Curiosity in Early Modern France and Germany

NEIL KENNY

OXFORD
UNIVERSITY PRESS

OXFORD

UNIVERSITY PRESS

Great Clarendon Street, Oxford OX2 6DP

Oxford University Press is a department of the University of Oxford.
It furthers the University's objective of excellence in research, scholarship,
and education by publishing worldwide in

Oxford New York

Auckland Bangkok Buenos Aires Cape Town Chennai
Dar es Salaam Delhi Hong Kong Istanbul Karachi Kolkata
Kuala Lumpur Madrid Melbourne Mexico City Mumbai Nairobi
São Paulo Shanghai Taipei Tokyo Toronto

Oxford is a registered trade mark of Oxford University Press
in the UK and in certain other countries

Published in the United States
by Oxford University Press Inc., New York

The moral rights of the author have been asserted
Database right Oxford University Press (maker)

First published 2004

British Library Cataloguing in Publication Data

Data available

Library of Congress Cataloging in Publication Data

Data available

ISBN 0-19-927136-4

1 3 5 7 9 10 8 6 4 2

Typeset by SNP Best-set Typesetter Ltd., Hong Kong
Printed in Great Britain
on acid-free paper by
Biddles Ltd.
Kings Lynn, Norfolk

*For my mother, my father,
and Leslie*

Preface

THIS project has received support from several institutions. Just as I was doubting whether I would ever undertake it, the award of a two-year British Academy Research Readership enabled me to do so: I am very grateful for this. Progress was also made during sabbatical leave granted by Cambridge University and Churchill College Cambridge, both of which provided research grants too. A Fellowship at the Herzog August Bibliothek Wolfenbüttel opened up new research vistas. Assistance was given by librarians at Wolfenbüttel (especially Christian Hogrefe), the Bibliothèque Nationale de France, Cambridge University Library (especially David Lowe), the Bodleian Library, and the British Library. When giving papers on this project I received helpful feedback from audiences at the Cabinet of Natural History seminar of Cambridge University's Department of History and Philosophy of Science, at the Neo-Latin Studies seminar of Cambridge University, at the Seminar on Social and Cultural History in Britain and Europe 1500–1800 (All Souls College Oxford), at the series on Curiosity and Wonder in the Early Modern Period (Modern History Faculty, Oxford University), at the French Department seminar of Glasgow University, at the Renaissance seminar of Bristol University, at the early modern French seminars of the universities of Cambridge and Oxford, and at colloquia at University College Cork ('Mapping the Course of Literary History') and Trinity College Cambridge ('The Early-Modern Encyclopedia').

Numerous people have generously shared with me expertise, thought, or information which—for however many years I have sat on it—is now present in this book in some way. They include Alison Adams, Kathryn Banks, Jill Bepler, Ann Blair, Pollie Bromilow, Emily Butterworth, Kevin Chang, Antonio Clericuzio, Nicolette David, Silvia De Renzi, Nick Dew, Simon Ditchfield, Thomas Elsmann, Tony Evans, Joe Freedman, Yasmin Haskell, Sirkka Havu, Judith Hawley, Marian Hobson, George Hoffman, Iris Hunter, Sylvia Huot, Kristian Jensen, Ross Kennedy, Liz Kenny, Dilwyn Knox, Nigel Leask, Jenny Mander, Hanspeter Marti, Pierre-François Mettan, David Money, Roger Paulin, Laura Preston, Wolfgang

Rother, Ulinka Rublack, Bill Sherman, Anne Simon, André Tournon, Franco Trevisani, Alain Viala, Margaret Whitford. The help given by some people included devoting time and energy to reading synopses or draft sections, which were improved by their judicious suggestions: Peter Burke, Terence Cave, Liz Guild, Nick Hammond, Sue James, Michael Kenny, Melissa Lane, Ian Maclean, Paul Nelles, Leslie Topp, Andrew Webber. The two anonymous assessments commissioned by OUP also led to improvements, while Sophie Goldsworthy has been a most supportive editor, with Frances Whistler ably shepherding the typescript into print, helped by Veronica Ions and Rosemary Dear. Indispensable support of other kinds has been lavished unstintingly by my family and friends.

Contents

List of Illustrations

Illustrations 2–5 are reproduced by permission of the British Library. (See Bibliography for shelfmarks.)

List of Figures

Introduction

W H Y did people write, talk, and argue so much about curiosity in the early modern period, much more than today? What were they trying to achieve? Why was curiosity such a fashionable and controversial topic in numerous orations, conversations, treatises, brochures, conduct manuals, university dissertations, sermons, letters, periodicals, newspapers, novellas, plays, operas, ballets, and poems? When I say that people endlessly mentioned it, I mean that they talked and wrote about 'curiosity', *curiositas*, *curiosité*, *Curiosität*, that they called people or things 'curious', *curiosus*, *curieux*, *curiös*, and so on—the list could of course be extended to other European languages beyond English, Latin, French, and German.[1]

The point of invoking curiosity was almost always to regulate knowledge or behaviour, to establish who should try to want to know what, and under what circumstances. Talking or writing about curiosity was very often a way of trying to stop some people from wanting to know or do something and a way of trying to allow—or even to force—other people to know or do it. Discourse about curiosity, while not confined to questions of knowledge, played a crucial role in the production, acquisition, control, and circulation of knowledge, as a recent overview of the social history of early modern knowledge has shown.[2] But what exactly was that role? Did discourse on curiosity serve above all as a salutary warning—disastrously ignored in modern times—that some kinds of knowledge are best left unpursued (Shattuck 1996)? Or, conversely, did it legitimize the so-called Scientific Revolution and even modernity itself, by helping to liberate human inquiry from theological constraints (Blumenberg 1988)? Or, in a similar vein, did it help 'social challengers' defeat 'conservative literary culture' (Benedict 2001)? Or did it give collectors access to invisible worlds by enabling them to piece together fragments of the visible world (Pomian 1987)? These

---

[1] By 'curiosity' I always mean this family of terms, for which I use the English noun as a shorthand throughout.

[2] Burke 2000, 26–7, 41, 43, 46, 84, 111, 190.

interpretations are fruitful; each finds some support in early modern discourse on curiosity. However, no single thesis of this kind is entirely borne out by that discourse, which is rich and contradictory. Moreover, given that those theses also contradict each other to some extent, how can I claim that they are all fruitful?

My own thesis is that people talked and wrote about curiosity for conflicting purposes, and that they could do so because there was an enduring lack of consensus about what exactly curiosity was. Viewed globally, early modern discourse on curiosity was a process whereby different interest-groups and individuals—as well as different institutions, disciplines, and genres—sought to impose their own understanding of curiosity but without ever succeeding entirely in doing so: the 'shapes'[3] that they gave to curiosity were always resisted either by intrinsic inconsistency and contradiction or else by other people. To talk or write about curiosity was usually to enter an arena within which some of the period's basic anxieties and aspirations about knowledge and behaviour were thrashed out. If no enduring consensus about curiosity emerged, does it follow that 'curiosity' could mean just about anything and that early modern discourse on it was so shapeless and diffuse that no shapely history of it can now be written? No: people often defined curiosity clearly and dogmatically, as being this rather than that. They often gave it shapes that they hoped would be definitive and universally accepted. My aim is to tell the stories of how those distinctively early modern shapes of curiosity came and went, of how they were constantly created and undone.

These are stories in the plural because they go in different directions depending on whose point of view one tells them from. Was curiosity good or bad or both? Was it considered to have been long undervalued or recently overvalued? Numerous conflicting answers to these and other questions were proposed. If the modern historian chooses to tell just one story, one grand narrative which purports to explain all early modern discourse on curiosity, then that amounts to taking sides between parties who were in conflict in the period. It amounts to implying, for example, that the church was either right or wrong to criticize new developments in secular culture as sinful curiosity. Indeed, even if the modern historian makes the apparently

---

[3] Writers sometimes referred to the *formæ* or *Gestalten* of curiosity or of curious knowledge (3.4.1 and 3.5.2 below). See also 3.4.4.3 (*formatæ*).

innocuous gesture of selecting one institution, locus, practice, or human type—such as the learned society, the coffee-house, travel, or Faust—as embodying the quintessence of early modern curiosity, then that involves privileging some period understandings of curiosity over others that contested them at the time. Such *parti pris* is perfectly legitimate if openly avowed—as it is in Shattuck's passionate essay, for instance—but it does necessarily involve renouncing any symmetry postulate,[4] preferring to participate retrospectively in early modern contestation about curiosity, seeking to resolve it now rather than to show that it was unresolved then.

My aim is to try and allow a range of conflicting early modern groups and individuals—clerical and secular, male and female—to have their say about curiosity, without letting any one voice drown out the others, as they often sought to do at the time. However, I do not seek merely to paraphrase these clashing voices, but to analyse the relations between them: when clerics and courtiers or men and women talked about curiosity so differently, were they really all talking about the same thing? Did they consider themselves to be doing so? The answer is often yes. But how is it possible for different groups to hold wildly incompatible views of something, in this case curiosity, and yet to consider nonetheless that they are talking about the same thing? To answer such questions, one needs to study not only the shapes which people tried to give to curiosity but also the process of shaping, not only what people turned curiosity into but also how they did so. That process of contestation is now only dimly accessible to us across the intervening centuries. But it is still visible in one medium—that of ordinary language. Only by paying attention to the language of early modern writers can we glimpse the process whereby they ceaselessly reshaped curiosity, often in an attempt to have the final word on its shape.

What exactly, then, did people mean when they talked or wrote about 'curiosity'? They often meant something like 'inquisitiveness' or 'desire for knowledge'. However, the term also had quite different meanings from its modern counterpart. Sometimes 'curiosity' was even defined in *contradistinction* to 'desire for knowledge'. Or else it meant something like 'diligent/anxious desire for knowledge': this reflected the continuing influence of its classical Latin etymon *cura*

---

[4] The phrase is used by historians of science: see Golinski 1998, 7. For a similar point, expressed in different terms, see Cave 1999, 52–3.

('care, diligence, anxiety, fastidiousness').[5] Indeed occasionally 'curiosity' was still near-synonymous with *cura*, involving little or no emphasis on a desire for knowledge. Also, 'curiosity' could denote or connote a 'desire to do or discover things that go beyond one's allotted role in life': this was roughly the sense of the classical Greek nouns *polypragmosyne* and *periergia*, of which the Latin noun *curiositas* was often considered to be a translation.

In all of those senses, curiosity was usually a passion, desire, vice, or virtue in human subjects. Yet the same word was also often used to denote the objects at which this passion was directed: they were often called 'curiosities' or 'curious' things. So curiosity was considered to be both something inside a person that made him or her desire certain objects and yet also something about those objects that made them desirable. This family of terms had both subject- and object-oriented senses.[6] And the two were often closely related to each other. To call an object 'curious' was often to represent it, variously, as 'rare', 'exotic', 'excellent', 'fine', 'elegant', 'delicate', 'beautiful', 'noteworthy', 'select', 'collectable', 'worth buying', 'small', 'hidden', or 'experimental', and so on.[7] Most of these meanings too have largely disappeared from modern usage. Elsewhere I have provided a fuller analysis of the changing histories of the 'curiosity' family of terms.[8] However, in themselves, divorced from the contexts in which they helped regulate knowledge and behaviour, those meanings tell us little about how and why they were constantly contested.

Two seismic semantic shifts begin to tell us more. First, whereas from antiquity through the sixteenth century curiosity had most often—but not always—been a vice, especially from the seventeenth century onwards it was often morally neutral or positive. Curiosity was still commonly considered a vice, but now also often a healthy passion. The knowledge and behaviour produced by curiosity had previously been considered largely defective, but it was now considered either defective, morally neutral, or admirable. Deciding between these became immensely controversial: as relative consen-

---

[5] On the 'curiosity' family's classical Latin roots, see Labhardt 1960; Lancel 1961; Mette 1956. On the spread and semantic history of this family of terms from antiquity to the early modern period, see N. Kenny 1998, ch. 3.

[6] I am using these terms rather than 'subjective' and 'objective' (used in N. Kenny 1998).

[7] Daston 1994, 43–9; Daston 1995, 17–18; N. Kenny 1998, chs. 3–5.

[8] In N. Kenny 1998 (a semantic survey that is a prolegomenon to the present study).

sus about the badness of curiosity disappeared, it became even more of a battle-ground for efforts to distinguish good knowledge or behaviour from bad. This made much discourse on it very highly charged. Its new capacity to be good or indifferent as well as bad made it encompass a much wider range of knowledge and behaviour than before: it entered the mainstream of human life, having previously often been on the disreputable margins.

Secondly, at the same time as curiosity was spreading to good knowledge and behaviour, it was also spreading to objects. It was especially from the early seventeenth century that people started talking and writing of 'curiosities' and 'curious' objects much more than before. These object-oriented senses had been fairly rare in antiquity and still not very widespread in the sixteenth century. They then proliferated dramatically. 'Curiosity' often came to encompass not only people's desire to know or possess something but also *what* they desired to know or possess. This verbal symmetry points to a new dream that seems to have existed in some quarters, according to which there was a whole world of curious objects out there, waiting to satisfy the every desire of the curious human subject. And yet this relation between the curiosity of subjects and of objects was often as fraught as that between good and bad curiosity: the question whether or not curiosity ought properly to be directed at curious objects was often controversial. Thus, curiosity became a key battle-ground for attempts to distinguish between not only good and bad desire, but also between good and bad objects of desire.

If one makes visible the process whereby these meanings were constantly contested through ordinary language, then it becomes impossible to argue that all or even some of them amounted to an early modern 'concept' of curiosity, at least in the sense usually given to 'concept' in everyday parlance or throughout most of the history of philosophy—that is, an entity (whether supersensible, mental, and/or linguistic) comprised of images, ideas, thoughts, meanings, or abstract objects that are included according to a definitive set of criteria.[9] Curiosity was understood in so many ways that it had no ineliminable core that always characterized it. Of all the semantic

---

[9] See Rey 1998; Weitz 1977, 3; Weitz 1988. The status of concepts has also been debated especially in the history of political discourse (e.g. J. G. A. Pocock, Quentin Skinner, German *Begriffsgeschichte*) and in political theory (e.g. Freeden 1996). See also W. B. Gallie's famous essay on 'essentially contested concepts' (1996), though I am not incorporating his specific criteria for definition of such a concept.

strands that ran through it, none was always present, not even 'desire for knowledge'. Its repertoire of meanings was not only variable but contradictory. 'Curiosity' was sometimes exclusively good, but sometimes exclusively bad. A 'curious' object was sometimes understood as a 'useless', 'uncommon', 'expensive', 'exclusive', 'learned', or 'short' one, but conversely at other times as a 'useful', 'common', 'cheap', 'popular', 'unlearned', or 'long' one. No concept, in the usual senses, is to be found amongst this mess of ordinary language.

Therefore, since the authors of recent major studies of early modern curiosity treat it, explicitly or implicitly, as a concept, or else as a group of concepts, they are obliged, to varying degrees, to distance themselves from ordinary language. Those studies are Hans Blumenberg's *Prozeß der theoretischen Neugierde*, Gérard Defaux's *Le Curieux, le glorieux, et la sagesse du monde* (on sixteenth-century France), Krzysztof Pomian's *Collectionneurs, amateurs et curieux* (on Paris and Venice from the sixteenth to the eighteenth centuries), Lorraine Daston and Katharine Park's *Wonders and the Order of Nature, 1150–1750*, the multi-authored *Curiosité et 'libido sciendi' de la Renaissance aux Lumières*, and Barbara Benedict's *Curiosity: A Cultural History of Early Modern Inquiry* (on England 1660–1820).[10] Each sets up a concept or concepts of curiosity as its object of study. Blumenberg understands 'theoretical curiosity' as inquiry of a rational, disinterested kind. Defaux understands curiosity as inquiry of an overweening kind. Benedict understands it as inquiry of many kinds, which all, however, shared a common denominator, an ineliminable core:[11] 'Even as the emphasis and shape of the attack on curiosity alters according to cultural circumstances, however, throughout the early modern period curiosity denotes the transgressive desire to improve one's place in the world' (Benedict 2001, 20).

---

[10] Benedict 2001; Blumenberg 1988; Daston and Park 1998, chs. 6–8; Defaux 1982; Jacques-Chaquin and Houdard (eds.) 1998; Pomian 1987. It is particularly difficult to generalize about *Curiosité et 'libido sciendi'*, since its contributors have differing approaches.

[11] Conceptual history often identifies even more emphatically a core that is judged to be an ineliminable part of the concept in question: e.g. see a recent study which treats 'public opinion' as an early modern concept: 'It does appear possible when writing of an idea to focus upon a core of meaning that does not vary with the telling. As I have argued elsewhere, some unit ideas are tidier and less prone to misreadings than are others.' (Gunn 1995, 8). On the question whether concepts have ineliminable cores, see Freeden 1996, 62–75.

Since many occurrences of 'curiosity' did not denote this transgressive desire, Benedict is here treating curiosity as a concept that was not coextensive with the period's ordinary language. Concept-based approaches can heuristically reveal much about the past, as all these important studies show. But they do so by tidying up the period's ordinary language. Certainly, most of these studies (except Blumenberg's) focus mainly on early modern texts that use the 'curiosity' family of terms. But they sometimes state or imply that their chosen concept of curiosity is also present in texts which do not explicitly use those terms: they thereby imply that there is a distinction between word and concept, and that the concept is even more widespread than the word. Conversely, they sometimes discount, openly or tacitly, as lying outside their chosen concept of curiosity, those meanings and uses of the 'curiosity' family of terms that do not meet the criteria by which they are defining that concept. Since that is also what early modern writers did, in a sense these historians are taking up where those writers left off, continuing to reshape curiosity now.

Such discounting or decontestation[12] of unwanted occurrences and meanings is practised unusually openly by one follower of Blumenberg: he distinguishes between certain early modern agents who, in his view, used the concept of *curiositas* incorrectly and others who used it correctly: 'The primary meaning of *curiositas* is the human impetus to know and research; subsequent degenerations of the concept prove to be a secondary misunderstanding.'[13] In this view, the proper, 'primary' meaning was the subject-oriented one; the degenerate, 'secondary' meanings found in some early modern discourse were the object-oriented ones. Decontestation by modern scholarship is usually more nuanced. Indeed, Benedict, Daston and Park, Pomian *et al.* have shown rich *connections* between meanings such as the subject- and object-oriented ones that are being hygienically separated in this quotation. However, the concepts that they study still emerge only at the price of some decontestation of unwanted meanings and occurrences.

The more one minimizes such modern contestation, by focusing instead on the ordinary language of early modern writers in all of its

---

[12] The term is from political theory. See Freeden 1996, 76, 82–3.

[13] '*Curiositas* meint in erster Linie den menschlichen Wissens- und Forschungsimpetus; spätere Degenerationen des Begriffs erweisen sich als sekundäres Missverständnis' (Daxelmüller 1979, 155).

untidy messiness, then the more visible becomes their own ceaseless contestation of curiosity. It would be tempting to call that early modern process concept-formation, but that would be misleading, first because the curiosity being reshaped had no ineliminable core, and secondly because the process, far from being teleological, did not culminate in a concept (in the usual senses). The ceaseless contestation often involved establishing apparently trifling but in fact crucial distinctions between highly charged words. So the only way to try to reconstruct that process is to pay attention to exactly what terms were used when and indeed to pursue the hypothesis that concepts do not exist independently of words, in contrast to the concept-based studies just listed, which implicitly assume that they do. Thus, by investigating how early modern discourse about curiosity was used to try and regulate knowledge and behaviour, I hope also to provide an empirical case-study in whether 'concepts' exist,[14] putting this to the test not of analytical philosophy or cognitive science but of history and ordinary language. As well as writing a history of curiosity, I hope to contribute to debates about historiography.

How did early modern writers go about this contesting? They all agreed that 'curiosity' denoted one or more things that did really exist, such as a passion or a quality of objects;[15] but they disagreed as to what exactly those things were, about the relation between them and the 'curiosity' family of terms. I am not claiming to judge whether or not those terms really did refer to something beyond language, such as a mental and/or bodily instinct or desire: that question is being left open, for the present reader to answer on the basis of his or her philosophical preferences.[16] What I am claiming to show is how writers selected some meanings from the 'curiosity' family's wide range in order to shape and reshape the thing or things that *they* considered curiosity to be. Could each of these various shapes of curiosity be called a particular 'conception' of it? No, at least not in the sense attributed to that term by John Rawls and other philoso-

---

[14] Cf. Fodor 2003; Putnam 1981, 17–21; Weitz 1977, ch. 1.

[15] I have encountered only one fleeting instance of explicit doubt about the existence of curiosity as a real thing: an obscure 1724 university dissertation on curiosity that was being particularly thorough about its own premises (1.1 below).

[16] For a fuller development of this point, see N. Kenny 1998, 23–8.

phers, since they define 'conceptions' as particular variations on an underlying 'concept' that does have an ineliminable core.[17] The constant reshaping of curiosity occurred in various ways. Some writers included in the thing that they called 'curiosity' as many meanings of that family of terms as possible. They argued that curiosity was a genus that consisted of many distinct 'species' or 'sorts'. For example, the curiosity of the traveller was distinct from that of the busybody, and yet each was a species of the same underlying passion. Academic writers provided systematic, discursive typologies of the various species of curiosity. Other writers showed the connections between the different species by resorting to allegory or exemplary tales.

Some shaped curiosity by using the semantic distinction between subject- and oriented-senses: they defined curiosity as a desire for curiosities, or alternatively as a desire that is specifically not directed at curiosities. For example, certain university writers argued that true curiosity is not directed at curious, collectable objects but, rather, that it is a noble desire to have knowledge of universals. But for others still, curiosity was anything *but* that: 'There is as much difference between someone who is a *curieux* in my sense of the term and a man who has a noble desire for knowledge as there is between a child who builds little castles out of cards and an architect who builds a palace out of marble.'[18] Some writers reshaped curiosity self-consciously and carefully, others more tacitly or casually. A few were so self-conscious that they even explicitly surveyed existing usage of this family of terms before declaring their own. A few tried to impose their version of what curiosity was by using this family of terms in ways that would have struck their contemporaries as odd, as remote from ordinary language. Many extended the scope of curiosity by applying it to experiences to which it had not previously been applied, or else by interpreting previous texts which did not mention it as being nonetheless about it.[19] On the other hand, even conventional, less

---

[17] See Rawls 1973, 5: 'Thus it seems natural to think of the concept of justice as distinct from the various conceptions of justice as being specified by the role which these different sets of principles, these different conceptions, have in common.'

[18] 'il y a autant de difference entre un curieux de la maniere que je l'entens, et un homme qui a un noble desir de sçavoir qu'entre un Enfant qui fait de petits Chasteaux de cartes, et un Architecte qui bastit un Palais de Marbre' (Scudéry 1979, 46).

[19] e.g. the Lutheran theologian Adam Rechenberg's interpretation of the writings of Johann Konrad Dannhauer (1.3.3 below).

self-conscious, and more casual usage also involved constant reshaping of curiosity: for example, in some church-based writing the controversial possibility that good curiosity exists was tenuously aired through recurrent, tortuous grammatical structures (such as *ne . . . que* or conditional sentences) or else through dissonance between the meanings of different parts of speech (such as the adjective 'curious' and the noun 'curiosity').

Thus, the relations between these various species or sorts of curiosity were unstable, judged variously to be close or distant. To adapt Ludwig Wittgenstein's term, each relation was one of family resemblance, hovering between similarity and difference. Indeed, I argue that the 'curiosity' family of words can be understood as a concept or concepts only in the sense in which the later Wittgenstein used the term, that is, as a rope composed of numerous interwoven fibres that are neither identical nor unrelated to each other, with no single fibre—that is, no ineliminable core—running through the whole rope. 'And the strength of the thread does not reside in the fact that some one fibre runs through its whole length, but in the overlapping of many fibres.' (1968, § 67, p. 32). What enabled contemporaries to treat multifarious kinds of curiosity as all being the same thing was the structure of curiosity as a network of family resemblances that was constantly being extended, though not according to any set of definable criteria. Although Wittgenstein uses the term 'concept' for such structures, I refrain from doing so, since it would be difficult to speak of an early modern 'concept of curiosity' without reintroducing involuntarily the unwanted senses of 'concept', since they are so deeply ingrained in modern usage.

It might seem anachronistic to describe the process of shaping as unresolved and to claim that this network of family resemblances ultimately resisted the many definitions of curiosity that early modern writers sought to impose. Certainly, many early modern writers insisted that they *had* described the definitive shape of curiosity. But every such claim was contested, directly or indirectly, by other writers and institutions: it would be anachronistic to ignore this. The conflicting parties usually agreed that they were disagreeing about the same thing. Some bishops condemned theatre, fashion, and astrology, while courtiers enjoyed these: yet both groups agreed to call these practices curiosity, the bishops understanding it as a bad thing and the courtiers as a good thing. Curiosity was relatively singular in this respect, since aggressive name-calling is usually one-way: one party applies a label (such as 'barbarian') that *only* has a pejorative sense and so is not recognized as applicable by the party denigrated (Koselleck 1985, 159–97). Overt asymmetry of that kind occurs even with the rhetorical figure of paradiastole, which redescribes an action as, say, a vice rather than a virtue. Paradiastole alters the application of a term, such as 'courage', but it does not turn 'courage' into the name of a vice.[20] But curiosity, being morally reversible, involved apparent symmetry that was however specious, since the bishops and courtiers, while discussing the same thing, understood it in conflicting ways, each struggling to give their own definition a meta-status in relation to their adversaries'.

Thus, although the 'curiosity' family of terms did not constitute a 'concept' (in the usual senses), that does *not* mean that it was just a set of terms that people used in disparate ways: rather, it was often the discursive glue that enabled people to disagree in the first place. The sharing of common terms by interlocutors is a prerequisite for disagreement as well as agreement. 'Curiosity' was a common arena for battles over meaning. Modern historians, while ignorant of so much that early modern agents knew, are at least better placed to study those battles between different early modern institutions or interest-groups rather than just to adopt the perspective of one of them. But modern historians do not have a monopoly of that broader perspective: some choose to side with just one of those clashing voices, while conversely a few early modern writers chose not to, preferring instead to highlight the unresolved process whereby curiosity was contested. The clearest example that I have encountered is Madeleine de Scudéry in her remarkable conversation-novella *Célinte* (1661).

The battles over knowledge and behaviour in which 'curiosity' and its cognates were implicated also involved many other neighbouring terms, for example 'desire for knowledge', 'interest', 'wonder', 'subtlety', 'singularity', 'difficulty', 'rarity', 'novelty', 'experiment', 'practice', and their cognates, or near-synonyms in specific languages, such as *polypragmosyne* and *periergia* (Greek) or *Vorwitz* and *Neugierigkeit* (German).[21] Periodic consideration of how these were used with or in contradistinction to curiosity will

---

[20] See Skinner 1991 and 1996, ch. 4.
[21] On the relation of 'curiosity' to these indigenous Germanic terms, see N. Kenny 1998, 93–102.

show what was distinctive about the latter. However, the 'curiosity' family of terms is the only one that I will be investigating in all of its ordinary-language uses, through both its presence and its significant absences, while avoiding using it in its modern senses in my own commentary. Certainly, this language-based approach could be fruitfully applied to numerous other terms too, but not simultaneously. Perhaps only by maintaining absolute critical distance from one limited set of early modern words at a time is it possible to uncover the vulnerable contestability, the flickering evanescence of the changing shapes which those words ascribed to things. If a historian excised from his/her own commentary all use, in modern senses, of all terms that were associated with knowledge in the early modern period, then he/she would barely have any words left with which to write.

Moreover, curiosity lends itself particularly well to this ordinary-language-based approach because it was especially highly charged, like other terms such as 'gallant', 'chaste', 'atheist', or *libertin*. At a time when many moral and evaluative terms were contested (as Quentin Skinner's work on paradiastole has shown), attributing curiosity to someone often involved strong evaluation—whether celebration or denigration—but rarely indifference. Often it was too potentially controversial a term to be used lightly: positive uses of it often gained seductive force from the frisson of interdiction which it could convey. 'Curious' became, for a while, a self-consciously modish label—indeed some people eventually complained about its modishness. Thus, many contemporaries were themselves particularly conscious of its presences and absences. However, even if they had not been, this language-based approach would still reveal distinctions that a concept-based approach might conceal. For example, if the object of my study was curiosity as bad desire for knowledge—that is, a tidied-up concept from which some of the ordinary-language meanings of 'curiosity' were excluded—then that concept could be denoted in German not only by *Curiosität* but also by *Neugierigkeit* and *Vorwitz*. But to treat these three as even rough synonyms would be to lose the distinctiveness of each. It would be to overlook, for example, the way in which the 'curiosity' family of terms enabled writers to link *Curiosität qua* bad desire for knowledge to many good species of 'curiosity', to objects *of* 'curiosity', to the *curiositas* discussed by Latin writers, and so on. *Neugierigkeit*, on the other hand, certainly did not create those same connections. It created different ones. Yet few early modern families of terms explicitly created so many, between so many practices, as did 'curiosity', which was singular in some respects, because of various factors—its extreme polysemy, its moral reversibility, its evaluative potential, its denotation of both subjects and objects, its modishness.

The continual contestation of curiosity was much more than a tiff over semantics. It involved conflicting uses of curiosity made by different groups, often for crucial ends, on two related levels, first on that of lexis, since early modern writers 'used' the terms *curiositas*, *curiosité*, and so on in their texts, and secondly on a rhetorical level, since groups were thereby 'using' curiosity to serve their own persuasive purposes,[22] countering others' uses of it, usually in order to try and regulate knowledge or behaviour in some way, for example to legitimize their own knowledge, to prevent others from acquiring or transmitting knowledge, to commodify and sell knowledge or material objects, to cement sociability, to control sexuality, to foster obedience, to manipulate public opinion, to promote ideologies such as absolutism, and so on.[23] Yet these general, modern labels—such as

[22] I am adapting the approach developed by Skinner and others who have applied J. L. Austin's speech act theory to the history of discourses. They stress that the illocutionary aims of texts can only be reconstructed if the surrounding contexts are taken into account. See the essays by Skinner in Tully (ed.) 1988*b*. See also Pocock 1996, esp. 53: 'There is an important sense, if I am right in this, in which a history of the concept of, for example, "the state" will in fact be a history of the various ways in which the words *status*, *Staat*, *état*, *estate*, *stato*, and so forth have been used. In this history, these words will not have been used on every occasion to convey the concept of the state in any continuous or cumulative sense whatever, so that the history of the language usages and speech acts in which the various cognates of *state* have been involved is not a history of the concept of the state, even if one can be abstracted from it. One may write a diversity of synchronic histories of the ways in which these cognates have been used and made to perform a diversity of linguistic and other historical contexts, and I have indicated that this is the kind of history that I prefer writing and know how to write.' This formulation describes my own approach too, except that I also give weight to the diachronic dimension of such uses. Early modern writers drew upon previous versions of 'the state' or of 'curiosity' in order to create new versions for new ends, while also often explicitly considering themselves, however, to be discussing the same thing as the previous writers. For example, many of the German university dissertations that constantly reinvented curiosity for almost a century, from 1652 onwards, did so by referring to—and yet radically departing from—versions of curiosity offered by previous dissertations (§ 1 below). The relation between the earlier and later dissertations is one of both continuity and discontinuity. Despite this mild difference of emphasis, my approach is closer to Pocock's formulation than it is to the kind of conceptual history—*Begriffsgeschichte*—developed by Reinhart Koselleck, since that kind deems concepts separable from words. For comparisons between Pocock/Skinner and *Begriffsgeschichte*, see Hampsher-Monk 1998; Pocock 1996.

[23] On the place of 'concepts' within ideologies, see Freeden 1996.

'sociability' or 'absolutism'—will serve here as approximations which in fact mask numerous highly localized and particular uses. My approach will be to recount micro-narratives of those uses, eschewing the kind of grand narrative fostered by concept-based approaches.[24] Only if language is studied in cultural, social, and intellectual contexts do such uses of curiosity become visible—or partly visible, since the contexts surrounding any text are so inexhaustible, so obscure to modern eyes, that its numerous speech acts are only partially recoverable.

It was because curiosity was always being put to so many new, specific uses that it was constantly reshaped. So my earlier question—'What did curiosity mean?'—can be answered thus: its meaning lay in its uses (Wittgenstein 1968, § 43, p. 20). Definitions of it, even ones offered in the period itself, were just one use among others: they were not definitive meta-statements. Certainly, some writers provided a careful, sophisticated definition of curiosity. They presented their definition as universally applicable and as logically and chronologically prior to the particular uses which they wished to make of curiosity. However, the definition was almost always demonstrably shaped, at least in part, by those uses. For example when, in the second half of the seventeenth century, the developing climate of absolutism in Brandenburg-Prussia led some of its universities to seek justification for a state-sponsored gathering of information about the territory's inhabitants, they did so by defining curiosity as being partly a good thing: in order to authorize this definition they sidestepped patristic condemnations of curiosity and ferreted out instead certain *loci* in Roman Law, moulding them to prove that some curiosity had indeed always been good. Newspaper publishers, educationalists, naturalists, and others similarly dressed up particular uses of curiosity as neutral definitions of it. If the modern historian only pays attention to the definitions, then they can be very misleading.

Is that to say that early modern writers merely pretended, out of cynical pragmatism, to believe in their own definitions of curiosity? No, not necessarily: many seem to have believed that it was definable. Does this make them naïve rather than cynical? No, at least not necessarily: permanent or provisional belief in the determinacy of a 'concept', and in a particular definition of it, may well be a prerequi-

---

[24] For a fuller development of this argument, see N. Kenny 1998, 44–9.

site for performing certain kinds of speech acts or for making certain kinds of practical decisions in social or political life.[25] Problematizing all definitions may be a luxury, one which cannot be afforded by texts that seek to instigate particular actions in the world (sales brochures, political tracts), but can be afforded by less instrumental texts, like Scudéry's *Célinte*,[26] or else by the modern historian. As Wittgenstein puts it: if we 'draw a boundary' around a concept it is because we have 'a special purpose' for it: but the concept thus delimited is only usable *for* that special purpose (1968, § 33, p. 69).

On the other hand, using curiosity in attempts to instigate precise actions in the world, believing thereby in its determinacy, did not have to involve defining it. Indeed, most often it did not. Preachers and storytellers who narrated exemplary tales of calamitous curiosity were often supremely unconcerned to define it. They did not even imply an unstated definition. That would not have assisted their rhetorical aim, which was not to make their addressees understand an abstract point, but to make them behave in certain ways. Indeed, many writers and readers, if asked what curiosity was, would have answered by reeling off particular stories about it rather than by defining it in general terms. Curiosity was often a 'plot summary',[27] an aggregate of examples linked by family resemblances that could be pointed out but not actually explained.[28]

The uses of curiosity varied according to context, for example according to which language one was writing in, at which date, within which institution, for which audience, about which sex, in which discipline or genre or register. The potential list is infinite. The present study samples such contexts. It ranges mainly from the late sixteenth to the mid-eighteenth century. Its geographical focus is France and the Germanic territories. These two are combined in order to introduce a comparative dimension and yet also because of

[25] See Freeden 1996, 76–7.

[26] It would be tempting to use the modern term 'literary' to characterize such texts that are less pragmatically instrumental, less concerned to instigate particular actions in the world. However, this would necessarily involve excluding from the category of the 'literary' many texts studied below—exemplary tales, moralizing dramas, school ballets, and so on—that are 'literary' in many usual senses and yet that do seek to instigate particular actions in the world.

[27] 'résumé d'intrigue' (Veyne 1979, 82, describing concepts).

[28] Wittgenstein 1968, § 75–6, pp. 35–6.

their close linguistic connections: not only were the German adjectival forms *curios*, *curiös*, and *curieus* influenced by the French *curieux*, but *curieux* and *curiosité* were among the many modish French terms to be widely used in unchanged form in German in the seventeenth and early eighteenth centuries because they connoted desirable, French-style courtly and urban culture. Since intellectual culture was still Latinate, much writing in Latin will also be considered.

Three kinds of context provide this study with its analytical structure: institution, discursive tendency, and sex/gender.

First I investigate the ways in which curiosity was used by various institutions: universities, the church, and many others.

My investigation of universities focuses entirely on the Germanic territories, where Lutheran universities latched on to the theme of curiosity spectacularly (Section 1): as soon as the Thirty Years' War had ended, from 1652 onwards, they explicitly devoted many disputations to it. This wave continued for almost a century. The resulting corpus has not previously been studied. Whereas in other sections I take soundings from a vast array of potential material, in this case I have attempted a survey of the corpus in question.

In most of these disputations, curiosity was presented as a passion. Whereas in previous centuries that passion had usually been considered a vice, here it was occasionally a virtue but more often something that was morally indifferent in itself but always operative in practice as either a virtue or a vice. Some of these disputations attributed to curiosity a much more central role in cognition than had previously been allocated to it. They made enormous, unprecedented claims about its importance.

Universities did not rest with one version of curiosity. The disputation system encouraged them to reshape it constantly, since the system relied on contestation and on the constant injection of a modicum of novelty. Curiosity had a finite shelf-life as a topic: it was explicitly presented as a novel theme in 1652, but by 1724 it was referred to explicitly as a much-treated one. One might expect its constant reshaping to have been in the service of disinterested, academic truth. But it was almost always demonstrably driven by the new professional, political, social, and intellectual uses to which these institutions were putting curiosity. These uses varied from one faculty or territory to another.

Although the participants in these disputations always reshaped curiosity, they often explicitly considered themselves to be discussing the same thing as each other. On the few occasions when they thought that they were discussing a different thing, then they usually felt obliged to say so carefully, arguing that the polysemic 'curiosity' family of terms refers to more than one thing. These university texts pore over the meanings of terms, and yet they also show that curiosity, however protean, was far more than just a repertoire of terms that were periodically used in different ways. It was a thing that the institution constantly sought to define while also tacitly acknowledging—through the disputation system—that it would always resist uncontestable definition.

My second institution is the church, both Catholic and Protestant, in both France and the Germanic territories (Section 2). Unlike universities, the church already had a long history of using curiosity—especially for purposes of prohibition, since church discourse had tended to make curiosity wholly reprehensible rather than virtuous or morally ambivalent. This tendency now continued. Indeed, it may be one reason why early modern church discourse on curiosity has received relatively little attention, since its newness compared with previous periods is less obvious than that of, say, the healthy curiosity that was now celebrated in many secular circles. And those who have studied early modern church attacks on curiosity have sometimes adjudicated against them as being, for example, a last-ditch reactionary stand against the progressive forces of modernity (Blumenberg).

However, those church attacks were neither pure repetitions nor last-gasp pleas. They remained vociferous and widespread well into the eighteenth century. Although they did sometimes repeat the constative message of patristic and other previous authorities who had condemned curiosity, only in a few contexts—such as that of monastic discipline—were those strictures now being *applied* in much the same way as they had been for centuries. Mostly this was repetition with a major difference, since the old strictures were now put to new uses that were often local or specific to the post- and Counter-Reformation world of print polemic: the aim was to discourage new philosophies (Cartesianism), heresies (*libertinage*, Socinianism), and fads (for luxury, for theatre), to try and uphold a Lutheran clergy's independence from the local city Senate, and so on.

Moreover, even church discourse was irrevocably changed by the new enthusiasm for curiosity that characterized much secular discourse. However different many church writers' version of curiosity was from the new secular versions, the church writers claimed that they were in fact referring to the same thing, but that their understanding of it was the correct one. When people happily described themselves in secular contexts as being 'curious', confident that this was now a respectable or innocuous label, some church writers aggressively reinterpreted that self-description as an incriminating confession.

On the other hand, church discourse sometimes conceded ground and was itself invaded by the new secular uses of curiosity, since they were too useful to miss out on. For example, one orthodox Lutheran theologian (Adam Rechenberg) mounted the astonishingly bold argument that even in the discipline of theology there existed a good species of curiosity, which he defined as care for the salvation of oneself and others. His reshaping of curiosity was one of those that was too highly innovative to catch on further afield. But the notion that it might be possible to rechannel curiosity rather than having to eradicate it was one shared, however tenuously, by even the most austere critics of this passion. Did that mean that some curiosity could be good? Good curiosity had a spectral presence in much church discourse, where it was a distant cousin of the robustly reified good curiosity of secular discourse. Even within church discourse, the battles fought over curiosity were so intense that it could not be defined and circumscribed according to definitive criteria.

My third examination of institutional uses of curiosity focuses on a cluster of institutions, in both France and the Germanic territories, that produced and disseminated knowledge outside the confines of university or church: some were relatively formal, such as academies or learned societies; others were more commercial, such as publishing houses; others were relatively informal, such as networks of savants, naturalists, collectors, travellers, and antiquarians (Section 3). What these institutions and groups had in common, from the point of view of curiosity, is that they introduced those two great semantic sea-changes into it. First, it was they that reshaped curiosity into something that was usually good, in opposition to church and even much university discourse. Secondly, it was they that turned a wide range of knowledge and matter into curiosities, into objects—whether material or discursive—whose role it was to satisfy people's curiosity. By contrast, both university and church, even when they were encouraging curiosity, tended to discourage people from directing it at curiosities, which they judged to be epistemologically unsatisfactory or morally dangerous.

The importance of curiosity within this cluster of institutions has been established by modern historians, who have studied curiosity far more in relation to them than in relation to university or church: so much so, that it has become tempting to equate those secular institutions' versions of curiosity with the period's as a whole—but that would be a misleading synecdoche.

This cluster of institutions included some that fostered the practice of collecting in a literal or proper sense, that is, the collecting of material objects in cabinets of curiosities and the like. However, more broadly, these institutions tended also to shape knowledge as a metaphorical collection of curiosities, of discursive fragments that did not add up to a coherent, systematic whole. Books were presented as figurative cabinets of curiosities or as collections of recipes, facts, anecdotes, news, and so on. Even where no collecting metaphor was explicit, many books on history, antiquities, nature, occult sciences, travel, and so on were presented as containing discrete, 'curious' items. This culture of printed curiosities was especially prominent in the Germanic territories in the late seventeenth and early eighteenth century. In order to reflect its distinctive emphasis on shaping *objects*, I label it the culture of curiosi*ties*, adapting the well-known phrase 'culture of curiosity' which Pomian coined to designate the world of early modern collecting. I am applying my version of the phrase to many practices and discourses beyond collecting proper, though the phrase is also designed to show that collecting proper became a metaphor for those other practices and discourses.

These institutions' uses of curiosity often involved commodifying knowledge, marketing it, popularizing it, purveying it in convenient form for practical manipulation (by territorial rulers, scholar-courtiers, bureaucrats, urban burghers, women, and others), promoting sociability within male networks of collectors or naturalists, and so on. This contrasts with some university uses of curiosity (especially in philosophy faculties), which were more inward-looking, aiming for example to keep prestigious knowledge situated firmly within their own walls. But any such generalizations are tenuous: within the culture of curiosities, curiosity could also be used in order to make knowledge the preserve of an elite few or else to aggrandize the individual competitively.

Indeed, it is even impossible to describe the culture of curiosities as a whole as being always positive about curiosity. However much these institutions celebrated curiosity, even they were still haunted by old anxieties surrounding it. They even sometimes made use of those anxieties: by calling the knowledge that they produced 'curious', they sometimes gave it an aura of the forbidden that made it all the more attractive and marketable. Although the culture of curiosities was relatively distinct from church discourse, it was no more immune from it than vice versa. Although each shaped and used curiosity in conflicting ways, there was an agonized, contested family resemblance between them. They were both often considered in the period to describe at least partly the same thing.

Following this survey of institutions, my second context for uses of curiosity is of a rather different kind: it is that of the two discursive tendencies which dominated writing about curiosity. Almost every time that a writer used this family of terms, one or both of these tendencies can be shown to have structured the textual environment immediately surrounding that occurrence. The first is what I am labelling the 'curiosity-collecting' tendency (Section 3): phrases such as 'full of curious details' or 'I am curious about antiquity' explicitly or implicitly presented curiosity as being the collecting of discrete objects, whether material ones such as clocks or shells, or else discursive ones such as recipes or news items. Second is what I am labelling the 'curiosity-narrating' tendency (Sections 4–5): phrases such as 'fatal curiosity' or 'curiosity led me astray' explicitly or implicitly presented curiosity as part of a narrative, as one stage in a linear sequence of events. So curiosity was usually either a process of accumulating fragments, often within a literal or metaphorical space (such as a cabinet), or else a passion (or vice or virtue) that was situated in a temporal chain of actions leading to a telos, usually a calamitous one.

On most occasions when curiosity was mentioned, at least one of these two tendencies was present, however embryonically. On a lexical level, they were embedded in the semantic structure of the 'curiosity' family of terms: for instance, object-oriented senses figured especially in the curiosity-collecting tendency. On a broader level, the structuring effect of either tendency often seeped into whole texts or discourses. The curiosity-collecting tendency often operated in texts that were collections, compilations, or lists; it permeated especially the culture of curiosities and usually involved celebration of curiosity. On the other hand, the curiosity-narrating tendency often operated in stories, ranging from novellas and five-act plays to one-sentence *exempla*; it permeated especially religious or moralizing discourse and usually involved denigration of curiosity—the chain of events usually led to a calamitous end.

Each tendency often shaped knowledge in a broadly distinctive way, whether as a spatial collection of fragments or else as a temporal process fraught with danger. But they did not do so systematically and so cannot be called epistemological or cognitive paradigms. Rather, they were, precisely, structuring tendencies within discourse. To return to Wittgenstein's metaphor: they were fibres or strands that ran through much but not all of the rope called curiosity. Obviously, texts that mentioned curiosity were not the only ones to present knowledge as a collection or as a process fraught with danger. I examine the collecting- and narrating-tendencies only insofar as they involved curiosity, though an examination of their broader role in early modern discourse, beyond the confines of curiosity, would certainly be worthwhile. Although one of these tendencies or fibres usually predominated in any discourse, the two were often intertwined, considered to be one and the same thing viewed in two different lights.

The relative prominence of the two discursive tendencies varied across decades as well as across discourses. For instance, when the culture of curiosities waned in some (but not all) discourses in about the mid-eighteenth century, the curiosity-collecting tendency gave way increasingly to an optimistic version of the curiosity-narrating tendency: in some discourses, curiosity was now less likely to be the unsystematic accumulation of particulars and more likely to be one stage in humanity's projected progress towards greater truth and wealth.

Which of the two tendencies predominated also depended partly on the lexis of the language in question: in French and Latin both tendencies thrived; in German the curiosity-collecting tendency predominated because the object-oriented senses of the 'curiosity' family (*curieus* and so on) were more prominent than the subject-oriented ones (since terms like *Vorwitz* were often used instead of

Curiosität in its subject-oriented sense). So I illustrate the curiosity-narrating tendency more often with French and Latin texts than with German ones.

My third and final route for detecting uses of curiosity is via sex and gender. Curiosity was used very differently when attributed to men (Section 4) and to women (Section 5). Although in the seventeenth century curiosity often became more positive than it had been previously, mostly it was male curiosity that was transformed in this way. The sex differential was actually increased: an even larger proportion of bad curiosity was now female. This illustrates the problems inherent in any grand narrative of the early modern liberation of human curiosity from previous constraints.

Curiosity was widely used to train the behaviour of both sexes. Boys were often trained to avoid all curiosity but sometimes how to spot the difference between bad curiosity, which was often deemed effeminate, and the good species, which would lead them to a glorious career in the public gaze. By contrast, girls were almost always trained to avoid all curiosity. The interdiction was used to discourage women from trying to know things that only men should know. Curiosity was also used in attempts to control sexuality. Men were persuaded not to investigate too curiously women's sexual behaviour: the motivation was not to safeguard female autonomy but rather to avoid the social calamity that inevitably follows such inquiry, since women can never be counted upon to be faithful in every circumstance. By contrast, women's own curiosity was often described as residing in their lack of chastity, rather than in anxiety about male chastity. Male writers were much more interested in reining in female sexuality and knowledge than they were in voicing female anxiety about men. However, these generalizations will—like all those I offer here—be nuanced by the example of particular case-studies. Even female curiosity was occasionally permitted, though this was often for purposes that suited male writers.

This study's tripartite division into three kinds of context—institution, discursive tendency, sex/gender—is necessary for the sake of analysis but it distorts the complexity of early modern uses of curiosity, in which all of these contexts and many more combined. In order to lessen the distortion, some of my sections simultaneously treat two contexts rather than one. Sections 1–2 are on one kind of context alone: institutions (university and church). On the other hand, Section 3 is on two kinds of context: institutions (those of the culture of curiosities) and yet also a discursive tendency (curiosity-collecting). Similarly, Sections 4–5 are on both a discursive tendency (curiosity-narrating) and also a sex (respectively male and female). This enables me to investigate how different kinds of context meshed together: for example, the institutions of the culture of curiosities drew heavily on the curiosity-collecting tendency of discourse.

Thus, the clearest representation of my structure is to be found not in the Table of Contents, which lists the actual sequence of sections, but in the following list of the three kinds of context:

Institutions	1.	UNIVERSITY
	2.	CHURCH
	3.	THE CULTURE OF CURIOSITIES
Discursive tendencies	1.	COLLECTING
	2.	NARRATING
Sexes	1.	MALE
	2.	FEMALE

Other kinds of context than these three are also examined throughout. Many of them I call discourses.[29] The various communicative situations within which curiosity was used, whatever their type—genres, discourses, discursive tendencies, institutional or sex-specific statements, and so on—can all be understood as Wittgensteinian language-games (*Sprachspiele*), each of which had specific rules.[30] The rules governing uses of curiosity changed from one game to the next, and yet the various games were linked by family resemblances. To call them games is not to suggest that they were trivial: the stakes were often high.

This project's aims compel me to range across many early modern disciplines and to study primary sources that might often be considered nowadays to fall under the remit of several modern disci-

---

[29] By 'discourse' I do not mean a Foucauldian deep structure that constitutes experience, but rather an academic discipline, a genre of writing, or else the texts produced by a specific institution, for a specific market, or in relation to a specific activity. ('Genre' is being used in the open-ended sense suggested by Cohen 1986). Discourses in this sense overlap with each other. They have broad affinities with what Pocock (1987 and 1996) calls languages (or sometimes discourses), though they do not all necessarily promote political ideologies. My aim is not to provide a theory or a typology of discourses, since the relation between them varies from one text or context to another, and some were more precisely defined in the period than others (see Maclean 1991).

[30] See A. Kenny 1973, ch. 9; Wittgenstein 1968, §§ 23–76, pp. 11–36.

plines too, such as intellectual, cultural, institutional, literary history, or the history of science, although I cannot hope to emulate the quality of contextualization that specialists in all those fields would be able to provide. Throughout, a similar technique of close reading will be applied. The 'curiosity' family will be studied not as discrete units or lexemes but as interacting with other features of texts—including non-lexical ones such as structure—as well as with their contexts. The meaning of texts is not confined to the meaning of individual terms.[31]

My focus on uses of language is designed to replace any approach that would see language as a mere epiphenomenon of underlying social, cultural, or intellectual contexts, as a mere 'effect' that is 'caused' by them. Language is inextricably bound up with such contexts. Yet, on the other hand, it is not coextensive with them. So, did the uses of curiosity extend into non-verbal dimensions of, say, physical or social reality? If they did, then that reality is even less accessible to us now than the words which were designed to affect it: who knows how many adolescents *did* commit, or refrain from, specific actions—whether physical (going to a place, looking at an object) or verbal (asking a question)—because they had been drilled to avoid curiosity? It is even impossible to identify a precise point at which the uses to which the 'curiosity' family was put shaded off into the non-verbal, whether one conceptualizes that point as where discourse becomes practice,[32] as where text or language becomes society,[33] as where meaning becomes experience or power,[34] as where concepts become structures,[35] as where the illocutionary becomes the perlocutionary,[36] or as where a language-game becomes a 'form of life'.[37] The surviving remnants of early modern discourse give us glimpses of how people attempted to use the 'curiosity' family of words to get things done, whether or not those attempts actually succeeded.

[31] See Hobson 1998, esp. 2–3, 234–5.
[32] On Michel Foucault's different attempts to grapple with this issue, see McNay 1994, 62, 69–72, 87, 108.
[33] See Burke 1987 (language); LaCapra 1983, 41–8 (text).
[34] See Dunn 1985, 2 (power); Toews 1987 (experience).
[35] See Richter 1996, 11 (on *Begriffsgeschichte*).
[36] See Austin 1962.
[37] See Tully 1988*a*, 23; Wittgenstein 1968, § 23, p. 11.

I

Institutions: University

Universities were keener than most institutions to provide definitions of curiosity that were careful, detailed, and coherent. But that did not make the definitions any more disinterested than those produced by other institutions. On the contrary, the definitions were driven by the universities' attempts to make curiosity serve their own specific ends.

The predominantly Lutheran universities of central and northern Germany were greatly preoccupied with curiosity for almost a century from 1652, that is, as soon as they began their revival in the aftermath of the Thirty Years' War. In these institutions curiosity became a favourite theme for debate, spectacularly acquiring a prominence that they had never given it before: it was judged to be either a good or a bad thing or both. Positive evaluations of it were influenced by the non-university, European-wide culture of curiosities which, by 1652, was already redefining curiosity as praiseworthy while glamorizing its objects as curiosities: some of the institutions associated with that culture—such as academies, learned societies, and networks of collectors—included university professors among their members. On the other hand, negative university evaluations of curiosity were influenced especially by the long history of church discourse on curiosity, in which many a professor also had a stake, and not only if he was a theologian. Notwithstanding these links between universities and other institutions, university discourse on curiosity was a distinct language-game: it did not merely repeat pre-existing discourses but, rather, struggled with them and with their contradictions, reshaping curiosity for new purposes.

'Curiosity' became one of the key families of terms with which these universities tried to regulate knowledge. There were various semantic reasons why it was now well qualified for this role. Whereas in previous periods 'curiosity' had denoted mainly a limited range of bad knowledge, now it often denoted knowledge in general, both good and bad (*bona/mala curiositas*). It often denoted not just knowledge-seekers (*curiosi*) but also the knowledge sought (*curiosa*) and indeed the relation between those subjects and objects, since *curiositas* was frequently understood as inquiry that was inappropriate to one's role in life, directed at objects that were pernicious not in themselves but only when sought by someone who had no business to seek them. When *curiositas* denoted this indecorous relationship between subject and object, between inquirer and knowledge, it was often understood in these university discussions—as it had been sometimes in antiquity—to be a close or partial translation of the Greek terms *polypragmosyne* and *periergia*.[1] Since these Greek terms were often explicitly defined in universities as denoting *curiositas*, in the present section 'curiosity' embraces them too.

A further reason for the new centrality of curiosity in these institutions was its newly extended capacity to be a reflexive topic. On the one hand, it was an object of study: a passion, or a virtue, or a vice that could be first defined and then shown to operate in many different spheres of life. As such, it was now claimed to have unprecedented importance: some even claimed it was *the* antecedent to all action or knowledge-acquisition. On the other hand, since those spheres of life included academic disciplines, curiosity drove university study as well as being an object of it: some disputants joked that they were being curious about curiosity. Given the continuing qualms about curiosity, such reflexivity was sometimes uneasy. But in previous decades it would barely have been possible, since any description of oneself as curious had usually been unadvisable.

This spread of curiosity was fostered by institutional as well as semantic factors. One distinctive practice of the Protestant universities of central and northern Germany was their printing of teaching-related material, including disputations, on an exceptional scale.[2] According to one conservative estimate, 80,000 pre-1800 German university publications are now held in large academic libraries

---

[1] See Cziesla 1989, ch. 4, esp. 120, 123; Quinn 1995.

[2] See Evans 1981, 176–7; Nelles 2000, esp. 34. See Freedman 1999, 17: 'From the end of the sixteenth century onwards, these disputations apparently began to be published in very large quantities at Protestant academic institutions in Germany, in moderate to large quantities in Switzerland and Scandinavia, in moderate quantities in the Netherlands and the Baltic region, and in relatively small quantities in Scotland. Such disputations appear to have been only very rarely published in England, in much of Eastern Central Europe, and south of the Alps.'

(W. Müller 1990, 93). It may be that the prominence of curiosity was no greater in those Protestant German universities than elsewhere but that we simply have more evidence of it in them because they left more printed records. Yet, on the other hand, it is more probable that their reliance on print created material conditions that fostered the sustained dissemination and constant reshaping of a topic such as curiosity. Most university discussions of curiosity were dissertations, many of which took previous printed dissertations on curiosity as their starting-point. As in the non-university culture of curiosities, curiosity was here a product of print.

Yet it was also a product of another material medium: speech. A few university discussions of curiosity were orations, and most were oral disputations, which are likely to have diverged significantly from the printed dissertations that accompanied them. Although oral university discourse on curiosity is lost to us, it seems also to have shaped curiosity (and other topics) in specific ways, by subjecting it to constant contestation. The oral disputation, the printed dissertation, and the oral or printed oration were all related but distinctive language-games.

For what purposes was curiosity used in them? Often for pressing, local ones. Certainly, most discussions of curiosity began with would-be universal definitions of it, as the disputation and dissertation genres required (1.2 below); but authors then went on to apply or illustrate those definitions with particular examples that often reveal the purposes underlying the apparently *a priori* general definitions (1.3). Not that those illocutionary aims are always clear: many are now inaccessible; some were more specific than others; not every definition can be precisely linked to particular aims. Moreover, investigating the pragmatic uses of curiosity often involves a delicate progression from a broadly 'internalist' level of analysis (what epistemological or moral truth-claims were made about curiosity?) out to a broadly 'externalist' level (what were the social uses of curiosity?). Controversies about the relative merits of these two levels of analysis have raged in recent years, especially in the history of science, where unremitting focus on truth-claims has been challenged by predominantly sociological or anthropological approaches.[3] I am trying to link the two, to show how epistemological and moral claims about curiosity had social uses.

---

[3] For a survey of these recent developments, see Golinski 1998.

The uses of curiosity varied by faculty. Whereas in faculties of philosophy, devoted to humble propaedeutic tasks, the uses remained largely within the ambit of the university itself, in the three higher faculties they also stretched out into the world beyond the university: this occurred to some extent with medicine (1.3.2), more with theology (1.3.3), and most of all with law (1.3.4), which is why I treat these faculties in that order rather than according to their usual hierarchy.

The uses of curiosity also varied by place. These universities were tied to local courts and élites; they were reshaping transnational discourses to fit regional needs, territorializing curiosity as well as institutionalizing it. The decentralized political structures of the Holy Roman Empire of German Nations fostered variety in intellectual life and, in this case, in the shapes of curiosity. However, this does not make these university versions of curiosity any less 'representative' of early modern curiosity than were, say, local versions produced in Paris or London, even if a few of the latter achieved wider European dissemination. Moreover, it would make little sense to call these German versions 'provincial', since in early modern Germany there was in any case no cultural 'centre' in relation to which they were ex-centric. German universities of this period have long been discounted as stagnant, provincial backwaters enlivened only by the new foundations (Halle and Göttingen) which soon became associated with the Enlightenment. This stereotype has recently been challenged with evidence that a range of technical, pedagogical, and intellectual innovations were being explored in them.[4] As a contribution to the history of universities, the present section offers one further small instance of those innovations, showing the extraordinary dynamism, creativity, and ingenuity with which curiosity was reshaped for new needs. As a contribution to the history of language-games, it explores what one kind of institution did with curiosity.

1.1 CURIOSITY AND UNIVERSITIES IN CENTRAL AND NORTHERN GERMANY

Curiosity became a burning topic not in lectures and textbooks, but in disputations, professorial orations, and lecture announcements.

---

[4] Nelles 2001, esp. 147. See also Evans 1981, esp. 169–70.

Between 1652 and 1744, at least 42 such items devoted to curiosity were printed in or just outside the Holy Roman Empire of German Nations, mostly in the central and northern territories (Table 1; Figure 1.1; Bibliography, Primary Sources 1).[5] None of these texts has been studied in modern times, to my knowledge.[6] Eight of the 42 were reprinted in the period—a further indication of the topic's popularity, which seems to have been especially high for sixty years from 1670, peaking in the first decade of the eighteenth century. Most of the institutions in question were Lutheran universities; a few were universities that were bi-confessional for a time (Erfurt, Frankfurt a.d. Oder, Rinteln); a couple were *Gymnasien* (in Gera and Danzig); a couple were outside the Empire but Germanic to varying degrees (in Strasbourg, annexed by France in 1681, and in the free Polish city of Danzig).

Of these 42 items, the vast majority—about 37—were dissertations, propounding arguments that were also defended orally on a particular day, in a particular hall. Following Hanspeter Marti, I refer to the printed version as a dissertation and to the overall event as a disputation, although the two terms were not distinguished so consistently in the period.[7] The vast corpus of early modern German dissertations has begun to receive expert attention,[8] but it still

[5] Table 1 includes only items in which curiosity is a sustained theme, with just 6 exceptions—the Rostock and Marburg dissertations and Friese/Ritter 1691—where it occurs little after the title. In many other cases (not included in Table 1), curiosity figures more tangentially as a label for dissertations themselves: many are called *curiosae*, e.g. Friedrich Hoffmann (*praeses*; Professor of Medicine at Halle), *Dissertationes physico-medicae curiosae selectiores*, 2 vols. (Leiden, 1733 and 1735). I have not included dissertations that were referred to in the period but are no longer, to my knowledge, extant. Nor have I included examples from further afield, such as a well-known dissertation by the famous Linnaeus (Carl von Linné) (*praeses*), with Olaus Söderberg (*resp.*), *Specimen academicum de curiositate naturali*, Medical Faculty, Univ. of Uppsala, 1748 (Stockholm, 1748; reprinted in 1749, 1786, and 1787; translated into German in 1778; for a modern French translation, see Linnaeus 1972, 124–43). The following items in Table 1 are omitted from certain aspects of my analysis, since I have not been able to consult them: Joch/Seyfart 1708, Mitternacht 1667, Rosteuscher 1692, Simon/Rühle 1675, Zeiblich/Feind 1700.

[6] The only study of curiosity in a university context seems to be Daxelmüller 1979. His aim—a vindication of Hans Blumenberg's thesis about 'theoretical curiosity'—takes his analysis in a very different direction from mine. Daxelmüller's rich study does not include the texts I am studying, except for a passing mention of 3 of them (123).

[7] Marti 1981, 118 n. and 1982, 16–17.

[8] See Allweiss 1979; Barner 1970, 393–407; Daxelmüller 1979, chs. 2–3; Evans 1981, 174–81; Horn 1893; Kaufmann 1898, 369–400; Komorski 1995 (the best survey of recent scholarship); Koppitz 1979; Kundert 1984, 53–67; Marti 1981; Marti 1982, 13–77 (the most helpful modern overview of the genre); Trevisani 1992, 41–53.

TABLE I. *German dissertations, professorial orations, and lecture announcements devoted to* curiositas, curiosa, polypragmosyne, periergia

Printed (reprinted)		University (or other institution)	Faculty
1652 (1690, 1713, 1735)	dissertation	Frankfurt a.d. Oder	philosophy
1667	dissertations	Gera (*Gymnasium*)	—
1668 (1675)	dissertation	Leipzig	theology
1670 (1670, 1672, 1691)	*dissertation*	*Frankfurt a.d. Oder*	*law*
1670	*dissertation*	*Strasbourg*	*philosophy*
1672 (1675)	dissertation	Leipzig	theology
1674–5 (1683)	dissertation	Jena	law
1676	oration	Danzig (*Gymnasium*)	medicine
1677 (1690, 1743)	dissertation	Frankfurt a.d. Oder	law
1685	*dissertation*	*Wittenberg*	*philosophy*
1685	dissertation	Marburg	philosophy
1686	dissertation	Marburg	philosophy
1687 (1708)	dissertation	Leipzig	philosophy
1687	dissertation	Erfurt	law
1688	dissertation	Erfurt	law
1691	dissertation	Leipzig	philosophy
1692	dissertation	Danzig (*Gymnasium*)	philosophy
1693	*dissertation*	*Leipzig*	*philosophy*
1696 (1702, 1710)	dissertation	Frankfurt a.d. Oder	law
1699	dissertation	Helmstedt	philosophy
1700	*dissertation*	*Wittenberg*	*philosophy*
1701	oration	Helmstedt	medicine
1703	dissertation	Rostock	medicine
1705	dissertation	Rostock	medicine
1705	*dissertation*	*Strasbourg*	*philosophy*
1706	dissertation	Erfurt	law
1708	*dissertation*	*Jena*	*philosophy*
1708	*dissertation*	*Leipzig*	*philosophy*
1709	dissertation	Halle	medicine
1709	oration	Jena	medicine
1711	dissertation	Rostock	medicine
1712	dissertation	Rostock	medicine
1713	dissertation	Rostock	medicine
1714	dissertation	Halle	medicine
1714	dissertation	Strasbourg	philosophy
1720	*oration*	*Altdorf*	*medicine*

TABLE 1. *Continued*

Printed (reprinted)		University (or other institution)	Faculty
1724	dissertation	Jena	philosophy
1725	*dissertation*	*Altdorf*	*law*
1725	*dissertation*	*Leipzig*	*law*
1730	*oration*	*Leipzig*	*law*
1740	dissertation	Rinteln	philosophy
1744	dissertation	Erlangen	philosophy

Note: Bold type means that the title of the item uses the noun *curiositas*. Normal type means that the title uses the adjective *curiosus*. Italics mean that the title uses *polypragmosyne*, *periergia*, or their cognates.

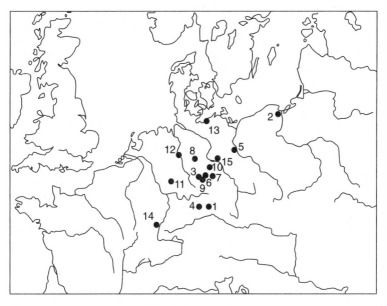

FIGURE 1.1. Institutions represented in Table 1. The map shows (1) Altdorf, (2) Danzig, (3) Erfurt, (4) Erlangen, (5) Frankfurt a.d. Oder, (6) Gera, (7) Halle, (8) Helmstedt, (9) Jena, (10) Leipzig, (11) Marburg, (12) Rinteln, (13) Rostock, (14) Strasbourg, (15) Wittenberg. Adapted, with permission, from an essay by W. Frijhoff in H. de Ridder-Symoens (ed.), *A History of the University in Europe*, ii: *Universities in Early Modern Europe (1500–1600)* (Cambridge: Cambridge University Press, 1996), 95–100.

remains a relatively untapped source and has been little used for the sustained study of specific themes or disciplines. The remaining five items in Table 1 are orations on curiosity, including professorial inaugurals (Schulze 1720, Seger 1676), an outline of a professor's lectures in the forthcoming semester (Schrader 1701), and invitations by a dean or vice-chancellor to a forthcoming disputation (Krause 1709, Scherzer 1730). All of these orations—with the possible exception of the invitations—seem to have been delivered orally as well as being printed.

This preoccupation with curiosity spread to many institutions: fifteen are represented in Table 1. Yet its epicentre lay in Brandenburg-Prussia and in neighbouring Saxony.[9] Not only did these two states together account for about half of these texts, but it was here that dissertations on curiosity were most frequently reprinted: all four of the Frankfurt a.d. Oder ones were reprinted (each of them more than once), as were three of the Leipzig seven.

The debate about curiosity spread to all faculties too, most of all to the lower faculty of philosophy or arts,[10] closely followed by two of the higher faculties—law and medicine—whereas theology was barely touched. All levels of student were involved, ranging from sophisticated candidates for doctorates in law (Cocceji/Lettow 1696, Streit/Kalckhoff 1706) and medicine (Stahl/Donzelina 1714) right down to *Gymnasium* adolescents producing 'little dissertations' (Mitternacht 1667).[11] In between these two extremes, curiosity was debated by licentiate graduands ([Brunnemann]/Henel 1691, Henrici/Frantz 1709) and, most often of all, in the *exercitationes academicae* which did not count formally towards a degree but which served as training for university students of all levels. Indeed, most early modern German dissertations belonged to this type.

The debate spread to both conservative and progressive faculties. The connection of curiosity to new developments in universities is suggested by the participation of some of the leading academic

---

[9] In general, more dissertations were printed in Saxony than in any other state (Evans 1981, 178).

[10] Philosophy accounts for the highest number of dissertations and orations on curiosity (18), which is all the more striking given that this faculty produced the fewest dissertations overall in German universities (Marti 1981, 120).

[11] 'Dissertatiuncula'. On Mitternacht, see Kelly 1996; *NDB*. On the 'luxuriant literary undergrowth' of printed orations and dissertations connected with schools as opposed to universities, see Evans 1981, 175.

reformers of the time. The physician Georg Ernst Stahl, the jurists Samuel Stryk and Heinrich von Cocceji, and the theologian and church historian Adam Rechenberg—whose two dissertations on curiosity date from his student days—were all progressive thinkers, not necessarily in the sense that they fit in with any linear narrative of progress through the so-called Scientific Revolution and pre-Enlightenment, but in the sense that they were keen to reform their discipline. Stahl and Stryk were especially famous, as was Stryk's fellow Roman lawyer Johann Brunnemann, who also participated in the debate, along with other professors who were famous but not quite to the same extent, such as the physicians Johann Ernst Schaper, Rudolf Wilhelm Krause, and Johann Heinrich Schulze.

Most of these professors acted as *praeses* for dissertations on curiosity, that is, they supervised them and chaired the disputation in which the student (as *respondens*) defended his arguments—sometimes with help from the *praeses*—against objections that were put by one or more opponents (*opponentes*). The contribution of the *praeses* to the printed dissertation could be anything from actual authorship to a cursory glance over a draft composed by the student. Authorship was often attributed to the *respondens* on the title-page[12] or else it was sometimes effectively attributed to either *respondens* or *praeses* by being subsequently included in collections bearing his name.[13] But these are not necessarily reliable indications of actual authorship, and in either case the topic and approach often bore the professor's general stamp.

What made curiosity an ideal topic—for a few decades—for orations and disputations? Its potential for reflexivity lent it to orations, which were often occasions to glorify or lament the nature of university study. Curiosity was entirely reflexive in the orations that were devoted to it, whatever the faculty: dominated by epideictic rhetoric, these praised or blamed the curiosity of scholars. In medical dissertations too, curiosity was purely reflexive:[14] the only *curiositas* for which they offered a pathology was that of physicians themselves, not of their patients.[15] In other faculties this reflexive potential of

[12] This occurs in 15 of the dissertations I am considering, in at least one edition.

[13] This occurs with 2 respondents (Pipping and Rechenberg) and one *praeses* (Stryk).

[14] Esp. Bierling/Pestel 1740; Fichtner/Puchelberger 1725; Rinder/Lasius 1699.

[15] Such pathologies are outlined notably in the 2 Halle dissertations, Henrici/Frantz 1709 and Stahl/Donzelina 1714.

curiosity to be one of the motives underlying the actual discipline added resonance to the main way in which dissertations treated curiosity—as part of the subject-matter of a discipline, for example as a passion to be described by philosophy. In philosophy and law dissertations, while curiosity was mostly treated as something to be studied by the discipline,[16] it was sometimes treated as a motive underlying it,[17] and usually in both these ways. In terms of the distinction that was developed from Aristotle and became prominent in Central European Reformed pedagogy, curiosity came under both *praecognita* (the nature of a discipline) and *systemata* (its contents) (Hotson 2000, 31–2).

Certainly, curiosity was not the only reflexive topic fashionable in disputations and orations: 'difficulty' was another. But curiosity was one of the few that was inside as well as outside disciplines: another was 'subtlety', since it was attributed both to practitioners of a discipline and to some of the objects studied, such as certain natural phenomena. Even *subtilitas* was nowhere near as semantically rich as *curiositas*, but these two topics and *difficultas*—each designated mainly by a feminine Latin noun ending in *-tas*—all gave the impression of being disputation- or oration-sized topics, unlike the vaster topics tackled in lectures or textbooks.[18]

Curiosity was also an ideal topic for disputations because, for a while, it seemed relatively new: it figured little in the traditional curriculum, whether in lectures or textbooks. The celebrated pedagogical reformer Christian Thomasius complained that curiosity was one of those affects that law students needed to understand and yet were simply not taught about (1713, 354). Contemporary textbooks on

[16] Esp. [Brunnemann]/Henel 1691; Cocceji/Lettow 1710; Olearius/Schlegel 1725; Siber/Jacobi 1685; Silberrad/Christann 1714; Stolle/Schlosser 1724; Streit/Kalckhoff 1706; Stryk/Lüedecke 1743; Succov/Haag 1744; Watson/Rose 1690; Zeiblich/Feind 1700.

[17] Esp. Friese/Ritter 1691; Hilscher/Cramer 1693; Rosteuscher/Schelgwig 1692; Westphal/Pipping 1708.

[18] e.g. Rudolf Wilhem Krause, Dean of the Medical Faculty of Jena, who devoted to *curiositas* one oration announcing a forthcoming doctoral promotion, also devoted 2 others to *difficultas* (*De difficultate in studio medico hodie emergente* (Jena, 1697) and *De scientiae physicae praestantia et difficultate* (Jena, 1707)). Friedrich Schrader, long before he devoted a *programma* to *curiositas*, devoted his inaugural to *subtilitas* (*De admiranda naturae in operibus suis subtilitate oratio*, Univ. of Helmstedt, 1683). All these are in the Herzog August Bibliothek, Wolfenbüttel (HAB).

ethics and moral theology did cover curiosity, but fairly succinctly, as one of many passions, virtues, or vices.[19]

In contrast to the limited place allotted to it as an object of study within the main curriculum, curiosity was beginning to enjoy much greater prominence as a reflexive, rhetorically seductive label *for* university study, especially of an innovative kind. The centuries-old pejorative association of novelty with curiosity, which was still strong in some university texts, was transformed in others into an alluring quality, so that 'curious' could virtually mean 'cutting-edge'.[20] This occurred particularly in universities that were introducing experimental natural philosophy into the curriculum. One of the first to do so, by 1680, was Helmstedt (Clark 1992, 97), where medical professors in particular, teaching both medicine and philosophy, described as 'curious' the new kinds of pedagogic activity that were now supplementing standard lectures: anatomical dissections, mechanical and other physical 'experiments' or demonstrations. They tried to drum up interest among the students and the local public by exploiting denotations which 'curious' was also acquiring in contemporary learned societies—'new', 'experimental', 'empirical'—as well as other connotations prevalent in the contemporary culture of curiosities: 'supplementary', 'visually exciting', 'of popular appeal'.[21] It might be argued that this curious knowledge had

[19] e.g. Becmann 1679, 67–9 (published while he was Professor of History at Frankfurt a.d. Oder); Buddeus 1719*a*, 214–16 (first published in 1711 and intended for his students at Jena: see the start of the liminary address to the reader).

[20] e.g. Pasch 1695. The 'curious devotion to novelty' ('curiosum novitatis studium') is divided into good and bad in Westphal/Pipping 1708.

[21] See 3.4.1 below. On the visual appeal of such 'experiments', see Clark 1992, 92–8. The 'experimental' demonstrations which Schrader held in his home away from the lecture hall, in semesters when there was sufficient student interest, were known as a 'collegium curiosum experimentale' (*Catalogus lectionum et exercitationum in Academia Julia*, [Helmstedt], e.g. Winter Semester 1692, [):(4']). *Collegia* seem to have been discursive gatherings. Like other forms of important private teaching in various disciplines, they usually had a more practical, empirical slant than lectures: see Nelles 2000 and 2001, 154–68. Schrader's medical colleagues A. Christian Gakenholtz and the celebrated anatomist Heinrich Meibom sought to attract students to dissections and mechanical demonstrations by calling both spectacle and onlookers 'curious': e.g. Meibom, *Programma . . . quo ad anatomen corporis foeminini in novo theatro primam omnium ordinum curiosos solemniter invitat*, Helmstedt, 1673, esp. [A1ᵛ], A2ᵛ, [A4ᵛ]. This invitation to '*curiosi* of all ranks' suggests that in this Helmstedt context the term could denote not only students but also other interested amateurs and perhaps medical professionals. In addition, this terminology is prominent in treatises by the Helmstedt medical professor Johann Andreas Stisser on botany (1697), where the 'exotic' connotation of curiosity was added to the others, and also

nothing to do with curiosity the passion, in other words that object- and subject-oriented senses were wholly distinct from each other; yet they were sometimes explicitly connected, for example in Friedrich Schrader's 1701 Helmstedt *programma* on *curiositas*.

So curiosity often connoted novelty in two ways: first as an appar- ently new object for study in itself; secondly, as a label for new kinds of knowledge. But it did not connote novelty wholly or continually: it did have at least some roots in the curriculum, especially in philoso- phy, however summarily it was treated there. Since disputation topics were supposed neither to replicate the curriculum nor to be so novel that they were singular (Marti 1982, 27), curiosity was there- fore an ideal topic for a while, especially in philosophy disputations. In jurisprudence, because it had 'barely been brought together by anyone else',[22] if anything it risked having too much 'singularity' as a topic.[23] This was even truer of theology, at least so far as any notion of *good* curiosity was concerned, since in theology—as opposed to, say, natural philosophy—such a notion remained shocking. Only Rechenberg attempted to defend it in a sustained way, and perhaps he could do this only because he had already proved his orthodoxy by devoting a previous dissertation to condemnation of *bad* curios- ity in theology. Conversely, bad curiosity in theology did not take off as a disputation topic either, probably because it was insufficiently novel. So the rise to prominence in universities of certain kinds of curiosity was due partly to the precise requirements of the disputa- tion genre. The eventual decline of curiosity as a disputation topic was an inevitable result of its own success: by 1724 it no longer looked suitably fresh: the stock of potential variations on it no longer looked inexhaustible.[24] It was perhaps in order to freshen up the

on mechanics (1686). Only Schrader seems to have extended the discourse of curios- ity from these supplementary areas of the curriculum into descriptions of his core lec- tures, not only in his 1701 *Programma* but also in 2 dating from 1683. All the above are in HAB; I am grateful to Paul Nelles for pointing me towards them.

[22] 'cum vix à quopiam . . . congestum sit' (Stryk/Lüedecke 1743, 289).

[23] 'I'll easily be able to show how *polypragmosyne* may be subjected to a jurispru- dential treatment . . . which I'll now explain, at least briefly, lest I be suspected of affected singularity.' ('De πολυπ[ρ]αγμοσυν a[u]tem, quatenus Jurisprudentiae quoque dispositioni subjicitur, acturus facilè quidem . . . ut, saltem paucis, ne singu- laritatis affectatae suspicionem incurram, eam explicem.' [Brunnemann]/Henel 1691, [A2ʳ⁻ᵛ]).

[24] 'When I began writing this exercise, I had seen and read few authors, who had subjected this matter to the anvil of their learned inquiry. However, when I was about to add the colophon to these pages, there occurred to me several other authors who—

topic that people started debating the less familiar-sounding *poly-pragmosyne* and *periergia* rather than *curiositas*: all but one of the disputations and orations on curiosity in the 1720s and 1730s high-lighted these Greek terms, which were also becoming increasingly useful for some purposes because they still harboured the pejorative meanings that had now become weaker in the Latin term.

University curiosity therefore emerged from an institutionally imposed tension between tradition and novelty. Giving new twists to a thing that had already been described for centuries necessitated a combination of rigour and creativity in the use of textual authorities. When sifting through authoritative texts, professors and students paid very precise attention to terminology, searching for occurrences of the 'curiosity' family of terms, and they deemed the adjective *curiosus* and the adverb *curiose* to be as potentially relevant to their purposes as the noun *curiositas*. This made it easy to authorize a nega-tive view of curiosity, with reference either to pagan antiquity (from Seneca to Plutarch) or to the patristic tradition. However, in com-parison with early modern theologians, most of these university authors played down the Church Fathers: even if they considered curiosity to be wholly or partly bad, they referred only occasionally to, say, St Augustine[25] and mainly mediated the patristic tradition indirectly through recent authorities, especially moral philosophers such as the Lutheran Johann Christoph Becmann[26] or the Calvinists Jean de L'Espine[27] and William Ames.[28] By contrast, the many uni-versity writers who considered curiosity to be wholly or partly posi-tive had a much more difficult task in authorizing this view with reference to older usage. Faced with the discrepancy between some current secular usage—which made curiosity positive—and the predominantly negative judgements provided by older texts, some

as I have now found out—had also discussed the theme of curiosity.' ('Paucos quidem, cum in limine adhuc versarer huius tentaminis conscribendi, & videram & legeram Auctores, qui hanc materiam doctae suae disquisitionis incudi subjecerunt[.] Vix tamen colophonem addituro paginis hisce, obtigerunt nonnulli alii, quos thema de curiositate tractandum sibi sumsisse, tum demum cognovi.' Stolle/Schlosser 1724, [3]–4). See also Bierling/Pestel 1740, 12: '*curiosity* itself has begun to be explored and explained more curiously in recent times' ('ipsa *curiositas* recentioribus demum tem-poribus curiosius indagari ac explicari coepit').

[25] e.g. Kromayer/Scherzer/Rechenberg 1675, C3^r, E2^r.
[26] e.g. Bierling/Pestel 1740, 7; Rinder/Lasius 1699, A[1]^v.
[27] e.g. Kromayer/Scherzer/Rechenberg 1675, E2^r.
[28] e.g. ibid., B[1]^v; Streit/Kalckhoff 1706, 22; Stryk/Lüedecke 1743, 291.

resorted to blatant asymmetry, authorizing only bad curiosity although they also proposed a good kind.[29] Others scoured old texts for positive occurrences. Rechenberg's bold and highly unusual claim that 'healthy curiosity' (*sana curiositas*) can exist in theology was authorized with reference to Tertullian, who was indeed one of the few Church Fathers to have accepted that *curiositas* could be good as well as bad.[30] More often, dissertation writers authorized positive senses of 'curiosity' with reference to Cicero, conveniently ignoring the fact that he also used these terms negatively.[31] The search for positive ancient occurrences also led to Roman Law (1.3.4 below). Or else writers tacitly dropped their terminological rigour and interpreted authoritative texts which did not mention good curiosity as being nonetheless about it. Rechenberg claimed that Johann Konrad Dannhauer had already described the proper role of 'healthy curiosity' in exegetic theology: Rechenberg was undeterred by the fact that the terms actually used by Dannhauer were quite different.[32] Others interpreted ancient texts such as Roman Law in this terminologically loose way. Indeed, even the existence of bad curiosity was sometimes proved with reference to earlier texts that did not explicitly mention it.[33]

By contrast, the ordinary language of contemporaries, in which 'curiosity' had new meanings, was not usually considered a proper source of authority for those meanings, however much the new university versions of curiosity were in fact influenced by them. Indeed, one writer, devoting his 1699 dissertation to a demonstration that curiosity is wholly good, explictly discounted 'the common meaning of the word', which he acknowledged to be still a 'disordered appetite to know': consequently, the 'curiosity' family of terms was

[29] e.g. the oration by Seger (1676).

[30] Kromayer/Scherzer/Rechenberg 1675, E[1]ʳ. On this aspect of Tertullian, see Meijering 1980, 8–11; Newhauser 1982, 570; Oberman 1974, 16–18.

[31] e.g. Cocceji/Lettow 1710, 6; Schrader 1701, A2ᵛ; Westphal/Pipping 1708. At least one dissertation did cite Cicero to illustrate the negative sense (Stahl/Donzelina 1714, 5). On *curiosus* and *curiose* in Cicero, see Labhardt 1960, 207–8. In fact it was Cicero who seems to have coined *curiositas*, using it on just one recorded occasion (Labhardt 1960, 209), which the dissertation-writers do not mention.

[32] Kromayer/Scherzer/Rechenberg 1675, [M3ᵛ]. The reference is to Dannhauer 1642 and 1654.

[33] Rechenberg supports his assertion that unhealthy curiosity has flared up in our time by referring to the orthodox Lutheran theologian Heinrich Höpfner, although the Höpfner passage in question does not actually mention curiosity (Kromayer/Scherzer/Rechenberg 1675, A3ʳ; Höpfner 1674, 280–1).

absent from whole swathes of his dissertation.[34] However, ordinary language eventually gained greater authority: a 1744 dissertation writer carefully checked his definitions of curiosity against it.[35]

In other words, these professors and students were seeking to define what they saw as a thing called curiosity and yet they did not consider it to be denoted by the whole existing range of meanings of 'curiosity' nor indeed only by that family of terms, though most tried to tie the thing to the family as closely as possible. They had little doubt that some of these meanings of the 'curiosity' family of terms did denote the same thing, whether a passion, virtue, or vice: only an especially thorough dissertation went so far as to worry momentarily whether any such 'thing' really did exist at all beyond words (Stolle/Schlosser 1724, 4). Another dissertation author, with somewhat circular logic, cited the fact that he and others had written about curiosity as proof that it does exist: 'It would certainly be foolish to want to debate or write about a thing which does not exist.'[36]

Similarly, there was not much doubt that this thing had always existed.[37] But why then were universities only discussing it in detail now? Two explanations were offered. The first was that curiosity had previously been ignored by universities precisely because it is everywhere in everyday life. This argument was put in the 1652 dissertation that inaugurated the new university preoccupation with curiosity: 'Curiosity has barely been discussed up till now, as is clear if we call to mind the exercises held in universities. For that which is ordinary, daily, or hourly tends to play at best a tiny part in academic concerns and discussions.'[38] The second explanation offered was that this passion was more prevalent now than in previous periods: the amount of curiosity in the world was not fixed but had actually

---

[34] 'communis vocis notatio', 'inordinato Appetitui sciendi' (Rinder/Lasius 1699, A[1]ᵛ).

[35] Succov/Haag 1744, 8, 27.

[36] 'Stultum vero esset, de re, quae non est, disputare aut scribere velle.' (Bierling/Pestel 1740, 4).

[37] There was a little doubt, however: Westphal/Pipping (1708, 12) hesitated as to whether curiosity was new or not.

[38] '*Curiositas* . . . hactenus penè fuit inaudita, si memoriam institutarum in Academiis Exercitationum quodammodo repetamus. Nempe id, quod est vulgare, domesticum, quotidianum, aut horarium, eruditarum curarum et tractationum pars aut nulla, aut valde exigua esse solet.' (Watson/Rose 1690, 746). On Watson, see Jöcher 1750–1.

increased. The preface to a 1677 dissertation gave this theory a formulation that became well-known and influential, being quoted with enthusiasm at other universities over the next generation: 'We have been preserved for a curious age, in which things that do not smack of curiosity are either little cared for or wholly neglected.'[39] The theory was applied to both good and bad curiosity: elsewhere it was argued that 'unhealthy curiosity' (*insana curiositas*) in theology had 'flared up again in our own time', with the Thirty Years' War being one implicit factor.[40]

Although there was a consensus that curiosity existed, there was enormous disagreement as to what exactly it was. This disagreement was not an accidental side-effect of university discourse on curiosity; rather it was the very condition of its possibility, since curiosity could only survive as a disputation topic by being constantly freshened up. The function of disputations was both to define things like curiosity and yet also to contest any such definition. They were inherently conflictual discursive situations in which the respondent's arguments were automatically contested by the *opponens*. Although the printed dissertations which have survived are necessarily more univocal than the unrecorded oral disputations, even the printed versions reveal traces of that unrecoverable oral plurivocality by anticipating and refuting likely objections to the definitions that they propose.[41] And although the survival of the printed versions may lead us to assume that they were more important than the ephemeral oral version, in fact the reverse was true: students were judged more by their on-the-spot oral performance than by the printed dissertation (Nelles 2000, 44). If the printed evidence suggests that definitions of curiosity were no sooner proposed than contested, then that is likely to have been even truer during the oral debates themselves, with curiosity being endlessly reshaped by respondents under fire.

[39] 'Ad curiosum reservati sumus seculum, in quo ea, quae curiositatem non redolent, aut curantur parum, aut plane negliguntur' (Stryk/Lüedecke 1743, 289). Most of this preface is quoted by Krause (1709,)(2ʳ) and by Westphal/Pipping (1708, [3]–4). For another example of this topos, see Silberrad/Christann 1714, 7.

[40] 'nostro tempore rursus accensam' (Kromayer/Scherzer/Rechenberg 1675, A3ʳ). Rechenberg is quoting from an anti-Catholic work by the Calvinist theologian Andreas Rivet (1634, 494). Rivet and Höpfner, to whom Rechenberg also refers for this point, were writing during the Thirty Years' War. Höpfner in particular connects social to intellectual strife.

[41] See esp. Stolle/Schlosser 1724 and Succov/Haag 1744.

So curiosity was profoundly institutionalized by universities. But that does not mean that they made it into a static, monolithic 'concept'. Nor on the other hand did they just let it mean anything to anyone. Rather, they constantly defined and counter-defined it with a rhetorical creativity that honed it for specific uses. Let us now consider the ways in which it was defined.

1.2 DEFINING CURIOSITY

1.2.1 *Passion*

The most extensive definitions of curiosity were given in philosophy dissertations. Yet even they gave varied, conflicting answers to the questions that recurred. Is curiosity a passion? Is it a virtue or a vice? Is it a big or a small part of us? Is it mental or physical? Do God and animals have it too? Does it involve doing as well as desiring? Is it directed only at certain kinds of knowledge? Is it directed at the present, past, or future?

The majority consensus was that it is indeed a passion (*passio*), that is, in the more usual terminology of these texts, an affect (*affectus*) or affection (*affectio*).[42] Like other passions, it is rooted in the body, and in particular in the heart.[43] Its very name proves this: *curiositas* derives from *cor urat* ('let the heart burn'). This fairly obscure etymology, which seems originally to have been Varro's idea, enjoyed unusual prominence in these dissertations, some of which vaguely combined it with the more usual etymon *cura* by quoting Cicero on the 'care which cooks' someone.[44] Curiosity can stop the flow of the blood, making us pale; it can heat the blood, making us go red; it can make us sluggish, or it can make us tremble, excited by too much spirit.[45] Even when directed at knowledge, curiosity is bodily and emotional. Indeed, no early modern philosophers, not even Cartesian ones, argued that human knowing could be free of

[42] On the passions in early modern philosophy, see James 1997, 1998*a*, and 1998*b*.
[43] C. Thomasius 1706, 120; Watson/Rose 1690, 746.
[44] 'curamve . . . quae nunc te coquit' (Cicero, *Cato Maior de senectute*, I.1; Cicero was in turn quoting Ennius). See Cocceji/Lettow 1710, 6; Streit/Kalckhoff 1706, 3; Westphal/Pipping 1708, 6. See N. Kenny 2003, 61–3. For Varro, see Labhardt 1960, 208. On other etymologies, see N. Kenny 1998, 35, 56.
[45] Watson/Rose 1690, 758, 760–1.

emotion: to attribute any such view to them is a modern projection, as Susan James has shown (1997).

If curiosity is a passion, is it moral or immoral? The traditionally dominant view was that curiosity is always a vice. That view still dominated in disciplines such as theology and moral philosophy[46] or else in vernacular genres such as cautionary tales. But it was now only rarely defended in university dissertations,[47] except in those which took *polypragmosyne* or *periergia* rather than *curiositas* as their prime focus.[48] The opposite, much more novel view was that curiosity is always a virtue. But it too was defended only rarely, in fact in just one dissertation, it seems: its Cartesian author could only reshape curiosity into an entirely good thing by explicitly spurning customary understandings of it.[49]

The much more common answer was that curiosity is morally indifferent in itself but always manifests itself in any given context as either a virtue or a vice.[50] This view was formulated in a well-known textbook by the great pre-Enlightenment jurist Christian Thomasius, from which at least a couple of these dissertations took their cue.[51] It involved either a modification or a rejection of scholastic moral philosophy, which had long designated *curiositas* as a vice of excess, as opposed to the vice of deficiency *negligentia*,

[46] See the textbooks by Becmann (1679, 67–9) and Buddeus (1719a, 214–16): Buddeus criticizes Becmann for making *curiositas* a weakness of the intellect rather than a passion. Both had a big influence on university dissertations on curiosity: the Becmann passage is referred to by Bierling/Pestel (1740, 7), Rinder/Lasius (1699, A[1]ᵛ), Silberrad/Christann (1714, 14) and the Buddeus passage by Stolle/Schlosser (1724, 6), while reference is also sometimes made to other passages on *curiositas* written by Becmann (Cocceji/Lettow 1710, 6) and Buddeus (Silberrad/Christann 1714, 9). But even these dissertations refused to follow the 2 moralists in making all curiosity bad.

[47] For an example, see the medical dissertation by Henrici/Frantz (1709). It could be argued that their constant references to *nimia curiositas* ('too much curiosity') imply that a good, non-excessive kind is possible, but they do not develop that possibility.

[48] Hilscher/Cramer 1693; Olearius/Schlegel 1725; Ortlob/Fuchs 1708; Schaller/Huber 1670; Scherzer 1730; Scherzer/Saltzmann 1705; Siber/Jacobi 1685.

[49] Rinder/Lasius 1699 (Helmstedt). Cartesianism affected some progressive Lutheran universities, such as Helmstedt and Jena, but its main centres in Germany at the turn of the century were Calvinist universities. See Clark 1992, 107–8; Hammerstein 1981, 257–9; Trevisani 1992. On its spread in European universities, see Gascoigne 1990, 215–20.

[50] e.g. Watson/Rose 1690.

[51] C. Thomasius 1706, 120. This passage is referred to by Henrici/Frantz (1709, 2) and by Stolle/Schlosser (1724, [3]). Thomasius later advised students to read it to find out what they needed to know about curiosity (1713, 354 n.).

with the virtuous mean *studiositas* sitting between the two extremes.[52] Some dissertations retained the Aristotelian framework
but simply reshuffled the cards. One suggested that *curiositas* might
itself be a virtuous mean.[53] Another made *sana curiositas* ('healthy
curiosity') the virtuous mean by identifying it with *studiositas,* which
degenerated into *insana curiositas* if excessive and into *negligentia* if
deficient.[54]

Although the passion of curiosity was always inserted into a moral
framework, occasionally that framework became less insistent, especially from the early eighteenth century onwards. In some dissertations, the goodness and badness of curiosity was now less directly
linked to virtue or vice: one writer advised how to 'curb this affect
through true love of virtue',[55] but that was not quite the same as calling it a virtue or vice in itself. By the mid-eighteenth century, it was
possible to understand as an 'instinct' that was, in itself, amoral.[56]
This greater loosening of the moral ties that bound curiosity had
already been evident since about the late seventeenth century in other
kinds of discourses, such as French vernacular prose fiction (4.4.3
and 4.4.5 below). Such loosening was occurring with other passions
too; it gradually turned curiosity, in some discourses, into something
more familiar to the many modern people who assume that psychology is very distinct from ethics.

Many of these dissertations defined curiosity as a desire, in particular as a 'desire to know'.[57] For most, this desire was a passion,

---

[52] e.g. see the Thomist commentary by the Jesuit Lessius (1605, 722–4), which was
well known in German universities: Stryk/Lüedecke (1743, 291, 295, 309) refer to this
passage by Lessius but drop the Aristotelian framework. Even the frequently anti-
scholastic Michel de Montaigne reiterates the topos in similar terms in about 1580,
making 'gravité' ('seriousness') the virtuous mean: 'Le vice contraire à la curiosité,
c'est la nonchalance' ('The opposite vice to curiosity is nonchalance', Montaigne
1962, 345). See Aristotle, *Nicomachean Ethics,* II.6.

[53] 'for in the moral virtues moderation cannot exist without curiosity' ('nempè in
virtutibus moralibus mediocritas sine Curiositate non sit', Watson/Rose 1690, 777).

[54] Kromayer/Scherzer/Rechenberg 1675, E2ʳ.

[55] 'ex vero virtutis amore hunc affectum compesces' (Bierling/Pestel 1740, 49).
There are still occasional, vestigial references here to *curiositas* as a vice (27, 44). For
another example, see Stolle/Schlosser 1724.

[56] Alexander Gottlieb Baumgarten's definition of 'curiositas' as an 'instinctus ad
cognoscendum, quae nondum cognovimus' ('an instinct to learn what we do not yet
know') is quoted with approval by Succov/Haag (1744, 2).

[57] 'desiderium sciendi' (Rinder/Lasius 1699, A[1]ᵛ). This Cartesian dissertation
thus echoes Descartes: 'la curiosité, qui n'est autre chose qu'un désir de connaître'
(1990, art. 88).

though by the mid-eighteenth century the tie binding desire to passion could also be loosened: one dissertation raises the possibility of
divine, passion-free desire by arguing that 'desire is even attributed
to God'.[58] While this possibility remained largely unexplored, many
of these dissertations did claim that the passion of curiosity was a
desire absolutely fundamental to normal processes of cognition. This
claim would have appeared misguided and dangerous to preceding
generations. It was one manifestation of the more general tendency
in late seventeenth-century philosophy to try and find a single
starting-point for all the passions: whereas for Spinoza that starting-
point was striving or *conatus*, in Cartesian and other strands of
thought it was desire, which became '*the* antecedent to action, the
driving force which shapes our responses and colours all our other
emotions', displacing from this role the previously dominant
Thomist duo of desire and aversion.[59] Whereas in the German
university world *curiositas* was still often understood as proceeding,
like all passions, from that Thomist duo,[60] nonetheless it was
increasingly seen as proceeding from this newly unified desire or
desiderium.[61]

One dissertation even presents curiosity not as a mere species of
desire, but as *the* other key passion besides desire: 'Curiosity urges
the soul to consent to the actions and objects which seem capable of
serving the preservation of the body; and it usually differs from other
affects, since it is only through desire [*cupiditas*] and curiosity that
we can be spurred to excellent actions.'[62] Here curiosity is fundamental not only to cognition, but to our very existence. It is not just
a desire for knowledge but a care—in the sense of its etymon, *cura*—
that we take in order to ensure our bodily survival. It is shared by animals too, for example by eagles and lions when they close their talons
when walking, lest contact with the ground blunt them or else leave
traces by which they can be hunted down (Watson/Rose 1690, 763).
The novelty of this argument can be gauged by the extent to which its
author is here reversing the meaning of an image used in the treatise

---

[58] 'quod [desiderium] *ipsi DEO tribuitur*' (Succov/Haag 1744, 9).

[59] James 1997, 145–56, 265–71 (269).

[60] Stolle/Schlosser 1724, 8; C. Thomasius 1706, 121.

[61] e.g. Succov/Haag 1744, 6.

[62] 'Curiositas itaque incitat animam, ut consentiat actionibus et Objectis quae
inservire posse videntur conservando corpori; Et in eo à reliquis affectibus ferè differt;
quod nullus detur, qui *nos ad actiones* re ipsa praestandas, *excitare* queat, nisi *per
Cupiditatem et Curiositatem*.' (Watson/Rose 1690, 757).

on curiosity by Plutarch, for whom this closing of talons teaches us that we should *restrain* our curiosity.[63] It remained unusual to attribute curiosity to animals: Montesquieu would do so in the following century, but even Thomas Hobbes—who judged curiosity central to cognition—denied it to animals.[64]

The new centrality of curiosity often rested, in these dissertations, on its ability to team up with several other passions, not only desire (*cupiditas* or *desiderium*) but also most typically pleasure (*voluptas*) and ambition (*ambitio*), as well as others such as love (*amor*), hate (*odium*), sorrow (*tristitia*), or greed (*avaritia*).[65] The scope of *curiositas* could be broadened so much that one writer, who used the Thomist distinction between concupiscible and irascible passions, implied, more unconventionally, that *curiositas* can be not only concupiscible, as is to be expected, but also irascible.[66] His reason is even more unusual: *curiositas* can be directed at future, remote objects and indeed, for that matter, at past ones, as well as at present, more accessible ones: 'there seems no doubt that curiosity is *preoccupied with the whole of time*'.[67] This remarkable claim goes well beyond more commonplace understandings of the passions as oriented towards future action, including Descartes's influential limitation of the scope of *désir* to a concern with the future.[68] For Christian Thomasius, *curiositas* is directed at the future and present, in contrast to wonder, *admiratio*, which is stuck in the present (1706, 121).

Indeed, curiosity was often displacing wonder in these German universities, as in some late seventeenth- and early eighteenth-

---

[63] Plutarch 1971, 66ᵛ. In Plutarch the image already has a slight ambivalence rather than being entirely negative: the talons—interpreted as *polypragmosyne* (*curiositas* in the Latin translations)—should be saved for when they really are needed. This ambivalence had been brought out even more in the imitation of the Plutarch passage by the moralist Jean de L'Espine (1588, 486).

[64] James 1997, 189. Montesquieu criticized Hobbes for this (1964, 1142).

[65] e.g. Stolle/Schlosser 1724, 9, 13, 26–8; Watson/Rose 1690, 760–1. For an influential definition (quoted by Stolle/Schlosser 1724, 6) of *curiositas* as a species of *voluptas*, see Buddeus 1719a, 214, 216–17.

[66] Watson/Rose 1690, 761. On the concupiscible and irascible appetites, see James 1997, 56–9. I am grateful to Sue James for making helpful suggestions to me about the Watson/Rose dissertation.

[67] 'extra dubium esse apparet, *circa omne tempus* eam [*sc.* curiositatem] *occupatam esse*' (Watson/Rose 1690, 758).

[68] Descartes 1990, art. 86. Some dissertations restrict the scope of *curiositas* or *polypragmosyne* to a concern with the future by making them a species of hope (respectively Bierling/Pestel 1740, 6; [Brunnemann]/Henel 1691, A3ʳ).

century philosophy.[69] Whereas *admiratio* had long been considered in the Aristotelian tradition to be the beginning of all philosophy, some university texts now attributed that role to curiosity.[70] They criticized Descartes for making wonder the first of the passions. Thomasius attacked Descartes for omitting *curiosité* from his list of six primordial passions, a criticism echoed by a medical dissertation at Halle, where Thomasius was teaching.[71] Descartes had only included curiosity—fleetingly—as one of the numerous species of *désir* (1990, art. 88), a strategy sometimes adopted in German dissertations too (Stolle/Schlosser 1724, 7).

Some of these Protestant university texts were deflecting accusations of superficiality from curiosity onto wonder, which they described as a soft option that does not commit one to investigating truth in the way that curiosity does, or at least should (Thomasius 1706, 120). Various strands may have fed into this suspicion of wonder: a Lutheran association of it with Catholic superstition;[72] Francis Bacon's qualms about it;[73] and a pre-Enlightenment version of the centuries-old Aristotelian tradition in which philosophy makes wonders cease, as opposed to the Augustinian tradition which privileged reverential wonder over arrogant curiosity.[74] For Thomasius, *admiratio* is the daughter of ignorance and is directed at *admiranda*, that is, at natural or praeternatural effects which are rare and irregular and yet which *admiratio* can mistake for supernatural ones—so-called miracles. He reduces the role of *admiratio* by arguing that it sometimes but not always occasions *curiositas* and that *curiositas* does not necessarily originate in it; *admiratio* does not always entail desire for knowledge, whereas *curiositas* does. Later followers of Thomasius persisted with this emphasis on *curiositas*, making it for example 'the affect that accompanies all principal affects'.[75] They resisted Cartesian attempts to replace good *curiosité*

---

[69] Daston and Park 1998, 316–28. On the relations between curiosity and wonder, see also ibid. 120–6, 303–15; James 1997, 188–91.

[70] Bierling/Pestel 1740, 10; C. Thomasius 1706, 119–21.

[71] Henrici/Frantz 1709, 2. See Descartes 1990, part 2.

[72] See Daxelmüller 1979, 158–72; Hsia 1989, 151–3.

[73] Daston and Park 1998, 228–9; James 1997, 188. These German dissertations were full of references to Bacon.

[74] See Daston and Park 1998, 39–41 and ch. 3.

[75] 'Est itaque curiositas affectus concomitans omnes affectus principales.' (Henrici/Frantz 1709, 2, quoting, without acknowledgement, from C. Thomasius 1706, 121).

in cognitive processes with something rather more steady and reliable—*attention*.[76] They seem to have continued to designate an enormous spectrum of knowledge-acquisition as curiosity not because they thought it was always good but precisely because it could be good or bad and so was uniquely placed to regulate the relation between good and bad knowledge, unlike *attention*—which was always good—or even *admiratio*, the history of which was certainly ambivalent but was not characterized by strong distinctions between *bona* and *mala* species of it, as was that of *curiositas*.

How could someone turn their bad curiosity into the good kind or else into something good that was not called curiosity? Some thought this could be achieved by training either one's reason, will, or body, depending on where curiosity was primarily situated.[77] Some thought it could be achieved by moderating this passion, in traditional Aristotelian fashion (Watson/Rose 1690, 790). But what was the difference between good and bad curiosity anyway?

1.2.2 *Genus and species*

There were two main ways of dividing up curiosity.

First, the unusual way was to divide it up into different meanings. According to this approach, the polysemic 'curiosity' family of terms denoted a range of different things which, however, were unrelated to each other, merely happening to share the same homonyms. This approach lent itself to particularly innovative versions of curiosity, since it enabled their authors to avoid having to connect them to more established versions. For example, the Helmstedt Cartesian for whom *curiositas* was wholly good found the negative 'meaning' ('significatus') given to *curiositas* by both Becmann and Francis Bacon 'narrower and, in a way, foreign to my theme'.[78] Or else the divisions between the meanings of *curiositas* correponded to those

---

[76] For the Cartesian Jean-Pierre de Crousaz (1720, 247) *admiration* (good or bad) leads either to *curiosité* (bad) or to *attention* (good). He was criticized by Bierling/Pestel (1740, 5) for making *admiration* the sole occasion of *curiosité*. On anxiety about the lightweight mobility of curiosity, see James 1997, 190.

[77] For the intellect, see Becmann 1679, 67–9. For the will, Stolle/Schlosser 1724, 7–8; C. Thomasius 1706, 120. For the body, see Lessius 1605, 723, whose argument that some *curiositas* is sense-based is taken up by Stryk/Lüedecke (1743, 309).

[78] 'Angustior itaque quodammodo ac alienus à meo proposito . . .' (Rinder/Lasius 1699, A[1]ᵛ).

between disciplines: '*Curiositas* does not have the same sense in law
as in the writings of philosophers; the same goes for *curiosus*'.[79]

The second, more dominant approach was to divide up curiosity
into different species, which were subdivisions of the same overall
genus. This approach involved tacit, informal realist claims: species,
unlike meanings, all necessarily belong to the same thing. It had been
common since antiquity to use the genus/species terminology—
derived from natural philosophy—as a way of dividing up moral or
psychological entities. The most extravagant instance in the history
of *curiositas* had been St Anselm's definition of it as a vice with forty-
four 'genera'.[80]

The widespread university understanding of curiosity as a genus
that is divided into multiple species created the conditions whereby
curiosity could be constantly reshaped while remaining, in the eyes
of contemporaries, recognizably the same thing. In each disputation
or oration, speakers were able to tinker with existing versions of the
genus by adding a species here, deleting one there, or else by changing the genus into one species of a new overall genus. Most new
versions were presented as if they were definitive, but occasionally it
was acknowledged that they were provisional, at least in their detail.
One writer on *periergia* explains that he will discuss both its licit and
illicit species, 'not because, when one species of a divided genus is
explained and known, we immediately know accurately the nature
of the opposite species, but rather because once it is known, we
understand that other things which are included under that genus
belong to its various species.'[81] The existence of the thing or genus
called curiosity is clear, as is its rough overall shape, whereas the
detail of its species is subject to elaboration and contestation. That
contestation was fostered institutionally, not only through disputation but also through print: previous disputations and orations on
the same topic remained well-known for many years after the oral
event because they were printed (at the respondent's expense, in the
case of dissertations). The printed versions found their way outside

[79] 'Sumitur quidem Curiositas non unâ eadem significatione tam in Jure, quam in
scriptis Philosophorum, sicut et verbum curiosus' (Cocceji/Lettow 1710, 6).
[80] See Defaux 1982, 81; Peters 1985, 91.
[81] 'non quidem ita, quod explicata et cognitâ unâ specie generis divisi, statim accurate cognoscamus naturam speciei oppositae, sed quod illâ cognitâ, intelligamus,
caetera, quae sub genere comprehensa sunt, ad species pertinere' (Fichtner/
Puchelberger 1725, 4).

their home institution to many other German universities and, occasionally, to other countries.[82] The methods of dissemination were various: respondents distributed them in the manner of modern offprints; they were actively collected by many professors; those professors' libraries were subsequently dispersed at auctions; and university libraries probably had reciprocal arrangements for supplying each other with their institutions' printed material.[83]

Dissertations and orations on curiosity contained many references back to their predecessors, showing how they were modifying or rejecting those earlier versions of curiosity. These references are indicated in Figure 2.[84] Their intricate web shows how curiosity spread from one institution to another, changing as it went, yet with professors and students from different universities, faculties, and decades nonetheless considering themselves to be all discussing more or less the same thing. Almost all of these references—thirteen out of seventeen—were to disputations and orations on curiosity that had been held in other universities, not in one's own. And most of these cross-institutional references—nine out of thirteen—involved the Brandenburg-Prussian and Saxon universities Frankfurt a.d. Oder, Leipzig, and Jena, suggesting that there were particularly strong discursive ties between them. Most references—ten out of seventeen—were made to discussions of curiosity emanating from disciplines other than one's own: thus, the circumscribed innovation demanded of a respondent could be demonstrated by describing how a thing familiar in one discipline also operated in another, in which it was unfamiliar.

Some dissertations added to or deleted species that they found in previous dissertations. For example, the *curiositas juridica* studied throughout the Stryk law dissertation is presented there as an additional new 'species' of curiosity, of which others, such as 'Curiositas Theologica', have been treated elsewhere, including in

---

[82] On the provenance of those in the Bodleian Library, see Evans 1981, 174–81.

[83] I am grateful to Howard Hotson and Paul Nelles for these suggestions.

[84] The dates used to plot Fig. 1.2 are those of first publication. Continuous lines mean that the later writer seems to have had first-hand knowledge of the text referred to; broken lines mean that there is a direct reference to the earlier text but that the later writer's knowledge of it seems to have been second-hand. In addition, 10 seems to have borrowed from 4 and 8 without acknowledgement. The 1740 entry for 'Neugierigkeit, Curiosität' in Zedler's *Universal-Lexicon* is also included.

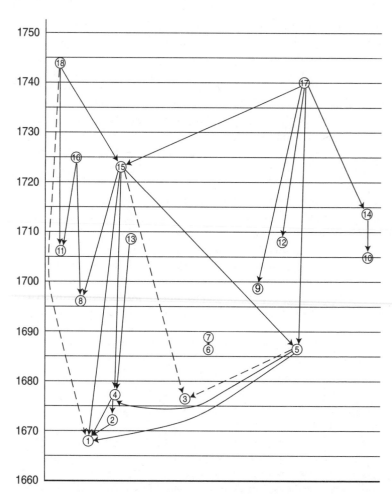

FIGURE 1.2. Cross-references between dissertations and orations. Texts are as follows: 1 = Kromayer/Rechenberg 1675; 2 = Scherzer/Rechenberg 1675; 3 = Seger 1676; 4 = Stryk/Lüedecke 1743; 5 = Westphal/Pipping 1708; 6 = Brückner/Brandis 1687; 7 = Brückner/Schultz 1688; 8 = Cocceji/Lettow 1710; 9 = Rinder/Lasius 1699; 10 = Scherzer/Saltzmann 1705; 11 = Streit/Kalckhoff 1706; 12 = Joch/Seyfart 1708; 13 = Krause 1709; 14 = Silberrad/Christannus 1714; 15 = Stolle/Schlosser 1724; 16 = Olearius/Schlegel 1725; 17 = Zedler 1961–4; 18 = Succov/Haag 1744.

dissertations.[85] On the other hand, Stryk deletes the species of 'Curiositas' studied by moralists, since it is inherently vicious and so cannot belong to his genus of curiosity, which is always morally ambivalent (291).

Another option was to take what previous writers had defined as a whole genus of curiosity and then turn it into a mere species of an enlarged genus. This strategy enabled existing, wholly negative versions of curiosity to be incorporated into newly ambivalent ones rather than being rejected or accepted wholesale. For example, one philosophy dissertation incorporated in this way the negative verdicts on *curiositas* given by Bacon, Becmann, and others. These earlier writers 'seem to have discussed not the general notion of curiosity, but rather the special, bad application of this affect to things which are contrary to our fixed purpose, selecting what is bad, not saying what is good in that thing'.[86] They had treated one of the species of curiosity as if it were the entire genus; they had mistaken part of the picture for the whole.

Thus were spawned numerous elaborate typologies of curiosity, which used other, existing typologies as building blocks. Almost all provided ways of distinguishing bad from good curiosity, but there was a tension between two models for doing so. One model involved a simple bipartite structure: good species of curiosity were listed, followed by bad, or vice versa.[87] In the second model, various rubrics of knowledge or action were listed; under each rubric, both a good and a bad species of curiosity were described. This second model suggested that good and bad curiosity, far from being separated by some reassuring contextual gulf, coexisted in many contexts, where they were separated only by a hair's breadth.

In practice, these two models often overlapped. In other words, there was some uncertainty as to whether bad curiosity was confined only to certain kinds of knowledge and action or else whether it could crop up in any. Many dissertations hesitated between these two possibilities: they judged that, while bad curiosity tended to occur especially in certain contexts, it could occur in any context. Certainly, they tried to suppress such hesitations by creating an

[85] Stryk/Lüedecke 1743, 290. Rechenberg's 2 theological dissertations are referred to (296).

[86] 'non de curiositatis notione generali, sed de mala affectus huius ad res fini nobis praestituto contrarias applicatione speciatim disseruisse, et excerpsisse quod malum est, quod vero bonum est in eadem re, non dixisse videntur.' (Bierling/Pestel 1740, 8).

[87] e.g. Watson/Rose 1690.

impression of certainty through the neat academic typologies that were a hallmark of the dissertation genre. Yet cracks in the typologies betrayed hesitations. For example, a Leipzig philosophy dissertation, which became quite well-known, mainly applied the second model to 'the curious devotion to novelty' (for which it frequently used 'curiositas' as a rough synonym).[88] The dissertation sketched a 'general economy' of *curiositas*, dividing it into 'genera' (12) which corresponded to the scholastic disciplines (Figure 1.3), each of which was further subdivided into a licit and an illicit genus.[89] The authors list scores of examples of innovations in grammar, rhetoric, logic, and so on; these are presented as the species of those 'genera'.[90] However, it is often unclear which is supposed to be licit and which illicit. Moreover, the genus of what is labelled 'common' *curiositas*— common people's appetite for hearing news and inventing gossip— should in principle include a licit sub-genus but in practice does not (39). Elaborate typologies had loopholes which would have provided *opponentes* and others with opportunities for contestation.

These typologies and their areas of uncertainty enabled bridges to be built not only between new and old versions of *curiositas* but also between *curiositas* and its Greek near-synonyms, *polypragmosyne* and *periergia*. For example, the Brunnemann law dissertation on *polypragmosyne* divides it into four 'genera' (also called 'specie[s]'):[91] first, straying from one's discipline or vocation (*polymatheia*); secondly, investigating the lives of others; thirdly, *periergia*—acting in matters which do not directly concern us; fourthly, assuming a function which is not ordinarily ours. Unusually for *polypragmosyne*, these genera are not necessarily bad, but can also be good. Although *polypragmosyne* is the designated name of this thing and officially has no Latin synonym (A2^r), in fact the *curiositas* family of terms (noun, adjective, adverb) is used as a substitute for it with increasing frequency in the dissertation,[92] even

---

[88] Westphal/Pipping 1708: 'curiosum novitatis studium'. As well as being reprinted, the dissertation got a positive mention in a 1703 number of the Leipzig periodical *Unschuldige Nachrichten* (1707, 586); also, it was referred to by a 1724 Jena dissertation and by Zedler's *Universal-Lexicon*. On Pipping, see Erler 1909, ii. 334.

[89] 'generalis οἰκονομίαῶ (11). The diagram has been deduced from the prose of the dissertation (10–11).

[90] 'we will now proceed to deduce its species, that is, to list examples' ('transimus jam ad specialem ejus deductionem, h.e. ad recensionem Exemplorum', 11–12).

[91] [Brunnemann]/Henel 1691, A3^r, E2^r.

[92] e.g. A3^r, B1^v, B2^v, B4^r, B4^v, C2^v, D2^r.

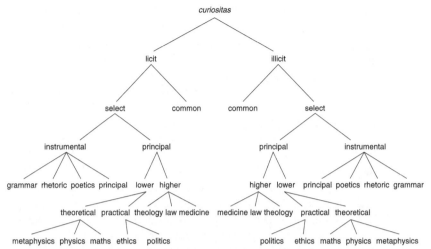

FIGURE I.3. *Curiositas* schema deduced from Westphal (*praeses*)/Pipping (*resp.*), *De curioso novitatis studio* (first printed 1687). For reasons of space, the right-hand side (below 'illicit') has been reversed.

becoming more prominent than the main Greek term except at points of transition between the genera. *Curiositas* was here absorbing some of the meanings of *polypragmosyne*, designating certain actions, whether or not they involved the acquisition of knowledge. This semantic contamination fed back into subsequent definitions of *curiositas*, making it involve doing as well as desiring (1.3.4 below).

The most important of all the distinctions made in these apparently definitive but ultimately fragile typologies was that between good and bad curiosity. But where exactly did the difference reside? In the desiring human subject? Or else in the actual objects desired?

1.2.3   *Subject and object*

The question of the relation of passions to objects was complex and vexed in early modern philosophy.[93] In most of these university discussions, curiosity consisted of a desiring subject and of desired objects (or knowledge of objects). In action-oriented definitions,

[93] See James 1997, esp. 103, 105, 107, 108, 110, 113–15, 173–4, 179, 186–7; James 1998*b*, 945 n.

curiosity consisted of an agent and of acts. There was fierce debate as to whether the goodness or badness of curiosity inhered in the subjects/agents or in the objects/acts. In fact, another explanation came to predominate: whether curiosity was good or bad was determined by the relationship of the subject/agent to the object/act. The most decisive issue became the appropriateness or inappropriateness of a particular person trying to know or do a particular thing. People could be either rightly or wrongly 'curious' depending on who they were and on what they were trying to know; certain objects of knowledge could be either licit or illicit depending on who was trying to know them. Obsessed with decreeing who can know or do what, the authors of these dissertations and orations were trying to contribute to the social regulation of knowledge and behaviour. This is perhaps one reason for their drive to maintain curiosity as a unified thing encapsulating an enormous range of human life: the single generic label strongly suggested that the desires or objects remained inherently the same, that their goodness or badness was perspectival, context-based, or, in scholastic terms, accidental not substantial,[94] or, in grammatical terms, adjectival not substantival: *mala curiositas* was opposed to *bona curiositas* rather than *curiositas* being opposed to *studiositas*.

Although this emphasis on the relationship between subject and object came to predominate, it was not the only possible way of judging curiosity. A minority of university writers considered its badness or goodness to inhere exclusively or primarily in the human subject: 'Morality is only relevant to decisions made by a free being insofar as they depend on his/her freedom. The objects which I mentioned in a previous section as being sometimes called curiosities cannot be classified among these.'[95] So, while one medical dissertation which presented *curiositas* as a knowledge-corrupting passion did also describe the resulting havoc—pernicious Paracelsianism, Epicureanism, and mechanical philosophy—nonethless these were

[94] 'For that goodness and badness, due to which curiosity is either allowed or forbidden in our laws, is only added to it *per accidens*' ('Illa enim bonitas et malitia, ob quam Curiositas in Jure nostro vel praecipitur vel prohibetur, per accidens eidem accedit', Stryk/Lüedecke 1743, 291). See also Kromayer/Scherzer/Rechenberg 1675, [C4ᵛ].
[95] 'Moralitas autem non competit nisi determinationibus entis liberi, quatenus a libertate pendent: quas inter referri nequeunt, quae §. cit. curiositates interdum vocari diximus, obiecta.' (Succov/Haag 1744, 5). The writer is arguing that *curiositas* should simply be defined as the desire to know, not as the desire to know this or that object.

its effects, not its cause (Henrici/Frantz, 1709). This approach was a secularized application of the Augustinian tradition which tended to see *curiositas* as primarily rooted in the human subject's turn away from God, however much it also characteristically involved certain pernicious objects of knowledge.[96] The even more unusual view that *curiositas* is wholly good was the only other one from which it was possible to argue that this goodness inheres primarily in the subject, while also having a characteristic object, in this case truth (Rinder/Lasius, 1699).

Also in a minority were those who saw the goodness or badness of curiosity as determined primarily by its objects. Here, concern for the moral well-being of the human subject got lost from view: the main purpose—attractive to universities—was to legitimize or outlaw certain fields of knowledge. For one medical professor, the defining characteristic of 'love of curiosity' ('Curiositatis amor'), that he understood as good, was its choice of apparently new rather than really new objects: 'it is directed not at phenomena which are new—at least in the estimation of the ignorant, inexperienced, and youthful—but at those things which . . . *seem* new, not so much because of the novelty of the thing as because of our ignorance of it'.[97]

Even for those who did not think that the goodness or badness of curiosity inhered primarily in its objects, there was still a great temptation to judge that goodness or badness by those objects alone, or at least to illustrate it mainly through them. Designating some knowledge as wicked or useless seems to have been easier than persuasively identifying as vicious the hidden motives of those who pursued it. Even Rechenberg, although he sets up a sophisticated framework for discussing far more than just objects, processing *curiositas* through the sausage-machine of Leipzig scholasticism, discussing for example not just the definition and genus of unhealthy *curiositas* in theology but also its difference (subdivided into subjects, causes, adjuncts), nonetheless ends up devoting to objects the lion's share of both his dissertations.[98] And yet he presents those objects of

---

[96] See Blumenberg 1988, 110. For varying medieval verdicts on the relative importance of subject and object in *curiositas*, see ibid. 128–9; Defaux 1982, 76; Newhauser 1982, 574–5; Oberman 1974, 29.

[97] 'non versatur circa nova φαινομυνῶσ saltim talia, prout ignaris, inexpertis, puerisque omnia, etiam quae . . . tamen nova videntur, non tàm ob novitatem rei, quàm ob ignorantiam' (Krause 1709,)(2ᵛ). See also Seger 1676.

[98] Kromayer/Scherzer/Rechenberg 1675, B[1]ᵛ–[C4ᵛ], G[1]ᵛ–[M3ᵛ].

knowledge as being merely the material cause of *insana* ('unhealthy') *curiositas*, that is, as just one subdivision of cause, which in turn is just one subdivision of difference. In the case of *sana* ('healthy') *curiositas*, although objects account for just one third of Rechenberg's scholastic grid for analysing it—since its subjects and actions account for the other two—they actually occupy over two-thirds of the dissertation.[99] The detailed discussion of *what* theological *curiosi* want to know has swollen out of proportion with its allotted role within the overall analytical framework.

Whether one's distinctions between good and bad curiosity hinged wholly or partly on deciding that certain objects (or acts) were licit or illicit, this rhetorical task was greatly facilitated by the object-oriented senses of the 'curiosity' family of terms, for these university texts tended to reserve those senses for bad objects, while avoiding the 'curiosity' family when denoting good objects. Stahl and his student, who had almost nothing good to say about *curiositas*, decried the medical study of 'curious phenomena that are devoid of actual practical use'.[100] These object-oriented senses of the *curiositas* family usually had similar pejorative force in these dissertations and orations. On the whole they denoted the kinds of knowledge—singular, rare, exotic, wondrous, useless, novel for novelty's sake—from which these universities were most anxious to distance themselves.[101] Academics for whom *curiositas* could be either good or bad usually reserved object-oriented senses for the bad kind,[102] except when they denoted the objects of new 'experimental' philosophy. The Schrader who ran a 'collegium curiosum experimentale' at Helmstedt echoed this positive sense in his oration on *curiositas*[103] but otherwise reserved object-oriented senses for pernicious, sensational medical *curiosa* (A2ᵛ, B3ʳ), which the physician should forsake for simple, clear, useful objects.

[99] 36 out of 52 pages.
[100] 'curiosa phaenomena usu reali & pragmatico destituta' (Stahl/Donzelina 1714, 37; see also pp. 51, 53, 59, 60 for further examples).
[101] See 3.3 below. Daxelmüller (1979, 117–25) similarly identifies 2 semantic strands in *curiositas*—one being Blumenbergian 'theoretische Neugierde' ('speculative curiosity'), aimed at truth, and the other being preoccupation with the macabre and sensational—but he does not make the point that the latter often emerged especially in the object-oriented senses.
[102] e.g. Seger 1676, 11; Stryk/Lüedecke 1743, 290.
[103] 'I love and value the curious, experimental investigations of more recent men' ('curiosas experimentales recentiorum inquisitiones amo et aestimo', Schrader 1701, A2ᵛ).

Whereas in the contemporary culture of curiosities the object-oriented senses of this family of terms seemed a gratifying mirror of its subject-oriented ones, promising that curiosity could be sated by 'curiosities', in universities such semantic symmetry had troubling implications and was often avoided, perhaps out of anxiety that the object-oriented senses would drag respectable curiosity into superficial pleasures.[104] Some university discussions of curiosity avoided its object-oriented senses altogether,[105] thereby maintaining conceptual hygiene by going against the grain of much contemporary usage. The *praeses* of one disputation remarks wryly that, while the candidate has sought to seduce readers by using the term *curiositas* in his title, in fact he has 'not dared promise new and curious discoveries'; all will be fine 'so long as it is possible to speak of curiosity without mentioning curious things'.[106] Similarly, the writer of the Helmstedt Cartesian dissertation had no wish to sully the reputation of his morally and epistemologically pure *curiositas* by giving it sensational *curiosa* as objects, rather than clear, self-evident truths (Rinder/Lasius 1699). For anyone hoping nonetheless to salvage the subject/object symmetry of the 'curiosity' family, making it correspond to a real cognitive symmetry between subjects and objects, the only way to safeguard against unwanted meanings was to resort to neologism, describing the simple and common object of healthy *curiositas* not as *curiosum*, which would imply it was difficult and rare, but as 'sanè-curiosum' ('healthily curious').[107]

Although most university teachers and students did not call the objects of curiosity 'curious', most did consider that the epistemological and social goodness or badness of curiosity was determined primarily by the relation between those subjects and objects, rather than by the subjects or objects in themselves. Decorum and context were all. Writers repeatedly guarded against things which, given our profession (*professio*) or vocation (*vocatio*) in life, it is not fitting (*non oportet*) for us to investigate or do, and which are foreign to us (*aliena*) and do not concern us (*nos non attinent, ad nos non*

---

[104] For university criticism (by Buddeus) of this semantic symmetry as a fantasy projection onto objects by the desiring subject, see N. Kenny 1998, 15.

[105] e.g. Krause 1709; Streit/Kalckhoff 1706; Watson/Rose 1690.

[106] 'Quamvis *Tu* novas curiosasque rerum inventiones promittere non ausis; dummodo de curiositate sine rerum curiosarum mentione dici aliquid possit' (Silberrad/Christann 1714, [3]).

[107] Kromayer/Scherzer/Rechenberg 1675, [F4^v], G[1]^v.

pertinent) (1.3.4 below).[108] This was the prime sense of the Greek terms *polypragmosyne* and *periergia*. The *locus classicus* for their treatment was Plutarch's treatise on *polypragmosyne*, always translated as *De curiositate*.[109] Plutarch's *polypragmosyne* involved prying into the lives of others, especially their secrets and vices. It was almost entirely reprehensible. Remarkably, however, in some early modern German universities, some *polypragmosyne* was legitimized. Meddling in areas which did not directly concern one—including the vices of others—was sometimes deemed not only permissible but even a duty. Just as *curiositas*, previously having been mainly pejorative, had mostly become ambivalent in these university texts, so too *polypragmosyne* sometimes now denoted both the good and the bad species of this meddling ([Brunnemann]/Henel 1691). And this newly ambivalent meddling sense in turn fed back into *curiositas*, where it joined that term's other ambivalent senses (Stryk/Lüedecke 1743). There was even an explicit perception that this was a peculiarly contemporary understanding of curiosity: 'I won't go wrong if, adapting *curiositas* to the ways of today, along with Plautus . . . and Horace I call it "preoccupation with other people's business".'[110]

This relational—rather than subject- or object-centred—understanding of curiosity sat uneasily alongside apparently egalitarian protestations that it is a passion common to 'every human age, sex, and condition'.[111] It was almost always thought that the actual workings of that passion should be judged according to social, political, and sexual decorum. While the notion of decorum was one of the most deeply ingrained regulators of behaviour in early modern society, universities were now using it to reshape curiosity in new ways. This decorum-based curiosity—whether *polypragmosyne*, *periergia*, or *curiositas*—was applied to two main contexts: first, to the university world itself, notably to the relations between the disciplines (should we stray beyond our own?); secondly, to the everyday social world outside the university (should we always mind our own

---

[108] Cf. St Augustine, *De utilitate credendi*, 9.22: 'curiosus tamen ea requirit quae nihil ad se adtinent'.

[109] See Defaux 1982, 143–9.

[110] 'Non aberravero, si *Curiositatem* ad hodiernos mores accommodatam, *cum Plauto . . . & Horatio* appellavero *studium rerum alienarum*' (Stahl/Donzelina 1714, 9).

[111] '*Curiositas . . . omni hominum aetati, sexui et statui inest*' (Watson/Rose 1690, 758).

business?) Universities were seizing the long history of curiosity, refurbishing it, and diverting it towards new uses.

1.3 'ADAPTED TO THE WAYS OF TODAY':[112] USING CURIOSITY

1.3.1 *Legitimizing the institution*

Dissertations and orations on curiosity were performative as well as constative: by defining curiosity, universities were trying to use it, for a wide range of purposes. One of those purposes was to legitimize the universities themselves, to justify, protect, and glorify the knowledge which they transmitted while also vilifying other kinds.

Prestige was something that these universities sorely needed.[113] They were in intense competition with one another for students and for the best teachers. Following the founding of new universities by territorial rulers who were anxious to accumulate both cultural capital and, in some cases, a training ground for their burgeoning bureaucracies, there were now barely enough students to go round. According to Charles McLelland, whereas on the eve of the Thirty Years' War 20 universities had shared nearly 8,000 students, by about 1700 there were 28 German universities (excluding Austria) sharing about 9,000 students, which represents a drop in average from 400 to less than 290. And the situation got worse thereafter.[114] In order to maintain prestige—thereby continuing to win the electoral, ducal, or municipal patronage upon which they depended—and also in order to attract students from as far away as possible, universities needed to demonstrate both their local utility and yet also, if possible, their significance in supra-regional, even international debates.[115]

---

[112] See n. 110 above.

[113] This account of the situation of German Lutheran universities draws on: Clark 1992, 90–2; Hammerstein 1981; McClelland 1980, 27–33; Hsia 1989, 116–21; Ridder-Symoens (ed.) 1996, 140–2.

[114] McClelland 1980, 28. Clark (1992, 91) counts all the universities in the Holy Roman Empire of German Nations as numbering about 36 in 1700 (16 of them Catholic), as opposed to 16 in 1500. See also Evans 1981, 169–70, 173.

[115] On the increasing regionalization of universities in the confessional age, see Hsia 1989, 116–21.

These collective interests meshed with more personal ones. Teachers and students constantly needed to glorify and justify their activity, since it was not always clear to the outside world that it was glorious or justifiable: although most students were drawn from what can loosely be called the bourgeoisie, they tended to be itinerant, somewhat rootless potential servants of the bureaucratic state, rather than representing local bourgeois interests.[116] Moreover, the development of new bureaucracies now made university training an alternative path to social elevation if one lacked noble credentials.[117] For teachers, an academic career was not easily won and, in extreme cases, it could even be an escape from poverty. Gottlieb Stolle, years before presiding as a well-known Jena politics professor over a dissertation on curiosity, had allegedly spent his late twenties living off bread as a student at Halle (Jöcher 1750–1).

Legitimation was sought in many ways. One way was through the prominent rituals of academic life,[118] whether the 'solemn' disputations for degree promotions—with their special carpets, flowers, and academic dress—or else the distribution of printed orations and dissertations as invitations not just to professors but also to the local great and good (Horn 1893, 87–8). Individual students, especially those who wanted an academic career, sought status in various ways: by getting friends and teachers to contribute congratulatory poems to their printed dissertation, by having it printed more than once (preferably with a claim that one was the author), or by drawing attention to any mention of it that had been made in the local press.[119]

This collective and personal legitimation was also sought through the *themes* of orations and disputations. Potentially reflexive themes such as curiosity were particularly effective, because they enabled speakers to praise university learning and to distance themselves from its opposite. Hence the attraction of curiosity, in universities large (Leipzig, Jena), medium (Frankfurt a.d. Oder), and small (Altdorf, Rinteln).[120] When the University of Erlangen opened,

---

[116] See McClelland 1980, 31–2.

[117] See Dahm 1972, 286.

[118] For a similar point, see Hammerstein 1981, 252. Cf. Clark's view of disputations as forensic theatre (1992, 93).

[119] All of this, and more, was done by Heinrich Pipping: see Westphal/Pipping 1708, [):(2ᵛ], 51–2. Of those students involved in dissertations on curiosity, Rechenberg too had his reprinted under his name.

[120] On the size of Lutheran universities, see Hammerstein 1981, 257–60.

among the very first philosophy disputations, setting out the new
institution's stall, was one on the morality of curiosity.[121] Orations,
largely epideictic, had an even more overt legitimizing function: 'On
*praise*worthy curiosity in medicine' is the title of one.[122]

The glory of this reflexive curiosity was sometimes tactfully
directed less at the institution than at its patrons: curiosity was
used to try and secure funding. When Georg Seger gave his 1675 inaugural as professor of physics and medicine at the Danzig *Gymnasium
academicum* (halfway between a *Gymnasium* and a university),
having arrived in the Polish city from Thuringia two years earlier, he
chose good 'curiosity about nature' (*curiositas physica*) as his theme.
Conflating intellectual with social pre-eminence, he argues at length
(13–30) that this *curiositas* has always befitted rulers most of all,
from Adam (monarch of the world) to Charles II (granter of the
Royal Society's charter): 'those with the most power have enjoyed
this curiosity of ours most'.[123] The 'curiosity about nature' of
philosophers is really that of their rulers. Whereas Steven Shapin has
argued that the likes of Robert Boyle took the credit, as gentlemen,
for work done partly by technicians and other servants (1994, ch. 8),
here it is the turn of the philosophers to have their work accredited to
the curiosity of social superiors. Aristotle is mentioned, not in his
own right, but only as someone who was paid by Alexander the
Great to research (22)! Seger ends sagaciously with glowing praise of
the way in which the municipal council of Danzig has sponsored
curiositas and with a plea for them to continue doing so (60–3),
thereby demonstrating their regal status. The councillors were probably there to hear the speech, since they regularly attended such special events (T. Hirsch 1858, 7–8). The quest for status was certainly
important for this institution of about 400 students, which printed
more dissertations than probably any other *Gymnasium* (Horn
1893, 77–80) and yet was now just past its heyday, destined
to decline in the early eighteenth century, failing in that century to
persuade the municipal council to let it seek a university charter
(Goldmann 1967, 82–3).

---

[121] Succov/Haag 1744. The Academia Fridericiana Baruthina, founded in Bayreuth
in 1743, was transferred in the same year to Erlangen.

[122] 'de curiositate in medicina laudanda' (Krause 1709).

[123] 'qui summam in Mundo potestatem habuerunt, Curiositatem quoque nostram
ut plurimum in deliciis habuerunt' (Seger 1676, 13). On Seger, see Jöcher 1750–1.

The legitimizing uses of curiosity sometimes clashed with its other uses. There were numerous reflexive jokes about 'a contagion of curiosity' that spread from topic to speaker,[124] or about speaker and audience directing their curiosity at curiosity.[125] But these were sometimes uneasy, especially when the body of the dissertation demonstrated that curiosity was largely bad.[126] The coherence of definitions was being sacrificed in order to exploit pragmatically the attractive aura that surrounded curiosity in much contemporary culture. Universities were doing the same as playwrights or authors of novellas who condemned curiosity in their plots while also explicitly appealing to their readers' curiosity.

The coherence of definitions was also challenged by uncertainty as to whether curiosity should be pleasurable. Answers varied depending on the uses to which curiosity was put. For the most part, curiosity was deemed to be bad if it involved pleasure (*voluptas*): it was then likely to be useless, impractical, and erroneous. According to one dissertation on the *periergia* of the learned, written in the conservative university of Leipzig, a scholar should not spend his time composing speeches in praise of the devil, donkeys, drunkenness, or baldness (Hilscher/Cramer 1693, B[1]ᵛ). These universities were anxious not to give the impression that they were self-indulgent havens of pleasurable curiosity, useless to society.

However, on the other hand, pleasure *was* sometimes associated with good curiosity if immediate purposes required this. Giving the impression that academic curiosity was devoid of pleasure was not going to attract students to lectures. So Seger, in his inaugural, emphasized that the difficult problems encountered when we are curious about nature give us immense pleasure—*jucunditas* rather than the more frequently pejorative *voluptas* (1676, 33–55)— although the endlessly reiterated condemnations of curiosity might not initially look too pleasurable to modern eyes. In fact respondents tried to make them as pleasurable as possible, since they sought to persuade listeners by entertaining them. Hence the numerous comic anecdotes about the bad curiosity of scholars who had inquired why Homer began the *Iliad* with a *m* but the *Odyssey* with an *a*, whether

---

[124] 'Curiositatis . . . contagio' (Westphal/Pipping 1708, 40).
[125] e.g. Bierling/Pestel 1740, 3; Rinder/Lasius 1699, A[1]ʳ; Seger 1676, 8; Stolle/Schlosser 1724, 3; Watson/Rose 1690, 749.
[126] Bierling/Pestel 1740, 2, 57.

Anchises had a wet-nurse, what the Sirens sang, how many rowers Ulysses had (Hilscher/Cramer 1693, A3ʳ), which foot Aeneas put in Italy first, what were the names of the men inside the Trojan horse.[127]

The distinctions between good and bad knowledge that were maintained by discourse on curiosity ran along institutional lines. One of those lines distinguished the male university world—'this place'—from the world outside.[128] The Leipzig dissertation which divided 'curious devotion to novelty' into 'select' (academic) and 'common' (everyone else) made the former good or bad and the latter entirely bad (Westphal/Pipping 1708, 39). Seger excluded 'rustic wits' from good *curiositas* about nature.[129] According to Stahl and his student, heeding medical advice from women is rash *curiositas* when deciding on a treatment (Stahl/Donzelina 1714, 59).

The lines of demarcation maintained by curiosity were also between faculties. Not surprisingly, the higher faculties were particularly keen to point this out. In the Stryk/Lüedecke law dissertation, good *curiositas* is, roughly speaking, the preserve of the higher faculties and bad *curiositas* the preserve of the lower faculty of philosophy: as the dissertation's survey of species of *curiositas* moves away from philosophy and then on to theology, medicine, and law, suddenly the species become largely good instead of largely bad (1743, 290).

Curiosity was used by professors to try and regulate firmly the relation between all faculties. The question whether interdisciplinary study should be encouraged was a burning one. The need to answer it was one reason why curiosity was so often defined as a transgression from one's proper domain into another, as a matter of context and decorum. Whether an inquiry or action was good or bad depended on its appropriateness to one's professed discipline. Some

---

[127] These last 3 questions are ridiculed both in [Brunnemann]/Henel 1691 (B[1]ʳ) and in Scherzer 1730 (4). For further examples, see Bierling/Pestel 1740, 40; Westphal/Pipping 1708, 15.

[128] Compare the use of curiosity in an Oxford University sermon preached in 1760: 'I have now, as I propos'd, pointed out some of the Evils arising from the Mis-use of Curiosity: And if they shall appear to be well founded, need I infer the Necessity of our being guarded against them? It is but strict Justice to say, that the salutary Rules and Discipline of *this Place* are most admirably calculated for this Purpose: The whole Circle of useful Knowledge which is here taught will afford strong Motives to Men to employ their Curiosity on some worthy Object' (Griffith 1760, 23–4; my italics).

[129] 'rustica ingenia' (Seger 1676, 13).

dissertations wielded *curiositas* (Stahl/Donzelina 1714), *polyprag-mosyne* ([Brunnemann]/Henel 1691), or *periergia* (Fichtner/Puchelberger 1725, A3ʳ–C2ᵛ) as batons with which to regulate the polymathy and polyhistory for which the German academic world was renowned but which, as we shall see, was far from being indiscriminately encouraged.[130] The decorum-based understanding of curiosity was thus transposed from the realm of personal ethics (Plutarch) to that of an institution's structure.

The *polymatheia* of those exceptional few who know many arts, sciences, and doctrines is praised by one dissertation, which presents it as a species of *polypragmosyne* ([Brunnemann]/Henel 1691, A3ᵛ–[A4ʳ]). The dissertation also praises the more usual and modest boundary-transgressions of students who are not spectacular poly-maths but who read either profane texts to help with their theological studies or else philosophical, theological, and medical texts to help with their legal studies. This is licit as long as the extra doctrine does not conflict with the home discipline (A3ᵛ). On occasion, curios-ity could be not the principle of transgression but rather the very practice that was carried across the boundary: Seger's inaugural shows how 'this usefulness of curiosity about nature' extends not only to its home discipline (physics) but 'most fruitfully to each and every faculty',[131] not only to medicine, but even to theology (where it clarifies biblical analogies with the natural world) and law (where it helps decide whether a baby born in the eleventh or twelfth month is legitimate).[132] Thus, in addition to the more widespread designa-tion of, say, 'philosophical curiosity' as a cousin of 'legal curiosity' (species of the same genus), the curiosity that was specific to one dis-cipline could also be transferred to others.

However, not all were so sanguine about such transgressions. In a medical dissertation, interdisciplinary cross-fertilization was con-demned as bad *curiositas*, even in cases where the imported doctrine was good in itself.[133] More usually, however, whenever transfer of doctrine across disciplines was condemned as *polymatheia* or *perier-*

---

[130] The 2 classic treatises on these phenomena were Joannes von Wower, *De poly-mathia tractatio* (Hamburg, 1603; republished 1665 and 1701) and Daniel Georg Morhof, *Polyhistor* (initial version Lübeck, 1688). See Deitz 1995; Grafton 1985; Waquet (ed.) 2000; Zedelmaier 1992, 286–307.

[131] 'haec . . . Curiositatis Physicae utilitas . . . ad omnes omninò Facultates uber-rimè se extendit' (Seger 1676, 55).

[132] Ibid., 55–60, esp. 55, 56–7.

[133] Stahl/Donzelina 1714, on which see 1.3.2 below.

gia, this was because the doctrine was judged both inappropriate *and* bad in itself, whether it was judicial astrology, other divination, or magic.[134]

So cross-faculty polymathic curiosity was certainly not indiscriminately encouraged: after all, the training of students in specific vocational skills—as lawyers, clerics, physicians, and so on—was one of the main purposes of these universities. Yet nor was polymathic curiosity banned. Rather, it was carefully regulated. By contrast, *non*-university polymathic curiosity was condemned much more whole-heartedly. When mechanical rather than liberal arts were considered, then transgression of vocational boundaries was condemned outright, even if the extra skill being imported was not in itself inherently bad. Artisans and craftsmen, trained in one art, must not practice a second simultaneously—or even subsequently—since then they are guilty of bad, even illegal *polymatheia* (that is, *polypragmosyne*) or *periergia*.[135] The purpose of long apprenticeships was precisely to discourage this ([Brunnemann]/Henel 1691, C1ᵛ–C2ʳ). This anxiety about artisans who try to diversify within the mechanical arts was not mirrored in the liberal arts. Universities were again proposing one law of curiosity for those inside the institution and another for those outside. A goldsmith could not be a cobbler but a professor of medicine could also hold chairs of history and poetry.[136]

In short, while these Lutheran dissertations and orations certainly did not promote the kind of systematic encyclopaedic ideal that had been cultivated in, for example, the Reformed pedagogy of Johann Heinrich Alsted at Herborn,[137] they did seek to permit some transgressions of discipline boundaries and to prevent others, calling that process of transgression—whether negative or positive—curiosity. Thus, curiosity operated as an open-shut valve, as a single regulatory

---

[134] See [Brunnemann]/Henel 1691, B3ʳ–[B4ʳ]; Fichtner/Puchelberger 1725, 26–9; Ortlob/Fuchs 1708; Siber/Jacobi 1685; Silberrad/Christann 1714, 12–13.

[135] See, respectively, [Brunnemann]/Henel 1691, [B4ᵛ]–C2ᵛ; Fichtner/Puchelberger 1725, 33–40.

[136] e.g. the anatomist Heinrich Meibom (d. 1700) was professor of all 3 at Helmstedt (Moller 1744, i. 304; iii. 431–43). During his Halle and Altdorf career, the polyhistor Johann Heinrich Schulze—who prefaced his 1720 professorial inaugural with the theme of *periergia*—taught botany, anatomy, Greek, Hebrew, and geography (Kaiser and Völler 1980, esp. 19). For these and other examples, see Evans 1981, 173–4; Nelles 2001, 168–75.

[137] See Hotson (forthcoming).

framework for the flow of knowledge, permitting it in some cases and preventing it in others. Medicine too was regulated by curiosity in this stop-go way.

1.3.2 Regulating medicine

Curiosity seems to have become central to the regulation of medicine in some universities for a brief period at the start of the eighteenth century. Whereas philosophy dissertations were devoted to curiosity for almost a century—from 1652 to 1744—virtually all of the German medical disputations and orations on it were held between 1701 and 1720. In that period, more disputations and orations on curiosity were held in medical faculties than in the other three faculties put together.

Medicine was felt to be in particularly urgent need of regulation. Many of the dilemmas underlying this need were centuries-old. How far should medical research go? To what extent was learned medicine a means to a therapeutic end or else an end in itself? To what extent could it explain the body as well as healing it? How much practical skill (*ars*) should physicians have? How much theoretical knowledge (*scientia*) should practitioners, surgeons, and empirics have? Yet such dilemmas were particularly urgent in turn-of-the-century German Lutheran universities, for various reasons. Not only was there general pressure on those universities to demonstrate their social usefulness, but such *Nützlichkeit* became especially desirable in those universities in which Pietism exerted a growing influence— most famously Halle, which opened in 1694:[138] Pietism gave academic medicine greater responsibilities for public health and the welfare of the poor. The need for regulation of university medicine was also felt to be acute because of a perceived danger that the heady new doctrines spawned by the so-called Scientific Revolution would make teaching self-indulgent and irrelevant.[139] Alongside battered but continuing Aristotelianism and Galenism were now not only Paracelsian iatrochemistry but also new kinds of empiricism, and mechanism in its various forms, from Cartesianism to Democritean

---

[138] On *Nützlichkeit* in Pietist writings, see Geyer-Kordesch 1990, 66. On the founding of Halle, see Boehm and Müller (eds.) 1983, 174–7; Hammerstein 1970.

[139] On the state of medical philosophy in the late 17th and early 18th century, see Cunningham and French (eds.) 1990; French and Wear 1989; L. King 1970 and 1978.

atomism, not to mention animist reactions against it. This added to uncertainty about the proper relation of medicine to other branches and about the proper structure of the medical syllabus: to what extent, if at all, should it include botany, pharmacy, surgery, anatomy as well as the traditional trio of physiology, pathology, and therapeutics?[140]

People tried to regulate this turmoil by shaping curiosity in ways that promoted or attacked certain kinds of medicine. But because these uses of curiosity conflicted with each other, there was conflict about what exactly it was. This university contestation of it was much more aggressive in medicine than in philosophy. In medicine, curiosity was almost always presented as either largely good or else largely bad, but rarely as half good and half bad, as it was in many a philosophy dissertation. Yet that is not to say that medical writers hived off one species of curiosity and disconnected it from the multi-species passion that was discussed in philosophy faculties. However absorbed the medical writers were in their specific polemical uses of curiosity, they still saw it as a passion which operated in many other spheres of life too and was, at least potentially, both good and bad.[141] Even in this fraught context, the notion that good and bad knowledge were intimately related to each other and came from the same source outweighed the propensity to dissociate them from each other by giving them different names. When an *entirely* bad passion was to be described, *periergia* displaced *curiositas* in the title (Schulze 1720).

Some used curiosity to promote recent, innovative medical research. Or rather—because it would have been unwise to claim outright novelty in medicine—they praised curiosity for producing insights which, because of humanity's previous ignorance of them, had at least the appearance of novelty.[142] These writers, like many in the culture of curiosities, cheerfully reversed the centuries-old opposition between *curiositas* and *utilitas*, emphasizing instead the

---

[140] On the reform of French university medical syllabi, see Brockliss 1987, 391–400. On the relation between university medicine and other medical practices in Germany, see Lindemann 1996.

[141] e.g. Henrici/Frantz (1709) acknowledge that *curiositas* is indifferent in itself (2), although their dissertation itself is entirely devoted to 'too much curiosity' (*nimia curiositas*): this constantly repeated phrase leaves open the possibility of a moderate curiosity, which is only momentarily glimpsed near the end (30). See also Krause 1709,)(2^(r–v); Schrader 1701, A2^(r–v); Seger 1676, 9–11; Stahl/Donzelina 1714, 10–13.

[142] Krause 1709,)(3^r. On Krause, see Steinmetz 1958, i. 158.

'usefulness of curiosity about nature'.[143] Others used curiosity to
attack certain kinds of medicine. For them, the danger was that
curiosity might leave usefulness behind and go off on its own useless,
speculative, error-strewn path instead of healing people: 'The deceitfulness of a prurient age lies in distinguishing the curious from the
useful and in concentrating and expending its energies . . . on things
which bring no practical benefit.'[144]

Among the prime targets in medical faculties for such denigration
and—more rarely—praise were the new corpuscular philosophies.
As William Clark has shown, in the German academic world there
was a general resistance to the hegemony of unvarnished ballistical
mechanism (1992, esp. 110). Schrader of Helmstedt, whose concern
with both good and bad curiosity was relatively unusual for a medical professor, viewed corpuscularianism as bad curiosity, not intrinsically—indeed in physics he was an anti-Aristotelian sympathizer
with it—but only insofar as it was systematically applied to medicine, since it then endangered the Hippocratic primacy of *observatio*,
experientia, and cure over claims to understand first causes.[145] In
Schrader's introduction to his lecture course on therapeutics, it is to
empirically oriented modern authorities—such as Giorgio Baglivi,
Thomas Sydenham, and the iatrochemist François dele Boë
Sylvius—that he refers his students when showing how to avoid such
bad *curiositas*.[146] However, while Schrader is using curiosity to stem
the flow of corpuscularianism into medicine, he also uses it to open
the floodgates to *observatio*.[147] For, as we have seen in another context, Schrader understands good curiosity as consisting in empirical
and experimental observation. He designates it mainly by the adjective *curiosus* but also on occasion by the noun *curiositas*: he concludes his oration by telling students that, important as lectures and
books were, their 'true places of learning' were 'patients' beds . . .
pharmacists' workshops, surgeons' rooms, and chemists' furnaces.
Be hunters after observations and skilled scrutineers of the particu-

---

[143] 'haec . . . Curiositatis Physicae utilitas' (Seger 1676, 55). See also Krause 1709,
)(3^r. On this opposition and its negation, see N. Kenny 1998, 115, 157–61.
[144] 'Seculi prurientis fallacia est curiosum contra distinguere utili, & industriam
suam . . . illis addicere & impendere quae nihil opis afferunt' (Schrader 1701, A3^r).
[145] Ibid., A2^v–[A4^r]. On Schrader, see Kestner 1971.
[146] Schrader 1701, A3^r, [A4^v]. On these 3, see L. King 1970, 93–133 and 1978,
244–50.
[147] I am grateful to Kevin Chang for help with this point.

lars that instruct the future practitioner and rapidly train his practical judgement. Let these things exercise your curiosity.'[148] Schrader is here using curiosity to open the polymathic valve—encouraging students to look about in 'places of learning' that were outside the usual university ambit—just as he uses it elsewhere to close the valve and keep out corpuscularianism. However, it was more common to use curiosity only to slam that valve shut.

Border disputes between medicine and neighbouring disciplines were nowhere more intense than in Halle, which provides my main case-study in how curiosity was used to reinforce those threatened borders. A substantial doctoral denunciation of bad curiosity was presided over by Georg Ernst Stahl in 1714.

Stahl (1659–1734) was professor in this new university from 1694 to 1715, alongside Friedrich Hoffmann. It was an extraordinary team. Indeed it has been argued that these two, along with Herman Boerhaave, were the leading medical innovators on the Continent in the early eighteenth century.[149] Stahl became famous in chemistry for the ill-fated phlogiston theory and in medicine for his theory of animism, which influenced subsequent vitalism and anti-mechanism in the German Enlightenment and in France.[150] Although the doctoral candidate who spoke on *curiositas*, Giovanni Francesco Donzelina, was no beginner,[151] Stahl is likely to have been closely involved in the disputation, given the relatively small number of medical students at Halle (Hoffbauer 1805, 109). Moreover, Stahl's own substantial address to the respondent was printed at the end of the dissertation (Stahl/Donzelina 1714, [65–76]). The dissertation straightforwardly propounds Stahlian animism. Its main originality, of the limited kind required by the genre, seems to lie in the way it systematically grafts the rhetoric of *curiositas* onto animism.

This dissertation seeks to bolster the borders between medicine and neighbouring disciplines by defining transgressions of those

[148] 'sed credite & aegrotantium . . . cubicula, & pharmacopaeorum officinas, & Chirurgorum conclavia & Chymicorum hypocausta, vera musea vestra esse. Observationum venatores ac solertes estote singularium scrutatores quae futurum Artificem instruunt & judicium practicum maturè formant. Haec curiositatem vestram exerceant . . .' (Schrader 1701, [B4ᵛ]).
[149] Geyer-Kordesch 1990, 75; L. King 1970, 3 (who also adds Baglivi). On Stahl's career, see Geyer-Kordesch 1990, 66–7; Hoffbauer 1805, 110–12. Kevin Chang is preparing a Ph.D. on Stahl at the University of Chicago.
[150] See respectively Geyer-Kordesch 1990, 82–7 and French 1990, 102–3.
[151] Donzelina had matriculated in the medical faculty in 1707 (Juncke 1960, 123).

borders as a species of bad _curiositas_, as _polymatheia_ (3–4), as an illness that takes the form of meddling: hence the title of this dissertation, 'a cure for curious medicine' (_Medicina medicinae curiosae_). It
could have been called 'a treatise on things not directly concerning
medicine'.[152] When what is imported from other disciplines involves
practice rather than theory, actions rather than thoughts, then this
curiositas can be called _polypragmosyne_ (11).

This attack on polymathic _curiositas_ is also a defence of Stahlian
animism, since this animism was grounded in the conviction
that organic life cannot be reduced to the explanatory principles
employed in neighbouring disciplines, such as physics or chemistry.
Although Stahl himself was a considerable chemist, that did not
make him an iatrochemist when it came to medicine (46–50). But the
greatest potential threat to the autonomy of medicine came from
mechanistic physics (25–32). The threat was coming from a familiar
direction: medicine had for centuries sought to assert its autonomy
from natural philosophy. For Stahl, mechanism was to be kept out of
medicine not because it was over-dogmatic and insufficiently empirical in a medical context—in Schrader's parlance: over-curious in
one sense and under-curious in another—but because it was unable
to explain what animates organic beings. Stahl considered that
although the motion of the body—bones, muscles, circulation of
blood—can be partly described by Newtonian physics (just as its
composition can be partly described by chemistry), that motion is
not determined by matter itself, as it is in the case of real pulleys,
levers, springs, or presses.[153] Rather, it is determined by soul (_anima_),
which teleologically organizes the body's motions through the will
and intellect, in a process which he calls life. Stahl thus stopped short
of any Paracelsian, vitalistic attribution of plastic power to matter,[154]
yet he did emphasize the inseparability of soul and matter as far as
the physician is concerned. His medicine was what would nowadays
be called holistic. The patient's reason, will, sensations, passions,
corporeal fantasy may all be part of any illness (Geyer-Kordesch
1990, 77). Indeed, the repeated insistence in this dissertation that

---

[152] '_Tractatio rerum Medicinam directè non spectantium_' (Stahl/Donzelina 1714,
14).
[153] On his animism, see French 1990, 89–93; Geyer-Kordesch 1989, 156–63 and
1990; L. King 1964, 121–4 and 1978, 143–51. On Stahl, see also Kaiser (ed.) 1985.
[154] I am grateful to Antonio Clericuzio for pointing this out.

'curious medicine' is an illness seems an application of Stahlian pathology to *curiositas* itself. That application had already been achieved five years earlier by another Halle medical dissertation, Stahlian in doctrine although he was not the *praeses*: it had defined *curiositas* as a passion—connected to *phantasia* (imagination)—that had vitiated all ancient and much modern philosophy, including mechanism.[155] These dissertations may have been influenced by the negative understanding of *curiositas* developed by Buddeus and published in 1711: Buddeus taught theology at Halle until 1705 and for five years up till then had co-edited a journal with Stahl and Christian Thomasius.[156]

The purpose of Stahlian *curiositas* was to attack not only far-flung mechanists but also one much closer to home: Stahl's Halle colleague Hoffmann, who was almost certainly present at both of these disputations. The well-documented philosophical antagonism between Stahl and Hoffmann rumbled on for decades, even beyond their deaths, since Hoffmann's treatise on their differences was not published until 1747.[157] The dispute has been called the archetype of those between animists and mechanists that recurred through most of the eighteenth century (French 1990, 90). For Hoffmann, matter was inherently mobile, not passive, thus the human body operated according to the laws of mechanics and so could be understood in terms of recent physics. To deny this would be to undermine the physician's ability to improve health through the management of non-naturals, such as diet and exercise, since the Stahlian soul could choose to ignore their effects (French 1990, 92). If organic bodies could perform tasks like reproduction that were impossible for inorganic ones, this was due not to soul but to an inherent, organizing plastic power (L. King 1964, 124–6).

In the 1714 dissertation, Stahl, perhaps sheltering slightly behind his student, indirectly but flagrantly accuses Hoffmann of bad *curiositas*, that is, of inappropriately importing into medicine not only mechanism but also anatomy (32–7), which is also here seen as belonging properly to physics, not to medicine:

Of what use is such anatomico-physical curiosity to medicine? None! So, to prevent useful, true, and worthy medicine from being abandoned and

---

[155] Henrici/Frantz 1709: for *phantasia*, see pp. 7, 17, 27, 32.
[156] I am grateful to Kevin Chang for pointing this out. See Kirchner 1958, i. 26.
[157] See French 1990; L. King 1964, esp. 124.

muddled, it is absolutely essential to separate these commonplace curiosities from the realm of medicine and to treat them in their own sphere . . .

   In order to dispel useless anatomical curiosity and yet make medicine benefit from anatomy—which, since it deals with the body as inanimate, belongs more to physics—it is enough to know the body's *general* constitution, that is, its organs and limbs, their number, location, connection, and general arrangement.[158]

The badness of *curiositas* resides here not in the object itself (the human anatomy), nor in the subject (the physician), but in the indecorous relationship between the two. By contrast, for the mechanist Hoffmann, anatomy had much greater importance for medicine, since every action and use of bodily parts depended upon their shape and size (French 1990, 96–8). For this reason, and because Hoffmann was professor of practical medicine, anatomy loomed large in his pedagogy, as did chemistry (Hoffbauer 1805, 110–12).

   The axe of *curiositas* was being wielded in this and other battles over the Halle medical syllabus. The role of botany was also controversial. According to Stahl, it too was over-imported into medicine (Stahl/Donzelina 1714, 37–9). But according to the Halle statutes, the faculty's second professor was supposed to teach botany in addition to medical theory: and the *secondarius* was none other than Stahl himself. Hoffmann was not keen to teach botany either, although the faculty had its own botanical garden. Only with the appointment in 1698 of Heinrich Henrici as supernumerary professor (*extraordinarius*) had the garden begun to be exploited (Hoffbauer 1805, 151).

   Stahl was also using *curiositas* to promote his brand of Pietism. As Johanna Geyer-Kordesch and Roger French have shown, Stahl is one of the most spectacular instances of the widespread interconnection between religion and medicine in this period. Hoffmann too was a Pietist, but of the 'enlightened' variety, whereas Stahl's Pietism was of the more radical, Enthusiastic kind. Stahl's animism can be under-

---

[158] 'quam tandem talis anatomico physica curiositas utilitatem conferet ad Medicinam? sane nullam! Unde ne utilis, vera, & digna Medicina destituatur & confundatur, necessarium omnino est, quo hae vulgares curiositates à Medico foro distinguantur, & in sua sphaera tractentur . . .

   Quo vero anatomica inutilis curiositas, repurgetur, & Anatomia ipsa, (quae dum cum corpore exanimato versatur, ad physicam tractationem magis pertinet) in usum Medicinae transferatur; sufficit nosse *generalem* corporis constitutionem, quoad partes, earundemque numerum, situm, connexionem, & dispositionem generalem' (Stahl/Donzelina 1714, 34).

stood as an attempt to keep God in medicine, to promote the free pursuit of spirituality through the inspired activities of soul, such as perception and feeling.[159] Three specific semantic strands of *curiositas* were enlisted to this cause: not just the decorum sense (already mentioned), but also two others.

First, the old opposition between *curiositas* and *utilitas*—that had recently been much contested—now received a shot in the arm from Pietist *Nützlichkeit*. Inappropriately imported knowledge makes 'medical curiosity useless'.[160] This rhetoric was the opposite of that found in some medical faculties where 'curious medicine' seemed attractive precisely *because* it was not purely utilitarian but, on the contrary, 'novel, difficult, controversial, interesting' and so productive of suitable disputation topics.[161] In the medical faculty of Rostock between 1703 and 1713, Johann Ernst Schaper gave his students a string of topics from 'curious medicine' on which to cut their teeth in practice disputations through which they worked their way up to licentiate level. 'Curious' here meant that each disputation took the form of (two) questions, which were 'curious and at the same time useful':[162] the careful formulation suggests that they had added value—pleasure, intrinsic interest—beyond the purely useful. Students debated why aversion can arise between two men without their knowing the cause (Schaper/Neucrantz 1703), whether phlebotomy is more likely to save a life if adminstered in a drastic, one-off way rather than repeatedly and modestly (Schaper/ Barnstorff 1711), and so on.

Secondly, the 'supplementary' connotation of curiosity[163] was used in the 1714 dissertation to attack 'curious medicine' as a superfluous supplement to true medicine. Stahl's aim was to strip this polymathic accretion away from medicine, thereby restoring it to an

---

[159] French 1990, 89–95, 109–10; Geyer-Kordesch 1990.

[160] '*inutilem* reddunt curiositatem medicam' (Stahl/Donzelina 1714, 14).

[161] Stahl himself was not above giving *curiosus* a positive, object-oriented sense, but he limited it primarily to the 'observation' meaning. e.g. Stahl, *Observationes physico-chymico-medicae curiosae* (n.p., 1709).

[162] 'Curiosa haecce et simul utilis quaestio' (Schaper/Neucrantz 1703, A[1ʳ]). These were 'circular' (*circulares*) disputations (see Daxelmüller 1979, 43), i.e. they involved a rotation of respondents among a small group of students. By contrast, the 'solemn' (*solemnes*) disputations which the same students eventually performed for the licentiate were more systematic discussions of a medical theme, via 50 or so carefully connected *theses*. On Schaper, see A. Hirsch (ed.) 1884–8; Kestner 1971.

[163] See N. Kenny 1998, 140–1.

imagined Hippocratic purity. When Hippocrates said that physics should be the basis of medicine, he had in mind only 'the very early and most simple conceptions', not the physics of Aristotle, Descartes, Gassendi, or the Eclectics.[164] (Stahl's actual position was often more nuanced: he certainly did not accept all ancient and criticize all modern medicine.) This rhetoric is remarkably similar to Pietist exhortations to strip away the dogmatic accretions of Lutheran orthodoxy, restoring the church to a devotional simplicity rooted in more direct contact with *the* ancient authority, the Bible. Medicine is to be similarly purged and its accumulated debris swept away: both of the Stahlian Halle dissertations on *curiositas* use the metaphor of cleansing the Augean stable.[165] Pietism shaped not only Stahl's pathology, but also his very conception of the reform which medicine needed: like the true church, true medicine lay buried beneath supplementary layers which had ended up making it ill, or 'curious'. Each could be restored to living praxis by peeling away lifeless layers, whether of mechanism or of Lutheran orthodoxy.

What would orthodox Lutherans have made of this rhetoric? For them, doctrinal supplements to the Bible were essential, not superfluous. So the one orthodox Lutheran theologian who undertook a detailed university study of curiosity found that Pietist condemnations of it told only half the story.

1.3.3 *Confessionalism in Electoral Saxony*

Faculties of theology were the ones that showed the least interest in reshaping curiosity through disputation. In theology, curiosity had for centuries been almost entirely bad, from Augustine and Aquinas to Luther and Calvin:[166] even nowadays, the only reference works likely to give a wholly negative definition of 'curiosity'—as distinct from 'the desire for knowledge'—are theological ones.[167] In these early modern theology faculties there seemed to be relatively little that was new to say about it—except insofar it could be used to bludgeon the latest heretics—and so it was not an ideal disputation topic. However, church discourse on curiosity was now showing some

---

[164] 'priscis simplicissimis conceptibus' (Stahl/Donzelina 1714, 18).
[165] Henrici/Frantz 1709, 27; Stahl/Donzelina 1714, 14, 40.
[166] See Blumenberg 1988, 65–144; Meijering 1980; Newhauser 1982; Oberman 1974; Peters 1985.
[167] e.g. *New Catholic Encyclopaedia* 1967.

signs of change initiated by its encounters with the new secular culture of curiosities, which it either condemned or—occasionally—
accommodated (2.3 below). Such change was more visible in church
discourse of a pastoral or commercialized kind than in theology
faculties. But there was one major exception.

Adam Rechenberg (1649–1721) produced two substantial dissertations on the role of curiosity in theology, the first on the unhealthy
(*insana*) species (1668) and the second on its healthy (*sana*) counterpart (1672). He was on his way to a career as a celebrated professor
of theology at Leipzig:[168] he obtained the baccalaureate in theology
in 1670 and the licentiate in 1678. The two dissertations were
reprinted together in 1675 with authorship being attributed to
Rechenberg rather than to his teachers: the attribution stuck. Both
dissertations became important reference points for two subsequent
treatments of *curiositas* which in turn proved influential, those by
Stryk (Stryk/Lüedecke 1743, 296) and Christian Thomasius (1706,
120), who was Rechenberg's brother-in-law. But the greater influence was had by the more conventional dissertation, on unhealthy
curiosity in theology: it was referred to in several other dissertations,
right up till an astonishing seventy-six years after its first printing
(Succov/Haag 1744, 3). The editor of a 1690 collection of texts on
curiosity, printed in Wedel, referred to it enthusiastically but said
that there was no need to reprint it since it was still readily available
(Hartnack (ed.) 1690, [):(6ʳ⁻ᵛ]). However, precisely because the more
innovative dissertation—on healthy curiosity in theology—did not
catch on to the same extent, it reveals more clearly the limits to the
new uses to which curiosity could be put: no single individual could
change a discourse single-handedly.

Rechenberg tries to bridge the gap between theological and secular versions of curiosity by transferring to theology the dominant
secular assumption that curiosity was divided into a good and a
bad species. Curiosity in theology therefore belongs to the same
generic family as philosophical, astrological, or political curiosity
(Kromayer/Scherzer/Rechenberg 1675, [A4ᵛ]–B[1ʳ]). What enables
Rechenberg to argue this was his revision of the venerable scholastic
opposition between *curiositas* and *studiositas*. He makes *sana
curiositas* synonymous with *studiositas* as the virtuous mean and

---

[168] On Rechenberg, see Hammerstein 1972, 272–4; Jöcher 1750–1; Rathmann
(ed.) 1984, 89–90.

replaces *curiositas* with *insana curiositas* as one of the two vicious, opposite extremes lying on either side of that mean, the other being *negligentia*. Rechenberg thus turns curiosity into a tool for defence as well as attack: it 'should be both set free and restrained'.[169] This was virtually unprecedented in theology. While some practices could, as ever, be attacked as bad curiosity, others could now be defended as good curiosity.

The attacks and defences for which Rechenberg shaped curiosity were in the service of Lutheran orthodoxy. Studying at the conservative university of Leipzig, from which nascent Pietism would soon be excised,[170] Rechenberg certainly did not intend to make any Pietist use of *curiositas* in order to restrict the role of reason in theology. On the contrary, he processed *curiositas* through the formidable machine of Aristotelian, neo-scholastic analysis, which was a characteristic weapon of Lutheran and Reformed theology faculties in the confessional age.[171] His orthodoxy was not of an extreme kind, as his notion of *sana curiositas* and his subsequent researches in church history suggest. Yet his intellectual world was that of the orthodox theologians. He referred to many of them in these two dissertations, especially to the major polemical theologian Johann Konrad Dannhauer (1603–66) and the influential Leipzig professor Johann Hülsemann (1602–61), but also to Johann Georg Dorsch, Leonhard Hutter, Abraham Calov, the great Johann Gerhard, and to the *praeses* of each dissertation, Hieronymus Kromayer and Johann Adam Scherzer.[172]

Rechenberg shows how *curiositas* could serve the orthodox cause in the age of confessionalism when, in the context of academia, polemics was the dominant mode, since it was crucial to distinguish one's Lutheran doctrines from Reformed (Calvinist) or Catholic ones, either by attacking the gratuitous intricacy of the other doctrines (their *insana curiositas*) or by defending the necessary intricacy of one's own doctrines (their *sana curiositas*).[173] Indeed, Rechenberg

[169] 'curiositas . . . laxanda ac restringenda' (Kromayer/Scherzer/Rechenberg 1675, [M3ᵛ]).

[170] See Boehm and Müller (eds.) 1983, 241.

[171] See Althaus 1967; McGrath 1986, 152–67; Petersen 1964; Preus 1955.

[172] On most of these, see Matthias 1995, 471–7. For an outline of the doctrine of these and other orthodox Lutheran theologians, see McGrath 1986, 150–78; Preus 1955. On Kromayer and Scherzer, see Jöcher 1750–1.

[173] On confessionalism in general, see Hsia 1989; Vierhaus 1988, 60–4; Wallmann 1992; Zeeden 1965.

shows that *curiositas* comes into its own especially in polemical theology. Although his systematic, scholastic approach leads him to claim that both *insana* and *sana curiositas* occur in all three parts of theology—didactic-polemic (or dogmatic), exegetic, and moral— in fact he devotes by far the most space to the first of those (Kromayer/Scherzer/Rechenberg 1675, B3^v–C3^v), to which he also devotes the whole of the dissertation on *sana curiositas*.[174]

Notwithstanding the confessionally eclectic sources which he cites as authorities to prove the existence of *insana curiositas*,[175] Rechenberg gives it a distinctively Lutheran stamp, defining it as 'a man's concern to busy himself investigating things which are neither revealed in Scripture nor need to be believed, done, or hoped for in order to achieve salvation; the motive for this concern is to show off one's intelligence or to pursue fame; it is divinely forbidden, danger- ous, rash, and quite useless.'[176] What 'need[s] to be believed' is limited to what is contained in the Bible and in the Lutheran articles of faith. These limits are transgressed by various groups who are or have been guilty of *insana curiositas*.

The main group is of late medieval scholastics, Thomas Aquinas et al. Their moral theology is obsessed with questions such as: whether a donkey would imbibe baptism if it drank holy water; whether a fly nibbling at the consecrated host nibbles at Christ's body; whether someone really is baptized if the syllables get jumbled up—'in the name of the therfa and the ons and the yhol itspir'[177]—or else are uttered by someone with a stammer.[178]

---

[174] He promises to show in future how *insana* and *sana curiositas* work in moral theology and claims that Dannhauer has already described the role of *sana curiositas* in exegetic theology ([M3^v]).

[175] They include not only St Augustine but also the Jesuit Cornelis van den Steen and the Calvinists William Ames and Jean de l'Espine (Kromayer/ Scherzer/Rechenberg 1675, B1^v, C3^r, [C4^v], E2^r). See Ames 1630, 75–9[= 77]; L'Espine 1588, Book 6. Rechenberg seems to have become aware of L'Espine's negative discussion of *curiositas* only after printing the *insana* dissertation, so it is not mentioned until the start of the *sana* one.

[176] 'Curiositas in Theologia, est studium scrupulosum, quo homo res, quae nec in S. Scriptura revelatae, nec creditu, factu aut speratu ad salutem sunt necessariae, percontari satagit, ostendandi ingenii & famam venandi gratia susceptum, quod divinitus interdictum, periculosum, temerarium & plane inutile est' (Kromayer/ Scherzer/Rechenberg 1675, [A4^r]).

[177] 'in nomine Trispa et Liifi et Ceisan Tuspriri'.

[178] Kromayer/Scherzer/Rechenberg 1675, C3^v. Rechenberg states that these ques- tions were asked by the Catholic moral theologian Martin Bonacina.

More contemporary targets are the latest heretics, amongst whom for orthodox Lutherans in 1668 the radical Protestant sect of the Socinians loomed very large, their denials of the Trinity and of the divinity of Christ spreading semi-visibly across Europe, not least among leading intellectuals. They went further even than orthodox Lutherans in their expectations that scripture-based doctrine should be accessible to reason:

What causes the Socinians today—as once the Arians—to impugn even the mystery of the Holy Trinity if not *damnable curiosity*? The words of Johann Crell the Socinian plainly attest what he babbled about this mystery. For the Socinians convince themselves that God would not have proposed anything for human belief that was not accessible to human curiosity . . . They should have realized that, when it comes to mysteries, our reason has to be captive to faithful obedience.[179]

A few months earlier, also in 1668, Rechenberg had acted as respondent in a disputation on this very topic—Socinian unitarianism—which was one of no fewer than 154 short anti-Socinian disputations, often held weekly, over which Scherzer, *praeses* of Rechenberg's subsequent *sana curiositas* disputation, was to preside at Leipzig between 1668 and 1672.[180] Devoting such resources to the attack must have seemed all the more imperative since some Socinians had been granted temporary refuge in neighbouring, more confessionally tolerant Brandenburg, following their expulsion from Poland in 1658 (Press 1991, 306). Ultimately the orthodox counterblast was successful: the Socinians gained few footholds in Germany (Wallmann 1985, 99–100).

However, the accusation of *insana curiositas* is not levelled only at those outside the orthodox fold. It serves to regulate orthodox as well as heterodox inquiry: even accredited Lutheran theologians sometimes take reason too far in their desire to show off:

---

[179] 'Quae alia caussa ob quam hodiè Sociniani, ut olim Ariani, adeò SS. Trinitatis mysterium impugnant, quàm *damnosa curiositas*. Expressa Joh. Crellii Sociniani id verba, quae de hoc mysteriô effutivit, testantur. Persuadent enim sibi Deum homini nihil ad credendum proponere, nisi quod curiositati humanae sit pervium . . . Ast nòsse debebant in mysteriis rationem nostram sub obedientiam fidei esse captivandam' (Kromayer/Scherzer/Rechenberg 1675, C[1ʳ]). On Socinianism, see Jolley 1998, 382–5; Preus 1955, 81–5, 89–90, 94; G. Williams 1962, 749–63, 857.

[180] These were published together: see Scherzer 1672. Rechenberg's dissertation is on pp. 114–21.

So those who are most responsible for care of our religion quickly restrain those theologifiers . . . Our most serene electors of Saxony have understood this, salutarily warning in a decree that 'disputations held by their theologians should all be on established points of doctrine; they should be grounded in those articles of Christian faith and in Holy Scripture'.[181]

Rechenberg is quoting from the constitutions of the universities of Leipzig and Wittenberg, where the theology faculty had indeed been severely weakened by internal disputes in the Reformation. He is confessionalizing *insana curiositas*, by attributing to the secular leaders of Electoral Saxony the power to define and identify it. In the confessional age, the university's authority in defining a particular vice or virtue was often borrowed ultimately from the territorial state. In any case, the two intersected in many an individual: Kromayer and Scherzer, for example, who presided over Rechenberg's two dissertations, also both acted as assessors for the consistory (Jöcher 1750–1).

Sana curiositas in theology is confessionalized even more sharply by Rechenberg. He defines it as the care that secular and ecclesiastical authorities should take for the salvation of the faithful, as well as the care which ordinary believers should take for their own salvation. The definition proved very influential not in theology but in jurisprudence: it was soon adapted by the great jurist Stryk, who decided that this kind of good curiosity could serve the Brandenburg-Prussian state. Rechenberg and the later jurists were putting the etymological *cura*—'care, diligence, solicitude'—back into the *curiositas* family, from which it had been gradually ebbing away in the seventeenth century, while always being available for a recall whenever needed.[182] *Sana curiositas* does not primarily concern knowledge, therefore, though inquisitiveness about doctrinal matters is one aspect of the legitimate care which secular and ecclesiastical authorities should take. When is such inquisitiveness 'healthy'? Again the answer is deeply political: decorum determines who should want to know what. Rechenberg elaborates a hierarchy of subjects (his word: 'Subjectum') of *sana curiositas*, in descending

[181] 'Quapropter ii, quibus religionis cura potissimum incumbit, hos Theologastros maturè cohibeant . . . Intellexerunt hoc Serenissimi Saxoniae Electores, saluberrimô planè decretô caventes: *ne disputationes aliae à Theologis suis, quàm Thematicae, eaeque uni ex Christianae fidei Articulis proportionatae &S. Scripturae dictis habeantur*' (Kromayer/Scherzer/Rechenberg 1675, D[iv]).

[182] See N. Kenny 1998, 35–6, 38–41, 55–8, 60–2, 65–6, 81–5, 90–1, 102, 128, 189.

order according to how much doctrinal inquisitiveness they should have: first university theologians—this is another self-legitimizing text—then cathedral theologians (such as bishops), then ordinary Christians who, whether learned or not, listen rather than teach. Among such listeners, rulers ('Principes') should have the most *curiositas*, witness David and Constantine (E2^{r-v}).

Rechenberg has carved out a species of *sana curiositas* not just so that he can defend it but also so that he can accuse others of lacking it or even—in the case of Catholics—of unjustly denying it to others. Rechenberg contrasts his own willingness to allocate a modest amount legitimate *curiositas* even to humble people with, on the other hand, the Catholics' reluctance to allow lay people any knowledge of their quasi-Eleusinian mysteries, lest the fraudulence be detected (E2^{v}–E3^{r}). This is an ingenious variation on the more standard theme in Lutheran universities that Catholics foster bad *curiositas*: according to one Halle dissertation, the excessive *curiositas* of common people was a direct result of the secretiveness of Catholic philosophy and theology, which so frustrated people that they turned to unhealthy *curiositas*, sometimes even becoming atheists (Henrici/Frantz 1709, 5–6).

However, a much more urgent target which his definition of *sana curiositas* enabled Rechenberg to attack was the Hohenzollern family. Since the conversion to Calvinism in 1613 of the Brandenburg Elector Johann Sigismund and then of most of the court, the ruling family of Brandenburg-Prussia, having first failed to persuade its overwhelmingly Lutheran populace to follow it into a second Reformation, had ruled with a policy of relative religious toleration, which extended also to Catholics and immigrant sects, including the Socinians (Fulbrook 1983, 87). Viewed from the Saxon city of Leipzig, entirely Lutheran, this seemed a gross dereliction of pastoral-political duty or, in Rechenberg's terms, a failure to exercise *sana curiositas*. While he does not mention the Hohenzollern by name, he quotes approvingly from a denunciation of their conversion by the Wittenberg professor Leonhard Hutter.[183] Borrowing a term which he seems to have derived from Dannhauer (E2^{v}–E3^{r}), Rechenberg calls such abrogation of *curiositas* Gallionism, after Gallio the proconsul of Achaja in the Acts of the Apostles

---

[183] Kromayer/Scherzer/Rechenberg 1675, E2^{r}. For the passage quoted, see Hutter 1614, (:)iv $^{r-v}$.

(18.12–16), who refused to adjudicate when the Jews brought a case against Paul, or even to let Paul defend himself, since he (Gallio) was not qualified in doctrine. Indeed, Rechenberg's 1672 title-page presents the whole dissertation as a vindication of *sana curiositas* against Gallionism and syncretism. While the argument that secular rulers should enforce orthodox Lutheranism was commonplace in Rechenberg's circles, the identification of this as *sana curiositas* seems to have been his own, inspired perhaps by a few pre-existing lexical scraps: a Dannhauer dissertation derides Gallio's excuse that he wished to avoid *polypragmosyne* and also accuses him of *incuria*,[184] a term which Rechenberg seizes upon as looking conveniently opposite to *curiositas* (E2ᵛ, E3ᵛ). These scraps help Rechenberg give the impression that his newly defined *sana curiositas* must really have existed all along.

He is using it to attack not only Gallionism but also a related phenomenon, equally topical and anathema to Lutheran orthodoxy: syncretism. Rechenberg's disputation was held at a time when German Lutheranism was in danger of being torn apart by a series of disputes over syncretism: these flared up especially in 1645–56, 1661–9, and 1675–86.[185] Georg Calixt—who died in 1656—and his followers were trying to bring the Lutheran and Reformed churches closer to each other, in the very years which saw the failure of the ecumenical colloquies in Thorn (1645), Kassel (1661), and Berlin (1662 and 1663) in which Catholics also participated. Calixtians emphasized the common doctrinal ground between the two main Protestant churches rather than the differences between them. They aimed to cut away what they saw as superfluous layers of orthodox doctrine by arguing that the essentials of Christian doctrine had been outlined in the Bible and the early church (the first five centuries). While the centre of syncretism was Helmstedt and the Lower Saxon Guelf principalities, it received support for political reasons from the Great Elector in Brandenburg-Prussia, Friedrich Wilhelm, and so was attacked for both religious and political reasons by Dannhauer and the orthodox Saxon heavyweights in Rechenberg's intellectual world—Hülsemann, Calov, Kromayer, and Scherzer.[186]

---

[184] Dannhauer/Pichler 1664, A2ᵛ, 44.

[185] See Matthias 1995, 477. My account of Calixtian syncretism is also based on Hsia 1989, 116–21; Press 1991, 306–7; Wallmann 1995, 552–9.

[186] For Kromayer and Scherzer, see the works by them listed in Jöcher 1750–1.

Rechenberg's contribution was to present syncretists as lacking *sana curiositas*: by consenting to the dilution of doctrine, they abandon the Lutheran doctrinal distinctiveness that is the only truth. The brunt of Rechenberg's outrage is not borne directly by Calixtians but by Arminians, the relatively liberal Calvinists who were the other side of the syncretist coin. Among these, the Dutch Remonstrant Simon Episcopius (or Biscop), who before his death in 1643 sought to systematize Arminian doctrine, is singled out for repeated attack. Rechenberg attacks the Arminians not only for lacking *sana curiositas*, but also for criticizing as bad *curiositas* the sound doctrinal edifices of orthodoxy. Given the centuries-old use of *curiositas* as a negative weapon in theology, this spectacle of a theologian vying to be more curious than his opponents is extraordinary. Like Calov before him (Preus 1955, 81–3), Rechenberg accuses the Arminians of pyrrhonism;[187] he demonstrates at every turn the solid biblical foundations of doctrinal points which they denigrate as 'more curious than useful',[188] 'more curious than necessary',[189] 'useless and perversely curious',[190] 'curious trifles',[191] 'curious questions',[192] or 'absurd curiosity'.[193] These points include: God's three attributes—simplicity, omniscience, prescience; the Trinity; the nature of pre-lapsarian human justice; whether baptism instils faith in infants; whether bodies will be resurrected individually.[194]

In the terms of Rechenberg's overall scholastic schema, the Arminian vice of lack (*negligentia*) is mirrored by the Socinian vice of excess (*insana curiositas*), with orthodox Lutherans providing the happy median (*sana curiositas*). 'Brothers' ('Fratres') in their opposing vices, Arminians and Socinians play down their doctrine so as not to offend each another (K[1ᵛ])—a somewhat disingenuous claim given that Rechenberg quotes from an anti-Socinian work by Episcopius ([G3ʳ]). They thus find themselves agreeing on some points both with each other and also with Lutheran syncretists.[195] A sorry, woolly-liberal sight, according to Rechenberg.

---

187 e.g. I4ᵛ, K[1]ᵛ–K2ʳ.
188 'tractationem curiosam magis, quam utilem dicunt Arminiani' (G2ʳ).
189 'curiosum magis quam necessarium dogma esse statuunt' (G3ᵛ).
190 '*inutile ac perversè curiosum*' (H[1]ʳ).
191 'Arminiani pro curiosis nugis habent' (H[1]ᵛ).
192 'curiosas quaestiones' (K2ᵛ).
193 'ineptae curiositatis' (L[1]ʳ).
194 See respectively sigs. G2ᵛ–G3ᵛ, G3ᵛ–H[1]ʳ, K2ᵛ–K3ʳ, L[1]ʳ⁻ᵛ, [L4ʳ].
195 e.g. [I4ʳ], K3ʳ⁻ᵛ, L[1]ʳ.

While the Saxon theological *curiositas* innovatively fleshed out by Rechenberg was profoundly confessional, it remained restricted to the level of doctrinal debate. It was Brandenburg-Prussia law faculties that supplied the most sustained university proposals to involve *curiositas* in the confessionalized regulation not just of doctrine, but of everyday social life.

1.3.4 *Social discipline and confessionalization in Brandenburg-Prussia*

The University of Frankfurt a.d. Oder spearheaded jurisprudential attempts in Brandenburg-Prussia to make curiosity descend from heights such as polemical theology and become a tool for making everyday activities either legal or illegal. To this effect, *curiositas* and *polypragmosyne*—in the traditional, pejorative sense of vicious prying into the secrets of others, worst of all into those of princes and the state[196]—were transformed into a desire or activity that could, if used properly, actually help society run more efficiently. Like other potentially subversive practices, such as Pietism, curiosity was thus turned into a potential friend rather than enemy of the new absolutist project of Brandenburg-Prussia. The notion that dangerous passions could be rechannelled for the common good was becoming familiar in the political thought of late seventeenth- and early eighteenth-century Europe (Hirschman 1977). It had particular appeal for those German territorial states which were developing forms of absolutism, using confessionalization as a means of social discipline and vice versa. Nowhere were these tendencies more pronounced than in Brandenburg-Prussia, as Gerhard Oestreich and others have shown.[197] Out of a cocktail of ideological ingredients including

[196] Curiosity in this political sense had been condemned from Plutarch to Bacon (Cziesla 1989, ch. 4). It was still discussed in some dissertations, e.g. Scherzer/Saltzmann 1705, 11–12.

[197] See Oestreich 1980, esp. 275–97 and 1982, esp. chs. 7, 15; Hsia 1989; Schilling (ed.) 1994. The modern concepts of confessionalization and social disciplining—like others such as 'commodification' in Section 3 below—are being used as heuristic rather than infallible labels: on the historiographical problems which beset them, see Ditchfield 1998. My account below also draws on histories of early modern Germany (Gagliardo 1991; Hughes 1992; Press 1991; Schilling 1989), of Brandenburg-Prussia (Mitchell 1980), of absolutist tendencies in early modern Germany in general (Raeff 1983; Vierhaus 1988) and in Brandenburg-Prussia in particular (Fulbrook 1983; Mittenzwei and Herzfeld 1987), and of the confessional politics of Brandenburg-Prussia (Dorwart 1938; Nischan 1994).

Lipsian neo-Stoicism, courtly Calvinism, older forms of church discipline, new Pietism—which the Hohenzollern fostered as a buffer against Lutheran orthodoxy—emerged a dominant set of values for civic life: frugality, austerity, obedience, duty, social responsibility, control of the passions.

This reshaping of curiosity was one of countless tasks which law faculties were performing for territorial states. Jurisprudence was gradually displacing theology as the key source of those states' legitimation and dethroning theology as the most prestigious university discipline.[198] The chanceries of German principalities were pouring forth a greater volume of decrees than any others in Europe.[199]

The potentially good curiosity which emerged can be broadly summarized as thorough investigation of—and/or action in—other people's business. It contained a strong strand of *cura*; although knowledge was also usually involved, it did not have to be, since this curiosity could involve action only. But what counted as other people's business? It was defined with legal precision as other people's possessions, interests, spheres of administration, and so on (Olearius/Schlegel 1725, 5). Whereas in the Plutarch tradition curiosity was bad because other people's business was out of bounds, now it could be legal to investigate it, or even illegal *not* to do so. The legality depended again on decorum, on who was trying to know what, in what circumstances, and for what purposes—it could be licit if the aim was to acquire a good or to avoid an evil.[200]

Three ancient terms were used to shape this new-style curiosity: *polypragmosyne*, *periergia*, and *curiositas*. The two Greek terms were the most obvious names to use, since in antiquity they had indeed denoted action-oriented, decorum-defined concern with other people's business. However, even in dissertations which did focus officially on the Greek terms,[201] *curiositas* was sometimes used informally as a synonym for them.[202] Thus, some of the Greek terms' meaning was transferred onto *curiositas*, not only because the Latin term was more familiar and comprehensible but also because it

---

[198] See Ridder-Symoens (ed.) 1996, 509–17.

[199] See Kitchen 1996, 107; Raeff 1983, part 2.

[200] See [Brunnemann]/Henel 1691, A3^r; Streit/Kalckoff 1706, 4; Stryk/Lüedecke 1743, 291.

[201] [Brunnemann]/Henel 1691; Olearius/Schlegel 1725, 4. See also Fichtner/Puchelberger 1725 and Scherzer 1730, which are more about *periergia* as a practice of jurists (and other scholars) than about legal judgments on it.

[202] e.g. [Brunnemann]/Henel 1691, B3^v–[B4^v].

enabled this new-look curiosity to be presented as just one more species of curiosity the universal and ancient passion, rather than as the creation of political expediency.[203] *Curiositas* also lent itself better than the emphatically pejorative Greek terms to division into a good and a bad species. *Curiositas* could operate more easily as an open–shut valve, making activities either legal or illegal. Occasionally, *polypragmosyne* too acquired this two-way function, its meaning changing through contamination with *curiositas*: the Greek term was explicitly extended beyond Plutarch's pejorative definition to denote a preoccupation with good as well as bad objects ([Brunnemann]/Henel 1691, A2ᵛ).

The key university in this reshaping of curiosity for the benefit of the state was Frankfurt a.d. Oder, where this new use of curiosity was initially mooted in a 1652 philosophy disputation[204] before being fleshed out in law disputations, one on *polypragmosyne*, presided over by Johann Brunnemann (1670), and two on *curiositas*, presided over by Samuel Stryk (1677) and Heinrich von Cocceji (1696): these three were among the leading jurists of the age. The printed dissertations that accompanied these disputations were all subsequently reprinted: taken together, there were at least fourteen editions of them, an astonishing total, and evidence that this new-style Brandenburg-Prussian curiosity had a considerable impact. It was imitated elsewhere, though on at least one occasion its radicalism was diminished in the process: one Saxon imitator could not bring himself to go so far as to make *polypragmosyne* a good as well as a bad thing.[205] The Brandenburg-Prussian jurists made curiosity about other people's business potentially good not out of any liberalism but because they thought this might benefit the state.

In shaping and authorizing this new-style curiosity, minimizing any impression that it was invented for current political expediency, the Frankfurt a.d. Oder jurists turned to Roman Law. In the *Corpus juris civilis* they found a few occurrences of *curiosus* and its cognates; they seized upon these and filled them out semantically by grafting

---

[203] See esp. Stryk/Lüedecke 1743.

[204] Watson/Rose 1690, 768–71, 777–8.

[205] I am referring to the Olearius/Schlegel dissertation against *polypragmosyne* (Leipzig law faculty, 1725), which refers emphatically back to the Cocceji/Lettow Frankfurt a.d. Oder dissertation as well as to an Erfurt dissertation by Streit/Kalckhoff (1706), which in turn made heavy, unacknowledged use of the Frankfurt a.d. Oder dissertations by Cocceji/Lettow and Stryk/Lüedecke.

them onto the other, much richer traditions of comment on *curiositas*.[206] No matter that in the original Roman Law context the noun *curiositas* barely occurred at all or that the forms which did occur more—*curiosus* and the adjectival noun *curiosa*—did not imply the existence of a passion called *curiositas*. The reception of Roman Law in early modern German universities and indeed courts was overwhelmingly oriented towards what was useful for contemporary practice rather than towards history and philology: in other words, the so-called 'Italian' tradition (*mos italicus*) dominated over the 'French' one (*mos gallicus*),[207] whereas in French universities, for example, there was more of a balance between the two.[208] No one embraced this localizing pragmatism more than Stryk, *the* civilian (civil lawyer) of his age, who formulated the famous principle 'he who applies the Justinian law to his own situation revels in its original intention'[209] and whose well-known eventual textbook, *The Modern Use of the Pandects*, had a strongly Brandenburgian slant.[210]

Prussian-style *curiositas* was built above all on a few decisive *loci* from Roman Law. One was a statement in the *Digest* (XV.III.3, 9) that a creditor should be circumspectly *curiosus* about his debtor.[211] This statement was the focus of the doctoral dissertation presided over by Cocceji, who taught that Roman—as opposed to customary Germanic—Law should be pre-eminent in all except public law.[212] Amplifying the *locus* from the *Digest*,[213] his student reshaped the

---

[206] In addition, curiosity could be extracted from Roman Law *loci* which made no use of this family of terms. e.g. Olearius/Schlegel 1725, which builds *polypragmosyne* out of the following *locus* from the *Digest* (L.XVII,§.36): 'It is wrong to get involved in a matter which does not concern one.' ('Culpa est, immiscere se rei ad se non pertinenti.')

[207] On this reception, see Dahm 1972; Eck 1893; Hammerstein 1972; Stintzing and Landsberg 1880–1910, iii. 32–70; Strauss 1986.

[208] Brockliss 1987, 289–90. On the teaching of law in French universities, see his pp. 277–334.

[209] 'qui legem Justinianeam pro se allegat, intentione gaudet fundata' (quoted in Hammerstein 1972, 82).

[210] *Usus modernus Pandectarum*, 1690–1712. See Koschaker 1966, 101; Stintzing and Landsberg 1880–1910, iii. 67. On Stryk, see also Eck 1893, 300–1; Hammerstein 1972, 155–61.

[211] 'curiosus igitur debet esse creditor, quo vertatur'.

[212] On Cocceji, see Hammerstein 1972, 182–3; Stintzing and Landsberg 1880–1910, iii. 112–17.

[213] This *locus* also serves as a key opening reference point in 2 other dissertations: Streit/Kalckhoff 1706, 4; Stryk/Lüedecke 1743, 289. It is also referred to in [Brunnemann]/Henel 1691, C3ᵛ.

occurrence of the adjective *curiosus* into a *curiositas* which is incumbent on people when they enter into a vast array of contracts, not just loans (Cocceji/Lettow 1710). As announced in the title, the aim is to make *curiositas* profitable ('proficua')—perhaps one tiny element in the drive towards greater economic efficiency and performance in the quasi-absolutist state (Raeff 1983, 87).

Other crucial *loci* were the laws—notably *Justinian Code*, XII.XXIII—that regulated *curiosi* and *stationarii*, that is, officers of the imperial postal system, the *cursus publicus*, which in the Roman Empire had transported couriers and letters by horse and carriage. It had been set up by Augustus primarily to communicate commands to all corners of the Empire. However, *curiosi* could denote 'spies' in late antiquity, and the *curiosi* of the *cursus publicus* may also have acted as undercover intelligence-gatherers, especially in times of civil disorder.[214] Whether or not this had actually occurred, the jurists of Frankfurt a.d. Oder, plus the odd philosopher there, were convinced that it had done, and they enthusiastically advocated this system as one species of *curiositas* or *polypragmosyne* which the modern Empire would do well to imitate[215] or which indeed—despite the absence of anything like an imperial police force[216]—was already 'employed, rightly, in some places today',[217] in order to counter threats to public peace. This line of thought seems to have been sparked by the discussion of *curiosi* and *stationarii* in Brunnemann's famous commentary on the *Justinian Code*, to which all these dissertations refer (Brunnemann 1663, 987–8). This was one instance of the admiration with which the Roman Empire's centralizing control systems, whether military or civil, fiscal or governmental, were regarded in those German territories which were undergoing rapid centralization (Oestreich 1982, 7).

Other Roman Law *loci* could be building-blocks for modern *curiositas* if adroitly handled. For example, it is stated in the *Digest*

---

[214] This is argued by Blum, though not all agree (1969, 34). On the *cursus publicus*, see also Jones (ed.) 1970, 145.

[215] Esp. Stryk/Lüedecke 1743, 289–90, 298. See also Streit/Kalckhoff 1706, 22; Watson/Rose 1690, 770–1.

[216] See Vierhaus 1988, 91.

[217] 'Unde adhuc hodiè in nonnullis locis rectè adhibentur' ([Brunnemann]/Henel 1691, C3ᵛ). According to one non-university source—Paul Marperger—it was in 'certain imperial cities' ('gewissen Reichs-Städten') that those latter-day successors to the 'Curiosi' of the Roman Empire now operated, spying and reporting back to magistrates (Marperger [1730?], 30).

(XXII.VI.6, 6), during a discussion of the extent to which a person can be expected to know about a law or a fact, that it is reasonable to expect neither 'dull-witted negligence' ('negligentia crassa') nor the 'curiosity of a spying reporter' ('delatoria curiositas'), but rather something in the middle. Stryk and his student gleefully seize upon this rare occurrence of the noun *curiositas*, pointing out that it is here explicitly ascribed to spying informers ('expresse Delatoribus Curiositas quaedam assignatur', Stryk/Lüedecke 1743, 289). However, such terminological sensitivity is dropped as soon as it no longer suits present purposes. When Stryk and his student themselves come to discuss people's obligation to know about published laws (300), they make this obligation part of proper *curiositas*, now conveniently ignoring that same *locus* which, in the original context of the *Digest*, was saying that a person's reasonable knowledge of published laws could *not* be expected to extend to *curiositas*. Or again, when they discuss the extent to which one can be expected to be aware of a given fact, they quote the *locus* in full but claim that *curiositas* is also the usual legal term for the happy median between negligence and spying *curiositas*: in other words, they make *curiositas* denote both excessive *and* moderate inquisitiveness (301), in the same way as Rechenberg had made it denote both moderation (when *sana*) and excess (*insana*), the trio again being completed by the corresponding vice of lack—negligence.

Further semantic finishing touches were sometimes made to this Prussian-style *curiositas* in order to fit it for use in the social world. When it involved desire for knowledge, the outcome actually sought was not contemplative knowledge itself but a particular action, plus also the effects of that action (291). Thus the imperial spies (*curiosi*) were not only finding out something but doing something, 'taking care' ('curas gerere vel agere') of public order, which is why they were also called 'Curagendarii' ('care-takers') in Roman Law (298). Their *curiosi* name was derived nonetheless from *curiositas*, not (as Andrea Alciato thought) from *curia*, as in 'Curia Principis' ('the ruler's court'),[218] since that etymology would destroy the crucial Prussian links between late-Empire spies and the *curiositas* incumbent upon citizens of the modern state. Finally, in order to show that decorum-based *curiositas* is a duty, it was argued that in Tacitus its

---

[218] Stryk/Lüedecke 1743, 289. The *curia* etymology is also denied by Streit/Kalckhoff (1706, 3), who trace it back to Lorenzo Valla.

root, *cura*, could mean *officium* ('duty, office') (Streit/Kalckhoff 1706, 3).

Defined thus, Prussian-style *curiositas* was ready for practical use. The richest, fullest, and most influential description of its actions was the substantial Stryk dissertation. The topic of the dissertation is *curiositas* as defined by law. After first relating this to the other species of *curiositas*, Stryk and his student discuss the various objects at which it is directed: religious matters (ch. 2), public matters (ch. 3), licit private acts (ch. 4), illicit private acts (ch. 5).

First, having *curiositas* about religious matters involves, for the territorial prince, taking care of the souls of his population in the way recently described by Rechenberg, on whose two dissertations on *curiositas* Stryk and his student draw extensively, with acknowledgement (294, 296). They put the arguments, characteristic of the Protestant confessional state, that the secular ruler has extensive responsibility for ecclesiastical administration and must punish heretics. However, unlike the Saxon Rechenberg, they nuance this zealous *curiositas* in ways that echo the relative religious tolerance of Brandenburg-Prussia: heretics should only be put to death if they arouse sedition, and private freedom of worship should be allowed when written into the constitution which the ruler has inherited (292–4). Such views coincide with those generally held by Stryk—who was sympathetic to Pietism—and his own teacher Brunnemann: both minimized the applicability to Germany of canon law, which was less tolerant on such points.[219] On the other hand, this does not mean that there is any the less need for what Gerald Strauss has shown to be the touchstone of early modern absolutism—plenitude of information. Although Stryk himself was not a radical absolutist,[220] the strong drift of this dissertation is towards centralization of both power and information. Stryk and Lüedecke propose drastic measures to assist this princely investigation into people's faith. They make the pastor the tool of the state, in typically confessionalizing vein (Hsia 1989, 18–22). They propose going beyond the practice of consistorial visitations of local parishes—common in Brandenburg since 1573 (Dorwart 1938, 277–8)—by insisting that, in order to hunt down error, pastors themselves should visit all homes in their parish, even those of magistrates. This inclusion of magistrates

---

[219] See Hammerstein 1972, 156–7; Stintzing and Landsberg 1880–1910, iii. 68–9.
[220] Stintzing and Landsberg 1880–1910, iii. 67–8.

reveals the absolutist determination to create hierarchies based on social discipline rather than on automatic privilege of rank: no-one was exempt from suspicion (Strauss 1986, 151–3). The spectre of people entering other people's houses to discover their vicious secrets seems uncannily familiar, for it is indeed what Plutarch had described as the vice of *polypragmosyne*: as if to banish this spectre, the Frankfurt a.d. Oder jurists add that the pastor

should not use this as a pretext to seek to meddle with the duties of others, to give orders to magistrates in matters concerning their office . . . to participate in the deliberations of princes themselves . . . So this species of prohibited curiosity, while it is unacceptable in anyone, is especially inappropriate to a minister of the church.[221]

This is the point at which good *curiositas* would go bad. When this dissertation assigns legitimate *curiositas* to individuals, it is usually leased out to them, ultimately by the territorial ruler, for the sake of a prince-defined common good—another touchstone of absolutist ideology[222]—and it can become vicious if used for personal gratification. An ancient private vice is being half turned into a new public virtue.

Curiositas about public matters (ch. 3) is mainly the magistrates' official handling of crimes. It begins with prevention: if only the kind of border-controls used by the Emperor Justinian had been introduced in recent years in 'our country' ('nostra . . . Patria')—presumably Brandenburg-Prussia—then how many foreign criminals would have been barred from entering: 'it would be useful if that former curiosity, which was ordered by the Emperor . . . was today practised once more and if inquiries were diligently made about the circumstances of strangers, so that those seeking admission to the community had their origins, life, character, and means of support examined.'[223] Foreigners should also continue to be under surveillance for possible criminal behaviour once admitted. The question

---

[221] 'modo non sub ejusdem praetextu alieno muneri se immiscere, Magistratibus in officio imperare . . . imo ipsis Principum consiliis interesse intendat . . . Haec enim prohibitae Curiositatis non postrema species, quemadmodum in nemine hominum approbanda . . . ita praecipue Ecclesiae Ministro neutiquam convenit' (Stryk/Lüedecke 1743, 293).

[222] See Kitchen 1996, 107; Strauss 1986, ch. 5; Vierhaus 1988, 100–1.

[223] 'utile foret, si pristina illa, & ab Imperatore . . . praecepta, curiositas hodie iterum exerceretur, in advenarum conditionem diligentius inquireretur, illique, qui in civitatem se assumi petunt, examinarentur de origine, vita, moribus & sustendandi mediis' (Stryk/Lüedecke 1743, 297).

arises whether investigation of possible crimes by them and others should be restricted to magistrates alone. On the whole, the answer is yes, except for those *curiosi* (spies) to whom the investigation could be officially (if secretly) delegated, as in late Roman times. The use of ordinary people as unofficial informants is largely frowned upon, because of the danger of calumny and of the bad, self-gratifying species of *curiositas*. In other words, while the dissertation is consistently happy to see the delegation of state-sponsored *curiositas* to people who have official functions—such as pastors, magistrates, or their spies—it reveals extreme nervousness about delegating it to people who have no official role: this reflects the deep-seated distrust of human motivation which permeated the laws of the early modern bureaucratic state (Strauss 1986, 151-2). But what if common people do happen to possess useful information? Reluctant to disallow all juridical use of such information, Stryk and Lüedecke argue that a person can denounce a crime—thereby 'assisting the magistrate's curiosity'[224]—if it is *about* to be committed rather than has been already committed, and that a person can be reasonably expected to know about notorious and repeated crimes in their neighbourhood, but not about hidden ones such as debauchery and adultery.

Similar ambivalence surrounds juridical use of information arising from another, even more dubious species of *curiositas*, that of Catholic priests, who insist on having every sin listed in the confessional 'in order to satisfy their impious curiosity'.[225] Bad curiosity is, as so often, projected onto other churches. While information obtained via the confessional is disqualified in principle from use in criminal investigations, this prohibition can be overridden in exceptional cases such as treasonable plots: the refusal of Catholic priests to reveal the details of the Gunpowder Plot in England which had been confessed to them is cited later (308).

The public matters at which *curiositas* should be directed are not only crimes. They include others which, to modern readers, are perhaps even stranger bedfellows, but which were crucial ingredients in the development of the Prussian military state.[226] One is war, where *curiositas* means not just the reconnaissance, spying, and intelligence-gathering that a military leader should organize, but

---

[224] 'Magistratus curiositatem adjuvare' (298).
[225] 'ut impiam suam curiositatem expleant' (299).
[226] On Brandenburg-Prussia as a military state, see Fulbrook 1983, 47-58; Vierhaus 1988, 101-2.

also his general readiness and circumspection. The complacent Swedes showed themselves lacking in all these qualities recently when ousted from Brandenburg by the Great Elector—presumably a reference to their defeat at Fehrbellin in June 1675, having invaded from Swedish Pomerania in 1674. 'In war, not troubling oneself with curiosity about the enemy's intentions is definitely harmful!'[227] Other public objects of *curiositas* are positive laws. Whereas people are not expected to find out about them prior to their publication, on the other hand 'Curiosity about published laws is more necessary'.[228] Obedient citizens' social discipline lies not only in obeying laws that happen to reach their attention—presumably by word of mouth, or from the pulpit, or by printed poster[229]—but also in being responsible for ensuring that they are not unwittingly transgressing others. Ignorance is no excuse.

Next, the private acts, licit or illicit (chs. 4–5), at which *curiositas* can be legitimately directed are ones which, even if they do not seem to concern us directly, may concern us in some sense: 'laws require curiosity of anyone who enters into a contract'.[230] For example, a fiancé can and should have *curiositas* about the exact state of his fiancée's dowry and virginity; in turn, she should have *curiositas* about his solvency. The same applies not only to creditors and guarantors of debts, but also to buyers. If a purchased item turns out to have defects which

could be seen and easily spotted by a more curious and diligent buyer, then there will be no grounds for seeking compensation through legal action or a plea . . . Indeed the laws are written for the vigilant, not for the negligent . . . Thus if a pig sold to a butcher has measles, there are no legal grounds for seeking compensation, for it will be easy for a practised eye to diagnose that disease through inspection of the palate and tongue . . . Note I said, 'if a pig is sold to a butcher'. For, if the buyer is someone else, who is not nor ought to be an expert in this field, then equity will recommend a different outcome.[231]

---

[227] 'Tantum scilicet in bello nocet de hostium consiliis neglecta curiositas!' (299).
[228] 'In legibus promulgatis magis necessaria est curiositas' (300).
[229] On these methods of publishing ordinances, see Raeff 1983, 46–7.
[230] 'in contrahentibus etiam Leges Curiositatem quandoque desiderant' (303).
[231] 'Nam si videri possint, & ab alio magis diligenti curiosove emtore facile deprehendi, redhibitoriae actioni vel exceptioni locus non erit . . . Jura quippe vigilantibus, non vero negligentibus scripta sunt . . . Hinc si lanioni porcus venditus sit grandinibus laborans, *das Finnen hat*, actioni redhibitoriae nullus relinquitur locus; Facile enim morbum isthunc per inspectionem palati & linguae dignoscere poterit artifex . . . Dixi

As the dissertation strays into the details of pig-buying and the like, actual occurrences of the *curiositas* family of terms become less frequent, often limited to the start of a discursive point, as if the writer is straining heroically to make *curiositas qua* contractual vigilance a species of the single overall genus *curiositas* that includes very different species such as, say, astrological, magical, or sexual inquiry.

And it is to the more familiar species that Stryk and student devote their closing discussion of illicit *curiositas* that is aimed at private acts (ch. 5): opening other people's letters, eavesdropping on their confessions, and so on (310). Adultery returns here, considered now not as a crime at which citizen-like *curiositas* should or should not be directed, but rather, with reference to Plutarch on *polypragmosyne*, as being in itself an act of illicit *curiositas* which the male adulterer directs at the cuckolded husband's *voluptas* or sexual pleasure (308–9).[232] In a further contortion of the argument, the precise relation between *curiositas* and *voluptas* in the male extra-marital transgressor is then discussed. Was the Jesuit theologian Lessius right to argue that, if a man touches in a forbidden place another man's wife but—presumably falling short of adultery—does so purely out of *curiositas*, not out of *voluptas*, then he is guilty only of a venial sin, not of a mortal one?[233] Stryk and student, while sweeping aside the casuistical notion that some sin is merely venial, can just about bring themselves to accept the theoretical possibility that *curiositas* might operate without *voluptas*, but this makes them no less keen to see this *curiositas* prosecuted in a civil court:

It is therefore obvious that he is sinning, since he is prying into something that does not belong to him, thereby doing injury to another . . . Although I concede Lessius's point (loc. cit.) that this curiosity is dangerous and that a few people could distinguish so exactly between curiosity and pleasure that it becomes possible to touch out of curiosity without simultaneously conceiving of pleasure, nonetheless, even if there are such people, I do not think that they should go entirely unpunished, in case their impunity draws others to that dangerous curiosity.[234]

---

vero, si lanioni venditus sit: Nam si alius, qui hujus rei peritiam nec habet, nec habere debet, emtor extiterit, aliud suadebit aequitatis ratio' (306).

[232] See Plutarch 1971, 65ᵛ: 'il semble que l'adultere soit une espece de curiosité, de rechercher la volupté d'autruy'.

[233] See Lessius 1605, 722–4.

[234] 'Quod autem peccet, exinde manifestum est, quia res ad ipsum non pertinentes cum injuria quadam alterius inquirit . . . Et quamvis cum Less. *all. l.* facile largiar, periculosam esse illam Curiositatem, & paucos inter Curiositatem et voluptatem adeo

These jurists are transporting painstakingly into a juridical framework the *curiositas* that had long been denounced by moral theology; they are imagining its every twist and turn in everyday life and trying to categorize each as legal or illegal. Sin is criminalized in the search for social discipline.[235] *Curiositas*, often just a passion, vice, or virtue, has here also become either a crime or else a civic duty, one of the many public tasks demanded of the citizens of the early modern confessional state.

These legal definitions of curiosity had considerable illocutionary force. Did they also have perlocutionary force? That is, did they really have any impact on people's lives outside their institution of origin? Or were they just speculative words whose impact remained confined within university walls?

They were certainly not laws. Nor can they be extrapolated directly onto the positive laws of Brandenburg-Prussia and other states, still less onto the application of those laws,[236] and still less onto social practices. Definitions of *curiositas* were not uppermost in the minds of farmers and adulterers. What the dissertations do reveal is an extraordinary, obsessive, perhaps semi-speculative interest, in academic circles, in regulating the chaos of everyday life by interpreting it in terms of curiosity. The sheer detail of these proposals, like the sheer volume of early modern German ordinances, could be interpreted as a sign that their authors assumed that there was widespread resistance to such confessional social disciplining and moral policing, rather than as a sign of its success. Such resistance did indeed exist. According to Rudolf Vierhaus, although German absolutism was 'a system of rule in which the sovereign acted as legislator and supreme judge and possessed military and supreme administrative authority', on the other hand it was far from being the unlimited exercise of authority by a sovereign territorial lord.[237]

Nonetheless, university jurisprudence was preoccupied with the social disciplining of everyday activities such as curiosity. These dis-

---

exactam facere distinctionem, ut, quando illius causa tangit, non hanc simul concipiat; Attamen si dentur tales, eos impunes plane relinquendos non esse autumo, ne alii quoque ad periculosam hanc Curiositatem impunitate alliciantur' (309).

[235] Cf. Hsia 1989, ch. 7, 'The Moral Police'.

[236] The same is true of the German ordinances richly documented by Raeff (1983).

[237] Vierhaus 1988, 88–9. Cf. also Hsia 1989, 135–42, 151–62; Oestreich 1982, 259–63.

sertations indicate a current of ideas that existed among the likes of Stryk, Brunnemann, and Cocceji who, at the universities of Frankfurt a.d. Oder and then Halle—where Stryk later taught, from its opening in 1694 until 1710—trained two generations of future judges, lawyers, princely legal advisers, and court officials of the growing Brandenburg-Prussian bureaucracy, fulfilling one of the main purposes for which the University of Halle had been founded, and using Roman Law broadly to legitimize absolutism.[238] All this at a time when, as Gerald Strauss has shown, university-trained lawyers in city courts had long since taken over the trial function of lay judges and sometimes even of rural courts in Germanic territories, while difficult decisions were often referred to faculty legists.[239] Moreover, the top professors dispensed legal advice at the highest political level: Stryk and Brunnemann were counsellors to the Elector. Johann Philipp Streit, who presided over a 1706 law disputation 'on the curious man' ('de viro curioso'), was at that time rector of the University of Erfurt and so almost directly answerable to the chancellor, who was also a Catholic Elector, the Archbishop of Mainz.[240] This dissertation's direct, unacknowledged purloining of Prussian-style *curiositas*—from the Stryk and Cocceji dissertations—can be compared to the widespread copying of the ordinances of the great states (Prussia, Hesse, Saxony) by other states (Raeff 1983, 54).

Finally, the writings of law professors could even be translated into law: Brunnemann's famous 1647 treatise on investigative procedures in criminal cases (Brunnemann 1672), which was referred to in his student's dissertation on *polypragmosyne* ([Brunnemann]/Henel 1691, E2^r), was eventually incorporated into Brandenburg criminal law in the early eighteenth century (*ADB*). While legal disputations

---

[238] This function would increasingly be taken over by natural law, with the likes of both Cocceji and Stryk's Halle colleague Christian Thomasius: cf. Dyck 1976; Gagliardo 1991, 94–5; Strauss 1986, 63–4. The crucial training function of the Halle and Frankfurt a.d. Oder law faculties would be further demonstrated in 1727 when Friedrich Wilhelm I established there the first chairs in Cameral Science, that is, public administration.

[239] Strauss 1986, ch. 3, esp. 77–84.

[240] Streit was rector or pro-rector for an exceptionally long period (17 years). The Elector was represented in Erfurt by a pro-chancellor of the university. Even while Streit was pro-rector, he was directly answerable to—and often acted for—the rector (Count Philipp Wilhelm von Boineburg), who also acted as the worldly ruler of the city of Erfurt, that is, as the Elector's *proprinceps*. See Kleineidam 1981, 76, 261–6.

were semantic battles among the legal elite, they show nonetheless that semantics was one important component of the acculturation that stood shoulder to shoulder with coercion in the processes of social disciplining and confessionalization.[241]

1.4   CONCLUSIONS

Several micro-narratives emerge from this survey of university discussions of curiosity. Most often curiosity was defined as a passion and/or a desire, rooted in the body, morally indifferent in itself but always manifesting itself as a virtue or a vice. Unprecedented claims about its importance were sometimes made: it was *the* other key passion alongside desire; it and not wonder was the beginning of all philosophy; it was directed at the whole of time—past, present, future; it ensured our very survival; even animals had curiosity. It usually involved wanting to know something but it could equally involve wanting to do something. Whether it was good or bad depended most often—at least in theory—not on the inherent goodness or badness of the desiring subject or of the desired object but rather on whether the relation between the two was appropriate: for example, under what circumstances was it licit to find out about other people's business, to meddle in it, or to import learning from one discipline into another? Context determined morality. This understanding of curiosity as a licit or illicit desire to know or act in a way that transgressed the boundaries separating other people's business from our own was explicitly described as being a distinctively contemporary version of curiosity—'adapted to the ways of today'—though it was strongly influenced by the ancient Greek terms *polypragmosyne* and *periergia*.

However, these are, precisely, micro- rather than macro-narratives, since not all of the university versions of curiosity fit even these generalizations about it. Moreover, even individual versions, however coherent at first glance, were often beset with inconsistencies or contradictions of the kind that were seized upon in disputations. Yet the ongoing contestation about the nature of curiosity was not an initial phase in the emergence of a definitive 'concept'; rather, it was the very condition that made possible the sixty-year-long life

---

[241] On acculturation in this context, see Hsia 1989, ch. 6.

of curiosity as a prominent theme in university debates. These institutions, obsessed with defining things, paradoxically required that things have a degree of indeterminacy, which they fostered through their practices of oration, disputation, and printing, through their habit of dividing things into species, and through their encouragement of rhetorical creativity within certain limits. The greater the number of professors and students who claimed that their definition of curiosity was definitive, the greater the indeterminacy fostered overall by these institutions.

Why did they foster this indeterminacy? To enable them to mould curiosity continually according to their changing needs. The very definitions of curiosity were driven, at least to some extent, by the multifarious purposes for which universities used it: to legitimize universities and discredit other sources of knowledge; to win funds by flattering patrons; to reinforce the superiority of the higher faculties; to attack one's own faculty colleague; to defend the autonomy of porous disciplines such as medicine and yet also allow a limited amount of polymathy, especially to professors rather than students; to attack perceived enemies of Lutheran orthodoxy, such as late medieval scholastics, Catholics, Socinians, Arminians, syncretists, or the Hohenzollern; to gather information for the benefit of the state through pastoral visits to homes, border controls, spies, or the confessional; to make ordinary people responsible for informing themselves about the laws to which they are subject and about the people with whom they enter into private contracts. Many more attempted uses of curiosity can now no longer be recovered. And the extent to which they effected actual changes in opinion or behaviour can mostly only be surmised.

Yet this does not mean that 'curiosity' was simply a multi-purpose set of terms. Most professors and students went out of their way to show that their version of curiosity was at least partly connected to others, not just through words but in reality. There was a collective effort to demonstrate that they were mostly all talking about the same thing, however differently they understood it. And however new the uses to which curiosity was being put, all agreed that it had always existed, even if some thought that there was now more of it around than in previous periods.

These powerful beliefs—in the longevity of curiosity, in its underlying unity whatever the diversity of its species, and in its enormous scope—were perhaps sustained for various reasons. Universities turned to authoritative texts from the past in their search for validation, however creatively they adapted those texts to their own needs. It was in the interest of universities to present their polemical tools—such as curiosity—as timeless, universal entities, since that detracted attention from the expediency with which they used them and so enhanced the persuasiveness of the use. Moreover, the cumulative academic and other descriptions of curiosity as a timeless, universal entity had turned it into an extraordinarily powerful and subtle framework for making distinctions between good and bad knowledge or action, and for making those distinctions often by judging the relation between desiring subjects and desired objects or else between agents and acts. These institutions' discourse on curiosity tells us much about how they treated topics and themes in general; but above all it tells us how and for what purposes they continually reshaped curiosity.

2

Institutions: Church

2.1 CURIOSITY IN CHURCH DISCOURSES

My second example of an institution which shaped curiosity for a variety of uses is the church. For the most part, early modern church discourse condemned curiosity, treating it as a sin, usually venial but sometimes mortal.[1] But no single semantic fibre ran through all discussions of curiosity in texts which claimed institutional affiliation to a church. Curiosity consisted usually in wanting to know too much, but sometimes in wanting to do something inappropriate (2.2.2, 2.2.4.1): in other words, *curiositas*, *curiosité*, and so on were again sometimes influenced by Plutarch and *polypragmosyne*, though less often than in university discourse. The notion that curiosity could be either good or bad depending on circumstances was also much less common in church than in university discourse.

Although university- and church-style curiosity were both shaped via authoritative texts from the past, that link to tradition was even stronger in the case of church discourse. Novelty was not a straightforwardly prized value in either institution, but whereas university discourse was sometimes positive about the association between curiosity and novelty, church discourse could not be so, since novelty smacked of heresy. Nonetheless, the most direct source of church versions of curiosity was not the Bible itself: after all, the 'curiosity' family of terms occurs only about a dozen times in the Vulgate, and the noun *curiositas* only once. Rather, the most direct source was the patristic tradition of discussion of *curiositas*.[2] Like the Church Fathers, early modern theologians then projected *curiositas* back *onto* the Bible: for example, the Calvinist William Ames authorized the statement 'We should also avoid all curiosity' by referring to

---

[1] Verbeeck-Verhelst 1988, esp. 349.
[2] On this tradition, see Blumenberg 1988, ch. 5; Defaux 1982, ch. 4; Meijering 1980; Newhauser 1982; Oberman 1974; Peters 1985.

Deuteronomy 29.29, Proverbs 25.1, 1 Timothy 6.20, 2 Timothy 2.23, Titus 3.9, John 21.22, and Acts 1.6–7, although the 'curiosity' family did not generally occur in these verses, whether in the Vulgate and the corrected versions of it or in new Protestant Latin translations.[3]

However, early modern church discourse on curiosity did not just repeat its patristic sources. Even when it quoted them directly, this repetition introduced a difference, since curiosity was often being put to new, distinctively contemporary uses. Moreover, church discourse was now deeply affected by rise of the secular culture of curiosities. Before the seventeenth century, churches had never been confronted with the existence of such an array of secular discourses which explicitly celebrated desires and objects as 'curious'. Whereas medieval critics of curiosity had often been monks attacking fellow monks who would not have accepted that label, which therefore functioned as what Reinhart Koselleck calls an asymmetric concept, early modern church critics were in a very different position, attacking as bad a curiosity that was happily flaunted, as good, by a much more autonomous lay philosophical culture.[4] In the face of this challenge, church discourse could not simply carry on as before. It responded mainly in two ways.

One response was to intensify the attacks on curiosity. Given the new-found popularity of curiosity in many quarters, it seemed more of a threat than ever to people's salvation (2.2 below). Moreover, its apparent innocence only seemed to provide new proof that St Augustine had been right to warn of its duplicity when he argued that 'the vain and curious desire to learn things through the flesh' is 'masked under the name of acquiring knowledge'.[5] Worldly rather than spiritual, curiosity seemed to reinforce the divide between church and 'world'. Indeed, it was so pervasive—an ex-Jesuit spotted 'curiosities everywhere' (2.3.3)—that it seemed to be virtually syn-

---

[3] 'Debemus etiam curiositatem omnem vitare' (Ames 1630, 76). By contrast, a few writers did seek to ground their condemnation of curiosity in Latin biblical terminology: e.g. Calvin presented his treatise against judicial astrology as an attack on the 'curiositez' of the world, echoing the attack in Acts (19.19) on the magical arts of the Ephesians, which were called *perierga* in the original Greek (as Calvin points out (1985, 99)) and *curiosa* in the Vulgate (though not in all 16th-century translations of Acts).

[4] Cf. Pantin 1998, 65.

[5] 'experiendi per carnem vana et curiosa cupiditas, nomine cognitionis et scientiae palliata' (Augustine 1968, ii. 174).

onymous with the world, at least until the culture of curiosities shrank in scope, from about the mid-eighteenth century. By contrast, nowadays the curiosity—as opposed to desire for knowledge—that is still condemned by some church discourse is no longer coextensive with the secular world or with mainstream science and learning but is limited to divination, pornography, and other people's private secrets.[6] The situation in the early modern period was very different: curiosity became one of the key flashpoints in the constant battle between church and world. It had played this role before—for example in St Augustine's writings—but never so extensively.

How should the church conduct its battle with the world? Opinion was divided, as Henry Phillips and others have shown with reference to Counter-Reformation France: some advocated spiritual withdrawal from the world, arguing that it was impossible to live a religious life in it; others argued that one should engage with the world and try to reform it spiritually (Phillips 1997, esp. 4–5). Curiosity was enlisted in both these strategies, but mainly in the more antagonistic one: worldly curiosity was to be entirely rejected.

Because of the rise of positive meanings of curiosity in secular culture, the clash was profoundly semantic: a church-defined meaning of the term needed to be imposed on secular meanings. For example, in 1678 the Danish ex-anatomist and dissector of the human brain, Nicolas Steno (Nils Stensen), wrote, now as a new bishop, to his friend and erstwhile collaborator Melchisédech Thévenot, urging him to abandon naturalist endeavour, to realize that 'all the curiosities of the world are mere vanities' (a rewriting of Ecclesiastes 1.1).[7] Steno was still speaking the language of *curiosité* that he and Thévenot would have shared previously as natural philosophers. But he was now changing that term's prime denotation to the patristic one. Yet this was not a wholesale change of meaning: the replaced denotation—'good researches into nature'—resonated on as a subservient connotation. Thus, even in church discourse, a secular perspective was included alongside the religious one in the term 'curiosity', which became an arena for the clash between the two perspectives instead of reflecting only the religious one. This dual perspective, distinctively early modern, made the 'curiosity' family of terms especially highly charged in church discourse. Occasionally,

---

[6] *New Catholic Encyclopaedia* 1967, q.v.

[7] 'toutes les curiositez du monde ne sont que vanitez', quoted in Dew 1999, 87.

even church critics of curiosity allowed the secular perspective such prominence in their use of the term that this begged the question whether bad curiosity could be rechannelled for good purposes or could at least serve as an image for good religious inquiry. Such ambivalent moments were not new: when St Augustine spoke of 'pia curiositate', was this merely an oxymoron, as Labhardt thinks (1960, 217), or an indication that pious curiosity really might exist? But the early modern prominence of positive senses made such questions arise much more often: many were not clearly answered but instead left grey areas in texts, blurred boundaries around curiosity.[8]

Whether or not this tenuous, phantom, good double of curiosity appeared in their discourse, church critics of curiosity—such as Steno the bishop—gave a meta-status to the pejorative religious meaning, which explained and relativized the secular meaning but did not eradicate it. Thus, Steno did not think that he was now talking about a different thing from what he and Thévenot would previously have called curiosity when conducting their researches. He merely thought that he now understood that thing better. Crossing over from secular to church discourse—from one language-game to another—usually involved creating a new hierarchy of meanings but not a new thing. Although churches understood curiosity very differently from, say, universities, learned societies, naturalists, or collectors, all of these institutions and groups usually considered each other to be referring to the same thing, not to unrelated meanings which happened to share the same homonym.

The second church response to the culture of curiosities was to accommodate it rather than condemn it out of hand (2.3).[9] Although, as we have just seen, even stern critics of curiosity hinted that a good species of curiosity might exist, only a few church writers pursued that possibility clearly. Doing so made them vulnerable to accusations that they were capitulating to the secular world. They saw themselves as seeking to reform the secular world through engagement with it, rather than giving up on it (2.3.1, 2.3.3). Engaging with the world could mean trying to spread religious mes-

---

[8] My approach to these grey areas is indebted to Terence Cave's analysis of conceptual disturbances in early modern texts (1999).
[9] For the notion of accommodation, see Phillips 1997, 5.

sages by entering the commercial book market: even books that condemned curiosity had to be advertised as appealing to curiosity, since that had become such a standard sales technique. Pragmatic imperatives created cracks in the churches' united front against curiosity (2.3.2, 2.3.4).

Thus, even the churches, although they mostly condemned curiosity, did not produce any single definition of curiosity that proved definitive in the sense that it was adopted by all church discourse, let alone by secular discourse. This was because, like universities, churches used curiosity, in countless ways. Although those uses sometimes took the form of definitions—most obviously in theology—on the whole they did so less than in universities. Conceptual coherence was often not a top priority. Much church discourse was concerned less to define curiosity than to teach people how to avoid it. This pragmatism was especially characteristic of pastoral discourse, such as that of priests, prelates, pastors, preachers, confessors, and spiritual directors. Preachers found that the best way to persuade their congregations to avoid curiosity was to bombard them with exemplary tales of it and metaphors for it rather than with theoretical definitions of it. The behaviour which people tried to instil by talking and writing about curiosity could be mental and spiritual more than physical, for example when novice monks were being trained in meditation (2.2.1).

These different uses to which curiosity was put arose from distinct genres and discourses: training manuals for novices, speechs about church administration, polemical tracts attacking secular or other religious groups, sermons, letters and other forms of spiritual advice, guides for pilgrims, popularizing compilations of religious doctrine. Selective examples of these will be studied, all written by men although often purporting to be about or for women too. These printed remnants are likely to have differed from the oral events—sermons, speeches, conversations—which some of them record, as was the case with printed university sources. Whether oral or written, each genre or discourse was a language-game that moulded curiosity according to its own rules. Even a single writer—such as the bishop Jean-Pierre Camus—gave a different version of curiosity according to which genre he was writing in.

Curiosity often bore distinctive confessional stamps. In some contexts, Calvinists were even less likely than Catholics to allow for the existence of a good species.[10] Curiosity was used by one Calvinist pastor to help people decide whether God had called them to certain actions (2.2.4.1); it was used by a Lutheran church administrator to try and give his pastors autonomy in relation to the local political regime (2.2.2); by a Pietist (Spizel: 2.2.3) to attack much learned culture as dangerous diversions of the kind which we earlier saw the Pietist Stahl condemning in medicine; by a Catholic bishop (Bossuet) to attack any theological inquiry that took place outside his church (2.2.4.3); by an ex-Jesuit to embrace worldly culture (2.3.3). However, on the other hand, each religious group did *not* have its own definitive and entirely distinctive 'concept' of curiosity. Calvinists and Lutherans did not seek to follow systematically everything that their founders had written about curiosity.[11] By no means all Jesuits accommodated curiosity.[12] Even Spizel's distinctively Pietist, apparently clear-cut condemnation of it leaves open the tenuous possibility that it has a good species too.

Catholicism and Calvinism are represented here mainly by texts written in French on *curiosité*. Lutheranism and Pietism are represented mainly by texts written in Latin on *curiositas*. There was a greater terminological gulf between German and Latin than between French and Latin, since fewer German writers used those terms' vernacular cognate—*Curiosität*—as the equivalent of *curiositas*; most preferred instead native Germanic terms such as *Fürwitz*, *vorwitzig*, and *neugierig*, which were all used by Luther[13] and were more comprehensible to non-Latinate readers, although *curiositet* (later *Curiosität*) began to arise in subject-oriented senses in the late sixteenth century.[14] The relation between those native Germanic terms and *curiositas* would repay further study. Terms like *Fürwitz*, while roughly synonymous with *curiositas* and with the French *curiosité*, also differed from them in crucial ways: for example, they too denoted a sin but without also connoting the culture of curiosities;

---

[10] e.g. in the philosophical poetry written in French from the 1550s to the 1620s (N. Kenny 1991*b*, 264–70).

[11] Curiosity in Luther and Calvin has been studied by Oberman (1974, 39–49) and Meijering (1980) respectively.

[12] See 2.2.3 below, on Garasse, who attacked curiosity, as did his contemporary and fellow Jesuit Nicolas Caussin (Valentin 1978, i. 95–7; Verbeeck-Verhelst 1988, 353–5). Thomist Jesuit treatises presented *curiositas* as the opposite of good *studiositas*: e.g. Lessius 1605, 722–4; Nicquet 1648, 88–9.

[13] Aland (ed.) 1974, 372, 387, 390.

[14] See N. Kenny 1998, 43, 93–101.

they therefore lacked the dual perspective mentioned above and the capacity to make, say, theologians and collectors seem to be talking about the same thing; moreover, they did not connect desiring subjects to desired objects in the way that the 'curiosity' family did. It was perhaps for such reasons that efforts were sometimes made, for example in academic theology, to make *Curiosität* the main vernacular equivalent of *curiositas*.[15]

My case-studies stretch from 1573 to the early eighteenth century, but they are not arranged in strict chronological order, since the precise date was not the most decisive factor determining the shapes and uses of curiosity: they depended even more on the kind of language-game to which they belonged, so I have roughly grouped cases together accordingly. I begin with a 1680 text in order to show that monastic discourse on curiosity, even by this relatively late date, remained much closer to its medieval precursors than did certain other, more worldly kinds of early modern church discourse.

2.2 AVOIDING CURIOSITY, MORE OR LESS

2.2.1 *A manual for the novice monk*

Even in the apparent stillness of monasteries, discourse on curiosity was used in attempts to get people to *do* things. The actions it promoted were not so much physical as mental and spiritual, part of what Mary Carruthers has shown to be the craft or ortho*praxis*—as distinct from orthodoxy—of monastic meditational rhetoric (1998, esp. 1–6). This discourse was, in contrast to much other church discourse on curiosity, largely untouched by the contemporary culture of curiosities. It was rooted in patristic authorities such as Augustine, Gregory the Great, and Bernard of Clairvaux.[16] Curiosity was overwhelmingly sinful, part of the world from which monks sought to

---

[15] e.g. the translator of Johann Franz Buddeus's *Institutiones theologiae moralis* translated *curiositas* as *Curiosität*, but even he still needed to explain the latter's meaning at the start of passages on *curiositas*, by including also the more familiar term *Vorwitz* ('die curiosität oder vorwitz', Buddeus 1719*b*, 229 = 1719*a*, 214; see also Buddeus 1719*b*, 466 = 1719*a*, 437).
[16] On the monastic tradition of *curiositas*, see Carruthers 1998, 82–91, 94, 99–101; Oberman 1974, ch. 4; Peters 1985, 91–2.

sequester themselves, though even in this tradition the possibility of a holy curiosity was very occasionally half-glimpsed.[17]

Numerous manuals written for the benefit of novice monks (and their masters) advised them how to avoid bringing curiosity into the cloister. Let me take as an example the *Neophyte's Guide, or Clear and Simple Instruction for the Novice Monk* (Augsburg, 1680) by Juvenal d'Anagni (1635–1714), a Franciscan belonging to the reformed Capuchin order, who was himself a novice master before serving as Provincial in his native Tyrol (Diaz y Diaz 1974). His manual is devoted to two activities: first mental prayer and secondly mortification. Each can only be performed if curiosity is avoided.

First, in mental prayer and meditation on the Passion, *curiositas* risks sidetracking the novice if his intellect rather than his will is stimulated. This risks occurring especially in the method of meditation which involves reflecting on the people involved in the Passion, then on their words, then on their actions. The novice's craft consists in progressing through the various rhetorical 'places' into which each of these objects of meditation is subdivided—for example, the *loci* for 'people' include their nature, affects, reasonings, internal virtues, external behaviour, conditions and circumstances. The danger is that the novice, instead of just using these headings to orient his will and emotions, will want to *know* something under each heading. That would be *curiositas*, as St Bernard and St Peter of Alcántara warned. However, novices are actually less at risk from it than the more learned, who have more baggage in the intellect that needs emptying in order for meditation to be possible.[18] Secondly, perfection through mortification can only be achieved if the novices become dead to both sensual and intellectual delights,[19] whether 'curious' words and fragrances—to which he should not turn 'very curiously'—or 'curious speculations'.[20] The sin of curiosity is thus inseparable from curious objects.

[17] Carruthers argues that the notion of holy curiosity existed, but all bar one of the medieval quotations that she uses as evidence for it involve the adjective or adverb, not the noun *curiositas* (Carruthers 1998, 99–101): this suggests that holy curiosity remained a grey area rather than a distinct notion.

[18] Juvenal d'Anagni 1680, 26–8. On the problem of the status of learning in monastic culture, see Leclercq 1957.

[19] Thomas Aquinas argued that *curiositas* was based either in the senses or in the intellect (Cabassut 1953, 2654–6).

[20] 'verba curiosa . . . odorifera . . . curiosa . . . curiosiùs . . . curiosae speculationes' (224–4; for further advice on avoiding *curiositas* in mortification and in preparation for mental prayer, see pp. 296, 15 respectively).

Juvenal d'Anagni was not concerned to define curiosity but to show novices how to avoid it. In other church discourses, avoiding curiosity also involved action, but of a much less interior kind.

2.2.2   *Pastors and politics: an oration by a Hamburg church administrator*

Curiosity could also be understood as meddling in other people's business. Whereas universities explored the possibility that such meddling could be justified under certain circumstances, church discourse did not. Invoking this kind of curiosity was often intended to keep people out of one's own business. For example, far from the monastic cloister, in the urban bustle of Hamburg, one Lutheran church administrator spoke about curiosity in order to prevent the city's supreme civic authority—the Senate—from meddling in church affairs, as well as to prevent his own clergy from meddling in municipal politics: in 1573 Joachim Westphal, the superintendent or spiritual leader of the city's clergy, gave them a speech about avoiding curiosity (*De vitanda curiositate oratio*). Probably present in the audience were Hamburg's chief pastors (*Hauptpastoren*), the junior clergy of the major parishes, and preachers of the minor chapels and churches in the city and its suburbs.[21] The choice of topic was not innocent.

As Joachim Whaley has shown, in 1573 the independent city of Hamburg was a major commercial centre, rapidly swelling with immigrants of different confessions and nationalities, while still trying to find political structures which would ensure stability and peace among the mainly Lutheran populace following the upheavals of the Reformation. Institutional instability reigned. The prime movers in the Reformation had been the parish clergy, and in 1532 the powerful post of their *Superintendent* had been established. Yet divisive doctrinal pronouncements made by successive incumbents fostered civil unrest, inducing the city's Senate, worried by the prospect of an uncontrollable clergy, to ban theological controversy in 1560, reduce the powers of the superintendent, and leave the post empty from 1562 to 1571. It was subsequently filled only in 1571–4—by Westphal—and 1580–93, after which the Senate's magistrates consolidated their administrative power over the church by

---

[21] On the composition of the Hamburg ministry, see Whaley 1985, 25.

replacing the troublesome post with a much weaker one. In 1580 they also consolidated their grip on doctrine by imposing the Book of Concord as the basis for Lutheran teaching. Orthodoxy had triumphed.[22]

In 1573 Westphal (1510–74) knew that he would have to fight to maintain the existence of his post and the relative autonomy of his clergy. For the previous nine years he had effectively been acting as superintendent although the actual post had been suppressed. Like his predecessors, he himself was a notorious controversialist, well known beyond Hamburg as a Gnesio-Lutheran, an anti-Philippist, bitterly opposed to doctrinal compromise with Calvinism.[23] However, he seems to have considered that in this instance it would be best to proceed through negotiation rather than confrontation with the Senate. Such was the urgency of the situation that—apparently on his own initiative—he revived an old tradition that had been dormant for thirty years, by convening the clergy to hear his speech: 'there occur, from time to time, occasions and causes which demand public disputation of some controversial article of doctrine, and in such cases I cannot refuse to do what is prescribed by ordinance'.[24]

He begins by announcing that his topic is the vice of meddling in what lies outside our calling or profession: *polypragmosyne*. The rest of the oration outlines its causes (pride, ambition, avarice, sloth), the virtues it opposes (modesty, humility), its evil effects, the biblical *loci* which forbid it, *exempla* of it (biblical and other) and, finally, ancient sayings which discourage it.

Initially, he gives only another Greek alternative (*periergia*) for *polypragmosyne*, 'since we lack a Latin equivalent, and the Latin word *curiositas* does not match the compound Greek term in emphasis and force'.[25] However, this official philological precision[26] is undermined by his own verbal practice: the printed version has

---

[22] Whaley 1985, 8–16, 23–5.

[23] On Westphal, see Moller 1744, i. 727–8; iii. 641–59; *Oxford Encyclopaedia* 1996; Wallmann 1985, 102; Whaley 1985, 117–18.

[24] 'fateor, posse aliquando incidere eiusmodi occasiones et causas, quae flagitant, ut de controverso aliquo doctrinae articulo publice disputando conferatur, in quo casu mihi, ut id quod exigit ordinatio, faciam, non sit recusandum' (Westphal 1573, A2^v–A3^r; see also sig. A2^{r-v}).

[25] 'cum latino vocabulo, quod ei respondeat careamus, et graecae vocis compositae Emphasim et vim, curiositatis vocabulum non assequatur' ([A7^v]).

[26] In earlier days, Westphal had briefly taught philology (*Oxford Encyclopaedia* 1996).

curiositas in its title, not a Greek term, and he sometimes uses *curiositas* and its cognates as if they were synonymous with *polypragmosyne.*[27] This is partly in order to use language that is more familiar to his audience and partly in order to enable him to authorize this vice through a biblical phrase, 'curiosè agentes'— 'acting curiously', that is, 'being busybodies'—which occurs in the Vulgate: St Paul, 2 Thessalonians 3.11 (A5ʳ). Curiosity is thus terminologically muddled by conflicting desiderata: philological precision, biblical underpinning, and comprehensibility.

But this imprecision does not hinder in the slightest the illocutionary purposes for which the superintendent is describing curiosity, for those purposes emerge less through the opening definition of *polypragmosyne* than indirectly through Westphal's *exempla* of it, or—to use Westphal's own terms—through 'histories' (*historiae*) rather than through 'precepts' (*praecepta*). His purposes are multiple: for example they include getting parish clergy to do their jobs more conscientiously. But the main purpose seems to be to urge the clergy not to meddle in politics and to urge the Senate—perhaps the prime intended audience for the printed version—in turn not to meddle in ecclesiastical affairs. His peroration states that this vice is menacing the church with specific dangers at present ([B4ʳ⁻ᵛ]). Perhaps referring indirectly to the recent and present trouble in Hamburg, he lists civil turbulence as one of the effects of curiosity, particularly of the kind that confuses the sacred with the profane ([A6ᵛ]–[A7ʳ]).

The clergy display *polypragmosyne* when they get involved in secular matters: not for nothing are they prohibited from wearing a sword (B3ʳ), and hence the instruction to St Peter, the first bishop, to put away his own (B[1]ʳ). Two of the three *exempla* from non-biblical history amplify this message: for example, a Count of Bichingen who was Bishop of Magdeburg, upon hearing that the Duke of Saxony was preparing to wage war on him, simply continued with his pastoral duties, saying 'I will look after my churches, God will do the fighting for me', at which point the Duke turned back his soldiers, saying he had no chance against an adversary who had God for an ally. The third such *exemplum* slips in the more controversial message that secular rulers should stay out of church affairs: Leontius, Bishop of the Danube province of Moesia, having observed his colleagues at a synod obsequiously asking the Emperor Constantine

---

[27] e.g. A3ᵛ, A5ʳ, [A6ᵛ], [A7ᵛ], B3ᵛ.

what the synod should do, then publicly admonished Constantine for not minding his own business, at which point the mighty Emperor withdrew: 'For just as a bishop should not take on the role of prince or magistrate, so a prince should not usurp the role of a bishop or minister.'[28]

For 'prince', read 'Senate'. Westphal was offering to renounce interference in civil politics in return for retaining the right to speak his mind about doctrine. However much the Senate magistrates may have applauded his general definition of *polypragmosyne*, seven years later they showed what they thought of his particular proposed applications of it by imposing the Book of Concord. Ultimately, the superintendent's illocutionary aims were not translated into perlocutionary success.

Westphal's specific historical circumstances—on the post-Reformation borderline between ecclesiastical and municipal authority—led him to see curiosity as a vice that could occur in both the church and the secular world but that was not inherent in either: rather, it consisted in confusing the two. By contrast, for many early modern church writers, curiosity was an inherently secular vice from which true Christian communities needed to distance themselves.

2.2.3 *Against libertines, scholars, clockmakers, and Rosicrucians: François Garasse, Johann Valentin Andreae, Gottlieb Spizel*

For different reasons, neither the Lutheran superintendent in 1573 nor the Capuchin advising novices in 1680 needed to cope with secular claims that curiosity was a good thing. Many church writers did have to, including members of the regular or secular clergy who wrote polemical tracts condemning the curiosity which they saw in the world around them. They had much more of a semantic battle on their hands: however keen they were to condemn curiosity, it had a distinctively early modern duality in their works, incorporating the perspectives of both church and world.

Among these critics were Catholics, such as the French Jesuit François Garasse, and Lutherans such as the pastors Johann Valentin Andreae and Gottlieb Spizel (the Pietist). All three were aiming to reform the secular world by helping people to avoid curiosity.

---

[28] 'Ut enim Episcopus officium principis aut magistratus non debet occupare, ita nec princeps Episcopi seu ministri officium debet invadere.' (B[1]ᵛ).

Echoing the patristic tradition, all three presented *curiosi* or *curieux* as enemies of the community who wish to be different from the crowd, cultivating a singularity—'in religion, learning, and other areas of behaviour'[29]—which, especially for Garasse and Spizel, leads in turn to atheism.

Andreae (1586–1654), influenced by Johann Arndt, became the outstanding Württemberg figure in the early seventeenth-century movement to consolidate Lutheran orthodoxy by reforming everyday life in line with Christian social precepts.[30] The movement may be seen as a precursor of Pietism. Andreae's *Treatise on the Pestilence of Curiosity* (1620), written while he was a pastor at Vaihingen, was one of several works sketching his ideal of what he often called 'a community of Christ'.[31] One big impediment to the ideal is 'curiosity . . . or that immodest thirst to know and do what lies beyond the customary cleverness of human beings'.[32] *Curiosi* include those who commission and buy elaborate paintings, statues, jewellery, clocks, or other automata, those who seek the secret of perpetual motion, fraudulent alchemists, and practitioners of magic and divination (10–26). The climax of the treatise is then devoted to heresies stemming from curiosity, notably of the mystical spiritualist kind: Andreae condemns the followers of the radical Saxon pastor Valentin Weigel (1533–88) and also the so-called Rosicrucian fraternity, to which Andreae gives special status as 'the inner core of curious people of our time'.[33] Thus curiosity is not confined to inquisitiveness: it involves both 'knowing and doing', both clock-makers and Rosicrucians.

Over fifty years later, Spizel's attack was on *curiositas* understood as 'knowing' rather than as 'doing', but its direct borrowings from Andreae's treatise suggest that Spizel considered himself to be denouncing the same vice as his predecessor.[34] Spizel (1639–91), after studying theology at Leipzig, spent thirty years as a Lutheran

[29] 'religione, literis, et moribus reliquis' (Andreae 1621, A2^{r-v}). See Andreae 1621, 7–11, 26–8; Garasse 1971, i. 167; Spizel 1676, 117–21, 954.

[30] Hsia 1989, 21. On Andreae, see Beeler 1996; Montgomery 1973; Wallmann 1985, 113.

[31] '*societas Christi*' (Andreae 1621, 37). On this notion, see Montgomery 1973, i. 63–4.

[32] '*Curiositas* . . . sive immodica supra quam solita hominum solertia admittit, sciendi, agendíque sitis' (3).

[33] 'Curiosorum huius temporis . . . viscus et offendiculum' (35; see pp. 33–7).

[34] Compare Spizel 1676, 950, 954–5 with Andreae 1621, 5–6, 12–13 respectively.

pastor in Augsburg, where, as a friend and follower of the Pietist leader Philipp Jakob Spener, he became instrumental in introducing Pietism to the southern German city while also becoming known further afield for his writings (Blaufuß 1977, esp. 93). In the wake of Spener's crucial programme of church reform, the _Pia desideria_ (1675), Spizel included two extended attacks on the curiosity of academics in his two treatises on the 'inhabitants of THE WORLD OF LEARNING',[35] _The Happy Scholar_ (1676, 948–1059) and _The Unhappy Scholar_ (1680, 816–42). Spizel's aim was spiritual reform of the institutions of learning, turning them from 'profane' into 'pious'.[36] Like many others (Evans 1981, 171), he criticized universities (1676, 985), and he proposed a syllabus of patristic reading for schools (1676, 1029–33): indeed _The Happy Scholar_ was itself studied as a textbook in at least one school (Blaufuß 1977, 93). Spizel seems to have been concerned less with analysing the individual psychology of curiosity than with laying bare quasi-anthropologically the social mechanisms of honour, glory, and flattery which produce it in the 'world of learning' (1676, 950–2). This profane 'world', against which Spizel's Pietism is pitted, is not limited to universities and schools, but also stretches much further into space and time: his list of scholars 'unhappy due to harmful curiosity' includes Cicero, Heraclitus, Cornelius Agrippa, Girolamo Cardano, Jean Bodin, Hugo Grotius, and René Descartes,[37] while the select few scholars who have escaped _curiositas_ and the other vices of learning include Moses, Seneca, St Augustine, Petrarch, Juan Luis Vives, Desiderius Erasmus, Justus Lipsius, Francis Bacon, and of course Spener himself.[38]

Curiositas is the last of the nine vices which Spizel attributes to scholars in _The Happy Scholar_, the others including impiety (or atheism), pride, jealousy, calumny, ambition, and avarice. Like his fellow Pietist Stahl, Spizel understands curiosity as the appetite for knowledge, insofar as it is excessive and is aimed at useless or incomprehensible objects (1676, 948). Although curiosity is not here equated with action, the influence of _polypragmosyne_ is still present in other ways, as with Stahl: the excessiveness of curiosity is sometimes

---

[35] 'LITERATI ORBIS incolae' (Spizel 1676, 971).
[36] For this terminology, see Spizel 1676, e.g. 1002, 1006, 1008, 1010, 1012.
[37] 'Infelices ex noxia curiositate' (ibid. 1125–6).
[38] Ibid. 1019–20, 1126–8.

defined as transgression of decorum, when a scholar goes beyond the bounds of his own discipline, as did Grotius when he strayed from jurisprudence into theology.[39] Spizel levels the charge of curiosity at scepticism, at irenic and syncretist theology, at some natural philosophy, at divination and magic, at new philosophical systems such as Cartesianism (1676, 955–88). His near-total unwillingness to countenance the possibility of good curiosity contrasts with the exploration of that possibility—also in the 1670s—by the orthodox Rechenberg, who had studied under the same teachers as Spizel at Leipzig (Kromayer and Scherzer) but had remained within the university world rather than switching his prime institutional allegiance to Pietism. Although both men encountered curiosity in the same educational setting and so would presumably have agreed that they were discussing the same thing, they developed conflicting understandings of it, even when both were applying it to the same phenomenon, such as Calixtian syncretism, their common enemy. Although both agreed that such syncretism was a betrayal of true religion, Spizel condemned it as curiosity while Rechenberg condemned it as a lack of healthy curiosity.

While the Protestant Andreae was levelling the charge of curiosity at Rosicrucians, in France the Catholic Garasse (1584–1631) was doing the same to those whom he called 'atheists' and *libertins*, enemies of true religion, and whose alleged leader, the poet Théophile de Viau, Garasse compared at some length to the mythic founder of the Rosicrucians, Christian Rosencreutz (Godard de Donville 1989, 129–32).

Garasse, a periodic teacher at Jesuit colleges and a preacher, was one of the Jesuits' foremost and most belligerent polemicists. He had been spearheading the campaign to have Théophile executed on charges of writing licentious poetry that reflected depraved morals.[40] Before Théophile's eventual sentence to banishment (1625, but not in fact fully imposed), Garasse published *The Curious Doctrine* (1623) as an attack both on Théophile and on other figures whose alleged free-thinking seemed to Garasse to be of the same ilk as the alleged sexual deviance of the poet. These figures belonged mainly to

---

[39] Spizel 1680, 837. See esp. 1680, 816–42, on the 'Wrongly curious, *polypragmon* scholar' ('Literatus male-curiosus et polypragmon').

[40] On Garasse, see Fouqueray 1910–25, iv, ch. 4; Jouhaud 1996; Marchand 1980; Phillips 1997, 233–4; Trooz 1947. On *La Doctrine curieuse*, see Godard de Donville 1989, 119–327.

the legal, parliamentary, and humanist circles which, whether noble or bourgeois, Catholic or Protestant, were largely hostile to the Jesuits: Étienne Pasquier, Justus Lipsius, Pierre Charron, the Scaligers, Isaac Casaubon, Pierre Du Moulin. Whereas Andreae and Spizel's uses of curiosity involved definition of it, Garasse largely bypasses definition, simply using *curieux* as a recurring term of abuse for *libertins*.[41]

The aims of these polemical tracts were problematized by the fact that some of the people whom they sought to label as 'curious'—such as Andreae's collectors and alchemists—would quite happily have accepted that label, seeing it as positive rather than pejorative.[42] Thus, even for these critics, the 'curiosity' family of terms was not univocal but rather an arena for a clash of meanings. This provided the critics with opportunities for irony but it also made it difficult for them to impose successfully their pejorative meaning or to dissociate themselves entirely from the very thing which they wished to condemn.

This potential complicity between attacker and attacked was a more general problem in such tracts. For example, Andreae has remained to this day a perplexing figure because, on the one hand, he wrote the *Chymische Hochzeit* (1616) and probably the *Fama fraternitatis* (1614)—the texts that triggered the Rosicrucian movement—while, on the other hand, he never acknowledged unambiguously authorship of Rosicrucian texts, denied writing some that were sometimes attributed to him, and castigated the movement in various treatises, including the one on *curiositas*.[43] Even Garasse, the scourge of *libertins*, could be argued to have created them as a category, giving them a collective identity—which they would not otherwise have had—by taking heterogeneous intellectual and literary figures and lumping them together as *libertins*, *athées*, and *curieux*.[44] The problem was exacerbated by what Andreae and Garasse allege to be the hidden or duplicitous nature of

---

[41] There is one exception: the few pages on 'le vice de curiosité' as an attempt to investigate fate (Garasse 1971, i. 337–42). On this passage, see Godard de Donville 1989, 222–5.

[42] Godard de Donville (1989, 220) makes a similar point about Garasse. For other reflections on his use of curiosity, see Jacques-Chaquin 1998*b*, 87; Merlin 1998, 126–8.

[43] See Åkerman 1998, 69–77; Montgomery 1973, i. 158–255.

[44] Godard de Donville 1989. See also Phillips 1997, 233–4.

the hated phenomenon: the dividing-line between uncovering it and creating it is tenuous.[45]

Garasse tries to make polemical capital out of the dual perspective that is embedded in curiosity. It offers him the opportunity for sustained irony, as in his full title—*La Doctrine curieuse des beaux esprits de ce temps, ou pretendus tels* (*The Curious Doctrine of Today's Self-Proclaimed Fine Minds*). Only the last three words—'ou pretendus tels'—would have revealed to the prospective reader that the terms 'curieuse' and 'beaux esprits' were meant pejoratively. The meaning of 'curieuse' initially appears to be object-oriented ('excellent, choice'), but then shifts ironically on closer inspection to an underlying subject-oriented one ('over-inquisitive'). Elsewhere, the *prima facie* meaning is the positive, subject-oriented one that was becoming widespread in natural philosophy: 'That only *libertins* have a good mind, being curious people who try to enter into the secret of natural causes'.[46] Garasse is exploiting rather than simply eradicating the misguided secular meanings of curiosity.

Spizel homes in even more precisely on a positive claim to be curious that is made by one of his misguided scholars. He then reappropriates it not for irony but as evidence to be used against that scholar. He quotes from a letter addressed to Johannes Trithemius by the famous occult philosopher Heinrich Cornelius Agrippa. Agrippa asserts—or, according to Spizel, 'confesses'—that 'from an early age he had been a CURIOUS [*sc.* diligent] INVESTIGATOR of wondrous performances and of actions full of mysteries'.[47] Agrippa, writing over a century before Spizel, when *curiositas* was almost always pejorative, would certainly not have considered that his use of the adjective *curiosus* amounted to a confession that he suffered from the vice designated by the noun *curiositas*, but that is how Spizel chooses to interpret the statement. By Spizel's own time, naturalists were calling themselves *curiosi* even more routinely. So, for church-based writers, the increased moral polysemy of curiosity was not just a threat but it actually provided them with incriminating evidence for the existence of this half-hidden vice.

[45] Garasse considers the 'curious doctrine' of *libertins* to be largely concealed in the newly formed private sphere (Merlin 1998, 126–8).

[46] 'Que les seuls Libertins ont l'esprit bon, comme personnes curieuses, qui taschent d'entrer jusques dans le secret des causes naturelles' (Garasse 1971, i. 176).

[47] 'fatetur, *ab ineunte aetate sese mirabilium effectuum et mysteriis plenarum operationum* CURIOSUM *fuisse* EXPLORATOREM' (Spizel 1676, 979).

Spizel ascribes so much significance to incriminating occurrences of this family of terms that he here puts Agrippa's key term in the upper case, just as he does when quoting—now more in the spirit of the source texts—Apuleius's narrator's confession that he was '*curiosus*'[48] or the admission, by the famous alchemist and physician Franciscus Mercurius van Helmont, that he had gone in for 'vain INVESTIGATIONS OF CURIOSITIES'.[49] Indeed, extraordinarily enough, although this single, climactic occurrence of the family of terms— 'CURIOSITATUM'—does not come until four sentences from the end of Van Helmont's confessional autobiography, it is apparently what motivated Spizel to reproduce the whole autobiography in his own *Unhappy Scholar* (842–56). Where a source texts lacks any incriminating occurrence of the 'curiosity' family, Spizel is happy to add one: when quoting with approval a denunciation by Maarten Schoock of 'pedlars of new dogmas', he inserts 'and curious' in between 'new' and 'dogmas'.[50] Spizel is a philological detective, uncovering terminological evidence in some texts, planting it in others, paying the same close attention to whether or not the 'curiosity' family is present as that which we encountered among some early modern university scholars.

However, the secular meanings of curiosity also posed problems for such church-based writers. Garasse had trouble imposing on curiosity the meanings that he wanted it to have. Like many French church-based writers,[51] he associated curiosity closely with magic. In his desire to prove that even apparently innocent occurrences of the 'curiosity' family of terms in fact refer to magical, diabolic practices, he argues that 'all ancient legal authors, whether Greek or Latin, confused the two terms *magus* and *curiosus*'.[52] The argument would not have convinced German university jurisconsults who pointed out that *curiosi* meant 'spies' in Roman Law. And it certainly did not convince one of the defenders of Théophile *et al.*, the abbé François Ogier, who attacked the argument as one indication of the Jesuit's philosophical and grammatical ignorance (1623, 198–9). These

---

[48] Spizel 1680, 818.

[49] 'vanas CURIOSITATUM INDAGATIONES' (Spizel 1680, 856).

[50] '*ab iis, qui institores sunt novorum* (curiosorumque) *dogmatum*' (Spizel 1676, 986).

[51] See Verbeeck-Verhelst 1988, 349, 352–5, 356–60.

[52] 'tous les anciens Autheurs qui ont traicté du droict, tant parmy les Grecs que parmy les Latins, ont confondu ces deux termes: *Magus* et *Curiosus*.' (Garasse 1971, i. 338).

philological battles had high stakes, since they determined whether claims to be *curieux* were incriminating.

Moreover, it could be argued that even Garasse *exploited* the attractiveness of curiosity for his own purposes rather than only condemning it through irony. By calling his book *La Doctrine curieuse*, was he not marketing it by giving the impression that it was full of 'excellent, choice' doctrine, as he did indeed presumably think it to be? There is evidence that his title was read in this sense by contemporaries. His fellow Jesuit René de Ceriziers, more indulgent of curiosity, included Garasse's title—without saying that it was ironic—in a list of books which served to illustrate the contemporary craze for curiosity (1643, [a viii^v]). Moreover, an unsigned liminary poem in Ogier's *Judgement and Condemnation of the Book 'Curious Doctrine'* speaks of 'that book' as 'more rotten [*cariosus*] than curious [*curiosus*]'.[53] Beyond its wordplay, this phrase assumes that Garasse had used the term 'curieuse' not only for the sake of polemical irony, but also to attract prospective readers to his own book, seeking to cash in hypocritically on the worldly senses of *curieux*. Whether or not this charge was justified, the polysemic slipperiness of *curieux* made it possible.

Even the terminologically precise Spizel faltered on the question which produced persistent grey areas in church discourse: did a good kind of curiosity also exist? The reforming nature of his project forced him to address this. Whereas Garasse and Andreae's rhetoric was largely demonstrative and judicial, condemning and accusing 'curious' people whom they considered to be mostly beyond redemption or cure,[54] Spizel's rhetoric had a much stronger deliberative component, advising readers how to rid themselves of harmful curiosity, how to convert the 'world of learning' rather than reject it. This begs the question: what should replace curiosity? The very fact that Spizel often adds the epithet 'harmful' (*noxia*) to *curiositas* could be read as implying the potential existence of a harm*less* kind. And yet he is probably mainly using the epithet to stop readers interpreting *curiositas* in the positive sense ascribed to it by much of their contemporary learned culture. Indeed, at one point he spells out that the Pietist conversion of the 'CURIOUS SCHOLAR' should be performed not with a 'NEW CURIOSITY' but with humility.[55] He is ruling

---

[53] 'magis | Quàm Curiosus, est cariosus hic liber' (Ogier 1623, e iii^v).

[54] See Andreae 1621, 1, 35; Trooz 1947, 116.

[55] 'CURIOSI LITERATI . . . NOVAE CURIOSITATIS' (Spizel 1676, 1010–11).

out the notion—which more accommodating church discourses espoused—that curiosity could be *rechannelled*. However, four years later, we find Spizel introducing Van Helmont's confessional auto-biography as a 'mirror for scholars who offer up first vain and then healthy curiosity'.[56] Where does this sudden, puzzling reference to *sana curiositas* come from? Certainly not from Van Helmont's text. Given that Spizel uses *sana* rather than the more common *bona*, has he now read or heard of—and been influenced by—Rechenberg's dissertation on *sana curiositas*, recently printed at Spizel's old university? It is as if even the Pietist Spizel can no longer keep the lid entirely shut on *curiositas* and stop a phantom good double emerging from it.

2.2.4   Pastors and flocks

Taking pastoral care of the faithful involved teaching them how to avoid curiosity. Spizel's tract had a pastoral dimension to it, but much writing was more emphatically pastoral, ranging from ser-mons to letters of spiritual direction or else to advisory treatises that were written for specific audiences. The pragmatic instrumentality of these language-games was overt: they were intended to affect the reader or listener's spiritual behaviour—what Fénelon called their 'practice'. In Counter-Reformation France, mortification became a goal for lay people as well as for monks: curiosity was often under-stood in an Augustinian sense, as an alluring worldly trap, and avoiding it helped one find the path to perfection. Since pastoral dis-cussions of it sought to effect specific changes in people's behaviour, they were preoccupied with particular applications of curiosity to everyday life rather than with academic-style definitions of it. Therefore, more common than definitions were *exempla*, taken from recent history as well as from the Bible and classical antiquity. If occasionally a general definition of curiosity was offered, it was ren-dered almost incoherent by the range of particular applications which were included under its aegis (2.2.4.1). When a prelate such as Bossuet did write about curiosity in systematic, theological terms, he did so not in a sermon but in a treatise which had no obvious pastoral aims and may have been written essentially to clarify his own thoughts.

[56] 'Speculum Literatorum, vanae primùm, dein sanae Curiositati litantium' (Spizel 1680, 842).

My case-studies include a Huguenot pastor in the late sixteenth century, a German Catholic sermon-writer in the early seventeenth, and three of the greatest prelates in Counter-Reformation France. The pastoral purposes of each forced him to address practical questions. Exactly how do we avoid curiosity? With what do we replace it? With something quite different, or with a good species of the passion curiosity? But does any such good species exist? (It was much more difficult for pastors than for university professors to answer yes.) Such questions gnaw away at the coherence of curiosity in pastoral writing, generating an unease that is evident in the interrogatory, conditional, hypothetical, or negative grammatical structures in which they are often couched.

2.2.4.1   A pastoral treatise: Jean de l'Espine

Curiosity was the theme of Book 6 of the *Excellent Discussions of the Soul's Tranquillity and Happiness* (1587) by Jean de L'Espine. Each of the seven books was devoted to one vice. Written and revised from about 1557 onwards, this was the major work by this Augustinian monk who had become a Huguenot minister and a personal friend of Calvin.[57]

L'Espine's aim was 'to teach us how to live well', as the polymath Charles Sorel put it in the 1660s, when he judged this widely read, much-printed treatise to be still just about usable for that purpose.[58] The original editor, the Calvinist publicist Simon Goulart, who added an extensive paratextual apparatus, presented the work not as a contribution to academic moral philosophy but as an accessible, vernacular source of meditations for people of both sexes—who should read 'a few pages' per day—and as a propaedeutic to private Bible reading.[59] Yet it also had academic readers: as late as the 1670s it was referred to in German Lutheran university circles for its treatment of curiosity.[60] It was known in Catholic France too: François de

---

[57] On L'Espine, see Hogu 1913; on the *Excellens Discours*, see Hogu's ch. 3, and see his pp. 112–16 for a paraphrase of the 6th book on *curiosité*.

[58] 'Il est besoin d'instructions précises pour nous apprendre à bien vivre. On peut se servir pour cecy des *Discours de Jean de l'Espine, du Repos et du contentement de l'Esprit*: on leur a donné le nom d'*Excellens*, mais je croy que c'estoit pour leur siècle: le nostre demande quelque chose de plus accomply.' (quoted by Hogu 1913, 96). The treatise was printed 8 times in French up till 1599 and was translated into Latin, English, and German (Hogu 1913, 125, 157–9).

[59] 'quelques fueillets' (L'Espine 1588, [*6ʳ]–[*7ʳ]).

[60] See Becmann 1679, 68–9; Kromayer/Scherzer/Rechenberg 1675, E2ʳ.

Sales possessed a copy, ostensibly for purposes of refutation (Hogu 1913, 125–6).

The semi-academic dimension of this pastoral handbook emerges in L'Espine's concern to sketch the relation of curiosity to other passions (442) and to define as well as discourage this passion, 'which we will call curiosity, for want of any more appropriate term for that illness and disturbance of the soul which goads us incessantly to want to know useless or unnecessary things, to get involved in many matters which are outside our vocation or contrary to it'.[61] Thus, as for Andreae, curiosity involves both knowing and doing. Like Westphal, L'Espine here reveals a dissatisfaction with ordinary language, since it does not name this passion perfectly. His use of the term *curiosité* will not necessarily simply mirror his reader's ordinary uses of it. And yet this independence from ordinary language clashes with L'Espine's pastoral, communicative purposes: because his discussion of curiosity (444–93) includes many referents that would not ordinarily be called *curiosité*, he often avoids using the term until the very end of the particular sub-section in question (454, for example).

Having started with a definition, L'Espine then proceeds to outline not a set of precisely related genera and species of curiosity—as an academic treatise might—but rather some broadly related 'groups' (*bandes*) of curious people.[62] However, not all of these 'groups' fall clearly within his opening definition of curiosity: the pragmatic, pastoral uses to which he is putting curiosity gradually erode academic neatness. Indeed, such fuzziness may have been what led Sorel to describe the *Excellent Discussions* as lacking in 'polish'.

Initially, L'Espine's 'groups' of curious people do illustrate his definition coherently: they are people who disobey their 'vocation'. L'Espine is confessionalizing curiosity, making it distinctively Calvinist, broadening the meaning of 'vocation' to encompass not only one's profession or social rank—which is how various Lutheran dissertations and the superintendent Westphal understood it—but any God-willed action that one might undertake: 'for where there is

---

[61] 'que nous nommerons Curiosité, dautant que nous n'avons point de terme plus propre pour exprimer ceste maladie et perturbation d'esprit: par laquelle nous sommes incessamment aiguillonnez à vouloir connoistre choses qui sont inutiles ou non necessaires, et à nous entremettre et soigner de plusieurs affaires, outre ou contre notre vocation' (442).

[62] For the term *bande*, see pp. 475, 476, 477.

no vocation, there is none of [God's] grace or presence'.[63] For instance, one apparently heterogeneous group of *curieux* to be condemned by L'Espine are people who go in for magic, divination, 'barbaric' (that is, non-humanist) law and medicine, and cabalistic theology: what unites them all is their attempt 'to do things which they have not been not called to do'.[64]

Whereas these examples of vocation-abuse all involve the acquisition of knowledge and so were customary referents of *curiosité* in 1587, other examples, involving actions alone, were less familiar referents of the French term. For instance, in order to investigate the problem of distinguishing false from genuine vocations, L'Espine discusses famous revolts: their outcome reveals whether they were genuine. The failed German Peasants' Revolts (1524–5) were wrong because undertaken 'without vocation',[65] whereas by contrast (456) the similarly subjugated Swiss peasants were called to their rebellion (when in 1291 they founded the Everlasting League for the defence of Uri, Schwyz, and Nidwalden against their Habsburg masters). Another example of false vocations is the very history of the Catholic Church, in which bishops usurped their posts by corrupt means and were incapable of acting in a pastoral rather than depraved manner, because they had not been genuinely called to that profession (452–4).[66] Although these examples come in Book 6 on *curiosité*, L'Espine cannot bring himself to apply that term directly to them.

On the other hand, some of the 'groups' whom L'Espine does emphatically call curious do not actually fall, even approximately, within his opening definition. Those whose 'curiosité' makes them want to know their neighbours' secrets (486–9) are included not because they transgress any vocation but merely because L'Espine, having just referred to Plutarch's treatise on *polypragmosyne* for another point (486), decides to continue imitating Plutarch here: L'Espine's passage on this group closely echoes Jacques Amyot's 1572 Plutarch translation.

---

[63] 'car là où n'est point la vocation, là n'est point sa grace ni presence' (454).

[64] 'essayer à faire les choses à quoy ils ne sont point appellez' (473). For the whole passage, see pp. 473–86. For 'barbarie', see p. 476.

[65] 'sans vocation' (455).

[66] The question of false vocations must have been especially burning for L'Espine, who himself changed profession from monk to minister and who as a Calvinist considered the order of things in France—where he was almost killed during the St Bartholomew's Day Massacre in 1572—to be a world upside down.

Another mismatch between L'Espine's opening definition of curiosity and his pastoral discussion of it hinges on the question whether all curiosity really is bad. Whereas his definition suggests that it is, on the other hand his deliberative pastoral rhetoric, even more strongly than that of Spizel, hints that curiosity can perhaps be rechannelled in a positive direction rather than being best avoided altogether (480–1, 485–6). L'Espine's editor Goulart, who took it upon himself to clean up any conceptual confusion in the manuscript (Hogu 1913, 99), has added paratextual comments that change L'Espine's hints into certainties: 'How to make use of curiosity' is his bald margin heading at this point.[67] And yet in L'Espine's actual text, this good double of bad curiosity remains much more tenuous and grey. Like Fénelon and Bossuet after him, L'Espine evokes it not through a straightforward assertion but through tortured formal linguistic structures, such as questions or concessive and negative clauses. We should contemplate God's words about how He looks after us and forgives us: 'Would not curiosity to seek and understand everything about *those* matters be more salutary than trying to know what He was doing before He created the world?'[68] The comparative and the interrogative conditional leave open the possibility that this is less a positive assertion of the goodness of some curiosity than a mildly ironic use of *concessio*, provisionally and strategically exploiting a term (*curiosité*) which readers may find alluring in order to persuade them to direct their attention to appropriate objects. Again, Goulart swats away such nuance in his margin heading: 'What we should be curious to know regarding the son of God'.[69] Later, it is a concessive clause that L'Espine uses to outline further his grey phantom: 'So, if we are curious to know, we should apply ourselves to things of which we are capable'.[70] This conditional sentence still does not quite amount to a positive encouragement to be 'curi-

[67] 'Moyen de se servir de la curiosité' (486). Goulart performed a similar distortion in his commentary (published 1581–1610) on another work by a fellow Huguenot, the famous philosophical poem *La Sepmaine* by Guillaume de Saluste du Bartas: the commentary gave good curiosity much more prominence than did the poem itself (N. Kenny 1991*b*, 272–3).

[68] 'La curiosité de cercher et entendre tout es ces choses ne seroit-elle pas plus salutaire que de sçavoir ce qu'il faisoit avant qu'il eust crée le monde' (480).

[69] 'Que c'est que nous devons estre curieux de conoistre touchant le fils de Dieu' (480). For another example involving a question, see p. 481. For a fleeting positive use of 'curieux', see p. 467.

[70] 'Il faut donc, si nous sommes curieux de conoistre, que nous nous appliquions aux choses dont nous sommes capables' (485).

ous'. The most positive phrasing L'Espine can find for good curiosity is the negative 'ne . . . que' ('only') construction: like hunters keeping hounds focused on the prey, 'So we should restrain our curiosity and only allow it to follow what it can understand.'[71]

Thus, the pastoral writer L'Espine seems happy to live with conceptual greyness. Not so Goulart, who even tries to interpret the whole of Book 6 as a systematic comparison of bad with good curiosity. Whereas L'Espine has divided Book 6 into three 'concerns' ('solicitudes', 422), of which the first two are good (concern for matters within our vocation and for the outcome of our actions) and only the third is curiosity (illegitimate concern for what lies outside our vocation), on the other hand Goulart reinterprets the first two as good curiosity, although there is nothing more than a single passing occurrence of the adjective 'curieux' in L'Espine's actual extensive discussions of those two concerns (422–44 (436)). Goulart's distorting margin-heading reads: 'Three kinds of concern, which are the sources of praiseworthy and vicious curiosity'.[72] This fleeting suggestion that proper concern with one's own vocation is a good form of curiosity anticipates the more systematic attempts made in some German university dissertations a century later to demonstrate exactly that. But some readers of the *Excellent Discussions* must have been left confused by this major discrepancy between its text and paratext. As the cases of Trithemius and Gaffarel will also show, the collaborative nature of early modern book-production meant that authors were not guaranteed sole control of how curiosity or anything else was presented in their works.

2.2.4.2 *Sermon culture: Matthias Faber and Jean-Pierre Camus*

Whereas pastoral treatises such as L'Espine's sought to define curiosity, however concisely and tenuously, on the other hand the language-game of sermons usually dispensed with definition altogether, focusing entirely on persuading the faithful to avoid curiosity and on showing them how to do so. Intellectual sophistication and moral complexity tended not to be priorities: simplicity and clarity were. Dispensing with good phantom doubles of bad curiosity, sermons presented curiosity as entirely bad, at least until the latter part

---

[71] 'Aussi faut-il que nous retenions nostre curiosité, et que nous ne lui permettions suyvre sinon ce qu'elle pourra comprendre' (485–6).
[72] 'Trois sortes de solicitudes, qui sont les sources de la curiosité louable et vitieuse' (422).

of our period: one 1760 sermon against 'misapply'd curiosity' encouraged a well applied kind too, but this unusual rhetoric was doubtless made possible by its setting—the university church of Oxford—and is unlikely to have had many antecedents.[73]

However, the relative simplicity of curiosity in sermons did not make it a static thing that was always described in the same way and for the same purpose. On the contrary, it is likely to have been end-lessly localized by preachers, applied to the specific circumstances of the occasion, their congregation and confession, their location.[74] Preachers all over Europe used popular printed collections of Latin sermons as models, but their actual oral performances, often in the vernacular and now lost to us, are likely to have been very different from the printed model (Herzog 1991, 161–9), just as oral disputa-tions were different from the corresponding printed dissertations. Moreover, the other kinds of printed aids which preachers plun-dered—notably commonplace-books—always actively reshaped curiosity rather than just passively transmitting a pre-existing 'thing' called curiosity: the actual term *curiositas* and its cognates were absent from many of the excerpted scriptural, patristic, and classical passages which such manuals interpreted as being about *curiositas* and marshalled under its aegis.[75]

Although the localized uses to which curiosity was put in sermons are now largely lost to us, we do have access to some of the printed raw materials that fuelled those uses. Let me briefly consider two case-studies: first one German model sermon and then one collection of commonplaces compiled by a celebrated French preacher.

A sermon on *curiositas* was included in the collection of sermons for feast days by the Bavarian Matthias Faber (1587–1653), who became a Jesuit in 1637, having first published in 1631 this popular collection, which was reprinted in Antwerp as well as in Germany.[76]

---

[73] More typical was the 1725 sermon in which a minister in the Canterbury diocese preached 'against unnecessary curiosity in matters of religion', contrasting it with good 'desire for knowledge' (Newton [1725], [1]).

[74] On this heterogeneity of the circumstances of sermons, see Bayley 1980, esp. 14–15; Herzog 1991.

[75] e.g. Buys 1608, 46–51 (*curiositas* is one of 83 vices for which the Jesuit Buys lists remedies); Dadré 1603, 130ʳ–131ᵛ (see Moss 1996, 133, 202–3; on the usefulness for preachers of this work by a Paris theologian, see Bayley (ed.) 1983, p. xi); Granada 1586, 399–403 (a Dominican).

[76] Faber 1643, iii. 152–5. On Faber, see *ADB*. His collection was reprinted in (at least) 1641, 1642, 1643, 1648, and 1663.

Localized versions of the sermon—probably turning *curiositas* into *Fürwitz*—are likely to have been delivered for many decades, perhaps in Protestant as well as Catholic churches: the sermon was summarized approvingly even in a Lutheran miscellany of 1690 (Hartnack (ed.) 1690,):(4ᵛ). The sermon was one of eight provided by Faber for the Feast of St John the Evangelist. It was a commentary on Christ's words of rebuke to Peter for asking what would eventually happen to John: 'what is that to thee? follow thou me' (John 21.22). These words were commonly interpreted in the early modern period as a rebuke to curiosity.[77] Indeed, Faber may have been surreptitiously amplifying an earlier Spanish sermon collection which interpreted them in this way.[78]

Faber gives a rhetorical rather than a philosophical structure to *curiositas*. He does not define it in terms of its roots in the human subject, for example via Augustine's doctrine of the three concupiscences, which is here mentioned in passing but does not operate as an organizing principle.[79] Rather, he spatializes *curiositas*, dividing it into five according to the location of its objects, which are either above us (difficult theological doctrine), below us (useless trifles), behind us (the past and also the future, when we try to know it through divination), to our right (other people's business), to our left (other people's vices), instead of straight ahead (the narrow path to Christ). After the exordium, each of the sermon's five points amplifies one of these locations with *loci, exempla*, and images. Faber makes no philosophical claims about the status of his spatial schema, unlike those German dissertation writers who presented their genera and species of *curiositas* as the true shape of this passion or else of knowledge. Instead, Faber's spatial schema seems designed above all to be clear, striking, and memorable, like the emblems or other pictures which Jesuits used abundantly in their sermons and pedagogy. Moreover, Faber makes his schema seem natural by basing it on the spatial metaphors, sayings, images, and examples which had described curiosity since antiquity and were still common: 'Quae supra nos, ea nihil ad nos' ('We should not concern ourselves with things above us': attributed to Socrates); Thales in the well; Icarus and Phaeton in the sky.[80]

---

[77] See Ames 1630, 76; Barker 1599; Camus 1613, vii. 451.
[78] Villavicencio 1566, 26ᵛ–27ᵛ.
[79] Faber 1643, iii. 153.
[80] On the early modern spatialization of forbidden knowledge in terms of height and depth, see Ginzburg 1976.

Curiositas is morally as well as spatially simple in Faber's sermon. There is no question of rechannelling it in a good direction: it must simply be avoided. Or, to use his metaphor: one must avert one's gaze (155). Certainly, even here there is a good double of bad *curiositas*, but it is emphatically not called *curiositas*: for example, it is permissible to gaze to the left at the sins of the wicked, but only for the sake of correcting or praying for them, not out of *curiositas* (155). Moreover, in contrast with those university legal dissertations which made fine distinctions between circumstances in which investigation of others' business was a licit or illicit species of *curiositas*, here it simply always involves illicit *curiositas*, whether reading others' letters, entering their house uninvited, prying into the daily ablutionary habits of one's bishop (in an entertaining *exemplum* taken from Robert Bellarmine), or being preoccupied with the alleged failings of a local magistrate or cleric rather than with one's own (154–5). Unconcerned with legal fine points, the sermon is using curiosity to foster harmonious relations between parishioners and also to keep parishioners at a respectful and obedient distance from their priests and politicians.

My second case-study is a chapter on curiosity in a work which was shaped by pulpit rhetoric and also promoted it: the *Diversitez* (1609–18) by Jean-Pierre Camus (1584–1652).[81] Camus became Bishop of Belley in 1609. At the outset of a career which saw him become, as Peter Bayley has observed, 'by far the most prolific preacher of early seventeenth-century France',[82] as well as a writer of sermon collections, a polemicist, an author of religious romances, and a pastorally active bishop (in characteristically Counter-Reformation style, like his friend François de Sales), Camus published this eleven-volume miscellany in which his own observations were mingled with extensive near-transcriptions from the personal commonplace books which he had compiled throughout his youth (Moss 1996, 256–7) and which he, like other preachers of the period, almost certainly drew upon in his own sermons.[83]

Although sermon culture is by no means the only context within which the *Diversitez* should be understood, ambivalently modelled as it is on Michel de Montaigne's *Essais*, nonetheless many of

---

[81] On the *Diversitez*, see Descrains 1985; Julien-Eymard d'Angers 1952. On Camus in general, see Descrains 1992; Robic-de Baecque 1999.

[82] Bayley (ed.) 1983, p. xvii.

[83] On this general practice, see Bayley 1980, 78; Bayley (ed.) 1983, p. xi.

Camus's chapters are rich stores—of examples, anecdotes, and parallels—which were not only of potential use to sermon-writers, especially with the help of the volumes' indexes, but are also remarkably similar to some sermons themselves, notably those which Bayley has dubbed the thesaurus kind. These had come to predominate in early seventeenth-century France. In them, 'the preacher's main function [was] the presentation and connexion of a wide range of anecdotes, illustrations and analogies'.[84] A chapter 'On curiosity'[85] was published in the *Diversitez* at a time (1613) when Camus's own sermon practice was tending to move from the thesaurus style to a distinctive, pruned-down version of it—influenced by Italian Counter-Reformation currents—in which examples, parallels, and the like were strung together in a compressed chain from which continuous argument was largely absent.[86]

Echoing that style, Camus's 27-page chapter offers no definition of curiosity nor even any overarching argument, but rather a sea of continuous French prose, interspersed with Latin quotations, in which biblical, patristic, and especially classical commonplaces are strung together, occasionally around familiar, informal thematic clusters or kinds (*sortes*) of curiosity,[87] such as heresy, magic, collecting, *curiosité* about the natural world, about the vices of others, or about uselessly speculative sciences.[88] Camus suggests a few contemporary applications: Geneva is a receptacle of thieves in the same way as 'the mind of the curious person' is a receptacle of the vices of others.[89] But mostly he offers stock examples rather than contemporary applications of those examples, presumably leaving such localization for his readers to inject as they re-use his store, for, just as some of Camus's sermons seem to have been intended both to be listened to as they were and yet also to be reworked by other preachers (Bayley 1980, 90–1), so chapters in the *Diversitez* such as this one on *curiosité* seem to have been intended both to be read and yet also to be recycled by their readers in other forms, such as sermons.

Although he does not spell out many precise contemporary applications of his examples of curiosity, he does offer general advice on

[84] Bayley 1980, 77; see pp. 77–85.
[85] Camus 1613, vii. 425–52 ('De la curiosité').
[86] Bayley 1980, 85–91, esp. 86.
[87] 'Encores une sorte de curiosité' (452).
[88] See respectively pp. 437–9, 452–3, 425–7, 427–8, 443–9. For a more extensive condemnation of magic as *curiosité*, see Camus 1609, ii, sigs. 256ᵛ–278ʳ.
[89] 'l'esprit du curieux' (429).

their moral applicability (just as he tended to spell out clearly the moral lessons to be drawn from parallels in his sermons):[90] Icarus is a 'fine symbol' of minds buried in paganism, Prometheus a 'fine painting of the person who is curious about matters too lofty', Pandora's box 'the true image of curiosity', while Uzziah (who dared to touch the priestly incense holder)[91] is a 'fine figure' for French laity who dare argue about doctrine and so fall into heresy.[92] The emphasis on visual 'image' and 'painting' again recalls the predilection for allusive use of emblems in Camus's compressed sermon style (Bayley 1980, 89). Indeed, elsewhere in the *Diversitez*, Camus himself demonstrates more precisely how his readers—who probably included preachers, confessors, spiritual directors, as well as lay people—could apply, for example in pastoral situations, the examples enumerated in the curiosity chapter: for instance, when admonishing a friend, in a letter, for being over-zealously mystical in his spiritual exercises, he paraphrases St Bernard and then reminds his friend of Icarus, Phaeton, Prometheus, Ixion—listing them in the same order as in the chapter on curiosity—as well as of Thales.[93]

This chapter from the *Diversitez* echoes the moral simplicity of many of Camus's sermons[94] by privileging images and applications of curiosity over complex arguments about it or even definitions of it: curiosity is here entirely bad, as in Faber's sermon. And yet, in other kinds of writing, Camus described some curiosity as good (2.3.2): even elsewhere in the *Diversitez*, in the very different, more epistemological than ethical context of a chapter on wonder, he goes so far as to interpret the famous opening of Aristotle's *Metaphysics* ('All men naturally desire to know') as a description of 'natural curiosity',[95] as also some contemporary writers on natural philosophy were beginning to do,[96] unlike many sixteenth-century writers who, like Montaigne, had paraphrased Aristotle as describing a

[90] Bayley (ed.) 1983, p. xvi.

[91] 2 Paralipomenon 26.[18.20].

[92] 'beau symbole' (432), 'Belle peinture du curieux des choses trop eslevees' (433), 'la vraye image de la curiosité' (436), 'belle figure' (449).

[93] Camus 1610, vi. 565–6. Cf. Camus 1613, vii. 431. On the mystical tradition's understanding of this particular temptation as *curiositas*, see Cabassut 1953, 2659.

[94] See Bayley (ed.) 1983, p. xvii.

[95] 'c'est elle [*sc.* l'admiration] qui donne la curiosité naturelle aux hommes: *Omnes homines natura scire desiderant*' (Camus 1620, iii. 15).

[96] e.g. Du Pleix 1635, a x^r.

desire for knowledge which they certainly did not equate with curiosity.[97]

In other words, curiosity changed as Camus crossed over from one language-game into another. However entirely he denounced it in sermon-style writing, elsewhere he could give it partial approval. This variability of curiosity within his writing derives not from any special inconsistency or incoherence on his part, but rather from the context- and discourse-bound nature of curiosity, which was variable because writers sought to use it for different purposes in different genres. It would be misleading to privilege some of these genres over others, to argue, for instance, that the systematic philosophical definitions of curiosity given in treatises are somehow more authentic or revealing than the more overtly rhetorical, suggestive, and example-rooted versions of it given in sermons. These two versions of curiosity were not authoritative original (treatise) and debased copy (sermon), but rather equal cousins, linked by family resemblances.

2.2.4.3 *Two prelates: Bossuet and Fénelon*

Let me now broaden the investigation of uses of curiosity to encompass a wider range of spiritual writing—mostly pastoral, including sermons—in particular by two French prelates: Jacques Bénigne Bossuet (1627–1704), Bishop of Condom (1669–71) and of Meaux (1681–1704), the greatest preacher in an age of great preachers, and François de Salignac de la Mothe Fénelon (1651–1715), Archbishop of Cambrai from 1695, though largely confined to his diocese from 1697 as a result of the Quietist controversy, in which Bossuet had become his bitter adversary.[98]

Whereas Camus shared the belief of his friend François de Sales that Christianity should penetrate secular action in the world rather than turning away from it,[99] on the other hand Bossuet and Fénelon, like many others in Counter-Reformation France in the second half of the seventeenth century, espoused brands of Augustinianism that advocated spiritual—and, in the case of Jansenists, material—turning away from a secular world that did not merely include curiosity

---

[97] See Montaigne 1962, 1041. For Montaigne, the 'curiosity' family of terms remained largely pejorative.

[98] See Adam 1969, 268–9; Calvet 1956, ch. 15; Lebrun (ed.) 1988, 532–3.

[99] On Sales, see Lebrun (ed.) 1988, 351–7; Phillips 1997, 17–20.

among its many vices but, according to some, was dominated by this particular vice.[100] According to these writers, one should seek to become dead to *curiosité* and to the world of which it is part: 'We think we are very far from the world because we have withdrawn from it, but we still speak the language of the world and we still have its feelings, its curiosities . . .'[101]

To many church writers of Bossuet's and Fénelon's generation, curiosity seemed to have gained a much stronger stranglehold over secular culture than in the heyday of Camus: *curiosité* and its cognates were now used as terms of praise for a much wider range of desires and activities. Both Bossuet and Fénelon responded to this spread of curiosity in two conflicting ways. On the one hand, they seized upon the innocuous appearance of curiosity as evidence that it was especially dangerous, since its innocent façade lured its victims to their downfall. On the other hand, more surprisingly, Bossuet and Fénelon also exploited the good secular meanings of *curiosité* for their own pastoral purposes. As in the case of L'Espine a century earlier, it remained uncertain whether this amounted to their stating that *curiosité* could be good. Let me consider these two responses in turn.

First, the duplicitous nature of curiosity was just one aspect of what struck many Augustinians as the radical gulf between the world and the church, appearance and reality. In the words of a French translation of a treatise by that most hardline of Augustinians, Cornelius Jansen, Bishop of Ypres in the Spanish Netherlands, curiosity is 'all the more deceitful [than concupiscence of the flesh] because it appears more virtuous'.[102] Similarly, for Bossuet, 'concupiscence of the eyes', which included curiosity, was 'a vice with a slightly more delicate appearance' than 'concupiscence of the flesh', but in fact it was 'basically just as coarse and bad'.[103] This discontinuity between the everyday experience of curiosity and the spiritual truth about it was milked for its shock value in pastoral discourse. One of Fénelon's pedagogical fables is about a 'fox who was pun-

---

[100] On Bossuet's Augustinianism, see Busson 1948, 373–83. On Fénelon's, see Gouhier 1977.

[101] 'On croit être bien loin du monde parce qu'on est dans une retraite, mais on parle le langage du monde, on en a les sentiments, les curiosités' (Fénelon 1983–97, i. 808; see also ii. 1128–9). See also Bossuet 1890–7, iii. 297; Bossuet 1930a, ch. 8.

[102] 'd'autant plus trompeuse, qu'elle paroist plus honneste. C'est cette curiosité . . .' (Jansen 1659, 40; see also pp. 42, 45). Cf. Jansen 1641, ii. 137.

[103] 'un autre vice un peu plus delicat en apparence, mais, dans le fond, aussi grossier et aussi mauvais' (Bossuet 1930a, 23).

ished for his curiosity'. Having decided to 'devote the remaining days of his life to curiosity', he went to the Escorial to admire the wild animals depicted in the tapestries: but while he gazed on, two of the palace's dogs strangled him.[104] The fable shocks because the punishment seems disproportionate to the innocuous crime. But the disproportion is only apparent, since even apparently innocent kinds of curiosity such as 'interest in fine arts' stem from sinful concupiscence. Fénelon is giving a distinctively late seventeenth-century Augustinian twist to the older notion that less heinous kinds of curiosity are a slippery slope to more heinous ones, that curiosity is spread across a continuum from 'superfluous and useless' to outright 'bad', as Calvin stated when warning his followers that judicial astrology leads to hardcore magic.[105] Whereas when Calvin was writing (in 1549) the choice was mainly between fairly and extremely negative senses of curiosity, a century later it was between positive and negative senses, so curiosity lent itself much more to shocking switches of perspective in pastoral discourse.

Even when the theme of duplicitous worldly appearances was not explicit, those shocking switches of perspective were still often embedded in church discourse on curiosity, especially when this family of terms was used on the fraught, widening borderline between religious and secular contexts, as we saw in the case of Steno writing to Thévenot in 1678 (2.1 above). The uses of curiosity in the *Pensées* by the friend of the Port-Royal Jansenists, Blaise Pascal, were also highly charged because of a similar clash of discourses rooted in his own life history. Not only did he interpret curiosity in Augustinian fashion as concupiscence of the eyes, but he identified that vice with the contemporary kinds of curiosity—usually deemed positive in a secular context—which he himself had enthusiastically practised through mathematics and physics and from which, by early 1659, he seems to have become fully detached.[106] The concupiscence of the eyes is the realm of 'curiosities and the sciences', as opposed to the concupiscence of the flesh (*la chair*) or the other concupiscence,

---

[104] 'Le Renard puni de sa curiosité'; 'donner ses derniers jours à la curiosité' (Fénelon 1983–97, i. 207).

[105] 'une curiosité non seulement superflue et inutile, mais aussi mauvaise' (Calvin 1985, 102; see also pp. 94, 98–9).

[106] Sellier 1970, 178–9. Pascal's sister Gilberte Périer described his previous researches into nature as 'curiosité' (Pascal 1963, 20).

pride (the realm of authority).[107] The concupiscence of the eyes, as the realm of 'curious minds' and of 'the curious and the learned', also corresponds, for Pascal, to the intellectual order of people, the other two orders being those of *charité* and *chair*.[108] The Augustinian critique feeds off the fact that the intellectuals criticized are now even openly calling themselves 'curious', shooting themselves in the foot even more than Agrippa, whose apparently innocuous use of *curiosus* in the 'diligent' sense was seized upon by Spizel as incriminating. Whereas from a modern perspective it might seem that new positive secular meanings were threatening old religious negative ones, from the perspective of the Jansenist Pascal and the Pietist Spizel the new positive secular ones were simply more grist to the mill of the old negative religious ones.

The Augustinian gulf between the appearance and the reality of curiosity was thus used in order to discredit a range of secular practices, among them theatre, which lent itself especially well to this critique, being an overtly illusory spectacle. The chapter on *curiosité* in the French translation of the aforementioned treatise by Jansen railed against 'all the vanity of tragedies and comedies'.[109] Bossuet, in an untitled 1694 treatise on 1 John 2.15–17, not printed during his lifetime, amplified in terms of Augustinian theology a powerful denunciation of the theatre which he had recently published.[110] The unprinted treatise discusses the verses from the first Epistle of St John ('Love not the world . . .') that outline the famous triad of sins—concupiscence of the flesh, concupiscence of the eyes, and pride—the second of which was sometimes referred to as *curiositas* by Augustine (notably in the very influential Book 10, chapter 35 of the *Confessions*).[111] However, Bossuet departs from both Augustine and Jansen by trying to subdivide 'concupiscence of the eyes' into two 'species' ('espece[s]'), of which curiosity is only one, the other being 'ostentation'. Theatre exemplifies 'ostentation' rather than 'curiosity', while still being closely related to the latter. Curiosity is here limited only to the cognitive desire to learn through the eyes (understood figuratively) and other senses (through history or the occult sciences,

---

[107] 'dans les curiosités et dans les sciences' (Pascal 1963, fr. 148, p. 520).

[108] 'des esprits curieux' (Pascal 1963, fr. 308, p. 540); 'les curieux et savants' (fr. 933, p. 624).

[109] 'toute la vanité des Tragedies et des Comedies' (Jansen 1659, 43).

[110] Bossuet 1930*a*; see p. ix. For his public attack, see Bossuet 1930*b*.

[111] On the considerable influence of the *Confessions* on 17th-century French religious writing, see Courcelle 1963, 383–460.

for example), whereas the purely and literally ocular vanities of theatre, fashion, and bibliomania are 'ostentation' rather than curiosity.[112]

Yet the case of theatre also shows that even French Augustinian uses of curiosity were not all uniform. Different translations of the *Confessions* reflected disagreements within religious circles about the desirability of condemning the theatre, in a period when many French bishops enjoyed reserved seats at court spectacles.[113] Unlike the Jansenist Robert Arnaud d'Andilly, who translated that Jansen treatise as well as the *Confessions*, the Jesuit René de Ceriziers sought to turn Augustine's fire away from contemporary French theatre by emphasizing that the Bishop of Hippo's targets were specific to late antiquity: in Ceriziers's exegetic translation of Augustine, the 'spectaculis' at which concupiscence of the eyes is directed become 'Gladiators' and the 'Amphitheatre' rather than 'spectacles' in general.[114]

The second response of Bossuet, Fénelon, and others to the spread of secular claims about the goodness of curiosity was, at first glance, much more surprising: they exploited those positive senses for their own pastoral ends. Going beyond the notion that a higher object should 'extinguish' curiosity, or that it should just 'exhaust itself',[115] or that it should—in Pascal's Augustinian formulation—change into wonder,[116] they sometimes seemed to verge on arguing that it should instead be changed into good curiosity. It is as if, notwithstanding their Augustinianism, they gesture towards the notion—which was beginning to gather greater momentum in the seventeenth century— that destructive passions can be harnessed for good purposes (Hirschman 1977, 14–20). As Nicholas Hammond has noted, even Pascal, who usually understands *curiosité* in Augustinian terms as concupiscence of the eyes,[117] argues at one point—in keeping with his general insistence that Christianity fits human nature—that God gave humans numerous figural, apparently diversionary routes to charity (such as Old Testament prophecies) 'in order to satisfy our

---

[112] Bossuet 1930*a*, chs. 8–9. Bossuet's terminology is not entirely consistent.
[113] On these debates, see Bossuet 1930*b*, 7–65; Dubu 1970; Phillips 1997, 59–65; Thirouin 1997.
[114] 'Gladiateurs . . . Amphitheatre' (Augustine 1659, 352). Contrast Arnaud d'Andilly's translation: Augustine 1671, 405.
[115] 'éteint', 's'épuise' (Fénelon 1983–97, i. 934; ii. 615).
[116] 'sa curiosité se changeant en admiration' (Pascal 1963, fr. 199, p. 526).
[117] e.g. Pascal 1963, fr. 933, p. 624. See Sellier 1970, 175–82.

curiosity, which seeks diversity through that diversity which always leads us to the one thing that is necessary to us'.[118] This *curiosité* is positive in people who seek the figurative sense, but negative in those—such as the Jews, in Pascal's anti-semitic perspective—who remain stuck with the carnal, literal sense of the figures.

Usually, however, such glimpses of positive curiosity in spiritual or pastoral contexts emerged only indirectly and tenuously (as in the case of L'Espine), via tortured formal linguistic structures, such as conditional tenses, questions, or negative constructions like 'ne . . . que'. The second point of a sermon delivered in 1660 by Bossuet to recent converts from Protestantism was an attack on *curiosité*,[119] and yet he asked 'Are you curious about the truth?' and said that, if so, 'let our curiosity go no further' than the church, which holds all the answers.[120] This ambiguous formulation can be interpreted as prescribing either a renunciation or a redirection of *curiosité*. These converts should learn 'to be curious only in the company of the church'.[121] Does this mean that the converts should redirect virtuously the passion which once led them to heresy? Or is this merely an opportunist effort to persuade the converts—by adopting a term likely to appeal to them—which does not, however, commit Bossuet to believing in the existence of good *curiosité*? In other words, is a thing at stake here or just a word? Good *curiosité* is being evoked in order to get the audience to act in a certain way (to obey), but, unlike bad *curiosité*, it does not necessarily exist in reality: it has only a grey, spectral existence.

Similar questions can be asked of Fénelon when, in a 1713 letter to a friend—probably the chevalier Destouches—in which he outlines his plans for an apologetic work, he contrasts people's futile, worldly curiosity with their lack of curiosity about why they are alive at all: 'A traveller goes to Monomotapa and Japan to learn something which is quite unworthy of his curiosity and which, once discovered, will not cure him of any of his ills. When will we find men who make,

---

[118] 'pour satisfaire notre curiosité qui recherche la diversité par cette diversité qui nous mène toujours à notre unique nécessaire' (Pascal 1963, fr. 270, p. 535). See Hammond 1994, 128–30 (esp. 130).

[119] Bossuet 1890–7, iii. 203–8.

[120] 'Etes-vous curieux de la vérité? . . . que notre curiosité n'aille pas plus loin' (205).

[121] 'apprenez à n'être curieux qu'avec l'Église' (207). For another use of 'ne . . . que' with 'curieux' in a positive sense, see Bossuet 1930*a*, 92. For an example with 'ne . . . pas', see Bossuet 1890–7, iv. 28 n.

instead of a trip around the world, the slightest effort of curiosity in order to unravel the mystery of their condition?'[122] Here the reality of this phantom good double of bad curiosity is attenuated because it emerges not through a direct proposition but through a question and a negative superlative ('the slightest').[123] A little earlier in the same passage, it was glimpsed via a comparison: 'Be just as curious to find Him who made you, and to whom you owe everything, as the coarsest men are curious to follow up a wicked suspicion, to satisfy their bestial passion?'[124] Is this pious double really a non-bestial passion that is also called curiosity? If not, it may be that Fénelon, far from reifying 'good curiosity' in this way, is instead grappling to find a vocabulary with which to describe the spiritual life, and is settling here, paradoxically, for the vocabulary of the vicious passions (jealousy, hatred, revenge are also mentioned) (806), using it as a counter-analogy for the spiritual life. Worldly life is at once an image and a counter-image for spiritual life. Bad curiosity is an image for something that is good but that may not be straightforwardly nameable as good curiosity. The ambiguity is produced by the fraught state of the border between church and world. To the extent that there is some continuity between the two, bad curiosity can perhaps be transformed into good. But to the extent that the two domains are discontinuous, it cannot.

When, a little later in the same letter, Fénelon refers to 'this pious curiosity' ('cette pieuse curiosité', 812), he seems after all to have reified and named more definitely that indeterminate something. However, this phrase could still be interpreted as an oxymoron rather than as a signifier denoting a 'thing': the problem raised by Augustine's use of the phrase 'pia curiositate', mentioned above (2.1), has not gone away.

Yet there is a major difference between such moments in Augustine and in Fénelon: curiosity now, in early modern France, also had far

---

[122] 'Un voyageur va au Monomotapa et au Japon pour apprendre ce qui ne mérite nullement sa curiosité, et dont la découverte ne le guérira d'aucun de ses maux. Quand trouvera-t-on des hommes qui fassent, non pas le tour du monde, mais le moindre effort de curiosité pour développer le grand mystère de leur propre état?' (Fénelon 1983–97, ii. 808–9; see also pp. 806–8).

[123] Fénelon used a similar phrase ('la moindre curiosité') in the same context in another letter (1983–97, ii. 797).

[124] 'Soyez aussi curieux pour trouver celui qui vous a fait et à qui vous devez tout, que les hommes les plus grossiers sont curieux pour suivre un soupçon malin, pour contenter leur passion brutale' (807).

more prominent positive meanings in secular contexts. Fénelon seems to have been exploiting and accommodating these when raising the spectre of good curiosity. Although, as has just been shown, the passions of jealousy or hatred could also occasionally be used alongside curiosity as counter-images for the spiritual life, it was far more common in church discourse for this kind of ambivalent counter-image to be based on key words which, like 'curiosity'—but unlike 'jealousy' or 'hatred'—often carried neutral, ambivalent, or positive (but not almost entirely negative) moral value in the period. For example, 'knowledge' and 'spectacle' are two of Bossuet's other favourites: 'It is to His knowledge, not our own, that we should give ourselves up . . . Do you wish to see a spectacle worthy of your eyes?'—then look up at God's handiwork, the skies, instead of at the theatre.[125]

Curiosity, then, provides an especially highly charged example of how moral and other vocabulary was made necessarily slippery and unstable by the constant switching between worldly and spiritual perspectives which is characteristic of pastoral discourse in the Augustinian tradition. Beyond church discourse too, moral labels were being subject to considerable re-evaluation more generally in this period, as Quentin Skinner has shown by focusing on the rhetorical figure of paradiastole, whereby a given action (such as saving money) is reassigned from a vice (such as avarice) to a virtue (such as prudence), or the other way round.[126] With curiosity, the problem was slightly different:[127] it involved deciding whether this thing was a vice or a virtue in itself. Yet, just as in cases of paradiastole, it often remained uncertain whether the redescription was a purely verbal strategy or else involved a claim about real things,[128] so with curiosity, even in pastoral discourses which overwhelmingly defined it as a vice, there was uncertainty as to whether fleeting positive uses of the term referred to a tenuous virtue or else were devoid of referentiality.

In contrast with curiosity the virtue, curiosity the vice had a much more solid, reified status for Bossuet and Fénelon. They frequently

---

[125] 'C'est [à] sa science, et non à la nostre, que nous devons nous abandonner . . . Voulez vous voir un spectacle digne de vos yeux?' (Bossuet 1930a, 28, 31). Fénelon uses 'science' in a similar way (Fénelon 1983–97, i. 936).

[126] Skinner 1991 and 1996, ch. 4.

[127] For a fuller discussion of this distinction, see N. Kenny 1998, 44–5.

[128] In addition to the works by Skinner, see Cave 1999, 101 n. 39.

evoked it pastorally, for pragmatic ends, that is, in order to get their flocks to behave in certain ways. The behaviour that they sought to promote was above all spiritual, rather than necessarily physical, material, or intellectual. For the mystically oriented Fénelon, as for monastic writers, real action can take place only in the realm of spirit. Curiosity involves apparent action, even hyperactivity, but in fact it is far removed from real action: indeed Fénelon routinely contrasts *curiosité* with *pratique*. For example, giving spiritual direction to the Duke of Burgundy some time before April 1711, he advises him to 'Read the Gospel without curiosity, with humble docility, in a spirit of practice'.[129] Fénelon and Bossuet were thus transferring pastorally to the everyday, lay world of the Counter-Reformation the centuries-old monastic ways of condemning curiosity.[130] In the written version of a Lenten sermon on death, delivered in the Louvre (22 March 1662), Bossuet first describes *curiosité* as one of the most violent of human passions, which makes people investigate nature's secrets and cultivate elaborate technical or political skills. Then, like any master teaching a novice monk how to meditate and avoid *curiositas*, he urges the Court to focus instead on the image of Lazarus's tomb and so 'gather back together within ourselves all those wayward thoughts'.[131]

There were differences in emphasis between Fénelon's and Bossuet's pastoral applications of curiosity. For the semi-Quietist Fénelon, *curiosité* belonged to the intelligence, which was to be suppressed in prayer: in a mystical piece (printed in 1713) on the necessity of knowing and loving God, he describes how abandoning himself to grace involves renouncing any attempt to understand grace rationally: 'God forbid that I should want to know anything more about it! the rest of it would only foster presumptuous curiosity in me.'[132]

On the other hand, for Bossuet, who eventually became the supreme French episcopal guardian of what he considered to be

---

[129] 'Lisez-vous l'Évangile sans curiosité, avec une docilité humble, dans un esprit de pratique' (Fénelon 1983–97, ii. 974; see also i. 561).

[130] On avoiding curiosity in order to achieve quasi-monastic mortification, see Fénelon 1983–97, i. 673, 808. For another pastoral contrast between mortification—that is, the 'practice' ('pratique') of self-renunciation—and 'vaine curiosité', see Camus 1637, a ii[r].

[131] 'recueillir en nous-mêmes toutes ces pensées qui s'égarent' (Bossuet 1890–7, iv. 163).

[132] 'À Dieu ne plaise que j'en veuille savoir davantage! tout le reste ne servirait qu'à nourrir en moi une curiosité présomptueuse' (Fénelon 1983–97, i. 711).

doctrinal orthodoxy, avoiding *curiosité* often meant avoiding any belief that was not sanctioned by the Gallican Catholic hierarchy. That was precisely what he argued in the second point of the sermon that he delivered on 14 February 1660 to the 'new converts' ('Nouveaux convertis'), rue de Seine-Saint-Victor in Paris. In the surviving written version, *curiosité* is presented primarily as a threat lurking not within the individual, nor within the Church, but outside it. The church—which, in the first point, is presented in classic Counter-Reformation terms as a house or ship buffeted by storms— is the sole haven from *curiosité*. The whole illocutionary force of the second point stems not from logical argument but from this chain of visual images with which Bossuet pounds the audience. As in Faber's model sermon, curiosity is here repeatedly spatialized, now less systematically but with Bossuet's characteristically dazzling arsenal of rhetorical figures. Whereas Faber had given curiosity five directions, Bossuet settles for two: 'there is nothing so high in the sky nor so hidden in the depths of Hell that they [*sc.* curious minds] do not imagine they can reach it'.[133] But he also repeatedly adds an inside/outside axis, with curiosity always being on the outside: 'The Church has spoken, that's enough. This man has gone outside the Church; he preaches . . . what is his doctrine?—Oh vainly curious man! I don't try and find out about his doctrine: it's impossible for him to teach well, since he doesn't teach in the Church.'[134] In this spatialized variation on decorum-based understandings of curiosity, where one is listening is more decisive than who one is, or even than what one actually listens to. Bossuet's rhetorical appeal to his audience, his *captatio benevolentiae*, then grafts this inside/outside rhetoric onto other oppositions, notably 'us/them' and 'present/past': 'Let's leave them to wander in error, my brothers . . . As for us, children of the Church, and you who had been left outside like stunted children but who have at last returned to her bosom, learn to be curious only with the Church.'[135] Bossuet is trying to make these ex-Huguenots—one

---

[133] 'il n'y a rien de si élevé dans le ciel, ni rien de si caché dans les profondeurs de l'enfer, où ils [*sc.* esprits curieux] ne s'imaginent de pouvoir atteindre' (Bossuet 1890–7, iii. 204).

[134] 'L'Église a parlé, c'est assez. Cet homme est sorti de l'Église; il prêche . . . quelle est sa doctrine?—O homme vainement curieux! Je ne m'informe pas de sa doctrine: il est impossible qu'il enseigne bien, puisqu'il n'enseigne pas dans l'Église' (205).

[135] 'Laissons-les errer, mes frères . . . Pour nous, enfants de l'Église, et vous que l'on avait exposés dehors comme des avortons, et qui êtes enfin rentrés dans son sein, apprenez à n'être curieux qu'avec l'Église' (207).

of the key constituencies in the Counter-Reformation attempt to re-
convert France—feel that *curiosité* is a thing of their past, which they
are shedding as they abandon one community for another. Yet, as we
have seen, Bossuet also strategically leaves open the possibility of
transforming that old bad curiosity into a new good kind, perhaps in
case the message should be too austere to be acceptable. Curiosity is
here being defined institutionally, as beginning at the point where the
true church ends. Whereas some universities divided curiosity
between themselves (good) and the outside world (bad), here it is
being projected almost wholly onto the world outside the institution.

2.3   ACCOMMODATING CURIOSITY, MORE OR LESS

Most church discourse, then, urged avoidance of curiosity, while
occasionally hinting that a tenuous good curiosity might also exist.
However, a few church-based texts did give that spectre of good
curiosity a more solid existence: worldly curiosity was to be accommodated rather than avoided. This was a minority view, but it serves
as an extraordinary reminder of the degree to which, even within
church discourse, curiosity was a site of contention as well as of
consensus.

2.3.1   *A pilgrim's guide*

Pilgrims were particularly vulnerable to curiosity, which they had to
avoid at all costs in order to concentrate on their spiritual aims.
Otherwise, they would get distracted by the worldly wonders that
they encountered en route. That, at least, was the advice of numerous
medieval and early modern guidebooks on pilgrimage.[136] Some of
them did see pilgrimage as an outlet for a natural human desire for
knowledge, but on the whole they certainly did not call that desire
'curiosity'.[137]

However, by the early eighteenth century, even that dominant
discourse could be undermined. Remarkably, at least one guidebook
for pilgrims now proposed accommodating rather than avoiding

---

[136] See Stagl 1995, 47–9; W. Williams 1998, 74–7, 90–3; Zacher 1976.

[137] e.g. Sigmund Feyerabend (*Reyßbuch des Heyligen Landes*, 1584) calls pilgrimage 'ein natuerlich begierd, lust und liebe viel und mancherley ding zu wissen unnd zu
erfahren' (in Simon 1998, 45).

curiosity. In 1713, Conrad Hietling, an Austrian Franciscan who had lived in Bethlehem, published his *Pilgrim Lovingly Led by Devotion and Curiosity through the Holy Land and Jerusalem*. In this allegory, the pilgrim, who is disappointed by illusory worldly hopes, reaches the Holy Land but is then unsure which path to take. He is accosted by Devotion and then his conversation with her is interrupted by another female figure, Curiosity, who says that she knows all the places to visit. Initially, 'she is rejected by Devotion as vain and dissolute', but then she is accepted as a guide on condition that she remains religious and modest.[138] The band of three sets off, with Curiosity usually first describing each place and then Devotion providing the more authoritative closing spiritual reflection on it. Curiosity also asks and answers numerous questions, such as why Christ came into the world to serve rather than to be served, why as a poor man (121), and so on. After the journey, the pilgrim spends the rest of his life with Curiosity and Devotion as his inseparable companions—as in the frontispiece to the present book.

A centuries-old tradition is being reversed: curiosity becomes the companion rather than the curse of the pilgrim. But, as if to minimize what must, to some readers, have been quite a shock, the reversal is represented by the narrative as being careful, conditional, gradual, and partial. This impression of gradual reversal is also created by the collocations of curiosity with neighbouring terms: having started by evoking the patristic coupling *vana curiositas*, Hietling eventually has Curiosity inveigh *against* her own patristic near-synonym, *vana gloria* (147). Curiosity, having almost always been inherently bad in pilgrimage writing, has here become not an entirely good passion, but one that is potentially good or bad. It is on constant probation.

2.3.2 *Marketing religion*

Accommodating curiosity also gave churches a way of getting their messages across. In the seventeenth century, when the 'curiosity' family of terms became so prominent in the advertisement of secular books (Section 3 below), some religious books—especially ones aimed at a broad readership that went beyond professional groups such as clerics and theologians—risked being ignored if they were not now advertised with similar new rhetoric, however much this

---

[138] 'veluti vana & dissoluta repellitur â Devotione' (Hietling 1713, 5).

conflicted with the overwhelming pastoral advice to avoid curiosity. Moreover, unlike, say, the confessional, the book market was riven with other, less pastoral agendas, such as those of printers and book-sellers who needed to make money out of the widespread public interest in religious matters. So the church in print found itself simultaneously appealing to and denouncing its readers' curiosity. Those who entered this fray, accommodating rather than rejecting curiosity, included some Benedictines[139] and some Jesuits,[140] not surprisingly given the Society of Jesus's practices of cultural, intellectual, moral, and rhetorical accommodation.[141]

This commercial/rhetorical appeal to readers' curiosity was at its most blatant in a very small number of religious books that brazenly highlighted the noun 'curiosity' as an alluring feature of their title. Titles like *Holy Curiosity* and *Useful Curiosity* aligned the noun with terms to which it was much more usually antithetical, especially in church discourse.[142] The accompanying epithets 'holy' and 'useful' served both to distinguish this curiosity defensively from a bad kind and yet also to entice readers by giving them an oxymoronic frisson.

Most of the religious books with 'curiosity' in their title were collections of questions. Two of these were entitled *La Sainte Curiosité*, one by the ex-Jesuit René de Ceriziers (2.3.3 below) and another by the canon lawyer Laurent Bouchel, who answered forty questions on the Old and New Testaments and on eschatology, such as whether resurrected men will all speak the same language (yes: Hebrew) or whether they will re-acquire all the hair and nails which have been clipped off them throughout their life (no . . .).[143] The bold title sits rather uneasily with the text itself, in which occurrences of the noun *curiosité* in fact remain negative, mildly positive, or cagily non-committal rather than stridently positive.[144]

Even more contradictory was the Benedictine marketing of another collection of questions. In 1621, the order reissued a 1508 work (*The Book of Eight Questions*) by one of its most famous reforming abbots, Johannes Trithemius, under the new title *A Ruler's*

---

[139] D'Assonleville 1625 (a commonplace-book designed especially for preachers); Trithemius 1621.

[140] Ceriziers 1643; Masen 1672.

[141] See the entries for 'accommodation' in the index of O'Malley 1993.

[142] e.g. Bouchel 1616; Ceriziers 1643; Masen 1672.

[143] Bouchel 1616, 470–86. On Bouchel, see *Dictionnaire* 1933–; Michaud 1843–.

[144] 3, 25, and 508.

Curiosity (*Curiositas regia*). These 'most delightful and useful' theological questions had allegedly been put to Trithemius by the Holy
Roman Emperor, Maximilian I.[145] But Trithemius himself might
have turned in his grave in response to the new title of 1621 since, as
Jean Dupèbe has shown, Trithemius considered *curiositas* to be a
vice present in demonic magic and shared by many humanists and
monks. Indeed, in this very work, the third answer given to the
Emperor condemns 'over-curious' people who perform magic with
the help of demons.[146] Dissociating himself from this vice was a crucial way for Trithemius to try and make respectable, on the other
hand, his own Neoplatonic thaumaturgy, spiritual and natural magic
(Dupèbe 1986). Yet even this careful dissociation did not prevent
Trithemius from being described by the Pietist Spizel as having been
damned for his occultist *curiositas* (1676, 981). Trithemius would
hardly have thanked his brethren for making him even more vulnerable to such accusations in 1621. But by then chinks were beginning
to open up even in churches' opposition to curiosity.

The titles of a rather larger number of religious books stopped
short of appealing to 'curiosity' but still presented the book's contents as 'curious', using phrases—such as 'curious questions' or 'curious researches'—that had long been pejorative in a religious context
and indeed, for some, still were.[147] In other words, these would-be
enticing titles included the adjective but not the noun. This was a
more attenuated, less brazen strategy, conveniently ambivalent for
writers who were still nervous of appealing outright to curiosity, or
at least of taking responsibility for such an appeal. If the book's contents were curious, did that mean that curiosity was being appealed
to? Usually the answer was unclear, but sometimes it was a clear
'yes', since the object-oriented occurrence in the title could either
lend itself to being read as a subject-oriented one[148] or else was

---

[145] 'iucundissimae simul et utilissimae' (Trithemius 1621, title-page).

[146] 'nimium curiosi' (Dupèbe 1986, 85).

[147] e.g. Brunfels 1520 (*Refutation of Sophistry and of Curious Questions*, by a
Lutheran pastor). Later, in 1661, Bossuet expressed outrage at people considering
Christ 'a subject for curious researches' ('un sujet de recherches curieuses', 1890–7, iv.
27–8; cf. also vi. 524); and Pascal's sister Gilberte Périer wrote that 'he never concerned himself with the curious questions of theology' ('il ne s'est jamais appliqué aux
questions curieuses de la théologie', Pascal 1963, 20).

[148] In phrases like 'curious question' and 'curious research' the adjective could have
either an object-oriented sense (e.g. 'noteworthy') or a subject-oriented one (e.g. 'pursued with inquisitiveness'): see N. Kenny 1998, 129–34.

echoed by a clearly subject-oriented one in the text itself. For example, the 1695 re-edition of a 1548 treatise by Lambertus Hortensius as *History of the Anabaptists, or Curious Account of their Doctrine, Rule, and Downfall* included engravings of punished, dismembered, naked Anabaptist bodies 'in order to satisfy the curious', giving them gratifying gore.[149] Or again, in the anonymous *Curious Conversations in the Realm of the Dead Between . . . Christian Gerber and . . . David Schwerd[t]ner* (1732), the adjective in the title is echoed in the text by extensive discussions not only of the *curieus* (here defined as 'paradoxical and rare') quality of Gerber's treatise on the rebirth of souls, but also of the moral worth of his *Curiositaet* in researching this topic (which is opposed to negative *Neubegier* or *Neugierigkeit*).[150]

The label 'curious' also gave readers of religious books other information about the contents. It often indicated that the book was relatively popularizing, that it contained selective rather than systematic doctrine, that it was divided into discrete little points or answers to questions, and/or that those points were offbeat, problematic, controversial,[151] or inessential[152] and so not to be found in standard catechetical works.[153]

---

[149] 'afin de contenter les Curieux' ([Hortensius] 1695, A4^r).

[150] The famous Lutheran pastor Gerber had died in the previous year (1731). Schwerdtner was a superintendent. On both of them, see Jöcher 1750–1. On Gerber, see *ADB*. The Lucianic genre of the dialogue of the dead flourished in Germany between 1680 and 1810 (Engelsing 1973, 49; Rutledge 1974). For about 20 years, there was a vogue for calling such dialogues 'curious' (18 examples of this are listed in Rutledge's appendix 1, 16 of them occurring between 1719 and 1732). The 'curious' label seems to have connoted not only polemic but also the other-worldliness of the settings.

[151] e.g. Fabricius 1707 (a pamphlet by a Helmstedt professor of theology, occasioned by the cross-confessional marriage of Elizabeth Christina of Brunswick to the Emperor Charles VI); [Fouillou] 1735 (a Jansenist attack on the claims of the *convulsionnaires*; other Jansenists were convinced by their claims; on the controversy, see Cognet 1964, 114–17). Sometimes 'curious' sheltered ironically under an innocuous denotation such as 'noteworthy' but in fact connoted controversy, polemic, or satire (N. Kenny 1998, 184–5): e.g. Jurieu 1682 ('entretiens curieux', title-page).

[152] Two editions (1727, 1731) of a 1704 English version of Pascal's *Pensées* were entitled *Thoughts on Religion, and Other Curious Subjects* because much of the material seemed alien to Pascal's main, apologetic purpose (Pascal 1727 pp. xxix–xxx). Pascal would presumably have hated having his text labelled 'curious'.

[153] Several of these meanings are combined in Anroux 1662; Baudrand 1815 (a hugely succcessful anthology of anecdotes and episodes from the lives of holy people, published from 1771 onwards); Osorio da Fonseca 1666.

2.3.3 *Questions to ask an accommodating*
ex-Jesuit: René de Ceriziers

Few of the church-based accommodators of curiosity went so far as to justify their strategy at length. A spectacular exception was René de Ceriziers in his *Holy Curiosity, or Curious Questions on the Main Articles of Faith, Religious Mysteries, and Church Ceremonies* (1643). Perhaps because it was so brazen and provocative, declaring so openly what others practised more implicitly, this work did not catch on. By its author's standards, it was a commercial flop, being apparently confined to one edition (by a minor printer),[154] of which only one copy is now extant, it appears. Modern critics too have largely ignored it.[155] Like Rechenberg's much more academic but similarly bold dissertation on healthy curiosity in theology, Ceriziers's collection seems to have had little subsequent impact, precisely because it stretched church discourse beyond what was more widely acceptable in its time. But, by the same token, it therefore reveals the outer edges of what was sayable about curiosity in church discourse.

Ceriziers (1603–62) had taught in various Jesuit colleges before leaving the Society of Jesus in 1641 and becoming chaplain first to the Duke of Orléans, then to Louis XIV. He was a clerical courtier: his was a worldly and powerful milieu, not an ascetic one. Writing from the 1630s onwards, he became well-known as a prolific and successful author of vernacular histories (secular and ecclesiastical) and fictions and as a translator of St Augustine. Accommodating secular to religious culture, he was adept at moulding church history to the narrative genres which sold well at the time, the romance and novella: his life of St Genevieve was a much translated bestseller which was still read in the nineteenth century.[156]

The curious questions to which Ceriziers offered answers covered Scripture and beyond. Unlike the Lutheran Rechenberg, the ex-Jesuit felt no need to claim that they were all grounded in the Bible. Most of Ceriziers's answers are drawn from the Fathers and other theologians. Some of the questions cover standard catechetical doctrine (why is Scripture obscure? how is God eternal? why can there only be

---

[154] On the printer, Estienne Danguy, see Renouard 1995, 112.

[155] The 2 exceptions of whom I am aware are Godard de Donville (1989, 220) and Chesneau (1946, ii. 260), who remark briefly that it accommodates secular curiosity.

[156] On Ceriziers, see *Dictionnaire* 1933–; Michaud 1843–.

one God?), whereas others go well beyond it and are the religious equivalent of contemporary miscellanies of curious questions about nature and art (why did the ancients live longer than us? where would Mary's soul have gone if she had died before Christ?)[157] He justifies his project in a Thomist spirit by arguing that, while faith cannot be founded on natural reason, it must be compatible with it and so the causes of the church's mysteries and ceremonies can be examined ([a vii^{r-v}]).[158] Also in a scholastic vein, and like Rechenberg, except more fleetingly and in less academic and formal terms, Ceriziers presents this good curiosity as a median between the two vicious extremes of, on the one hand, bad curiosity and, on the other, culpable 'negligence' of such virtuous inquiry ([a viii^r]).

It is in the rich, extensive preface that Ceriziers explains and justifies his accommodation of secular curiosity ([a v^r]–e iv^v). It begins very defensively: Ceriziers seems well aware of the stern criticism that his accommodation of secular curiosity is likely to draw. He describes (after Pliny) a Greek Temple of Diana fronted by a statue of the goddess so ingeniously carved that it looked melancholic to anyone entering and joyful to anyone coming out: similarly, 'I have no doubt that, when the reader first glances at the frontispiece of this work and reads the curiosity title, he will judge the title disagreeable and unpleasant, since that thing [Curiosity] has been judged by the wise to be most dangerous and has been condemned by Scripture and the Church Fathers.' Yet when the reader has read the book, 'he will find that the face of that Curiosity has a quite different demeanour from what he previously thought it to be' and that what at first scared him in fact delights him.[159] The commonplace metaphor of an unalluring architectural façade that conceals hidden riches is here used to make this book a space for the transformation of bad curiosity into good. Like Hietling's pilgrimage narrative of Curiosity's shift to respectability, Ceriziers's miscellany can be read as a brazen amplification of those more customary, fleeting moments in religious writing when the possibility of good curiosity is tenuously glimpsed.

[157] Questions 3, 40, 42, 83, 199 respectively.

[158] For praise of Aquinas, see sig. [a viii^r].

[159] 'Je ne doute point que d'abord le Lecteur jettant les yeux sur le frontispice de cet ouvrage, et y lisant le tiltre de Curiosité, ne le juge desagreable et mal plaisant, comme chose fort dangereuse au jugement des sages, et condamnée par l'Escriture et Peres de l'Eglise. . . . il trouvera que la face de telle Curiosité aura tout un autre air qu'il ne pensoit' ([a v^{r-v}]). See also sig. e iv^r.

Those moments were usually couched in tortuous linguistic structures—such as 'ne . . . que' negatives—and Ceriziers writes those
structures large in order to dissociate himself from bad curiosity: he
embarks on a series of parallel negative sentences telling readers
what his curiosity is not: 'For the Curiosity which I am addressing in
this book is not', he argues, an attempt to investigate mysteries
reserved for God, secrets reserved for Nature, or occult philosophy.[160] This extended preterition, followed by a definition of what his
curiosity *is* ('not *x* but *y*'), shares the same 'from negative to positive'
movement that is often found fleetingly in church discourse on
curiosity, except that elsewhere the dominant element is usually the
negative one (*x*), whereas here it is the positive one (*y*):

> The subject which I am treating in this book does not include those areas, yet
> I am still calling it Curiosity, not interpreting the latter term in a strict sense;
> indeed it is not always understood in a bad sense in our language, but is used
> for precise attention and diligence which is aimed at obtaining some praise-
> worthy knowledge.[161]

The distinction between bad and good curiosity is here conceived
as one between a sense which is stricter—both semantically and
morally—and one which is looser. Ceriziers thus avoids connecting
good and bad curiosity to each other via the more systematic vocabulary of genus and species that is favoured in university dissertations,
for example treating them as opposite routes taken by the same passion. Instead, good curiosity is here boldly detached from its customary moorings in sinful human nature.

In the definition quoted above, Ceriziers has shorn curiosity of all
senses except 'diligent desire for good knowledge'. To stress the 'diligence' strand of curiosity was a ploy commonly used by those who
wished to make it positive, as we saw in the case of some German
university dissertations. However, in Ceriziers's case the ploy is devi-
ous: it does not correspond to his actual semantic practice, but simply serves to reassure readers who are anxious about indulging in
curiosity about religion.[162] In the rest of the preface, this apparently

---

[160] 'Car la Curiosité que je me suis proposée en ce livre, n'est pas . . .' ([a v^v]).

[161] 'Le sujet que je manie en ce livre, n'est point de ces matieres, je l'appelle neant-
moins Curiosité, ne prenant pas la signification du mot à la rigueur, aussi ne se prend-
il pas tousjours en mauvaise part parmy nous, mais passe pour une estude et diligence
exacte qui se travaille à la recherche de quelque loüable cognoissance' ([a vi^v]).

[162] Similarly, he openly acknowledges that the epithet 'holy' ('sainte') in his title
also has this function ([a vi^v]).

purified curiosity in fact re-acquires a rich set of connotations characteristic of contemporary secular discourses on curiosity, such as 'rarity' and 'collecting discrete objects'. For example, Ceriziers tacitly grafts object-oriented curiosity onto the subject-oriented 'diligent desire' sense, referring to his book's contents as 'Curiositez' (e ii[v]) and as 'concerning the most curious points of Christian doctrine'.[163] He is thus spelling out the link between object- and subject-oriented curiosity which most 'curious' books on religion repressed or else hinted at more vaguely, since they were nervous of appealing unambiguously to their reader's subject-oriented curiosity.

The rest of the preface describes Ceriziers's two motives for writing this book in this form. Determined to situate the book on the cusp between church and world, he makes the first motive ecclesiastical and the second secular. The first is his duty, as a 'Pasteur', to edify both himself and others ([a vii[v]]–[a viii[r]]). The second motive is much more surprising: it is the curiosity of the age. (The term used—'siecle'—also strongly connotes the secular world). Perhaps only someone steeped in Jesuit culture could so unabashedly take from the secular world his cue for a religious work. Moreover, his description of this second motive is full of excitable enumerations and extended metaphors, as if the affective force of Ceriziers's prose is granting more importance to this motive than to the ecclesiastical one:

The second motive which prompted me to compile this collection is the incredible Curiosity of the age in which we live. There's strange curiosity in everything, in everyone. One person directs his Curiosity at buildings, another at gardens, another at flowers, another at fruit, another at paintings, this person at fashionable clothes, that person at sauces and feasts. Everyone is tickled only by Curiosity: people speak and write today of nothing but Curiosities, of *Curious Doctrine, Unheard-of Curiosities, Natural Curiosities, Curious Conversations,* Curiosities everywhere.[164]

Curiosity is not an age-old fixture: it is peculiarly contemporary. As we have seen, the same claim was made in German universities, a

---

[163] 'touchant les plus curieux points de la doctrine Chrestienne' ([a vii[r]]).

[164] 'Le second motif qui m'a poussé à dresser ce recueil est l'incroyable Curiosité du siecle où nous vivons. Estrange curiosité en tout, en tous. Qui porte sa Curiosité aux bastiments, qui aux jardins, l'un aux fleurs, l'autre aux fruicts, celuy-cy aux peintures, celuy-là aux habits à la mode, quelque autre aux saulses et festins. Tout le monde n'est chatoüillé que de Curiosité; on ne parle, on n'escrit aujourd'huy que de Curiositez, *Doctrine curieuse, Curiositez inoüyes, Curiositez naturelles, Entretiens curieux,* Curiositez de tous costez' ([a viii[v]]).

little later. For this clerical courtier, the contemporary phenomenon is entirely positive. Nowhere does he condemn collecting and the like as sinful concupiscence, although he himself had translated Augustine. In the discussion of bad curiosity at the outset of Ceriziers's preface, he peremptorily acknowledges Augustine's qualms about curiosity but thereafter they are ignored, although the fads which Ceriziers enumerates—such as gastronomy and fashion—flagrantly go beyond the 'diligent desire for knowledge' to which he earlier confined good curiosity.

Ceriziers makes curiosity into a single thing composed of multifarious desires and objects—'a strange curiosity in everything, in everyone'—such as collecting, fashion, gastronomy, and also a wide range of publications, whose titles he quotes here. The first two titles are those of treatises well-known at the time, by Garasse against *libertins* (2.2.3 above) and by Jacques Gaffarel on Persian talismans (3.4.10 below); the third recalls the title of a collection of questions on natural philosophy by Scipion Du Pleix (*La Curiosité naturelle*; 3.4.2 below); the fourth was a generic title used in several works, of which the best-known to Ceriziers was probably the controversial defence of regular, as opposed to secular, clergy by Jacques de Chevanes (2.3.4 below). These works, first published in 1623, 1629, 1606, and 1634 respectively, were thus being used by Ceriziers in 1643 as evidence of the ubiquity of a thing called *curiosité*.

Having made curiosity into such a wide-ranging thing, and a peculiarly contemporary one, Ceriziers then boldly claims that it has become widely directed at religion too, and that there is nothing wrong with that. He claims that it has become especially impossible for clerics to socialize, whether in upper-class or modest households, whether in the city or the country, without being asked, by women as well as men, 'an infinite number of curious questions' about religion:[165] 'So, in order to satisfy all of those Curiosities more easily and to *accommodate* the habits and humours of today's people, I have sought out and gathered together these [Curiosities?] from the infinite number that exist, making them into something like a bouquet of different flowers'.[166] If, as seems most likely, 'celles-cy' does indeed

---

[165] 'une infinité de Questions Curieuses' (e[i]ʳ).

[166] 'Or pour plus aisément satisfaire à toutes ces Curiositez, et m'*accommoder* aux maeurs et humeurs des personnes du temps, j'ay recherché et recueilly celles-cy entre un nombre infiny, et en ay fait comme un bouquet de differentes fleurs' (e[i]ʳ⁻ᵛ; my italics).

refer back to 'Curiositez', then Ceriziers is here presenting his book as a miscellany of 'Curiositez'-objects which will satisfy the 'Curiositez' of reading subjects. So this seems to be one of those rare moments in seventeenth-century discourse when the fantasy of a blissful symmetrical union between subject- and object-oriented curiosity—characteristic of what I will later call the culture of curiosities—is actually made explicit.

Whereas many religious writers stressed the duplicity of curiosity, that is, the discontinuity between its innocuous everyday appearance and its noxious spiritual reality, by contrast Ceriziers grounds his celebration of curiosity in the everyday forms it takes, notably in *mondain* conversation. Not only does it arise from the questions that have been put to him in conversation, but also it will feed back into his readers' future conversations, enabling them to perform well in social gatherings (e iv[r–v]):[167] this work is one of many Jesuit-influenced contributions to the genre of the conversation manual. Far from treating everyday curiosity with suspicion, Ceriziers is—to use modern terminology—helping to produce ideology by naturalizing his own discourse, by claiming that it is a transparent reflection of the everyday.

The preface culminates in a lavish reflexive description of his book, which he compares, through a series of metaphors, to the real or imaginary collections, edifices, and spaces of the contemporary secular culture of curiosities. This textual collection of religious information is like an Indian temple built from feathers and honey; its contents are like fruit picked from orchards, precious stones retrieved from mines, fine drapery from shops, golden objects from treasure houses, paintings in a temple (e ii[r]–e iii[v]). Whereas Bossuet and Fénelon rejected such secular curiosity but occasionally used it as a fleeting counter-image for a tenuous, good, spiritual kind of curiosity, conversely Ceriziers is largely using secular curiosity as a positive, celebratory image for good, spiritual curiosity. However, even in his case, there is a residue of unresolved ambivalence in the attitude towards secular curiosity. In the dedication (addressed to a cardinal) that precedes the preface, he had sought to dissociate 'this holy Curiosity' ('cette sainte Curiosité') from the secular 'fashion,

---

[167] Similarly, Bouchel presents his *Sainte Curiosité* as arising from conversations with his friend Paul Scarron (1616, a ii[r]–a iv[v]), while Nazare Anroux's miscellany on the Holy Family contains 'answers to the curious questions' put to him by nuns (1662: see sigs. a ii[r]–[a iv[r]]).

adornment' sense by personifying it as a woman wearing a simple dress, *without* pearls or stones (a ii^r–a iii^v). And yet those repressed stones and pearls now return with a vengeance at the end of the preface. Not that the closing celebration of curiosity in the preface embraces all of the term's contemporary secular connotations: Ceriziers is compelled to rule out at least one of them—'novelty', a connotation that had reached hyperbolic heights in Gaffarel's famous title, *Unheard-of Curiosities*. By contrast, 'these must not be called unheard-of Curiosities, since after all they can be heard every day in schools and read in books.'[168] The 'novelty' connotation may be fine for objects discovered by collectors or natural philosophers, but even Ceriziers judges it incompatible with a miscellany of religious truths culled from ancient, authoritative sources. Even Ceriziers does not manage to make holy curiosity an exact replica of its secular cousin.

2.3.4   *Secrets of mendicants, mystics, inquisitors*

Ceriziers did not conceive of his curious religious facts as secrets. However, some writers did claim to reveal secrets about certain Counter-Reformation religious groups, all for the sake of what they called the public's curiosity. But these writers' motives in construing the public as having curiosity were never innocent: secrets were revealed through forensic rhetoric, that is, aggressively or defensively, by enemies or friends of the religious group in question. Public curiosity served as an alibi for these revelations; it was used in order to legitimize and justify them. If religious polemicists had simply continued to condemn curiosity outright, that would have deprived them of invaluable propaganda opportunities: accommodating curiosity was the price they had to pay to get their message across. Printed polemic was thus a distinct language-game within church discourse: it produced its own versions of curiosity rather than exactly replicating theological ones. The secrets of religious organizations, as of political ones, were being desacralized in France in this period: increasingly they were revealed or concealed for strategic rather than transcendental reasons.[169]

---

[168] 'Il ne les faut donc pas nommer les Curiositez inoüyes, puis qu'en effet tous les jours on les oyt dans les Escholes, on les void dans les livres' (e iii^v).

[169] For politics, see Merlin 1998, 118–24.

Let me consider this construction, accommodation, and use of public curiosity in relation to three controversies: the first concerns mendicant orders; the second concerns the Inquisition and the Freemasons; the third concerns mystics.

First, public curiosity was a weapon brandished by both sides in the fierce confrontations that took place in the 1630s between Jean-Pierre Camus and defenders of the religious clergy. This was one episode in the long-running antagonism between the secular and regular clergy in Counter-Reformation France.[170] Considerable resentment was often felt by French bishops like Camus about the existence, within their parishes, of the religious houses of orders— especially the Jesuits and Capuchins, the fastest-growing new Counter-Reformation arrivals—who owed direct allegiance to the Pope and so were largely exempt from episcopal jurisdiction. While this non-Gallican presence spearheaded the fight against Protestantism, on the other hand it often gallingly attracted the support, money, and Mass attendance of the richest parishioners.

Initially, Camus defended the regular clergy.[171] But he then turned against them by publishing anonymously in 1631 his vehement attack on monastic communities, *The Disinterested Spiritual Director*. (The last straw for him may have been the defection of one of his own penitents to a Capuchin confessor).[172] A counter-blast, the *Curious Conversations between Hermodorus and the Unknown Traveller*, was published anonymously in 1634, written by Jacques de Chevanes, a Capuchin whose religious name was Jacques d'Autun. Camus in turn attacked that work in his anonymous *Light Cast by Meliton on the Curious Conversations of Hermodorus* (1635). The dispute reached the attention of Rome, which denounced Camus's works, and of the Cardinal Richelieu, who in 1633 ordered Camus to desist, fearful of the propaganda gains being handed on a plate to European Protestants. Both the *Curious Conversations* and the *Light Cast by Meliton* were banned in France, but this and other related disputes involving Camus rumbled on into

---

[170] On the Camus controversy and its broader context, see Adam 1969, 27–9; Butterworth 2002, ch. 2; Chesneau 1946; Fouqueray 1910–25, v. 42–3.

[171] Chesneau 1946, 45–6. See Camus 1640.

[172] Fouqueray 1910–25, v. 42–3.

the early 1640s. From 1631 to 1636 alone, eighteen pro-Camus tracts—by him or by others—were printed.[173]

Chevanes openly acknowledges that his choice of the term *curieux* in his title was carefully calculated. He sees himself and Camus as battling for control of the 'curious minds' of readers: he regrets that they 'have been fired up to read' *The Disinterested Director* and states that the best riposte is for *him* to wrest control of them by giving them curious knowledge, that is, the true secrets of cloisters:

If I have given the attractive title *Curious Conversations* to all of the questions discussed in my book, this is because I think there is nothing which people today desire more passionately to know than the secrets of cloisters and the ways in which they are run. If that were not the case, then the *Disinterested Director* and many other books which he has written would not have deceived so many people. So, in order to satisfy the curiosity of those who have been so badly informed by reading this bad director, in the present work I am refuting all the lies which have been told about this matter . . .[174]

This accommodation of readerly curiosity is all the more remarkable for being made by a Franciscan mendicant: in the language-game of polemics, with his order's reputation under threat, this Capuchin is quite happy to drop the monastic tradition of antagonism to curiosity. Chevanes could have chosen to counter-attack Camus by arguing that the sacred secrets of cloisters should not be tainted by public curiosity. But such an argument was unlikely to win any points in print polemics. Instead, Chevanes tries to correct the calumnies of Camus by divulging mendicant secrets, explaining, for example, why coenobites have long beards.

However, Camus, in his subsequent *Light Cast by Meliton*, argues that Chevanes may only have pretended to want to satisfy public curiosity. It is as if any reluctance to do so has now, by the 1630s, become indefensible:

[173] For these details, see Adam 1969, 28; Chesneau 1946, 159–60, 191–2; Fouqueray 1910–25, v. 42–3.

[174] 'n'ont peû empescher . . . que . . . les esprits curieux ne se soient eschauffés apres sa lecture. . . . Que si j'ay qualifié toutes les questions, qui s'y traictent, du titre aggreable d'*Entretiens curieux*; je pense, qu'il n'est rien aujourd'huy, que l'on desire de sçavoir avec plus de passion, que les secrets des Cloistres, et l'intelligence de leur police. Si cela n'estoit, les livres du *Directeur des-interessé*, et quantité d'autres, qui sont partis de sa plume, n'auroient pas abusé tant de personnes. Afin donc de satisfaire à la curiosité de ceux, qui en sont si mal informés, par la lecture de ce mauvais Directeur, je refute en cest Oeuvre, tous les mensonges, qui concernent ceste matiere' (Chevanes 1634, a2ʳ⁻ᵛ).

You say that you have given your work the title *Curious Conversations* in order to satisfy the curiosity of those who desire nothing so much as to penetrate the secrets of cloisters; but, whether you were speaking in the spirit of those who have been egging you on, and who usually say the opposite of what they think, or whether you have just failed to achieve your aim, in either case you have poured such dense darkness over the monastic mysteries.[175]

By contrast, the light to be shed by Camus *will* satisfy this deceived public curiosity. These two opponents actually agree about the rules of the language-game they are in: each presents himself as the champion of public curiosity and as the only one who can truly satisfy it. Also, each takes for granted that to call one's book *curieux* is to appeal to the reader's *curiosité*: that leap from object to subject may appear self-evident but, because it was theologically controversial, it was far from taken for granted in the market for non-specialist religious books. Camus had not hesitated to make the same leap in his own earlier defence of regular clergy, against Protestants.[176] And yet this is the same Camus who, in a different language-game, devoted an entire chapter of his *Diversitez* to showing that *curiosité* is a wholly sinful passion (2.2.4.2 above).

My second example comes from over a century later, when secrets of religious organizations were still being aggressively revealed in the name of public curiosity. One such organization was the Inquisition, whose arch-enemy Freemasony similarly relied on secrecy. An exposé of the Inquisition's secrets, in the voice of one of its Masonic victims, John Coustos, was translated from English into French as *Curious Investigative Procedures used by the Portuguese Inquisition against Freemasons* ([1756]).[177] The object-oriented term 'curious', denoting roughly 'noteworthy' and designed to attract readers, also

---

[175] 'Vous dites que vous avez donné à vostre Ouvrage le titre d'*Entretiens curieux*, pour contenter la curiosité de ceux qui ne desirent rien tant que de penetrer les secrets des Cloistres; mais soit que vous ayez parlé conformément à l'esprit de vos Instigateurs, qui disent ordinairement le contraire de ce qu'ils pensent, soit que vous ayez manqué à vostre dessein, vous avez versé de si espaisses tenebres sur les mysteres Cenobitiques' (Camus 1635, i, sig. e ii").

[176] *Le Voyageur inconnu. Histoire curieuse, et apologetique pour les religieux* (1640; 1st edn. 1630). The 'curieuse' of the title is immediately echoed, in the first sentence of the Preface to the reader, by an approving mention of the latter's 'curiosité' (a ii").

[177] The work was also translated into German, as *Curieuses Verfahren* (n.p., [1756]). Coustos was apparently born in Berne and was subsequently naturalized in England ([Coustos] [1756], 1–2).

connoted 'controversial', as in numerous other non-specialist works on religious matters.[178] It was used in the same way by the Inquisition, now against the Masons: an anti-Masonic book by an Inquisition supporter was denounced in the *Curious Investigative Procedures* as containing 'many investigations' about Freemasonry which were 'most curious according to their author, but in fact pitiful'.[179] Each of these enemy organizations assumed that its own secrecy was justified and that its opponent's was not. According to Coustos, the Inquisition has a 'love of secrecy' because its secrets are shameful, whereas Masons, who have no evil to hide, are secretive for the purely strategic reason that 'secrecy excite[s] curiosity' and so draws many people to join the society.[180] So public curiosity could here be maximized by secrecy rather than—as in the Camus/Chevanes dispute—satisfied by revelation of secrets.

My third example, that of mysticism, shows that in the case of some groups, although neither their defenders nor even their attackers were keen to divulge the group's secrets, both did nonetheless divulge them, however reluctantly. Especially in the context of late seventeenth-century Counter-Reformation polemics, the burgeoning discourse about public curiosity seems to have exerted a pressure of its own which few keepers of religious secrets were in a position to resist.

Mystics, unlike the religious clergy or the Inquisition, were not part of a formal organization. Nonetheless, the tradition of which they were part dictated that the secrets of its techniques and practices should not be publicly divulged, for fear of abuse and fraudulent imitation. Opponents of mysticism also preferred to keep its secrets under wraps, if for different reasons: they feared that its heretical practices would spread.

---

[178] § 2.3.2 above. Curiosity in a *subject*-oriented sense could also be used, in an ironically disingenuous way, in the polemical hunt for the alleged secrets of religious societies, e.g. in Pascal's *Lettres provinciales* (1656–7): 'je fus visité par M. N., notre ancien ami, le plus heureusement du monde pour ma curiosité; car il est très informé des questions du temps, et il sait parfaitement le secret des Jésuites' ('I was visited by our old friend M. N., extremely fortunately as far as my curiosity is concerned, for he is very well up on contemporary issues and has perfect knowledge of the Jesuits' secrets', Pascal 1963, 375).

[179] 'quantité de recherches pitoïables, mais très-curieuses, selon l'Auteur' ([Coustos] [1756], p. v).

[180] 'l'amour du secrèt' (15); 'le Secrèt excitoit la curiosité' (34). The Masonic victims of the Inquisition refused 'to satisfy the odious curiosity of their torturers' ('contenter l'odieuse Curiosité de leurs Boureaux', [Coustos] [1756], p. iv).

However, many secrets of mysticism were let out of the bag in France, for example, in the controversy surrounding Quietism which, in the closing years of the seventeenth century, signalled the decline of the interest in mysticism that had grown through much of the century.[181] At the height of the controversy, Quietist doctrine received widespread publicity, as a result of what both attackers and defenders of the doctrine conceived as public curiosity. Both now felt obliged to publicize the doctrine's secrets even more, since half-knowledge of them would lead the public to disastrous misconceptions. For both attackers and defenders, public curiosity was to be accommodated not in Ceriziers's celebratory mode, but as an exercise in damage-limitation.

The dilemma faced by opponents of mysticism can be illustrated by a 1688 Jesuit tract that denounced Miguel de Molinos's Quietist doctrine of the inner way. The tract takes the form of a letter by someone who thanks his correspondent for having 'satisfied my curiosity'[182] by sending a copy of the famous sixty-eight propositions of Molinos. In return, the helpful sender of the propositions has asked for an explanation of the whole affair. Whereas the letter-writer's initial private curiosity about the doctrine was unproblematic, on the other hand answering this request by his correspondent might risk infringing the 1687 decree by the Pope (Innocent XI) banning anyone from speaking or writing about the propositions. But the letter-writer finds a way round this impediment: 'since those propositions, which [His Holiness] had thought he was burying under rigorous silence, have *become public through natural curiosity*, I thought that if I provided an analysis of that pernicious doctrine then, far from going against his ban, I would on the contrary be supporting his good intention.'[183] To ban any further public curiosity would be to shut the stable door when the horse has bolted. An extra dose of what presumably also counts as public curiosity—the ensuing printed analysis of the doctrine—is now a necessary 'antidote' ('contrepoison') to be administered to feeble minds (5). Whether the Jesuit writer of this tract was sincere or disingenuous in using the

---

[181] On the controversy, see Bayley 1999; Le Brun 1986.

[182] 'contenté ma curiosité' (*Lettre* 1688, 4).

[183] 'come ces Propositions qu'Elle [*sc.* sa Sainteté] croyoit ensevelir par un rigoureux silence, sont d[e]venûes publiques par une curiosité naturelle; j'ai cru, que bien-loin de contrevenir à sa défense, ce seroit au contraire seconder sa bonne intention si je faisois l'Analise de cette pernicieuse Doctrine' (5).

existence of previous publicity as a pretext for this publication matters less than the fact that public curiosity is here ambivalently presented as both culprit and cure.

Similar ambivalence towards public curiosity about mystical secrets is evident in the pro-mystical work which proved to be the turning-point of the Quietist controversy, the *Explanation of the Saints' Maxims on the Inner Life* by Fénelon. It appeared in January 1697 and helped prompt his banishment from the court on 1 August that year. Twenty-three propositions drawn from the work were subsequently condemned by Pope Innocent XII (1699). The semi-Quietist Fénelon abhorred the doctrine of Molinos but was defending, against Bossuet and others, his own spiritual guide Madame Guyon, who had been in prison since 1695 because of her Quietist teaching. Fénelon began the preface to the *Explanation* by saying that he had always thought that mysticism, the pursuit of inner paths, is a subject which 'requires a kind of secrecy':[184]

That is what persuaded me that it was necessary to stay silent about this subject as much as possible, *for fear of over-exciting the curiosity of the public*, which has neither the experience nor the light of grace that is necessary in order to examine the works of the saints. . . . But *since that curiosity has recently become universal*, I think that it is as necessary to speak as it would otherwise have been desirable to keep quiet.[185]

In the wave of publications preceding and following the papal condemnation of Molinos, the mystical horse has now bolted. Like a modern government minister confronting the *fait accompli* of a leak, Fénelon is forced to break his silence.[186] Faced with the practical impossibility of continuing to discourage public curiosity about the secrets of mysticism, he is forced to collude in the stimulation of that curiosity. We have already seen Fénelon being occasionally, tenta-

---

[184] 'demande une espèce de secret' (Fénelon 1983–97, i, *Explication des maximes des saints sur la vie intérieure*, p. 1001).

[185] 'Voilà ce qui m'a persuadé qu'il fallait garder autant qu'on le pourrait le silence sur cette matière, de peur d'exciter trop la curiosité du public, qui n'a ni l'expérience ni la lumière de grâce nécessaire pour examiner les ouvrages des saints. Car l'homme animal ne peut ni discerner ni goûter les choses de Dieu telles que sont les voies intérieures. Mais puisque cette curiosité est devenue universelle depuis quelque temps, je crois qu'il est aussi nécessaire de parler qu'il eût été à souhaiter de se taire' (1001–2).

[186] On 1 March 1695, at the ecclesiastical commission investigating Madame Guyon (the 'Entretiens d'Issy'), Fénelon had had to abandon his previous defence of the notion of a strictly secret spiritual tradition being transmitted down the ages (Fénelon 1983–97, i. 1550).

tively, and tenuously positive about curiosity, but that was part of his search for a vocabulary with which to describe the spiritual life (2.2.4.3 above). Now, by contrast, there is nothing uplifting about the resigned acceptance of curiosity which opens this 'Explanation', this unveiling of mystical secrets. Rather, it is an admission that, by the end of the seventeenth century, the Counter-Reformation language-games of printed polemic imposed different rules from those which prevailed in, say, pure moral theology, where curiosity could still be straightforwardly condemned.

2.4　CONCLUSIONS

If any early modern institution might be expected to produce a monolithic, stable 'concept' of curiosity, it would surely be the church. Indeed, that seems to be why church discourse is largely omitted from Hans Blumenberg's narrative of the rehabilitation of 'theoretical curiosity' (1988): for why focus on an institution that seemed only to be repeating what it had already been saying for centuries and that, in Blumenberg's narrative of the emergence of modernity, provided only a reactionary counter-weight to new, positive secular understandings of curiosity?

In fact, church discourse on curiosity was far more pervasive, complex, and heterogeneous than that account implies. Although on the whole it condemned curiosity, it often hinted that, once bad curiosity had been avoided, a good kind might ensue. But was that good kind just a rhetorical effect of condemnations of curiosity, or was it a real thing? The real existence of such good curiosity was often left unclear; it was glimpsed via tortured grammatical constructions that were perhaps a symptom of the anxiety that the newly positive status of curiosity in secular discourse was causing in church discourse. Occasionally the existence of good curiosity was asserted more clearly by church-based writers.

This variability indicates the problems—and the opportunities— that were created for church discourse by the rehabilitation of curiosity in many secular discourses in the period. The growing gulf between the general tenor of much church and secular discourse on curiosity was brandished with relish by many church writers as proof of the illusory nature of the ways of the world, that seem pleasurable and innocent but are in fact spiritually disastrous. These church writers considered themselves to trump secular discourse with a meta-discourse.[187] They re-read secular discourse against the grain, claiming for example to find a pernicious noun-thing (*curiositas*) lurking implicitly in texts that had used only an apparently innocuous adjective (*curiosus*). On the other hand, a few church writers sought rather to bridge the gulf between church and secular discourse, to accommodate the latter rather than give up on it. In either case curiosity was especially highly charged in church discourse because, unlike medieval curiosity, it almost always incorporated the perspective of both church and world, whether the aim was to make one obliterate the other (Steno's 'curiosities of the world'), to juxtapose the two ironically (Garasse's 'curious doctrine'), or else to merge the two (Ceriziers's 'holy curiosity').

The clash between church and secular discourse was not the only reason for the absence of any monolithic church 'concept' of curiosity. Another reason was the absence of any monolithic 'church', especially in this age of splintering confessions. Yet nor is conceptual uniformity to be found among single confessions (such as Calvinism) or single intra-confessional institutions (such as the Jesuits). Certain characteristics emerge—Jesuit accommodations of curiosity; Calvinist definitions of curiosity as action that exceeds one's predestined vocation—but not uniformly. Why not? Because curiosity varied endlessly according to the uses to which it was put in different language-games. Curiosity was evoked in order to produce or suppress behaviour that was material (making luxury clocks), social (theatre-going; meddling in politics), commercial (book-buying), cognitive (divination; useless scholarship), or spiritual (mental prayer and meditation). These uses were often quite independent of any explicit or even tacit definition of curiosity. Pastoral discourse usually bypassed such definitions altogether: pastors wished to influence people's behaviour, not to educate them academically. Indeed, those pastoral treatises that did include definitions of curiosity often then departed from them in practice anyway (L'Espine). Although theological definitions were part of church discourse, it would be inappropriate to measure the rest of church discourse against them.

---

[187] Only from the mid-17th century did an equivalent, secular counter-discourse seek to develop this kind of meta-status: Thomas Hobbes argued that religion had actually *originated* in curiosity (Zarka 1998, 164–5), and Voltaire later identified the church not with good curiosity but with bad (futile concern with the afterlife, miracles, and so on) (Delon 1998, 194–6).

On the contrary, the power of much church discourse on curiosity derived from the way it eschewed academic definitions in favour of ordinary language, with all of its untidy incoherence ('All curiosity is bad, yet you should direct your curiosity at spiritual matters'; 'All curiosity is bad, but do buy this curious book').

But were these really contradictions or else did 'curiosity' simply have different meanings? That is, were the different uses of curiosity in church discourse simply unrelated uses of the same words, or were they underpinned by a sense that the same thing was always at stake? No single answer to that question is possible, precisely because early modern church writers were themselves constantly and anxiously grappling with it. Yet, on the whole, there was remarkable consensus—even between opponents, such as church critics of worldly curiosity and secular defenders of it—that they were indeed all talking about the same thing, although there was no monolithic 'concept' of curiosity, even within the church. From the point of view of early modern, church-based writers, their understandings of that thing were correct and other people's were incorrect. From the retrospective point of view of the modern historian, curiosity was a crucial discursive arena within which conflicting understandings clashed. It is tempting for the modern historian to adjudicate within that arena, as does Blumenberg in favour of the secular understandings, making them more distinctively early modern and therefore, implicitly, more correct. If, however, one abstains from such adjudication, then it is clear that no early modern writer, group, or institution ultimately had discursive control of curiosity. Indeed, even within church discourse, individual writers' understandings of curiosity were always liable to be wrested from their control by other factors, such as the book industry: L'Espine's curiosity was deformed by his editor Goulart, Trithemius's by his posthumous Benedictine publishers. Such deformation became more extreme whenever curiosity crossed from one institution to another. In other words, curiosity was a supra-personal, supra-institutional arena within which different individuals and institutions clashed, projecting wildly different understandings onto what they all usually considered to be the same single thing. Viewed as a collective arena, curiosity had a life of its own, behaving in ways which no single person or institution could control, however much they tried.

3

Institutions: The Culture of Curiosities

Discursive Tendencies: Collecting

3.1 THE CULTURE OF CURIOSITIES

My third look at the institutional uses of curiosity focuses on a group of institutions, some relatively formal, official, and regulated (academies, learned societies, publishing houses), others looser and more informal (networks of savants, naturalists, collectors, travellers, and antiquarians). These communities were often fostered by 'mediating institutions such as the laboratory, cabinet, museum and library',[1] the coffee house, the newspaper stall, the salon, even the court. They were distinct from both university and church, although their membership overlapped with that of those two institutions.

It was within these largely secular institutions and communities that there developed, especially from the early seventeenth century onwards, the worldly discourses of curiosity that were attacked in much church discourse. The two most distinctive semantic features of these worldly discourses were, first, their tendency to make curiosity more positive and, secondly, their enthusiasm for curiosities— that is, they were responsible for the rapid proliferation of relatively new, object-oriented usages of this family of terms, alongside the continuing subject-oriented ones. This semantic shift in emphasis may seem trivial, but it had profound epistemological and moral dimensions. It has prompted me to label this cluster of institutions and communities the culture of curiosities.

[1] Nelles 1997, 43.

3.2   COLLECTING AND NARRATING
AS DISCURSIVE TENDENCIES

The tendency within the culture of curiosities to call objects 'curious' often entailed shaping matter or discourse into a collection of fragments. In other words, when several material or discursive objects were described as 'curious' or as 'curiosities', it was stated or implied that they were fragments belonging to a literal or metaphorical collection.[2] This was a distinctive obsession within the culture of curiosities. It was sometimes couched in terms other than curiosity; but it was often grounded in the object-oriented semantic thread of the 'curiosity' family of terms. In cases where it was, I am labelling it the curiosity-collecting tendency (or thread or strand). In cases where it was not, I am simply labelling it the collecting tendency.

However, this was only one of two discursive tendencies which often accompanied any given occurrence of the 'curiosity' family of terms. Secondly, in other instances, especially when 'curiosity' was used in a subject-oriented sense, the surrounding text stated or implied not a collection of objects but rather a narrative, a story. Phrases like 'my curiosity' or 'she was curious' often denoted one stage in a narrative which then led to a happy end ('my curiosity led me to learn one of nature's secrets') or an unhappy one ('she was curious and so was punished'). The narrative could be fictional or true; it could last a sentence or a whole volume. Again, in cases where this narrating tendency was grounded in the subject-oriented thread of the 'curiosity' family of terms, I am labelling it the curiosity-narrating tendency (or thread or strand). In cases where it was not, I am simply labelling it the narrating tendency.

Curiosity, then, usually entailed either collecting or narrating, in the senses I have outlined. In the culture of curiosities, it entailed especially collecting, which is why the present Section 3 operates on two axes, studying the uses of curiosity made both by a set of institutions and communities (those of the culture of curiosities) and also within one discursive tendency (curiosity-collecting). On the other hand, in other institutions and discourses—university, church, moralizing fiction and theatre—the curiosity-narrating strand was dominant. It will be studied especially in Section 4.

---

[2] For a highly condensed version of the present analysis of this tendency, see Kenny (forthcoming).

Obviously, the curiosity-collecting strand was prominent in the discourse of those who collected material objects, whether in cabinets, museums, or libraries. But it also spread to a wide range of other discourses—on nature, history, the news, and so on—even when the only objects being collected were discursive rather than material ones. In other words, the collecting of material objects may have operated as the literal term of a metaphor that spread to other discourses.[3] However, the shape of discursive collections may have influenced that of material ones, as well as vice versa. Indeed, even my working distinction between material and discursive objects is tenuous, since the discursive objects—facts, recipes, anecdotes, and so on—that were collected in books and periodicals were also partly material, composed of print and paper. So I differ from those who have argued that the 'privileged sites' of curiosity were the eclectic cabinet and the *Wunderkammer*[4] or that the 'privileged image' of the early modern *curieux* was the collector:[5] there were other important sites and images of curiosity not only in other institutions (university and church) but also elsewhere within the culture of curiosities itself.

The collecting and narrating strands of curiosity were not entirely distinct. They often cooperated with each other within a single text: for example, some travelogues were driven forwards by the subject-oriented curiosity of the traveller that led him from one place to the next, but they also came to long halts when the object-rooted curiosities or curious features of a place were enumerated, turning narration into collection.

On the other hand, the relation between the two strands was often agonistic. In 1665 the mechanical philosopher Robert Boyle eloquently privileged narrating over collecting: he associated narrating with subject-oriented curiosity (but did not, in this instance, associate collecting with curiosities). If you have been reading Aesop's fables, he says,

or some other *collection* of apologues of differing sorts, and independent one upon another; you may leave off when you please, and go away with the pleasure of understanding those you have perused, without being solicited

---

[3] A similar point is made in relation to Britain by Benedict (1990, 93), but I differ from her in that she has the metaphor encompass the whole of a period instead of certain discourses within it: 'eighteenth-century curiosity fractures culture into a cabinet of curiosities'.

[4] Olmi 1992, 191 ('i luoghi d'elezione').

[5] Jacques-Chaquin 1998a, 14 ('l'image privilégiée').

by any troublesome itch of *curiosity* to look after the rest, as those, which are needful to the better understanding of those you have already gone over, or that will be explicated by them, and scarce without them. But in the book of nature, *as in a well-contrived romance*, the parts have such a connection and relation to one another, and the things we could discover are so darkly or incompleatly knowable by those, that precede them, that the mind is never *satisfied* until it comes to the end of the book; till when all that is discovered in the *progress*, is unable to keep the mind from being molested with impatience, to find that yet concealed, which will not be known, till one does at least make a further *progress*. And yet the full discovery of nature's mysteries is so unlikely to fall to any man's share in this life, that the case of the pursuers of them is at least like theirs, that light upon some excellent romance, of which they shall never see the latter parts.

Even 'the pleasure of making physical discoveries' is always accompanied by 'both anxious doubts, and a disquieting curiosity'.[6] Thus, natural philosophy is not a collection of discontinuous fables but rather a linear narrative, whose telos is deferred beyond the life of any single philosopher-reader. Just as the 'connection' between 'the parts' of the romance is only partially perceived, so the experimental search for causal understanding is necessarily provisional and conditional.[7]

Still more cautious than the Royal Society founding member Boyle was Bernard le Bovier de Fontenelle in his 1702 preface to the first volume of the official history of its French counterpart, the Académie des Sciences. Without resorting to the vocabulary of curiosity, he *embraces* rather than rejects the collecting metaphor, at least as a first step:

Hitherto the Académie des Sciences has grasped Nature only in *small chunks*. There is no general *system* . . . Today one fact is established, tomorrow an entirely *unconnected* one. Conjectures about causes continue to be hazarded, but they are just conjectures. So the annual *collections* which the Académie presents to the public are composed only of *detached pieces*, independent of each other.

The possible second step and telos will be not the long-awaited dénouement of a romance but rather the integration of everything collected: Fontenelle imagines this by projecting a narrative structure

---

[6] *The Excellency of Theology, Compared with Natural Philosophy* (Boyle 1744, iii. 428; my italics). 1st edn. 1674. Probably written in 1665.
[7] On Boyle's epistemology, see Shapin 1996, 101–6.

onto collecting, imagining a future progress towards integration, and thereby blissfully fusing the collecting and narrating tendencies: 'Perhaps the time will come when we will join together these scattered members into a regular body; and if they are as we wish them to be, then they will somehow assemble themselves of their own accord.'[8] This is, after all, only the first volume of the history of the Académie, on a par with the first volumes of Boyle's imagined romance.

These examples show that the collecting and narrating tendencies of curiosity often had an epistemological or cognitive dimension. 'Let's constantly amass items of knowledge—one curiosity at a time', as one mid-eighteenth-century pedagogue put it.[9] They could also have a moral dimension, especially in the case of narrating ('she was curious and so was punished'). However, they were not coextensive with any such dimension, which is why I am labelling them discursive rather than, say, epistemological or moral. And they were tendencies, not fixed paradigms: even the curiosity-collecting tendency was endlessly variable, as writers shaped curiosities for different uses. Although curiosities were often novel and difficult, the theological ones offered by Ceriziers lacked novelty (2.3.3 above), while l'abbé Bougeant's 'curious observations' on physics lacked difficulty (3.4.2 below). Discursive curiosities cannot therefore all be explained by recourse to any single modern theory, such as Pomian's anthropological thesis that the objects in early modern collections gave people access to invisible worlds.[10] Such theories are powerful heuristic tools, but they can only be matched occasionally, not systematically, with the period's terminology. The object of my study is not a mentality or a paradigm but rather ordinary language, the language-games played with it, its dominant discursive tendencies, and the battles fought over them, which made it intrinsically

---

[8] 'Jusqu'à présent l'Académie des Sciences ne prend la Nature que par petites parcelles. Nul Système général . . . Aujourd'hui on s'assure d'un fait, demain d'un autre qui n'y a nul rapport. On ne laisse pas de hasarder des conjectures sur les causes, mais ce sont des conjectures. Ainsi les Recueils que l'Académie présente tous les ans au Public, ne sont composés que de morceaux détachés, et indépendants les uns des autres . . . Le temps viendra peut-être que l'on joindra en un corps régulier ces membres épars; et s'ils sont tels qu'on les souhaite, ils s'assembleront en quelque sorte d'eux-mêmes.' (Fontenelle 1989–, vi. 49–50). On this passage in the context of the Académie's predilection for strange facts, see Daston and Park 1998, 246.

[9] Juvenal de Carlencas. See 3.4.5.1 below.

[10] Pomian 1987, 15–59. For an example of this argument's influence, see Olmi 1992, 166.

variable, rough at the edges, contradictory, and—in short—resistant to any single, overarching explanatory theory.

For this reason, I differ from the major modern scholars who have interpreted early modern curiosity in terms of an overarching paradigm. Hans Blumenberg privileges curiosity in the subject-oriented sense that is most germane to what I am calling the narrating tendency: he focuses on early modern texts which claim curiosity as a crucial first or intermediate stage in a linear quest for knowledge (1988, chs. 8–10). On the other hand, he gives little attention to the object-oriented senses ('a curious object', 'curiosities') which were so prominent in the period and which were central to what I am calling the collecting tendency. He gives 'curiosities' a very subordinate role, in which they benefit from the recent legitimation of curiosity and are swept along by it, hanging on to its coat-tails (210). A more antagonistic relation between what I am calling the collecting and the narrating tendency of curiosity is described by Krzysztof Pomian who, in contrast to Blumenberg, focuses on the senses of 'curiosity' which were most central to the activity of collecting 'proper', from about 1550 to 1750. Although he ascribes far more importance than does Blumenberg to those senses, Pomian too interprets them as being ultimately overtaken by 'science': 'curiosity was an interregnum between the reigns of theology and science' (1987, 80). His thesis does dovetail partly with mine: as can be deduced from some of his examples, the demise of what he calls this interregnum involved—to translate into my terms—a certain victory of the narrating over the collecting tendency of curiosity. In 1754, the *Encyclopédie* condemned in one article the curiosity of the person who collects drawings, painting, and engravings, while its main article on curiosity praised it as the necessary first step in the path to knowledge of causes, in other words as a stage in a narrative. And, remarkably, not a single object-oriented occurrence of curiosity is to be found in that main *Encyclopédie* article. So, although Pomian argues that 'science' replaces 'curiosity', in fact the third stage in his schema—'science'—does still include curiosity after all, only now shorn of its object-oriented senses and of its collecting connotations.[11]

The fact that some curiosity does continue in Pomian's third, 'science' stage, although it is not supposed to, shows that such grand

[11] On curiosity in the *Encyclopédie*, see N. Kenny 1998, 74–81; Pomian 1987, 155–62.

narratives cannot take account of the complexity of ordinary language. They have to ignore those semantic strands which do not suit them. For example, one modern study of curiosity in early modern German universities and learned societies seeks to interpret those institutions in the light of Blumenberg's narrative but can only do so by denigrating some of the 'curiosity' family's connotations (such as 'odd', 'sensational') as degenerate offspring of its supposedly 'true' connotations (such as 'rational', 'empirical', 'experimental'), thereby privileging those meanings that are conducive to the narrating tendency (an impetus leading to progress), as opposed to the collecting tendency (a non-progressive accumulation of sensational facts).[12]

While the division of curiosity into 'true' and 'degenerate' meanings is here particularly explicit, it is also the implicit precondition of all grand narratives of curiosity. Blumenberg has to sideline more early modern meanings of curiosity than does Pomian, which itself indicates how prominent was the curiosity-collecting thread in the period. Blumenberg's 'theoretical curiosity' and Pomian's 'culture of curiosity' can certainly both be grounded in the early modern terminology of curiosity, but Blumenberg has to look among, say, members of the Académie des Sciences—such as Fontenelle or Pierre-Louis Moreau de Maupertuis—while Pomian has to look mainly among collectors.[13] Yet these two influential modern critical constructions become less helpful when they are understood—as they have often been—as describing not specific discourses (of academicians or collectors, for example) but rather the whole of early modern discourse. Even the 'culture of curiosity', as described by Pomian, was certainly not ubiquitous within early modern discourse, nor even within discourse on curiosity, as my analysis of university and church has shown: Ceriziers was being more hyperbolic than accurate when claiming in 1643 that curiosities were 'everywhere'. Yet Pomian's 'culture of curiosity' has sometimes become so identified with the period as a whole that anyone now studying early modern curiosity is often presumed to be working on collecting and its neighbouring discourses.

So I am certainly not claiming to describe *en bloc* an early modern *epistêmê* of curiosity, akin to Michel Foucault's Renaissance

---

[12] Daxelmüller 1979, 155. See Introduction above.
[13] Blumenberg 1988, 219–30, 303 n.307; Pomian 1987, 61–80 ('La Culture de la curiosité').

epistémê of similitudes (1966, ch. 2). Rather, the aim of the present section is to explore the uses of curiosity in those institutions and discourses in which the curiosity-collecting tendency was especially prominent (sometimes in conjunction with the narrating one): academies and learned societies, pedagogical works, how-to books, miscellanies, newspapers, and other periodicals, as well as books on nature and art, luxury and fashion, collecting, antiquarianism, travel, history, occult sciences. In their uses of curiosity, these discourses often had much more in common with each other than with university and church discourse. And yet there was also variation between them.

The examination of the relations between some of the discourses in this culture of curiosities is already underway, thanks to Barbara Benedict, Lorraine Daston, and others.[14] But many connections between the discourses listed above still remain to be investigated. And those connections have not yet been studied through exclusive focus on the language of curiosity, in all of its richness, contestedness, and contradictoriness.[15] If Blumenberg and Pomian have been able to deduce such different paradigms from their sources, that is partly because the 'curiosity' family of terms encapsulated the dilemma between discursive tendencies. And that is why it is often impossible to characterize leading proponents of new philosophy, such as Francis Bacon, Galileo Galilei, or René Descartes, as being baldly pro- or anti-curiosity, unless by 'curiosity' one means something less—or more—than the full range of meanings which the philosopher in question actually gave to that family of terms.[16] Even

[14] Benedict 1990 and 2001; Beugnot 1988; Daston 1994 and 1995; Daston and Park 1998, esp. 231 and ch. 8; Frühsorge 1974, 193–205; Merlin 1998; Whitaker 1996, esp. 75.

[15] For a language-based approach to curiosity in one text from the culture of curiosities—Antoine Furetière's *Dictionnaire universel* (1690)—see Blair 2003. Several studies have distinguished between the subject- and object-oriented senses of 'curiosity', but only sporadically: see Benedict 2001; Beugnot 1988, 21; Daston 1994, esp. 35–6; Daston 1995, 18; Eamon 1994, 314–18; Nelles 1997, 43–4.

[16] It would be worth studying systematically the role of curiosity in the discourse of such figures. Both Blumenberg (1988, 191–200) and Daston and Park (1998, 228, 307, 310, 311), present Bacon as being relatively positive about curiosity notwithstanding some misgivings about it, but the 'curiosity' family of terms itself does not always appear in the evidence which they quote, and insofar as it does, it seems more negatively than positively charged and does not suggest that Bacon associated curiosity prominently with the advancement of learning or—as has also been pointed out by DaCosta Kaufmann (1993, 184–6)—with the natural-historical collecting of particulars. On curiosity in Bacon, see also Harrison 2001, 279–82. Galileo represents for

proponents of new philosophy did not simply embrace the curiosity-narrating tendency and reject the curiosity-collecting one. The latter too played an important role in the discourses associated with the so-called Scientific Revolution, notwithstanding Pomian's opposition between 'science' and 'curiosity'—by which he largely means curiosity-collecting. The Scientific Revolution was not just about thundering towards a telos; it also involved the collecting of knowledge, sometimes without any view to a telos (a dimension which is obscured by the very term 'Revolution').

That is not to say that major innovative philosophers such as Bacon, Galileo, Descartes or, for that matter, Thomas Hobbes or Nicolas Malebranche, were representative of the period as a whole in their pronouncements on curiosity (which were especially enthusiastic in the case of Hobbes).[17] Just like the pronouncements of lesser writers, theirs were discourse- and context-specific, sometimes explicitly so: Malebranche was upbeat about curiosity in philosophy but more wary of it in theology (Jacques-Chaquin 1998*a*, 20–1). The rich life of curiosity in contemporary discourses, both inside and outside the culture of curiosities, cannot be reduced to the status of a mere secondary, diluted or degenerate echo of canonical thinkers, as it is implicitly for Blumenberg. Even canonical thinkers were led by contemporary discourses as well as leading them. Moreover, whereas theorists of the passions—such as Hobbes, Descartes, or the more obscure writers of university philosophy dissertations—were concerned to define coherently curiosity and its place in human psychology or physiology, this was not the concern of the vast majority of contemporary discourse involving curiosity. As in much church discourse, when curiosity was being used to do things—for instance

Blumenberg (1988, 203–9) an important instance of the legitimation of 'theoretical curiosity', but only Galileo's early biographer supplies Blumenberg with an explicit interpretation of Galileo's activity in terms of *filosofica curiosità* (209). By contrast, Galileo himself was scathing about *curiosi* who collected objects (Olmi 1992, 180). As for Descartes, his *Recherche de la vérité par la lumière naturelle*, written in the 1640s, is selected by both Bernard Beugnot and Pomian as a key text on curiosity, but they interpret it in opposite directions, as praising curiosity (Beugnot 1988, 25) or as condemning it (Pomian 1987, 78–9). My own reading would see Descartes as grappling with the complex heritage of this family of terms by reinscribing the centuries-old 'bad/good curiosity' opposition, which now becomes an opposition between the bad, infinite curiosity of orthodox learning and the good, finite curiosity of Cartesianism.

[17] See Daston 1994, 41; Daston and Park 1998, 307; James 1997, 189–90; Zarka 1998.

to sell books or to give someone an aura of social distinction—theoretical definitions of it were probably far from many writers' and readers' minds.

3.3   CALLING OBJECTS 'CURIOUS'

Within the culture of curiosities, different discourses or language-games used curiosity in ways that were, to a degree, specific to them, which is why I distinguish between them below (3.4). However, on the other hand, they often had in common certain discursive tendencies that, on the whole, were avoided or criticized by church and university discourse: notably, the tendency to shape matter and discourse into a collection of objects. They also often commodified these curious objects, endowing them with financial value. Curiosities—whether material or discursive—were often used in attempts to make money or else to boost their owner's prestige. Exchanging them was sometimes a way of creating sociability. These modern labels—'commodification', 'sociability', and so on—are helpful if applied selectively and heuristically as tools which can reveal some of the uses to which curiosity was put. But, like similar heuristic labels adopted above—such as 'confessionalization' and 'social discipline' (1.3.4)—they cannot function as all-encompassing theories since, as consideration of ordinary language shows, curiosity was used in ways more variable, contradictory, specific, or else vague than they can allow for. Ordinary language reveals tensions and even incoherence within the culture of curiosities.

What were the characteristics commonly attributed to curious objects within that culture? Curious objects were variously 'rare', 'uncommon', 'exotic', 'excellent', 'fine', 'elegant', 'delicate', 'beautiful', 'new', 'useless', 'extraordinary', 'strange', 'wonderful', 'entertaining', 'interesting', 'noteworthy', and 'select'.[18] Often, to call an object 'curious' was to say both something about the way in which a human subject had crafted it and something about the way in which it was an object of human attention: a discursive object such as 'a curious remark' (*une remarque curieuse*) could be both 'punctilious'—via a metonymic projection from the human subject who had crafted it 'carefully', *curieusement*—and also 'uncommon' (in

---

[18] Daston 1994, 43–9; N. Kenny 1998, 113–15, 119–22, 134–43.

the more straightforwardly object-oriented sense).[19] This simultaneous combination of subject- and object-oriented senses provides linguistic evidence for arguing that curious objects did not exist
objectively as such, but instead were crafted by subjects for other
subjects, by humans for humans. The combination also shows that
to call an object 'curious' was to conjur up not a logical 'concept' but
rather a loose, polysemic cluster of meanings, subject- as well as
object-oriented. Some of those meanings were overt denotations,
others shaded off into covert but powerful connotations, such as
'collectable', 'worth buying',[20] 'small' and 'hidden',[21] or 'experimental' (that is, objects of experimental philosophy and of empirical
observation).[22]

Just as many kinds of material objects were called curiosities
in 'literal' collections such as cabinets, many kinds of discursive
objects were similarly labelled in textual collections: for example,
one periodical was presented as a 'Saxon cabinet of curiosities' containing 'occurrences . . . cases . . . inventions . . . letters . . . descriptions'.[23] Other discursive objects commonly called 'curious' were
'observations', 'remarks', 'notes' (*Anmerkungen*), 'narrations'
(*Erzählungen*), 'questions', 'researches' (*recherches*). When applied
to these, 'curious' usually had an object-oriented meaning but sometimes also a subject-oriented one: *recherches curieuses* could be ones
that were not only 'uncommon' but also 'conducted with care'.

The discursive construction of curious objects was symmetrically
matched by that of curious subjects who were the clientèle for them.
Readers in the culture of curiosities were called *curieux, curiosi,
curieuse Leute* ('curious people'), *curieuse Liebhaber* ('curious amateurs'), or *die curieuse Welt* ('the curious world'). In the context of
one particular discourse, that of natural history and natural philosophy, Daston and Park have demonstrated that the term 'curious'
(along with 'ingenious')

defined a new community of inquirers primarily by sensibility and object,
and only secondarily by university training or social status. Disposable time

---

[19] N. Kenny 1998, 128–34.
[20] For these 2, see N. Kenny 1998, 169–83, 186–7.
[21] Daston 1994, 45.
[22] Daston 1995, 17–18.
[23] 'Begebenheiten . . . Casus . . . Inventiones . . . Briefe . . . Beschreibungen'
(*Sächsisches Curiositäten-Cabinet* 1731, 'Vorrede').

and income as well as education were to some extent assumed by the avocations of empirical inquiry, voluminous (and usually polyglot) correspondence, and collecting, but they were not the core qualifications of 'the curious'. More central was a highly distinctive affect attached to equally distinctive objects: a state of painstaking attention trained on new, rare, or unusual things and events. . . . The 'curious' or 'ingenious' constituted themselves as a self-declared, cosmopolitan elite, one which spanned national and confessional boundaries, and which was the immediate ancestor of the Republic of Letters of the Enlightenment. The new community of the curious was nearly as socially diverse as it was geographically far-flung, embracing aristocrats and merchants, physicians and apothecaries, lawyers and clergymen of all denominations; but it was united in its preoccupation with the marvels of art and nature.[24]

Being curious in precisely this way was to some extent *specific* to natural history and philosophy, rather than characterizing all discourses, even those within the culture of curiosities. Nonetheless, the application of the same epithet to readers and inquirers in so many discourses—from natural philosophy to newspapers—built bridges between those discourses. The symmetry between the label applied to reading subjects and to the objects read suggests a fantasy that objects could satisfy subjects. Publishers were happy to foster this fantasy by declaring that their curious books were for curious readers, since this would help sell them, while readers in turn were happy to be addressed by publishers as 'curious' since this seemed to include them in the kind of élite described by Daston and Park. The language of curiosity enabled publishers to persuade and readers to aspire. It gave readers a way of imagining that they were part of an élite club, however few credentials they might seem to have, for example in terms of erudition, socio-economic position, contacts, or participation in correspondence networks. The community of the curious was a phantom informal institution to which many thousands of readers belonged—at least in their own heads.

Vagueness sometimes shrouded not only the question of who counted as curious, but also of what did. The above-listed epithets which were often applied to curious objects were not a fixed set. Not only were some of them sometimes specifically excluded—by Ceriziers, Bougeant, and many others—but curious objects were also sometimes described as being the *opposite* of what was expected, for example as being 'old' rather than 'new', 'useful' rather than

---

[24] Daston and Park 1998, 218. See also Daston 1994, 49–54.

'useless', 'common' rather than 'uncommon', or else (on the level of connotation) 'cheap' rather than 'expensive', or 'popularizing' rather than 'learned'.[25] Such reversals sometimes had deliberate shock value, especially in the earlier part of the period when they also had more novelty value: the Minim friar Marin Mersenne, who was the hub of a wide network of philosophers and naturalists, polemically defended the culture of curiosities when unconventionally suggesting in 1634 that 'the main curiosities which preoccupy men'—which he initially contrasted conventionally with 'the arts which are necessary to human life'—might actually be of 'utility' even to those necessary arts.[26] Such polemical reversals point to tensions within particular discourses. For example, the question whether objects which were curious could also be 'useful' was especially fraught in natural philosophy and natural history, where there was often a guilty conscience about non-utilitarian investigations into curious objects. That is why both opponents and defenders of naturalist inquiry argued respectively that such inquiry was, or was not, 'mere curiosity', thus revealing both the attempt to make curiosity compatible with utility and also the difficulty of doing so.[27] The habitual claim that a book was 'both curious and useful' could imply a range of possible relationships between those two terms,[28] as slippery as those between the two terms of that closely related, longer-lasting collocation, 'pleasurable and profitable'.

Further uncertainty surrounded the status of curiosities as fragments. They were widely presented not just as objects but as fragmentary ones, in contradistinction to some notional whole. The whole in question could be conceived as, for example, a branch of knowledge, an animal species, a foreign country or continent, a

---

[25] For an analysis of these semantic reversals in terms of linguistics rather than in their historical and discursive contexts, see N. Kenny 1998, 114–17.

[26] Question 1 ('Quelles sont les principales curiositez qui occupent les hommes?') in *Les Questions theologiques, physiques, morales, et mathematiques* (Mersenne 1985, 211–14): 'les Arts qui sont necessaires à la vie humaine' (211), 'l'utilité' (213). Daston (1994, 43–4) also discusses Mersenne's *question*, from a different angle. In similar vein, Mersenne presents another 1634 collection of 'Questions curieuses' as 'Utiles aux Predicateurs, aux Theologiens, aux Astrologues, aux Medecins et aux Philosophes' (1985, [515]). On Mersenne, see Dear 1988.

[27] Gedner defends the study of nature against the charge that it is 'a mere curiosity, which only serves as an amusement for the idle' (1762, 162). Pluche denies that his enumeration of nature's resources is motivated by 'la seule curiosité' (1732–51, ii, p. xiii).

[28] N. Kenny 1998, 159–61. On this claim, see also Benedict 1990, 60–2.

period of history. In the case of cabinets and museums, Pomian conceives of that whole as an invisible world (another place or time) to which the visible, collected curiosities (such as medals of Roman Emperors) could give access. Without systematically espousing any such anthropological theory, I will be exploring some of the relations of fragment to whole that were stated or implied in the culture of curiosities. Uncertainty often surrounded the question whether the curious fragments, if collected in sufficient number, would eventually add up to a coherent whole or else would always remain just a disparate collection of fragments.[29] To the extent that eventual integration was deemed possible, the collecting tendency could be overtaken by the narrating one, as we saw in the context of the new philosophy with Boyle and Fontenelle, whose imagined whole was a fully satisfactory physical account of nature. Some publications implied that their curious fragments could add up to a whole, but many—such as miscellanies—implied that they could not.

The shaping of knowledge into curious fragments often had specific epistemological and social purposes. For example, as Gottfried Frühsorge and Wilhelm Kühlmann have shown, in the late seventeenth and early eighteenth century a burgeoning German market of vernacular publications offered knowledge that was *politisch*, that is, of practical use to territorial rulers, to scholar-courtiers, to *bürgerlich* (or even aristocratic) bureaucrats in the court administrations of the developing absolutist states, as well as to non-functionary

---

[29] By contrast, a germane comment by Benedict (2001, 257 n.24) emphasizes just one of these two possibilities: 'curiosity . . . as a cultural category fragments or decontextualizes impressions and observations without recombining them into a meaningful shape'. Whereas for Benedict curiosity is a 'cultural category' that can be partly separated from period terminology and so inserted into a modern explanatory narrative, I am studying curiosity as a family of terms characterized by conflicting semantic threads which contemporaries constantly contested as they sought to use it for different purposes. In contrast to Pomian's 'invisible world' thesis, but without referring directly to it, Merlin (1998) argues that the curiosities accumulated in cabinets and newspapers were a collection of visible, immediate appearances which did *not* add up to any transcendent totality (117) but only gave at best tantalizing glimpses of nature, God, or the absolutist king. She ties her thesis partly but not systematically to the 'curiosity' family of terms and is suggestively mapping the 'culture of curiosity' (118) onto another political context, that of 17th-century France. Merlin and Pomian differ as to the ratio of presence/absence which they find embodied in collected curiosities or—to put the same point differently—as to the residue of continuing desire which they find amidst the gratification afforded by curiosities. In my perspective, adjudication between their two general theories can take place only on a local, text-by-text basis.

urban burghers, enabling them to act prudently in the public or private sphere. So-called *galant* theorists such as Christian Thomasius and Christian Weise contrasted such *politisch* knowledge with pedantry, by which they largely meant scholastic, metaphysics-based systems of knowledge which were taught in Latin in traditional universities.[30] Frühsorge has demonstrated that this *politisch* knowledge was often called *curieus*, and that it was sometimes broken up into alphabetically ordered fragments, for example in lexicons. The preface to one very successful *Lexicon of the Curious and Real*—which contained entries on many disciplines and skills, such as physics, medicine, mechanics, building, navigation—set out its epistemological premises clearly. A discipline can be presented using two methods:

With the systematic method the material hangs together; its pieces are presented in such an order that they follow on from each other.

By contrast, with the alphabetical method nothing hangs together; instead, all the knowledge is ripped up into small pieces and presented, without connections, in a sequence determined by the twenty-four letters of the alphabet.[31]

There are remarkable echoes here of the vision of fragmented knowledge sketched in the different context of natural philosophy by Boyle and Fontenelle. Yet whereas those two academicians envisaged at least the future possibility of the 'pieces' becoming a whole, here the whole is being enthusiastically dismantled in the service of immediate, practical actions of many kinds. The readership of this lexicon is *die curieuse Welt*: 'we would like to investigate . . . how the curious world came by this alphabetical method'.[32] Two explanations are given: first, the amount of knowledge available has proliferated,

---

[30] See Frühsorge 1974 (largely on the private sphere); Kühlmann 1982 (largely on the public, civic sphere). See also Smith 1994, 42–4; Steinhausen 1895.

[31] 'Nach der Systematischen Methode hänget die Materie an einander, und die Stücke davon werden in solcher Ordnung vorgetragen, daß eines aus dem andern fleust.

Nach der Alphabetischen Methode hingegen hängt nichts an einander, sondern die gantze Wissenschafft wird in kleine Stücke zerrissen, und ohne Connexion in einer solchen Reihe vorgetragen, wie es die Ordnung der vier und zwantzig Buchstaben erfo[r]dert.' (Marperger 1727, preface by Johann Hübner,)(2ʳ; first published in 1712; quoted in Frühsorge 1974, 203 (see also pp. 202–5)).

[32] 'wir wollen . . . nachforschen, wie denn die curieuse Welt auf diese Alphabetische Methode gekommen sey?' ( )(3ʳ).

especially in the vernacular; secondly, 'the current age has such curiosity, that each person wants to know everything or, at least, something about everything'.[33] This subject-oriented curiosity has produced curious objects of knowledge in the image of its own desire, that is, as selective bits rather than as a whole.

Antagonism between systematic and unsystematic (or alphabetical) arrangements of knowledge was certainly not new: for example it had flourished in late sixteenth- and early seventeenth-century French miscellanies which rejected encyclopaedic classifications of branches, occasionally in the name of curiosity.[34] Indeed, the ever-increasing difficulty in establishing satisfactory, coherent, metaphysically grounded encyclopaedic systems, even in learned German culture,[35] may be another context—more intellectual than political—that helps to explain the rise of *curieus* knowledge in *politisch* discourse. Ultimately, encyclopaedias themselves would have to be alphabeticized. And yet there was no *exact* precedent for the *politisch* representation of knowledge as curious fragments—dislocated from their place within a branch, just as 'exotic' objects in cabinets were dislocated from their original setting—that is, as particulars which were immediately accessible to people with a moderate education (rather than only to those who had progressed step-by-step through preliminary axioms and principles), and which were often ordered alphabetically or indeed numerically (since, as we shall see, curious fragments of knowledge also differed from systematic knowledge in that they could be counted and quantified).

Calling objects 'curious' also often involved making them spatiotemporal, that is, making them fragments of times and spaces, often remote, at which subject-oriented curiosity was directed. Even in university and church discourses, although they mainly focused on curiosity rather than on curiosities, this passion was sometimes described as unusual because directed at all dimensions of time—present, past, and future (1.2.1 above). Bossuet conflated as one and the same passion 'all those vain curiosities to know what's going on

---

[33] 'endlich führet das jetzige Seculum eine solche Curiosität bey sich, daß ein iedweder alles, oder doch zum wenigsten von allem etwas wissen will' (){3ᵛ; quoted in Frühsorge 1974, 203).

[34] N. Kenny 1991*a*. For curiosity, see pp. 214–15.

[35] On 17th- and 18th-century encyclopaedism, see Dierse 1977; Loemker 1972; Schmidt-Biggemann 1983; Vasoli 1978.

in the world' (present), the historical curiosity which 'reaches out to the most distant bygone eras' (past), and arts of divination (future).[36] This overarching temporal framework lumped together gossips, historians, and astrologers. It explains how curious objects could be both very old ones (antiquarianism) and very new ones (newspapers), but in either case far removed from the present. The curiousness of objects was thus a relative, relational attribute rather than an inherent one, produced by factors such as their position in time.

The position of objects in space could also make them curious. Curious fragments tended to be ones that were dislocated from their proper place, whether literally (in cabinets of curiosities) or figuratively—when they were bits of knowledge divorced from the context of the discipline to which they belonged.[37] Their curiousness was thus a function either of their own position in space or else of the location—literal or figurative—of the person perceiving them. Indeed, this can still be the case today when, in a greatly reduced number of discourses, objects are called 'curious': what is a curiosity for a foreigner can be a familiar, daily menace for a local.[38] Moreover, in the decades when the 'curiosity' family was beginning to be fêted in many discourses, not only was it sometimes dependent on spatial perspective in this way, but it also had the power to *denote* spatial dependency, thereby reflecting back on itself. A celebrated 1638 treatise on optics by Mersenne's fellow Minim friar Jean François Niceron was entitled *La Perspective curieuse*. An object is viewed in a 'curious perspective' when, by tricks of anamorphosis, catoptrics, and dioptrics, it appears to be something that it is not: it is changed by the way in which it is looked at. Instead of being 'well proportioned', it now seems 'deformed and out of proportion'.[39]

As Niceron's title-page indicates, for him the phrase 'curious perspective' primarily denotes 'uncommon' optical effects, as opposed

---

[36] 'toutes ces vaines curiositez de scavoir ce qui se passe dans le monde . . . Cette curiosité s'étend aux siècles passez les plus éloignez' (Bossuet 1930*a*, 24–5).

[37] Cf. Benedict 2001, 12.

[38] ' "Curiosity? Bugger curiosity", an irate Ravishankar Raval told reporters in his home town of Jotana. "It may be a curiosity to you, but it's terrifying if you live here. Let me tell you, if it wasn't sacred, we'd slit its throat tomorrow." Raval was complaining about the huge black goat which has menaced the inhabitants of Jotana, north Gujurat, for the past three years' (*India Today*, 15 February 1994; quoted in *Private Eye*).

[39] 'difformes et sans raison . . . bien proportionnees' (Niceron 1638, table of contents).

to standard ones. Such curious deformations did not have to be spatial; they were also sometimes aural, as in music, where 'curious' harmonies were unusual, seemingly dissonant ones.[40] So Niceron's 'curious perspective' is not representative of all curious deformations. Nor—despite Ernest Gilman's fruitful application of Niceron's phrase to the many ingenious, witty tricks of perspective in seventeenth-century painting and writing—can all such tricks really be understood as 'curious perspective' if one respects the contours of the period's terminology, since the phrase was not common. (Gilman (1978, 40–50) quotes just one other similar occurrence, from Hobbes.) And yet there is a resonant similiarity between the transformation of objects by Niceron's 'curious perspective' and the transformation of objects in cabinets by the 'curious gaze' of collectors, for whom they too become 'deformed and out of proportion'. Indeed, Niceron celebrates the curiosity of Parisian cabinet-owners in his treatise (77). The 'curiosity' family, as well as shaping objects in more discourses than previously, could now also reflect on that process of perspectival shaping.

Although curiosity often involved both time and space, one of the two was usually dominant. In those discourses in which the curiosity-collecting tendency was prominent—that is, which were either on collecting 'proper' or else used collecting as a metaphor—the spatial axis was the more prominent. To present a book as a 'curious collection' of disparate knowledge was to use a spatial metaphor. Not that the collecting tendency was only spatial: the time that is involved in compiling a collection—whether of material or discursive objects—was also sometimes stressed. Conversely, in those discourses where the curiosity-narrating tendency was prominent—such as moralizing stories about the perils of curiosity or else histories of the progress of human curiosity throughout the ages—the temporal axis predominated. Again, however, that is not to say that the narrating tendency was only temporal: the places through which curious heroes or villains progress were also sometimes stressed. Whether as a passion or as a quality of objects, curiosity was both spatial and temporal.

---

[40] This musical usage of the adjective occurred in English, Italian, and Spanish. It was sometimes applied to guitar chord-shapes that transgressed the standard harmonic rules governing other instruments, such as lute and keyboard. Francesco Corbetta's 'very curious sonatas' for guitar, published the year after Niceron's optical treatise, were of this kind (1639: see title-page).

Objects were made 'curious' not only by time and space but also by economics. But the relation of curiosity to economics was far from straightforward. Indeed, it illustrates some of the contradictions at the heart of the culture of curiosities. On the one hand, curiosity was inseparable from markets, conspicuous consumption, the display of wealth, and the rise of what is now referred to as a consumer society, especially when the European economy as a whole began to come out of the contraction that had prevailed for much of the seventeenth century.[41] For those with the means, in towns and courts, this was a period of 'money-guzzling curiosity' or, as Bossuet ironized, 'spendthrift curiosity: one can never have too many rarities, precious jewels and stones, paintings, curious books'.[42] Commodification affected not only such material curious objects, but also the discursive ones contained in publications, just as many kinds of other, non-curious knowledge were increasingly being endowed with monetary value, partly as a long-term result of the introduction of printing and the rise of the book market, but now on a greater scale than ever (Burke 2000, ch. 7). The frenetic selling of books, periodicals, journals, newspapers, and pamphlets was a far cry from the scholastic and humanist dictum 'Knowledge is a gift of God and so cannot be sold'.[43] To call a publication 'curious' was just one marketing device among many, but it became a particularly common one and was explicitly recognized as such, even by Christian Thomasius, who favoured *curieus* and *politisch* knowledge yet still complained in 1689 that publishers ('Verleger') believed that they could get rid of a book more quickly if they put 'Curiositäten' or 'curiös' in the title (N. Kenny 1998, 186). The title-page of a mock catalogue of curiosities—called *Curieuser Misch-Masch*, in a sardonic translation of *Miscellanea curiosa*—declared 'Buy it or leave it'.[44]

Thus, to call a material or discursive object 'curious' was often to connote expensiveness, but sometimes, more surreptitiously, to con-

---

[41] See Parker (ed.) 1997, 191; Powell 1988, ch. 4.

[42] 'Geldfressende Curiosität' (*Das neugierige und veränderte Teutschland* 1988, 217); 'une curiosité depensiere: on ne scauroit avoir trop de raretez, trop de bijoux precieux, trop de pierreries, trop de tableaux, trop de livres curieux' (Bossuet 1930a, 28). On the links of curiosity to consumerism, greed, and the market, see Benedict 1990 and 2001, ch. 2; Daston 1994, 36, 43–5, 51–2; Daston 1995, 17; Daston and Park 1998, 305–10; Pomian 1987, esp. 53–5.

[43] 'Scientia donum dei est, unde vendi non potest'.

[44] 'Wers nicht kauffen will kans bleiben lassen' ([Wohlrab] 1733).

note the exact opposite—cheapness—since miscellanies, periodicals, journals, and popularizations of learning were often presented as providing curious discursive objects in cut-price form for 'those that are desirous of knowledge, but are not in a capacity to buy a multitude of Books' (as a volume devoted to the 'admirable curiosities' of the British Isles put it (Crouch 1682, A2^v)).

A second, more major contradiction at the heart of curiosity arises from its ability to connote neither 'expensive' nor 'cheap' but rather the absence of any monetary consideration whatsoever. In other words, to equate curiosity with consumerism tells only half the story; the other half is the sustained attempt made by many to dissociate curiosity from financial gain. In academies and learned societies, aristocratic circles, or among the many who aped aristocratic values, there prevailed the notion—whatever the reality—that material or discursive curiosities should be freely exchanged, cementing ties of what Christian Licoppe has called 'sociabilité curieuse' (with reference to the *mondain* civility of amateur French naturalists, whether in Paris or the provinces).[45] More broadly, the ideal of freedom from financial considerations also underpinned claims that noble or genteel researchers into nature were the most believable ones since they had no financial interest, as Steven Shapin has demonstrated in relation to England (1994, ch. 2). The ideal of free exchange was also compatible with the ever-growing notion that knowledge should be put to the service of the public good rather than of private gain: this often did involve striving for greater collective prosperity, but the latter was often dissociated from curiosity. The minister Louvois was brutally clear about this in 1686, three years after Colbert's death had given him control of the Académie Royale des Sciences. He wanted the academy now to give up 'curious research which is only pure curiosity or, as it were, amusement for chemists' and turn instead to 'useful research which can be relevant to the service of King and State'.[46]

Curiosity therefore denoted either pure motives, devoid of financial gain, or else the exact opposite: concern with such gain. In this contradictoriness, curiosity resembled 'interest', which became another fashionable theme, especially from the late seventeenth

[45] Licoppe 1996, 122; see also pp. 86–7.

[46] 'recherche curieuse, ce qui n'est qu'une pure curiosité ou qu'est pour ainsi dire un amusement des chimistes . . . recherche utile, celle qui peut avoir rapport au service du roi et de l'Etat' (quoted in Ornstein 1963, 157).

century. Knowledge could be pursued either 'purely out of interest' or else, by contrast, because one had a (self-seeking) 'interest' in it.[47] In the case of both curiosity and interest, the contradiction seems to reveal anxiety about the economic dimension of knowledge, which was sometimes flaunted, sometimes repressed. Those modern histories—such as Blumenberg's—which focus on early modern philosophical texts on curiosity that are largely devoid of object- and finance-oriented meanings, represent curiosity as implicitly transcending economic considerations, in contrast to Pomian's curiosity which, like the collectors who embody it, has its feet firmly in the market. Early modern curiosity was in fact both inside and outside economics; it both embraced and rejected it, depending on the context. Whereas Blumenberg seems to have attributed to 'theoretical curiosity' the disinterestedness often trumpeted by protagonists in the so-called Scientific Revolution,[48] the fact that the 'curiosity' family also often connoted financial gain perhaps reveals a latent financial substratum underlying that apparently money-free curiosity. The 'legitimation of theoretical curiosity' (Blumenberg) may also have been a proto-capitalist legitimation of various kinds of moneymaking. In this interpretation, from a modern perspective the church may cease to be entirely the villain of the piece—an obstacle to intellectual freedom, as it is implicitly for Blumenberg—and its attacks on diviners for swindling the curious poor out of their money may even be praiseworthy.

Aristocratic discourse that suppressed the economic connotations of curiosity sublimated financial value—that was deemed vulgar—into other kinds of more acceptable social value. Ownership of material curiosities was sometimes—though not always—a badge of social distinction. The same could apply to mental ownership of discursive curiosities, that is, of fragments of knowledge which could be offered up and exchanged in civil conversation at court or salon, just as material curiosities were exchanged between collectors. Wit could be displayed like material wonders (Shapin 1996, 126), and both were called 'curious'. Numerous manuals were presented as containing conversational curiosities of this kind, not just in the *curieuse Welt* of German *politisch* discourse, but also in the French world of

---

[47] On the connections between curiosity and interest, see Frühsorge 1974, 197–9; N. Kenny 1998, 143–55.
[48] On these claims of disinterestedness, see Shapin 1996, 161–5.

honnêteté which was its explicit model. More particularly, 'curious' was also often a badge of learning, serving to distinguish an imaginary, exclusive, pan-European community of learned naturalists, collectors, and so on from the common herd.

Again, however, that is only half the story, since this 'distinguished' connotation of 'curious' also spawned its opposite—'vulgarizing'—in the same way that 'expensive' spawned 'cheap'. It was in the interest of printers and booksellers to offer as many buyers as possible the chance to imagine that they belonged to the community of the curious. But this meant that many curious publications were popularizing: they were explicitly directed at those who were *not* rich or learned. Indeed, the splintering of knowledge into curious fragments in many such publications seems to have been specifically designed to include those with no trained-up attention span and with little leisure time for reading: one weekly periodical full of 'curious reports' of extraordinary facts and events was designed for anyone, whether 'learned or unlearned', who might want to spend the odd 'quarter of an hour' reading it.[49]

Finally, there was yet another contradiction within the culture of curiosities. Curiosity could be seen as either solipsistic or collective, as either an anti-social or a social activity. On the one hand, material curiosities could be hoarded by an individual; on the other hand, curiosities—material or discursive—could be exchanged in order to cement social relations, whether in aristocratic or courtly circles or else, in urban places that promoted the exchange of curious information, notably the coffee-house, for which Gottfried Frühsorge has claimed what other scholars have claimed for the cabinet, by making it into an emblem of a culture, 'the authentic location of *curiosité*'.[50] After all, curiosity was often associated with articulation and communicative interaction, with speech and writing. Even in moral discourses that condemned curiosity, it was commonplace to say that this vice of trying to know other peoples' shameful secrets was motivated by the desire to have the pleasure of spreading them. In the culture of curiosities, to the extent that curiosity had an aesthetic dimension, it can be contrasted with the later, more silence-oriented 'sublime', as Katie Whitaker has suggested (1996, 80). Whereas

---

[49] 'gelehrt noch ungelehrt . . . eine viertel Stunde Zeit' (Happel 1683–9, i [1683], sig. [ii]ʳ).
[50] 'der genuine Ort der "Curiosité"' (Frühsorge 1974, 200).

'curious' most often connoted 'short' when applied to discursive objects—as we saw with the periodical designed for fifteen-minute readings—on the other hand it could also connote 'long', especially in collocations like 'curious description', which appeared in countless book titles and indicated that the contents were 'written with care' and so 'thorough, detailed' (that is, 'long'). So the articulation of curiosity in writing and speech could produce either a plethora of small discursive curiosities or else a few large curious descriptions.

Thus, while the act of calling objects 'curious' often served epistemological and other purposes, it cannot be reduced to any single, coherent epistemology, ideology, or purpose. It made knowledge elitist and popular, useless and useful; it made objects money-based and money-free, expensive and cheap; it isolated individuals and yet also produced communities. These battles over curiosity and contradictory uses of it reveal broader anxieties and tensions concerning knowledge: was it public or private, for pleasure or utility, for financial or philosophical gain? Did it foster the superiority of a few people or else the participation of many in a societal enterprise?

3.4   DISCOURSES

The culture of curiosities, then, tended to shape knowledge as a metaphorical collection of curious objects. Yet its uses of curiosity, while having certain common characteristics, were not uniform, but variable and even contradictory. In other words, struggles to impose one understanding of curiosity over others occurred not only on the border between, say, the church and the culture of curiosities, but also within that culture itself, since each of its constituent discourses or language-games made specific uses of curiosity, as also did different users operating within even a single such discourse. Moreover, the precise chronology of the rise and fall of curiosity as a prominent theme varied from discourse to discourse within the culture of curiosities. For these reasons, I will now study one discourse at a time.

Although contemporaries did not refer in so many words to a culture of curiosities, many did presuppose the existence of a cluster of secular discourses and practices in which curiosity played a prominent role. They disagreed as to its exact extent, but their common assumption that it existed became a topos, for example among clerics, most of whom made that cluster the latest manifestation of the passion that the church had condemned for centuries. In other words, many people in the early modern period would have understood my Sections 1, 2, and 3 as all being about the same thing, rather than being about different things that happened to be denoted by the same word.

Among clerics who identified in a hostile spirit what I am calling the culture of curiosities, Bossuet grouped together as curiosity not only gossip, history, and divination (as we have seen), but also new fiction, poetry, and theatre, some aspects of philosophy, theological questions, and the 'spendthrift curiosity' of collecting (1930*a*, 24–8).[51] Among those fewer clerics who also identified the culture of curiosities, but in a more sympathetic way,[52] Mersenne listed the 'main curiosities [i.e. unnececessary arts] which occupy men' as including the cultivation of tulips; the collecting of medals, engravings, paintings, precious stones, shells, exotic fruit, fish skeletons, and insects; silk-making, teaching birds how to speak, making and playing musical instruments; games and sport; divination, optical tricks, and chemistry (1985, 212).

3.4.1 *Academies and learned societies*

Among the several academies and learned societies that were founded in the second half of the seventeenth century, several shaped nature and art into curiosities and investigators of them into curious people.[53] These new institutions tended to be far more enthusiastic than universities or churches about shaping knowledge as a metaphorical collection of curiosities. But that shape was far from uniform, even among academies and learned societies. Even within a single institution, curiosity could have conflicting meanings, revealing anxieties about the knowledge produced. The 'curiosity' family was polysemic: it had a cluster of meanings that were linked more by habit than by logic. Indeed, as in universities, it was this protean

---

[51] Bossuet's hostile list echoed those of other clerics, e.g. Jansen (1659, 42–6) and Nicolas Caussin (Merlin 1998, 127–8). For a secular version, see La Bruyère 1962, 393–8 (398) (1st edn. 1688).

[52] See also 2.3.2 above (Ceriziers).

[53] A similar point is made by Daston and Park (1998, 219). General, Europe-wide studies of the period's academies and learned societies include McClellan 1985; K. Müller 1970; Ornstein 1963; Voss 1980; for a general study of France, see Brown 1934; for one of Germany, see Evans 1977.

quality that kept curiosity at the heart of institutional debates about knowledge for a few decades, since it was a key terminological medium within which conflicts concerning knowledge could be articulated.

Two new German institutions even incorporated curiosity into their name. First, 1652 saw the founding of an 'Academy of those curious about nature' (Academia naturae curiosorum) following the circulation in 1651 of a proposal by a Schweinfurt physician (Johann Laurenz Bausch).[54] The academy was for physicians only, its aim being to advance medicine and ancillary subjects such as pharmacy, botany, anatomy, chemistry, pathology, and physics, not by holding meetings but by encouraging and collectively vetting the production of monographs by its members (Evans 1977, 170–1). It was thus a relatively loose institution, having no headquarters other than where its current president happened to be. However, largely thanks to a new member (Philipp Jacob Sachs), the academy then became more official: it obtained imperial recognition and status in 1677 and 1687, achieving a membership of 150 by 1686 and of 250 by 1702 (Winau 1977, 122–4). In 1670 it launched a learned journal—the first in Germany[55]—which ensured its visibility on a European stage: the *Miscellanea curiosa*, modelled on the *Philosophical Transactions* of the Royal Society and the *Journal des sçavans*, which had both started in 1665.

Secondly, in 1672 a professor of mathematics and physics at Altdorf, Johann Christoph Sturm, who was renowned as perhaps the most skilled German experimenter, created a 'Curious or experimental conference' (Collegium curiosum sive experimentale) as a framework for devising or repeating experiments with his students and friends.[56] This club was far from an official academy. It lasted only till Sturm's death in 1695 and seems to have grown out of his private teaching; it was perhaps a more extensive version of the kind of private lectures and demonstrations which Schrader gave under the same title in the early 1690s at another university with innovative tendencies, Helmstedt (1.1 above). The focus of Sturm's *collegium* was probably the collection of instruments (especially air-pumps) which he had in his house. What gave this grouping a wider visibility

---

[54] On this academy, see—in addition to the general studies mentioned above—Daxelmüller 1979; Stern 1952; Winau 1977.

[55] See Kirchner 1958–62, i. 18–19.

[56] On this institution, see Evans 1977, 136; Ornstein 1963, 175–7.

and status was, as in the case of the 'Academy of those curious about nature', the medium of print: Sturm published, in 1676 and 1685, two volumes of experiments performed by the *collegium*, which was grandiosely compared (in the liminaries) to the recent great European academies.

These two German institutions arose respectively outside universities and on the fringes of them. In 1662 the twenty physician members of the 'Academy of those curious about nature' still included no university teachers of medicine (Winau 1977, 121). Yet, despite grave university qualms about the culture of curiosities, it would be wrong to present universities as being entirely antagonistic to academies and learned societies. To some extent, there was a division of labour between them, with universities and *Gymnasia* being more oriented to teaching and academies to research (Gascoigne 1990, 251–2). One *Gymnasium* oration declared in 1675 that the new European academies were an important manifestation of curiosity (1.3.1 above). Moreover, universities and academies began seizing upon curiosity, albeit in very different ways, at exactly the same time, when the treaties of Westphalia were at last restoring peace to the Empire. The year 1652 saw both the start of the wave of university disputations on curiosity (Frankfurt a.d. Oder) and also the founding of the 'Academy of those curious about nature' (Schweinfurt).[57]

In France and England, investigators and their objects were widely dubbed 'curious' in the discourse associated not only with the chartered bodies—the Académie Royale des Sciences (founded 1666)[58] and the Royal Society (founded 1660)—but also with the other groups or informal circles devoted to the study of (especially) nature which preceded or coincided with those chartered bodies.[59] To take but one famous example: the Royal Society founding member Robert Boyle referred constantly to curiosity, usually enthusiastically, when describing both the motivation and the objects of

---

[57] Indeed, 1652 was also the year in which another, now more obscure academy with exactly that title may also have existed in Madrid (Evans 1977, 137). There had been at least one precursor to such titles, an Academia curiosorum hominum (or Academia secretorum naturae) which had met in the Naples home of the natural magician Giovanni Battista della Porta (d. 1615) (Ornstein 1963, 73–4).

[58] In addition to the general studies mentioned above, see Hahn 1971.

[59] On these other groups or informal circles in France, see Brown 1934; Dear 1988, 3; Phillips 1997, 176–80.

'curious naturalists' such as himself.[60] Why was curiosity given such pride of place by these academies, learned societies, and informal networks? For what purposes did they invoke it? The most obvious surface denotations of 'curious'—such as the subject-oriented sense 'inquisitive' or the object-oriented sense 'worth being inquisitive about'—in fact tell us little about the force which the term had in these contexts, and which derives much more from its rich *connotations*. Indeed, it was through the connotations rather than the denotations of such key terms that knowledge was often shaped in early modern institutions, as closer study of the 'Academy of those curious about nature' reveals.

Officially calling its members 'curious' was part of the academy's attempt to connect itself to a Europe-wide project for the advancement—or, as I will argue, the collecting—of knowledge: the main vehicle for that attempt was eventually the academy's learned journal, which fast gained an international profile. Although the academy became the Empire's representative on the learned international stage, by calling its members 'curious' it sent out the signal that it shared the aims of the self-styled 'curious' of all Europe rather than being primarily national, imperial, or confessional. Indeed, the rise of learned societies in the Empire as a whole has been interpreted as an attempt to restore tolerant civility to the world of learning after the Thirty Years' War—in contrast with the confessionalism of universities—picking up from the earlier utopianism of Johann Valentin Andreae and others (Evans 1977, 132–3). Whereas for Andreae individuals suffering from curiosity and 'singularity' excluded themselves from his 'Christian society' (2.2.3 above), now here was a community in which curiosity was a badge of membership. The role of curiosity in the construction of ideal communities had been inverted.

The academy founded in Schweinfurt called its objects 'curious' as well as its members. What meanings was *curiosa* used to convey in the title of the periodical (*Miscellanea curiosa*) which, to a certain extent, this institution became? A member who joined in 1675—Christian Mentzel—gave his answer in a letter: when considering articles for inclusion (he wrote), the editors should verify 'whether

---

[60] Boyle 1744, v. 440. This work (*Some Considerations of the Usefulnesse of Experimentall Naturall Philosophy*, 1663) provides many examples of these recurrent uses. On Boyle and his English contemporaries on curiosity, see Harrison 2001.

they are curious cases; otherwise these *Ephemerides* would be a heap of medical cases which were already sufficiently known here and there. If there was nothing rare, then the *Ephemerides* would vegetate: they must contain and make public something curious and new about all the topics which they treat.'⁶¹ 'Curious' cases are here above all 'rare' and 'new' ones. This is borne out by the actual contents of the periodical, which was full of monstrous, marvellous, strange medical cases and natural objects (Evans 1977, 137). So this academy and its periodical were participating, like the Académie des Sciences and the Royal Society, in what Daston and Park have described as the reform of natural history and natural philosophy through the collecting of curious, praeternatural particulars and wonders for which these institutions were often not seeking to provide even specific explanations, let alone global ones. Although members of these institutions did seek to study natural laws, they were also undermining the Aristotelian exclusion of abnormalities from natural philosophy, thereby dislocating the smooth scholastic passage from experiential particulars to universals.⁶² As Peter Dear has shown, only when the Royal Society started to adopt Isaac Newton's physico-mathematical explanations of its experimental practice did that institution start to promote one overall natural-philosophical framework, within which experiments were granted token rather than independent significance.⁶³

The very title of the *Miscellanea curiosa* locates that periodical firmly within what I am calling the curiosity-collecting tendency, as one contribution to that broader European project of reforming natural history by collecting curious particulars. The term *miscellanea* was routinely associated in the period with collections of discursive objects. When Mentzel feared that the periodical might become a 'heap' or collection of common medical cases, he was not, I would argue, denigrating the notion of collection in itself, but rather expressing preference for a dynamic collection over a static, 'vegetating' one. The ongoing renewal of the periodical through 'new'

⁶¹ 'obs auch curiose casus sein; anders würden die Ephemerides eine congeries casuum medicinalium sein, die hin und her genugsam bekandt. Und wan es nichts rares wehre, würden die Ephemerides vegetieren. Es müssen darin von allen materien curiosa et quidam nova sein und offenbahrt werden' (quoted in Winau 1977, 129). On Mentzel's contributions to the *Miscellanea curiosa*, see Winau 1968.
⁶² Daston and Park 1998, ch. 6. See also Eamon 1994, ch. 8.
⁶³ Dear 1995, ch. 8 and pp. 246–7.

medical cases makes the collection dynamic by injecting into it a latent narrative axis, driven by the subject-oriented curiosity of the curious members, contributors, and readers. The periodical genre itself fosters this constant renewal which is not progressing towards any eventual telos, unlike naturalist knowledge as described above by Boyle and Fontenelle.

Mentzel's letter makes clear the assumption that the *miscellanea curiosa* contained in this periodical were empirical fragments ('cases') rather than, say, systematic university-style dissertations. Indeed, the periodical's first title-page described it only as 'containing observations'.[64] Each 'observation' was typographically distinct from the rest and, for the most part, between one and five sides long. This relative brevity, together with the fact that these discursive fragments could be read on their own rather than as just one cog in a larger theoretical machine, was what enabled the contents of this and other such learned journals to be popularized so widely in other kinds of publications (3.4.2 below). The shape of curious cases and observations lent itself to popularization much more readily than that of, say, Aristotelian natural philosophy. As Daston and Park have argued, the fragmentary shape of curious knowledge about nature may also have promoted civil dialogue between naturalists more than did universities, not only because the latter fostered disputational wrangling, but also because disagreements about fundamentals in universities necessarily produced disagreements about particulars, whereas curious cases and observations could circulate without being attached to fundamentals.[65]

However, within the academy there was a conflict between this connotation of 'curious'—'a collection of short, free-floating fragments'—and others. By calling its members *curiosi*, this institution was also representing them as 'diligent', since that etymological sense, common in antiquity, continued to thrive in this period. *Curiosus* was understood as a synonym with the founding motto of the academy, 'Never idle'.[66] This 'diligence' was institutionally defined: it involved not only the collection of cases and observations, but also the painstaking, would-be exhaustive description of natural

---

[64] 'continens . . . observationes' (*Miscellanea curiosa* 1670).

[65] Daston and Park 1998, 240–6. See also Shapin 1996, 133–5.

[66] 'Nunquam otiosus' (K. Müller 1970, 138). Since the members of Della Porta's Academia curiosorum hominum were known as 'Otiosi' (Ornstein 1963, 74), this motto was probably a dig at them.

objects, notably in the monographs which members published. Thus, 'curious' could connote not only 'short' discursive objects, but also 'long' ones.

These Latin monographs were usually devoted to a plant or animal. They described it systematically and cohesively, not in a fragmentary way. Typically 200–300 pages long, they resembled university treatises, indeed their authors eventually included at least one professor.[67] Yet although their form was very different from that of the academy's periodical, they too were often called 'curious': *Cynographia curiosa* (on the dog), *Lagographia curiosa* (on the hare), *Lilium curiosum* (on the lily), *Oologia curiosa* (on the egg).[68] While 'curious' here still vaguely connoted the 'rarity', 'novelty' and indeed 'beauty'[69] of the natural object—all helpful for marketing purposes—it also connoted 'diligent, thorough', as was demonstrated by the collocation with -*graphia* ('thorough writing about X'). 'Thoroughness' shaded into 'accuracy': the alternative title for the 'Curious lily' was 'or, an ac*cura*te description of the white lily', harking back to the *cura* etymon.[70] Moreover, the author's 'curious labour' is spelt out in the liminaries to these monographs.[71]

'Curious' was here an institutional guarantee of quality. It connoted not any 'thoroughness', but specifically those modes of 'thoroughness' which were laid down in the academy's constitution: monographs should describe an object's names and synonyms, its manner of generation, its natural location, its differences from other objects, its species, the effects of remedies derived from it, and so on (Winau 1977, 118). Herein lay the 'method and laws' or the '*norma* ['pattern'] of the Academy of those curious about nature', to which the works cited above, plus others not entitled *curiosa*, were advertised as conforming (on their title-pages).[72] 'Curious' became the most prominent shorthand for this *norma*. When readers

---

[67] Matthias Tiling, who taught in the medical faculty at Rinteln.

[68] Respectively: C. F. Paullini 1685 and 1691; Tiling 1683; Garmann [1691].

[69] One liminary poem describes as curious (i.e. 'delightful') the scent of the lily, taking care to italicize the key term and thus connect it wittily to the monograph's title ('*curiosos . . . odores*'; Tiling 1683,)(5ʳ).

[70] 'seu accurata lilii albi descriptio' (Tiling 1683).

[71] 'curioso labori' (C. F. Paullini [1688], [][7ʳ]). See also Tiling [1679],)(2ᵛ: 'Rhabarbarum curiosè examinanti'.

[72] A typical phrase was 'juxta methodum et leges illustris Academiae Naturae Curiosorum descripta' (C. F. Paullini [1688]). See also C. F. Paullini 1685, 1686, 1691, 1695; Tiling [1679], 1683.

encountered the title of these monographs, the *norma* was perhaps the dominant message which the term 'curious' conveyed to many of them. 'Curious' here certified that a book was reliable and that its author was a member of a learned élite. Indeed, some publications seem to have tried to steal its authority by presenting themselves fraudulently as being 'by a member of the *collegium* of the curious in Germany'.[73]

This sense of 'curious' was made explicit in a 1674 monograph, *Curious Scurvygrass*: 'I am calling that [scurvygrass] curious, not because it is curiously polished, but because it is being described according to the PATTERN AND RULE LAID DOWN BY THE ACADEMY OF THOSE CURIOUS ABOUT NATURE.'[74] This author excises the 'polished, beautiful' meaning from 'curious', as if ashamedly acknowledging that over-use of the term for marketing purposes has damaged its philosophical authority. Such anxiety is even more evident fourteen years later in a monograph on sage which now drops 'curious' from its title but still tells the reader: 'And I do not want you to be angry that our little plant is described by the term "very curious". We have called it curious not because you will reckon it "curiously" adorned, but rather because it is described according to the laws and method of OUR CURIOUS *COLLEGIUM*.'[75] However, such attempts to impose a philosophically respectable meaning on 'curious' by defining it carefully were always liable to be undone. For example, when the scurvygrass monograph was translated into English, the original Latin title was both retained and glossed: *Cochlearia curiosa, or: The Curiosities of Scurvygrass*. The English title still connoted the 'beauty' and probably 'novelty' of scurvygrass, but again it was the more respectable, *cura*-oriented sense that was officially sanctioned by the translator: 'it is both a learned and accurate work, so that it may deservedly be called *Cochlearia Curiosa*' (Moellenbrock 1676,

---

[73] 'von einem . . . Membro des Collegii Curiosorum in Teutschland' (*Curieuse Gedancken, von der wahren Alchymia* 1702): no author, printer, or place is given.

[74] 'CURIOSAM voco illam, non quòd curiosè expolita sit, sed quia ad NORMAM ET FORMAM ACADEMIAE NATURAE CURIOSORUM est tractata' (Moellenbrock 1674,):(3ᵛ).

[75] 'Ne excandescas autem, velim, quòd *curiosiori* crenâ descriptam plantulam nostram nominem. Non est quòd rearis, eam *curiose* esse ornatam; quia tamen secundùm leges et methodum *COLLEGII NOSTRI CURIOSI* . . . descriptam est, *Curiosam* diximus eam' (Paullini [1688],)[(4ʳ⁻ᵛ). The temptation for modern scholars is to follow such writers in trying to excise unwanted senses of 'curious'. While for Evans (1977, 137) it denotes the 'exotic' and 'odd' in the context of the 'Academy of those curious about nature', on the other hand the Blumenbergian Daxelmüller (1979, 155) reaches the contrasting conclusion that these academy members were called 'curious' because they were devoted to reason, experiment, and empiricism.

A3^v). Yet there is no longer any mention of the German academy, so for this translation's readers this work was *not* 'curious' in the sense that it followed the rules of a particular institution. So, even when 'curious' stayed within a single discourse—here naturalist—it could never be apprehended in purely 'typical' form but was always partly embedded in local conditions.

Further tensions regarding naturalist knowledge were articulated through the varying role assigned to curiosity within this German academy. Especially problematic was the relation of curiosity to usefulness. Now that the centuries-old opposition between these two categories was being partially eroded in certain discourses, the 'Academy of those curious about nature', while choosing curiosity rather than 'utility' as its guiding principle, nonetheless sought to claim that some of the knowledge which it produced and transmitted was 'useful'. The first volume of the *Miscellanea curiosa* declared that the academy's three goals were 'the virtuous, the curious, the useful', whereby if not synonymy, then at least compatibility between the three was claimed.[76]

However, this compatibility was later increasingly challenged, notably by the most celebrated German philosopher of the time, Gottfried Wilhelm Leibniz. He too partly understood curiosities in institutional terms, associating them especially with naturalist academies: in a letter of 1672 he distinguished 'belles lettres' (history, politics) from what he variously called 'curiosités', 'Curiositäten', and 'Curiosa': '*Curiosa* are . . . things philosophical, mathematical, physical, and medical, for the investigation of which the King founded the Académie Royale des Sciences some years ago.'[77] Yet elsewhere Leibniz was less benign about such institutionalized *curiosa*: his attitude to curiosity was as context-bound and as difficult to summarize globally as was Descartes's. He attacked the monographs produced by the 'Academy of those curious about nature' for being on topics which were 'of curiosity rather than of practical applicability' and for 'following a method which was better suited to establishing a repository than to providing openings'.[78] He

---

[76] '*Honestum, Curiosum, Utile*' (*Miscellanea curiosa* 1670, 8).

[77] '*Curiosa* sind . . . Philosophica, Mathematica, Physica, Medica, zu deren aufnehmen vom König die Academia regia scientiarum vor etlichen jahren gestifftet worden' (Leibniz 1923–, i. 296).

[78] 'plustost de curiosité que de practique, et suivants une methode qui estoit plus propre à ce qui doit servir de repertoire, qu'à donner des ouvertures' (quoted in Winau 1977, 129).

was thus rejecting the curious *norma* of the academy precisely because its discourse and practice was stuck in a collecting tendency ('repository') rather than a narrating one, in which the monographs might create 'openings' leading to future new knowledge. By contrast, the Berlin 'Society of Sciences' (Societas Scientiarum Brandenburgica) or Prussian Academy, which Leibniz founded in 1700, was to include utilitarian focus on agriculture, manufacture, commerce, and so on, avoiding 'mere curiosity' and 'useless curiosities'.[79] Subsequently, especially from about the mid-eighteenth century, following the arrival in many quarters of a new metaphysics which once again stressed nature's *regularities* (Daston and Park 1998, 252), even the 'Academy of those curious about nature' also joined in with this institutionalized demotion of the 'curious': the term was dropped as the academy was increasingly known by its German title—*naturae curiosi* became *Naturforscher*. So there is some truth in the assertion that the 'Academy of those curious about nature' and the 'Society of sciences' were founded under the respective banners of 'curiosity' and 'utility' (Winau 1977, 130). But before we turn that contrast into an overly simple modern narrative, it should be noted that neither the older academy's name change nor Leibniz's attack necessarily involved a wholesale rejection of curiosity, but rather a diminution of its relatively recent compatibility with 'usefulness'. The distinction might seem minute, but it is a reminder that the lurching dance of constantly changing relations between key terms in the shaping of knowledge is not one from which this or that term can be eliminated at a stroke. Rather, in German as in French academician circles, there was what Licoppe has called a 'tension between curiosity and utility', which was made explicit by the famous naturalist René-Antoine Ferchaut de Réaumur in a treatise on how to transform wrought iron (1722): 'People are often too quick to divide knowledge into curious and useful. This division is not as easily made and as secure as they think, especially in relation to the present topic. If properly considered, the useful always has something curious about it, and it is rare for the curious, if pursued properly, not to lead to the useful.'[80] In this case, each category is

---

[79] 'bloße Curiosität', 'unnützer Curiositäten' (quoted in Winau 1977, 129). See Ornstein 1963, 177–97.

[80] 'Souvent on hésite trop peu à partager les connaissances en curieuses et en utiles. Cette division n'est pas aussi aisée à faire et aussi sûre qu'on pense, surtout en cette matière. L'utile bien considéré a toujours du curieux et il est rare que le curieux bien suivi ne mène pas à l'utile' (quoted in Licoppe 1996, 121).

geared to a different institutional readership, the 'useful' to members of the Académie des Sciences who were collaborating with engineers on public projects and the 'curious' to networks of *curieux* who were keen on quasi-aristocratic, free exchange of knowledge (Licoppe 1996, 121–2).

However, curiosity was used not only to shape or exchange knowledge about nature, but also to sell it.

3.4.2   *Nature and art: telling and selling 'the most curious things in the universe'*[81]

Especially in the late seventeenth and early eighteenth century, in Germany and France there was a vigorous market for books purporting to popularize knowledge of the curious objects of nature—and also of art, as we shall see. Such books were mostly in the vernacular. Some declared that their aim was to popularize the specialist curious observations of the new academies, for example by translating into German the reports of the 'Academy of those curious about nature', which was particularly slow to give up publishing in Latin, owing to anxiety that this would limit its readership to German-speaking lands. These popularizing books also drew on other sources, such as the author's other reading or his own medical practice. Most of them shared with the early naturalist academies the tendency to shape knowledge as an unsystematic, empirically grounded collection of curious fragments.

Yet curiosity also partly changed as it crossed over from learned to popularizing genres, from one language-game to another. Whereas in the context of an academy curious knowledge was associated with a distinguished elite, these popularizing publications suggested that any readers could join that élite, and so curious knowledge came paradoxically to be, connotatively, 'popular' and 'inexpensive'. In contrast to quasi-aristocratic networks of *curiosi* or *curieux*, these publications dispensed with the ideology of free exchange, making it clear that they were commodifying and selling curious knowledge.

Only from the late seventeenth century was there a vogue for these popularizing works that presented nature and art as a collection of curious objects. Certainly, already in early seventeenth-century France naturalist miscellanies were marketed under the aegis of

---

[81] Francesco Colonna called a work of his 'L'HISTOIRE NATURELLE DES CHOSES LES PLUS CURIEUSES DE L'UNIVERS' (Colonna 1734, ii. 298).

curiosity, which was just now becoming a more positive term in much naturalist discourse, following tentative and ambivalent gestures in that direction in genres such as philosophical poetry.[82] A bestselling 1606 'collection'[83] of naturalist questions by Scipion Du Pleix was called *La Curiosité naturelle*, while Pierre Bailly's medical *Questions naturelles et curieuses* appeared in 1628. Each resembled later collections of discursive curiosities in that it divided knowledge into discrete, alphabetically arranged marvels: Why do we yawn when we see others yawning? How can water rise above its source?[84]

However, these works do not fully belong to the culture of curiosities. Notwithstanding their titles, neither presents natural knowledge as an unsystematic collection of curious fragments. The 'curiosity' family barely figures in either work, whereas 'wonder' *is* prominent in Du Pleix's collection.[85] Moreover, these early collections use the 'curiosity' family only in subject-oriented senses: at this date, the 'curieuses' in Bailly's collocation with 'questions' almost certainly means 'inquisitive' rather than 'odd' (N. Kenny 1998, 132–3). Nature contains 'wonders' but not curious fragments. Although Daston and Park—with reference to another work by Du Pleix, his treatise on physics—have included him among their 'praeternatural philosophers' because of his concern with wonders, some of which he considered resistant to philosophical explanation,[86] nonetheless he was seeking wherever possible to insert them into an Aristotelian framework of causal explanation. Indeed, this collection of questions is explicitly conceived as a supplementary sequel to his systematic treatise on physics—itself part of a projected corpus of Aristotelian treatises—to which he refers back for the 'general precepts' which he is here applying to the questions.[87] Moreover, even subject-oriented curiosity is not wholly good according to Du Pleix, who still participates in the old naturalist discourse which was wary of it: on a rare occasion where he does evoke 'curious minds', it is a pejorative label for those who try to explain the inexplicable.[88] It

---

[82] On curiosity in philosophical poetry, see N. Kenny 1991*b*; Pantin 1995, 123–5, 133–4.

[83] 'Recueil' (Du Pleix 1635, a iv[r]). By 1640 it had been reprinted at least 13 times.

[84] Du Pleix 1635, 30, 99.

[85] e.g. 99, 187.

[86] Daston and Park 1998, 160, 221, 228.

[87] 'les preceptes generaux' ([a xi[r]]; see also pp. 4, 71). See N. Kenny 1991*a*, 44.

[88] 'esprits curieux' ([a viii[r]]).

was not until about the mid-seventeenth century that curiosity and wonder became, temporarily, more closely aligned in some naturalist discourse (Daston and Park 1998, 311–15). Du Pleix's positive use of curiosity in a title probably had mild shock value in 1606—as, *a fortiori*, did Bouchel's 'holy curiosity' in the title of his theological questions of 1616 (2.3.2 above)—but it did not yet involve representing nature as a collection of curious fragments which floated free of any secure explanatory framework. Nature remained for him largely an interlocking system.

By contrast, a century or more later, curious fragments did happily float more or less free of secure explanatory frameworks in French publications which popularized the knowledge of learned naturalists. L'abbé Bougeant initiated in 1719 a sequence of volumes of *Curious Observations On All Parts of Physics, Extracted and Collected From the Best Memoirs*. His preface explained that the English *Philosophical Transactions*, the Leipzig *Acta eruditorum*, other learned journals, and publications of the Académie des sciences are

full of curious observations on physics. However, these excellent works can barely be found except in libraries, being very long and expensive. And, because the most curious observations which they contain are necessarily mixed in with other material, less interesting or too advanced for most readers, few people read them. That is what made me think of giving the public a collection of the most curious observations, which I had initially extracted from these Memoirs for my own private use.[89]

As 'curious' crosses over from one language-game (learned societies and periodicals) to another (a digest), the connotation 'selecting' is added to that of 'collecting': whereas the 'observations' contained in periodicals are curious in the sense that they are 'collected', 'new', 'rare', 'empirical', and sometimes 'experimental', digests like this one added 'select' to those meanings.[90] If one meaning is added,

---

[89] 'remplis d'observations curieuses sur la Physique. Cependant ces excellens ouvrages ne se trouvent gueres que dans les Bibliotheques; parce qu'ils sont fort longs, et qu'ils coutent cher; et comme les observations les plus curieuses y sont necessairement mêlés avec d'autres matieres moins interessantes, ou qui passent la portée de la plupart des Lecteurs, ils ne sont lûs que de peu de personnes. C'est cette consideration qui m'a fait naître la pensée de donner au Public un Recueil des plus curieuses observations, que j'avois d'abord tirées de ces Memoires pour mon utilité particuliere' ([Bougeant] 1730–7, i, sig. a ii^{r-v}).

[90] On the 'select' meaning of 'curious', see N. Kenny 1998, 140.

others are subtracted in the transfer from one genre to another: going against the standard 'beautiful' connotation of 'curious', Bougeant admits that his 'curious observations' are not the most 'beautiful' ones to be found in the periodicals, since the latter are often the most difficult and so are inappropriate for his digest (i, sigs. [a iii^v]–[a iv^r]).

The claim to contain only the most curious bits was a topos among these popularizing naturalist works. For book-buyers, 'select' contents were necessarily cheaper than merely 'collected' ones, as Bougeant points out. They could also reach a broader audience. Rejecting the 'long' for the 'short' connotation of 'curious', Bougeant says that he has abbreviated periodical articles to make them accessible 'to people whose occupations or particular taste prevents them from knowing physics in depth and yet who are delighted not to be entirely ignorant of it and to know at least, so to speak, the news of what's going on in the Republic of Sciences'.[91]

The construction of this specific kind of knowledge—understood as somewhere between learning and ignorance—as 'news', reveals a structural analogy between different discourses within the culture of curiosities, between Bougeant's 'curious observations' about physics and the 'curious news' offered by contemporary newspapers (3.4.8 below). Bougeant's curious fragments of nature are less similar in shape to physics as taught in universities than to news or else to curious fragments collected in other discourses, such as antiquarianism. Bougeant sees his sources as constituting not primarily a linear narrative called 'the Scientific Revolution' but rather a spatial landscape from which he can collect endlessly, since 'the land of observations is vast and fertile enough to supply material to satisfy [my reader's] curiosity'.[92] Antiquarians used the same metaphor: one described himself as collecting objects from 'the vast and curious land of antiquity' (3.4.6 below). Only when he is forced to answer charges of philosophical incoherence does Bougeant gesture towards integration of his fragments into a whole: he claims that, 'by collecting them together into one single body', he has turned the discoveries of others not into a system, but at least into 'a kind of history of

---

[91] 'aux personnes à qui leurs occupations ou leur goût particulier, ne permet pas de sçavoir la Physique à fond, et qui sont cependant bien aises de ne la pas ignorer tout-à-fait, et de savoir du moins, pour ainsi dire, les nouvelles de ce qui se passe dans la Republique des Sciences' (i, sig. [a iii^{r-v}]).

[92] 'le Pays des Observations est assez vaste et assez fertile pour fournir de quoi satisfaire à sa curiosité' (ii, sig. a iii^v).

physics since its restoration'.[93] But his volumes give the impression that even this history of physics is more on the model of natural history—as a collection of particular observations—than of linear narrative.

Such works often had to answer charges of incoherence and superficiality: to popularize natural knowledge as curious fragments was certainly controversial. After a volume or two had appeared, authors were sometimes forced into stating more clearly whether or not they really thought that nature consisted of nothing but curious fragments. In the preface to his third volume, Bougeant concedes that he does not think this: his 'collection' is only half of 'the work'—a notional whole which would include secure physical explanations, whereas Bougeant has often omitted explanations, even where the source author had proposed them. But Bougeant's concession certainly does not take him back to Du Pleix's position. Bougeant has collected 'observations' rather than 'dissertations' because no single system can yet explain the many 'extraordinary [i.e. praeternatural] facts' which he includes.[94] He quotes not only the sceptical words about systems included in Fontenelle's preface to the history of the Académie des Sciences,[95] but also a statement by Johann Jacob Scheuchzer that 'even Descartes would have done better to hold fire'![96] Bougeant is intent on letting his 'curious observations' float freely for a good while yet. In this he may have been motivated by commercial concerns as much as epistemological ones, since his 'curious observations' could be enjoyed by far more people when not attached to a demanding philosophical system.

The same can be said of a four-volume work by the French-based praeternatural philosopher and occultist Francesco Colonna, his Pliny-inspired *Natural History of the Universe, in which Physical Explanations are Reported for the Most Curious and Extraordinary Effects of Nature* (1734). With the guilty conscience of the rampant plagiarist, he claims that out of respect for the Académie des Sciences he has used only 'the observations of the societies of London, Italy, Germany'.[97] While venturing 'physical explanations for all these

[93] 'en les rassemblant en un seul corps . . . une espece d'Histoire de la Physique depuis son rétablissement' (iii, sig. [a ii^r]).

[94] 'faits extraordinaires . . . Recueil . . . l'Ouvrage . . . Dissertations et non pas des Observations' (iii, sigs. [a i^r]–[a ii^r]).

[95] [Bougeant] 1730–7, iii, sigs. [a ii^v]–[a iv^r]. See 3.2 above.

[96] 'Descartes lui-même auroit gagné à differer' (iii, sig. [a v^r]).

[97] 'des Observations des Societez de Londres, d'Italie, d'Allemagne' (Colonna 1734, i, pp. ix–x).

curiosities' more readily than does Bougeant and while acknowledging that much of nature is not curious, nonetheless he is supremely unconcerned with that ordinary course of nature, since his probabilistic approach to praeternatural curiosities licences a luxuriant, anti-Cartesian eclecticism.[98] Works like this, in which the 'curiosity' family is glamorously ubiquitous, conveyed to their readers the subliminal message that, even if curiosities were only one part of nature, it was the only part worth bothering about. Half a century later, any such message was much more muted in the collections of 'the most beautiful and curious' animals, plants, and minerals published by the botanical physician Pierre Joseph Buc'hoz, despite their seductively lavish visual illustrations, for Buc'hoz was also the author of numerous other works of standard rather than curious natural history, to which he referred as appropriate.[99] By contrast, Colonna's readers, despite his disavowals, could be forgiven for taking away the impression that nature *was* effectively a collection of curiosities.

Digests were not the only publications in France to disseminate learned naturalist knowledge beyond academician circles by dressing it up as curious. Treatises described 'very curious experiments' on, for example, magnetism and other physical topics, arising from specific empirical events, such as the discovery of some magnetic iron when the belltower of Chartres Cathedral was demolished in 1690.[100] Paolo Boccone obtained a privilege in France for several books, one of which appeared in 1671, his *Curious Researches and Observations on the Nature of White and Red Coral*. It contained findings which, according to the title-page, had previously been examined in sessions of the academy that met in the house of l'abbé Pierre Michon Bourdelot.[101] The term 'curious' in the title connoted the world of cabinets and *naturalia*-collecting to which Boccone presented himself as belonging (1671, 26–7).

The case of the Sicilian Boccone shows how the polysemy of 'curiosity' enabled it to appeal to the worlds of both academia and commerce. Erstwhile botanist to the Grand Duke of Tuscany, Boccone had come to Paris seeking patronage and clients—that is,

---

[98] 'les raisons Physiques de toutes ces curiositez' (i, p. ix). See also i, pp. vii, xi–xii; ii, pp. 297–8; iii, p. 7.

[99] 'les plus belles et les plus curieuses' (Buc'hoz [1790?], title-page).

[100] Le Lorrain de Valmont 1692: 'Expériences trés-curieuses' (title-page). See also Le Lorrain de Valmont 1693, preface.

[101] On this academy, which started in 1665, see Brown 1934, ch. 11.

money—and he called such potential buyers of his expertise 'curious' in the handbill which he had printed as a calling card, entitled *Notice for the Intelligent and Curious*. In it he offered to run fortnightly meetings which would be 'free to anyone who is curious and knowledgeable in the study of botany' and at which he would sell 'the seeds of the most curious plants which he [had] brought from Italy', adding that herbalism was 'so agreeable, so curious' that even women were invited along.[102] This classic sales pitch involved making his clients, his wares, and his profession all 'curious'. Subject- and object-oriented senses were combined not into a logical 'concept' but rather into an associative cluster of meanings. That cluster was designed to flatter potential clients—by paradoxically admitting a wide range of them to an exclusive club, thereby combining the 'distinguished' with the 'popular' connotations of 'curious'—and also to make the purchase of curious objects the apparently natural seal of their own status as curious people, exploiting the widespread fantasy that there existed a satisfying fit between curious objects and subjects. The apparently generous offer to include women in this male club was the most striking manifestation of these shifty paradoxes. By offering free entry only to the curious, Boccone was managing to combine a vestige of the quasi-aristocratic ethos of free exchange of curiosities with, on the other hand, overt commercialism. And who can blame him? Debating coral at Bourdelot's academy was all very well but it was not possible to live off that kind of presumably free (that is, gratis) exchange.

Books appealing to both an academic and a less learned audience also appeared in Germany, where dissemination of naturalist knowledge as a collection of curiosities again took various forms, ranging from at least one digest[103] to many treatises and miscellanies. Some of these were written in Latin and sought not to choose between curiosity as 'accuracy' and as 'rare novelty' but rather to yoke the two together: Gottfried Voigt's collection of *Physical Curiosities*—such

[102] *Avis aux personnes d'esprit, et aux curieux* (n.p., n.d.): 'L'entrée en sera libre à tous les curieux et intelligens dans l'estude de la Botanique'; 'Il vendra les semences des Plantes les plus curieuses qu'il a apportées d'Italie'; 'si agreable, si curieuse' (quoted from the transcription of the handbill given by Brown 1934, 283–6). On Boccone, see Brown 1934, 237–41; Findlen 1994, 107–8.

[103] Ferdinand Albrecht, Duke of Braunschweig-Lüneburg, gave the title *Collegium curiosorum* to his 2 volumes (1667) of abstracts in German of the work of the Royal Society and the Académie des sciences (Bepler 1988, 191).

as the generation of new species from the decayed remains of dead old animals—were 'described, by an accurate method, together with other delightful, rare, and new things'.[104] These curiosities were 'made public for the sake of those curious about nature', thereby granting readers membership of a kind of virtual academy.[105]

By contrast, in some vernacular, German-language works which popularized naturalist knowledge, curiosity acquired a different shape: the 'brief, fragmentary' connotation of 'curious' replaced the 'long, accurate' one. These works were compiled especially by town physicians,[106] who constituted an important group among the readership of learned journals and yet whose daily practice must have given them a close idea of what a range of literate but less educated people would find comprehensible and compelling. Among these physician authors was at least one member of the 'Academy of those curious about nature', whom we earlier encountered writing official Latin monographs for that body, and who also wrote other curious Latin naturalist monographs:[107] Christian Franz Paullini. Among his vernacular miscellanies—containing far more than just naturalist knowledge—is *Pleasant Boredom*, which draws heavily on the academy's *Miscellanea curiosa*. It contains 'fine, select, rare, and curious discourses, questions, and occurrences': there is no mention of 'accurately' or 'thoroughly' described ones, indeed its discontinuous sections average only four sides each, devoted to topics such as green milk, hair-eaters, a living snake pulled from inside a woman's breast.[108] Another connotation that Paullini now drops is the understanding of curious, discursive objects as being freely exchangeable. Here, the reality of the book market requires that they had better be worth the asking price: 'I presume that the German-speaking reader will be satisfied with the wares he gets for his money'.[109]

---

[104] 'aliisque rebus jucundis raris, novis, accurata methodo conscriptae' (Voigt 1668, title-page).

[105] 'in gratiam naturae curiosorum publicae luci expositatae' (title-page).

[106] e.g. Hellwig 1710–11 and 1711; Maurer 1713. Maurer's preface ([)( )(6ᵛ]) made several of the same points about his *Observationes curioso-physicae* as Bougeant later made about his *Observations curieuses*.

[107] e.g. C. F. Paullini 1699, 1703*b*.

[108] *Anmuhtige Lange Weile oder Allerhand feine, außerlesene, seltene und curieuse Discursen, Fragen und Begebenheiten* 1703*a*, §§ 8, 23, 80. C. F. Paullini published a similar collection of naturalist and other 'Curiositäten' (title-page) 3 years later (1706).

[109] 'wird vermuhtlich der redlich-teutsche Leser für sein Geld vergnügsame Waar bekommen.' ()(3ʳ).

However, for Paullini curiosity is not stable: rather, its slipperiness reflects anxieties about the status of the knowledge that he is offering. When, in another vernacular work, he wants to refer to curious people of the more learned sort—who, he is arguing, could learn much about nature from farmers—he clarifies the category by resorting to Latin, calling them 'die Herren Curiosi' (1705*a*, 4). While keeping one eye on 'the German-speaking reader', Paullini has to keep the other on 'die Herren Curiosi', since his popularization of such vast quantities of naturalist knowledge was criticized as unreliable. In another vernacular treatise—a 'curious account' of the benefits of massage (with 'curious' mainly meaning 'novel')—Paullini, now a 55-year-old physician of his home town of Eisenach, was stung into establishing his credentials by enumerating his university studies, his travels and work experience, and even a university job offer at Pisa twenty-five years earlier.[110] Paullini had also been involved in other learned societies such as the Fruchtbringende Gesellschaft.[111] Even within the output of this single, prolific author, curiosity is torn in different directions as it shuttles between language-games, reflecting the various institutions and discourses which Paullini's own career straddled insecurely.

Naturalist knowledge that was popularized as 'curious' was not always shattered into fragments. For example, in 1671 René Bary published his *Physics, which—Following Ancients and Moderns—Discusses Everything that is Most Curious in Nature*. In contrast to the works just surveyed, this was a systematic 'body of physics', not a selection of curious and marvellous fragments, despite the title's similarity to that of Colonna.[112] But 'curious' still meant 'popularizing' for Bary, a royal counsellor and historiographer who was mainly mediating knowledge not for urban burghers in the Holy Roman Empire but for the self-styled urbane sophisticates, the 'honnestes gens' (i, sig. [a viii^r]) who either frequented the court at Versailles and the salons of Paris and the provinces or else wished that they did so. He was promoting physics less for direct study of nature than for *mondain* conversation. For him, as later for Bougeant, what is curious in nature is what is most easily communicable and yet also—in contrast with Bougeant—what is most beautiful, so long as it is not

---

[110] 'curieuse Erzählung' (C. F. Paullini 1698, title-page; see sig. B5^{r–v}).
[111] On Paullini's career, see Dünnhaupt 1990–3, iv. 3080.
[112] 'corps de Physique' (Bary 1671, i, sig. a ii^r).

totally superficial (i, sigs. [a vii^v]–[a viii^r]). So some connotations of 'curious' are back in ('beauty'), while others are out ('rare'). What is 'most curious in nature' is what goes down best in conversation. This definition just takes to a shameless extreme the anthropocentric circularity evident in all of the naturalist popularizations surveyed.

Although I have described these popularizing works as being on nature, they were also on art, that is, human skill. Indeed the Aristotelian distinction between nature and art was considerably blurred in the seventeenth century by cabinets which included *artificialia* alongside *naturalia* and by the new conviction that instruments, practical skills, and experimentation were indispensable to knowledge of nature.[113] While many vernacular works which were called 'curious' included both sides of this blurred boundary, some focused mostly on art, that is, on techniques—for, say, civil architecture or military installations—which were curious because 'new' and 'elaborate, ingenious', like Niceron's 'curious perspective'.[114] Indeed, as Daston has shown, the understanding of curious objects as 'elaborate' ones—combining what I would call both a subject- and an object-oriented sense—further blurred the distinction between natural and artificial objects, since it was applied to both (1994, 46–7).

However, whereas most of the popularizing works on nature and art discussed so far were presented as collections of curious discursive fragments, by the 1730s that tendency was waning, although Bougeant's digest continued to be printed. Curiosity was still prominent in various popularizing books on nature and art, but its shape was changing: it now emerged increasingly through the narrating rather than the collecting tendency of discourse. To some extent this shift was discourse-specific: it did not occur uniformly or simultaneously throughout the culture of curiosities. New experimental techniques were now integrated less into metaphorical curious collections than into narratives of human curiosity's progress into the future—an interpretation much more familiar to modern ears. The meanings of curiosity which are privileged by Blumenberg were now overtaking those which are privileged by Pomian. Grammar was the medium of this shift: subject-oriented curiosity was reasserting itself against the decades-long hegemony of curiosities.

---

[113] See Clark 1992, 92–8; Daston and Park 1998, ch. 7; Rossi 1970.
[114] e.g. Böcler [1664]; Wohlhausen 1677.

An example of this displacement is provided by an anonymous prospectus printed in Paris in 1739, which invoked curiosity to try and raise finances for a projected series of experimental demonstrations involving aerostats—vessels which might fly, having been emptied by a vacuum pump or the like. The prospectus, entitled *Fruitful Curiosity*, was addressed not to experts but to potential backers, the 'interested curious',[115] who, having paid 24 *sols* for their prospectus, would enjoy up to six free entries to the eventual demonstrations—should they ever materialize: I do not know if they did—and they would also have first place in the queue to join the royal-supported fund-raising company which the author hopes subsequently to found for the production of the machines (38–40). Not until a two-page note at the end, following a much longer sales pitch, is the reader given the slightest idea that the proposed experiments concern aerostatics: as for the actual new technique which the author proposes using, it remains shrouded in mystery. Money-making by similar means was common in Paris: in the previous year (1738), 7,500 people had each parted with three *livres* to hear a concert of flute music performed by an automaton, described by the duc de Luynes in his diary as 'une machine digne de curiosité'.[116]

The 41-page sales pitch in the *Curiosité fructueuse* is entirely devoted to the two motives for the proposed experiments: interest and curiosity. Thus, as in much early modern writing—on alchemy, for example—the representation of motives for knowledge far outstrips the representation of knowledge itself. The author was banking on people enjoying reading a prolonged account of their own curiosity.

Although curiosity is crucial to this prospectus's attempt to raise funds, three related factors now differentiate it from the culture of curiosities. First, far from celebrating curiosity unequivocally, the prospectus reintroduces the centuries-old moral qualms about it, which had never abated in church discourse and moral philosophy but had been played down in much early modern naturalist discourse. Secondly, the prospectus ignores the object-oriented senses of 'curiosity'—which would surely have been prominent had it been written thirty years earlier—just as the *Encyclopédie*, a few years later, tried to disengage those object-oriented senses from proper

---

[115] 'aux Curieux intéressés' (*La Curiosité fructueuse* 1739, [1]).
[116] Benhamou 1987, 91. Benhamou's study is not primarily terminological.

philosophical curiosity (3.2 above). Thirdly, curiosity now emerges through the narrating rather than the collecting tendency of discourse.

Curiosity is here primarily the motor of two potential narratives, one happy, the other unhappy. The difference between the two lies in whether curiosity is harnessed to interest, which is understood as the commercial and utilitarian self-interest of society as a whole. If curiosity is not harnessed to interest, then our projects get snarled up in unhappy narratives ('Histoires') leading to our downfall, as the fate of Pandora and other secular and biblical protagonists shows (8–9). On the other hand, if we are curious because it is in our interest to be so, then we will be protagonists in a happy narrative stretching into the future:

the curiosity of the physicist, the mechanist, the architect, and of even the least craftsman is usually aimed at perfecting their art by perfecting themselves; this produces universal benefit which is all the more perpetual because, far from diminishing, it can only go on increasing, for the good of posterity.

Such are the *Curiosities* which can rightly be called *Fruitful*.[117]

The odd vestige of the collecting tendency survives: the happy narrative arising from the invention of aerostats will bring men accumulation, not of curious objects but of wealth—'no other invention will have procured more riches and wealth for them'.[118] On the other hand, the collecting of curiosities is implicitly condemned: of the curious traveller the author asks: What? Would he really have wanted to impose upon himself all that travel and risk if it was merely to satisfy his eyes through the diversity of objects offered up to them by the various climates in which he might find himself?'[119] At least some travellers writing from within the culture of curiosities would in fact have answered 'yes': they would have been satisfied

---

[117] 'la Curiosité du Phisicien, du Mécanicien, de l'Architecte, et jusqu'à celle du moindre Artisan n'a d'ordinaire pour but, que la perfection de leurs Arts, en cherchant à se perfectioner eux mêmes, d'où il résulte un avantage universel, et d'autant plus perpétuel, que loin de diminuer, il ne poura jamais aller qu'en augmentant au profit de la postérité.
Telles sont les *Curiosités* qu'on peut nomer à juste titre *Fructueuses*' (22).

[118] 'jamais invention ne leur aura procuré tout à la fois plus de richesses, et plus de comodités' (23).

[119] 'Quoi donc ne voudroit-il se doner tous ces mouvemens, et courir tous ces risques, que pour satisfaire ses yeux par la variété des objets que leur ofrent les divers Climats où il peut se trouver?' (17).

with a landscape full of immediate curiosities, rather than with subsequent 'utility', as the reward for their curiosity.

In similar vein, one can speculate that, if preceding proponents of aerostatic experimentation—who are listed at the end of the prospectus ([43–4])—had been asked why they wanted to conduct such an experiment, some might have answered 'because it is curious', implying a match between their curiosity and the 'curiousness' of its object, characteristic of the culture of curiosities. (The list includes some figures whom we have already encountered describing 'curious experiments': Sturm and Pierre Le Lorrain, abbé de Valmont). But the author of this prospectus inhabits a changed discourse: he never describes such experiments as 'curious', nor even as 'curious and useful', but as 'useful'.[120] While this confirms Licoppe's argument about the shift towards 'utility' in early eighteenth-century technological discourse in France (3.4.1 above), it certainly does not confirm any replacement of curiosity by utility. After all, even to describe as 'fruitful' the role of curiosity in happy narratives is still to invert a long-standing association between curiosity and fruitlessness.[121] Rather, what has disappeared here is the capacity of curiosity to encompass both objects of knowledge and the desire for them, in a cosy loop of gratification. The newly prominent partner in the terminological dance surrounding good knowledge of nature—alongside very old partners such as 'utility' or more recent ones such as 'curiosity'—is 'interest', which in this prospectus, as in many other texts of the 1730s, is entirely good, just as curiosity had often been in secular discourse from the early seventeenth century onwards. And just as curiosity had often seemed to be *the* dominant passion in the culture of curiosities—and even sometimes in university discourse— here it is 'interest' that is explicitly granted that status (4).

Nonetheless, this is not the end of curiosity, even in popularizing discourse on nature and art. Far from it. Although the culture of curiosities is here disintegrating, curiosity is still used to bind together a remarkable range of discourses and practices as being so many 'kinds of curiosities', that is, manifestations of a single passion. Certainly, these discourses and practices are no longer bound together by dint of the similarities of shape between their curious

---

[120]   e.g. title-page, [43].

[121]   e.g. a follower of Francis Bacon felt obliged to deny that his master's 'Experiments' were 'Curious and Fruitlesse' (W. Rawles, in Bacon 1626, A[1]ᵛ).

objects; moreover, some discourses and practices that were previously familiar in contemporary summaries of the culture of curiosities—newspapers, book-collecting, antiquarianism—are now dropped. But the list is still long: it includes astronomy, geodesy, travel, ethnography, natural history, chemistry, botany, anatomy, physics, mechanics, architecture, crafts.[122] Curiosity has changed shape, but it is still so rhetorically powerful that this author believes that the best way of raising funds is to devote almost the whole of a prospectus to the role played by curiosity in other disciplines, almost entirely ignoring the actual experiments proposed.

3.4.3   How-to books

Closely related to popularizing works on nature and art were books that showed readers how to perform specific practical tasks. As William Eamon has shown, these too became entangled, for a finite period, with what I am calling the culture of curiosities.

How-to-do-it printed books had come into existence well before the rise of the culture of curiosities, and they outlasted its fall. In Germany they dated back to the 1530s (Eamon 1994, 112–20). Their contents were often presented as 'secrets', and the heterogeneous genre which Eamon has therefore called 'the book of secrets' lasted well into the eighteenth century, when it was gradually displaced by the ideal of public, open knowledge.[123] 'Secrets' of nature and art, which had long been avidly devoured by less educated readers, had since the fifteenth century also been enjoying much more attention from some naturalists (especially physicians), and then increasingly in the sixteenth and seventeenth centuries from collectors and those natural philosophers who had the anti-Aristotelian notion that some knowledge was accessible only through experience and not through reason, for example because it involved chance occurrences or occult properties. In the seventeenth century, 'secrets' then sometimes became identified with curiosities, on the model of those prized by empirically oriented naturalists and collectors.[124] This identification peaked between about the mid-seventeenth and the early eighteenth century. Let me briefly investigate exactly

---

[122] 'especes de Curiosités' (21); see pp. 11–22.
[123] Eamon 1994, part 2, esp. ch. 10.
[124] See Daston and Park 1998, ch. 4; Eamon 1994, chs. 8–9, esp. pp. 314–18.

how the language of curiosity remoulded for a while the book of secrets.

The range of how-to books that were presented as curious or as containing curiosities was very wide. They included books devoted to domestic household tips (known in German scholarship as *Hausväterbücher*),[125] to land and agrarian economy as well as to domestic economy,[126] specifically to gardening and agriculture,[127] to cookery,[128] to the manufacture of ornamental artefacts,[129] to chemical and medical recipes,[130] to metallurgical ones,[131] or else to a mixture of these categories.[132] Also wide-ranging were the readerships envisaged for these curious how-to books. They included non-specialists of all social ranks[133] (such as lower-class or *kleinbürgerlich* urban burghers),[134] women and men,[135] craftsmen, inexperienced medical professionals,[136] and nobles needing to run an estate, to make a good impression at court, or to organize a self-improving voyage.[137] The compilers of these largely practical curiosities included a town physician (Christoph von Hellwig), a court physician (David Kellner), nobles,[138] and even one eventual member of the Académie des Sciences (Nicolas Lemery), albeit an unusual one—partly self-taught, the former pupil of an apothecary—who was so enthusiastic about popularization that he held the academy's only known experimental demonstrations (of chemistry) for non-specialists, including women.[139] Through the likes of Lemery, curious how-to books had links both with less educated people and also

---

[125]   e.g. Hellwig 1718.
[126]   Hohberg 1715–16 (first published 1682), a bestseller (Dünnhaupt 1990–3, iii. 2151–9).
[127]   e.g. Le Lorrain de Valmont 1708 (first published 1705; at least 8 edns. by 1715: see Debus 1991, 160–1).
[128]   Wolley 1674.
[129]   e.g. *Der curieusen Kunst- und Werck-Schül erster [anderer] Theil* 1759–60.
[130]   e.g. *Der curiose Chymicus . . . Der curiose Medicus . . . Der curiose Chirurgus* 1706.
[131]   e.g. Kellner 1701 and 1715.
[132]   e.g. Lemery 1684; *Schatzkammer* 1686 (first published 1684).
[133]   See *Schatzkammer* 1686, title-page.
[134]   Eamon 1994, 121–6.
[135]   See Lemery 1684, *3ᵛ; *Schatzkammer* 1686, title-page.
[136]   See *Der curiose Chymicus* 1706, A2ʳ.
[137]   For all of these, see Hohberg 1715–16. For estates, see Hohberg 1715–16.
[138]   François Du Soucy, sieur de Gerzan, and Wolfgang Helmard von Hohberg.
[139]   Ornstein 1963, 158. Lemery joined the academy in 1699. He also wrote a very successful chemical textbook (Debus 1991, 147–8).

with the learned world of the academies, just as other go-betweens connected the world of artisans to that of universities.[140]

Certainly, even before the emergence of the culture of curiosities, how-to books were conceived as reference books full of discrete particulars that did not offer readers systematic understanding of a branch of knowledge. As recent scholars of 'secrets' have argued, adapting Carlo Ginzburg's notion of a cynegetic paradigm, the epistemology which secrets implicitly fostered was—as in practical medicine, collecting, or much of the new natural philosophy—closer to that of the hunter who uses particulars (clues) as a way of finding other particulars (quarries), than to that of philosophy, which reasons via universals.[141] However, now that these books contained not only 'secrets', 'experiments' (tried and tested techniques), and 'recipes' but also curiosities, they were represented even more emphatically as unsystematic collections of fragments. This was reflected in their typographical presentation: the curiosities were described in discontinuous chunks of prose, just a few lines long, or else in framed visual pictures of techniques, again several to a page.[142] The curiosities were sometimes the actual objects described, sometimes the techniques used to manipulate them, sometimes the descriptions of those techniques, and sometimes more than one of these. Techniques became 'curious things' which could be possessed, just like material objects in cabinets, or just like the discursive curiosities which *honnêtes gens* and *die curieuse* Welt collected for display in conversation: 'The finest and *most curious things* are often neglected and abandoned because they are so difficult to *acquire*. Among these can be counted the *method* for making sundials.'[143] Curious how-to books shaped knowledge very similarly to other discourses within the culture of curiosities. Indeed their titles were sometimes indistinguishable from those of cabinet catalogues, periodicals, and miscellanies: *Treasure Chamber of Rare and New Curiosities, New and Curious Treasure Chamber, Curiosities of Nature and Art, Collection of Rare and New Curiosities,*

[140]   e.g. Johann Joachim Becher (Smith 1994).

[141]   See Daston and Park 1998, 159; Eamon 1994, ch. 8; Ginzburg 1990.

[142]   For details, including photographic reproductions of pages from 2 such works (*Schatzkammer* 1686; Lemery 1709), see N. Kenny 1998, plates 7, 8, 10, 11.

[143]   'Les choses les plus belles et les plus curieuses sont souvent negligées et delaissées à cause des difficultez qu'on trouve à les acquerir; Entre lesquelles on peut bien mettre la Methode de faire les Quadrans' (Du Heaulme 1641, 5). In its 2nd edn. (1654) this treatise was renamed *Principe curieux*.

Miscellaneous and Collected Chemical-Metallurgical Things.[144] If such volumes included a systematic treatment of an object, it was pointedly *not* described as a curiosity: appended to the *Treasure Chamber of Rare and New Curiosities* was *A Treatise which Describes the Nature of Coffee, Tea, Chocolate, and Tobacco.*[145]

Curiosity was used partly to market how-to books more effectively. The commercialization, through print, of allegedly unique recipes and techniques—'secrets'—had debased the aura of uniqueness surrounding such knowledge (Eamon 1994, ch. 7), which was therefore in need of a fresh image. In the mid-seventeenth century book market, curiosity had exactly the requisite aura of freshness: hence in 1649 Du Soucy seized upon the hyperbolic title of Gaffarel's notorious 1629 occultist treatise (*Unheard-of Curiosities*)[146] for his own volume of how-to treatises for nobles (*Profitable Unheard-of Curiosities*), a blatantly attention-seeking publication which was financed by the author himself, apparently in hope of patronage since it also included a project for a further work (on the creation of the world).

Du Soucy also sought mild shock value by collocating 'Profitables' so baldly with 'Curiositez', reversing the curious/'useful' opposition which was still dominant in most discourses at this date.[147] The utility of how-to books needed no demonstration. But, by starting to present them as 'curious' too, writers like Du Soucy were trying to give techniques, recipes, and secrets an aura of fun. Thus began a few decades of edgy cohabitation between curiosity and utility in such books. It was common to stretch the boundaries of utility in order to make it compatible with curiosity, trying to have it both ways. Even if games and party tricks were included among the household tips in a book, it was still claimed that 'nothing it contains is useless, be it for entertainment and galantry or else for the money to be earned depending on the skill with which one masters them', as one printer put it when presenting Lemery's *Collection of Rare and New Curiosities*, which was announced on the title-page to be a 'Work

---

[144] *Schatzkammer* 1686; Hellwig 1718; Le Lorrain de Valmont 1708; Lemery 1684; Kellner 1715.

[145] 'Ein Tractat Naturgemässer Beschreibung der Coffee, Thee, Chocolate, Tabacks' (*Schatzkammer* 1686, title-page).

[146] See 3.4.10 below.

[147] Du Soucy had a penchant for controversy: he had earlier been involved in the promotion of Paracelsianism in Paris (Debus 1991, 70–1).

very useful and necessary to all kinds of people for the preservation of their life'.[148]

However, in the early eighteenth century, it was increasingly difficult to maintain this cheery proximity of curiosity to utility in how-to books, as is shown by changes in the strategies used to market Lemery's bestseller. In the major early editions (1684, 1685), curiosity colonized the how-to genre to the point of displacing altogether the more expected term 'secrets' from the title (*Collection of Rare and New Curiosities*): the title now situated the book clearly within the culture of curiosities.[149] Certainly, this marketing strategy did not wholly reflect the terminology used within the book itself, where 'Curiositez' sometimes specifically denoted those techniques that were not life-preserving (such as how to represent the four elements in a glass phial),[150] rather than being an umbrella term for all the techniques described. Indeed, this slipperiness of 'curiosity'—denoting both a whole book and yet also only some of its contents—was widespread in the how-to genre and beyond. All techniques were curious, but some were more curious than others. In this perspective, the techniques which *were* more 'useful' and life-saving were at once curious (coming under the book's global title) and not curious (since not specifically designated as such within the book). However, although the 'curious' and the 'useful' were therefore even now not identical, no firm division between them was embedded in the arrangement of these early editions of Lemery's manual.

This soon changed. Over the next decades, the publishing industry stopped labelling the whole range of Lemery's techniques 'curiosities'; it now exempted medical remedies in particular from that label, calling them secrets once again instead. Secrets made a comeback, first alongside curiosites, but then as the dominant label. A new hierarchy was established, with medicine at the top and curious techniques regarding beauty, nature, and decorative arts at the bottom.[151] As in some German universities at this time (1.3.2 above), medicine proved to be a branch relatively resistant to curiosity: publishers

---

[148] 'rien de ce qu'il contient n'est inutile, soit pour le divertissement et la galanterie, soit pour les émolumens que l'on en peut tirer selon le genie de ceux qui en acquerront la pratique' (Lemery, *Recueil des curiositez rares et nouvelles . . . Ouvrage trés-utile et necessaire à toutes sortes de personnes, pour la conservation de leur vie*, 1684, [*4ʳ]).

[149] One provincial edition of Lemery's book did resort to a more conventional title (*Recueil de secrets*, Toulouse, 1692).

[150] Lemery 1684, ch. 10 ('Curiositez rares et admirables').

[151] See Lemery 1694, 1709, and 1737.

seemed to feel that readers desperate to cure their sick child did not want to be titillated by promises that this or that remedy would be fun or intrinsically fascinating. Indeed, even in a 1706 how-to book for inexperienced medical practitioners that *was* still insistently marketed as 'curious', the author was at pains to excise such unwanted connotations, clarifying that the book would not necessarily satisfy the reader's 'Curiosität', that its doctrine was long-established rather than newfangled, 'so that we won't get bogged down in curiosities and constant doubt, which are of little use in practice'.[152] This introductory book is curious because it selects material from more systematic treatises (A2^r). Like some naturalist popularizers, its author tries to shape the curious to his own needs, in this case making it 'selective' but neither 'exotic', 'new', nor 'difficult'.

The decline of curiosities in the how-to genre entailed a renewal of the prominence of secrets, at least for a while. As for curiosity in the context of artisan techniques, by 1787 it had become, for the satirical poet John Wolcot, the watchword only for George III's aimless, rambling, magpie-like collecting of trivial data about beer-making on a royal visit to a brewery.[153]

3.4.4   Pedagogues

What about the less overtly commercial world of education? Did pedagogues too appropriate the culture of curiosities for their own ends, encouraging curiosity in learners or else dressing up knowledge as curious? There is no single answer: educators were deeply divided by curiosity. Whereas for centuries students had been urged to avoid it, the likes of John Locke now stressed that it was in fact essential in education.[154] For others, the new culture of curiosities threatened more harm than good to students. We have already seen this view expressed in some German Lutheran universities (Section 1). It would be tempting, in a Blumenbergian narrative, to represent these battles over curiosity as ones between pedagogical progressives and reactionaries, with curiosity being on the side of the angels, but in fact they were more complex.

---

[152] 'damit man nicht bloß in Curiositäten und stetem Zweiffel, welche in der Praxi wenig Nutzen geben, stecken möge' (*Der curiose Chymicus* 1706, A2^{r-v}).
[153] [Wolcot], *Instructions to a Celebrated Laureat; alias The Progress of Curiosity*, 1787, pp. [iii], iv, 18, 19, 28, 30, 32.
[154] Locke 1989, 167, 182–6. 1st edn. 1693.

3.4.4.1   Claude Fleury

Great anxiety about the role of curiosity in education was expressed by the abbé Fleury in his *Treatise on the Choice and Method of Studies*. Fleury, now celebrated above all as an ecclesiastical historian, was tutor (from 1672) to the two orphans of Armand the Prince de Condé and (from 1680) to the legitimized son of Louis XIV and Mademoiselle de La Vallière. He wrote his treatise on education in 1675, probably at the instigation of Madame de Longueville, for the tutor of her illegitimate grandson.[155] It then circulated for a while in manuscript (Goré 1957, 252n.), before Fleury revised it, publishing a printed version in 1686, now catering not just for aristocratic males but for a wider range of potential pupils, including women (ch. 34).

The treatise is profoundly ambivalent about curiosity in education, constantly chewing over it, caught between the culture of curiosities and the more traditional church discourse of Fleury's associates, Fénelon and Bossuet.[156] And yet the treatise was not just a doomed, one-off, reactionary backlash against the spread of positive curiosity into pedagogical discourse. For one thing, it was influential: it affected Fénelon's writing on the education of girls,[157] and it was still being reprinted in 1724. More importantly, it had a strong utilitarian bent—relative to the Jesuit syllabus, the *Ratio studiorum*, for example—as part of the ambitious programme of dissent from Louis XIV's government which Fleury, Fénelon, and others developed, based on agrarianism in opposition to the mercantilism of Colbert.[158] If related to this context, Fleury's treatise may seem progressive rather than reactionary. His attacks, in the manuscript version, on contemporary French education as pedantic and useless to society have led one historian of education to interpret it as innovative for its time, as reflecting the aspirations of the newly developing bourgeoisie.[159] Fleury was also mixing those aspirations with the more traditional ones of the nobility, which often scorned studies deemed curious and superfluous.[160]

---

[155] Dainville 1978, 44. On Fleury's life, see the *Dictionnaire de biographie française*.

[156] Bossuet attacked curiosity not only as pastor and preacher (2.2.4.3 above), but also as tutor to the dauphin when the latter was 17 (1709, 228–36).

[157] Goré 1957, 252n. See 5.1 below.

[158] See Goré 1957, 252–6; Lougis 1976, 176; Rothkrug 1965, ch. 5.

[159] Dainville 1978, 43–52, esp. 50–1.

[160] See the treatise—primarily for young nobles—by the Huguenot La Primaudaye (1581–90, i, sigs. 2ʳ, 13ʳ, 22ᵛ, 23ᵛ, 48ᵛ–51ᵛ).

For Fleury, curiosity should not play a major role in the acquisition and application of knowledge. However, it is a problem that will not go away, returning constantly in his treatise, mainly in three ways.

First, echoing many centuries of pedagogical discourse, Fleury calls it 'dangerous' (249), a 'passion' (252) that leads students away from 'necessary' and 'useful' learning. The survey of the history of learning with which the treatise starts gives various examples of curiosity corrupting erudition in this way over the ages. Franks, medieval nominalists, and Renaissance humanists all directed excessive 'curiositez' at the beauty or complexity of language: 'the curiosity which always spoiled [the Franks] emerged from that time'.[161] So Fleury, far from presenting knowledge as collectable curious fragments, is writing within the curiosity-narrating tendency: curiosity always marks an unhappy twist in his historical narratives, invariably followed by a happy one when curiosity is dispelled. 'From that time . . . learning re-awakened too'.[162] This is a narrative, but not the kind in which curiosity leads to an advancement of learning.

Fleury then turns from the history of learning to one's choice of studies. He argues that the wrong choice at a young age can lead to a wasted life consumed by hobbies, in other words to (what I am calling) the culture of curiosities: 'Some people find [life] too short for the study of history; others spend their life on the pure curiosities of travelling, of expertise in the fine arts such as painting and music, of seeking out rare things. Yet when will you learn to live, and when will you inform yourself about the matters which are specific to your profession?'[163] By presenting curiosity as that which lies beyond the bounds of one's 'profession'—whether noble or other[164]—Fleury is applying the ancient, decorum-based understanding of curiosity (and, behind it, of *polypragmosyne*) which continued to be so strong in early modern church and university discourse and which, by contrast, was quietly dropped in the culture of curiosities, where we have

---

[161] 'la curiosité qui les a toûjours gâtées, s'y mêloit deslors' (29; see also pp. 45, 75–6).

[162] 'Depuis ce temps . . . les études se réveilloient aussi' (29).

[163] 'Il y a d[e]s gens qui la trouvent trop courte pour l'étude de l'histoire: il y en a qui la passent à de pures curiosités de voyages; d'intelligence dans les beaux arts, comme la peinture et la musique; de recherches de choses rares. Cependant quand aprendrez-vous à vivre, et quand vous instruirez-vous des choses particuliéres à vôtre profession?' (85–6).

[164] See also pp. 167, 203–4, 264–5, 274–5.

already seen writers and printers trying to earn money and fame by offering their discursive curiosities to as broad an audience as possible, not just to a particular profession or social rank.

Secondly, however, curiosity can nonetheless play a positive role in the acquisition of knowledge, but only under certain circumstances, notably in young children, since 'curiosity and teachability are never so great' as at their age, when it is fine to employ, say, paintings and other techniques—such as the holding of conversations in front of them—'to exercise their curiosity'.[165] Here this relatively new topos of the natural curiosity of children is more circumscribed than for Locke, since Fleury, echoing the Port-Royal moralist Pierre Nicole,[166] makes it clear that curiosity should not continue to be stimulated in this way in older children and young adults. It is fine for young nobles to read Cicero, Livy, and other ancients as part of the jurisprudential part of their education, but almost only if they do so in a strictly pragmatic spirit, to help them with future management of their lands and wealth: 'But in all of these observations one must avoid the continual temptation of curiosity, except if it is insofar as it can serve as an appetizer to awaken the desire for knowledge.'[167] As in much church-based pastoral discourse, the possibility of good curiosity is here tightly ringfenced by the conditional syntax.

Thirdly, notwithstanding this concern to minimize the curiosity of older children and young adults, Fleury does permit some 'curious studies'. These come third in a hierarchy of four: at the top are 'études nécessaires',[168] followed by 'études utiles',[169] then 'Études curieuses',[170] and finally 'Études inutiles'.[171] 'Necessary' studies are indispensable; 'useful' ones are desirable but not absolutely indispensable (209); 'useless' ones are always 'bad' in themselves.[172] The third category—curious studies—is particularly elusive and problematic, resisting such clear definition. Nevertheless, it is enormous, covering poetics, ancient poetry, music theory, fine arts, mathematics

---

[165] 'jamais la curiosité ni la docilité ne sont si grandes'; 'pour exercer la curiosité' (89, 98).

[166] Of children: 'Cette curiosité n'est pas un vice à leur âge' (Nicole 1670, 42).

[167] 'Mais il faut éviter, en toutes ces observations, la curiosité qui tente continuellement; si ce n'est entant qu'elle peut servir, comme d'un ragoût pour réveiller l'appetit de savoir' (199–200).

[168] 209; see pp. 111–208.

[169] 215; see pp. 209–45.

[170] 245; see pp. 245–53.

[171] 253; see pp. 253–8.

[172] 'mauvaises' (253).

(beyond the elements of arithmetic and geometry), optics, astronomy, antiquarianism, reading travel books, studying languages— 'for, apart from Latin, the rest can be classed as curiosities'[173]—theoretical knowledge of artisan crafts, natural history, chemical experiments, physics: 'I call all of that curiosity'.[174] Not only does Fleury's list include practices characteristic of the culture of curiosities, but by using the phrase 'curious studies'—applying the adjective to desirable objects of knowledge—the cleric is himself now drawing on phrasing that is also characteristic of that culture, in which he is therefore implicating himself to an extent.

Fleury's anxiety surrounding these 'curious studies' is evident from their uncertain status. They are neither 'useful' nor 'wholly useless' ones (253). The zone that they inhabit, between two contraries—'useful' and 'useless'—is thus a logically impossible one (unless those contraries are understood as mediate ones).[175] Also tortured and contradictory is the way in which Fleury discusses 'curious studies'. He presents them as 'curiosities [which are] good and praiseworthy in themselves',[176] but he talks himself into dismissing his very first example—poetics and reading ancient poetry—as too time-consuming: 'the utility or pleasure which one derives from it is not, in my view, worth the effort, given the great amount of knowledge which it is more necessary to acquire'.[177] This balancing of considerations produces plentiful double negatives, reminiscent of the tortuous formal linguistic structures characteristic of pastoral religious discourse on curiosity: 'It is not that there is not profit to be had if one understands [these ancient poets] ... But ...'[178] For Fleury, 'curious studies' are often to be ruled out because they involve expenditure of limited time and energy: the learning process is the management of an economy of resources. People's personal economies differ, depending on their profession, so the appropriateness of 'curious studies'—as of most 'useful' ones and even of some 'necessary' ones—varies from person to person. Thus, Fleury gives the phrase

---

[173] 'car hors le latin, le reste se peut mettre au rang des curiosités' (248).

[174] 'J'apelle tout cela curiosité' (252).

[175] On the role of logical oppositions in the construction of curiosity, see N. Kenny 1998, 113–17.

[176] 'ces curiosités loüables et bonnes d'elles-mêmes' (253).

[177] 'l'utilité, ou le plaisir qui en revient, ne me semble pas digne de ce travail: veu le grand nombre de conoissances qui nous sont plus nécessaires' (247–8).

[178] 'Ce n'est pas que quand on les entend bien il n'y ait à profiter ... mais ...' (247; see also p. 248).

'curious studies' some of the positive weight that it had in the culture of curiosities while also partly applying to it the tradition of negative church comment on curiosity. Of language-learning, for example: 'the most dangerous curiosity of this kind is that for oriental languages',[179] since adepts inevitably suffer from pride in their erudition and singularity.

Fleury concludes his discussion of 'curious studies' on a note of remarkable moral ambiguity. The pursuit of oriental languages and other dangerous curiosities by a small number of people can be useful for society as a whole—to enhance trade, for instance: 'It is this passion of curiosity which is the most harmful to learned people, however much it may also often serve the pursuit of in-depth knowledge. But to achieve that end it is sufficient for just a few individuals to let themselves be carried away by it.'[180] For the good of society, moral harm to be done to a few individuals, who serve as sacrificial lambs. This ecclesiastical pedagogue's tentative foray into the culture of curiosities remains tortuously unresolved.

3.4.4.2   *Noël Antoine Pluche*

However, other pedagogues, while not entirely dispelling anxieties about the encroachment of the culture of curiosities into education, nonetheless were much more enthusiastic about it, especially in the early eighteenth century. For them curiosity was not so much the first stage in a linear sequence leading children to knowledge as the process whereby children *collected* items of knowledge. In other words, these educators exploited the collecting more than the narrating strand of curiosity.

The most famous example was the pedagogical manual, in several volumes, by the abbé Pluche, one of the most widely read works in eighteenth-century France (Mornet 1910, 460). Its very title advertised its epistemological immersion in the culture of curiosities: *Nature's Spectacle, or Conversations on the Particulars of Natural History which have seemed Best Suited to Make Young People Curious and to Train their Minds* (1732–51). This is not a systematic treatise, but rather an accumulation of 'particulars', of 'natural

---

[179] 'la curiosité la plus dangereuse en ce genre, est celle des langues orientales' (249).
[180] 'C'est cette passion de curiosité, qui nuit le plus aux gens de lettres; quoy que d'ailleurs elle serve souvent, pour mener bien loin certaines conoissances. Mais il suffit pour cela, de quelques particuliers, qui s'y laissent emporter' (252–3).

curiosities' that will gratify the 'curiosity' of the young.[181] Thus curiosity inheres in both the learning subjects and in their objects: the optimistic Pluche[182] gives full rein to the fantasy of symmetry between subject and object that is characteristic of the culture of curiosities. The manual is certainly not a collection of curiosities in the sense of a miscellany mixing different kinds of knowledge apparently at random. Indeed, it covers in a fairly coherent order the 'natural curiosities' of animals, plants, the sky, humans. Yet nor is it a systematic treatise on physics, since it starts with particulars, not with principles: 'Instead of proceeding methodically from general knowledge and universal ideas to particular ones, we thought we had better imitate here the order of nature itself and begin directly with the first objects which we find around us and which are constantly within reach: I mean animals and plants.'[183] Pluche begins with 'natural curiosities' that the hand can pick up: insects, shells, birds, fish. These relatively small material objects are turned into relatively short discursive ones thanks to Pluche's use of the dialogue form, which he calls the opposite of a boring 'continuous discourse'.[184] This recalls the short discursive segments of popularizing naturalist publications, which also establish the same relation between their natural objects as does Pluche: they are not explanatorily connected via aetiology and universal principles of physics. Instead, they are accumulated, collected alongside each other: 'When we have *collected* what is most curious in the sea . . .', as the advance summary of one volume's contents has it.[185] Pluche's children find themselves in a similar position to that occupied by the non-specialist readers of naturalist miscellanies, as well by academicians themselves in the early years of their institutions (whose publications Pluche is moreover using):[186] they are offered few causal explanations, since 'our aim is not to give a system'. To 'penetrate . . . Nature' more deeply

---

[181] 'curiosités naturelles' ([Pluche] 1732, i, p. xv).

[182] Hampson (1987, 81–2) recalls Voltaire's characterization of Pluche as an early Enlightenment, Candide-like figure, convinced that we are in the best possible of all worlds.

[183] 'Au lieu de passer méthodiquement des connoissances générales et des idées universelles, aux particulieres, nous avons crû devoir imiter ici l'ordre de la Nature même, et débuter sans façon par les premiers objets qui se trouvent au tour de nous, et qui sont à tout moment sous notre main: je veux dire les animaux et les plantes.' (i, p. vi).

[184] 'un discours suivi' (i, p. xi).

[185] 'Après avoir rassemblé ce que la mer a de plus curieux . . .' (iii, p. xx).

[186] See i, p. xiv.

will be given subsequently only to a few clever people (implicitly male).[187] In other words, the possibility that curiosity might be part of a narrative is here momentarily glimpsed, only to be passed over. Instead, readers are given 'only surfaces or that which strikes the senses':[188] hence the 'Spectacle' title, which shows that Fleury's limited concession to visual aids in child education has now been expanded to the whole of nature, which is one great big visual aid[189] to the stimulation of curiosity, or even to its production, as Pluche's wording sometimes suggests.[190]

The emphasis on spectacular visual surfaces recalls contemporary discourse on cabinets of curiosities. Pluche's manual is implicitly presented as resembling a cabinet—not a cabinet of antiquities, nor of unusual natural or artificial objects, but rather a natural history cabinet of the kind which gradually became dominant in France as the eighteenth century progressed (Pomian 1987, 143–62). Although Pluche often uses a particularly striking feature of one of his 'natural curiosities' to initiate the curiosity of his young readers—why are some birds' beaks and legs long and others' short? (i. 287)—nonetheless the main aim is to incite curiosity about the common and the everyday, not about the rare. So the culture of curiosities is changing as it enters the language-game of pedagogy: the ties that bind it to 'rarity' are being loosened. Yet some aspects of it are just reappearing in modified form. For example, to become curious about common objects in nature is to see them in a new way—in a 'curious perspective', one might almost say: 'You have led me into another world, into an enchanted world', gushes the young fictional *curieux* to his tutor after one volume's worth of revelations.[191] This is one cabinet-like text which does explicitly support Pomian's anthropological hypothesis that collections provide access to invisible worlds.

Fleury would have been horrified to hear a preceptor compliment his pupil that it is no longer necessary 'to attempt to make you curious. It's done: I see that the desire for knowledge has become your

---

[187] 'pénétrer le fond même de la Nature' (i, p. x). The sexing has been noted by Stafford (1994, 233–4).

[188] 'uniquement les dehors ou ce qui frappe les sens' (i, p. ix).

[189] The manual's appeal to the visual is analysed by Stafford (1994, 233–4), who emphasizes some of the same passages.

[190] e.g. title; i, pp. iv, 5.

[191] 'Vous m'avez conduit dans un autre monde, dans un monde enchanté' (i. 490).

dominant passion'.[192] And yet, despite everything, even Pluche still surrounds curiosity with vestiges of anxiety, especially in his repeated insistence that one should 'enclose curiosity within its proper limits', which partly coincide with the limits of 'each individual's social rank'.[193] A main difference between Pluche and Fleury is that what exceeds proper curiosity is no longer described as curiosity by Pluche, who no longer uses the centuries-old vocabulary of bad curiosity with which Fleury designates the excessive kind. Although the anxieties expressed by Fleury are still active here, they are greatly muted.

3.4.4.3 *Jesuits*

Pluche was certainly not the first to incorporate the culture of curiosities into pedagogical discourse. Others to have done so already included Christian Weise, director of the *Gymnasium* in Zittau (3.5.2 below), and one institutional group in particular: the Society of Jesus. As we have seen, the Jesuits had no single attitude towards the culture of curiosities: they either accommodated or spurned it. And I have found no evidence of knowledge being shaped as curiosities in the actual Jesuit classroom. However, many works—especially on natural philosophy—that dress up nature and art or else their own discourse as curiosities were written by Jesuits, including active teachers. These works are not always aimed at students; yet they mostly share a Jesuit pedagogical ethos: that is, they present knowledge less according to its internal logic than in a form that is likely to prove most attractive to the reader—which, for this period, often meant making it curious—and then using it explicitly or implicitly as a means of bringing the reader closer to God.[194] Pluche's own pedagogical strategy—starting with what initially strikes children rather than with the principles of physics, and emphasizing the visual appeal of nature—seems to owe much to the Jesuits (despite his own Jansenist sympathies).[195]

Thus, many Jesuits used secular curiosities to promote religion. They constantly chopped and changed curiosity to suit their

---

[192] '. . . de travailler à vous rendre curieux. C'est une affaire faite, et je vois bien que le désir de savoir est devenu votre passion dominante' (i. 494).

[193] 'renfermer la curiosité dans ses justes bornes'; 'l'état de chaque particulier' (i. 495–6).

[194] On Jesuit pedagogy, see Dainville 1940 and 1978; Scaglione 1986.

[195] On the role of sensory spectacle in Jesuit education, see Stafford 1994, 38–9, 47–9.

immediate rhetorical purpose. Many of them understood curiosity as a contemplation of the world's wonders that was designed to improve one spiritually. This alignment of curiosity with wonders ran counter to the preference expressed by some Lutheran philosophers for curiosity over wonders, motivated by a suspicion of wonder as redolent of superstitious Catholic miracles (1.2.1 above). Jacques Lambert, teacher of rhetoric and philosophy and rector of two Jesuit colleges in France,[196] published under various titles a work on natural philosophy in which each introductory 'discourse' was followed by moral 'applications'—the sun teaches us constancy, and so on. According to one title, the work described 'the marvels of nature' and 'the finest curiosities of natural philosophy'.[197] According to another, it contained 'The morals of the saints, established through explanation of that which, in the main parts of the world, is most worthy of the curiosity of good minds'.[198] Thus, both subjects and objects were curious in Lambert's schema.[199] For him, as for Pluche, what is curious in nature is not so much what is inherently 'rare' or 'singular' as simply that which lends itself well to the ulterior persuasive purpose. The shape of curiosity was more pragmatic than philosophical.

In many other Jesuit works, the ulterior spiritual purpose—bringing readers closer to God—was left largely or wholly implicit. Professors in Jesuit colleges from German-speaking areas to Hungary and Poland shaped the curious according to the uses that they made of it. The most famous among them was perhaps Kaspar Schott, who taught mathematics and physics at the *Gymnasium* in Würzburg. He maintained the characteristic Jesuit alignment of curiosity and wonder in his pair of treatises *Curious Physics, or Marvels of Nature and Art* (1662) and *Curious Techniques, or Marvels of Art* (1664).[200] Indeed, wonder not curiosity was the dominant category in the texts themselves. By calling his physics 'curiosa', Schott was, like some German academicians over the next two decades, trying to have the best of both worlds, on the one hand

---

[196] See Sommervogel (ed.) 1890–1911, iv. 1409–10.

[197] *Les Reflexions du sage. Sur la consideration des merveilles de la nature. Ou les plus belles curiositez de la philosophie naturelle sont mises en entretiens pour la conversation*, 1662.

[198] *La Morale des saints, establie sur l'explication de ce qu'il y a de plus digne de la curiosité des bons esprits dans les principales parties du monde*, 1661–2.

[199] See also Lambert 1661–2, i. 2, 11; iii. 2.

[200] On Schott, see Duhr 1907–28, iii. 589–92; Dünnhaupt 1990–3, v. 3810–23.

attracting readers with the 'rare' and 'hidden' quality of the objects he was describing (angels, demons, monsters, spectres, portents, meteors), and yet on the other hand claiming—with the help of the *cura* lurking in *curiositas*—to describe such potentially controversial objects according to the demanding empirical standards of the new natural philosophy, since nothing is 'worthier of human curiosity, i.e. of ac*cura*te and careful scrutiny'.[201] Indeed, having blatantly exploited the 'rarity' connotation on the title-page, he then explicitly denies that connotation in his preface, claiming that readers are going to be surprised to find that these 'curious and wondrous things' are in fact 'common' in nature.[202] The polysemy of curiosity enabled it to be pulled in conflicting directions while seeming to be a unitary quality.

Schott also highlighted the 'ingenious' and 'new' (indeed 'unheard-of') connotations of curious, especially in his *Technica curiosa*,[203] in which he disseminated the 'experiments' or recent technical innovations of his erstwhile Würzburg teacher and subsequent collaborator, Athanasius Kircher, and of others, such as Otto von Guericke, whose air-pump is included. The Jesuits' preoccupation with the status of experience and experiment—as they sought to incorporate data which had been artificially produced by new experimental practices into the old Aristotelian category of naturally occurring 'experience'[204]—led to 'curious' increasingly meaning 'empirical' or 'experimental' for Jesuit naturalists: three years before Sturm founded his Collegium curiosum sive experimentale, Wojciech Tylkowski, professor of philosophy at the Jesuit college in Warsaw, was calling his treatise on meteors *A Curious Meteorology, or: Meteors Described Through Empirical Observations*.[205]

Jesuit teachers also used curiosity to shape knowledge in other ways. The title of another textbook by Tylkowski acknowledges that making knowledge curious was a self-conscious strategy designed to

---

[201] 'rara, arcana, curiosaque' (Schott 1667, i, title-page); 'dignius humanâ curiositate, hoc est, accuratâ ac sollicitâ perscrutatione' (i, sig. d3ʳ).

[202] 'mira . . . curiosa . . . Trita' (i, sig. d3ʳ).

[203] 'curiosa, ingeniosa, magnamque partem nova et antehac inaudita' (Schott 1664, title-page).

[204] This is a simplifying summary of the complex account given by Dear (1995, chs. 2–3). This may explain Schott's dilemma over whether his curious phenomena are 'common'—which would make them more compatible with Aristotelianism—or else 'rare'.

[205] 'Meteorologia curiosa. Seu Meteora per experientias deducta' (Tylkowski 1669*b*, 1).

enhance pedagogy by accommodating intellectual fashion, in the same way as the courtly pastor Ceriziers accommodated cultural fashion: *Curious Philosophy, or: Curious Questions and Conclusions from the Universal Philosophy of Aristotle, Shaped ['formatae'] and Arranged to the Taste and Inclination of this Age* (1669).[206] The textbook provides a highly selective route through the Aristotelian canon: its sections—'Curious logic', 'Curious physics', and so on—are divided into briefly answered questions, which require a shorter attention span than would a systematic treatise and are typographically separated, making the book superficially re-semble many contemporary collections of discursive curious frag-ments.[207] The Jesuit classroom practice of neo-scholastic questions (Nelles 1999, 143) here meets the culture of curiosities.

Although the evidence of Schott and others[208] seems to show that Jesuit efforts to make knowledge curious focused on the 'new', exciting discoveries emanating from academies and so on, in fact Tylkowski and others show that these efforts could extend to the whole philosophy curriculum—at least in publications that dissemi-nated that curriculum to a broader audience, and also possibly in the classroom. Marton Szentivanyi, who taught at the Jesuit college of Tirnau in Hungary, periodically published—under the running title *Very Curious and Select Miscellany of Various Sciences* (1689–1709)—volumes of his 'dissertations' on physics, mathemat-ics, astronomy, and other branches. Showing the usual keen aware-ness of the potential polysemy of 'curious', he explained to his dedicatee that the contents were indeed

curious, very curious, yet neither playful nor vain; curious because they are rare, because they are far removed from common knowledge, not because they are collected all at one go, but rather because they are selected one by one from the most select authors; not, admittedly, because they are wholly new or unheard-of, but because they have been arranged and collected with

---

[206] The *Philosophia curiosa* includes a one-page advertisement for the *Meteorologia curiosa* (following the 'De anima' section), which presents the *Meteorologia* as one part of the *Philosophia*, although it is not actually printed with it.

[207] 'Curiosa logica', 'Curiosa physica'.

[208] e.g. [Bougeant] 1730–7 (3.4.2 above) and the popularizing, much reprinted *Entretiens physiques* by the college professor of mathematics and physics Noël Regnault (1745–50; see esp. i, p. x[= xiv]. 1st edn. 1729).

great labour from a huge number of extremely rare books in distinguished, famous libraries.[209]

Navigating his way through the sea of wanted and unwanted connotations of 'curious', Szentivanyi first—even at this late date—feels obliged to repudiate the centuries-old *vana curiositas* connotation, and then feels obliged in all honesty to drop any claims to the 'new' and 'unheard-of' connotation, before finally settling for 'selective' (which is here, as ever—and as he spells out—the deluxe version of the 'collecting' connotation).[210] Even within the discourse of the Society of Jesus, the language-games whereby curiosity added value to knowledge—rendering it worthy of illustrious dedicatees[211] as well as attractive to students or purchasers—changed endlessly.

3.4.5   *Collectors of material objects*

Curiosity served to ascribe value not just to discursive objects but also to material ones, such as those collected in cabinets. Such material collections might seem to be the heart of the culture of curiosities, its 'privileged site' (3.2 above), since they were apparently the literal term of the metaphor upon which it was based. However, my aim is to show how that metaphor spread to a host of other discourses. The operation of the curiosity-collecting tendency within the discourse of collecting 'proper' needs little demonstration: largely self-evident, it can be ascertained from the voluminous existing scholarship on early modern collecting.[212] Moreover, the tendency to shape matter and discourse into a collection of curious fragments did not necessarily

---

[209] 'curiosa, curiosiora, non tamen aut ludicra, aut vana; verùm ex eò curiosa, quia rara; quia à vulgi notitia abstrusa, et remota, nec obiter collecta, sed ex selectissimis Authoribus singulariter selecta; et licèt nec nova omnino, nec inaudita, tamen non parvo labore, nec nonnisi ex ingenti librorum rarissimorum copia, praecipuisque ac nominatissimis Bibliothecis concinnata, et accumulata' (Szentivanyi 1689–1709, i, dedication).

[210] For an early, non-Jesuit example of 'curieux' meaning above all 'selective' in a quasi-pedagogical work—which explains philosophical terms, presumably for students and/or courtiers—see Marandé 1649 (first published 1647). On Marandé, see Michaud 1843–.

[211] Compare the dedication to the Elector of Mainz in Schott 1664.

[212] Important, recent, general studies include Balsiger 1970; DaCosta Kaufmann 1993, esp. ch. 7; Daston and Park 1998, ch. 7; Evans 1973, 176–82; Findlen 1994; Hüllen 1994; Impey and MacGregor (eds.) 1985; Lugli 1983; Olmi 1992, esp. 165–92; Pomian 1987; Schnapper 1988 and 1988–94; Whitaker 1996. See also Schlosser 1908.

originate within the world of collecting 'proper'. Writing about nature, travel, history, news, and so on may have influenced collecting 'proper' as well as vice versa. It is in order to leave open this possibility that I am discussing collecting 'proper' now, halfway through this survey of the culture of curiosities, rather than at its outset.

Let me explore the uses of curiosity in the discourses of collecting 'proper' first through some general comments and secondly through a case-study of one particular practice: book-collecting.

For a while, the practice of collecting material objects was intimately bound up with the discourse of curiosity. One wag even called it 'curiosomania'.[213] However, although some recent scholarship has given the impression that curiosity was sometimes virtually coterminous with the collecting of material objects, in fact it was not. Not only did the discourse of curiosity extend far beyond the practice of curiosity but, conversely, not all collecting of material objects was conceived as curiosity. When, in the fifteenth century, the practice of collecting had begun spawning a related literature of guides, manuals, and descriptions (Pomian 1987, 9), curiosity was not yet a prominent theme in them. When, especially from the late sixteenth century onwards, a huge number of French, German, Italian, and English collectors did start being known as 'curious', as did their objects, even then not *all* collectors and objects were named thus, nor was the naming straightforward, especially initially: early seventeenth-century collectors still sometimes felt obliged to acknowledge that curiosity was half vice, half virtue, and to dissociate their activity from the vicious half.[214] Although the traditional negative sense of curiosity was subsequently largely suppressed within the discourse of collecting, it continued to be applied to collectors by others, not just by clerics, *philosophes*, and university professors but also by satirical playwrights (4.4.4 below).

However, although curiosity was not coterminous or coextensive with the practice of collecting, the French terms *curieux* and *curiosités*, German terms such as *ein curieuser Liebhaber, ein*

---

[213] *La Curiosomanie*. A play by C.-A. Coypel (d. 1752), listed in Brenner 1947 (p. 51, no. 5019).

[214] e.g. the Poitiers apothecary Contant (1609; probably first published 1600), who prefaces the poetical description of his botanical garden and naturalist cabinet by recalling that philosophers have much debated whether 'la curiosité' should figure among the virtues or vices (a iʳ). On Contant, see Balsiger 1970, 144–7; Schnapper 1988–94, i. 222–5.

curieuser, curieus, and *eine Curiosität,* as well as the Latin plural *curiosi*—used in German as in English at the time—were eventually widely applied to both the objects and the subjects of collecting, constructing a cosy loop of gratification between the two. The referentiality of 'curiosity' within collecting was rich and shifting. The term could denote the whole of a collection or else just some of the objects within it. Probably most of the collections that were described in the late sixteenth and the seventeenth century as containing curiosities belonged to what has been called the 'eclectic' type:[215] that is, whether or not they contained mainly one kind of object, they deliberately mixed and juxtaposed categories such as natural and artificial, antiquarian and new. Their 'curiosities' included coins, medals, precious stones, shells, crocodiles, elephant tusks, paintings, drawings, books, manuscripts, busts, clocks and other mechanisms. Such curiosities in eclectic cabinets were often understood as 'rare', 'uncommon', and 'singular'.

On the other hand, throughout the eighteenth century in France and Germany there was a trend (again with many exceptions) towards collecting one category of object, such as archaeological or, most often—at least in France—natural-historical ones (shells, minerals, anatomical specimens), with decreased emphasis on their 'singularity'.[216] This shift in emphasis did not expel the discourse of curiosity from collecting—it was still applied to natural-history collections (Pomian 1987, 161–2)—but it did call it into question and diminish its prominence, beginning at roughly the same time that curiosity was also being either reshaped or relegated in certain other discourses too (such as naturalist, technological, and how-to books). For example, what exactly it meant to call a collector *un curieux* was explicitly questioned. Did the label denote a learned antiquarian who studies his medals or else a rich courtier who finds his medals aesthetically tasteful? (asked the publisher of a 1739 numismatics treatise which was addressed to the latter group) (Pomian 1987, 148–9). For some mid-eighteenth-century *philosophes, un curieux* was, in the context of artistic objects, an ignorant collector, as opposed to a knowledgeable *connoisseur,* whereas in the late seventeenth century little distinction had been made between those two as terms for collectors.[217]

[215] Olmi 1992, 193. See also Pomian 1987, 64–5; Whitaker 1996, 87–8.
[216] See Bepler 1988, 27–8; Pomian 1987, 64–5, 143–62.
[217] See Pomian 1987, 155–62; Saisselin 1970, 61–2.

Within the discourse of collecting 'proper' the 'curiosity' family of terms varied enormously in function as well as in referentiality. It was used for many different purposes. Some were similar to those that we have encountered in other discourses of the culture of curiosities, such as the constitution of object-fragments and subjects as both 'curious', in a gratifying symmetry. Material objects in cabinets were not pre-existing givens: they needed to be constituted *as* objects. For example, they had to be selected, separated from their physical attachments to surrounding matter in their natural habitats, and then—to echo the recurrent terminology of the period—'brought from' that habitat to a cabinet.[218] This process of dis-location was consecrated by language, by terms like 'curious', echoing the phrase 'curious perspective' with which Niceron denoted trick dis-locations in optics. The trick process by which the objects in cabinets were constituted was highlighted especially in parodies, since they sought to uncover and disrupt the usually tacit processes involved in collecting. For example, some of the jokes in a *Fashionable Raffle of One Hundred Very Curious and Highly Valuable Items* showed by counter-example that collectable objects had to be material, small, preservable, portable, separable from their home context—as opposed to moral or inseparable from the person or thing to which they may be attached. One of the 'very curious' items to be raffled was a 'marine periwinkle [or, punningly: 'a pickled virginity'], found intact on the coast of the island of Chíos and brought to France out of curiosity'.[219]

The title of this parody also makes explicit that the 'curious' label, along with others, commodified collectable objects, giving them a financial price, just as it commodified the discursive objects collected together in publications on nature, for example. As in the culture of curiosities in general, this economic dimension was double-edged: it could be either flaunted or repressed. On the one hand, a market in curiosities and other objects became increasingly organized in the sixteenth and seventeenth centuries (Pomian 1987, 53). 'Curiosity', when it denoted the collecting of material objects, widely connoted money. Colonna, recalling his purchase, from the Moscow ambassador, of a furry skin derived from a famous 'lamb-plant' ('Plante-Agneau'), wrote ruefully: 'He made me pay for my curiosity, selling

---

[218] See Hüllen 1994, 123; N. Kenny 1998, 169–70.
[219] 'Un Pucelage mariné, trouvé entier sur les coste[s] de l'Isle de Chio, aporté en France par curiosité' (*Lotterie à la mode* [1620–30?], 6).

[the skin] to me at a high price'. Yet on the other hand, curiosities were often considered to be objects dis-located not only from their home context but also, precisely, from the market, since their owners often wanted to hoard rather than trade them (Pomian 1987, 18). Moreover, when they did part with them, it was sometimes in a way that ostentatiously denied economics, perhaps cementing social relations or a self-image of quasi-aristocratic liberality. Colonna continued: 'I kept it for a long time and gave it away in the end to someone who wanted it.'[220]

This ambivalent economic status of curiosities—both inside and outside the market—is one of the factors which makes it notoriously difficult to determine the extent to which they were used by their owners to accrue social prestige and distinction. For, if the main message transmitted by a splendid collection of curiosities was the wealth and therefore social importance of the owner, then the purely financial value of the collection often had to be implied rather than spelt out, lest the message defeat itself through vulgarity, especially in the case of aristocrats, who in England were calling themselves *curiosi* and *virtuosi* as one way of counteracting the general decline in their social status.[221] This was identified as duplicitous in the period itself. For example, as Michael Moriarty has persuasively argued, La Bruyère's scathing attack on 'la curiosité'—by which he understood the obsessive collecting of objects ranging from tulips to paintings—was designed to reveal that 'curieux' were abjectly dependent on the fashion system and on the market, however much they sought to mask that dependence by refusing to act in rational economic terms (for example by selling when they could make a profit).[222] On the other hand, because some contemporaries like the *moraliste* La Bruyère thought that some collecting/curiosity masked self-glorification by economic means, that does not mean that that was necessarily the dominant motive for all curiosity/collecting: hence the disagreement on this issue among historians of early modern collecting.[223]

---

[220] 'Il me fit payer ma curiosité, en me la vendant fort cher. Je l'ai gardé long-tems, et enfin je la donnai à une personne qui désiroit l'avoir' (Colonna 1734, iii. 231–2).

[221] See Eamon 1994, ch. 9.

[222] Moriarty 1988, 161–3. On La Bruyère's attack, see also Leplatre 1998; Mazaheri 1991.

[223] The case for interpreting collecting as an attempt to acquire social or political prestige is put by: Benedict 1990 (in relation to Britain); DaCosta Kaufmann 1993, ch. 7 (with nuance); Eamon 1994, ch. 9; Shelton 1994, 186–8. For a sceptical attack on such arguments, see Schnapper 1988.

One kind of curiosity which was a variation on the practice of collecting and was explicitly attacked by contemporaries as self-glorification by economic means was the acquisition of luxury objects, ranging from fine clothing to ornate trinkets. For a while, curiosity was a pivotal focal point in the decades-long debate about luxury which became prominent from the late seventeenth century. Indeed, the fortunes of the 'luxury' family of terms were set to echo partly those of the 'curiosity' family: the newly positive reputation which 'luxury' enjoyed in some discourses from the late seventeenth century onwards—when it became associated with a healthy, wealthy, trading society—echoed that which 'curiosity' had been enjoying especially from the early seventeenth, though the re-evaluation was no more universal or unequivocal in the case of luxury than in that of curiosity.[224] Curiosity was ambivalent enough to serve the purposes of both defenders and attackers of luxury. Its Janus-like potential made it pivotal in this as in so many other debates (such as the one surrounding the occult sciences). Whereas some seventeenth-century discourses sought to undermine the centuries-old opposition between 'curiosity' and 'necessity' (or 'usefulness'), on the other hand the old 'superfluous' or 'supplementary' connotation of 'curious' continued to thrive in many discourses (N. Kenny 1998, 140–1). Luxuries were described by both their defenders and their attackers as 'curious' in this sense, the former intending the term positively and the latter pejoratively.

Although 'curious' had become a largely positive term in the culture of curiosities, its much longer negative history could always be readily reactivated, even in works which were largely defending curiosity *qua* the acquisition of luxury goods.[225] In Germany, protectionist voices were raised against the craze for importing luxury goods, especially from France: indeed, concern about the craze's economic effects had led the Emperor to ban (ineffectually) first all French imports (1676) and then all commerce with France (1689, 1702).[226] The author of one such mercantilist tract (1684) homed in on two relatively new, frequently positive connotations of curiosity—'finance' and 'social distinction'—using the old negative force

---

[224] On the luxury debate, see Berry 1994, chs. 5–6; Galliani 1989.
[225] e.g. *Letter on the Nature and State of Curiosity* 1736. On this work, see Benedict 1990, 75–7.
[226] Hughes 1992, 123. On the craze for French culture, see Hoffmeister (ed.) 1983, 262, 362; Vierhaus 1988, 59.

of the term to turn them too into negatives, as he condemned 'money-guzzling curiosity' and people (especially in cities) who sought 'curious esteem' by purchasing such goods. He also reactivated the older, decorum-based understanding of curiosity—which was still prominent in church and university discourse—by attacking spendthrifts 'of low social rank' who were buying such goods 'out of an uppity curiosity which is out of all proportion with their rank'.[227]

On the other hand, German defenders of luxury—whether or not they actually used the vocabulary of 'luxury'—called material and discursive objects 'curious' in order to sell them to self-styled urban and courtly sophisticates as supplements, as aids not to survival but to politeness. That is what *curieus* mainly signals in the collections of discursive objects by the likes of August Bohse—often considered the founder of the so-called *galanter Roman*—such as his *Curious Manual of Various Select Letters and Verbal Compliments in the Newest Style, for the Use of People of High Social Status, Patrons, Women, and the Like* (1700).[228] 'Curious' here connotes not 'popularizing' but 'exclusive': it flatters readers into believing that they are members of *die curieuse Welt*. (The specific association of this kind of curious superfluousness with women put women in the same ambivalent position as curiosity itself (5.1 below).) 'Curious' here also connotes 'exotic', as much as in any inventory of curious objects from other continents, except that here 'exotic' means Italian or (especially) French rather than, say, Chinese or Brazilian. Bohse's manual of etiquette includes a glossary of French and Italian terms: its readers, like those of many such manuals, sought to ape the use of French terminology or language that was in vogue at the courts of many German territorial rulers who, in turn, were aping Versailles.

Curieus (like its cognates) did not merely serve to shape matter into sophisticated objects which were—to echo the discourse of material collecting—'brought from' France to Germany: it was itself one such object, a term widely perceived as being French rather than indigenous. Indeed many a German sentence even included the French form *curiosité* rather than the Germanicized *Curiosität*. Like *galant* and other modish terms, 'curiosity' regularly stood out

[227] 'Geldfressende Curiosität'; 'curiösen aestim'; 'Niedern Stands-Personen'; 'aus üppiger und seinem Stande gar nicht gemässer Curiosität' (*Das neugierige und veränderte Teutschland*, 1988, 217, 325–7).

[228] On Bohse, see Dünnhaupt 1990–3, i. 713–57.

typographically from the surrounding, Gothic-script text (Illustration 1), for example in translations or pseudo-translations of French texts, such as one collection of fairy-tales, which was presented as 'translated into German because of its odd curiosity'.[229] *Curieus* could figure both as an item in German lexicons of foreign words and also in their overall title, as a label for the lexicon's 'exotic' contents.[230] According to other lexicographers, who wished to purify the German language of such foreign imports, *curieus* was itself superfluous to needs (N. Kenny 1998, 93–101). So this battle over the word mirrored the battle fought over some of its referents: luxury goods imported from France. *Curieus* and its cognates had special resonance in German because they not only denoted the importation of 'exotic' objects but also embodied it.

Thus the uses of curiosity within the practices of material collecting were rich but patchy, rather than fixed or systematic. Calling objects 'curious' also arguably made some of them gateways to invisible worlds—in the terms of Pomian's anthropological thesis—but this too occurred patchily and in endlessly variable ways.

For instance, in 1670 the inventory of the collection of a nobleman of La Rochelle was printed. The title characteristically indicated that the objects were constituted through dis-location: *Collection of Curious Pieces Brought from the Indies, Egypt, and Ethiopia and Which are Now in the Cabinet of Léonard Bernon*. The cabinet was of the eclectic type. Among its animals, shells, and fossils, fifteen items are grouped together in the inventory under the rubric 'Various curiosities personally used by a commander of the savages'. These include 'The bed in which the great commander of the savages slept; a triumph made from the teeth of Christians killed in battle and of the enemies whom he ate; . . . his pipe (in which he smoked tobacco), hewn from marble and most curious.'[231] These curiosities are arranged—here discursively, and presumably materially in the cabinet—to evoke metonymically not a whole invisible world (if by that one means a whole culture or geographical area) but a particular person in an absent place. There is no indication of where that place

---

[229] 'wegen ihrer sonderbaren Curiosität . . . in das Teutsche übersetzet' ('Vallon' 1743, title-page).

[230] e.g. Belemnon 1728 (see p. 61).

[231] 'Diverses curiositez servant à la personne d'un General des Sauvages . . . Le Lict où couchoit le grand General des Sauvages, Un Triomphe de dents des Chrestiens tuez en guerre, et des ennemis qu'il a mangé . . . Sa Pipe où il prenoit du Tabac, faite d'une pierre de Marbre, fort curieuse.' (Bernon 1670, 13).

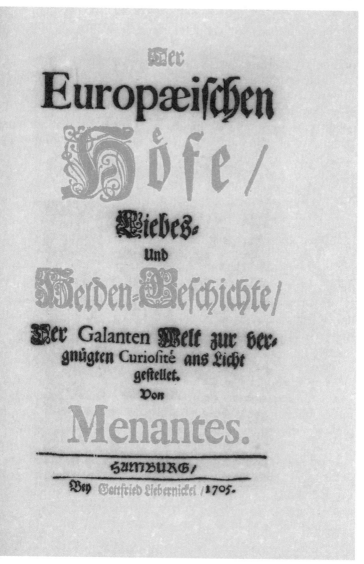

ILLUS. 1. Hunold, *Der Europaeischen Höfe, Liebes- und Helden-Geschichte* (1705).

is, except for an indication that one of the objects is Brazilian. In reality the curiosities may well have come from different individuals, perhaps even from different cultures, as visitors to the cabinet were probably well aware. But the collection pieced them together as fragments not of a whole culture but of a particular, absent, probably fictitious person. As in most material collections of curiosities, the evocation of absence was more spatial than temporal. Yet the language of the inventory also situates the absent person in time, if more shakily. As the tenses in the quoted passage show, he is largely associated with a vague, past period, as a historical figure. But this construction of a past breaks down when a couple of slips into the present tense make the fictionality obtrude: 'Rackets with which he walks on the snow . . . Castanets which they use during their celebrations.'[232]

A broad parallel can be drawn with Niceron's 'curious perspective': half close your eyes, look at fifteen discrete curiosities, and you can almost see them deformed into a particular person from another place and time. The use of the 'curiosity' family here resembles that by which antiquarians, historians, travel-writers, and journalists also sought to evoke, piecemeal, other places and times, via collections of discursive curiosities. Some material collections of curiosities may have been intended to symbolize whole invisible worlds—in accordance with Pomian's thesis—whether the macrocosm (especially up till about the mid-seventeenth century)[233] or else one area of nature (especially in the eighteenth century). But the other times or places which material collections of curiosities evoked were often themselves deemed very particular. A torn shoe could be deemed significant because it evoked not a whole past period, but an extraordinary past event (Bepler 1988, 169–70). For us now it is impossible to say whether, or in what sense, curiosities did or did not give people access to other times and places: but the language in which curiosities were represented shows at least that they were certainly sometimes considered to do so.

3.4.5.1   Book collecting

Even within the practice of collecting, curiosity—although usually considered to be one and the same passion and/or quality of

---

[232] 'Des Raquettes avec lesquelles il marche dessus la neige . . . Des Castagnettes, dont ils se servent en leurs réjouïssances.' (13).

[233] See Balsiger 1970, 552–60; Evans 1973, 176–7; Lugli 1983, 93–8.

objects—was endlessly reshaped because used for so many different purposes. Some of its chronological shifts were specific to particular kinds of collecting. This can be illustrated by the changes that occurred in how it was used within the world of book-collecting, in France. Here the 'curious' label endowed books with value that, increasingly, was narrowly financial in character.

Books were collected in various settings. Some were included in eclectic cabinets, alongside other objects. On the other hand, collections devoted principally to books—or to books and manuscripts—pre-dated the culture of curiosities and thrived throughout it. They can be classed roughly according to a typology elaborated by Jean Viardot. Largest and organized on the most scholarly lines were the libraries founded by great families of the legal nobility from the late sixteenth century onwards. Much smaller, but still arranged for intellectual and moral usefulness was what was known as the 'select library' (*bibliothèque choisie*) of the urbane *honnête homme*. From the late seventeenth century, this could shade into a different category, that of the *cabinet choisi*, where some of the books were included not only for their contents but also for features deemed more extrinsic, such as typography, binding, illustrations, paper. Collecting books primarily as material artefacts was sometimes known, from about the mid-seventeenth century, as 'bibliomania'. Where bibliomania—rather than reading—was the owner's sole motive, then the collection was sometimes called a *cabinet curieux* or a *cabinet de raretés*.[234]

With what values did 'curiosity' endow books? In the early seventeenth century, in the milieu of the Gallican humanist Gabriel Naudé—author of a famous treatise (1627) which advised the parliamentary legal nobility how to compile a library—books were 'curious' if 'rare', that is, as Paul Nelles has argued, either 'numerically scarce' or 'on an unusual or difficult topic', or even just 'good'.[235] To call a book or manuscript 'curious' was primarily to describe its intrinsic worth, not its price, even if price was connoted remotely because curious books were often likely to be relatively expensive ones.

Similarly, when almost a century later the Jesuit Claude-François Ménestrier published a manual advising *honnêtes gens* how to

---

[234] See Viardot 1984 and 1988.
[235] See Nelles 1997, 43–4.

compile both a *bibliothèque choisie* and a *cabinet choisi*, he made
'curious books' or 'books of curiosities' one of the fourteen categories of books which should be included, but he ignored the question of their monetary value. He called them 'curious' not primarily
because they were expensive but because they contained 'travels . . .
secrets . . . particular questions . . . facts . . . historical anecdotes', in
other words curious discursive fragments—rather than pedantic or
specialist expertise—which could then be elegantly recycled by the
library owner in '*honnête*, free, pleasant, and curious' conversations,
such as those in which the reader of Bary's compilation of what is
most curious in nature would also participate.[236] Such conversational exchanges of discursive curiosities mirrored the free, civil
exchange of material curiosities in the same aristocratic and quasi-
aristocratic circles. To collect books was to collect conversational
nuggets: curiosity was here inseparable from volubility. Although
Ménestrier is happier than La Bruyère to see the *honnête homme*
dabble thus in the culture of curiosities, he too ensures that curiosity
does not taint the *honnête homme* with vulgar economics, such as
explicit consideration of how much the 'curious books' will cost him.

Subsequently, however, in some circles, the label 'curious' served
increasingly to endow book collectors and their objects with specifically economic motives and values. Central to this shift was one
enormous descriptive checklist of the books that were sought by
bibliomaniacs: it was compiled by the French market's dominant
dealer in old printed books, Guillaume-François Debure le Jeune
(1763–82).[237] Debure systematically used *curieux* as the label both
for the most valuable books and also for their bibliomaniacal collectors (whom he also called *amateurs*, occasionally *connoisseurs*), as
opposed to those who wished to use books for scholarly purposes
(whom he called *savants*, *gens de littérature*, or, in the singular,
l'homme de Lettres). Paradoxically, Debure's apotheosis of *curieux*
thus coincided with their marginalization from mainstream learning,
for he was in fact reinstating an opposition—between the 'curious'
and the 'learned', as also between the 'curious' and the 'useful'[238]—
which had flourished for centuries, to the detriment of the 'curious',

---

[236] See 3.4.2 above. '*Les Livres Curieux*' (Ménestrier 1704, i. 50); 'les Livres de
Curiositez' (i. 93); 'Voïages . . . Secrets . . . Questions particulieres . . . Faits . . . Histoires
Anecdotes' (i. 50); 'des conversations honnêtes, libres, agreables et curieuses' (i. 44).

[237] On this work, see N. Kenny 2000*a*, 267–70; Viardot 1984, 458–63.

[238] e.g. Debure 1763–82, volume on theology (1763), no. 16.

before being undone in, for example, much naturalist discourse of
the second half of the seventeenth century, where being 'curious'
could involve being 'learned'. What Debure's *curieux* bibliomaniacs
know about is not learning itself but rather 'the trade in learning',
that is, the monetary value of books. 'Knowledge of books' is (he
argues) neatly divided into two halves: whereas the first half relates
to the content of books, 'The second, which is strictly speaking typographical, makes up the *science* [i.e. theoretical knowledge] of a
libraire: it consists in the exact and certain knowledge of books with
respect to their current trading value' and also with respect to other
factors, such as the books' 'rarity', 'singularity', authentic or pirated
status, and so on.[239] This *science* takes many years to acquire; it is
structured in a similar way to the *science* of nature as cultivated by
a Colonna: *curieux* covet not the vast number of 'ordinary books'
but rather 'these singular and extraordinary books'.[240] Just as
praeternatural philosophers like Colonna prized what went against
the ordinary course of nature, so bibliomaniacs prized what went
against that of book production.

Moreover, just as some experimenters produced curiosities by artificially suspending the ordinary course of nature, some printers and
bibliomaniacs produced them by tampering with routine book production. Not content with just collecting the few curious books that
had been unintentionally produced by the contingencies of mass production and distribution—printing errors, political suppression of
most copies, and so on—they sometimes actively and intentionally
fabricated books in a way that would make them curious, especially
after the spectacular and enduring rise in the prices of such books on
the Paris market from the early 1720s onwards.[241] Printers sometimes printed, 'for the curious', a small number of copies differently
from the main run of a book, whether on large paper or in a smaller
format.[242] Alternatively, some bibliomaniacs practised do-it-yourself

[239] Debure 1763–82, volume on theology (1763): 'le Commerce des lettres' (466);
'La connoissance des Livres ... Le second, qui n'est purement que Typographique,
fait, à proprement parler, la science d'un Libraire; elle consiste dans la connoissance
exacte et certaine des Livres, par rapport à leur valeur actuelle dans le commerce ... à
leur rareté ... à leur singularité' (pp. [iii]–iv).
[240] Debure 1763–82, volume on theology (1763): 'les Livres ordinaires' (p. v); 'ces
Livres singuliers et extraordinaires' (p. vii).
[241] On this rise, see Bléchet 1991, 51–2; Viardot 1984, 451.
[242] See Debure 1763–82, volume on theology (1763), no. 24 ('pour les Curieux');
volume on *belles lettres* (1765), no. 2696.

fabrication of curious books, for example by buying two editions of a work, one of which was more beautiful but had fewer plates than the other, and then ripping out the extra plates from the less beautiful edition and transferring them to the more beautiful one.[243] They were simply doing more flagrantly what other kinds of collector did surreptitiously—making objects curious by dis-locating them from their home context or transforming them in other ways, for example spraying bird-wings so that their feathers would not rot. In the discursive world of Debure, the point of making an object *curieux* was to make it worth more money.

Because 'curious'—in the context of book collecting—now served primarily to endow bibliomaniacs and their objects with financial motives and value, the term's application to *other* kinds of book collecting faded. In contrast with Naudé and his circle in the 1620s and 1630s, scholarly collectors, librarians, and bibliophiles in the mid-eighteenth century, who wished to distance themselves from bibliomaniacal *curiosité*, seem largely to have given up on the term, preferring to call themselves *bibliographes* or *littérateurs*[244] and to call their practice not *curiosité* but, say, *bibliologie*,[245] while only occasionally adopting Debure's terminology of *curieux* and *connoisseurs* (and then only in order to dictate what such bibliomaniacs really ought to collect).[246] Bibliomaniacs gained a monopoly of *curiosité*, but only at the expense of its being relegated within other discourses of book collecting. In the case of other terms—notably *rare* and *rareté*—which were claimed by both opposing camps, there were prolonged and bitter disputes over exactly what they meant when applied to books (Viardot 1984, 458–63).

Thus, whereas in some collecting practices of the mid-eighteenth century *curieux* became opposed to *connoisseurs*, in the context of book collecting those two terms gravitated towards each other, since *curieux* bibliomaniacs were in fact credited (at least by the likes of Debure, who sold books to them) with a systematic, specialist body of knowledge—of books insofar as they were market commodities.

[243] Debure 1763–82, volume on jurisprudence, sciences, and arts (1764), no. 1737.
[244] e.g. Mercier de Saint-Léger (1783, [3]), who wrote the most detailed of the attacks on Debure's system for attributing value to books (N. Kenny 2000a, 268–9; Viardot 1984, 458–63).
[245] The term used by the abbé Jean-Joseph Rive (Viardot 1984, 460).
[246] e.g. Mercier de Saint-Léger 1763, pp. 1645, 1655, 1680.

Once the bibliomania industry had largely succeeded in imposing a definition of curiosity that suited its own interests, it then tried to calibrate curiosity in even more precise financial terms. Debure gives his readers a rough idea of the financial value of each book or manuscript by using a small number of recurring, gradated phrases, starting with *assez rare*, then moving up to *rare, curieux, recherché*, then up to *fort rare*, or *très recherché des curieux*, and culminating in books which are *de la plus grande rareté* or *dans la classe des livres les plus curieux*.[247] Curiosity was thus integrated into a sliding financial scale. The integration then became even more specific in an *Essai de curiosités bibliographiques* published by the librarian and historian Étienne Gabriel Peignot in 1804. Judging from this catalogue (1804, p. [ix]), the 'Bibliophiles' whom it addressed were the readers whom I have been describing as bibliomaniacs. The books it listed were quite simply ones which had fetched more than 1,000 francs. Peignot was attempting nothing less than an integration of the two notoriously incommensurable value systems inherent in language and money,[248] describing 'the items which we know to be the most curious, financially speaking'—an extraordinary phrase.[249] Although in subsequent works Peignot listed books which qualified as 'curieux' on other grounds—mostly reminiscent of Debure's criteria[250]—here he was beginning with this sovereign financial criterion (of 1,000 francs) 'because we believe that the rarest and most curious objects must be in this category'.[251] Previously, to call a book 'curious' had involved implying indirectly that it was expensive. Now it involved stating explicitly that not only that it was expensive, but also how much it would fetch.

Curiosity helped make books into fragments of a virtual whole not only within book-collecting but also within a neighbouring discourse: the history of learning, known as *historia litteraria* from the start and then especially from the end of the seventeenth century. The relations between book collecting and the various kinds of *historia*

---

[247] e.g. Debure 1763, 13; Debure 1763–82, volume on theology (1763), nos. 1, 6; Debure 1763–82, volume on jurisprudence, sciences, and arts (1764), no. 1358; Debure 1763–82, volume on *belles lettres* (1765), nos. 2448, 3418.

[248] On this incommensurability in the case of curiosity, see N. Kenny 1998, 161–3.

[249] 'ce que nous connaissons de plus curieux sous le rapport de l'estimation pécuniaire' (p. xlii).

[250] See Peignot 1804, p. ii.

[251] 'parce que nous croyons que c'est dans cette classe que doivent se trouver les objets les plus rares et les plus curieux' (p. iv).

litteraria were complex and have only recently been elucidated.[252] Whereas *histoire littéraire* and related histories or bibliographies of *lettres, belles lettres, poésie,* or *auteurs* were often presented, well into the eighteenth century, in primarily spatial terms—especially as metaphorical libraries—the eighteenth century also saw that spatial model being increasingly displaced by a temporal one, as time-lines became the prime organizational principles and *histoire* replaced *bibliothèque* in the titles of such works.[253] This profoundly changed the relation of *historia litteraria* to the curiosity-collecting metaphor.

Initially, that metaphor sometimes contributed to the shape of *historia litteraria*. As long as past book production was represented in predominantly spatial terms, it was possible for it to be represented as a sprawling body of knowledge that was a collection of curiosities. For example, the author of one pedagogical manual (first published 1740–4) declares:

Let's constantly amass items of knowledge—one curiosity at a time—which combine real usefulness with much pleasure . . . But our writers have divided up their task: they have given us *histoire littéraire* piece by piece, instead of giving it in its entirety and full scope. While we wait for some skilful hand to take the trouble to collect together those scattered materials, in the mean-time I am presenting to young people . . . a short introduction to that history.[254]

A little later still, he speaks of 'the various pieces of *histoire littéraire* which we possess'.[255] The discourse is remarkably similar to that with which the academicians Boyle and Fontenelle described the current state of naturalist and experimental knowledge: as with Fontenelle, this pedagogue's description of spatial fragmentation is leavened by a glimpse of a future narrative in which the scattered pieces will eventually be integrated into a whole by a skilful hand.

---

[252] Nelles 1997, 2000, and 2001; Zedelmaier 1992, ch. 4.

[253] For a study of this shift which does not focus on the fortunes of curiosity within it, see N. Kenny 2000a.

[254] 'Curiosité pour curiosité, amassons toûjours des connoissances qui à une utilité réelle joignent beaucoup d'agrément . . . Mais nos Ecrivains se sont partagés leur tâche: ils ont donné l'Histoire Littéraire piéce à piéce, au lieu de la donner en entier et dans toute son étenduë. En attendant qu'une main habile veuille bien se donner la peine de ramasser ces matériaux épars, je présente aux jeunes gens . . . une courte Introduction à cette Histoire' (Juvenel de Carlencas 1749, i, pp. viii–xii).

[255] 'les différens morceaux que nous avons de l'Histoire Littéraire' (i, p. xv).

In fact, that skilful hand was already at work, in the person of Dom Rivet (André Rivet de La Grange) and the collaborators on his *Histoire literaire de la France*, published in Paris from 1733 to 1763 by the Benedictines of the Congrégation de Saint-Maur, before being taken up in 1814 by the Académie des Inscriptions et Belles-Lettres.[256] They saw themselves primarily not as metaphorically collecting 'one curiosity at a time', but as unravelling a narrative thread, from the Gauls onwards. Although the rich incidental details in their narrative are described at one point as 'curious things',[257] this phrase is now but a vestige of the curiosity-collecting metaphor, which, while still dominant in the discourse of bibliomania in the second half of the eighteenth century, was now down but not quite out in *histoire littéraire*.

3.4.6 *Antiquarianism*

in the vast and curious land of antiquity[258]

Another discourse and practice which was inseparable from collecting was antiquarianism, which—to borrow Anthony Grafton's metaphor—'bloomed outrageously' in sixteenth- and seventeenth-century Europe, having budded earlier (1997, 176).[259] The practice of collecting ancient medals, coins, statues, manuscripts had become particularly widespread from the second half of the sixteenth century (Pomian 1987, 49). Especially during the seventeenth century, the curiosity-collecting metaphor was widely used to shape antiquarian knowledge. This occurred so much in the late seventeenth century that it is easy to forget that antiquarianism had long been conceived as collecting but not as curiosity. Indeed, among Renaissance humanists—who were the main catalysts for early modern antiquarianism—*curiositas* was usually still a vice, that of aimless and disordered erudition (Gilbert 1960, 72). Sixteenth-century antiquaries did not systematically call themselves or their objects 'curious', preferring terms like 'singularities' for their objects. By contrast, in 1681 a guide for French visitors to the antiquarians in Rome and their

---

[256] On this work, see N. Kenny 2000a, 280–4; Moisan 1990, 69–71.

[257] 'choses curieuses' (*Histoire literaire* 1733–, i, p. xviii).

[258] 'dans le pays vaste et curieux de l'Antiquité' (Spon 1683, [a4ᵛ]; see also p. 1).

[259] For introductions to early modern antiquarianism, see Grafton 1997, 176–89; Momigliano 1990, ch. 3.

collections was presented as listing 'all the *curieux* and . . . all the main *curiosités*'.[260] By a century later still, with the new wave of antiquarianism initiated by Johann Winckelmann and others, preoccupied above all with supposedly universal aesthetic values, curiosity had been banished from much antiquarian discourse.

Given that antiquaries were fixated on the distant past, one might have expected them to write in a way that would enable them to construct historical narratives. However, they were not primarily concerned with writing chronological narratives of classical antiquity or the Middle Ages: that task was left largely to what Arnaldo Momigliano called post-Herodotean historians, who wove narratives to serve political and religious ends.[261] Antiquaries made comparatively little use of the capacity of curiosity to drive narratives forward: they did not tend to describe either ancient cultures or their own practice in terms of a happy or unhappy progression that was motivated by curiosity. Eschewing this temporal model, they adopted instead the predominantly spatial model of the curiosity-collecting metaphor. In this respect they were closer to other collectors than to narrative-based historians. They were also close to travel-writers, especially to ones who represented themselves more as collecting sights than as progressing temporally through them. Antiquaries described themselves as labouring not just in another time but in another place, 'the vast and curious land of antiquity', as the famous Lyonnese antiquary Jacob Spon put it. Thus, collecting and travelling were not just practices that were indispensable to antiquarianism (Spon practised both):[262] they were also images *for* it. They were not just metonymically contiguous to antiquarianism but also metaphors for it. These three practices were connected by terminological bridges, of which the most important was 'curiosity', especially in the second half of the seventeenth century.

'Curiosity' also helped to build bridges between antiquarianism and new natural philosophy. The two might be expected to have little in common. Yet, as Momigliano brilliantly demonstrated, the

---

[260] 'tous les curieux, et . . . toutes les principales curiositez' ([Huguetan and Spon] 1681, title-page). The list, compiled by Spon, was first published in 1673 (Pérez and Guillemain 1993).

[261] Momigliano 1990, 57, 61–2. Occasionally, antiquaries too became involved in religious or dynastic arguments (1990, 72–3).

[262] On Spon, see Étienne and Mossière (eds.) 1993, esp. the contribution by F. Bayard.

antiquarian focus on isolated objects, unrelated facts, and detailed description of them also characterized new natural philosophy of the empirical kind (3.4.1–2 above). Scepticism about philosophical systems was popular in the antiquarian circle of Nicolas-Claude Fabri de Peiresc. And it is no coincidence that many seventeenth-century antiquaries—such as Spon and his friend Charles Patin—were also physicians, for whom immediate, discrete problems were more pressing than complete theories. In antiquarianism, 'the individual facts were collected and set aside with a view to a future general survey of those institutions, customs, cults, for which coins and inscriptions were regarded as the most important evidence': but the survey, the anticipated whole, rarely came.[263]

The curiosity-collecting metaphor played a crucial role in uniting antiquaries with certain naturalists (non-Cartesians, pre-Newtonians, and so on). Both saw themselves as collecting curious fragments, whether material or discursive or (in the case of inscriptions, for example) both; the fragmentariness of objects was indeed at its most overt in antiquarianism, which often studied ruins, remnants of mosaics, or shards of unidentified artefacts. Because antiquarian knowledge was divided into objects, it could be numbered and counted: the engraved frontispiece in Spon's *Recherches curieuses d'antiquité* (1683) depicts a landscape—implicitly the 'vast and curious land of antiquity' mentioned in his preface—in which a collection ('amas') of fourteen 'fine pieces of antiquity' is being inspected by travellers; the objects are numbered, enabling Spon to describe them one by one (Illustration 2).[264] Antiquarianism was not the only discourse in which curiosities were countable: miscellany-periodicals which offered 'forty *galant* and learned curiosities' per quarter may seem worlds away, but in fact they structured knowledge in a broadly similar manner (3.4.9 below).

Both antiquarians and empirical naturalists considered that the curious fragments they collected did not quite add up to a whole, at least not yet. Certainly, much antiquarian writing was intended to be systematic (Momigliano 1990, 61–2). And some antiquarians indulged in overtly imaginary representations of a whole, as in Spon's frontispiece, which was a composite of objects from different times and places, akin to imaginary composite figures in cabinets of

---

[263] Momigliano 1990, 55–9 (58).
[264] 'un amas de plusieurs beaux morceaux d'antiquité' (Spon 1683, e2ʳ).

ILLUS. 2. Spon, *Recherches curieuses d'antiquité* (1683).

curiosities, such as Bernon's probably imaginary 'commander of the savages' (3.4.5 above). But antiquaries generally represented themselves as making local 'discoveries [*découvertes*] in the vast and curious land of antiquity' (Spon 1683, [a4ᵛ]) rather than as comprehensively surveying it. They thereby mirrored the self-representations of many naturalists in relation to the physical world, which was similarly described by Bougeant as a 'land of observations ... vast and fertile enough' to satisfy curiosity (3.4.2 above). Because the apparently bland and uninformative epithet 'curious' could in fact connote and convey this informal epistemology, its application to objects ranging from magnets to inscriptions established a degree of equivalence between them. Such equivalences were established by other terms too: the 'pieces of antiquity which curious travellers consider and examine'[265] were akin to the naturalist 'detached pieces, independent of each other' offered up by the Académie des Sciences (3.2 above) or indeed, in another discourse, to 'the various pieces of *histoire littéraire* which we possess' (3.4.5.1).

For antiquaries, curiosity was not a definable 'concept', but a polysemic cluster. Like naturalist academicians, they mainly used two of its semantic strands, which were connected habitually rather than logically: 'diligence' and 'fragmentation'. The two strands were united in the polysemic phrase *recherches curieuses*, which was common currency in antiquarian writing, for example in the titles of Claude Bouteroue's treatise on numismatics, the *Recherches curieuses des monoyes de France* (1666) and of Spon's *Recherches curieuses d'antiquité*. In this phrase *curieuses* had both a subject-oriented sense, denoting the 'diligence', 'thoroughness', or 'accuracy' of the researches, and also an object-oriented sense, denoting their 'singularity' or 'novelty' while also telling readers connotatively that the text described not a whole ancient custom or institution but discrete objects, a selection of the 'thousand curiosities' deciphered by antiquaries.[266] Through its ambiguity, the phrase *recherches curieuses* encapsulated the gratifying fusion of subject and object— the one seeking, the other sought and found—that was such a

---

[265] 'morceaux d'antiquité que des voyageurs curieux considerent et examinent' (ibid.).

[266] 'mille curiositez' (ibid., [a4ᵛ]). The meaning of phrases like *recherches curieuses* could be oriented more in one direction than the other through collocation with another, clarifying epithet: e.g. Laurenberg's *Graecia antiqua* (1660) was translated as *Description exacte et curieuse de l'ancienne et nouvelle Grèce* (1677).

widespread fantasy in the culture of curiosities and was also sustained in antiquarian writing by the constant switching from subjects (antiquaries, their readers) to objects (ancient artefacts, antiquarian treatises) as the referents of 'curious' and 'curiosity'.[267]

Not all books within the culture of curiosities looked the same. Whereas many represented their curious fragments typographically as relatively brief, discontinuous chunks of prose,[268] others were continuous treatises, especially ones which emphasized the 'diligence' or 'accuracy' in curiosity. Antiquarian works were mostly of the latter kind,[269] like naturalist monographs written by members of the 'Academy of those curious about nature'. Some sought to have it both ways, to make their work curious in the sense of both 'accurate' *and* 'fragmentary'. For example, the town physician Christian Franz Paullini, whose curious publications included both 'thorough' academy monographs and 'fragmentary' popularizing miscellanies, also compiled a directory of antiquarian information about German districts, the title of which—*Gaeographia curiosa*—both connoted its division into alphabetically ordered entries (mostly just a few lines long) and also denoted the fact that it had been collected with 'curâ' (and so was reliable): 'I am calling this *Geography* 'curious' because those [districts] have been collected with matchless thoroughness [*cura*] and application from ancient writers and registers.'[270] Paullini also stated that he had adopted alphabetical order to stop his 'curiositas' degenerating into the vice of disorder ()(3ʳ): even in 1699, the ghost of aimless erudition had not been entirely expelled from praiseworthy antiquarian curiosity.

So keen were some antiquaries to stress their affinities with new natural philosophy that they even sometimes inserted themselves and it into a single narrative of progress. Spon compared recent 'discoveries in the . . . land of antiquity' to 'new inventions' in physics (weighing air, measuring heat), medicine (the circulation of the blood), jurisprudence (new codes and laws), and so on;[271] his own antiquarian research was thus contributing to the general 'advance-

---

[267] e.g. Bouteroue 1666, a iiᵛ, e iiiʳ; Spon 1683, [a4ᵛ], e[1]ᵛ, e2ʳ, e2ᵛ, 1, 2, 299, 300.
[268] See 3.4.2–3, 3.4.9.
[269] e.g. Spon's *Recherches curieuses d'antiquité* contained 31 *dissertations* by himself and friends.
[270] '[*Gaeographiam* ajo . . .] eamque *curiosam*, quòd singulari, curâ studioque istos è . . . Scriptoribus tabulisque antiquis collectos' (C. F. Paullini 1699, [)(2ᵛ]).
[271] 'nouvelles inventions' (Spon 1683, [a4ʳ⁻ᵛ]).

ment of learning'.[272] Antiquaries were thus staking claims to Baconian rhetoric, presenting their knowledge not only as progress-oriented but also as 'useful' and 'necessary',[273] thus seeking to make those epithets compatible with 'curious', as did many a naturalist. The lack of total compatibility was still apparent from Spon's distinction between his antiquarian 'curiosité' (crammed into the odd spare minute) and his 'more essential studies' (medicine), which continues the centuries-old 'supplementary' connotation of curiosity.[274]

Spon was at this point writing not a collection but a narrative, describing not the periods which antiquaries studied but the antiquaries' own progress through time into a more knowledgeable future. However, Spon's narrative of progress did not involve curiosity. Whereas proponents of naturalist discoveries, especially in the eighteenth century, increasingly did attribute (what they saw as) progress to human curiosity, antiquarians seem not to have done so. Even when, for a finite period (especially the late seventeenth century), they were able to hitch themselves to the progress bandwagon, they seem not to have described that progress as the unfurling of curiosity. In antiquarianism, curiosity was used primarily to shape knowledge as curious fragments which gratified curious antiquaries but did not quite add up to a whole.

3.4.7   Travel

In the mid-seventeenth century, travel-writing as well as antiquarianism was being structured increasingly as a collection of curious fragments. Yet this curiosity-collecting tendency was never ubiquitous in travel-writing, any more than it was in naturalist discourse. For example, it was not prominent in the most famous German travelogue, by Adam Olearius (1647 and 1656), although that work was eventually dressed up in translation as *Most Curious Voyages*.[275] Moreover, although the centuries-old condemnation of curiosity as a vice had now become less prominent in travel-writing and even in the odd pilgrimage manual (2.3.1 above), nonetheless it was still considerably more prominent than in, say, antiquarianism. It was still not

---

[272] 'l'avancement des belles Lettres' ([a4ᵛ]).
[273] 'utile . . . necessaire' ([a4ᵛ]–e[1]ʳ).
[274] 'mes plus essentielles études' (e[1]ᵛ–e2ʳ).
[275] Olearius, *Voyages très-curieux*, 1727.

always self-evident that the curiosity of travellers was good, so some writers defensively disentangled good from bad curiosity.[276] Or else they pointedly omitted curiosity from the catalogue of travel-associated vices but still stressed that it was on probation, acceptable only insofar as it was directed at 'useful knowledge'.[277] The agonized early modern attempt to make curiosity 'useful' characterized this language-game as well as several others.

Nonetheless, the greatly increased popularity which travel genres enjoyed in this period[278] coincided with a large-scale injection of the language of curiosity into them. Most travel accounts drew on both of the discursive tendencies that I have identified: they both narrated the writer's progress through various places and also collected information about those places. Curiosity was used within both tendencies: on the one hand, it was occasionally described as driving travellers on through time and from place to place or else as driving readers to follow the travel narrative;[279] on the other hand, more usually it denoted the collecting of material or of discursive objects of knowledge, by both traveller and reader, at this or that place. Indeed, curiosity was a crucial bridge that linked the narrating and collecting tendencies.

However, it was collecting more than narrating that curiosity fostered in travel-writing. Most travel accounts were not only narratives but also lists, catalogues, or inventories: 'curiosity' denoted inventory more than narrative. A similar point has been made by Barbara Benedict in relation to the overall structure of printed collections of travel accounts, except that she argues that they suppress narrative more generally: 'each collection erases narrative coherence

---

[276] e.g. Biron 1703, pp. xx–xxi. See Bepler 1988, 25–6.

[277] 'la curiosité . . . les connoissances utiles' (Du Soucy 1650, 'L'art de voyager utilement', 22). As late as 1770, even the ethnographer Guillaume Raynal condemned as immoral the 'curiosité' of travellers (Van der Cruysse 1986, 14–15).

[278] See Bepler 1988, 31–40. Dew (1999, 105–12) shows that reading travel accounts became fashionable in France especially from the 1660s. The curiosity-collecting tendency also became rife in topography, whether exotic (e.g. Daulier Deslandes 1673) or local (e.g. *Curiosités de l'église de Notre-Dame* 1753; Behrens [1703]) and it continued to be so well into the 19th century. Like the curiosities of so many other discourses, topographical ones were sometimes arranged alphabetically (e.g. Crouch 1682).

[279] Travel books often included not just voyage narratives but also representations of the means by which those narratives were communicated, such as letters. This seems designed not just to stress the authenticity of their sources but also—as in cognate discourses such as journalism or naturalist pedagogy—to foreground, *en abysme*, their own readers' curiosity: e.g. Crespel 1742, preface.

by formal disjunctions, yet links its collected contents under the rubric of curiosity' (1990, 65). In my view this is to argue one step too far: narrative *is* often present, but it is not often propelled by the language of curiosity. The predominant association between curiosity and the collecting tendency within travel discourse is one of the factors that created close affinities between that discourse and others within the culture of curiosities, ranging from antiquarianism to journalism.

As practices, collecting and travelling were contiguous not only with antiquarianism, but also with each other: collectors and their agents travelled to find objects (Hüllen 1994, 132–4). On a more figurative level, collecting and travelling functioned as metaphors not only for antiquarianism but also for each other. Many a book which included a travel account was presented primarily as a collection of curiosities and secondarily as a travel narrative, such as Claude Biron's *Curiosities of Nature and Art Brought Back from Two Voyages to the Indies... With an Abridged Account of the Two Voyages* (1703). This work limits curiosity to the collecting and dislocating ('brought back from...') of objects. It also shows that Benedict's thesis about the suppression of narrative holds good for *some* texts, since even the report ('relation') of the voyages in fact consists mostly not in narrative but in a letter to Biron from Le Lorrain de Valmont (an adept of the culture of curiosities) urging Biron to study nature in the 'Orient'.

Yet many other travelogues *did* contain plenty of narrative. Some were presented primarily as narrative and secondarily as collections, but curiosity usually referred to their collecting dimension, that is, to the discrete objects (some of them antiquarian) which were encountered along the way and were 'numbered', that is, *enume*rated, by the author (recalling the literal 'numbering' of curious items in some contemporary periodicals).[280] When the editor, commenting on the traveller's progress, inserted the rubric 'His curiosity' in the margin of such a book, this was less likely to herald a new twist in the linear narrative (leading to happiness or downfall, as in moral fictions) than—in the words of the traveller—yet another 'thing which seemed quite curious to me', such as 'the way in which Christian

---

[280] e.g. Valle, *Les Fameux Voyages... avec un denombrement tres-exact des choses les plus curieuses, et les plus remarquables qu'il a veuës dans la Turquie, l'Egypte, la Palestine, la Perse, et les Indes Orientales* 1665–70, e.g. i. 341; iii. 304–6, 313–14 (and corresponding index entry).

women dress' in Constantinople.[281] To an extent, such books were inventories of these gratifying encounters between curious subjects and objects.

Other travel books, although they still contained much narrative, were presented primarily as collections of curiosities, or even, in an extreme case, as one single curiosity. A work by an Italian Capuchin was translated into German in 1692 as *The Moor Brought to Venice, or: A Curious and True Narration and Description of all the Curiosities and Noteworthy Things Which . . . Father Dionigi Carli Came Across in his Several Years as a Missionary in all Four Parts of the World, Africa, America, Asia, and Europe*. Whereas many a missionary report was more a 'curious description and news' of one particular culture than a narrative of travels from one culture to another,[282] the diverse curiosities which Carli describes ('Beschreibung') are embedded in a 'narration' ('Erzehlung') of his travels, showing that the discursive tendencies of narrating and collecting could be almost fused through curiosity. But it is the single curiosity which Carli actually collected—the Moor 'brought to' Venice from its (his) own home location—that (who) serves as a synecdochic advertisement for the whole work. Carli explains that, whereas 'it is customary' for anyone travelling far abroad 'to collect various curious things', his monastic Rule prevented him from collecting 'any slaves or other countless curiosities', but that he did allow himself to bring 'a Moor from Ethiopia'; this enabled Carli to 'represent and describe bodily to you [the Moor's] morals, customs, and religious observances'.[283] Carli has gone one better than the La Rochelle noble Bernon, who could show not the actual body of the 'commander of the savages' but instead various curiosities that represented him *in absentia*. By bringing back a human curiosity, Carli is claiming to do what parodies of collecting—with their talk of transported virginities—implied to be impossible: to transport immaterial objects, such as morals and customs. The Moor looms large in the presentation of the book: his dis-location and objectifi-

---

'Sa curiosité'; 'Une chose me parust là assez curieuse, qui est la maniere dont s'habillent les femmes Chrestiennes' (Valle 1665–70, i. 15).

[282] e.g. Böving, *Curieuse Beschreibung und Nachricht von den Hottentotten* 1712.

[283] 'er . . . ein und andere curiose Sachen einzusammlen pfleget'; 'keine Sclaven noch andere unzehliche Curiositäten'; 'einen Mohren aus ᴀᴇthiopien'; 'daß ich dir . . . seine Sitten, Gebräuche, und Gottesdienste leibhafftig vorstellen und beschreiben möchte' (Carli 1692,)3($^{r~v}$).

cation are spectacularly represented in an engraving before the title-page (Illustration 3). Yet he does not seem to feature at all in the work itself. He serves above all as a synecdoche not for material curiosities (since Carli claims to have brought back none) but for the many discursive ones which the text brings back to the reader in the form of knowledge. The Moor, this human curiosity, is especially resonant because he reveals the religious and cultural mastery of Western Europe: in the engraving he kneels before a monk.[284] One curious object is here serving as a shorthand for many others as well as for an extended narrative.

The curiosity-collecting tendency often had specifically pedagogical uses in both the discourse and practice of travel. Especially for young males from noble or otherwise wealthy families, the relatively unsystematic encounter with a wide range of curiosities (*naturalia, artificialia*, customs) which the Grand Tour to Italy and elsewhere provided was viewed as an important supplement to—or indeed a partial substitution for—systematic classroom tuition (Bepler 1988, 110–11). Manuals were specifically written for this category of 'curieux' travellers.[285] The 'curiosités' which they encountered had the same pedagogical function as those which some such travellers collected at home; indeed many of those encountered abroad were also housed there in collections.[286] For a young noble, reading a travel book was the pedagogical and epistemological equivalent of reading, say, Pluche's noble-oriented treatise on nature's curiosities (3.4.4.2 above). Travel of this kind, like the practice of collecting and like Pluche's treatise, gave young nobles (and others) prudential training in empirical, first-hand observation,[287] which was deemed important not just for professional naturalists. On the other hand, curiosity does *not* seem to have been a specific stage in the learning process in such pedagogical discourse, as if in some prototypical

---

[284] Like 'commodification', 'sociability', 'social distinction', or 'confessionalization', 'mastery' is an approximate, generalizing, and inevitably distorting modern label for one common use to which curiosity was put in discourse. While the drive to master other cultures has been studied in relation to the discourses of travel (e.g. Neuber 1991 for German representations of America) and collecting (e.g. Shelton 1994, esp. 189–203), its specific relation to the language of curiosity merits a detailed study, perhaps akin to Greenblatt's study of the role of mastery in representations of the 'wonders' of the 'New World' (1992).

[285] e.g. Du Soucy 1650, 'L'Art de voyager utilement', 2.

[286] Ibid., 24.

[287] See Bepler 1988, 351.

ILLUS. 3. Carli, *Der nach Venedig überbrachte Mohr* (1692).

Bildungsroman narrative. It was a collection of discrete encounters with objects, not a phase of a narrative.

Those discrete encounters were often voluble: curiosity was used in order to produce recyclable discourse. Travelling and reading about travel were widely considered to train noble or wealthy young men in conversation. They were to converse with the foreigners they visited, with their travelling tutor—whose ability to show and properly discuss curiosities and other sights had to be carefully vetted[288]— and also with people back home in salons and courts after their return, since travel was to provide life-long material to dine out on. Given the cultural prestige which was now attached to travel-talk, some non-travellers were determined that their omission from the practice of travel should not also omit them from its discourse. At least one fantasy travel game was explicitly designed to give those courtiers and officials whose duties kept them at home 'an understanding of the most curious things to be found in all the world's states, lands, and seas', that is, 'all that a gentleman needs' for conversation.[289] There were several ways for an *honnête homme* to collect 'curious things' for conversation: by travelling, by playing at travelling, by browsing in the library which he had compiled according to the advice of the likes of Ménestrier, or else by reading summaries of branches, such as Bary's epitome of physics. Manuals of travel-talk curiosities may well have had a specific appeal to aristocratic women too, who were largely excluded from the actual practice of the Grand Tour.

Some of these manuals seem so strange to modern eyes that it is difficult to gauge exactly how they were intended to be used. For example, *Le Voyageur curieux qui fait le tour du monde* (1664) is divided into three parts. The first, 'The curious traveller and his conversations', takes the reader on a present-tense journey round the world, starting and finishing in Dieppe. But this is not systematic cosmography: we sail round coastlines and up estuaries—having the cities encountered there described to us—but we do not venture inland. The remaining two parts are presented as 'Conversation material for the curious traveller'. The 'first material' (Part 2) is 'Curious philosophy', consisting in six treatises (on God, each of the four elements, and man). Again unsystematic, these are mostly thematically oriented towards travel, discussing sail-winds under 'air',

---

[288] See Du Soucy 1650, 'L'Art de voyager utilement', 23–5.
[289] 'le seul necessaire d'un Gentil-homme' (Jaugeon 1684, title-page and [a iv^r]).

Mexican volcanoes under 'fire'—without however being practical travel tips. Last comes 'Curious history' (Part 3), which includes brief historical narratives, heraldic information, and *exempla* from around the world (grouped under moral headings).[290] Unsystematic again, Part 3 could hardly serve as a historical guide to places to be visited.

It seems very unlikely that this handsomely printed quarto book of 784 pages was designed for travellers' luggage—in contrast to books such as Huguetan and Spon's 1681 duodecimo guide to Italy. Yet it is constantly presented as providing things to talk about—curious discursive fragments—along the way. That may indeed have been part of the intent. On the other hand, it may well have served non-travellers too (especially courtly and other aristocratic ones)[291] as a fantasy travel manual which could enable them to converse about travel-related matters or indeed about other topics, since travel is here also being used as a metaphorical framework for the collection of unsystematic, conversation-oriented learning—philosophical and historical as well as cosmographical—of the kind that was widely fostered within the culture of curiosities. Moreover, as in some antiquarianism, this distaste for system is fostered by a Christianized scepticism which casts doubt on all human knowledge.[292] The miscellaneous, curious materials of this work are presented not as the fixed truth but as ways of reflecting on truths. The author makes this clear at the start of the philosophical section:

I hope that, among the material given below, where I have *collected* all that is most curious and agreeable in nature, the reader will find not only subjects that are capable of satisfying his curiosity or of giving him some new knowledge, but also something that will help him converse and speak soundly on the most necessary and important truths.

But before proceeding I must advise my reader to reflect on the title of this work and to note the difference between the raw material for a conversation and, on the other hand, a finished conversation or speech. For example, Monsieur Du Chesne composed in many volumes various 'Collected pieces and memoirs' which can aid the history of France,[293] but he did not write a history of France. Similarly, in order to aid conversation, I have *collected*

---

[290] 'Le Voyageur curieux et ses entretiens'; 'Les Matieres d'entretien du voyageur curieux. Premiere Matiere. La Philosophie curieuse'; 'Histoire curieuse'.

[291] The aristocratic-sounding author ('le S' le B.') having already died, the printer dedicated the work to the royal architect Louis Le Vau.

[292] 'La philosophie curieuse', 257–8.

[293] Du Chesne 1609.

together in philosophical French, as I found it and without changing the language, much material written by various authors; but I have not written finished speeches, carefully structured and phrased.[294]

'Curious'—as in 'Le Voyageur curieux', 'Philosophie curieuse', and 'Histoire curieuse'—thus shapes knowledge as a collection of discrete items which is kept in a raw, discontinuous state primarily so that it can be more easily recycled by conversationalists, but also so that it does not make illusory claims to systematic truth. Making knowledge into curious fragments here has both pragmatic and epistemological purposes. Although this work is supposedly about travel, its use of the curiosity-collecting metaphor to shape knowledge brings it close to several other contemporary discourses and genres, such as periodicals (3.4.9 below) or—as the author here points out—antiquarian historiography (3.4.6).

Yet the culture of curiosities was not an entirely homogeneous bloc. Although in some of its discourses curiosity served to commodify knowledge, that use was often contested in travel-related writing. For example, the commodification of some controversial imports—such as tea, chocolate, coffee—could be both criticized and praised almost within the same breath. Spon starts his treatise on coffee by lamenting that, whereas God has put everything that is necessary for life within the environment of each community, nonetheless 'curiosity, or rather man's natural anxiety', combined with 'avarice', drives humans to seek in far-off lands that which 'may be less useful to them'. Yet he then states that we can thank this 'avarice' for coffee, whose 'usefulness' he will now demonstrate in a treatise which, mirroring its object, is 'new and curious': 'avarice . . . has *collected* everywhere rare, new, salutary, and delicious things by *digging*

---

[294] 'J'espere que dans les Matieres suivantes où j'ay recueilly tout ce qu'il y a de plus curieux et de plus agreable dans la Nature, le Lecteur trouvera non seulement des sujets capables de satisfaire sa curiosité, ou de luy donner quelque nouvelle connoissance: mais encor dequoy former des entretiens et des discours solides sur les veritez les plus necessaires et les plus importantes.

Mais avant de passer outre, il faut que j'advertisse mon Lecteur, de faire reflexion sur le Tiltre de cét Ouvrage, et de remarquer qu'il y a une difference entre la Matiere d'un Entretien, et un Entretien ou Discours composé[. P]ar exemple Monsieur du Chesne a fait Imprimer en plusieurs Volumes diverses Pieces ramassées et Memoires, qui peuvent servir à l'Histoire de France; mais il n'a pas fait l'Histoire de France. De mesme j'ay ramassé en François de Philosophe et en mesmes termes plusieurs Matieres de divers Autheurs, telles que je les ay trouvées pour servir à la conversation et à l'entretien; mais je n'ay pas fait des Discours composez et estudiez pour la liaison, ou pour le langage' (*Le Voyageur curieux* 1664, 'La Philosophie curieuse', 258–9).

them up in both of the Indies'.²⁹⁵ Spon's language suggests that he considers coffee and other such objects to be partly equivalent to the other, antiquarian curiosities to which he devoted so much time. The persistence of 'superfluous' and 'anxious' (as in *cura*) as negative connotations of curiosity are what still prevents it and 'avarice' from being more straightforwardly rechannelled, Enlightenment-style, for good commercial ends.

The continuing substratum of suspicion about the morality of travellers' curiosity was partly also a perception that some of them were just out to enrich themselves, by collecting exotic curiosities for their own private enjoyment and self-distinction, like some other collectors (such as bibliomaniacs). To counter this perception, some travel writers presented themselves as donating to the public the value of the 'curiosities of nature and art' which they brought back or described: this value resided in 'the use which men can gain from them for their health and life'.²⁹⁶ Even where 'usefulness' was not especially emphasized, the producers of curious travel books felt obliged to dissociate them from private, material collections and the display of personal wealth. Carli did this by citing his Capuchin Rule, which he interpreted as forbidding the purchase of numerous curiosities but not the bringing back of one single curiosity (the Moor) in order to educate others. Often, the ghost of private hoarding was not laid to rest so easily: the editor of a reissue of the vast *Accounts of Diverse Curious Voyages*, initially edited by Melchisedech Thévenot, went out of his way to define Thévenot as 'curious' in the 'member of a community of learning' sense, as opposed to the 'private collector' sense:

It cannot be said that all the delays which he created in order to perfect his work were due to any desire to keep to himself that which was most rare and curious in his possession, since he had a well-known keenness to communicate to the public what he had in his hands. And the vast correspondence

---

²⁹⁵ 'la curiosité, ou plutôt l'inquietude naturelle de l'homme'; 'qui leur est peut être moins utile'; 'l'utilité'; 'l'avarice . . . a ramassé par tout des choses rares, des choses nouvelles, des choses salutaires, et des choses delicieuses. Elle a foüillé pour cela dans l'une et l'autre Inde' (Spon, *Traitez nouveaux et curieux du café, du thé et du chocolate* 1685, 2–5). The treatise on chocolate is based on the one by Colmenero de Ledesma, an earlier French translation of which had also been presented as 'curieux' and as satisfying the reader's 'curiosité' (Colmenero de Ledesma, *Du chocolate. Discours curieux* 1643, a ii^r).

²⁹⁶ 'des Curiositez de la nature, et de l'art'; 'l'utilité, que les hommes en peuvent tirer, pour la santé, et pour la vie' (Biron 1703, pp. xxi–xxii).

which he maintained in order to obtain his extraordinary material with a view to publishing it clears him of that jealous possessiveness which is only too common among the curious.[297]

The famous case of Thévenot—who indeed had a vast personal collection of books as well as being involved in projects to disseminate knowledge (such as this edition or his informal academy)[298]—illustrates the 'private'/'public' ambiguity of 'curious' and the anxious need to distentangle those two semantic strands in certain speech acts. The disentanglement was always compromised: curiosities, allegedly freely given to the public, were in fact being sold, in the form of the printed travelogue, a genre subject to a variety of marketing strategies (Neuber 1991, 224–75), one of which was to advertise them as 'curious'.

Moreover, even if a traveller's curiosity was established to be free of private, mercenary aims, it was still inseparable from his financial status: indeed, paradoxically, the wealth of a curious traveller was sometimes judged to be the pre-condition for his lack of selfishly commercial motives. This lack removed obstacles from his travelling path. The Roman nobleman Pietro della Valle, for example, 'was no less rich than he was curious; making friends everywhere through his liberality, he had routes opened to him which had perpetually been closed to poor or greedy travellers'. Unlike Jason, Ulysses, and AEneas, he was not motivated by 'interest' of any kind.[299] Presumably, his aristocratic credentials also made his travel testimonies more believable, since they too were unsullied by commercial 'interest', like the observations of English experimentalists who were gentlemen (Shapin 1994). A century or so later, at least in late eighteenth-century British scientific travel writing, the opposition between curiosity and 'interest' had strengthened: curiosity was the

---

[297] 'On ne peut pas dire que tous les retardemens qu'il apportoit à rendre son Ouvrage entierement parfait, vînt d'une envie qu'il eût de conserver pour luy ce qu'il avoit de plus rare et de plus curieux, puisqu'on connoissoit assez le zele qu'il avoit pour faire part au public de ce qui étoit entre ses mains; et les correspondances qu'il entretenoit par tout pour en tirer ce qu'il avoit d'extraordinaire afin de le publier, le justifient assez de cette jalousie qui n'est que trop commune entre les Curieux' (Thévenot (ed.) 1696, i, sig. *[i]ʳ).

[298] On Thévenot, see Dew 1999, ch. 2. On the *Relations* (first published 1663), see Dew 1999, 88, 105–12; on Thévenot's academy, see pp. 95–104.

[299] 'Il n'estoit pas moins riche, que curieux; et se faisant par ses liberalitez des amis par tout, il s'ouvroit facilement des passages éternellement fermez à des Voyageurs, ou pauvres, ou avares'; 'l'interest' (Valle 1665–70, i, sig. a iiʳ).

one motive which (so it was tenuously claimed) could be untainted by commercial, financial, and other exploitation of the lands visited (Thomas 1994, 126–7). Perhaps only now, at least in some travel discourse,[300] did curiosity begin to resemble the modern-looking, 'theoretical curiosity' attributed by Blumenberg to the seventeenth century. These scientific writers were freeing curiosity from its associations not only with commerce but also with 'usefulness' (at least of the narrowly instrumental kind): but they show that the eventual return of curiosity to its pre-seventeenth-century opposition to 'usefulness' did not always necessarily diminish the status of curiosity.

3.4.8 History and news

The historical wonder-tree of notable curiosities[301]

Especially in the late seventeenth and early eighteenth century, curiosity was often used to shape both history and news as a collection of fragments. Whereas discourse on travel was characterized by tension between a spatial and a temporal axis, one might expect discourse on history and news to privilege exclusively a temporal axis. However, they were both often shaped as *spaces* by the curiosity-collecting tendency: as early as 1609, Pierre de L'Estoile called his memoirs 'the store of my curiosities'.[302] Curiosity was one of the rhetorical means by which similar shapes were imparted to items of history (*histoire, Geschichte, Historie*) and to items of news (*Nachricht, nouvelle, Novelle*), as well as to items from other discourses (such as travel or antiquarianism). The distinction between history and news was not absolute: relatively recent events were sometimes called 'newly historical' (*neu-historisch*).[303] Curiosity was used to lend an equivalent structure—that of a collection of frag-

---

[300] On the other hand, late 18th- and 19th-century Romantic travel-writing looked back nostalgically, and controversially, to the culture of curiosities (Leask 2002).

[301] [C. F. Paullini?], *Historischer Wunder-Baum merckwürdiger Curiositäten* 1705*b*.

[302] 'le Magazin de mes Curiosités' (L'Estoile 1880, [226]).

[303] e.g. Dexelius, *Colloquia historica curiosa[.] Das ist Neu-historische curiöse Gesprächs-Lust . . . Denen Liebhabern neu-historischer Curiositäten wohlmeynend ertheilet* 1699 (excerpts from 1697 newspapers); [Fassmann], *Curieuse Nachricht . . . zum bessern Verständniß der neueren Englischen Historie* 1718. C. F. Paullini's 'Historical wonder-tree' had 'old- and new-historical branches' ('alt- und neuen historischen Aesten', 1705*b*, title-page).

ments—not only to the remote and the recent past but also to the past and the future: one almanac—the *Hamburg Calendar of Curiosities*—divided many pages into a printed left-hand column (full of past events) and a blank right-hand one (for future events, to be written in by the reader, aided by astrology).[304]

Not all historiography shaped the past as a collection of curiosities.[305] For example, the mode of historiography that was politically dominant in Louis XIV's France did not do so: history-writing that transmitted moral and political messages (often in favour of the King) via a strong narrative thread, subordinating the role of erudition and documentation, indeed hiding their traces beneath a smooth, uniform rhetorical surface, uninterrupted by heavy citation of sources. This was the kind that Fénelon and Bossuet favoured. They denounced its main rival, which had affinities with antiquarian discourse and *did* often shape the past as a collection of curiosities: history-writing that cited its sources and documents directly, giving far more detail about past events and persons, not subordinating the detail to overarching moral schemata, striving less for eloquence than for erudition, and including many brief, discontinuous, or fragmentary narratives but not any single, over-arching one.[306]

In a letter of 1714 Fénelon tried to persuade the Académie française to promote the eloquent over the antiquarian kind of historiography:

He who is more a scholar than a historian and has more erudition than true genius does not spare his reader a single date, a single superfluous circumstance, a single dry and discrete fact. He follows his own taste without paying heed to the public's. He wants everyone to be as curious as he is about the minutiae at which he directs his insatiable curiosity. By contrast, a sober and discerning historian omits these tiny facts, which do not lead the reader to any important goal. Cut out those facts and you remove nothing from the history. They only interrupt, prolong, and make history that is, so to speak, chopped up into little bits, lacking any living narrative thread. That superstitious precision ought to be left to compilers. What matters most is to introduce the reader to the fundamental things, to make him discover the

---

[304] Halcke [1718], A3ʳ–[D4ʳ].

[305] For surveys of the different kinds of historiography pursued in early modern France, see Chézodeau 1997; Mellot 1998, 553–9.

[306] For an overview of the early modern—and modern—tension between documentary and narrative historiography, see Grafton 1997.

connections between them, and to waste no time in getting him to the dénouement.[307]

The curiosity of the pedantic antiquarian scholar takes the form of collecting minutiae—that is, fragments that will never be integrated into a polished whole. However, Fénelon is not here condemning all curiosity, but only curiosity *qua* collecting;[308] by contrast, he celebrates curiosity *qua* narrating. A little further on, he adds that good history-writing should have a strong *dispositio* or linear structure, like that of an epic poem, since Homer's chosen 'order constantly excites the reader's curiosity'.[309] Fénelon is concerned to make curiosity the motor of a narrative rather than the collecting of particulars. To some extent, this historiographical dispute took the form of a battle between the narrating and collecting tendencies of curiosity.

The terms used by Fénelon suggest that the role played by curiosity in shaping and sifting knowledge in this historiographical context was broadly similar to that which it played in some religious and naturalist discourse. First, the terms in which he condemns here the curiosity-collecting tendency recall his own pastoral condemnations of curiosity as an archbishop, for whom it is also a diversion from essentials, that is, from God (2.2.4.3 above). Secondly, his condemnation of erudite historical curiosity exploits negatively the same 'thorough, accurate' sense (derived from *cura*) that was used so positively by many contemporary naturalists. Moreover, his condemnation of the curiosity-collecting tendency to the Académie française closely echoes the celebration of that tendency by Fontenelle, twelve years earlier, on behalf of that institution's naturalist counterpart,

---

[307] 'L'homme qui est plus savant qu'il n'est historien, et qui a plus de critique, que de vrai génie, n'épargne à son lecteur aucune date, aucune circonstance superflue, aucun fait sec et détaché. Il suit son goût, sans consulter celui du public. Il veut que tout le monde soit aussi curieux que lui des minuties vers lesquelles il tourne son insatiable curiosité. Au contraire, un historien sobre et discret laisse tomber les menus faits qui ne mènent le lecteur à aucun but important. Retranchez ces faits, vous n'ôtez rien à l'histoire. Ils ne font qu'interrompre, qu'allonger, que faire une histoire pour ainsi dire hachée en petits morceaux, et sans aucun fil de vive narration. Il faut laisser cette superstitieuse exactitude aux compilateurs. Le grand point est de mettre d'abord le lecteur dans le fond des choses, de lui en découvrir les liaisons, et de se hâter de le faire arriver au dénouement' (Fénelon 1983–97, ii. 1178–9; first published 1716).

[308] Here I differ from the excellent account of these historiographical disputes given in relation to Pierre Bayle by Labrousse (1968, 62–70), who associates 'curiosité' wholly with mindless compilation, opposing it to critical historical analysis.

[309] 'un ordre qui excite sans cesse la curiosité du lecteur' (1196).

the Académie des sciences (3.2 above): whereas Fénelon rejects chop-
ping history into 'petits morceaux', into 'fait[s] sec[s] et détaché[s]',
Fontenelle had enthused that the Académie des Sciences offered
naturalist knowledge as 'morceaux détachés'; whereas Fénelon
advocates narrative history which makes 'liaisons' between events,
Fontenelle had accepted that there was 'nul rapport' between the
discrete pieces but that they might one day be joined together ('l'on
joindra'). To some extent, these two famous voices were reflecting
epistemological differences between discourses on nature and history in early eighteenth-century France: on the whole, it seemed
more possible to write a narrative about history (complete with
'dénouement') than to write the 'well-contrived romance' of nature
which Boyle tentatively imagined. But both discursive tendencies—
collecting and narrating—were present in writing about both history
and nature, as also in work produced under the aegis of both of these
French academies.

The shaping of history as a collection of curiosities, rather than as
a one continuous narrative, occurred in various ways. In other
words, the curiosity-collecting tendency was, precisely, a tendency,
not a fixed and rigid template. Whereas it sometimes made objects of
historical knowledge into 'thorough, accurate' ones—as did antiquarian historians as portrayed by Fénelon[310]—it could also make
them 'selective', as did many publications which suggested that readers liked their history in the form of fragmentary, discontinuous
highlights.[311] Curiosity was employed to shape historical knowledge
in a way that maximized its appeal to *honnêtes gens* and members of
the *galante Welt*. The 'Curiosité' of the *galante Welt* was explicitly
targeted by the private tutor and (later) pastor Johann Gottfried
Gregorii in his *Curious and Learned Historian*, a thousand pages of
'histories' ('Geschichten') in discrete prose segments (averaging three
to four pages each).[312] Gregorii formulates the headings of most of
these histories as questions: history, like nature in the naturalist 'curious questions' genre, has here become a set of answers to discrete

---

[310] For a later example, see *Curiosités historiques* 1759.
[311] Even existing works of prose fiction, as well as existing historical sources, were
sometimes reprocessed in this way. The Lutheran pastor Männling, compiler of historical curiosities, also anthologized the famous romances of Daniel Lohenstein: e.g.
his *Lohensteinus sententiosus* (1710) included stories, speeches, and 'curieuse Sachen'
(Dünnhaupt 1990–3, iv. 2624, 2627).
[312] [Gregorii] 1712,)(3[v],)(5[v]. On Gregorii, see *DBE*.

questions. History is also spatialized here, a set of discrete and small objects set out in synchronic space, rather than a diachronic progression through time: this is implied by Gregorii's description of his histories as precious stones,[313] a topos whose implications were spelt out even more by the French royal confessor and preacher Jacques Lefebvre who, in his *Most Curious Loci [Places] of History*, had 'collected together' famous utterances which 'occupy within history the same position as that occupied within nature by the most precious pearls'.[314]

The criteria governing the selection of these 'selected' historical curiosities recall those used for natural curiosities: the curiosities included in historical anthologies were discursive objects—such as Martin Guerre, or the most expensive diamonds ever[315]—that were deemed especially 'agreeable' (Lefebvre 1689, [2ʳ]), 'exotic',[316] 'extraordinary', or 'wonderful'.[317] Even where the contents were not explicitly called 'curiosities', the epithet 'curious' in the title could be used connotatively to shape history as selected fragments[318] or as extraordinary or unusual cases:[319] for Ménestrier, *'Curious books* include history books, but especially ones on more unusual histories'.[320] Ménestrier was thus using curiosity to find and shape raw material for the *honnête homme*'s conversational répertoire: such material could be culled from history as well as from travel. For some compilers, what defined a historical object of knowledge as a curiosity was precisely its appropriateness for polite conversation: bar-

---

[313] This passage ()(3ʳ⁻ᵛ) is quoted more fully in N. Kenny 1998, 121.

[314] Lefebvre 1689: 'recueillies . . . ramasser' ([2ʳ⁻ᵛ]); 'elles tiennent le même rang dans l'Histoire, que les perles les plus précieuses ont dans la nature' ([3ʳ]).

[315] Respectively: [Gregorii] 1712, 156; [C. F. Paullini?] 1705*b*, no. 32.

[316] e.g. Männling 1738 (first published 1720–1), which includes an 'Indiens Curiositäten-Compendium' (ii. 1–98) alongside more home-grown 'Curiositäten' ([)(4ᵛ]). 'Histories' and 'exotic curiosities' were also combined among the sources for Männling's collection of world 'superstitions', the *Denkwürdige Curiositäten . . . Aus denen curiositatibus exoticis[,] erbaulichen Historien* 1713.

[317] e.g. [Gregorii] 1712; [C. F. Paullini?] 1705*b*.

[318] e.g. at the end of the 17th century the Leipzig publisher Johann Ludwig Gleditsch inaugurated a short-lived 'new fashion for historical calendars' ('neue Mode von Geschichts-Calendern') which were called 'curious' in order to indicate that they devoted just a few lines to each key event of the century (*Curieuser Geschichts-Calender* 1698, A3ʳ). The entries were chronologically ordered but not joined up into narrative. See also Halcke [1718].

[319] e.g. *Die Niederländische Amazone oder Curieuse Lebens-Beschreibung und Helden-Thaten einer gewissen Weibs-Person* 1717; Schäffer 1748 (anti-Catholic).

[320] 'Les Livres Curieux sont tous les livres d'histoire, mais particulierement ceux de certaines Histoires plus recherchées.' (Ménestrier 1704, i. 50).

room bore topics—such as whether the Cremonese invented the *Bratwurst*—therefore did not count as curiosities (Männling 1738,)(4^[r–v]).

In the hands of these compilers, history consisted not of an unfolding narrative but of discrete particulars, which did not have to be ordered chronologically. Some compilers arranged them in the alphabetical order that was now popular 'in this kind of writing',[321] as it was in other discourses within the culture of curiosities. Like antiquities in antiquarian discourse, the discrete particulars could be quantified and counted, enabling writers to assure readers that they were getting their money's worth, as did Gregorii when pointing out that the histories in his book numbered over three hundred (1712,)(3^v), which indeed outdid the mere two hundred offered by C. F. Paullini (1705*b*). Each of the two hundred had a number attached to it: Paullini thus presented history as a sequence of numbers, though not of years. Even in systematic treatments of a single historical topic—such as the evangelical martyr Peter of Dresden— the title *Curious Thoughts* indicated that the work was divided into a sequence of reader-friendly, numbered paragraphs, many only a few lines long (J. Thomasius 1702).

If one purpose of making history into a collection of curiosities was to fuel conversation, another was to provide imaginary access— through reading—to other times and places. This purpose was certainly not ubiquitous. But it was occasionally explicitly avowed, suggesting that, although Pomian's anthropological thesis that curiosities gave people access to invisible worlds does not describe historiographical compilations precisely, any more than it does the material collections to which Pomian applied his thesis (since the concept of 'invisible worlds' is largely a modern one), nonetheless, when used as a heuristic tool, this thesis does help reveal an illocutionary purpose of some of those early modern works which made history into curiosities. Some of their contemporary detractors certainly identified that as the purpose: Bossuet thought that the 'curiosité' which 'stretches to the most distant past eras' is dangerous precisely because it stimulates not just the memory but also the imagination, taking the mind to other times, which in fact it vividly represents as places:

---

[321] 'in dieser Art von Schriften' (Männling 1738,)(3^r). The 1st edition of this work was entitled *Curiositäten-Alphabeth* (1720–1).

One is transported mentally inside the courts of ancient kings, inside the secrets of ancient peoples. One imagines oneself joining in the deliberations of the Roman senate . . . If this is in order to draw out some example that is useful to human life, then fine . . . But if it is to feed the imagination on these vain objects—as can be observed with most of the curious—then what is more useless than to dwell so much on that which is no more . . . ?[322]

Mental time-travel is here closely analogous to physical travel, since the mental kind too ends up in specific places, which the imagination presumably makes the reader experience in an illusory present.

Some works of history which called themselves, their readers, and their objects 'curious' do seem to have used curiosity to try and provide their readers with this kind of imaginary transport. As Malina Stefanovska has shown, even the *Mémoires* of Saint-Simon, mainly composed from 1740 to 1750, were close to the genre of collections of historical curiosities, offering the reader unsystematic glimpses of the court, privileging—like antiquarian history—the singular event and eschewing the epideictic narratives of official royal historiography. This interpretation is all the more persuasive because Saint-Simon uses the 'curiosity' family as a constant label for the events, protagonists, readers, and for the historian himself. Writing historical curiosities here involves resisting not just a systematic epistemology but also a political system: absolutism.[323]

Saint-Simon's curious reader was granted access to a place that was, usually and literally, inaccessible to him or her. Or, to extend Niceron's phrase beyond its intended scope of reference: Saint-Simon created a 'curious perspective', opening up an extraordinary visual field that was not accessible in ordinary conditions. Indeed, in some history-writing, curiosity connoted less the fragmentation of history into collectable objects than this extraordinary access to an otherwise inaccessible place or time. For example, many a 'dialogue in the realm of the dead' was marketed as 'curious' in Germany, espe-

---

[322] 'Cette curiosité s'étend aux siècles passez les plus éloignez . . . On se transporte en esprit dans les cours des anciens rois, dans les secretz des anciens peuples. On s'imagine entrer dans les deliberations du senat Romain . . . Si c'est pour en tirer quelque exemple utile [à] la vie humaine, [à] la bonne heure! . . . Mais si c'est, comme on le remarque dans la pluspart des curieux, pour se repaistre l'imagination de ces vains objets, qui a[-]t[-]il de plus inutile que de se tant arrester [à] ce qui n'est plus' (Bossuet 1930*a*, 24–5).

[323] Stefanovska 1999. The impact of absolutism on the construction of private secrets—of monarchs and subjects—at which curiosity was often directed has been analysed by Merlin (1998, 128–33).

cially between 1719 and 1732 (2.3.2 above): these present-tense, imaginary conversations between pairs of protagonists, many of whom were only recently dead, combined history with fiction, making overt the role of the writer's and reader's imagination in staging the conversation.

Curiosity also connoted imaginary historical reconstructions in another genre that overtly mixed history with fiction: books on present and recent European courtiers which claimed to lay bare their 'secrets' (their term, as well as Bossuet's), sometimes again in a spirit of political opposition, since, especially under absolutism, acquiescence or resistance to political authority was largely channelled through the verdicts of public opinion on any given ruling figure (Gunn 1995, chs. 1–2). Some of these books used crude allegory to dramatize these courts' switch of 'curious perspective' from inaccessibility to accessibility: dialogues between talking animals were published as *Curious Conversations Touching Upon the Most Secret Affairs of Several European Courts*, at the end of which a key revealed the identities of the interlocutors (the Emperor, Spain, 'the Turk', and so on).[324] No key was needed by many of the thousands of readers of Christian Friedrich Hunold's allegorical romance of 1705, which recounted scandals perpetrated by lightly anagrammatized protagonists over the previous fifty years—his *Amorous and Heroic History of the European Courts, Published to Satisfy the Curiosity of the 'galante Welt'*.[325] (As so often, 'Curiosité' and 'galanten' stand out on the title-page, emblazoned in non-Gothic type: Illustration 1). Here the reader's curiosity is not held back by even a whiff of 'utility': it is all pleasure. The titillation resides not just in the scandals themselves but in the fact that to reveal them thus is allegedly 'as dangerous as it is curious'.[326] Curiosity here has a cluster of connotations—'secret', 'forbidden',[327] 'previously unpublished', 'pleasurable'—all of which culminate in 'sex', perhaps the most effective marketing connotation of all. Curiosity was helping to sell these books by connoting 'sex'. Although 'curious' did not *always* primarily connote 'sex' in the genre of court secrets,[328] it did so

---

[324] *Entretiens curieux* 1674, [249].

[325] Hunold 1978. It was printed at least 9 times up till 1744 (i. 10*).

[326] 'so gefährlich als curieus' (i, sig.)(2ᵛ).

[327] 'eine . . . verbotene Sache' (i, sig.)(2ʳ).

[328] e.g. in the 'very curious letters' allegedly written by Mazarin to Louis XIV the king's love life is just one of many topics, and the titillation level remains low (*Lettres du Cardinal Mazarin . . . Avec d'autres lettres tres-curieuses* 1690).

increasingly, as it did also in more overtly fictional works or even in the odd medical treatise,[329] becoming in the eighteenth century a prime *de*notation (N. Kenny 1998, 167–8). The fantasy of the 'satisfaction' (Hunold's term) of curiosity which was so widespread in the culture of curiosities, almost invariably in works written by men, here became a male sexual fantasy, often all the more titillating because directed at female protagonists who had the names of real historical figures and so could be imagined really to have done this or that (just as the addition of scholarly apparatus to eighteenth-century pornographic novels about royalty presumably enhanced titillation (Grafton 1997, 111)). A *Collection of Some Curious Pieces Which Help Clarify the History of the Life of Queen Christine* (of Sweden) ended with the words: 'These truths have been communicated to you only to satisfy curiosity'.[330] Scenes of promiscuity did not make up the whole work, but they may have been its prime selling point. Curiosity was equated even more strongly with 'sex' by 1734, when a bibliography described another 'history' devoted entirely to Christine's love life as 'Curious; but not everything was included'.[331]

Two or three decades into the eighteenth century, curiosity was being used more and more to sell pornography but less and less to sell other books on history. Certainly, some historical miscellanies continued to be billed as curiosities but others were abandoning the label, like some how-to or naturalist books. Männling's historical *Alphabet of Curiosities* (1720–1) dropped the term from its title when reissued in 1738. Curiosity was losing its power to market history. Some history continued to be written as fragments, but now less as a metaphorical collection of curiosities.

Whereas history could be written in either systematic or fragmentary form, news lent itself even more specifically to presentation in the form of fragments. In France and Germany it was therefore presented even more often as a metaphorical collection of curious objects, again especially in the late seventeenth and early eighteenth

---

[329] For an early example, see Ferrand, *De la maladie d'amour . . . Discours curieux* 1623 (First published under a different title in 1612).

[330] 'ce n'est que pour satisfaire [à] une curiosité, qu'on vous fait part de ces veritez' (*Recueil de quelques pieces curieuses* 1668, 166). For a less salacious example, on Louis XIV's mistress, see *La Vie de la duchesse de la Valiere où l'on voit une relation curieuse de ses amours* 1695.

[331] 'Curieux; mais on n'a pas tout mis' ([Lenglet-Dufresnoy] 1734, ii. 121).

century, but beginning (at least in France) from about the 1630s. Again, printed news had pre-existed this metaphor, which was never applied to *all* news, even in its heyday: the news and its readers were often described not by the 'curiosity' family of terms but by neighbouring ones, especially the 'novelty' family (*nouvelles, Novellae, Novellen, Novitäten, Neuigkeiten, Neugierigkeit, Neugierde*). Indeed, the 'novelty' family was one of the few which shared the capacity of 'curiosity' to denote both objects and subjects of knowledge and so create a fantasy of gratification, of absolute harmony between the two, whereby plentiful 'Neuigkeiten' could satisfy the 'Neugierigkeit' of someone who asks 'was gibts Neues?' (*Der curieuse Kayserliche Staats-Courier* 1741, 2).

However, recent news events, write-ups of them, and their readers, were all often also described as 'curious'. This appellation gave to the news a broadly similar structure to that of other discourses within the culture of curiosities: when Peiresc said in 1633 that he enjoyed discovering 'particularités' and 'curiosités' in printed news-sheets imported from Venice and Amsterdam,[332] he was giving these discrete objects of knowledge a broadly similar structure to that of his beloved antiquities and *naturalia*. Likewise, religious or moral critics of newspapers saw the desire for news of politics and foreign events merely as yet another manifestation of curiosity rather than as a distinct phenomenon. Jansen gave a specifically seventeenth-century update to St Augustine's roll-call of 'curiosité' by adding the desire for news to the patristic list (Jansen 1659, 46–7). Whereas the dominant focus within the culture of curiosities was on curiosity as a quality of *objects*, such critics focused on it as a passion of subjects. Moreover, the moral theologian Johann Franz Buddeus debunked the apparent, gratifying symmetry between curious objects and subjects as being a mere effect of language rather than a real state: he argued that it is because 'curiositas' is directed at whatever delights the intellect and that people label as 'curiosa' the 'new and unusual things' ('nova, insolita') which are its 'object' ('Objectum'), such as the contents of 'newspapers and histories' ('novellarum et historiarum').[333]

Together with many other discursive objects within the culture of curiosities, curious news items acquired their shape from one new

---

[332] Quoted in Feyel 1987, 104.
[333] Buddeus 1719*a*, 216. Fuller version quoted in N. Kenny 1998, 15.

genre in particular: the printed periodical. This genre disseminated knowledge more rapidly and, on the whole, more cheaply than books, more widely than correspondence, in discourses ranging from politics to natural philosophy, and in new shapes—especially the bite-sized chunk—as we saw earlier in the case of popular anthologies that were based on learned journals.[334] There was no global early modern term for the heterogeneous genre of the 'periodical' (Vittu 1994, 106–7), which took more than a century after the invention of printing to emerge, and which can be defined at the most general level (Martens 1968, 16) as a publication that was intended to appear more or less regularly for general sale, possessing a recognizable degree of continuity of external form, and containing a plurality of items, as opposed to the single event to which one-off broadsheets and pamphlets like the French *canard* and *relation* or the German *Zeitung* had often been devoted previously and to which the *Nachricht* or *Bericht* continued to be devoted into the eighteenth century.[335] Nor did entirely consistent labels exist at the time for the various sub-genres of the periodical, such as the ones which I am labelling newspapers (often printed weekly, mainly on political and military news), learned journals (such as the *Journal des sçavans*), and miscellany-periodicals (on heterogeneous topics, from news to wonders of nature and art, but without the sustained moral and satirical perspective of the moral weeklies which became popular in the early German Enlightenment), as opposed to specialist periodicals (devoted to one discipline or profession). The modern German distinction between *Zeitung* (newspaper) and *Zeitschrift* (periodical handling other fields) only became consistent in the late eighteenth century (Lindemann 1969, 131–2). Newspapers were known generically in French as *gazettes*, *avis*, *nouvelles*, *relations*, and in German as *Zeitungen*, *Gazetten*, *Avisen*, *Relationen* and, especially from the late seventeenth century, also as *No[u]vellen* and *Courrier*. They appeared in Germany from the late sixteenth and early seventeenth

---

[334] § 3.4.2 above. See Lindemann 1969, 125; McClellan, 1985, 53.

[335] For *canards*, see Seguin 1964. For general studies of the early modern printed periodical in its various forms, including the newspaper, in France and Germany, see Bellanger *et al.* 1969–76, i. 83–249; Bogel and Blühm 1971–85; Censer 1994; Harris 1996, ch. 3; Kirchner 1958–62, i; Klaits 1976, ch. 3; Lindemann 1969; Popkin 1991; Powell 1988, 64–70; Sgard 1984; Sgard (ed.) 1991; Vittu 1994. The relation of (English) periodicals to curiosity is also studied by Benedict (2001, 93–103), whose approach differs from mine.

century[336] and in France from 1631 with the *Gazette*, though most French-language newspapers were oppositional ones flourishing in places like Holland, especially from the 1680s as Huguenots were being expelled from France (Harris 1996, 53).

French newspapers used curiosity virtually from the outset. In January 1632 Théophraste Renaudot launched the new monthly supplement to his weekly, recently founded *Gazette* and *Nouvelles ordinaires* with the following words: 'Now that even those who are the least curious for news are beginning to demand some, and that those who *were* curious about future things are finding more certainty in past ones, and that the past ones furthest from our own era are acknowledged to belong to us the least.'[337] In other words: the news has replaced divination and antiquarianism. Renaudot is using curiosity to transport readers not to the future or the remote past but to the recent past. This soon became a topos: in a variation on it in 1711, a single-item *Nachricht* was presented as giving the recent past a curious commemorative form so that a *future* community of readers would have access to it: the *Very Curious and Noteworthy News* of the marriage between the Tsar Crown Prince of Russia (Alexei) and the Princess of Braunschweig and Lüneburg (Charlotte Christine Sophie) makes this 'recent' event accessible 'not just to the living, whether they were absent from the actual event or present at it, but also to the *curiose Welt* to come'.[338] The *Nachricht* becomes like a dialogue of the dead in reverse, giving the unborn access to the living instead of giving the living access to the dead: in both cases, 'curious' connotes that switch of 'curious perspective' from one temporal 'world' ('Welt') or 'realm' ('Reich') to another.

So it was partly the relation of news items to time that made them curious. Their curiousness, like their novelty, was therefore a relational, evanescent quality rather than an intrinsic one. It depended partly on their own position *in* time as well as on their giving readers

---

[336] Bogel and Blühm 1971–85, i, p. vii. The 1st German daily newspaper appeared in Leipzig in 1660 (Press 1991, 314).

[337] 'Maintenant que les moins curieux de nouvelles commancent à en demander, que ceux qui l'estoyent des choses à venir trouvent bien plus de certitude aux passées, et que de celles-cy les plus esloignées de nostre siecle sont reconnuës nous appartenir le moins . . .' (*Recueil des gazettes . . . de toute l'année 1632*, 'Relation des nouvelles du monde, receuës tout le mois de janvier 1632', 43).

[338] *Sehr curiose und denckwürdige Nachricht* 1711: 'jüngsthin' (title-page); 'nicht alleine die so wohl ab-als answesend Lebende, sondern auch die nachkommende curiose Welt' (2).

access *to* recent times. An old news item could only be republished if updated with new, additional information which ensured that it stayed curious.[339] Conversely, news items were made into curious discursive objects by their relation not only to time, but also to space. Like material curiosities, they were explicitly used to transport readers mentally to other places and to bring those places to readers' minds. As Jean-Pierre Vittu has pointed out, the reader of a French newspaper in the 1690s worked his or her way through an ordered sequence of places (and also dates), starting with the furthest and ending up in Paris (1994, 140). Indeed, maps or geographical guides were printed specifically to help newspaper readers.[340] Although they might suggest that newspapers therefore gave readers access to a coherent whole world, it seems more likely that they imagined different places as discrete, unintegrated fragments: the places and dates through which the 1690s reader worked were not linked in the text by any single, over-arching narrative; newspapers jumped from one mini-narrative to the next; they were for the 'curiositas' of the person who likes constant change (Buddeus 1719a, 216), that is, discontinuity.

Nonetheless, the language of curiosity and of novelty conveyed the powerful notion that newspapers somehow embodied remote places and brought them to, say, the square kilometre around the Pont Neuf where French ones were sold most densely (Vittu 1994, 141–2) or to the coffee-houses of imperial cities and market towns where German ones were read and discussed.[341] A 1741 pamphlet entitled *The Curious, Imperial, State Courier*, mainly devoted to the forthcoming election and coronation of a new emperor (Charles VII, who was crowned in February 1742), takes the form of a fictional dialogue in a coffee-house of Frankfurt a. Main, where people sit talking and reading when a soldier enters. A merchant, seeing that 'I have before me a member of the Saxon officers' corps', seizes the chance to ask him 'for some news, since we're still waiting every day for the Saxon

---

[339] e.g. a 1711 description (by Johannes Philipp Eysel) of a sighting of osier roses was reprinted with observations from new sightings as a *Curieuse Nachricht von den schon vor vielen Jahren, auch in diesem 1747. Jahre zum Vorschein gekommenen Weyden-Rosen* [1747].

[340] On maps, see Vittu 1994, 141. For a guide, see Weise 1703, 421–90.

[341] See Bepler 1988, 219; Frühsorge 1974, 200–1. Obsession with news is one of the satirical targets of Sinold von Schütz (author of numerous devotional works) in his *Curieuse Caffe-Hauß zu Venedig* (1698), a precursor of the moral weeklies (Frühsorge 1974, 199–200).

newspapers to arrive'. The soldier duly obliges, with the wooden pre-
amble: 'The news from Saxony will be, so far as I'm aware, as follows
. . .'³⁴² Thus the pamphlet fictionally embodies its news in the transported soldier: as in many discourses in the culture of curiosities, a
fictional frame both emphasizes the gratifying symmetry between
desire and its objects and also authorizes knowledge, making it seem
to come from the horse's mouth.³⁴³ Although the language of 'novelty' has by this point largely displaced that of curiosity, the soldier
has a similar epistemological function to that of human curiosities in
the discourses of travel and collecting, such as the transported Moor
(3.4.7) or even the imaginary 'commander of the savages' (3.4.5): all
were supposed to embody an unfamiliar place and bring it to a familiar one.

The uses of curiosity in relation to the news were not stable or
fixed: rather, they were constantly contested. Proponents and opponents of the newspaper often used curiosity respectively to legitimize
or condemn this controversial new genre.³⁴⁴ As with, for example,
travel or the occult sciences, the moral reversibility of curiosity made
it a key lexical site for polemic, with each camp seeking to impose
their own understanding of curiosity on the opposing one. When
Renaudot tried to impose his, in the 1630s, such boldly positive definitions of curiosity were still precarious, and not yet reinforced by
the welter of object-oriented applications of the term to newspapers
which later took hold.³⁴⁵ Negative definitions such as that of Bishop
Jansen were probably still, if anything, more familiar to many
readers, which may have ensured that claims to satisfy curiosity were
all the more effective as marketing ploys, since they surrounded
newspapers with an aura of the forbidden, as they did even more
in discourses on court secrets or occult sciences.

Decorum-based understandings of curiosity were used both to
condemn and to legitimize newspapers. Critics of the newspaper

---

³⁴² 'da ich doch . . . einen Officier vom Sächsischen Corps vor mir habe'; 'etwas
Neues fragen, da man doch alle Tage Zeitungen aus Sachsen erwartet'; 'Die besondere
Neuigkeiten aus Sachsen werden, so viel mir bewust, folgende seyn' (*Der curieuse
kayserliche Staats-Courier* 1741, 2).
³⁴³ Curious collections of news were often in dialogue form (e.g. Dexelius 1699;
Le Mercure voyageur 1693).
³⁴⁴ On German polemic about the newspaper, see Hagelweide in Stieler 1969,
pp. xii–xiii; Locher 1990, 63–119. Neither study focuses on the language of curiosity.
³⁴⁵ Renaudot's early editorial statements (1631–3) use 'curiosity' only in a subject-
oriented sense.

genre argued that it made politically sensitive information available to too broad a readership.[346] Like church and university critics of other kinds of contemporary curiosity, these critics emphasized the centuries-old understanding of curiosity as *polypragmosyne*, as transgression of decorum, as interference in what does not concern us, given our estate or profession. Jansen (as translated into French) argued that, for people who are not in government, nothing can justify 'curiosité' for 'nouvelles' about what is happening 'outside our country, whether on land or at sea'.[347] He and others were drawing on the traditional interdict against delving into the secrets of rulers (*arcana imperii*), which had long been formulated as an interdict against *curiositas*.[348]

Decorum-based curiosity was also used to legitimize newspapers. Most defenders of newspapers did not reject decorum; they did not argue—as modern journalists might—that almost all citizens should have the right to almost all information. Rather, they claimed that newspapers respected decorum by communicating different information to different groups, depending on what they needed to know given their role in life: only boys and maids ought to be excluded, according to Kaspar Stieler (1695), who wrote of 'Neugi[e]rigkeit' rather than of *Curiosität*.[349] Some went so far as to describe legitimate, decorous inquiry as curiosity, thereby reversing its long-standing denotation of indecorous inquiry. One to do so was the pedagogue and *galant* theorist Christian Weise, not in any spirit of political opposition but because he considered newspapers to be an important tool with which to train students and professions of all kinds for their social duties: whereas 'state servants and courtiers' have the benefit of correspondence that tells them what is happening in the world, 'the majority of curious people have to use newspapers'. The latter were an unsystematic source of education, akin to travel. Weise's language of curiosity connotatively presented knowledge in newspapers as fragmented, new, attractive, and indeed useful, for instance when he outlined 'the use of newspapers for all kinds of curiosities' (such as theology, law, medicine, trade, the military arts). His chapter on the use of newspapers in political education is a careful balancing act, first reasserting that some *arcana imperii*

---

[346] Solomon 1972, 153–4; Vittu 1994, 105.
[347] 'au dehors de nostre païs, sur la terre ou sur la mer' (Jansen 1659, 46).
[348] See Kenny 2000*b*, 291, 300.
[349] Stieler 1969, p. xvi. See also Locher 1990, 69–70.

are out of bounds and then conditionally defending 'political curiosity', which can learn from newspapers 'what is most curious and useful in politics' on controversial topics such as the laws governing rulers (and their prerogatives and inheritances).[350] Weise was using curiosity to legitimize the transmission of knowledge by newspapers to their growing urban readership, composed of merchants, financiers, clerics, magistrates, students, or scholars from diverse social backgrounds.[351] Promoters of the new genre sought to establish its respectability by listing the instrumental uses that it had for different groups.

Not everyone who used curiosity to defend newspapers did so in the same way as Weise. Others were happier than the Zittau pedagogue to accept that, in order to be legitimate, curiosity did not always have to involve instrumental utility. They made curiosity rather fuzzy, sometimes encompassing all reading of newspapers but at other times encompassing only that kind of reading which sought 'satisfaction' rather than utility.[352] It would have been too controversial to identify pleasure as the aim of such reading that went beyond the bound of what one needed to know for utilitarian purposes. But it was sometimes acceptable to call such reading curiosity, which was therefore crucial to the effort made by some early modern newspapers to make it respectable to want to know certain things that exceeded the bounds of what decorum decreed that one needed to know.

For example, Paul Marperger—cameralist, economist, and member of the Prussian Academy—mainly emphasized the uses that newspapers had for specific groups: artisans, householders, clerics, historians, genealogists, physicians, merchants, generals ([1730?], 24–31). But his list also includes 'Curiosi'. This category is anomalous in this list because it is not defined by any particular rank or profession: indeed 'a curious newspaper-reader' is one who 'only

---

[350] Weise 1703 (first published in Latin in 1685), 'Curieuse Gedancken': 'Staats-Bediente und Hof-Leuthe' ()(4ᵛ); 'Dahero denn die meisten curieusen Leuthe sich der Zeitungen bedienen müssen' ()(5ʳ); 'Von dem Nutzen der Zeitungen in mancherley *Curiositaeten*' (ch. 6); 'politischen Curiositaet' ()( )( )(7ʳ); 'was in der Politique curieux und nützlich ist' ()( )( )( )(3ᵛ).

[351] Vittu 1994, 127–30, 142–4. See also Lindemann 1969, 123–5. Less research seems to have been done on the extent to which newspapers were also read by women.

[352] e.g. Renaudot: 'les curieux, par leur propre contentement' (*Recueil des gazettes … de toute l'année 1632*, 'Relation des nouvelles du monde receuës tout le mois de septembre 1632', 393).

stands out in any place in everyday life because of their rank, office, family, or estate'.[353] These 'Curiosi' have a precise set of reading aims, which Marperger describes in terms of neither profit nor pleasure:

Curiosi note in newspapers the inconstancy of all affairs of the world, the reversals and incidents which occur now and again and which no one had expected, at least not so soon; they note what is reported from this or that place as being new in nature and art, what great . . . people are acting on the great stage of world and state, what new inventions emerge and are put into practice now and then, what phenomena and other unusual things have been experienced and seen, what new books have been printed or are promised as forthcoming, and similarly what is written of noteworthy births, weddings, illnesses and deaths, new foundations, commissions, regulations, and so on.[354]

This body of knowledge may seem random to modern eyes, but it is constituted by distinct criteria: most of it is 'new' and 'unusual' (the two qualities singled out in Buddeus's attack on such curious knowledge); moreover, it is described in terms of discrete fragments (incidents, people, inventions, phenomena, books, births, laws), all of which are time-bound: that is, they have specific dates attached to them. However, while the knowledge enumerated here has this degree of internal coherence, it is also quite simply what tended to be lumped together in newspapers (and also miscellany-periodicals): Marperger, like newspapers themselves, is partly projecting the knowledge supplied by newspapers onto a new kind of reader, as evidence for what that reader's desires must be. Newspapers may have created these 'Curiosi' no less than the demands of the 'Curiosi' created newspapers.

---

[353] 'ein curioser Avisen-Leser (der nur irgends seinem Stande, Amt, Familia und Haußhaltung nach in gemeinen Wesen eine Figur machet)' (29). On Marperger, see Dünnhaupt 1990–3, iv. 2638–72.

[354] 'Curiosi bemercken aus denen Avisen die Unbeständigkeit aller Welt-Händel, die Revolutiones und Vorfälle, welche sich hin und wider ereignen, und worauf so leicht niemand, oder doch nicht, daß es so bald geschehen solte, gedacht hätte; was in Kunst- und Natur-Sachen von diesem oder jenem Ort gemeldet werde; was vor grosse . . . Personen auf dem grossen Welt- und Staats-Theatro agiren; was hin und wieder vor neue Inventa an Tag und in Praxin gekommen; was vor Phaenomena und andere ungewöhnliche Dinge erlebet und gesehen, vor neue Bücher gedruckt, oder doch noch künfftig heraus zu geben versprochen worden: Ingleichen, was von merckwürdigen Geburten, Heyrathen, Kranckheiten und Sterbe-Fällen, neuen Fundationibus, Commissionibus, Constitutionibus etc. geschrieben werde' (29).

'Curiosi' are a problem category, as their anomalous status in Marperger's otherwise rank-, profession-, and utility-based list of categories of readers shows. As so often, 'curious' encompasses both one particular part of a discourse and also the discourse as a whole. On the one hand, 'Curiosi' seem tacked on to the list as an after-thought, corresponding to a small percentage of readers. On the other hand, presumably any of the readers Marperger listed earlier could also belong to the 'Curiosi' category if they are not acting purely *as* merchants, generals, and so on. This is confirmed by his description of one of the prime physical locations for the reception of newspapers:

Later, inside such newspaper-shops, stalls, or kiosks—especially if they are spacious—there gather and converse many curious people from all ranks, learned and unlearned, state officials, merchants, soldiers, foreigners, and locals. There you can enjoy listening to debates about all kinds of state and world affairs, particularly in Holland and in the ports, where free speech is less tricky than elsewhere.[355]

The people in these ephemeral, informal huddles in Hamburg or Amsterdam have just one thing in common—being curious. 'Curious' is here being used to create communities just as it did in the Republic of Letters and among academicians, though here it con-notes 'inclusive' rather than 'exclusive' ones. Marperger, who was himself firmly embedded in structures of princely authority—as mer-cantile counsellor to the court of Saxony—does not develop this into a sustained argument for the right to 'free speech' in the public sphere. Yet, in an embryonic way, his 'curious people' are practising 'free speech' by breaching the repressive decorum which curiosity itself had bolstered for centuries and was still bolstering in, for example, the legal faculties of Brandenburg-Prussia (1.3.4 above). Although Blumenberg's thesis about the legitimation of 'theoretical curiosity' does not accurately reflect much early modern discourse on curiosity, it does here receive a little support.

[355] 'Solche Zeitungs-Buden, Boutiques oder Comptoirs, wann sie zumahl fein geraum seyn, dienen hernach zur Versammlung und Entretien vieler curioser Leute von allerhand Ständen, Gelehrten und Ungelehrten, Staats- Kauff- und Kriegs-Leuten, Fremden und Einheimischen; Wobey mann dann mit Lust das raisonniren über aller-hand Staats- und Welt-Händel, sonderlich in Holland und in denen See-Städten, wo das freyen Reden nicht so verfänglich als anderer Orten ist, anhören kan' (21). Also quoted in Lindemann 1969, 125.

Marperger's 'Curiosi' were not, in his account, consciously practising any political resistance to the regimes that prevented free
speech. However, some did understand curiosity as involving such
resistance, especially in French-language news that was printed outside absolutist France. One of the surveys of international political
news printed in Cologne—*Mercury the Voyager and the Man who is
Curious about Politics, Both Disinterested*—is a dialogue between
the two eponymous protagonists in which the winged messenger,
having just completed his regular three-monthly tour of Europe, now
gives (we are told) a more disinterested account than those he gave
previously (perhaps an allusion to the Parisian *Mercure galant*).[356]
The absence of 'interest' guarantees the truth of what curiosity
reveals (in contrast to later naturalist discourse, where curiosity was
only acceptable if harnessed to 'interest' (3.4.2 above)).

'Curious' also connoted political resistance when used in *object*-
oriented senses in discourse on news. In France this first occurred on
a large scale during the Fronde revolts (1648–53), when 'curious'
figured in the titles of numerous Mazarinades (pamphlets written
against Cardinal Mazarin), such as a *Curious Letter About the Most
Notable Occurrences in Paris since Epiphany*, where it denoted
'rare, excellent' and so on but also—more tellingly for readers—
connoted 'polemical, satirical', that is: 'giving the true story of what
happened' (which was also the sense exploited in the politically
motivated versions of the genre of salacious court secrets).[357] These
object-oriented occurrences do not add up to modern claims that citizens have the right to be curious about the truth of public affairs, but
they are part of the pre-history of those claims.[358]

However, even good curiosity about news was double-edged: it
could be used not only on the side of free speech and political resistance but also on the opposite side, for hegemonic propaganda as
well as for dissent. The church was not the only institution to exploit
occasionally the attractiveness of curiosity from about the 1630s
onwards despite having a long track record of condemning it: the
French government did the same through the *Gazette*. As I have

---

[356] *Le Mercure voyageur* 1693, 'Avis au lecteur'.
[357] *Lettre curieuse sur ce qui s'est passé de plus remarquable* 1649. On the
Mazarinades, see Carrier 1996. On the satirical connotations of curiosity, see 3.5.1
below.
[358] For the notion of pre-history, see Cave 1999.

argued elsewhere,[359] Renaudot's claims to be generously satisfying a France which is 'so curious for news' do not have to be taken wholly at face value.[360] Certainly, it is tempting to explain the rise of the *Gazette* and of other periodicals as responses to growing public curiosity for news (as well as for technological discoveries, and so on). Indeed, Élisabeth Labrousse has argued persuasively that this 'curiosité' was stimulated by the relative scarcity of such information, notably in the French provinces.[361] However, this interpretation still begs the question: why did periodicals, including newspapers, not emerge earlier? After all, it was not as if information had suddenly became even more scarce in France. It was a different story in Germany, where the need for news during the Thirty Years' War led to a steep rise in the production of periodicals, while that of books fell (Engelsing 1973, 42). True, the *Gazette* was read most of all in times of war,[362] and it too had its origins in the Thirty Years' War, since in the months preceding its first appearance (May 1631) Richelieu's attempts to take France into the war were meeting with internal opposition, with both sides printing their declarations in order to give them maximum exposure (Feyel 1987, 103). But the *Gazette*—of which Richelieu very soon secured control, whether or not he actually put Renaudot up to founding it in the first place[363]— provided an even more powerful way of justifying his foreign policy to the public, not of responding to the public's cries for information, although it was politic to dress up the new publication as being such a response. So the public curiosity which the *Gazette* claimed to satisfy was at least partly a construct, an ideological mystification. That is not to say that many readers did not consider themselves to be curious: but, in doing so, they may have been influenced partly by government discourse.

Subsequently, the appropriate objects of such government-sponsored curiosity for news, in France and the Holy Roman

---

[359] The remainder of this paragraph is a compressed version of Kenny 2000*b*, 292–5.

[360] 'la France, si curieuse de nouveautez' (*Recueil des gazettes de l'année 1631*, 3; from the opening sentence of the dedication to Louis XIII of the first annual collection of weekly issues).

[361] Labrousse 1968, 54–9. See also Feyel 1987, 104–5.

[362] Sgard (ed.) 1991, i. 446.

[363] On this question, see Jubert 1981. On the *Gazette*, see Haffemayer 2002; Sgard (ed.) 1991, i. 443–9. On its founding, see Solomon 1972, ch. 4.

Empire, were also shaped as 'curious'.[364] Just as, in the modern world, brainwashing by mass media is the flipside of widespread access to information, so seventeenth-century big government sought control of public curiosity at the moment of the latter's birth. Curiosity about public matters was—to use Blumenberg's term— legitimized, but partly by powerful institutions, in a sleight of hand intended to aid the manipulation of public opinion.

Moreover, this partial legitimation of curiosity served commercial as well as political purposes. Renaudot was an entrepreneur as well as a servant of the crown.[365] The more copies he sold, the more money he made, and the more Richelieu's messages were disseminated. In Germany, whether or not they pursued specific ideological agendas, the majority of founders of periodicals were printers,[366] merchant capitalists for whom this new form often guaranteed a more regular income than the one-off book (Popkin 1991, 209). Periodicals caused a heightened commodification of news (Burke 2000, 168–9), their sales rhetoric of curiosity being one strategy amongst others. While some merchants produced news, other merchants were among its major receivers and users, putting less commercial groups such as students to shame (according to Weise), 'since it is rightly a scandal if [students] are sometimes outdone in the study of this curiosity even at times by merchants, who can justifiably be called custodians of the news.'[367] Although the widespread presentation of the news as curiosities gave it structural affinities within other discourses, the commercial, political, and moral stakes in controlling the news were so high that the battles to control the curiosity generated by it were exceptionally intense.

---

[364] e.g. *Curieuser Bericht* 1706 (reporting the Emperor's ostracization of 2 Electors); [Mayolas] 1669–71 (*mondain* broadsheets, in epideictic prose and verse, containing 'ce qui se passe de plus curieux dans l'Europe' [title-page], i.e. Louis XIV's military successes and events at the French court).

[365] On Renaudot's life, see Solomon 1972.

[366] Hagelweide in Stieler 1969, p. xviii.

[367] 'da es [Studierenden] billig eine Schande seyn muß, wenn sie in dem Studio dieser Curiosité, auch jezuweilen von Kauffleuthen, welche man mit allem Recht Custodes Novellarum nennen kan, übertroffen werden' (Weise 1703,)(4[r–v]).

3.4.9 Miscellany-periodicals and miscellanies

ungrounded curiosity[368]

Newspapers were not the only periodicals that sometimes shaped their knowledge as collections of curiosities. Multidisciplinary periodicals also did so even more emphatically, especially in Germany in the decades when new periodicals were appearing thick and fast.[369] Indeed, by announcing that they contained curiosities, such multidisciplinary periodicals signalled to readers that they were not the kind that specialized in one area, such as recent political and military events (newspapers) or a single discipline. For example, one was called a *Saxon Cabinet of Curiosities, Where One Can Find Notable Items from Political, Ecclesiastical, and Mixed History, from the History of Arts and Learning, as well as from Genealogy, Physics, Estate and Household Management, Mechanics, and Nature.*[370]

Among multidisciplinary periodicals, it was especially ones that appealed explicitly to a less learned readership that shaped their knowledge as a collection of curiosities. Certainly, in relatively learned journals—such as transactions of academies or publications containing news from the Republic of Letters—curiosity was constantly used to shape the subjects and objects of knowledge.[371] However, with the occasional exception—such as the *Miscellanea curiosa* of the 'Academy of those curious about nature'—these more learned journals were not wholly presented as being collections of discursive curiosities.

On the other hand, like books on nature and art, so multidisciplinary periodicals were presented as collections of curiosities especially in order to popularize their knowledge, to appeal—rather like newspapers as described by Marperger—not only to a 'learned', socially 'high' readership but also to an 'unlearned', socially 'low'

---

[368] 'ungegründete Curiosité' ([Huhold] 1716, 12).

[369] In Germany, new, often short-lived periodicals of all kinds were produced at a remarkable rate between 1680 and 1720 (Kirchner 1958–62, i. 37, 39–53).

[370] *Sächsisches Curiositäten-Cabinet* 1731.

[371] On such publications, see Goldgar 1995, ch. 2. Some shaped their knowledge as curious objects to be exchanged between 'friends', cementing sociability: e.g. Tentzel (ed.), *Curieuse Bibliothec, oder Fortsetzung der monatlichen Unterredungen einiger guten Freunde...allen Liebhabern der Curiositäten...heraus gegeben* 1706 (published 1704–6; see Kirchner 1958–62, i. 27–8). The most influential German model for this genre of periodical was the 1688–90 *Monatsgespräche* of Christian Thomasius (Kirchner 1958–62, i. 23–5; Lindemann 1969, 187–91). On sociability and the learned journal, see Goldgar 1995, 59–69.

one, which could not afford many books but could buy Eberhard Werner Happel's four sheets of (German-language) *relationes curiosae* every week.[372] I am labelling these kinds of publication miscellany-periodicals. They broke knowledge down into discrete curiosities partly in order to include readers who were unable or unwilling to understand whole systems (geographical, historical, or philosophical) as opposed to particulars or else to read for hours on end (as opposed to 'a quarter of an hour').[373] The brevity of such curiosities was seized upon by critics of the periodical genre: should a reader attempt volubly to recycle one of these curiosities in conversation, 'If discussion of a matter lasts long, then one is amazed to see and hear how silent the initially voluble man falls'.[374]

Some miscellany-periodicals were quite explicit in calling themselves collections of curiosities. They had titles such as *Curious Cabinet of Foreign and Other Notable Things* (A. Paullini 1717–18) or *A Saxon Cabinet of Curiosities*. Moreover, each volume of the *Saxon Cabinet* was a 'repository'.[375] This miscellany-periodical extended the metaphor from the periodical itself to the topographical space of Saxony, presenting it as a fictional cabinet, a collection of various local curiosities, discursive and material, such as a 'curious description' of the Luther fountain in Wittemberg, the death of a Dresden baron and his 'curious mathematical inventions', or the curious, body-contorting dance of a girl in Grossenhain.[376]

---

[372] Happel 1683–9, i (1683), p. [406]; ii (1684), p. [801]; *Sächsisches Curiositäten-Cabinet* 1731, ii, sig. [2ʳ] ('von Hohen und Niedern, Gelehrten und Ungelehrten'). The distinction between learned and less learned journals was fluid: many learned journals too popularized knowledge, probably reaching not only highly educated men but also women and other moderately educated, non-graduate groups. Indeed, those journals are criticized for this (Goldgar 1995, 54–9, 61–2).

[373] 'eine viertel Stunde Zeit' (Happel 1683–9, i (1683), sig. [ii]ʳ).

[374] 'Bleibt man in Discours bey einer Sache etwas lange bestehen, so wird man mit Verwunderung sehen und hören, wie stille der vorhin beredte Mann werden wird' ([Huhold] 1716, 10–11). Most curiosities in the *Sächsisches Curiositäten-Cabinet* occupied 1–4 pages. When Happel claims that his periodical gives 'a curious description of the whole world, short and to the point' ('eine curieuse Beschreibung der gantzen Welt kurtzbündig') he is playing down the 'thorough' connotation of 'curious description' (which was highlighted in learned monographs by academicians), meaning instead a description which takes the form of discrete, selected highlights (Happel 1683–9, i. [406]).

[375] 'Erstes Repositorium' (*Sächsisches Curiositäten-Cabinet* 1731, p. i, title-page; see also p. i, 'Vorrede').

[376] 'Curieuse Beschreibung' (i. 170), 'curieusen Mathematischen Inventis' (i. 220), 'curieusen Tantz' (ii. 29).

The curious discursive objects contained in these miscellany-periodicals, like the curious material ones in literal cabinets, could be counted. Like alphabetical order, this numbering served to cut off one object from those surrounding it, reducing any discursive continuity between objects, and thereby making knowledge into a quantifiable commodity. Every quarter, Gottfried Zenner's *Spring [Summer, etc.] Parnassus, or Discussion of Forty 'Galant' and Learned Curiosities* offered the same ration: four international news items, eight biographies, six new 'particulars' (on topics such as war, religion, politics, learning, commerce, the arts), eight propositions from a range of disciplines, ten new European curiosities, and four book reviews.[377] Each of these categories became like a place (*locus*) in rhetoric, a fixed pigeonhole awaiting regular refilling with changing material. Such counting also gave knowledge a precise price: divide the price of an issue by forty and you could see exactly how much each curiosity cost. Sometimes the numbers were not so round but still equally precise: the two issues of the 'Saxon cabinet' advertised 86 and 82 curiosities (title-page).

Were these discursive curiosities marketed as useful? Their relation to utility was as fraught and variable as that of naturalist curiosities. A small number of miscellany-periodicals claimed to be useful, such as the *Curious and Useful Observations on Histories of Nature and Art . . . Collected by Johann Kanold* (1728–9), a member of the 'Academy of those curious about nature', but this periodical was called 'curious' mainly to signal that its miscellaneous material was a *supplement* to Kanold's more systematic 'collection' periodical (*Sammlung*, 1718–36). This status as supplements, shared by several other curious periodicals, did not mean that they were unsuccessful. On the contrary, one such supplement was the extremely successful *World's Greatest Notable Things, or Curious Reports* (1683–91) by Happel (continued by others after his death in 1690), which popularized sources such as learned journals, new natural philosophy, and travelogues.[378] Happel was employed by the publisher Thomas Wiering to compile this as a weekly supplement to Wiering's

---

[377] 'Particularitäten . . . Curiositäten' (Zenner 1695, title-page). On another 'curious' Zenner periodical, see Kirchner 1958–62, i. 32. Counting characterized other kinds of periodical too: 'nearly 1,000' news items were offered in Dexelius 1699 ('fast . . . Tausend', title-page).

[378] See Happel 1683–9. On Happel, see Dünnhaupt 1990–3, iii. 1952–68; Kirchner 1958–62, i. 47–8; Wagener 1968.

newspaper, the *Relations-Courier*.[379] Happel's contents are called 'curious' in order to designate them as miscellaneous, thereby distinguishing them from political and military news, which was covered by the *Relations-Courier*. For the ex-student Happel, commodifying knowledge as curiosities (he returns constantly to the term) was a way out of chronic poverty, which had driven him to write prolifically for the likes of Wiering. In this periodical, curiosity was not emphatically harnessed to 'utility'. But that is not to say that curiosity was therefore merely 'recreational',[380] for it was presented in stronger terms, 'to satisfy to some extent many honest Germans in whom the desire to read such curious material is growing powerfully, since they do not have Latin and other foreign languages'.[381] That is not the same as saying it is purely to entertain or to pass the time, which 'curious' could suggest in other genres (3.4.10 below). 'Curious' has an irreducible meaning here (roughly: 'a desire-satisfying, supplementary collection of singularities'), no more synonymous here with 'pleasure' than it was with 'useful' in discourses which sought to harness it to 'usefulness'.

However, those who thought that periodicals should be entirely 'useful' did seek to condemn curiosity by aligning it with pure 'pleasure'. The author (probably Marcus Paul Huhold) of a much reprinted treatise on *The Legitimate Use of Periodicals* argued that it was wrong to read them if one's motive was 'To satisfy one's curiosity and desire for pleasure' ('*Expletio curiositatis voluptatisque*').[382] The pastor Huhold was attempting to wrest periodicals away from the culture of curiosities at the same time as the more utility-oriented moral weeklies were emerging. Yet because *curieus, Curiosität*, and so on now had such positive connotations in much discourse on periodicals, Huhold's treatise—to which it is tempting to give a modern label such as 'early-Enlightenment', implying that it looks forward—in fact has to go back to the centuries-old pejorative association between *curiositas* and *voluptas*, which was still alive and well in

[379] See Happel 1683–9, i (1683), sig. [i]ᵛ. See Prange 1978, 182–4.
[380] *Pace* Powell (1988, 15–18 [18]) on the *Gröste Denckwürdigkeiten*.
[381] 'um dadurch manchen ehrlichen Teutschen, deme in Ermangelung der Lateinischen und anderer frembden Sprachen, die Begierde dergleichen curieusen Materie zu lesen, gewaltig anwächset, einiger massen zu vergnügen' (Happel 1683–9, i (1683), 'Vorrede' by Wiering, sig. [i]ᵛ; also quoted in Prange 1978, 183).
[382] [Huhold] 1716, 1 ('De legitimo usu ephemeridum'), 9. The treatise was printed in 1715 (already as a 2nd edn.?), 1716, 1717, 1718, 1724; Huhold was a pastor in Miedzichod in Poland (Adelung 1784–1897).

church and university discourse.[383] Although writing in German, Huhold even has to resort to the Latin term (and the French term, which here connotes pseudo-sophistication) in order to make clear that he understands curiosity pejoratively, shifting word family to 'Neugierigkeit' (and 'Wollust') when he moves into German (11).[384] Huhold is giving up as a lost cause Weise's attempt to inflect the culture of curiosities in the direction of utility when it came to reading newspapers. According to Huhold, 'inopportune *curiosi*'—whether they are uneducated and hope to use periodicals as a replacement for systematic, 'grounded studies' or else are educated and just want to supplement such studies—are trying to 'build something solid on sandy ground'; such people 'do not apply the hard work required to learn a discipline properly': they know a little about everything but not a lot about anything and so 'cannot be called learned'.[385] The dominance of the curiosity-collecting discursive tendency in periodicals leads Huhold to present himself as a prophetic voice in the wilderness: 'Yet I almost doubt if the grounded proof which I have just given will be accepted at the present time, since people consider such ungrounded *curiosité* to be one characteristic of a noble, virtuous disposition.'[386]

Did the likes of Huhold win their battle? Not if one applies Rolf Engelsing's controversial hypothesis of a bourgeois reading revolution in the second half of the eighteenth century, which saw the widespread displacement of 'intensive' reading and re-reading of a few texts (such as religious ones) by 'extensive', quicker reading of many texts (1974, ch. 12). This generalizing modern hypothesis—like

---

[383] Huhold's treatise, which appeared in Jena, may have derived this association from the Jena professor Buddeus, whose brief attack on people's curiosity for news was in a treatise first published in 1711 (3.4.8 above).

[384] Even Happel, for whom 'curiosity' is almost always positive, occasionally resorts to the Latin 'Curiositas' when meaning it pejoratively: iv (1689), p. 295; see also i (1683), sig. [ii]ʳ.

[385] 'unzeitige Curiosi', 'Grund ihrer studiorum', 'was solides auf einen sandigen Grund bauen', 'wenden keinen Fleiß an, diejenige Disciplin recht zu lernen', 'kein Gelehrter heisen kan' (10–11).

[386] 'Doch ich zweiffle fast, ob diese Beweiß-Gründe bey der itzigen Zeit, da man solche ungegründete Curiosité für einen Character eines hohen tugendhafften Gemüthes hällt, durchdringen werden' (12). Some works sought to undo this opposition between the curious and the 'grounded': e.g. Weidling's treatise on why natural law obliges us to virtue was called a *Curieuse und gründliche Moralité* (1701) because it was systematic and yet also took the popularizing form of brief, discrete answers (mostly under a page long).

Pomian's about the invisible world—can be fruitful if open to modification by each case it considers (Popkin 1991, 208). On the other hand, in another sense Huhold did win his battle: although attacks like his failed to stop the heterogeneous range of reading practices which can be provisionally labelled 'extensive', nonetheless they did herald the eventual diminution of the contribution made (in certain discourses) by the culture of curiosities to that rise of 'extensive' reading.

In the late seventeenth and early eighteenth century, the curiosity-collecting discursive tendency also invaded the miscellany, a genre very close to the miscellany-periodical except that it was not intended to be published periodically. Miscellanies were textual collections of discrete discursive fragments—not just of one sort (such as wonders of nature and art, how-to recipes, or extraordinary historical anecdotes), but of many sorts—which did not add up to any philosophical or other system. Whereas earlier miscellanies had been full of 'prodigies', their place was now increasingly taken by 'curiosities', which were not so automatically understood as divine signs to be interpreted (Schenda 1963, 695–8). Although versions of the inherently heterogeneous genre of the miscellany had existed since antiquity, a particularly large number were printed during the heyday of the culture of curiosities in Germany. (They are now often associated with what it has become customary to call the German Baroque, though that is one generalizing modern label that I am leaving aside.)

As in miscellany-periodicals, so in miscellanies the purpose of the curious knowledge offered to readers was nuanced in that it tended to be neither wholly useful nor wholly useless: the relation of curiosity to utility was fraught here too. Although the contemporary and Enlightenment critics of these miscellanies of curiosities called them 'useless'[387] and even their compilers often emphasized their 'usefulness' relatively little (in comparison with how-to books), on the other hand only a minority of them were advertised as being for 'pleasure' alone (3.4.10 below). Indeed, some were actively claimed to be 'useful', especially those whose curiosities were wholly or

---

[387] Yet miscellanies of curiosities had a long shelf-life, furnishing sources for many German subsequent writers. In the 1780s Jean Paul Richter recycled their material with loving irony (Grafton 1997, 119).

partly intended as material for conversation.[388] Many were themselves written as conversations, letters, or answers to discrete questions.[389] Some, like periodicals, counted and quantified their curiosities.[390] Some amplified the curiosity-collecting metaphor by describing the compiler as having 'brought together' these objects.[391] Some situated their collected objects not just within metaphorical cabinets,[392] but within other figurative spaces too: the *Jolly Theatre of All Kinds of Curiosities* (1663 onwards) was one of the most reprinted miscellanies of the time, compiled by Erasmus Francisci (or von Finx), another of the early professional writers who (like Happel) wrote for publishers on demand.[393] Some, like certain periodicals, in order to emphasize that they were imposing the uniform shape of curiosities on a heterogeneous range of disciplines, enumerated those disciplines on the title-page:[394] whereas some German universities used curiosity to regulate and restrict polyhistory or polymathy, especially in its extra-university manifestations (1.3.1 above), by contrast these miscellanies were using curiosity to *connect* disciplines, as a conduit for rampant polymathy.

By using curiosity to hurl together discursive objects that were taken from so many disciplines, most miscellanies of curiosities, like popularizing anthologies of curious naturalist knowledge, also practised philosophical eclecticism rather than promoting any single, coherent philosophical system. If a curiosity was excerpted from a source complete with a philosophical explanation of it, then the compiler often offered no verdict on that explanation (Wagman 1942, 49–50). Happel acknowledged that some of the causes of natural phenomena adduced in his miscellany-periodical were only probable.[395] Johann Georg Schmidt made some curiosity even more openly conjectural in his *Curious Speculations During Sleepless Nights*, tackling questions such as when the Last Judgement will

---

[388] e.g. 'Tranquillus' 1705.

[389] e.g. Ernst 1694; Francisci 1673–4; [Schmidt] 1707. For an early French miscellany of 'questions curieuses', see La Barre 1644.

[390] e.g. Ernst 1694; [Schmidt] 1707.

[391] e.g. Ernst 1694, title-page ('zusammen getragen'). Cf. also Neiner 1734 (title-page), a miscellany for householders and preachers in which 'usefulness' is more prominent than curiosity.

[392] e.g. 'Tranquillus' 1705, [)(vii^r] ('Schatz-kammer').

[393] Francisci 1673–4 (first published 1663–73). On Francisci, see Dünnhaupt 1990–3, ii. 1516–49.

[394] e.g. [Schmidt] 1707.

[395] Happel 1683–9, i (1683), sig. [i]^r.

occur, whether birds and animals were created to die for man's good, whether a buck's blood can soften diamond.[396] Thus, although such miscellanies were at the popular end of the philosophical reading-market and although their motivation for avoiding systems may have been as much commercial (to sell books) and ideological (to make knowledge more available to the less educated) as epistemological, nonetheless they they were effectively joining some academicians and antiquaries in using the curiosity-collecting tendency to promote mild scepticism about systems.

Only in the late seventeenth century did it become common to present miscellanies explicitly as collections of curiosities. Certainly, these were not the first miscellanies ever to be packaged in terms of curiosity. As soon as it had become possible in discourses like natural philosophy to speak of 'good' as well as of 'bad curiosity', the cathedral canon François Béroalde de Verville had published his multidisciplinary *Palais des curieux* (1612).[397] It shared many features with later miscellanies—a spatial framework, explicit rejection of system, and association of curiosity with conjecture. But in other ways it differed from the subsequent culture of curiosities: as its title indicates, curiosity was still here primarily a subject-oriented passion, not a circle of comforting symmetry between subjects and objects. Moreover, Verville still had to grapple to distinguish the curiosity that he was promoting from 'bad curiosity' which, although it continued to figure in German university discourse, made only rare appearances in later German miscellanies of curiosities, which tended to use other terms (such as *fürwitzig*) for overweening inquiry.[398]

However, one unusual miscellany of curiosities—the thrice-printed *Curiosa theologica* or *Theologische Curiositäten* (1690) by Daniel Hartnack—did attempt to integrate good with bad curiosity, uneasily weaving together church, university, and secular discourse, thereby making explicit the assumption that the curiosity that each described so differently was in fact one and the same thing.

Hartnack's 'theological curiosities' were twenty-one German and Latin tracts, mostly moral denunciations of decadent contemporary

---

[396] [Schmidt] 1707, 5, 185, 253.

[397] On curiosity in this work, see N. Kenny 1991*a*, 214–15, 234. For exceptionally early descriptions of miscellanies as 'curious', see the title-pages of Medrano 1583 (a conversation manual) and Sydrac 1531 (a collection of questions).

[398] e.g. [Schmidt] 1707, 5. But see also p. 296 (for bad 'Curiosität').

mores (such as dancing, duelling, fancy wigs, the craze for French culture), all but a couple probably by Hartnack himself,[399] a fiery and controversial Lutheran pedagogue and pastor who left a series of posts as teacher or rector under a cloud, accused of various transgressions, such as financial fraud and excessive violence (his idea of disciplining one boy was allegedly to break his ribs).[400] In some respects this miscellany anticipated the moral weeklies. The final 'theological curiosity' in it was none other than the 1652 Frankfurt a.d. Oder philosophy dissertation by Michael Watson and Andreas Rose on curiosity as an affect, virtue, and vice. This had a special role in the recent history of curiosity in that it had inaugurated the wave of German dissertations on the theme (1.2.1 above). Hartnack may indeed have attended the actual disputation 38 years previously, having matriculated at Frankfurt a.d. Oder in the same year (1652) as the young *praeses* Watson.[401] With nonchalant semantic slippage, Hartnack now presented this study of the curiosity of subjects as itself an object of curiosity, useful for lawyers and physicians as well as for theologians and philosophers.

Hartnack chooses the overall title for his miscellany with great care: he devotes his entire preface ('Von der Curiosität') to explaining why he had called it *Theological Curiosities*. 'Curiosität' can be understood in two ways: first (echoing St Augustine), as punishable, flesh-oriented, worldly behaviour or over-inquiry into matters of faith; secondly, as the 'good, curious thoughts and speech of the pious, who practise their faith with holy care'.[402] Like the writers of several university dissertations, Hartnack is making some curiosity good by restoring it to its roots in *cura* (here 'Sorge'). Hartnack then tells the reader that both the good and the bad 'theological' kind are described in this miscellany, 'as distinct from other curiosities' such as those which are pursued very properly in other 'disciplines and faculties', for example in the 'famous *collegium curiosorum*' (the 'Academy of those curious about nature').[403]

Hartnack therefore belongs to that bold but tenuous strand of church discourse which attempted the problematic feat of

---

[399] Faber du Faur (ed.) 1958–69, i. 181.

[400] Jöcher 1750–1. See also Wallmann 1992, 410.

[401] Friedlaender (ed.) 1887–91, ii. 28.

[402] 'guten Gedancken und Reden der Frommen, die in heiliger Sorgfalt ihren Glauben üben' (Hartnack (ed.) 1690,):([1]ᵛ).

[403] 'zum Unterschied anderer Curiositäten', 'Disciplinen und Facultäten', 'das berühmte . . . Collegium Curiosorum' ():(2ᵛ).

legitimizing some curiosity. Indeed, when he recommends other recent accounts of curiosity, he includes Adam Rechenberg's dissertation on 'unhealthy curiosity in theology' (which gave a glimpse of 'healthy curiosity', albeit not as much as the other Rechenberg dissertation, of which Hartnack seems unaware (1.3.3 above)). He also summarizes Matthias Faber's sermon against the five forms of bad curiosity (2.2.4.2 above), but he subtly alters it by also calling their opposites 'five good curiosities', whereas Faber had carefully refrained from naming them thus:[404] Hartnack thus puts flesh on what was for Faber merely a ghost of good curiosity.

On the other hand, Hartnack appears at first to dissociate himself from the culture of curiosities: he includes its bad part in the bad kind of curiosity and excludes its good part (naturalist academies) from the good kind of curiosity which he is discussing. However, this dissociation is partially belied by the very presentation of the miscellany: 'I am calling this book "Theological curiosities" and so must begin by saying something about curiosity.'[405] By slipping so easily— in this first sentence and throughout the preface—from the object- to the subject-oriented sense and back, Hartnack is half speaking the language of the culture of curiosities. His title, like those of more conventional miscellanies, must have struck his readers as advertising curious discursive objects which would satisfy curiosity. Indeed, he himself was also the author of a treatise of *Curiosa of Nature, or Physical Wonders* (Hartnack 1685). And his commercial awareness of his miscellany's need for 'buyers' ('Käuffer') is very apparent from its preface, which even incites readers to support his 'Collegio Curiosorum'—that is, this miscellany—by turning up at the publishers to demand a sequel ():(3ʳ). He was both attacking much of the culture of curiosities and yet also using it to get people to read his book.

3.4.10   *'Curious amusements' and 'curious sciences'*

A glance forward beyond the chronological scope of the present study suggests that, as the eighteenth century wore on, the collecting-curiosities metaphor was increasingly displaced, losing its centre-stage cultural position in many a relatively prestigious discourse

---

[404] '5. Gute Curiositäten' ():(5ʳ).
[405] 'Ich nenne dieses Buch Curiosa Theologica. Muß derowegen nothwendig hiebey etwas zum Eingang von der Curiosität erwehnen.' ():([1]ʳ).

and becoming the preserve of discourses—such as 'sex', 'entertainment', 'occult sciences', 'Romantic travel'—which, at least on the face of it, were more marginal, controversial, or less officially institutionalized.

Already from the late seventeenth century, books of 'amusements' and 'entertainment'[406]—often interlaced with philosophical, mathematical, and optical tricks (Stafford 1994), salon or parlour games, historical anecdotes, and short genres such as the riddle and epigram—were often 'collected'[407] as discrete curious objects and/or objects of curiosity, sometimes in the familiar alphabetical order,[408] and including women more emphatically among their addressees than did most discourses in the culture of curiosities.[409] These were curiosities designed to pass the time, to 'shorten' it (as was often said in German),[410] rather than to give access to other times. The customary promise of gratifying symmetry between subjects and objects was sometimes at its crudest here: an eighteenth-century manuscript collection of entertainments was simply called *The Curious Person Satisfied*.[411] Even works which were originally intended more to unsettle than to satisfy could be re-processed as 'curious amusements': that was the title, for example, of an English version (1714) of La Rochefoucauld's *Maximes* which included songs and verse.

Even these amusements sometimes doggedly refused to dissociate their curiosity entirely from 'usefulness', claiming both, in the same way as they often claimed to be serious as well as comic. A 1712 entertainment included how-to tips (but especially ones which were fun or showy).[412] Nonetheless, these 'curious amusements' were perhaps both a cause and a symptom of the disrepute into which curiosity was beginning to fall in some discourses—such as how-to and

---

[406] e.g. La Rochefoucauld, *Curious Amusements: Fitted for the Entertainment of the Ingenious of Both Sexes* 1714.

[407] e.g. *Nouveau Meslange de pieces curieuses* 1664, [1ᵛ] ('recueilly').

[408] e.g. *Schola curiositatis* [after 1670]. (*Curiositas* had not figured in the title of earlier editions).

[409] e.g. La Rochefoucauld 1714, title-page; *Nouveau Meslange* 1664, [1ʳ⁻ᵛ]; Tipper (ed.), *Delights for the Ingenious: or, A Monthly Entertainment for the Ingenious of Both Sexes* 1711.

[410] e.g. *Schola curiositatis* [after 1670], title-page ('zu . . . Zeit-Passirung'); [Schmidt] 1707, title-page ('Zu . . . Zeit-Verkürtzung').

[411] *Le Curieux satisfait* n.d.

[412] *L'Esprit curieux* 1712: see p. vi ('un grand nombre de choses très-curieuses et très-utiles').

naturalist books—in which utility was becoming both more important than curiosity and also less obviously compatible with it.

If 'curious amusements' were marginal to mainstream discourse, then this was doubly the case when they involved the occult sciences and arts. Battles over conflicting uses of curiosity were nowhere fiercer than in discourse on these. How did curiosity change from being, in the sixteenth century, a weapon used to condemn dangerous occultist practices, to become, by the eighteenth century, a marketing label for harmless occultist parlour games?

Although occult sciences and arts—such as magic, astrology, divination, alchemy—had been granted a greater degree of philosophical respectability by late fifteenth- and sixteenth-century humanist study of their ancient sources (Neoplatonism, the texts attributed to Hermes Trismegistus, and so on) which lay outside the scholastic canon, nonetheless they were never far from controversy, and occultist malpractice was called 'curiosity' both by opponents of all occult philosophy and also by practitioners of it who wished to dissociate themselves from its evil versions. For instance, as Jean Dupèbe has shown, for the abbot Johannes Trithemius *curiositas* was always a pejorative term: he used it to denounce diabolic magic, as distinct from his own theurgy (angelology and demonology).[413] Such attacks were mainly on curiosity in its subject-oriented sense, as a passion which led to attempts to know or do things by sinful means. As Nicole Jacques-Chaquin has shown in an excellent study of curiosity and demonology, curiosity seems to have become if anything more central to such attacks in treatises of the Reformation (such as Jean Calvin's 1549 attack on judicial astrology) and the Counter-Reformation (such as the Jesuit Martin Anton del Rio's 1599–1600 demonstration that occult curiosity produces heresy).[414]

Such denunciations of occult curiosity continued well into the eighteenth century and beyond. Indeed, when curiosity had long since become much more positive in many other discourses, it continued to be used as a pejorative term for abuses not just by opponents of occult philosophy[415] but also by its defenders.[416] The negative history of curiosity continued to weigh more heavily on

---

[413] Dupèbe 1986. See 2.3.2 above.
[414] Jacques-Chaquin 1998*b*: on Del Rio, see her pp. 76, 85–6, 89 and Walker 1958, 178–85. See Calvin 1985, 51, 63, 74, 84, 94, 99, 100, 102.
[415] e.g. Bordelon 1710*a*, *3*ᵛ.
[416] e.g. Pernety 1758, 312.

occultist discourse than it did on post-sixteenth-century naturalist discourse. However, from about the early seventeenth century some occult writers did also begin to claim and vaunt curiosity—in both subject- and object-oriented senses—instead of disavowing it.[417] Whereas occult sciences had been pejoratively termed 'curiosities' since antiquity (for example in Apuleius and the Old Latin Bible),[418] and whereas magic had been a prime focus of medieval scholastic attacks on curiosity (Eamon 1994, 59–65), now the phrase 'curious sciences' became a standard positive—as well as pejorative—shorthand for occult sciences.[419] Through this astonishing volte-face, even occult writing was beginning to be shaped by the emergent culture of curiosities. Some German occult writers sought respectability by claiming membership of the new naturalist academies of those who were curious about nature or else by giving their books titles that evoked such academies.[420]

The title of one of the most notorious occult books of the century—the *Unheard-of Curiosities* (*Curiositez inouyes*, 1629) by Jacques Gaffarel, a doctor of theology—emphasized that the author's reflections on 'oriental' culture, Persian talismans, astrology, and the cabala amounted to fragments rather than to any unified, coherent, whole philosophical system. The final sentence reinforced the message: 'Thus do I suspend my judgement yet again—as much on all these last curiosities as on the others proposed in this book—until I have found either weaker or stronger explanations.'[421] By making these sceptical noises, Gaffarel (who was friendly with the likes of Peiresc, Naudé, and Gassendi)[422] was putting his curiosities—which were ancient in one sense (116) and new in another (a4ᵛ)—on a par with the antiquities or news items

---

[417] e.g. Purling 1657, 6; [Runckel] 1727, [3], 4; Trismosin 1613, A iiiᵛ (this translation first published 1612); 'Valentine' 1624, a iiʳ⁻ᵛ. See Jacques-Chaquin 1998*b*, 102.

[418] See Labhardt 1960, 58; Lancel 1961.

[419] e.g. *Curieuse Gedancken, von der wahren Alchymia . . . von einem Liebhaber der curieusen Wissenschafften* 1702; [Job], *Anleitung zu denen curiösen Wissenschafften* 1717.

[420] e.g. *Curieuse Gedancken, von der wahren Alchymia . . . von einem . . . Membro des Collegii Curiosorum* 1702; Praetorius [= Schultze], *Collegium curiosum privatissimum physiognom-chiromant-metoposcop-anthropologicum* 1713.

[421] 'Par ainsi je suspends encore mon jugement, tant sur ces Curiositez que sur toutes les autres advancees dans ce livre, jusques à tant que j'aye trouvé des raisons ou plus foibles, ou plus puissantes' (Gaffarel 1637, 314; see also sig. a3ᵛ). On the treatise, see Rizza 1996, 205–40.

[422] Rizza 1996, 214, 216–17.

which the sceptic Peiresc called by the same name: all were fragments which did not add up to a whole. The association between curiosity and conjecture (3.4.9 above) thus enabled Gaffarel—who was in fact widely accused of credulity, not of scepticism—to reduce his responsibility for these controversial discursive objects. Making occult knowledge into curiosities rather than into a dogmatic system made them less likely to be universally censured. Indeed, although the Sorbonne forced Gaffarel to retract the book (Rizza 1996, 215–16), the editor of the later Latin edition (Gregor Michael), while critical of Gaffarel on many points, was effectively taking his cue from the author himself when, instead of condemning or accepting 'these *Curiosities*' outright, he invited 'very erudite men to discuss' them.[423]

But what exactly did Gaffarel mean by 'curiosities'? He mainly meant discursive objects—'Curious thoughts'—rather than material ones, although in his discussion they also became metonymically associated with material ones (especially in Part 2, on talismans). On the other hand, his curiosities were not entirely objects: they were partly the products of human subjects, which is why Gaffarel called them 'Curieuses pensees' ('inquisitive/diligent thoughts') rather than *pensées curieuses* ('odd thoughts').[424] Most of his uses of the term 'curiosities' are ambiguous and can be read with the emphasis on either subject or object.[425] The same goes for the title of the Latin editions—*Curiositates inauditae*—whereas the more expected *Curiosa inaudita* would have had an exclusively object-oriented sense. The ambiguity between the two senses was characteristic of French in the early seventeenth century, when object-oriented senses of 'curiosity' were still establishing themselves, whereas the subject- and object-oriented senses were more clearly separated later and indeed earlier: when in 1549 Calvin railed against judicial astrology and other 'curiositez', he meant 'kinds of curiosity', not 'objects of curiosity'.[426] To the extent that Gaffarel's curiosities were 'investigations' (rather than 'objects investigated'), they were conjectural and open-ended and so did not in fact offer the immediate gratification (of curiosity by curious objects) which was soon so much on offer in the culture of curiosities.

The fortunes of Gaffarel's treatise show the difficulties which beset seventeenth-century occultist attempts to make curiosity positive.

---

[423] 'eruditissimos Viros ad discutiendas *Curiositates*' (Gaffarel [1676], [)(7ʳ]).
[424] Gaffarel 1637, a2ᵛ.   [425] e.g. a2ʳ, a3ʳ, a4ᵛ, 3, 27, 112, 314.
[426] Calvin 1985, 45 (full title).

Realizing that his appropriation of the controversial term and of 'oriental' learning could not go without some defensive comment—his dedicatee was after all a bishop (of Nantes)—Gaffarel urged any critics to bear in mind that 'the most holy of the Church Fathers did not disdain the curiosity of the Gentiles'.[427] At a stroke, he thereby swept under the carpet the long patristic history of condemnations of *curiositas*. But even his later editor Michael did not allow him to get away with this. In contrast to what any linear, teleological, progress-based history of curiosity (such as Blumenberg's) might lead us to expect, Michael's extraordinary preface of 1676 (which still figured in the 1706 edition) pulled the Fathers back out from under the carpet, giving a long list of patristic (as well as biblical and classical) denunciations of *curiositas* (or of what Michael interprets as *curiositas*) (Gaffarel 1676,)(3^r-)(6^r). The list is followed not, as one might expect, by an indication that, on the other hand, *curiositas* can also be understood in a good sense, but merely by an acknowledgement that 'the curiosities of Gaffarel'—'signs of an idle disposition or curious mind'—'have been to people's taste'.[428] It is as if Michael can only risk editing this controversial work by proving his orthodox credentials through a blanket condemnation of *curiositas*, which downright contradicts the 'showy title' of the very work that he is presenting.[429] Indeed, translating the title into Latin had made it all the more provocative, since *curiositas* was still more negatively charged than *curiosité*, connoting the patristic tradition more strongly.

At the same time as Michael was writing his preface, less tortured gratification was beginning to be offered by the *mondain*, vernacular, occultist entertainments which were coming into vogue. Some were, if not metaphorical collections, then at least metaphorical edifices offering immediate satisfaction, whether a *Palace of the Curious* (frequently reprinted; by a member of the French royal household) or a *Palace of Games, Love, and Fortune, where the Curious will Find Answers to Questions of Love and Fortune*.[430] Unlike some treatises

---

[427] 'les plus saincts des Peres n'ont pas desdaigné la Curiosité des Gentils' (a2^r).

[428] 'otiosi ingenii aut curiosi animi portenta'; 'ad gustum fuere Curiositates *Gaffarelli*' ([)(7^r]).

[429] 'Specioso . . . titulo' ()(3^r).

[430] [Vulson de La Colombière] 1655 (1st edn. 1646); Colletet 1663. On La Colombière, see Gunn 1995, 55. See also Comiers 1694 (reprinted several times in the 18th century).

on divination that were still daring to claim that, for example, curious chiromancy was, if not 'useful', then at least 'not useless',[431] these books of games steered clear of any claims to 'usefulness', since that would have involved claiming that the answers they offered were true. Instead, these books were presented as pleasurable means of sociability, like other conversational games of this period. By aiming 'merely to contribute to the entertainment of the curious'[432] rather than to tell the truth, they defused church suspicions of them: one popular manual for confessors stated that physiognomy and chiromancy are mortal sins if we believe in them but only venial if we practice them out of curiosity, without actually believing in them (Verbeeck-Verhelst 1988, 365). Divorcing divination from philosophy, 'curiosity' from 'usefulness', was the price paid in order to avoid condemnation or ridicule.

Certainly, many courtiers or others who played these games may well have taken the answers at least half seriously: that is as impossible to determine as the exact degree to which readers of newspaper horoscopes believe in them nowadays. And the language of curiosity may have been retained in those books of games in order to commodify the books by giving them an aura of the risqué and the forbidden. Indeed, the money-making opportunities which 'curious' and controversial occultism afforded were explicitly recognized in the period. A 1706 editor of Gaffarel's bestseller glossed a comment made in 1632—that 'There is well-founded suspicion and conjecture that the publishers of Rouen printed this curious book repeatedly in the hope of profit, with no small detriment to its sense and style'—by recalling that this anonymously printed book had indeed 'immediately found so many buyers and was read so avidly'.[433] This was a new version of the centuries-old topos that occultists trick people out of money by exploiting their curiosity.[434] The corresponding oppo-

---

[431] Peruchio 1657, 2 ('elle n'est plus appellée . . . inutile'; 'nous l'appellons . . . curieuse').

[432] 'celle [fin] de ce livre n'étant que de contribuer au divertissement des Curieux' (Comiers 1694, A3ᵛ).

[433] 'tot statim emtores reperit, tam avidè est lectum . . . *Ac suspicio est . . . nec fallit conjectura, Rhotomagenses Bibliopolas spe lucri semelatque iterum non sine magna tum sensus tum styli corruptione curiosum hunc librum edidisse*' (Gaffarel 1706,)(2ʳ⁻ᵛ; the italicized words are by 'Allatius in Apibus Urbanis' (reference not identified), the others by Johann Albert Fabricius). Gaffarel's treatise was printed in French in 1629, 1631, 1632, 1637, 1650, in Latin in 1676, 1678, 1706.

[434] For an alchemical example, see Tahureau 1981, 183 (1st edn. 1565).

site argument, characteristic of the culture of curiosities—that occult truths are worth good money—was still being used in a 1793 fortune-telling book which argued that, just as we find earlier kings 'paying liberally for the answers they received', so 'the same curiosity is yet alive' (*Every Lady's Own Fortune-Teller* 1793, [i]).

However, by 1793, the times when defenders and attackers of such occult curiosity saw it as part of the same 'thing' as, say, naturalist or historical curiosity were long gone. The philosophical disrepute into which much occult philosophy had already fallen by the late seventeenth century was severing the connections between occult curiosity and not only 'usefulness' but also more respectable kinds of curiosity.[435] Occult curiosity was often being either trivialized as a harmless pastime in company or else driven into the private sphere. For example, in a dialogue of the dead by Fénelon, Marie de' Medici taunts Richelieu for his hypocrisy in criticizing her horoscopes while he himself had been obeying the following advice, allegedly proffered by Tommaso Campanella: 'When one wishes to play the great man, one affects to despise astrology; but although in public one pretends to be above such beliefs, in secret one is curious and credulous.'[436]

Nonetheless, it was no easier for critics of occult philosophy to dissociate its curiosity from their own that it had been, conversely, for occultists such as Gaffarel to dissociate their curiosity from its negative history. Curiosity was like a discursive glue which bound together apparently opposed perspectives and in which efforts to separate them became stuck. As Jacques-Chaquin has shown, on the one hand demonologists condemned the way in which occult writers explicitly appealed to their readers' curiosity through seductive narratives of occult practices; on the other hand, these critics used exactly the same technique themselves in order to draw in readers (1998*b*, 98–105).

Similar double standards characterized the packaging of some anti-occultist works. They encouraged and exploited curiosity *about*

---

[435] There were still many exceptions to this tendency, especially in Germany where academic study of occult philosophy long remained vigorous, e.g. Schwimmer, *Ex physica secretiori curiositates* 1672 (by a Jena professor of philosophy; 'curiositates' is the largest word on the title-page).

[436] 'Quand on veut faire le grand homme, on affecte de mépriser l'astrologie; mais quoiqu'on fasse en public l'esprit fort, on est curieux et crédule en secret' (Fénelon 1983–97, i. 483).

occult philosophy while discouraging the curiosity *of* its practitioners. One 1641 French treatise emphatically condemned the curiosity underlying judicial astrology and styled itself an 'antidote' to it, but its title made it more like a homeopathic one, curing curiosity with curiosity: *Curious Treatise on Judicial Astrology . . . In which Many Curious Questions are Resolved, for the Satisfaction of Curious Minds.*[437] The distinction between these two kinds of curiosity—illness and cure—was sometimes deliberately blurred, for rhetorical and marketing purposes. To the superficial browser, the titles of some of these anti-occultist works were remarkably similar to those of the works which they condemned. One of the works which followed Christian Thomasius's attack on belief in witchcraft and related phenomena was Johann Jakob Bräuner's *Physically and Historically Explained Curiosities, or Devilish Superstition Unmasked . . . Together with Other Odd Things . . . Presented as Fifty Curious Topics.*[438] The illusory beliefs themselves are now packaged as numbered objects of curiosity—like discursive curiosities in miscellany-periodicals—though the strategic parody of occultist collections also seems designed to draw in unreconstructed readers who will (initially at least) treat the werewolves, love potions, and ghosts (rather than the illusory belief in them) as curiosities, in the time-honoured manner, before then being disabused. Such works created an ironic discrepancy between these two senses. Like many church writers, from Hartnack to Fénelon, some early Enlightenment, anti-occultist critics of curious people found that the best way to beat them was to accommodate them, whether seriously or ironically.

3.5 ACROSS DISCOURSES

Although the culture of curiosities put a broadly similar stamp on curiosity across a wide range of discourses, those discourses also used curiosity in ways that were specific to them. Having emphasized those discourses' specificity by surveying them one by one, let me now return to the culture of curiosities as a whole. What bound it

---

[437] Pithoys 1641, 5 ('contrepoison'); see also pp. 2–4.
[438] 1737 (first published 1735). On this work, see Bausinger 1963, 346–7. For another example, see Bordelon, *De l'astrologie judiciaire. Entretien curieux* 1710a.

together? How did the broad shape of curiosities migrate from one discourse to another? This question can be answered on different levels. So far I have concentrated on two levels: that of certain institutions and that of discursive tendencies, in particular the curiosity-collecting tendency, which functioned as the agent of contagion between discourses, spreading the metaphor of collection of curiosities from one discourse to another as an organizing principle, thereby tightening the links between discourses. For example, miscellanies incorporated a wide range of discourses—natural philosophy, antiquarianism, history, news, and so on—softening, but not eradicating, the distinctions between them by breaking them all down into similarly shaped curiosities.

This contagiousness of curiosity across the various discourses of the culture of curiosities was also fostered—and exploited—by other means, for example by discursive modes such as satire and parody, by individual writers, and by one institution that I have not yet considered: the publishing house.

3.5.1   Satire

Satire and parody often transferred the language of curiosity from one context, in which it was familiar, to another, in which it was unfamiliar, comic, or surprising. Not all satire and parody involving curiosity operated in this way: some simply satirized or parodied a discourse of curiosity by remaining firmly anchored within it.[439] However, so many books parodied a discourse of curiosity in order to satirize something outside that discourse that 'curious', in these book's titles, came to mean 'satirical', at least by connotation:[440] that is what one bibliographer meant by saying of John Barclay's famous *Euphormionis Lusinini Satyricon* (1603–7) that 'Il y a du curieux dans ce Livre'.[441] Like the related connotation 'sex' (3.4.8 above), but usually for different reasons, the 'satire' connotation was veiled to varying extents: both sheltered behind a more innocuous

---

[439] For examples from material collecting and from the occult sciences, see 3.4.5 and 3.4.10 above. See also Reuter's famous parody of travel romances (Reuter 1964, esp. 7) and an obscure parody of a collector's inventory ([Wohlrab] 1733).

[440] For complementary remarks, see N. Kenny 1998, 184–5.

[441] [Lenglet-Dufresnoy] 1734, ii. 254.

denotation of 'curious' (such as 'noteworthy'), which however often told readers much less about what a book was really about. Both connotations—'sex' and 'satire'—became stronger as the eighteenth century went on: they rose to prominence within the culture of curiosities but long survived its heyday.

For example, the discourse of curious travel sometimes operated as a veil for satire of something else. One *Curious Account of Various Newly Discovered Countries* was in fact a medical satire, though the reader would not have known this from the title-page. The Princess 'Nalasté' (*la santé*) rules over different territories from the empire of 'Celanedime' (*la médecine*), and so on.[442] However, the most common cover denotation behind which both 'satire' and 'sex' lurked was 'material collecting.'[443] Many an anonymous political satire took the form of a parodic inventory of curiosities. A manuscript of the *Many Curiosities Found in the Cabinet of the Chevalier de Fourilles* itemized objects such as 'a hazelnut shell inside which, according to a medical report, one could fit the whole brain of D. D. L. F. [the duc de La Feuillade]'.[444] An English *Catalogue of Curious but Prohibited Books* ([1745?]) included among its 111 numbered items 'British Interest, (abridg'd). Sells abroad' (no.109). In the late eighteenth century such satires often masqueraded as collections of antiquarian documents, such as the *True Origins of Ecclesiastical Wealth: Historical and Curious Fragments Containing the Different Ways in which the Secular and Regular Clergy of France has Enriched Itself.*[445]

The satire was sometimes of a more general, moral, and/or social nature rather than specific and political. And it was dressed up not just as a cabinet but also as other containers associated with curiosity, such as the art gallery[446] or the raree-show (a peep-show hawked

---

[442] *Relation curieuse* 1741, a5ʳ.

[443] For a 'sex' example, see *Pieces echapees du feu ou La Curiosité, la rar[e]té* [1750?] (an erotic anthology).

[444] 'La Coque d'une Noise ou l'on pourroit mettre toute la cervelle du D. D. L. F. suivant le raport des Medecins' ('Plusieurs curiositez' [1682?], 43ʳ).

[445] *Veritable Origine* 1790. See also *Curious and Authentic Memoirs Concerning a Late Peace, Concluded Between the Rooks and Jackdaws* 1763 (on the Treaty of Paris between Britain and France).

[446] e.g. 'Bon-temps', *La Gallerie des curieux; contenant en divers tableaux, les chef-d'œuvres des plus excellens railleurs de ce siecle* 1671 (first published 1646; a comic anthology).

round fairs, villages, and cities and also standardly known in French as *une curiosité*). A German treatise against many forms of lying and boasting was styled as a *Curious Raree-Show, in which Wind-Making is Represented*. An engraving depicts five men peering inside, some imagining that they see something and beginning their windy descriptions of it, while a wiser man walks off, rejecting such nonsense (Illustration 4). This conceit partly validates—by satirically inverting it—Pomian's model of curiosity as giving access to invisible worlds. The onlookers claim to think that they have access to things which remain invisible, but in fact those things either do not exist or else have not been experienced by the onlooker. For example, one of the windbags satirized is he who returns from European travels claiming to have been shown 'all the antiquities and other *curiosa* of Rome' and 'all the curiosities of the Louvre in Paris'.[447]

In such works, the culture of curiosities was a kind of sugared pill, which sweetened satire or semi-concealed it. Although it was not the only such sugared pill, it was a particularly favoured one, partly because it was so prominent—like the internet nowadays, the terminology of which is often transferred parodically to non-internet topics—and yet also partly in the later eighteenth century because it was increasingly perceived as trivial, footling, dry, boring, in ironic contrast with the momentous political and moral stakes of the satire. Moreover, some satirists were drawn to the culture of curiosities because of its capacity to assert mastery over its objects (3.4.7 above): enemy brains could be cut down to hazelnut size, just as a collector's beliefs could be represented as being the same size as his diminutive material curiosities[448] or 'superstitious' beliefs could be represented as odd objects of curiosity in themselves (Bräuner (3.4.10 above)).

Satire that parodied a discourse of curiosity relied on readers perceiving the clashes between that discourse and another one. Such satire therefore indicates that, although the culture of curiosities was

---

[447] 'alle Antiquitäten und andere Curiosa', 'alle Curiositäten im Louvre zu Paris' (*Curieuser Raritäten-Kasten* 1733, 138). See also *La Curiosité; or, The Gallanté Show* 1797.
[448] 'toute la science, toute la profession, et même toute la Religion du bon-homme Oufle étoient renfermées dans les curiositez, dans les tableaux et dans les livres dont on vient de parler' (Bordelon 1710*b*, 7).

ILLUS. 4. *Curieuser Raritäten-Kasten* (1733).

often perceived by contemporaries as a broadly homogeneous whole, there was also a sharp awareness of the limits, the outer edges of this or that discourse within it, of the points at which one discourse's jurisdiction ceased and it gave way either to another discourse (or—in the period's university parlance—'species') of curiosity or else to another kind of discourse that lay outside the culture of curiosities. The crossovers between cognate but distinct discourses or 'species' of curiosity were effected mainly by the curiosity-collecting tendency but also sometimes by the curiosity-narrating tendency, especially through allegory: a fable on a fox's curiosity about fine art could represent human curiosity about neighbours, the future, or theology.[449]

3.5.2   *Writers, printers, publishers, booksellers*

Printed in Curiosenburg[450]

Certain writers in particular contributed not just to one but to several discourses within the culture of curiosities. Although the present study, rather than giving a decisive role to individuals, emphasizes instead the role of institutions or discursive tendencies—notably the tendencies towards collecting and narrating—in shaping curiosity, nonetheless it is undeniable that some individuals played an especially crucial role in mediating the spread of the curiosity-collecting tendency to several discourses within the culture of curiosities.

For example, Le Lorrain de Valmont helped spread it to natural and occult philosophy, agriculture, and horticulture. German writers spread it even more spectacularly than French ones, perhaps because they were operating in a cultural climate more sympathetic on the whole to polymathy. Not only professional writers like Happel and Francisci—who were the equivalent of the Venetian *poligrafi* and their Dutch counterparts (Burke 2000, 162–3)—but also physicians like Hellwig and C. F. Paullini and pastors like Männling and

---

[449] § 2.2.4.3 above. See 4.1, 4.4, and 4.4.2 below.

[450] *Wie stehts in Bender? . . . Gedruckt in Curiosenburg, im Jahr 1611* (in fact late 17th-/early 18th-century) (*National Union Catalog*).

Gregorii (who was also a teacher) each shaped several discourses as 'curious'.[451] They sometimes drew explicit attention to this recurring shape, whatever the discourse. Hellwig pointed out in both a chemical 'curious' collection and a miscellaneous one that he was using this key term to denote the brevity and discontinuity of the knowledge presented. He added that in the future he intended to write 'not only *curiosa* of this kind but also more extensive treatises'—'more extensive' here means 'not curious'.[452] He also compiled a how-to book, a calendar, one collection of medical cases and observations, another of exotic *naturalia*: he presented all of these too as 'curious' and/or as 'curiosities'.[453]

The most discursively contagious kinds of curiosities in Germany were the 'odd, singular' ones. However, Weise spread a less sensational kind across many discourses. In terms of modern historical labels, his were less 'Baroque' than 'early Enlightenment'.[454] This influential secondary-school director promoted a politics and a rhetoric based on practical prudence, an aesthetics derived from French neo-classicism, and a clear, student-friendly pedagogy which included new sources (such as newspapers), all in the form of 'curious thoughts' or 'questions', that is, as collections of points which were set out as a single series of relatively brief, discrete, numbered paragraphs, in contrast with the exhaustive textbooks which they were designed to supplement, in characteristic 'curious' manner.[455]

However, the 'shape' or—to adapt Weise's recurrent term—the *Gestalt*[456] of 'curious thoughts' and other curiosities was not determined by writers alone, but also by other factors such as the marketing imperatives of the book industry, as has been suggested

---

[451] Especially geography and history in the case of Gregorii (1712, 1713, 1715), some of whose works went to more than 10 editions (*DBE*). On Männling, see Tworek 1938.

[452] 'nicht allein auf diese Art, Curiosa, sondern auch, in weitläuffigern Tractaten' (Hellwig 1704, a2ʳ; see sigs. a[1]ᵛ–a2ᵛ). See also Hellwig 1738,)(2ʳ–)(3ʳ).

[453] Hellwig 1718, 1702, 1710–11, 1711.

[454] On Weise in this perspective, see Hoffmeister (ed.) 1983, 362–3.

[455] 'Wer sich aus diesen curieusen Fragen erbauen wil, der muß sich zuvor in einem Compendio Logico wol umbgesehen haben.' (Weise 1700, 18; 1st edn. 1696). For *Curieuse Gedancken*, see Weise 1693, 1698, 1701, 1702, 1703.

[456] e.g. Weise, *Curiöse Gedancken von der Imitation, welcher gestalt die lateinischen Autores von der studierenden . . . mit Nutzen gelesen . . . werden* 1698. See also Weise 1693 and 1700 (title-pages).

throughout Section 3. This occurred especially in certain cities. Books of curiosities were printed and published throughout much of Germany, but most of all in a triangle of which the three corners were Frankfurt a. Main, Leipzig (plus nearby Dresden and Erfurt), and Nuremberg (along with nearby Augsburg), though others were published in the north (Hamburg, for example). Publishers—many of whom were also printers and/or booksellers[457]—had considerable impact on the shaping of knowledge as curiosities, often counteracting the shapes given to curiosity by other institutions, such as universities and churches.

Many German printers and publishers specialized in certain kinds of curiosities. The book industry thus contributed to the rough and variable divisions of the culture of curiosities into sub-discourses, which were partly distinct and partly connected. In Leipzig, for example, the Gleditsch publishing and bookselling dynasty—especially Johann Friedrich and his son Johann Gottlieb[458]—produced 'curious' books which, although belonging to different genres, provided similarly shaped snippets of eloquence and alphabeticized knowledge for urban and courtly men and women who saw themselves as a sophisticated, French-oriented, *curieus*, and *galant* elite (Illustration 5).[459] Up in Hamburg, the curiosities published by Gottfried Schultze were more down-to-earth, how-to recipes.[460] Artisanal techniques loomed large among the curiosities which Karl Christian Neuenhahn both published and sold in Nordhausen.[461] The compiling pastors Hellwig and Gregorii had success in Erfurt, where 'curious' works by both of them were produced and sold by two publisher-booksellers (whose books were also published in Frankfurt a. Main and Leipzig): Hieronymus Philipp Ritschel and the heirs of Johann Christoph Stössel.[462] The recently deceased Stössel had also produced both Latin and German 'curious' works by the more famous polyhistorical academician C. F. Paullini,[463] who

---

[457] See Paisey 1988, p. X. Following Paisey, I state if the publishers in question also printed or sold books but I just use the term 'publisher' where it is not known if they did (although in most cases it is likely that they did).

[458] See Paisey 1988, 78.

[459] e.g. Bohse 1700; Corvinus 1715; [Marperger] 1727; Weise 1693.

[460] e.g. *Schatzkammer* 1686; Wolley 1674.

[461] e.g. Behrens [1703]; Kellner 1701. On Neuenhahn, see Paisey 1988, 186.

[462] Ritschel: Gregorii 1713, 1715; Hellwig 1710–11. Stössel heirs: [Gregorii] 1712; Hellwig 1711. On Ritschel and Stössel, see Paisey 1988, 210, 254.

[463] C. F. Paullini 1703*b*, 1703*c*, 1705*a*, 1706.

ILLUS. 5. [Corvinus], *Nutzbares, galantes und curiöses Frauenzimmer-Lexicon* (1715).

was published all over Germany. The example of the Stössel dynasty therefore suggests that the 'curious' works of Hellwig, Gregorii, and Paullini (in both his more learned and more popularizing vein) were seen as being of the same, curious ilk. On the other hand, an indication that *some* marketing distinctions were nonetheless made between Paullini's more learned and more popularizing curiosities is given by the fact that some publishers specialized in one or the other of them.[464]

Other book producers ranged much more widely across the culture of curiosities, giving the impression that that culture—whatever the differences between its sub-discourses—was perceived as a rough whole, as a super-discourse, so to speak, which structured a heterogeneous range of knowledge in broadly homogeneous ways. For example, within the space of seven years the Dresden publisher and bookseller Johann Christoph Mieth brought out: an anthology of 'curious' excerpts from recent newspapers; a 'curious' popularizing collection of chemical and medical recipes; and at least three books of 'curious thoughts' (two of them by Weise, one by Jakob Thomasius, which suggests that this short-lived genre was a product of the book industry as well as of Weise).[465] But the most striking example of all is provided by the Endter dynasty of Nuremberg, probably the most important such dynasty in the whole of the Empire, with scions who were variously publishers, printers, and/or booksellers.[466] They produced some of the key publications of the culture of curiosities, whether drawn from the new philosophy (Schott's *Physica curiosa* and *Technica curiosa*), from the new societies (the transactions of the 'Academy of those curious about nature'[467] and also Sturm's *Collegium experimentale, sive curiosum*, which arose from his teaching at Altdorf, just outside Nuremberg), from the popular end of the market (the *Lustige Schau-Bühne von allerhand Curiositäten* by Francisci, who was employed by the Endters), and even from the landowning, agrarian world (Hohberg's bestselling *Georgica curiosa*).

---

[464] Laurenz Kroniger and Gottlieb Göbel (Augsburg): C. F. Paullini [1688], 1691 (learned). Friedrich Knoch (Frankfurt a. Main): C. F. Paullini 1698, 1703a (popularizing). On these publishers, see Paisey 1988, 135, 144.
[465] Respectively: Dexelius 1699; *Der curiose Chymicus* 1706; Weise 1701, 1702; J. Thomasius 1702. On Mieth, see Paisey 1988, 176.
[466] See Evans 1977, 138–9; Paisey 1988, 53.
[467] Plus at least one of this academy's monographs (C. F. Paullini 1685).

Like the German learned societies themselves, this publishing dynasty—based in a Lutheran free city but not disdaining Jesuits such as Schott—raised up out of the ashes of the Thirty Years' War a culture of curiosities which was a largely cross-confessional phenomenon,[468] in contrast with the curiosity which Lutheran universities were busy confessionalizing in this period. On the other hand, university curiosity and the culture of curiosities did share some common ground, including their very medium: both were largely products of print. Just as the printing of dissertations disseminated and endlessly modified curiosity in universities, so the printing of an enormous range of curiosities shaped knowledge outside the universities as unsystematic fragments. Although it is tempting to think of the 'culture of curiosi*ty*' (*à la* Pomian) as primarily involving material objects (natural and artificial) in collections, the broader phenomenon of the culture of curiosi*ties* (as I have defined it) primarily involved printed objects, that is, artefacts which were at once discursive and material. It was created, for multiple uses, by the book industry as well as by other institutions.

3.6   CONCLUSIONS

The culture of curiosities consisted of institutions, groups, practices, genres, and discourses that tended to use curiosity very differently from the ways in which universities and churches used it. The culture of curiosities often used curiosity in order to commodify knowledge, to attribute financial value to it, to popularize and disseminate it, to legitimize and market it, to make money, to manipulate public opinion, to give people social credentials and practical know-how, to promote mild epistemological scepticism, to satirize, to entertain, and so on. All this it often did by presenting knowledge in predominantly spatial terms, as a metaphorical cabinet of curiosities—as a periodical entitled *Saxon Cabinet of Curiosities*, for example—or else as a collection of discrete, 'curious' fragments which did not add up to any systematic whole: book-buyers knew that a work entitled *The Curious and Learned Historian*, although not overtly presented as a

[468] See Evans 1977, 138–9.

metaphorical collection, was more likely to be a compilation of discrete facts and anecdotes than a single, over-arching narrative. Thus,
within the culture of curiosities, this curiosity-collecting tendency
(as I have labelled it) far outweighed the other strong early modern
discursive tendency of curiosity—to be part of a narrative chain
unfolding in time.

However, just as the culture of curiosities, however extensive, constituted only one part of early modern discourse on curiosity, so the
culture of curiosities was itself divided into numerous sub-discourses
or language-games—naturalist, antiquarian, journalistic, and so
on—each of which tended to use curiosity for different, specific purposes, whatever the broad similarities between them. The culture of
curiosities was neither wholly homogeneous nor simultaneous: it
rose and fell at different times in different discourses. For example,
while curiosities were starting to be sidelined in some how-to-do-it
books and periodicals in the early eighteenth century and then in
some *histoire littéraire* in about the mid-eighteenth, on the other
hand they were becoming more prominent in bibliomania, erotica,
and books of entertainments, while maintaining their prominence in,
say, the occult sciences. However, since some of the latter discourses
were less intellectually prestigious, this second wave marked in a
sense a relegation of curiosities when compared with the central,
peculiarly resonant position which they had enjoyed in such a wide
range of mainstream secular discourses in the late seventeenth and
early eighteenth century. Curiosities continued to figure in various
discourses—as they still do today—but no longer on such a large
scale and in a way that bound so many discourses together under
their aegis.

This erosion of the culture of 'curiosities' weakened the gratifying
symmetry—between the curiousness of objects and the curiosity of
subjects—that had been its bedrock. For example, as the eighteenth
century wore on, curiosity continued to be considered crucial to the
study of nature and technology, but increasingly it did not have
curiosities as its main object. Curiosity came to be viewed less as
a collection of gratifying encounters between subject and object
and more as one stage in a narrative of progress towards improved
technology and understanding of nature: in other words, the curiosity-
narrating tendency came increasingly to the fore in naturalist
discourse. While this kind of curiosity about nature may seem more

familiar to modern eyes, it was still distinctively early modern, notably because it was explicitly considered—for example in a 1739 prospectus—as just one manifestation of the same passion which also drove the traveller, the craftsman, the ethnographer, the architect.

The broad similarities between the uses of curiosity in different discourses of the culture of curiosities—such as travel-writing and miscellany-periodicals—were relations not of strict identity but rather of family resemblance. Although the culture of curiosities often imposed a broadly similar shape on disparate kinds of knowledge, it certainly did not homogenize them entirely or eradicate all distinctions between disciplines. Miscellany-periodicals were so spectacular because they imposed a similar shape upon diverse disciplines, but not because they reduced all disciplines to one. Moreover, works which parodied the language of one discourse within the culture of curiosities (such as antiquarianism) in order to transfer it satirically to another (such as court secrets) relied on readers distinguishing between those two discourses as well as juxtaposing them. Even just within the culture of curiosities—leaving aside university and church discourse—there was no single use of curiosity that was always present, no ineliminable core of what could be called a 'concept' of curiosity. Indeed, curiosity was used in flatly contradictory ways within the culture of curiosities: to embrace or repress economics, to promote useful or useless practices, to make knowledge élitist or popular, to prioritize individuals or communities.

And yet, although even within the culture of curiosities curiosity was not a 'concept' in any usual sense, since it was not subject to any definitive set of criteria, nonetheless it was more than just a polysemic family of terms that were used in innumerable different ways. Certainly, some contemporaries argued that some evocations of curiosity were chimerical—empty words that were used to sell books. But the view of most writers and readers within the culture of curiosities was that curiosity had a very real existence, that it was an actual thing. It was just that they constantly disputed and modified what exactly that thing was—for example a passion, or a quality of certain objects, or both?—and whether it corresponded to all or just to some of the meanings of the 'curiosity' family of terms. Individuals in isolation had relatively little power to impose their own definitions over those promulgated by institutions, practices, and discourses. For example, even Gaffarel, whose notorious *Unheard-*

of Curiosities contributed towards making it possible to be 'curious' about occult sciences, had his attempt to erase the history of patristic condemnation of curiosity reversed by the book industry, when later Latin editions of his treatise carried a cautionary preface which reinstated that history with a vengeance. But even institutions, practices, and discourses always failed ultimately to impose definitively and coherently their own definitions, since they were riven by dissent and by conflicting pressures. The contours of curiosity were at their most contested and strained in works (such as those by Fleury and Hartnack) that had one foot in church discourse and another in the culture of curiosities, or else in discourses (such as those on travel, luxury, and the occult sciences) in which traditional qualms about curiosity sat alongside newer enthusiasm about it. However, even writers who felt no need to address moral anxieties about curiosity constantly modified its shape in accordance with the uses that they made of it: whereas certain naturalists were happy to broaden the appeal of their scholarly monographs by entitling them 'curious'— connoting 'odd', 'uncommon', or 'beautiful'—in the text proper they disavowed such connotations in favour of the serious, scholarly meanings 'diligent, thorough, detailed'.

Despite such variability and contestation, contemporaries continually stated that it was one and the *same* curiosity that characterized not only many of the discourses within the culture of curiosities but also often even church and university discourse. For example, church critics equated the curiosity of collecting with that of newspapers, luxury goods, fashion, natural philosophy, and so on; the book industry put a homogenizing 'curious' stamp on very different books; certain writers processed very different branches of knowledge in a similar, 'curious' way in their successive publications. People proposed endlessly different versions of what did and did not count as curiosity and of which phenomena labelled 'curious' really did share the same quality as opposed to just happening to share the same label. Certainly, the culture of curiosities was united by internal family resemblances, which were stronger than those which also linked it to its more distant cousins, university and church discourse on curiosity. And yet even within the culture of curiosities, curiosity was always contested, because it was now put to innumerable uses.

This is the end-point of my survey of institutional uses of curiosity. But it is only the halfway-point of my investigation of the two discursive tendencies that dominated early modern uses of curiosity:

4

Discursive Tendencies: Narrating

Sexes: Male

'All those disturbances were caused by curiosity', said
Cleandre, 'but since they serve to entertain this gathering,
we should not yet repent altogether of being curious'.[1]

These 'disturbances' referred to in 1661, within a conversation
written by Madeleine de Scudéry, are all ones that she embeds in
narratives, that is, in stories, anecdotes, and examples that recount
a sequence of events or actions in which the curiosity of protagonists
figures at the start or in the middle and then always causes an
ending—usually calamitous. In countless other early modern texts
too, the mere mention of curiosity conjured up a narrative. This
powerful propensity was one of the most prominent semantic fibres
that ran through the 'curiosity' family of terms. It also structured the
sentence, paragraph, or pages that surrounded many an occurrence
of 'curiosity'; it can therefore be called a discursive thread, strand,
or tendency.

Yet this curiosity-narrating tendency was not ubiquitous. When
an occurrence of 'curiosity' did *not* conjur up a narrative, then the
chances are that it conjured up instead the collecting of discursive or
material fragments. It is arguable that most early modern occurrences of the 'curiosity' family of terms conjured up one (or both) of
these two language-games at some level—narrating or collecting.
Although these two discursive tendencies often co-existed, one of
them was usually dominant in any given discourse or institution. The
curiosity-collecting tendency was dominant in the culture of curiosities, as we have seen. On the other hand, the curiosity-narrating

---

[1] See 4.4.5.1 below.

tendency was dominant in church and university discourse, as well as in practices such as theatre, opera, and ballet, and in various genres of prose fiction and poetry, which all recounted what happens to curious people. These texts make curiosity a link in a narrative chain rather than a process of amassing discursive or material objects. Some of the church and university discourse that we have already encountered will now be briefly revisited in order to see how curiosity was embedded in narratives within it (4.3). But most of the present section goes beyond those two institutions, investigating how curiosity was used in a wide range of overtly fictional narratives that were designed to be watched, heard, and read (4.4).

The uses of curiosity were thus inflected not only by institutions but also by these two major discursive tendencies, towards collecting and narrating. On another level, they were also inflected by sex and gender. Curiosity was rarely—if ever—neutral in terms of sex and gender. It was almost always—perhaps always—tacitly or explicitly described as male or female, as masculine or feminine. This occurred not just in *certain* particular institutions, practices, discourses, or genres, but in *all* of those considered in the present study. Curiosity will be investigated as it was attributed to men (Section 4) and to women (Section 5): the end of the present section (4.4.5) acts as a bridge between the two in that it investigates curiosity as attributed to both. The sections on sex and gender focus on narrative but they could fruitfully have been extended to include the less narrative-based texts of the culture of curiosities too.

What, then, was the point of telling so many stories about male curiosity? What were its *uses*? They were too multifarious to be summarized en bloc, but many involved regulating various activities, including the acquisition of knowledge. Curiosity was often used in attempts to induce certain kinds of behaviour in men and boys. However, in addition to such pragmatic and instrumental uses, geared towards producing purportedly ethical action in the everyday world, some other uses of curiosity in narratives became increasingly aesthetic and cognitive: especially from the second half of the seventeenth century, curiosity came sometimes to be highlighted self-consciously as the motor that propelled forward the aesthetic artefacts that were narratives, as the thread that pulled readers forward through them. As these reflexive, aesthetic uses grew, the ethical uses sometimes waned or were even directly undermined.

Each different *use* of narrative-embedded curiosity entailed reshaping curiosity, which was not, therefore, a definable 'concept'. But nor was curiosity merely a set of terms that were periodically used for different purposes, for the reshaping often involved, precisely, a new or a renewed claim about what this thing called curiosity *was*, about which kinds of knowledge or activity came under its aegis and which did not. These claims were frequently conflictual: the shape and contours of curiosity were constantly contested in narrative, as in other kinds of writing. For example, in certain eighteenth-century French plays that satirize collectors of curiosities, the protagonist's curiosity, which he sees as the process of accumulating fragments, is ultimately represented as being in fact one phase in a sequence of actions that leads to his downfall: in other words, the curiosity-narrating tendency is triumphantly superimposed on the curiosity-collecting tendency. Note that in these plays, as so often, the curiosity that is shaped by these two tendencies is aggressively and polemically understood as being in fact one and the same thing. But that was not the only view possible. Collectors of curiosities would have argued that their curiosity was entirely unrelated to that described by moralizing stories about the dangers of curiosity or, at most, that it was a distant species of the same passion.

So the distinction between the narrating and collecting tendencies was one of several points of potential division within curiosity, that is, one of several boundaries that could be used either to link two types of curiosity together as being the same thing or else to partition them off as being distinct things. The position of such boundaries within curiosity depended partly on the language in question. In French, the narrating and collecting tendencies of curiosity were often closely intertwined (as also in Latin and English), because *curiosité* denoted both the inquisitiveness or acquisitiveness that propelled subjects through sequences of actions and yet also the kind of object that attracted them: the subject-oriented senses of *curiosité* tended to dominate within narratives whereas its object-oriented senses tended to dominate within the curiosity-collecting tendency. On the other hand, in German the link between those two discursive tendencies was much weaker, since *Curiosität*, *curieus*, and so on referred very often to objects but less often to the inquisitiveness or acquisitiveness of subjects (since they were more usually termed *Vorwitz* or *Neugierde*): so, whereas the curiosity-collecting tendency was extremely prominent in German discourse, there were far fewer German narratives of curiosity[2]—the nearest equivalent were narratives of *Vorwitz* or *Neugierde*. For this reason, the narratives of curiosity to be studied here will be mainly French, plus a few published in Germany but written in Latin.

There were several other kinds of boundary within early modern curiosity that enabled writers either to disaggregate or to aggregate it. Some that we have already encountered elsewhere were also used in narratives: the division of curiosity into 'species'; the grafting of new meanings of curiosity onto old; the dismissal of some usages of the term 'curiosity' as misnomers. However, two other kinds of dividing/joining-line within early modern curiosity were specific to narrative. First, narrative induced readers to connect different realms of experience, especially via exemplarity and allegory: an exemplary story which showed curiosity operating in one realm could be explicitly presented as applicable or transferable to several other realms too; an allegorical story about curiosity was similarly transferable to other realms. Second was the boundary between diegesis (the world represented by a narrative) and extradiegesis (the narrator or author's comments on elements outside the narrated world, such as the reader): this also sometimes became a boundary between two kinds of curiosity, that of protagonists on the one hand and that of reader, audience, or narrator on the other.

The extent to which these narrative-specific boundaries within curiosity were actualized depended not only on the uses to which curiosity was put and on the genre of writing in question, but also on the date. These boundaries have their history: they emerged and shifted over time. Exemplarity shaped curiosity continuously from the sixteenth to the eighteenth century, but in changing ways. Whereas in the late sixteenth century the moral of a narrative *exemplum* of curiosity—such as Poissenot's tale of the philosopher Secundus (4.4.3.3 below)—could be applied to a wide range of other contexts, ranging from divination to travel, because curiosity was still considered a vice in most contexts, on the other hand by the late seventeenth century the range of contexts to which any such *exemplum* of curiosity could be applied had become more limited and problematic, because of the new uncertainty as to whether curiosity

---

[2] One exception is the work of Aegidius Albertinus: see Locher 1989. Although J.-D. Müller (1984) describes *curiositas* as the focus of his excellent study of early German prose romance, this family of terms barely figures in the material he actually quotes.

was a vice or virtue or both or neither. Moreover, although both exemplarity and allegory continued to thrive in some genres into the eighteenth century, in certain genres and texts they became increasingly undermined over the course of the seventeenth century. The very notion that readers could be morally improved by cautionary tales of curiosity (or anything else) was either attacked (Lafayette) or ignored (Diderot).

Similarly, the relation between intra- and extradiegetic curiosity can also be historicized. On the whole, in the sixteenth century, whereas the curiosity of protagonists was frequently represented and condemned, the desire of readers or audiences to know what happens to protagonists next was not called curiosity. However, by the middle of the seventeenth century, that desire of readers or audiences was sometimes celebrated as curiosity, even if the actual story at which their curiosity was directed showed that curiosity was a dangerous thing: the exact relation between this extra- and intradiegetic curiosity sometimes remained unspecified or unresolved. But by 1661 it was possible for at least one writer—Madeleine de Scudéry— to draw explicit attention to this awkward boundary, revelling playfully in it in the sentence quoted in the epigraph to the present section, in which Scudéry wittily suggests that intra- and extradiegetic curiosity are in fact the same thing—siblings linked by an embarrassing family resemblance.

My own account of these historical shifts in the boundaries that shaped curiosity within narratives is necessarily provisional, deduced from the highly selective case studies offered here and liable to be nuanced by others that could be added. In order to emphasize these shifts, my account is structured partly along chronological lines, for example beginning with a 1600 exemplary tale of curiosity (4.4.1) and ending with Lafayette's 1678 demonstration of the impossibility of such tales (4.4.5.2), or else following the metamorphoses of the 'curious impertinent' from Cervantes to Diderot. However, my structure is not entirely chronological; it is partly based on genre, in order to show that these historical shifts did not affect all genres in the same way: in the eighteenth and even early nineteenth century, well after some narratives had demonstrated that it was problematic to represent the *curieux* as a universal type, nonetheless theatrical comedies (4.4.4) and Jesuit school ballets (4.4.2) continued cheerfully to do precisely that. The shapes of curiosity continued to be determined as much by local uses as by broader historical shifts.

4.1 NARRATING AS A DISCURSIVE TENDENCY

Nowadays the statement that one is working on early modern curiosity sometimes elicits requests for clarification along the lines: 'Do you mean as in "cabinet of curiosities" or as in "curiosity killed the cat"?' The question shows that vestiges of the early modern curiosity-collecting and curiosity-narrating tendencies are still present in modern discourse, and that the relation between the two still causes unease. Did the death of the cat have anything to do with the cabinet of curiosities? Or were they entirely separate?

Although the proverb 'curiosity killed the cat' is probably modern, it is a variation on an Elizabethan proverb which shared its *cura* etymon: 'care will kill a cat' was used by William Shakespeare, Ben Jonson, and many others, well into the eighteenth century.[3] Even if there had been an original, underlying story, it had most likely faded from view when the proverb was disseminated, like the forgotten, literal term of a dead metaphor. But the proverb still transmitted the basic elements of a narrative: a furry hero, a sticky end. And it postulated a relation of cause and effect between the 'care' and the end, as with Scudéry's 'disturbances . . . caused by curiosity'. Such proverbs were (and still are) one of the narrative forms by which passions, vices, and virtues can be represented. These various forms use narration to bypass definition. Instead of representing a passion through a universally applicable definition that hinges on abstract nouns and can be broken down into species and sub-species—as we saw in university dissertations—they tell a story, whether of what might happen ('care will kill a cat'), of what did happen ('curiosity killed the cat'), or of what tends to happen. The widespread recourse, then and now, to such stories in order to represent passions, virtues, vices, and vices suggests that 'concepts' are not so much general categories delimited by definable criteria as 'summaries of plots' (as Paul Veyne terms them).[4]

In early modern discourse, those plot summaries often took the form of *exempla*, of specific instances of virtue or vice, taken usually, but not always, from the Bible or classical antiquity.[5] Such *exempla*, often following a definition of a virtue or vice, had cognitive, pragmatic, and ethical uses, serving both to illustrate the virtue or vice

---

[3] e.g. Jonson 1998, 28.
[4] 'résumé[s] d'intrigue[s]' (Veyne 1979, 82; see pp. 89–91).
[5] See Hampton 1990; Lyons 1989.

and also to persuade readers to avoid or espouse it. The illustrative use was particularly prominent in university dissertations, where *exempla* of curiosity were usually subordinate to definitions of it, although in turn the examples sometimes exceeded or reshaped the definition. On the other hand, in much church discourse, especially pastoral rather than theological, exemplarity was more prominent than definition. Jean-Pierre Camus's sermon-oriented discussion of curiosity contained 'summaries of plots': numerous *exempla* of the vice but no definitions of it.[6]

If proverbs such as 'curiosity killed the cat' condensed narratives, then *exempla* could do so even more. Camus and countless other writers only had to mention a proper name—such as Icarus—for a particular narrative of curiosity to be evoked in the minds of many readers or listeners. 'The curiosity of Icarus' evoked not a theoretical definition or proposition but a story. Curiosity was equated not just with the figure of Icarus in himself but with what he did and with what happened to him. Such condensed exemplary narratives could also take visual form, notably in emblems.[7]

The plots, whether old or new, that were summarized as 'curiosity' in the early modern period continued to be predominantly unhappy ones. Although in many discourses, especially those of the culture of curiosities, curiosity had now been transformed into a virtue or a morally indifferent passion, in narratives it remained on the whole a vice. Certainly, many stories and historical anecdotes were promulgated enthusiastically within the culture of curiosities, but there they were largely marketed as curiosities, rather than being narratives about curiosity. It was only when, in discourses such as those on nature and art, the culture of curiosities and its discursive tendency towards collecting were on the wane, that curiosity could be transformed into a stage of a happy narrative (as in the 1739 *Fruitful Curiosity* prospectus—3.4.2 above). Previously, in the culture of curiosities it was the curiosity-collecting tendency that was used most often to encourage and legitimize certain kinds of knowledge

---

[6] For other discussions of curiosity that take almost entirely the form of *exempla* rather than of definition, see Garzoni 1586, 68ʳ–71ʳ (a contribution to the Theophrastian 'characters' tradition); Weber 1673, 459–66.

[7] However, not all visual representations of curiosity took narrative form. In Jean Baudouin's 1644 translation of Cesare Ripa's famous *Iconologia* (1593), whereas the image 'Curiosité d'amour' represents a moment from a narrative (Cupid and Psyche), on the other hand the image for 'Curiosité' is a non-narrative, allegorical, feminine personification. For these images, see Désirat 1998, 522–3.

and activity, whereas in other discourses the curiosity-narrating tendency was used most often to *discourage* them. In stories—from *exempla* to novellas or plays—the shapes of curiosity were usually closer to those given to it by theology and moral philosophy than by, say, natural philosophy.

Remarkably, even in texts which declared, on one level, that curiosity was divided into good and bad, the bad usually came to the fore once stories started being told. This discrepancy may point to a more general one in the period between discursive definitions of the passions and, on the other hand, narrative—or what are usually now called 'literary'—representations of them, which were frequently more tragic and negative in character.[8] Even today, there remains a discrepancy of moral evaluation between what many people might say about curiosity if pushed to make a general, non-narrative definition of it and, on the other hand, the darker tenor of the narrative phrase which actually comes more immediately to mind—'curiosity killed the cat'. In the case of both periods it could be argued that narratives, whether proverbs or examples, tend to be more negative because they have (and had) been around longer than more recent, positive reappraisals of curiosity: they are (and were) anachronistic sediments of an archaic view. Yet the argument can also be turned on its head: the persistence of negative *exempla* of curiosity throughout the early modern period—and not just in church discourse—perhaps points to continuing anxieties about it which refused to go away even when the culture of curiosities sought to eradicate them. Besides, even new unhappy narratives of curiosity were also produced in the period, most famously that of Doctor Faust, who quickly became an *exemplum*.

However, of the small, finite number of exemplars of curiosity who recurred constantly in early modern discourse, most were ancient, from myth or history. Most were male, a few female. Most had *not* been described as 'curious' in their ancient source texts (Apuleius's Psyche was the spectacular exception), nor would that label be an obvious one for them in most modern readers' eyes. Yet by the early modern period all were interpreted as 'curious', just as several biblical *loci* which did not mention *curiositas* were subsequently interpreted as being nonetheless about it (2.1 above).

---

[8] This conjecture, for which I am indebted to Sue James, would repay more systematic investigation.

The main ancient male exemplars were as follows. Icarus: his wax-cemented wings melted when he flew too near to the sun, plunging him into the Aegean. Phaethon: he heeded neither the discouragement nor the instructions of his father the sun (Phoebus) before joyriding the latter's chariot out of control, prompting Jupiter to kill him with a thunderbolt. Ixion: for attempting to seduce Juno, he also found himself on the end of one of Jupiter's thunderbolts before being tied to an eternally revolving wheel in hell. Prometheus: his theft of fire from the gods prompted Jupiter to have him tied to a rock where a vulture fed continually on his liver. Epimetheus: by agreeing to marry Pandora, he became the recipient of another punishment initially intended for Prometheus, when Pandora inquisitively opened the jar of woes which Jupiter had given her as a present for her bridegroom. (In some early modern versions, Epimetheus did the opening.) Ulysses's companions: they opened other receptacles—the barrels given to their master by the wind-god Aeolus—releasing winds which wrecked their fleet. Actaeon: having chanced, while hunting, upon Diana bathing naked in a stream, he was turned by her into a stag and hunted to death by his own hounds. Orpheus: he lost Eurydice to Hades by glancing back at her. Oedipus: his desire to know the truth led (in this interpretation) to his downfall. The astronomer Thales: he fell down a well while observing the stars. Others possessed curiosity that was, if not calamitous, then at least futile: Archimedes, Archytas, and Daedalus failed in their respective attempts to square the circle, to fly, and to build a running-machine to replace horses. Biblical males who were interpreted as exemplars of curiosity were rarer: I have encountered just one—Uzziah, who was smitten with leprosy as punishment for usurping the functions of the priests in the Temple (2 Chronicles 26.18–19). As for more recent stories that came to be interpreted as *exempla* of curiosity, one was provided by Ludovico Ariosto: Ariodant, in the misguided belief that he had seen his beloved Guinevere embracing his rival, leaped off a rock into the sea, claiming that he would have lived happily if only he had been blind (*Orlando furioso* 5.58).[9]

[9] e.g. see Andreæ 1621, 12–13 (Archimedes, Archytas, Daedalus), repeated by Spizel 1676, 954; Boissard 1588, 16–17 (Prometheus); Camus 1613, vi. 565 and vii. 431–6 (Thales, Icarus, Phaethon, Prometheus, Ixion, Epimetheus); Dacier in Aristotle 1692, 270 (Oedipus); Garzoni 1586, 68ʳ–70ʳ (Actaeon, Ariodant); [La Santé] 1737, 6 (Orpheus, Ulysses's companions). For Actaeon, see [Conti] 1627, 664 (and index entry); Estienne 1603, 11ʳ. For Uzziah, see Stryk/Lüedecke 1743, 295. Curiosity was

In France, from about the late sixteenth or early seventeenth century onwards, the culture of curiosities was beginning to emerge, with its positive re-evaluation of curiosity. One might therefore expect to find that cautionary tales of curiosity were on the wane at that time. And yet the opposite is true. Exemplary tales warning of the dangers of curiosity became no less insistent and, if anything, lengthier. Cautionary tales of curiosity, like church attacks on it, seem to have been energized by the secular rise of allegedly good curiosity. In a sense, the culture of curiosities, far from carrying everyone along with it, created even more opposition to curiosity in many quarters. But why was narrating so crucial to that opposition? What could narrative achieve that lay beyond the powers of more abstract, discursive, or definition-based representations of curiosity?

If the point was to persuade readers to change their lives and behaviour, then the *pathos* and memorableness of narratives of curiosity gave them far more rhetorical force than dry definitions of it. Narratives also gave people the means to make sense of their particular experiences by identifying them with textual *exempla* and thereby subsuming them within a universal—such as the passion or vice of curiosity—which those *exempla* explicitly illustrated. This transition from particular experiences to universals was also facilitated for readers by allegorical interpretation, which was sometimes closely related to exemplarity: Actaeon was both an *exemplum* of curiosity—figuring in standard lists alongside other *exempla* from the Bible or antiquity—and yet also an allegorical sign which could be interpreted as denoting curiosity or indeed other failings. Readers' applications of *exempla* to other contexts could thus turn them into allegories: for example, Fénelon's prose fable of the fox (2.2.4.3 above) seems to be about other species of curiosity than the apparently innocuous enjoyment of art in which the doomed fox indulges by visiting the Escorial. Nonetheless, exemplarity was also often distinct from allegory, since allegory created a greater discontinuity between its literal and figurative meanings than that which separated an *exemplum* from its universal meaning.[10]

a common—but not the most common—allegorical interpretation of the Actaeon myth among humanists (Brumble 1998, 5). For Ulysses and Oedipus, see Plutarch 1971, 64ʳ, 67ᵛ. Defaux (1982, 37) does demonstrate that Ulysses was sometimes interpreted by humanists as *curiosus*, but the 'curiosity' family of terms is absent from almost all the evidence he cites (chs. 1 and 3). Ulysses seems not to have become as near-synonymous with curiosity as, say, Icarus and Phaethon.

[10] Cf. Lyons 1989, 250 n. 45.

Yet the specific usefulness of narrative lay not only in the way in which it subordinated particulars to universals, making the former illustrate the latter, but also in its capacity sometimes to make particulars exceed or even resist universal definitions. Narratives gave curiosity dimensions that were virtually absent from generalizing definitions. Above all, narratives often showed that curiosity was not a discrete, self-contained passion or vice (or even virtue) within a human being, but rather that it was always part of a sequence of passions, actions, and events. Instead of being static and autonomous, curiosity always followed on from something and gave rise to something else, in a linear chain of cause and effect. The chain linked it not only to the subject's other passions but also to specific social outcomes: it affected both the individual and those around him or her. Whatever the precise composition of this chain of curiosity, most narratives represented it as unbreakable: once protagonists were curious—whether by free choice or not—their progression through the subsequent set of links was usually both inevitable and calamitous. I am calling this sequence a 'chain' in order to highlight not only its strict, linear order but also this constriction. I have drawn the metaphor from a description by Miguel de Cervantes of Anselmo, his hapless 'curious impertinent', who became one of the most prominent early modern exemplars of curiosity: 'Anselmo . . . persisted thus with a belief that was quite contrary to the truth, forging little by little the *chain* which was binding him to inevitable dishonour: the more Lothario wronged him, the more Anselmo thought he was obliged to Lothario.'[11] Chains do not just link, they also inexorably bind.

Someone can be trapped in such a chain without realizing it. Extended narratives in particular were sometimes used to demonstrate the ironic discrepancies between the iron reality of a chain and protagonists' perceptions of it. Anselmo has no idea that he is caught in a chain. A century later, the heroine of Eliza Haywood's *Masqueraders; or Fatal Curiosity*, awaiting her friend's lover, would—if she reflected—think she is on one link (curiosity) of a chain, whereas in fact she has already progressed to the next (love):

[11] Since I am concerned with the story as it circulated in France, I cite the first French translation of *Don Quixote*: 'Anselme . . . alloit ainsi par une croyance toute contraire a la verité, forgeant petit a petit la chaisne qui l'attachoit a une honte inevitable, de façon que tant plus Lothaire luy faisoit tort, tant plus il pensoit luy estre obligé' (Cervantes 1614, 467).

'Had PHILECTA ask'd herself the Question, when the Hour of his approach drew near, her beating Heart had soon inform'd her it was to something more than Curiosity she ow'd her present Agitations . . .'[12] Indeed the notion that a woman's curiosity leads to 'FANCY' and then to sexual 'DESIRE' was a topos of eighteenth-century fiction.[13] The chain-links which tended to precede and follow curiosity were also its metonymic connotations: 'curiosity' connoted 'love' or 'sex' because it was so often contiguous with them, preceding them psychologically or chronologically or both. A protagonist's denial that he or she had reached a phase—such as 'love'—beyond curiosity often made curiosity slippery and ironically charged, since eroticism was thus displaced onto it. Curiosity was metonymically linked in this way not only to other passions but also to its outcomes. Even brief titles such as *Fatal Curiosity* designated not just a particular species of curiosity but a chain, that is, a plot, complete with dénouement. Narrative made the *outcomes* of curiosity an integral part of what curiosity was.

Although the chain-bound status of curiosity emerged especially in narrative, it was also evident in discursive treatises. Indeed, philosophical treatises regularly discussed the normal sequences in which passions and actions occur in practice.[14] Theologians debated the precise sequence in which the triad of Augustinian concupiscences— one of which was curiosity—attacked a person.[15] Different metaphors were used. Calvin wrote not of a chain but of an 'awful, no-exit labyrinth' in which people, having once 'released the reins of their curiosity' by toying with judicial astrology (which is merely 'superfluous and useless'), then 'burrow even further forward into all kinds of divination' (which are downright 'wicked').[16] This slippery slope argument—to add a modern metaphor—underlies numerous treatises and narratives which contrast the apparently innocuous beginnings of curiosity with its calamitous endings, thereby echoing

---

[12] [Haywood] 1724, 19. On curiosity in Haywood's fictions, see Benedict 2001, 139–41; K. King 1998.

[13] *Tristram Shandy* ([Sterne] [1759]–67, viii. 14). See N. Kenny 1998, 168.

[14] See James 1997, 58–9, 73, 113, 255, and part 4 (e.g. 258, 260, 268, 291).

[15] e.g. Bossuet 1930a, 83–4; Jansen 1659, 40, 49. See Sellier 1970, 170.

[16] Calvin 1985: 'Or, comme c'est un horrible labyrinthe et sans yssue que des folies et superstitions, desquelles les hommes s'enveloppent depuis que ilz ont une fois lasché la bride à leur curiosité, beaucoup d'esprodvolages, apres s'estre amusez à la divination des astres, se fourrent encore plus avant, assavoir en toutes especes de divinations' (94); 'une curiosité non seulement superflue et inutile, mais aussi mauvaise' (102).

the Augustinian theme of its duplicity. The argument was put by Jesuits as well as by Calvinists; Garasse turns the labyrinth into a voyage: 'The devil . . . takes him first to idleness, then from idleness to gluttony and drunkenness, thence to sensuality, from sensuality to insensibility, from insensibility to curiosity, from curiosity to magic and witchcraft, thence to atheism: that is the voyage which all of those would-be fine minds usually undertake.'[17] Thus, with their labyrinths or voyages, even some treatise-writers virtually burst into narrative when trying to describe curiosity.

The specific usefulness of narrative also lay in its capacity to represent the temporality of curiosity. Whereas within the culture of curiosities usually it was spatial metaphors—such as that of a collection—that described curiosity, on the other hand the curiosity-narrating tendency was largely temporal: the chain of passions, actions, and events—in which curiosity was a link—unfurled inescapably in time. Narrativized curiosity could only be apprehended within a temporal framework, as something that came later than its causes and earlier than its effects, as something that was inherently transitional, existing only in relation to what preceded and what followed it. To translate this point into the language of Paul Ricoeur: the ultimate referent of narratives of curiosity was the temporal structure of human existence.[18] Certainly, the temporality of curiosity was not stressed only in narratives: even discursive treatises, dissertations, and sermons represented curiosity as an attempt to transgress the temporal structure of human existence by aiming to know the past or the future.[19] And the common designation of curiosity as *intempestiva*[20] or *unzeitig*[21]—'untimely' or 'unseasonable'—contained a latent or explicit suggestion that it breached not only decorum in general but temporal decorum (or *occasio*) in particular: it

---

[17] 'Le Diable . . . le mene premierement à la feneantise, de la feneantise à la gourmandise et yvrognerie, de celle-cy à la luxure, de la luxure à l'insensibilité, de l'insensibilité à la curiosité, de la curiosité, à la Magie et sortilege, de celuy-cy à l'Atheisme, et voyla le voyage que font ordinairement tous nos beaux esprits pretendus.' (Garasse 1971, 342; also quoted in Jacques-Chaquin 1998b, 87). Compare the simpler chain in Spizel (1676, 117–21), for whom curiosity leads to 'singularity', which leads to 'atheism'.

[18] Unlike Ricoeur (see White 1991, 143–4), I am including not only relative extended narratives, but also ones that are embedded in single phrases ('fatal curiosity') or words ('Icarus').

[19] §§ 1.2.1, 2.2.4.2, and 3.3 above.

[20] e.g. Becmann 1679, 17; Buddeus 1719a, 437; Stryk/Lüedecke 1743, 307.

[21] e.g. Buddeus 1719b, 466.

sometimes involved wanting to know something at the wrong time. However, only extended narratives privileged the theme of time's revenge against such curious, would-be escapers from its structures.

Compared with definitions and treatises, narratives also gave readers far more help in learning how to recognize curiosity when they came across it in life, whether in themselves or in others. Taken as a whole, the chain of events, usually culminating in calamity, often furnished proof that curiosity had occurred at some point earlier along the chain, whereas the curiosity on its own would have been difficult to apprehend directly and at the moment of its operation. The plot that surrounded curiosity was therefore analogous to other symptoms of curiosity such as the bodily 'external . . . signs of this affect'—facial pallor or redness, sluggishness, trembling, and so on—which tell us that someone is in its grip.[22] Indeed, such bodily symptoms could themselves be incorporated into narrative: a strange cluster of them—appearing care-worn, skinny, lamb-like, and dehydrated—formed the basis of one imaginative amplification, by François Rabelais, of what Plautus and others wrote about *curiosi* (N. Kenny 2003). The problems involved in directly detecting curiosity (and other passions) were—as we have already seen in the case of Haywood—explored particularly in late seventeenth- and early eighteenth-century fiction. Passion detectives, whether readers or protagonists, needed all the indirect clues that they could get, and narrative gave them many.

However, narratives did not merely function as practical guides to diagnosing curiosity. More than any other mode of writing, narrative could even undercut any such pragmatic use of curiosity by demonstrating the impossibility of diagnosing and judging it definitively, of mastering it discursively through definition and sub-division into neat species. In many narratives, distinctions between 'good' and 'bad curiosity' or between different species of curiosity—such as the lover's and the collector's—became blurred or erased. This occurred not in all narratives, but especially in those which went beyond the more rigid and transparent forms of exemplarity and allegory. For example, it was through comic fantasy that Rabelais transformed exemplarity when narrating the adventures of the *curieux* Panurge in *Pantagruel*.

---

[22] '*externa* quaedam *huius affectus signa*' (Watson/Rose 1690, 760; see pp. 760–1, 765).

In late sixteenth- and early seventeenth-century France, although some genres continued to use relatively transparent allegory (4.4.2 below), in others allegory had either waned or else had become more opaque and less communicative of moral or philosophical certainties.[23] The polymathic cathedral canon François Béroalde de Verville allegorized curiosity partially and opaquely in various philosophical fictions, such as *Le Cabinet de Minerve* (1596), *Le Voyage des princes fortunez* (1610), and the 'Recueil steganographique' which prefaced his 1600 version (*Le Songe de Poliphile*) of Francesco Colonna's 1499 *Hypnerotomachia Poliphili*. These were composed at a time when writers were beginning to use the 'curiosity' family in French in much more positive senses, at least in philosophical contexts, while always still having to keep an eye over their shoulder on the negative patristic senses: good curiosity still often had to be accompanied by the epithet 'good' in order to distinguish it from what would otherwise be assumed to be 'bad curiosity'. This ambivalence contributes to the opacity of Verville's allegories or 'partial' allegories.[24]

The curiosity of Verville's first- or third-person male protagonists often seems to propel them towards a telos of some kind, which is variously signalled to be philosophical, alchemical, erotic, moral, or an equivocal combination of these.[25] Along the way, the curious protagonists enjoy discrete moments of gratification—being shown rare objects, often inside cabinets—which, like the encounters with more discursive objects in Verville's miscellany *Le Palais des curieux* (1612), anticipate the flowering of the culture of curiosities. However, on the whole, in Verville even these discrete 'encounters' (*rencontres*)[26] between subject and object are often—unlike standard ones in the culture of curiosities, which are ends in themselves— subordinated to that broader quest (philosophical, moral, and so on): in other words, the curiosity-collecting tendency ultimately seems subordinated to the curiosity-narrating tendency. The same

---

[23] See Cave 1999, 160 n. 38; Jeanneret 1994.

[24] On *Le Voyage* as 'en partie un récit allégorique' (159), see Cave 1999, 155–64. For an earlier, more uniform and transparent allegory of curiosity, see the neo-Platonic *Discours philosophiques* by Pontus de Tyard, in 4 of which (1555–8) the ambivalent figure of the 'Curieux' is a major interlocutor (Huot-Bokdam 1986).

[25] On the relation between such levels of meaning in (respectively) the 'Recueil steganographique' and *Le Voyage*, see Mauri 1992 and 1996.

[26] See N. Kenny 1991a, 106–9.

goes for analogous episodes in Verville's fictional and historical romances.[27]

But the exact relation between the two tendencies—therefore the very status of curiosity—often remains unclear. The discrete encounters with knowledge variously seem to be either essential staging posts on the journey to the ulterior telos which need to be stopped at and then passed through, or else damaging diversions from that journey, or else harmless and pleasurable supplements to it.[28] How can one decide which is which? The problem is dramatized in the narratives themselves, since protagonists often get it wrong, not least because they are not always sure what their ulterior telos should be; nor is the reader sure, since, as Terence Cave has shown, Verville—evoking various versions of the sovereign good without committing his narrative to promoting any single one—gives no definitive representation of that telos which would enable one to put the various suggested levels of meaning into a stable allegorical hierarchy (1999, 163).

After the period of Verville, narratives that went out of their way to undermine any clear-cut definition of curiosity tended to be engage oppositionally more with the tradition of exemplarity than with that of allegory. In France, especially from the second half of the seventeenth century, curiosity was a major motor of some narratives without, however, being easily decipherable any longer as an *exemplum*. To an extent, this was just one symptom of the general (but not universal) decline of exemplarity in the period. That is not to say that abandoning exemplarity always involved abandoning clear-cut morality: several eighteenth-century plays were satires of curiosity whose protagonists were, if not exemplary or counter-exemplary in the injunctive sense, then certainly types that illustrated general moral (and social) categories.

Those narratives that *had* begun to resist the incorporation of curiosity into stable moral categories can be interpreted as logical extensions of the sheer uncertainty, anxiety, and excitement that surrounded the status of curiosity in other contemporary discourses, where it was no longer taken for granted that curiosity was 'fatal'. The increased moral ambivalence of curiosity may have given narrative fiction a more prominent and distinctive role in representing it,

---

[27] e.g. Verville 1592, 86ᵛ–90ᵛ and 1597, 131–2 (called a 'rencontre').
[28] See N. Kenny 1991a, esp. ch. 5.

since the more narrative fiction cut loose from exemplarity, the more it could represent and leave unresolved a conflicting array of moral and affective responses to curiosity.

This was partly because the potential split between curiosity as extra- and as intradiegetic made curiosity especially prone to ambivalence in narrative. This split had its equivalents in discursive texts which made human curiosity their theme while also appealing to their reader's curiosity, as we have seen not only in the culture of curiosities but also in church and university discourse. The split could be particularly uneasy in church discourse which both condemned and appealed to curiosity. That unease was even more widespread in narratives, which also sometimes reflected much more richly on the relation between the curiosity of reader and of protagonist. When Verville claims that the architectural descriptions in *Le Songe de Poliphile* are designed to satisfy those who are 'light in their curiosity and do not delve beyond the surface'—as opposed to those seeking the hidden alchemical meanings—he is describing what Cave has called the vertical axis of allegorical interpretation, as opposed to the horizontal, intradiegetic plot axis along which Poliphile is faced with similar problems of interpretation.[29] If, in the sixteenth century, the pre-history of suspense sometimes intensified claims that readers experience desire (Cave 1999, 129–41), then it was especially in the seventeenth century that that desire often became curiosity.

The spread of curiosity from the intra- to the extradiegetic level of narration provided a structure for exploring—without necessarily resolving—the aporias of curiosity. The extradiegetic level, instead of defining curiosity definitively, sealing it off with a conceptual lid which would make it comprehensible and controllable, in fact often reopened it, like some Pandora's box. This did not occur only in overtly fictional narratives. For example, as Nicole Jacques-Chaquin has shown, late sixteenth- and early seventeenth-century demonologists used the seductive vocabulary of curiosity to hook people into reading *exempla* and thereby be persuaded to condemn occultist practices as curious (1998*b*, 98–105). However, whereas the instrumental, ethical aims of these treatises forced their authors to play down the paradoxicality of such a strategy, Scudéry was freer to play it up in her fiction, which aimed more to question what curiosity was

[29] 'légers en leur curiosité, n'enfoncent point outre la superfice' ([Colonna] 1600, ** i^r). See Cave 1999, 139.

than to use it pragmatically. Not all fictional texts complicated curiosity in this way. Many remained concerned to keep it firmly under control. But some fictional texts texts did give full rein to a puzzling, troubling curiosity which transgressed not only social decorum but also—more disturbingly—efforts to define that decorum and uphold it discursively.[30] That is one of the many reasons why Lafayette's *La Princesse de Clèves* and Diderot's *Bijoux indiscrets* are still widely read today, whereas many exemplary fictions are not. Neither work necessarily 'typifies' its period's uses of curiosity more or less than texts which sought conceptual closure, but each is more consonant with modern anxieties about the instability of moral categories.

4.2   MALE AND FEMALE, FEMININE AND MASCULINE

Curiosity was used differently in relation to men and to women. It was not merely attributed to each sex, male and female, but it was also described in ways that implied that it was itself masculine or feminine. In other words, it was part of the culturally, socially, and linguistically acquired set of characteristics which has come to be called 'gender'. In a gender-inflected language such as French, *curieux* and *curieuse* did not neatly account for half of the population each. *Curieux* could be either universal ('men' in the sense of 'humanity') or particular ('men' in the sense of 'males'): the term often alternated surreptitiously between the two. By contrast, *curieuses* always denoted women in particular. Sometimes, both men and women were described as being prone to negative curiosity (albeit in different ways). And sometimes negative curiosity was described as being specifically found in women. On the other hand, positive curiosity was almost always attributed to men alone, rarely to women, except if they were implicitly included in general eulogies of *curieux*, though often it is not clear that they were. For example, the apparent seventeenth-century rehabilitation of curiosity took place only in discourses and practices, such as naturalism and collecting, in which *curieux* were usually assumed to be men. Any grand narrative—such as Blumenberg's—of the early modern legitimation

---

[30] This argument is inspired by the characterization of 'literary' texts as disturbed or disturbing in Cave 1999, esp. 15.

of curiosity overlooks the fact that there was little such legitimation for women, as for various other social groups, such as those excluded by universities from the good curiosity which they claimed to pursue. Such grand narratives can only be told by occluding sex and class as well as economics.

Curiosity had a lopsided relationship to gender as well as to sex. When the good curiosity of men went bad, then it was described as feminine. In his treatise on physics, Bary justifies his inclusion of causal explanations—which some readers would find difficult— by saying that, however *mondain* the treatise might be, it does not descend to the level of its *most* lightweight readers: 'a treatise on physics is exposed to everyone's curiosity, so I must not give up working for tireless *curieux* just in order to pander to effeminate *curieux*'.[31] *Curieux* who like their physics superficial are effeminate here.

On the other hand, real physics was for real men, that is, masculine ones, whereas its objects were often feminized: in his 1667 ode 'To the Royal Society', Abraham Cowley describes (natural) philosophy as a 'Male Virtu' which teaches the 'curious Sight' to 'press' Nature 'Into the privatest recess | Of her imperceptible Littleness'.[32] The curiosities collected in cabinets were sometimes feminized too, as was the knowledge sought by the curious gossip.[33] In erotic narratives, male curiosity was directed not only at feminized objects but at females themselves, often unattainable or inscrutable ones which, like curiosities sought by a collector, seemed to resist 'possession'.

Yet curiosity itself, whether good or bad, in addition to connoting femininity because denoted by a feminine noun (in French, Latin, German, and so on), was also often explicitly personified as a feminine allegorical figure, as on the cover of the present book. The implications of this gendering varied. Where the curiosity represented was bad, then the femininity of the personification became metonymically associated with the wickedness of the curiosity.[34] Where the

---

[31] 'une Physique est exposée à la curiosité de tout le monde, et il ne faut pas pour les curieux effeminez, se défendre de travailler pour les curieux infatigables' (Bary 1671, i, sig. [a viii^r]).

[32] Sprat 1959, B[1^r], [B3^r]. Quoted in Eamon 1994, 314–18.

[33] L'Espine compares curious people who gossip about their neighbours, instead of reading good books, to a man who sleeps with ugly prostitutes instead of with his beautiful wife (1588, 488–9).

[34] e.g. Lipsius 1615, [A3^{r-v}]. 1st edn. 1607.

curiosity personified was good, then the relation of the allegorical feminine persona to actual male *curieux* or *curiosi* was more metaphorical than metonymic. Far from showing the contiguity of women to good male inquisitiveness or curiosity, she was an apt figure for the latter precisely because she belonged to a different realm.[35] For example, it was her chastity and modesty, not her intellect, that figuratively stood for good male curiosity.[36] It is no good having a metaphorical figure that comes from the same realm as what it represents. As modern feminist theory has demonstrated, the exclusion of women from actual practices is often the pre-condition of the centrality of feminine figures in the order of symbolic representation.

These were the norms that dominated early modern discourse on curiosity. Variations on them appeared in countless male- and female-authored texts, though it was particularly some women writers, such as Scudéry and Lafayette, who also challenged them to a degree.

4.3   NON-FICTION

4.3.1   Exempla

history is full of nothing but curious people undone by curiosity[37]

Narratives of curiosity were rife not just in overtly fictional genres but also in church and university discourse, mainly in the form of brief *exempla*. As Timothy Hampton (1990) and John Lyons (1989) have shown, exemplarity had always had its problems, such as the irreducibility of particulars to universals, but awareness of them seems to have become especially acute in some works in the late sixteenth and seventeenth century, from Montaigne's *Essais* to *La Princesse de Clèves*. And yet this crisis of confidence in exemplarity was not ubiquitous.

The early modern rhetoric of exemplarity was either injunctive (persuading readers to imitate some models of behaviour and to

---

[35] e.g. [La Santé] 1737, 2.
[36] e.g. Ceriziers 1643, a ii[r], e iv[v]; Hietling 1713, esp. 5.
[37] 'l'Histoire n'est remplie que de Curieux, que la Curiosité a perdus' (Scudéry 1979, 55).

eschew others) or illustrative (persuading readers that such and such is the case) or both.[38] Which of these tendencies dominated depended partly on genre. For instance, in L'Espine's Calvinist pastoral treatise, the *Excellent Discussions of the Soul's Tranquillity and Happiness* (1587), the narrative examples of curiosity were intended primarily to enjoin good behaviour. By contrast, in university philosophy dissertations, roll-calls of examples of curiosity were designed primarily to illustrate and demonstrate the real existence of numerous species of the passion (as well as the author's cleverness in locating them).

Examples were there to be used, that is, applied to everyday contexts. So, in academic discourse, exemplarity often overlapped with casuistry—the method for applying the principles of a discipline to specific cases, mediating between the abstract and the concrete, the universal and the particular.[39] Law dissertations on curiosity, such as the one supervised by the famous Stryk, were casuistic in their attempts to match numerous imaginary cases to legal principles (1.3.4 above). In moral theology, by the mid-seventeenth century casuistry had both reached an apogee and also, like exemplarity, was coming under considerable attack. Its two main functions broadly mirrored the illustrative and injunctive roles of exemplarity: casuistry was used both to illustrate general moral principles through particular cases (case casuistry) and also to study how to apply those principles to everyday life (practical casuistry). Examples of curiosity were explicitly placed in a casuistic framework by Becmann who, in his *Outlines of Moral Doctrine, on the Nature of Morals and their Various Cases*, stated that the modes or species of curiosity have been enumerated by casuists.[40] He was doubtless thinking of fellow Calvinists like Ames (*Conscience with the Power and Cases Thereof*) and L'Espine: indeed he refers a little later to both their discussions of curiosity.[41] Although Lutheran casuistry waned especially from the early eighteenth century, partly under the influence of Pietism, nonetheless even the 'examples' of good and bad learned curiosity reeled off by a Lutheran Pietist like Spizel were so many particular

[38] Lyons 1989, esp. 20–1 (modifying the exclusive emphasis on injunctive examples in Suleiman 1977).
[39] My account is based on *New Catholic Encyclopedia*, i. 195–7.
[40] 'Eius modi seu species à Casuistis recensentur' (Becmann 1679, 67; see pp. 67–9).
[41] Ibid. 68–9. See Ames 1630, 75–9[= 77] (and its English translation: Ames 1975, 49).

'cases' of general moral principles.[42] By contrast, the later, moral-theological discussion of curiosity by Buddeus—the Pietist-leaning professor who was key to the Lutheran turn away from casuistry—was free of examples and 'cases' (1719a, 216).

Application—crucial to both exemplarity and casuistry—involved either the application of general principles to particular cases or of old examples to new contexts. Some examples were more firmly rooted in specific contexts than others. For instance, each of the entertaining stories enumerated in a Leipzig dissertation on 'the curious devotion to novelty' illustrates just one of its species—'grammatical' in the case of a schoolteacher who taught Latin by an excessively novel method, getting his pupils to lick porridge off spoons when learning the verb *lingere* ('to lick up') (Westphal/Pipping 1708, 15). Other examples—such as that of Adam and Eve's curiosity—were much more mobile, more easily separable from one kind of curiosity and transferable to others.[43] They were closer to allegories of curiosity, which could be applied to more than one context when interpreted.

Casuistry and exemplarity also both highlighted narrative chains, even in discursive texts. In injunctive mode, this was in order to improve persuasion. It would have been rhetorically feeble to claim that learned *curiosi* were 'unhappy', if readers were not then scared with deterrent true cases of unhappiness produced by *curiositas*, such as that of Edmund Castell, who worked 16–18 hours a day on his *Lexicon heptaglotton* (eventually published in 1669) only to see much of it burnt, along with a large part of his library, in the Great Fire of London in 1666 (Spizel 1676, 998–9). Thus, even single phrases like 'the unhappiness of those who are wrongly curious'[44] were, like 'fatal curiosity', compressed narratives. The French term *effect*, meaning both 'effect' (or 'outcome') and 'action', was used to show that the end of such narrative chains was an action or event that was caused by the links that preceded it: 'Judge curiosity by such dangerous *effects*' wrote Camus, referring to the gruesome ends—being buried and burnt—which Aristotle and Empedocles's curiosity allegedly led them to.[45]

---

[42] Spizel, *Felix literatus ex infelicium periculis et casibus . . . 1676.*
[43] e.g. Becmann 1679, 68.
[44] 'de . . . male-curiosorum . . . infelicitate' (Spizel 1676, 960).
[45] 'Jugez de la curiosité par de si dangereux effects.' (Camus 1613, vii. 440).

Narrative chains were not only injunctive, however. They could also be used as diagnostic or forensic tools for detecting curiosity, not least for lawyers, who wished to be tough not just on crime but on the causes of crime, amongst them curiosity. Much of the crime analysed by Stryk was not curiosity in itself but rather 'the *effect* of curiosity in illicit private acts'.[46] Such jurisprudential nuance partly explains why, in moralizing drama or in commentaries on drama, relatively innocuous kinds of curiosity were deemed to merit apparently disproportionate punishments.

Yet some works—discursive ones as well as narrative fictions—emphasized that detecting curiosity in this way was not easy. L'Espine raises the question, in his pastoral treatise: if you are under the thumb of tyrants, how do you know whether a rebellion would be God's 'calling' for you or else godless curiosity? By the time that you find out, you may well have died in the process: 'it is difficult, and most often impossible, to know this divine calling except through the action's outcome [*les effects*]'.[47] The key difference between the revolts of the German and Swiss peasants is that the former lost and the latter won: the Swiss rebellion was

a similar case with a quite different outcome . . . From which we can deduce—given that they achieved something so difficult in such a short time and that their plans succeeded even better than they had dared hope at the outset—that they had a secret calling from God, whose power then constantly guided and strengthened them to fulfil it.[48]

Successful insurgents win not only their earthly cause but also the certainty that they were always meant (predestined) to do so. In 1587 this doctrine had immediate application for French Calvinists like L'Espine, caught in the middle of the unfolding chain of events that was the Wars of Religion, looking forward anxiously to the eventual outcome of their own insurgence against the monarchy.

---

[46] 'De curiositatis effectu in actibus privatorum illicitis' (Stryk/Lüedecke 1743, 307).

[47] 'il est difficile, et le plus souvent impossible de conoistre ceste divine vocation, autrement que par les effects' (L'Espine 1588, 456).

[48] 'en pareil cas eut une issue toute diverse . . . Dont est à presuposer, veu le peu de temps qu'ils furent à parachever une chose si difficile, et que leurs conseils leur succederent encores mieux qu'ils n'eussent osé esperer au commencement, qu'ils furent appellez par une secrette vocation de Dieu, et depuis tousjours conduits et fortifiez par sa vertu pour la pouvoir executer.' (456).

Some discursive texts did not just include discrete mini-narratives of curiosity, in the form of *exempla*, but they even incorporated a narrative of curiosity into their macro-structure. Whereas most discursive texts began with definitions before going on to list the causes, effects and (sometimes) punishments of curiosity,[49] on the other hand a few writers began with specific examples rather than finishing with them. For instance, for the Lutheran pastor Andreae, curiosity (pernicious) is an effect, the outcome of a narrative chain, not a cause within it. He is certain that curiosity is all around him. Detecting it is easy, but discovering its causes has been more difficult. The ultimate cause resides neither in Fate, nor in the wickedness of the world, but in the *curiosi* themselves (argues Andreae, as if rehearsing various possible plots for the Faust story, which had recently become well known in Germany). He describes this detection metaphorically in medical terms, claiming that he can diagnose the source and causes of the 'plague' or 'contagion' of curiosity that is carrying off the best minds, among them former friends of his, who serve as his prime example.[50] The point of this etiology is to seek a possible cure. Unlike most extended cautionary tales of curiosity (such as that of Faust) which recount a linear progression towards an inexorable end, Andreae's treatise begins at the middle or end—with the wretched curiosity of his former friends—and then works back to the beginning, trying to reconstitute the chain of events that led to it. He is using the discursive equivalent of the *in medias res* narrative technique.

4.3.2 *Histories of the arts and sciences*

Thus, even in the heyday of the culture of curiosities, *exempla* of curiosity continued to be overwhelmingly negative. However, especially from the second half of the seventeenth century, a few new, non-fictional, unprecedentedly happy narratives of curiosity were also written, in attempts to break the chain that usually led inexorably to calamity.

The authors of these narratives—ranging from a *Gymnasium* professor to French *philosophes*—rewrote the history of learning and

---

[49] e.g. Westphal 1573, A3^v (definition), A3^v–A4^v (causes), A4^v–[A7^r] (effects), B2$^{r–v}$ (punishments).

[50] Andreæ 1621, [1]–2 ('pestis . . . contagione').

culture as a linear progression of good curiosity throughout the ages. Some used *exempla* to integrate particular instances of good curiosity into this universal picture. For Seger, addressing his Danzig *Gymnasium* audience in 1675 (1.3.1 above), not only does history— from antiquity to the present—offer a chronological panorama of happy naturalist *curiosi*, but, on a micro-level, pleasure, wealth, and utility 'arise' from each labour of curiosity.[51] Like the author of the *Curiosité fructueuse* brochure of 1739 on aerostatic experiments (3.4.2 above), Seger saw himself and his contemporaries as moving through the middle of a such a fruitful chain, ensuring that it extended into the future. These narratives were both retrospective and prospective.

The same goes for the 1725 'Speech on the motives which should encourage us in the sciences' by Montesquieu. He describes the second motive as 'a certain curiosity that all men have and that has never been so justifiable as in our time. Every day we hear that the limits of men's knowledge have just been pushed back, that those with knowledge are astonished to find themselves having so much of it.'[52] As real advances in knowledge are made, so curiosity becomes increasingly justifiable: morality is dependent on history. That is quite different from Seger's iterative enumeration of instances of curiosity throughout the ages. By the eighteenth century, *some* of these histories of the progress of curiosity are at last beginning to lend limited support to Blumenberg's thesis about the early modern legitimation of 'theoretical curiosity'—a thesis which finds much less support in the seventeenth century, as we have seen.[53] For many Enlightenment figures, it is curiosity that pushes back 'limits'

---

[51] Seger 1676, 14–30, 55 ('emergens').

[52] 'une certaine curiosité que tous les hommes ont, et qui n'a jamais été si raisonnable que dans ce siècle-ci. Nous entendons dire tous les jours que les bornes des connoissances des hommes viennent d'être reculées, que les savants sont étonnés de se trouver si savants' (Montesquieu, 'Discours sur les motifs qui doivent nous encourager aux sciences': 1964, i. 54).

[53] Other such histories include Giambattista Vico's 1725 fable of the origins of human curiosity (Jacques-Chaquin 1998a, 21–2) and Maupertuis's 1752 *Lettre sur le progrès des sciences* (1752, 327–52), which is central to Blumenberg's case (1988, 219–26). However, although the 'curiosity' family of terms is always positive in the *Lettre*, it is often used within the curiosity-*collecting* tendency, i.e. to denote discrete encounters between subject and object, in which the object is sometimes sensational or extraordinary (Maupertuis 1752, [329], 331, 336, 338, 348, 349, 350). Even Maupertuis has not yet fully disentangled curiosity *qua* motor in the progress of sciences from, on the other hand, the rhetoric of the culture of curiosities.

('bornes') over time, rather than simply stopping at them and letting other, more respectable motors—such as 'desire for knowledge'— push progress forward. Curiosity became understood as a central driving force in the history of aesthetics as well as in that of natural philosophy. For the celebrated dramatist Beaumarchais (in 1767), 'men' (such as Columbus) would never have 'advanced in the arts and sciences' if they had 'respected the illusory limits' prescribed by predecessors: the 'curious genius' is he who transgresses such 'known limits', breaking the rules of theatre, for example.[54] Beaumarchais says 'men' advisedly, giving no suggestion that this 'curious genius' club includes women.

On the other hand, the role of curiosity within the history of human learning could still be understood as unhappy rather than happy. In the history of learning composed by the cleric and peda- gogue Fleury (3.4.4.1 above), episodes of curiosity (such as human- ism) led to calamities (such as the Reformation), before true learning was returned to:[55] those episodes were structurally similar to dan- gerous, curiosity-induced diversions within quasi-allegorical quest narratives. As late as the mid-eighteenth century, Jean-Jacques Rousseau inserted 'vain curiosity' even more precisely than Fleury into a specifically causal, historical chain in his 1750 *Discours sur les sciences et les arts*, describing curiosity as a vice which has 'caused' many 'evils' such as physics, an apparently good discipline which, however, together with the rest of the sciences and arts, has produced moral depravation.[56]

But histories of the arts and sciences were perhaps the only narra- tive genre in which defenders and attackers of curiosity slugged it out on a relatively equal footing. In other kinds of stories about curios- ity, the chain leading to calamity was usually unbreakable.

---

[54] 'Les hommes eussent-ils jamais avancé dans les Arts et les Sciences s'ils avaient servilement respecté les bornes trompeuses que leurs prédécesseurs y avaient pre- scrites? . . . Le génie curieux . . . s'élance au delà des bornes connues' (Beaumarchais 1957, 7–8).

[55] Fleury 1686, 2–82, esp. 78.

[56] 'les maux causés par notre vaine curiosité'; 'la Physique, [est née] d'une vaine curiosité' (Rousseau 1964, 9, 17). Blumenberg (1988, 230–3) acknowledges Rousseau's resistance to the notion that curiosity meant progress.

4.4 FICTION: EXEMPLARITY AND BEYOND

Just at the time when curiosity was becoming good in some discourses, a golden age of exemplary narratives against curiosity was also getting under way in France. Certainly, injunctive *exempla* cautioning against curiosity had been common in discursive texts for centuries. Yet, especially from the late sixteenth century, *exempla* of curiosity now began to be writ large, as extended, self-standing narratives, whether in the form of novellas or plays. In some quarters, this continued well into the eighteenth century. In others, it was increasingly problematized from the second half of the seventeenth century onwards.

Perhaps the most famous of these new, extended cautionary tales against curiosity was that of Faust. His story quickly crossed into France: 1598 (or earlier) saw the appearance of Pierre-Victor Palma-Cayet's French translation—subsequently much reprinted—of the anonymous *Faustbuch*, that had been published by Spiess in Frankfurt a. Main in 1587. Palma-Cayet made Faust curious: that is, he injected into the story the 'curiosity' family of terms, which had not been used in the original German.[57] Faust's 'appalling, terrifying end' was 'a good example', enjoining one 'not to imitate it but to take precautions against it'.[58] A few years earlier, one of the first humanist-style French tragedies with a biblical plot had emitted a similar exemplary message: in Jean de La Taille's *Saül le Furieux* (published in 1572, probably written in 1562),[59] the hero's collusion with the 'curiosité' of necromancy in trying to consult the spirit of the dead Samuel—with the help of the Witch of Endor—is amplified and condemned by the chorus. It is part of a chain of actions leading to his punishment at the hands of God (1972, 39).

As these two instances show, curiosity was often used in extended tales to caution specifically against dabbling in occult sciences. It was also used to caution against illicit sex. (This sometimes backfired: the later use of curiosity to sell occult or pornographic books made this association of curiosity with forbidden fruits into a source of titillation.)[60] Indeed, sex and occult sciences often overlapped in narratives.

---

[57] e.g. Palma-Cayet 1982, 45, 52, 57, 60, 77.

[58] 'la fin abominable et effroyable . . . un bon exemple pour ne l'imiter et par cy apres s'en donner garde' (Palma-Cayet 1982, 206).

[59] See Hall and Smith in La Taille 1972, 2.

[60] §§ 3.4.8 and 3.4.10 above.

However, readers' applications of curiosity extended beyond the surface themes—occult sciences, sex, or others such as travel[61]—of the narratives in which it was embedded. Further applications were sometimes suggested extradiegetically by the narrator, but even if they were not then, it is extremely likely that they would have been made by readers, given the reading habits associated with exemplarity.

And what of readers' or audiences' enjoyment of the stories themselves? Was it considered to be curiosity too? In 1572 the likely answer was no, but in much of the seventeenth and eighteenth century it was yes. La Taille, in the short treatise on tragedy which was appended to *Saül le Furieux*, disavowed—as something to be left to theologians—'curiosité' about whether the apparition he showed in Act 3 represented Samuel's actual spirit or else just an illusory figment of the imagination (1972, 23). Indeed, having condemned 'curiosité' in the play, on the extradiegetic level of the chorus, it would have seemed inconsistent to advocate it in the commentary. It could be argued that Act 3 itself does flagrantly exploit the audience's curiosity through its sensational representation of a forbidden necromantic ritual. However, although such double standards did doubtless add greatly to the play's appeal, La Taille pointedly avoids describing the audience's reaction to the play as one of curiosity. In 1572 it would still have been highly unusual to break the united front against curiosity in this way. To argue that La Taille in fact 'really did' tacitly exploit the audience's curiosity would be to erase these historical distinctions through a confidence that modern readers can locate 'things', such as curiosity, even where the words for them are absent. While that approach would be legitimate—indeed it characterizes most intellectual and literary history, including my own treatment of some themes here other than curiosity—I am avoiding applying it to curiosity, in an attempt to retrace its changing shapes exactly as they were ascribed to it in the period.

4.4.1   *Du Souhait*, The Happiness of the Wise/The Unhappiness of the Curious[62]

In 1600, two years after Faust was translated into French, a less well-known publication demonstrated the new power of curiosity to be

---

[61] e.g. 2 of La Fontaine's fables, 'Les deux pigeons' and 'La tortue et les deux canards' (1966, 241–3 [242], 269–70 [270]), first published in the 1679 edition.

[62] § 4.4.1 is a résumé of N. Kenny 1995a. Full references are provided there.

the anti-hero of extended, exemplary, novella-length narratives, ripe for application and use by readers in many spheres of life—politics, ethics, religion, education, manly vocations, and so on. François Du Souhait published together, as a symmetrical pair, two cautionary tales, *Le Bonheur des sages* and *Le Malheur des curieux*. A *gentilhomme* from Champagne, Du Souhait published over thirty works, largely directed at a noble readership. The antithetically symmetrical plots of the two 1600 stories can be summarized as follows.

The Happiness of the Wise is set in late sixteenth-century Germany. An unnamed prince has inherited his recently deceased father's worldly goods. Wishing to acquire his father's virtues, he consults his guardian, who advises him to go to Mainz to acquire good learning; but he should not be 'curious about hidden knowledge'.[63] So the prince lodges with the most celebrated pedagogue in Mainz, where he befriends six young noble co-students. One of these declares that they will only attain outstanding academic excellence if they go incognito to another university, where they will be treated according to merit rather than status. The young nobles, having obtained their fathers' permission, go to Paris, where they are educated by the Jesuits. They become the top students and, after revealing their status, they are presented to the French king. A young man at court offers some magical secrets to the prince, who refuses to be 'curieux' (72) and helps redeem the young man. The prince and his six friends receive recompense for all their virtue, variously becoming landowner, King, Archbishop, Imperial Ambassador, Imperial Governor, and so on. *The Unhappiness of the Curious* is set in Spain in the same period. Seven friends, including the comte d'Aite, highly accomplished in letters, are introduced to a demon, who divulges some secrets—such as that of rejuvenation—on the understanding that one of the friends be sacrificed, but d'Aite reneges on this deal and so the demon arranges a gruesome end for all seven. Thus is 'curiosité' punished.[64]

In these narratives, curiosity is always sinful, punished, and distinct from a good, moderate desire for natural (as opposed to occult) knowledge. On one level, Du Souhait purports to be proposing positive and negative *exempla* which are universally applicable to all humans. However, on another level, this universalization is a smoke-

---

[63] 'curieux d'une science cachee' (Du Souhait, *Bonheur* 1600, 21).
[64] Du Souhait, *Malheur* 1600, 79.

screen: the application of *exempla* turns out to depend entirely on sex and social rank. Du Souhait is using curiosity to help bolster the hereditary nobility after the ravages of the Wars of Religion, as well as to promote ultramontanism, the Jesuits, and the interests of the Holy Roman Empire (as opposed to Gallicanism or exclusively French patriotism). He does this both by his choice of dedicatees— whom he describes as *exempla* of wisdom ('sagesse') as opposed to curiosity—and also in the diegesis: in *The Happiness*, the Holy Roman Empire becomes a cause which can be served by those who are *sages* and avoid *curiosité*. An unnamed Jesuit establishment in Paris, presumably the Collège de Clermont, becomes the place where non-*curieux* education is to be had (71).[65] In *The Unhappiness*, Philip II is a pious king who praises 'Les sages' and chastises his erring subject for being 'trop curieux' (51–2). But the main opponents of curiosity are noblemen who obey their fathers and are truly noble, truly masculine, especially those from houses and dynasties close to Du Souhait's political allegiances, such as the Habsburgs and the Lorraine House of Haraucourt. Far from being a universal vice, *curiosité* is presented as ignoble and effeminate, associated with inauthentic noblemen, their social inferiors, and—with the exception of one dedicatee—with women of any rank.

Exemplary narratives like these were designed to train readers to speak, reason, and act in certain ways. Du Souhait's aristocratic, young, male readers who, together with fathers and mothers, are his implied readership, are being taught how to avoid curiosity and attain 'wisdom' by foreseeing chains of actions. Like *exempla* in sermons, these narratives are designed to get readers not so much to understand curiosity philosophically as to want to flee it and to know how to do so, by having the provision—*prevoyance*: part of prudence—to plot a chain of actions deliberatively. 'Learn by our examples', urges d'Aite's wretched steward.[66] Yet the mode of learning fostered by extended narrative is different from that fostered by *exempla*-laden treatises. The narrative amplification of example immerses readers in the page-by-page process whereby protagonists deliberate as to what course of action would be *sage* and what

---

[65] The Collège de Clermont had opened in 1563. Du Souhait seems to be advocating the return of the Jesuits to France, from where they had been expelled by Henri IV in 1595 and to where some would be allowed to return on probation by the 1603 Edict of Rouen. See Huppert 1984, 107–8; Scaglione 1986, [111].

[66] 'Apprenez par nos exemples' (*Malheur*, 79). See also pp. [7], 38, 80.

curieux, successfully in the case of the seven virtuous noblemen deciding whether to ask their fathers' permission, and unsuccessfully in the case of the comte d'Aite deciding—unwisely on his own instead of communally—whether to visit the demon. Once they have gone too far down the wrong chain, protagonists cannot go back, even if they now foresee their dire end (*Malheur* 22). The chains are not only temporal, but also spatial, whether metaphorically—as with Du Souhait's stock metaphor of the path of virtue—or literally: male *sagesse* involves waiting in the right place (Mainz, Paris) for the right time (till your father arrives, till you have finished two or three years of study) until you reap the reward by expanding into space (Empire and beyond) for ever (the virtuous characters are not re-presented as dying). On the other hand, *curiosité* is, as for St Augustine,[67] a denial of our finitude in time, or, as the demonologists argued, an attempt to skip time.[68]

Within his exemplary plots, on a diegetic level, Du Souhait maintains a united front against *curiosité*, using the term and its cognates 50 times over the two works. It is therefore all the more surprising to see a few extradiegetic cracks appear in that front, early signs of the moral splintering of curiosity that became prominent in narrative later in the seventeenth century: when *The Unhappiness* ends and the extradiegetic world beckons, the narrator enjoins parents to keep their children within the bounds of 'common and licit curiosity';[69] moreover, the dedicatee is told 'You have been *curieux*, but not like these *curieux* . . . They were *curieux* in a way which disdained God, whereas your *curiosité* only respects and glorifies Him'.[70] As in church discourse which glimpsed the possibility of good curiosity, here the tortuous form of expression—oxymoronic parallelism—indicates jokey unease: hardly surprising given that Du Souhait is envisaging a good species of a passion which he spends scores of pages denigrating as wholly evil. Already in 1600, there is one law for intradiegetic protagonists, another for extradiegetic ones. Du

---

[67] Blumenberg 1988, 113–14.

[68] Jacques-Chaquin 1998*b*, 83–4. Cf. Faber 1643, iii. 154. Martin Heidegger revives St Augustine's argument and applies it to *Neugierde*, which he similarly understands as an attempt to escape death, but by over-immersion in the *present* rather than in the imagined future (Ritter and Gründer (eds.) 1984, 735–6).

[69] 'la commune et licite curiosité' (79).

[70] 'Vous avez esté curieux, non pas comme ces Curieux . . . Ils estoyent curieux au mespris de Dieu, et vostre curiosité ne tend, qu'à son respect, et à sa gloire' ([3]–[4]; see also p. [7]).

Souhait does, however, stop short of asking this dedicatee to direct his *curiosité* at the anti-*curiosité* tale itself: *that* reflexive move—which Scudéry will make in 1661—would push moral coherence to its limits, and it is not yet possible in 1600, at least not in pragmatically instrumental works such as these, that use curiosity to train the young males of one group (the hereditary nobility) to dominate and obey, while virtually denying reading positions to other groups (inferior ranks; women, except as mothers).

4.4.2   *A Jesuit ballet for boys*

Although, 137 years later exemplarity and allegory had both fallen into disrepute in some quarters, it was still perfectly possible, at least in certain genres, such as the *ballet moral*, to compose exemplary-cum-allegorical narratives that enjoined avoidance of curiosity. As in Du Souhait's two stories, the main point was again to train young males: and exactly the same Jesuit institution as the one to which he had alluded was now involved once more.

At noon on Wednesday 7 August, 1737, a large section of Parisian and Versailles high society, numbering perhaps as many as 5,000, sat down to watch some schoolboys—twenty-three dancers, plus a few actors—provide a tangible, bodily, visual, and musical representation of curiosity on stage. The venue was the Jesuit college of Louis-le-Grand. The *ballet moral* on curiosity was scripted by a professor of rhetoric at the college, probably Gilles Anne Xavier de La Santé.[71] It served as the intermezzo to La Santé's tragedy *Regulus* and culminated in the college's annual prizegiving ceremony. It was customary for lavish, 'moral' ballets of this kind to be performed at this climax of the academic year: in 1736, the previous year, 'wisdom' (*sagesse*) had been the theme; in 1691 it had been the passions in general; back in 1671 it had also been curiosity.[72]

The life of this ballet was not confined to the event itself but was also extended through print, like that of numerous university dispu-

---

[71] See *Mercure de France* 1968, Sept. 1737, p. 2047. Brenner (1947) and Dupont-Ferrier (1921–5, iii. 265) attribute it to Charles Porée (also professor of rhetoric at Louis-le-Grand). On the college's ballets, see Dupont-Ferrier 1921–5, i. 294–303 (252 on attendance figures).

[72] Dupont-Ferrier 1921–5, i. 295. For the programme of the 1671 ballet, see Boysse 1880, 158–61. A *comédie-ballet* entitled *Les Curieux* was also performed at the Jesuit college of La Flèche in 1688 (Sommervogel (ed.) 1890–1911, iii. 777).

tations: a commemorative *placard* of the 1737 ballet was published by the college's *libraire*, while in the month after the performance the main organ of society news, the *Mercure de France*, printed a review of the ballet which described it in almost as much detail again.[73]

The ballet sought to show what curiosity is, and 'to correct the vicious, reprehensible part of that passion',[74] by telling stories about it. In a distinctively Jesuit way, the resources of rhetoric and of non-verbal media were milked for moral ends. The performers enacted a sequence of *exempla*, either mythological, historical, or drawn from everyday life. A brief, light definition of curiosity was also provided—this was an academic institution, after all—but even that took the form of a narrative.

The ballet is divided into four parts, each consisting of three scenes or *entrées*. The 'sources' or 'beginning' of curiosity are represented (Part 1), then its 'objects' or 'species' (Part 2), then the 'course' that it takes and the 'dangers' to which it exposes us (Part 3), and finally its 'consequences' and 'punishments' (Part 4).[75] This overall, chronological, and linear 'design' ('Dessein', 2) or 'sequence' ('suite')[76] *is* curiosity: no more direct definition than that is offered. Each *entrée* is therefore one example of one of those four consecutive stages through which curiosity unravels itself and reveals itself to be what it is. For instance, 'dangers' are illustrated by astrological moon-gazers who end up as lunatics, hallucinating that the moon is orbiting inside their head; punishments are illustrated by the shooting, in cross-fire, of a German religious solitary who was curious to see a battle (5–6).

The *entrées* are not static tableaux but mini-narratives. For example, an *entrée* in Part 1 shows how an 'Idle life' ('Vie oisive') is one source of curiosity: hawkers shout out 'curiosity' and 'rarity' in the street, offering objects for sale to the idlers who gather round, while the hawkers' accomplices then pick their pockets unnoticed (5). The scene in fact represents not just a source of curiosity but also its whole 'sequence' thereafter: objects, dangers, and punishments. So although the audience's attention is pushed towards one link in the chain at a time—here to the first one, the source—that link is almost always represented as inseparable from the rest of the chain.

---

[73] *Mercure de France* 1968, Sept. 1737, pp. 2045–56.

[74] 'de corriger ce que cette Passion a de vicieux et de blâmable' ([La Santé] 1737, 2).

[75] 'le Principe, l'Espece, le Cours, et les Suites', that is, 'Les sources . . . Les objets . . . Les Perils . . . Les Punitions' (2).

[76] *Mercure de France* 1968, Sept. 1737, p. 2054.

The hawkers' scene also shows how this ballet, like many moralizing attacks on curiosity, attacks the curiosity-collecting tendency by containing it within the curiosity-narrating tendency, superimposing the latter on the former as an explanatory framework for it, and thereby assuming that both involve one and the same curiosity. The 'curieux dupés' whose pockets are picked belong, like the news-hungry crowd in the 1671 ballet,[77] to the culture of curiosities in that they seek satisfaction by collecting discrete, curious objects, whether material (the hawkers' trinkets) or discursive (news). Whereas that collecting is an end in itself in their curiosity-collecting tendency, in the narrating tendency which the ballet imposes on them it becomes just one stage in an overall chain leading to punishment.

The ballet also shows how, even in the 1730s, by when curiosity was good in so many discourses, nonetheless bad curiosity was still often thought to produce better stories than did good curiosity or, at least, lent itself to story form much more than good curiosity. This ballet is supposed to demonstrate that curiosity is, 'like the other passions, fairly indifferent in itself, only becoming good or evil' through its object, motive, and degree of intensity.[78] However, despite this avowed even-handedness, eleven of the twelve *entrées* are in fact mini-narratives of *bad* curiosity. Moreover, this proportion was on its way up, not down: the earlier, 1671 ballet had included a greater number of positive stories, carefully dividing its four parts (and twenty *entrées*) equally between good and bad curiosity. So much for any notion that curiosity was progressively becoming rehabilitated. What perhaps explains this difference of emphasis between the 1671 and 1737 ballets is the greater role of narrative in the latter. The overall 'design' of the 1671 ballet had no narrative dimension: its four parts were 'so many species of curiosity'[79] rather than consecutive links in a chain, whereas in 1737 the species of curiosity together formed just one link in such a chain. The less strong the narrative structure, the more likely it was that curiosity could be good as much as bad. Certainly, both ballets included one attempt to rewrite old allegories of bad curiosity more positively: the 1671 Prometheus, by inspiring humans to learn the uses of fire, exemplifies the invention

[77] Boysse 1880, 159.

[78] 'comme les autres passions, est d'elle même assés indifferente, et ne devient bonne ou mauvaise' (2).

[79] 'autant d'espèces de curiosité' (Boysse 1880, 158).

of the arts, a good species of curiosity,[80] while in 1737 the misfortune of Epimetheus—which in 1671 had been an *exemplum* of bad curiosity[81]—is emphasized not to be the whole story, since the allegorical figure of Curiosity inspires travellers by pointing out that Hope is still at the bottom of Pandora's jar (2). But even in this instance, the attempt to deny that an old story is all about doom serves to evoke that doom as much as to dispel it.

The 1737 ballet was not merely designed to train boys to avoid bad curiosity: it also represented that training *en abysme*, making a spectacle out of it. The spectators saw schoolboys not only project themselves imaginatively into good and bad *exempla*—as Du Souhait encouraged young male readers to do—but actually embody those *exempla* as they acted them out. As well as training pupils and audience morally, the ballet showed off to its influential audience the college's moral training of its pupils, identifying good curiosity with a pedagogical institution's syllabus, as did university dissertations and at least one university sermon. Moreover, this was the same Jesuit institution as that which had kept Du Souhait's protagonists away from bad curiosity 137 years earlier: Louis-le-Grand had until 1682 been the Collège de Clermont. Like Du Souhait's protagonists and implied readers, many of the dancers were young male nobles. For instance, the 14-year-old Marc René de Voyer de Paulmy d'Argenson started off the performance by declaiming the prologue; he then became, in different scenes, a spirit (*génie*), a shepherd, a hawker, a consulter of astrologers, an alchemist, a sailor, a soldier in the battle scene, and then, in the finale, a spirit of poetry. This member of the powerful Voyer d'Argenson family, whose twelve-year-old brother Louis-Auguste was also in the cast, later became *Lieutenant-Général* of the King's armies and Governor of the château de Vincennes: his real career echoed the ones assigned by Du Souhait to his fictional protagonists as a reward for avoiding curiosity.

Although in almost all of the ballet's *entrées* curiosity was bad, as in so many narratives (including Du Souhait's) it suddenly became good when it stepped into the extradiegetic world. The 1737 prize-giving ceremony itself was sandwiched by the final dance, in which the enthroned Minerva, flanked by the personified figures of 'Useful Curiosity' and 'Emulation', awarded prizes to those who had sought—through a 'recherche curieuse'—to adorn their mind (8). As

80 Ibid. 160. 81 Ibid.

the fifty or so winners in the annual composition competition received their prizes—which usually included beautifully bound folios and editions of Latin classics[82]—they too became actors in a narrative of good curiosity which had reached its happy dénouement—reward rather than punishment. (Indeed they may have been the 'young people devoted to learning' who figure in the cast list for the final dance.)[83] The process of applying and using *exempla* was thus spectacularly dramatized: curiosity stepped out from myth and history and into the auditorium. That application was entirely masculine: there was not a girl in sight among the dancers, actors, or other pupils. 'Useful Curiosity' might be 'the mother of knowledge' but she, like all the figures in the ballet, including the other feminine personifications, was played by a boy and applied only to boys.[84] Lower social ranks were also implicitly excluded from 'Useful Curiosity': the hawkers' dupes were 'idle *petits bourgeois* and unemployed artisans'.[85]

The curiosity for which the prizewinners were being rewarded was not any modern-sounding, disinterested pursuit of the truth, nor Blumenberg's 'theoretical curiosity', but rather—as in Du Souhait—the intellectual and ethical training necessary for a public, patriotic role in civil society (8), the élite of which in fact sat watching them that very day in the shape of the Prince de Conti, the Cardinal de Polignac, many prelates and ambassadors, the Prince d'Elbeuf, as well as foreign princes and nobles.[86] And the boys' ultimate patron was the ultimate male, the King, who always paid for the prizes (8).[87] Louis XV had virtually displaced God as the great adjudicator waiting at the end of the narrative chain of curiosity.

4.4.3 *Triangles of curiosity*

One of the enduring uses of fictional narratives about curiosity was rather different: it consisted in giving men ways of coping with their

---

[82] On the annual prizegiving, see Dupont-Ferrier 1921–5, i. 250–2.

[83] 'JEUNES GENS dévoüés aux Belles Lettres' (8).

[84] It was perhaps to offset anxieties about the effeminizing effect of ballet and theatre that the college's professors of rhetoric who wrote pieces in this period preferred Corneille to Racine, finding the former more virile (Dupont-Ferrier 1921–5, i. 290).

[85] 'de petits Bourgeois oisifs et des Artisans desoeuvrés' (3).

[86] See *Mercure de France* 1968, Sept. 1737, p. 2056.

[87] Compare the praise of royal-sponsored curiosity in a Danzig *Gymnasium* oration in 1675 (1.3.1 above).

anxiety (*cura*) about women. In many a story, the hero is a man who wonders curiously whether a particular woman had slept with another man or even whether she might do so.[88] Exemplary or cautionary versions of this story urge men to avoid curiosity and to try not to worry about this. But some versions seem to exacerbate rather than dispel anxiety, compromising exemplarity by suggesting that there is no neat recipe for avoiding calamity. Although the gradual decline of exemplarity in some quarters happened over time, that is not to say that it was entirely chronological: in some cases—such as that of Cervantes—it was the earlier versions of such plots that exacerbated male anxiety most, with subsequent rewritings of them trying to dispel that darkness.

What makes many of these stories so forceful is that they advise men to avoid such curiosity not because it is ill-founded but because it is well-founded. The stories are frequently based on firm misogynistic assumptions about female nature: women are all the same, potentially unchaste; given half a chance, they would all sleep with other men. The question whether universal truths about female nature could be inferred from stories about particular women is richly problematized in early modern French fictions by women, from Marguerite de Navarre's *Heptaméron* (published 1558) to Lafayette's *Princesse de Clèves* (1678), whereas male-authored stories of male curiosity about women's sexual behaviour more often answered in the affirmative.

This question about the fixity of universal female nature was also a question about narrative. If women really are all the same, then every time a man tests a woman's chastity then the same dire result will ensue: the plot will always unfold in the same way. The woman will always turn out to have slept with another man or to be willing to do so under certain circumstances. Indeed, for exemplarity to work, for male readers to be persuaded not to be curious about such matters, then it is necessary to posit such an inexorable narrative chain of curiosity, since otherwise the reader might nourish the hope that, although calamity has engulfed other men who, like him, acted on their curiosity, it might not engulf him. Only with the decline of exemplarity in some quarters, especially from the second half of the

---

[88] For an exceptional case, where it is a woman who is described as feeling such anxious curiosity about a man, see the reference to Ovid's Procris by Garzoni (1586, 69^{r-v}).

seventeenth century, did the outcomes of such plots begin to become less predictable at times, like those of some other 'grand' moral and social narratives.[89]

Many of these stories of male curiosity about women involve a love triangle in which the desire of an interloping third party—whether real, imagined, or faked—displaces, replaces, or invades the hero's desire for the beloved. This is what René Girard has called 'triangular desire'. Although no single modern hypothesis can entirely explain why such tales were (and are) so haunting, Girard's interpretation of them as revealing the mimetic nature of all desire—our tendency to desire what we imagine a rival Other desires rather than what we simply want ourselves—is perhaps the most powerful available.[90] Whereas 'triangular desire' as defined by Girard figured in narratives from Cervantes to Marcel Proust, the stories that I am considering belong to a more historically specific version, that lasted for about 200 years, from the late sixteenth century onwards, when the hero (or anti-hero) in the triangle was often diagnosed as suffering from curiosity. Numerous variations on the triangle of curiosity were narrated, but many clustered around certain privileged figures who wandered from genre to genre, such as the 'curious impertinent'—whom Girard saw as the model of 'triangular desire'—and Oedipus.

4.4.3.1   The 'curious impertinent'

The 'curious impertinent' first appeared in Cervantes's exemplary novella *El curioso impertinente*, that was included in Part 1 of *Don Quixote* (1605). The novella became a remarkable hit in France. In 1608 it appeared both in Spanish, within a miscellany published in Paris, and also on its own in a bilingual French–Spanish version, before then being included in the first French translation (1614) of Part 1 of *Don Quixote*. Other versions of the story, but with the same distinctive title, were then produced in various genres, especially theatrical, at least up until the late eighteenth century. The influence of the story also extended to more distant variations on it which had other titles.[91]

---

[89] See Cave 1999, 139.   [90] Girard 1973, esp. ch. 1.
[91] On the Cervantes story, see Bataillon 1947; Girard 1973, 54–7; Neuschäfer 1990. On the story and its French fortunes, see Crooks 1931, 116–27; Fumaroli 1984, 108–14. One English example is Aphra Behn's *The Amorous Prince, or, The Curious Husband* (1671), on which see Benedict 2001, 122–4.

Cervantes's plot runs as follows. Anselmo marries Camilla and would be perfectly happy were it not for an 'illness'—his curiosity to know not whether she *will* be unfaithful to him, which might depend on contingent circumstances arising or not, but whether she *would* be, given tempting circumstances. (He thus seeks to know not the actual future but the conditional, potential future, since only the latter can tell him what his wife is really like.) He compels Lothario, his best friend, to test Camilla by pretending to try to seduce her. Lothario, initially reluctant, eventually goes beyond his remit and does actually seduce her. Only after the new lovers have eloped does Anselmo learn the truth. Lothario repents and dies on a battlefield, causing Camilla in turn to die of melancholy. Her husband also dies of grief: 'Anselmo's impertinent curiosity cost him his life'.[92]

Cervantes's novella was itself a variation on pre-existing narratives of triangular desire—in Ariosto, Boccaccio, Ovid, Herodotus, and so on—which recounted, for example, wagers on a wife's fidelity, seduction tests performed by husbands disguised as strangers, or a husband's revelation of his naked wife to another man in order to prove her beauty.[93] Such plots retained their fascination in the early modern period, from Shakespeare's *Cymbeline* to Mozart and Da Ponte's *Così fan tutte*. But Cervantes seems to have been one of the first to turn the husband-figure's desire into curiosity,[94] and it was he who made the phrase 'curious impertinent' denote—even when people used it without direct reference to his novella—not just this type of man but this particular chain of actions and events.[95]

As Girard has shown, this novella was particularly resonant within *Don Quixote* because of the parallels between the curiosity of Anselmo and that of the Don himself, whose own desire is (in Girard's terms) similarly mediated by others (1973, 11–12).[96] Yet why did the novella also exert such fascination independently of *Don Quixote*, in so much early modern culture? Perhaps because of the

---

[92] Cervantes 1614, 433–99 ('il en couta la vie a Anselme d'avoir eu une curiosité si impertinente', 499; 'maladie', 450).

[93] Examples include Herodotus 1966, i, 1.8–12 (Candaules); Ovid, *Metamorphoses* 2.36 (Procris).

[94] For a 1583 example (Poissenot), see 4.4.3.3 below.

[95] At least 2 subsequent French plays used the phrase to evoke the basic plot-line of *El curioso impertinente* without giving any details of it (Crooks 1931, 47). Like Faust, the 'curious impertinent' became a new exemplary narrative which could be evoked just by mention of its protagonist.

[96] On curiosity in *Don Quixote*, see also Weiger 1983.

tragic darkness at the heart of the tale's exemplarity. Although the novella can be argued to enjoin men not to be curious like Anselmo, it does so explicitly not implicitly, perhaps because the causes and origins of Anselmo's curiosity remain, as Marcel Bataillon has shown, mysteriously unexplained and perhaps inexplicable (1947, 132–3). How can narrative offer male readers a cure for an ailment that is not understood? Narrative here produces an enigma of the kind which discursive definitions of curiosity, whether in treatises or subsequent university dissertations, strove to dispel through their exhaustive explanations of what causes curiosity. Anselmo has not the slightest reason to be curious. For instance, nothing in his wife's behaviour gives rise to suspicion. Indeed, it is virtually implausible that he should be curious. Cervantes wryly hammers home this point by having the priest—although it is he who has just repeated the tale—complain that the tale would have been more plausible if Anselmo and Camilla had been lovers, not spouses.[97] This is presumably because it would have made his anxious curiosity more plausible than it is in the Edenic state which the two seem to have reached when they marry. Related to this inexplicability is the shocking disparity between the initial, perfect heterosexual love and homosocial friendship, which are both emphasized at length, and, on the other hand, the protagonists' eventual destruction of each other. Unmotivated curiosity can unleash a terrifying chain of events for no apparent reason. Far from simply preventing male readers from being curious, the tale perhaps inspires fear in male readers that they might become curious.

Also shocking is the disparity between the apparently innocuous, almost casual quality which Anselmo's curiosity sometimes assumes and its tragic outcome. When, although he has in fact already been betrayed, he is deluded into thinking that Camilla's fidelity has now been proved, he urges Lotario to persist with the test nonetheless, 'if only for the sake of pleasure and curiosity'.[98] Curiosity thus has two, interconnected dimensions: gnawing anxiety or light, supplementary, gratuitous amusement. The dangerousness of the latter recalls the Augustinian diagnosis of curiosity as especially dangerous because deceptively innocent. The discrepancy between these two

---

[97] Fumaroli's argument that Cervantes's novella remains within the limits of *vraisemblance* therefore seems problematic (1984, 110).

[98] 'quand ce n'auroit esté que par plaisir et curiosité' (463).

dimensions lent itself to both exemplarity and tragedy, since the pathos of the gruesome outcome was all the greater for arising out of incongruously light and trivial pursuits.[99] Cervantes's very title evoked only light, inconsequential curiosity: François de La Mothe Le Vayer explicitly distinguishes 'curieux' who are merely 'impertinents' (such as the news-hungry) from ones who are 'coupables' ('guilty'), since the 'guilty' go in for black magic and the like (1662, ii. 464). To describe curiosity as 'impertinent' was to call it ridiculous, wayward, and senseless rather than downright wicked in itself.

One measure of the darkness that contemporary readers found at the heart of Cervantes's exemplary curiosity is the fact that subsequent writers sought to dispel it. As Marc Fumaroli has shown, French theatrical adaptations of this novella played down its tragedy by replacing Anselmo's mysterious, melancholic illness with comedy and Cornelian voluntarism (1984, 111–14). Fumaroli takes pains to rule out the possibility that this rewriting was motivated by any fear of the irrational (114), but it is precisely this possibility which I wish to explore, as if Anselmo's anxiety was subsequently doubled by an anxiety to cover it up.

Pierre Corneille's play *La Place Royale ou L'Amoureux extravagant* (1635) was based, as Fumaroli shows (111–12), on Guillén de Castro's 1618 stage adaptation of Cervantes's novella.[100] Dark exemplarity has turned into troubled, non-exemplary comedy. Corneille's hero is Alidor, who loves Angélique but, worried at the loss of his will and freedom that this entails (ll.204–8), 'gives' her (ll.296, 1528) to his friend Lothaire in order to 'cure' himself (l.248). Anxious curiosity has been displaced by another illness—love: Alidor's strategy, far from being designed to discover 'What if?', is brutally instrumental and self-preserving. However, in a subsequent twist, not mentioned by Fumaroli, Alidor, having demonstrated to himself his independence, his ability to do without what he wants, then does want Angélique back, but it is too late. In giving Angélique away, Alidor has asserted his will, but only at the price of not getting what he wants. His will gives him no more control over events or

---

[99] e.g. Lillo's play *Fatal Curiosity* (1737), in which a virtuous son, returning home to his elderly parents after undertaking a 7-year voyage to the Indies to make his fortune and alleviate their poverty, decides to 'Indulge my curiosity' (31) by disguising himself initially as a stranger in order to maximize the pleasure of reunion, but his desperate parents then murder the 'stranger' for his money.

[100] See Castro 1991.

over women than curiosity gave Anselmo. Whereas Alidor's avoidance of curiosity sidesteps Cervantes's conclusion that all women are the same and can therefore ruin homosocial friendship, it nonetheless relies on another kind of misogyny: the exclusion of women as too threatening to masculinity (except as gifts to be exchanged between men, cementing their friendship).

Fumaroli argues that constant Cornelian heroines like Angélique become worthy partners of men in a victory of mind over passion (113). Yet whereas the men remain free to roam anywhere, her free will can only lead her to a convent, where she retires from a 'world' (l.1488) in which she has no place, since it is full of men asserting their own will. The choice seems to be between uncontrollable male curiosity (Cervantes), which allows women enough rope to hang themselves and men with, and the controlled male will (Corneille), which avoids that calamity by excluding women. *La Place royale*, which explicitly makes its hero exceptional rather than an example to be followed (ll.201–2), is less a cautionary tale than perhaps a troubled thought-experiment aimed at investigating what would happen if men managed to stop being curious about women's sexuality.

On the other hand, subsequent French theatrical adaptations of Cervantes's story often minimized its darkness by reinforcing its exemplarity, as if to reassure males that all will be well as long as they do abstain from curiosity about female chastity, which should be perfectly possible for them. That was, for example, the cautionary message of a popularizing, mythological version performed at the Saint German fair in 1711, with Jupiter as the 'curious impertinent' and Mercury as the seductive tester ([Fuzelier 1711]). In this version, the core assumption of Cervantes's misogyny—that 'Women are all the same'—remains in place. Other versions modulated the misogyny somewhat. By changing the genre from tragedy to comedy, they also reconfigured reassuringly the chain of events triggered by curiosity, so that it no longer led inevitably to calamity. And yet they still sought to instruct male audiences by example.

For instance, in *Le Curieux impertinent ou Le Jaloux* (1645), a comedy allegedly written by Brosse when only 13 years old,[101] the friend (Lotaire) quickly reveals to the wife (Clindore) her husband (Ancelme's) testing strategy. She intends to be unfaithful, not out of

---

[101] Brosse 1645, [a iii^v–a iv^r]. On the play, see Crooks 1931, 117–21.

the weakness ascribed to women by Cervantes, whose heroine never realizes that she is being tested, but in this case out of revenge. However, circumstances divert her from this and she ends up rejecting Lotaire, forgiving her husband, and being reunited with him. In keeping with the conventions of comedy, the plot teeters on the brink of various potential tragic endings before its actual happy resolution: the worst conditional futures—what might happen—are avoided, as the conditional tense reminds us: 'You now love someone [Clindore] who should [*devroit*] hate you', says Lotaire to Ancelme at the dénouement.[102] Female infidelity is presented as resulting from spite rather than from weakness (whereas in Cervantes the wife never learned that she was being tested). Eventually satisfied of his wife's constancy, a repentant Ancelme concedes that 'My curiosities are no longer legitimate'.[103] But 'no longer' implies that they once were, that he can only repent now because the results of his test have given him the benefit of hindsight. So, although there is an exemplary message (a ii r), the hero's repentance does not quite coincide with it. A vestige of Cervantes's darkness remains, since the play shows that avoiding male curiosity is less easy than its own injunctive gloss claims.

That darkness is dispelled even more thoroughly by a later comedy, which both reduces the misogyny further and also gives still more reassuring advice to men who are curious about women's chastity. *Le Curieux impertinent*, by Philippe Néricault Destouches, was first performed in 1706.[104] Whereas in the Cervantes original the marriage came near the start, Destouches delays it until the end, effectively responding—a century later—to the criticism which Cervantes put ironically in the mouth of his priest-narrator, who wished for greater plausibility. The change turns the Anselmo figure (now called Léandre) into the obstacle that is required of comic plots and that is here eventually overcome through the happy marital union of his friend (here Damon) with the woman tested (Julie). Indeed, from the late seventeenth century this transformation of the Anselmo figure into the comic dupe became one way of banishing the darkness from Cervantes's tale.[105] The fact that Damon in this

---

[102] 'Vous aymez maintenant qui vous devroit haïr' (95).
[103] 'Mes curiositez ne sont plus legitimes' (95).
[104] Destouches 1757, i. [1]-120.
[105] e.g. John Crowne's Restoration comedy *The Married Beau: or, The Curious Impertinent* (1694) and [Senne], *Les Curieux punis, comédie en prose et en un acte, mêlée d'ariettes* (1787).

version already loves Julie at the start, even before the test, also diminishes the tragic distance between outset and outcome which Cervantes emphasizes so much.

Compared with earlier versions, that of Destouches both mitigates the misogyny—by ironizing it directly—and demystifies the curiosity. Julie, far from being weak, only stops loving Léandre when she learns of the test. Her change is motivated not only by anger (as in Brosse) but also by a gradual realization that Léandre does not really love her, since his calculating test is incompatible with love. The fact that Damon does have long-standing love for her also makes her seem less fickle than Cervantes's Camilla who, although generally virtuous, would have fallen for any man who courted her persuasively. Whereas in the Cervantes tale curiosity was troubling because it dwelled within perfect love, here love and curiosity are, on the whole,[106] more reassuringly opposed to each other. The comforting exemplary message—'be loving, not curious'—can be given more wholeheartedly than to readers of Corneille or even Cervantes.

And yet doubts are still nourished by continuing misogyny... The only constantly loving character is male (Damon), and the theme of woman's ominous unknowability is as present here (37) as in other versions. The onus is still on her to prove her constancy, not on the men to prove theirs. A woman is a merchandise which a man ends up with by chance and can only know through use (says a character who is represented as commonsensical (38)). Although generations of French writers have by now tried in different ways to dispel the darkness of Anselmo's anxious curiosity, it still lurks beneath even this relatively happy rewriting of his tale.

4.4.3.2   *Diderot,* The Indiscreet Jewels

Although the mysterious curiosity of Anselmo was reassuringly demystified as plain ridiculous by one early eighteenth-century playwright, enabling him to dispense clear moral advice to men, a few years later the 'curious impertinent' shook off all claims to exemplary status as he reappeared in a rather different genre—the pornographic novel. Advising men morally what to do about their curiosity is the last thing that Diderot attempts in *Les Bijoux indiscrets* (1748), and yet, even in this apparently frivolous setting, the latest descendant of Anselmo remains prey to a troubling anxiety

---

[106] With one exception (19).

that cannot now be dispelled by libertine nonchalance any more than it could previously by cautionary moralizing. Neither moralizing nor pornography can fully tame this kind of curiosity.

Diderot's rewriting of the 'curious impertinent' story drops that appellation but is still explicitly about curiosity. The hero is now a Sultan, Mangogul, who has no need of a male friend to test the fidelity of the women in his court and city, since he possesses a magic ring which, when directed at a woman's genitals, forces those 'indiscreet jewels' to confess their secrets. Diderot is taking to a fantasy extreme the desire of the 'curious impertinent'. Here at last is a foolproof way of discovering the truth about women.

On the surface, this is not an anxious text, though the strenuousness with which it denies anxiety perhaps indicates otherwise. The Sultan starts using the ring not because he is anxious to find something out but because he is 'bored to death': his masculine curiosity is a thirst for erotic stories, since those with which his favourite concubine Mirzoza regales him have for the moment run out.[107] Thus does Diderot implicate his reader in the position occupied by his hero. Remnants of traditional cautionary discourse remain ('Some curiosities are misplaced'),[108] but these mainly serve to heighten the titillation, like a dominatrix's stern cry of 'naughty boy'. The same goes for the remnants of pedagogical and philosophical curiosity: the statement 'youth is curious' might evoke the pedagogue Pluche but in fact here means that young people are susceptible to seduction.[109] Curiosity seems here to have been reduced to those less respectable and prestigious connotations which, following the decline of the culture of curiosities, were often dominant in the mid-eighteenth century: sex, entertainment, and occult tricks. The ring obligingly produces numerous confessions: whereas Corneille imagines solving men's dependence on women by excluding women, Diderot imagines solving it by humiliating them. The ring humiliates numerous women in public, much to the amusement of the Sultan—and of the

---

[107] 's'ennuie à périr' (Diderot 1951, 7). Erotic curiosity is here always masculine (e.g. 11, 16, 46, 99, 172), except when it is projected by a male sub-narrator onto young girls (177, 191). Such projection was common in 18th-century pornographic narrative: e.g. when Cervantes's phrase was feminized (in *La Curieuse impertinente*, 1789), it denoted not some female equivalent of Anselmo but a sex-crazed chambermaid.

[108] 'il est des curiosités mal placées' (10).

[109] 'Jeunesse est curieuse' (191). The parodic 'curiosité des savants' (23) is directed at the philosophical question of how the ring can make matter speak.

implied reader—who has a detachment never shown by any 'curious impertinent'.

Yet the Sultan *is* dependent on one of his concubines, Mirzoza. The one source of suspense in a narrative otherwise based on pre-dictable repetition is whether or not the Sultan will renege on his agreement not to turn the ring on her (since that distrust would ruin their happy relationship) and, especially, what he would hear if he did. Both she and he are in fact anxious that his 'silly curiosity' might induce him to do this.[110] Whereas in Cervantes's tragic novella curiosity was mainly anxiety but occasionally switched to amuse-ment, in this pornographic novel it is mainly amusement but occa-sionally switches to anxiety. The Sultan's curiosity is not entirely unlike Anselmo's after all. Diderot's prolepsis includes a teasing hint that Mirzoza may indeed have something to hide: if that was true, then this would turn out to be a 'curious impertinent' story. Whereas in cautionary tales curiosity led to foregone conclusions—whether its chain unravelled in a tragic or a comic direction—here the fixity of those grand narratives has broken down.[111]

In the event, the Sultan does turn the ring on his favourite in a last-ditch effort to prevent her from dying when she has fallen ill. It suc-ceeds, and her 'jewel' speaks of her fidelity. Far from mitigating the text's suggestion that '(almost all) women are all the same', she becomes only the second counter-example, an exception that proves the rule.[112] As Mirzoza recovers consciousness, she hears her jewel speak, realizes what the Sultan has done, and reproaches him for mistrusting her. He replies: 'do not ascribe to any shameful curiosity the impatience which was only induced in me by despair at having lost you. I did not do the ring test on you but, rather, I thought that I could—without breaking my promises—use an expedient that would restore you to me.'[113]

---

[110] 'sotte curiosité' (11; see also p. 16).

[111] On the link between such breakdown and the rise of 'suspense', see Cave 1999, 138–41.

[112] The first exception is Zaïde (223–5). The rule is established by the 28 other occa-sions on which the ring is used. For a fuller, more nuanced account of Diderot's repre-sentations of women, see Goldberg 1984, chs. 4–6.

[113] 'n'imputez point à une honteuse curiosité une impatience que le désespoir de vous avoir perdue m'a seul suggérée: je n'ai point fait sur vous l'essai de mon anneau; mais j'ai cru pouvoir, sans manquer à mes promesses, user d'une ressource qui vous rend à mes voeux' (234).

A narrative driven by curiosity ends with the main protagonist emphatically denying any curiosity. Mirzoza says that she believes the Sultan's protestation, but the reader does not necessarily have to. After all, only a few pages earlier he was overwhelmed with anxiety that he, Mirzoza's lover, might not be as happy as the lover of the only woman so far proved to be faithful (Zaïde). And the Sultan is so delighted to hear what Mirzoza's jewel is saying that at first he does not even notice that she is recovering consciousness (234), as if his curiosity momentarily outdoes his concern to save her life. Moreover, Mirzoza immediately gets him to return the ring to the genie, calling it a 'fatal gift',[114] as if it still had a destructive potential she feared. The Sultan has managed to have it both ways, to find out what he was curious to know but not to find it out (so he protests) through curiosity. The question whether he protests too loudly is left hanging in the air. In *The Indiscreet Jewels*, curiosity is both gleefully, pornographically indulged and yet also feared for its tragic potential. The ghost of Cervantes's sexually fearful Anselmo still stalks even the libertines.

4.4.3.3 *Oedipus*

Oedipus, on the other hand, while inhabiting the most famous of all triangles of desire, is surely not, on the face of it, a 'curious impertinent': after all, it is not as if he sets out to test his mother in the way that Anselmo tests Camilla or Mangogul tests Mirzoza. However, even Oedipus got caught up in the misogynistic early modern drive to rewrite even apparently inappropriate stories as ones that caution curious men not to investigate female chastity lest they get a nasty shock. Let me explore these rewritings through two case studies. The first, dating from 1583, shows how, through exemplarity, the curiosity of Oedipus could be invoked in an attempt to regulate the behaviour of readers in many different spheres, all of which were still understood at this date as involving one and the same curiosity. The second, dating from 1659, shows what could happen when exemplarity was on the wane in some quarters: the Oedipus story is used by the dramatist Pierre Corneille to show, if anything, the difficulty of curing curiosity.

Shortly before Cervantes's *El curioso impertinente* first appeared, Bénigne Poissenot included in *L'Esté*, his 1583 collection of short

---

[114] 'son fatal présent' (234).

histoires, the story of the 'folle curiosité' of the philosopher Secundus.[115] Debating one day in Plato's Academy the question whether any wife could remain chaste all her life, Secundus is appalled by the majority verdict: no—women are too weak and imperfect. So, in order to try and prove the philosophers wrong, he decides to test his own mother, whom he has always considered one of the chastest women on earth. He returns home in disguise, propositions his mother, and is horrified to find that she is willing to sleep with the 'stranger' that he pretends to be. After an inactive night spent with his head on her breast, he reveals his identity. She dies of shock; he regrets the test and punishes himself by never speaking again, since his speech caused her death.

The story is told by a narrator (Prefouché) who is conversing with fellow students. Using Secundus as an *exemplum* that both enjoins against curiosity and illustrates it, Prefouché frames the story, both before and after, with briefer mentions of a few other examples:

So there you have the whole account of the curiosity of the philosopher Secundus and the fat lot of good that it did him. He should have been made wise by the example of Oedipus who, initially tranquil, then could not rest until he had discovered who his father was. Investigating this too curiously, he found that he himself had killed his father and, worse still, that his marriage was incestuous, since he had wed his own mother.[116]

This compresses Plutarch's already compressed exemplification of Oedipus as curious. Poissenot ignores the disparities between Secundus and Oedipus: he chooses not to point out that Secundus is investigating and semi-realizing a conditional future, Oedipus the determinate past; nor that Secundus's mother is knowingly unchaste, Oedipus's unknowingly. Instead, Poissenot creates similarities between the two: for the curious Secundus—as for Cervantes's Anselmo—a calamity that might happen is as bad as one that already has happened, such as Oedipus's; and blame now shifts to Jocasta who, although she has no idea that she is marrying her son, implicitly illustrates female unchastity as much as Secundus's mother does.

---

[115] Poissenot 1987, 82–90. On Poissenot's probable source, see p. 82 n. 48.

[116] 'Voilà l'entier discours de la curiosité du Philosophe Secundus, et le bien qui luy en print. Il devoit estre faict sage par l'exemple d'Œdippe qui, estant à repos, n'y peut jamais demeurer qu'il ne decouvrist qui estoit son Pere: de quoy s'enquestant trop curieusement, trouva qu'il estoit mort par sa main et, qui pis est, que son mariage estoit incestueux, ayant espousé sa propre mere.' (88). The source for this interpretation of Oedipus is Plutarch (1971, 67ᵛ), on which *locus* see Cave 1988, 146–8.

In both *exempla*, curiosity leads to calamity which leads to punishment: Secundus's voluntary aphasia echoes Oedipus's self-blinding. This three-segment chain of events is the common denominator which enables these two particular examples to enjoin and illustrate the same general message. Details of the links between the segments of the chain become—from the point of view of exemplarity—irrelevant. It does not matter that it could be argued that Oedipus's calamity began well before his curiosity; what matters is that within Prefouché's diegesis the curiosity is narrated before the calamity, thereby presenting curiosity as the trigger of calamity and punishment. Brief *exempla*, because they were stories narrated in highly condensed form—as in Poissenot's above-quoted version of the Oedipus myth—emphasized these crude sequences of segments instead of amplifying the chronological or causal nature of the links between them. For the purposes of exemplarity, Oedipus's curiosity in trying to know what already had happened is, implicitly, just as calamitous as if that curiosity actually caused parricide and incest which would not otherwise have happened. So strong is the modern tendency—shared by Sophocles's Oedipus—to assume that it is best to know family truths, whatever the cost, that this early modern insistence (echoing Plutarch) that Oedipus would have been better off ignorant is now difficult to understand.

Poissenot can use the curiosity of Oedipus and Secundus for many purposes because he makes them exemplary, widely applicable to various spheres of life. He uses their stories to enjoin against curiosity that is directed not only at family matters, but also at a wide range of others not mentioned in the diegesis itself. He surrounds the story of Secundus with diatribes against the curiosity of divination,[117] of natural philosophy, of ancient Gauls—who, according to Caesar, bombarded strangers with demands for news—and even of the French, Spanish, and Portuguese explorations of the 'New World'

---

[117] This attack on 'curieux' who want to 'sçavoir ce qui leur doit avenir' (82) presents Secundus's test as being very close to divination. Oedipus's recourse to divination is not directly mentioned but also implies this proximity. For Prefouché, divination sometimes tells the truth, but it then deprives us of 'repos' (83)—the term that is also used for the 'tranquillity' which Oedipus loses. The connection between divination and male testing of female chastity was common in early modern stories, such as that of a Frenchman who is tricked into thinking that he has successfully secured the services of a friend's familiar demon in order to check up on the behaviour of his courtesan while he is absent (Weber 1673, 461–2; Schott's *Physica curiosa* is cited as the source).

insofar as they went beyond what was strictly useful (82–4, 88–90). Thus, in the late sixteenth century, divination and male sexual curiosity were two closely related species of curiosity, either of which could serve, through exemplarity, to represent numerous other species of the vice. The contemporary tales of Faust and of Du Souhait's *curieux* could be read—and perhaps were read—as enjoining against curiosity directed at magic and much else, just as the tale of Secundus enjoined against curiosity directed at sex and much else.

This extensive exemplary transferability of Oedipus and Secundus was made possible by the relative moral homogeneity that in 1583 still surrounded curiosity, which was still a vice in most discourses. Certainly, that homogeneity was beginning to fracture: a few of Poissenot's students argue that curiosity can be good. But most of them still argue that curiosity is always bad and useless, quite distinct from 'a praiseworthy desire to learn'.[118] However, by about the mid-seventeenth century, that homogeneity had disappeared: curiosity, still hated in some discourses, was now widely fêted in others. This inevitably lessened the capacity of any single *exemplum* of curiosity to be applied so widely. Unlike Poissenot's tale or the partial allegories of Verville, later narratives of sexual curiosity were mainly about . . . sexual curiosity. Diderot does connect sexual curiosity to other, philosophical kinds in *The Indiscreet Jewels*, but in a ludic vein which ironizes those connections (without necessarily dismissing them altogether). Scudéry does connect the sexual species of curiosity to several others in 1661, but in an ambivalent and tangential way.

This scope of application of curiosity thus gradually narrowed down in narrative, both because curiosity was becoming more morally ambivalent and also because of the more general waning of allegory and injunctive exemplarity in some quarters. However, exemplarity was not considered to be the only story-telling method that could improve people morally: in mid- and late-seventeenth-century French neoclassical theatre, Aristotelian purgation of the passions was often considered to be another such method. Could catharsis purge curiosity? Corneille used Oedipus to raise that question but ultimately refrained from giving a reassuring affirmative answer.

---

[118] 'un louable desir d'apprendre' (88).

As Terence Cave has noted, Pierre Corneille, commenting in his *Discours de la tragédie* (1660) on the discussion of Oedipus in Aristotle's *Poetics*, argues that Oedipus induces the tragic emotion of pity but not fear, since few people would really fear killing their father and marrying their mother: in seventeenth-century terms, the plot is too *invraisemblable*. However, Corneille then rectifies this implausibility and salvages catharsis by claiming that

If the representation [of Oedipus] can imprint some fear in us, and if that fear is capable of purging some reprehensible or vicious inclination in us, then it will purge the curiosity which seeks to know the future and it will prevent us from resorting to predictions, which usually only serve to plunge us into the predicted misfortune via our very efforts to avoid it.[119]

Corneille goes on to explain that he is referring here not to Oedipus himself but to Laius and Jocasta, who caused Oedipus's misfortune by seeking to avoid it—once it had been predicted by the Delphic oracle—through their attempt to kill him as a baby. With the kind of chronological precision that brief *exempla* elide, Corneille points out that the audience's curiosity will thus be purged, through fear, not by what happens during the action of the play but rather by the vague 'image of an error' which was committed by Oedipus's parents forty years before the play's action begins.[120] The tortuousness of Corneille's discussion suggests it may be 'a kind of pre-Voltairean joke' (Cave 1988, 101), showing scepticism not just about the cathartic qualities of the Oedipus story but also about 'superstitious' fear of divination.

However, if it is a joke, it is an uneasy one. Corneille's analysis of divinatory curiosity as creating the very misfortune that it seeks to avoid was not implausible in 1660, but was widely shared;[121] it also echoes the way in which the 'curious impertinent' creates the outcome that he most fears—a plot that Corneille suppressed in *La Place royale*, as we have seen, but arguably in a spirit of anxiety

---

[119] 'Si sa représentation nous peut imprimer quelque crainte, et que cette crainte soit capable de purger en nous quelque inclination blâmable ou vicieuse, elle y purgera la curiosité de savoir l'avenir, et nous empêchera d'avoir recours à des prédictions, qui ne servent d'ordinaire qu'à nous faire choir dans le malheur qu'on nous prédit par les soins mêmes que nous prenons de l'éviter' (Corneille 1971, i. 38). I am working within the framework set up by the excellent discussion of Oedipus and curiosity in Cave 1988, 101–2, 118–26, 146–8, 314 n. 46.

[120] 'l'image d'une faute' (38).

[121] Cf. a year later (1661): Scudéry 1979, 51.

about it. To return momentarily to Girard's terms: desire in these triangles was imbued with fear. Moreover, the description, in the *Discours*, of divinatory curiosity as backfiring on itself is echoed in Corneille's own tragedy *Œdipe* of the previous year (1659). In the play the finger of blame is pointed not at Laius and Jocasta but at the two shepherds and at Œdipe himself, all of whom are explicitly described as having produced what oracles predicted by seeking to avoid it.[122] It is as if Corneille is indeed trying to maximize the production of fear, which he ascribes in the *Discours* to the actions of Laius and Jocasta, by ascribing it in the play to other characters. And Dircé, the one protagonist who is 'not very curious' to hear the dead Laius's pronouncement via Tirésie, is used by Corneille as a moral counterpoint, herself predicting that Œdipe will be punished for this necromancy.[123]

But Dircé does not have the last word. If her moralizing message coincided with that of the play as a whole, the audience's curiosity would perhaps be purged through fear but there would be no room for the Cornelian *admiration* (amazement) which œdipe increasingly inspires as he gains in heroic stature towards the end of the play (Cave 1988, 319–20). In fact *Œdipe* is far from being an extended *exemplum* cautioning against curiosity, even if at least one contemporary interpreted it in this way: as late as 1692, André Dacier, commenting on the *Poetics*, attributed Oedipus's misfortunes to his curiosity, thereby extending the discourse of exemplarity into tragedy, interpreting Sophocles's version as a cautionary tale, as if it were an extended equivalent of Plutarch's exemplification of Oedipus, to which Dacier alludes indirectly.[124] By contrast, Corneille's *Œdipe* is not explictly called 'curious'. Moreover, even his centrality is diminished, since he functions partly as a temporary obstacle to the union of lovers (Dircé and Thésée) in this generically ambivalent play (Cave 1988, 314–16). His truth-seeking actually helps the lovers, in the same way as the figure of the 'curious impertinent' was reduced to being a temporary obstacle to the happy union of two other lovers in some later comic adaptations which, from the

---

[122] Corneille 1971, iii. 68 (ll. 1758–60), 71 (ll. 1831–2). This emphasis on human agency contributes to what Cave describes as the play's questioning of the fatality usually associated with Oedipus (1988, 318). On Corneille's *Œdipe*, see Cave 1988, 314–22.

[123] 'assez peu curieuse' (p. 28, l. 546; see ll. 555–60).

[124] Aristotle 1692, 270. Quoted and analysed in Cave 1988, 118–19.

late seventeenth century onwards, sought to contain the disturbing, destructive power of his curiosity by making it the flaw that enables others to be united.

Any interpretation of *Œdipe* as a cautionary tale against curiosity is also perhaps compromised by Corneille's own avowed stimulation of his audience's curiosity. Whereas in 1583 Poissenot keeps curiosity largely bad by carefully referring to his reader's desire to know what happens next in terms of 'suspense' rather than of 'curiosity',[125] by 1660 it has become common to attribute curiosity both to protagonists and to readers: even the moralizing Dacier does so in 1692 (Cave 1988, 120). Is the curiosity of readers good, unlike the bad curiosity of protagonists? The question was uneasy, as is shown by the witty irony of Scudéry's suggestion in 1661 that the fact that tales of calamitous curiosity tickle our own curiosity means that curiosity cannot be *all* bad. Corneille does not make such an explicit link between intra- and extradiegetic curiosity. He leaves it open and unclear whether there is any relation between them at all. Are they simply two separate things that happen to share the same name? The strong similarity between them suggests otherwise: both protagonists and readers want to know the future. For protagonists, this is calamitous; but for readers and audience, it is purely pleasurable. In the *Discours du poème dramatique* (1660) Corneille advises playwrights how to maximize the pleasure of audiences by stimulating their curiosity about what will happen at the end of the tragedy. The calamitous dénouement should be delayed as long as possible, even within the fifth act:

The more one defers [the catastrophe], the more minds are held in suspense, and their impatience to know in which direction it will unfurl causes them to experience it with greater pleasure; that does not happen when the catastrophe begins at the start of the fifth act. An audience that knows the catastrophe too early has no more curiosity; its attention languishes for the rest of the play, which teaches it nothing new.[126]

This curiosity is certainly not bad: the audience will not be punished for it. But nor is it explicitly good, however enthusiastically it is

---

[125] 'Pour ne vous tenir plus longtemps suspens' (Poissenot 1987, 84).

[126] 'Plus on la diffère, plus les esprits demeurent suspendus, et l'impatience qu'ils ont de savoir de quel côté elle tournera est cause qu'ils la reçoivent avec plus de plaisir: ce qui n'arrive pas quand elle commence avec cet acte. L'auditeur qui la sait trop tôt n'a plus de curiosité; et son attention languit durant tout le reste, qui ne lui apprend de nouveau.' (Corneille 1971, i. 30–1).

described. Rather, it is a cognitive, aesthetic operation that is some-how freed from explicit ethical investments.

For the duration of their stay in the auditorium, audiences are freed from the injunction against curiosity about the future that Corneille himself gives both in the *Discours de la tragédie* and within the diegetic world of *Œdipe*. Although Corneille does not say whether or not the curiosity of protagonists and audiences is the one and the same thing, nonetheless his explicit stimulation of audiences' curiosity about the future seems to sit uneasily alongside his own claim that *Œdipe* is designed to purge audiences of their curiosity about the future. Within Corneille's writing, the uses of curiosity are part ethical, part aesthetic, and the relation between the two is awkward, neither clear nor resolved.

4.4.4   *Still typecast: comic* curieux *on stage*

However, in some other theatrical genres, stories of curiosity contin-ued to be narrated in order to draw moral lessons from them or, even more, to illustrate and satirize certain moral or social types.

This kind of illustrative rather than injunctive exemplarity contin-ued to thrive in a number of minor French one-act comedies that offered sustained 'satyre' (Planard 1807, 13) of one or more *curieux*. Let me consider three such plays, ranging from 1698 to 1807. Certainly, curiosity has by now reduced in its scope of application when compared, for instance, with Poissenot in 1583. These plays are not attacking a wide range of species of curiosity, nor are they presented as allegories or *exempla* that are applicable to other species than the ones that they actually depict. By now, the distance separating different species of curiosity—such as nosiness and natu-ralism—has widened. However, these plays still lump together some kinds of curiosity—that today are usually considered to be wholly distinct—as being in fact one and the same thing: in particular, they seek to demonstrate that the curiosity of the collector is also the passion that leads to calamity. In other words, they conflate the centuries-old kind of curiosity (the calamitous passion and vice) with the kind that had more recently become prominent within the culture of curiosities. They shape curiosity in this way in order to attack the culture of curiosities. They depict ridiculous characters whose dis-course is grounded in the curiosity-collecting tendency, that is, who are either collectors of material objects or else who seek to accumulate other kinds of discrete, 'curious' gratifications. And these plays then show that this collecting-based curiosity in fact triggers a calamitous chain of events, usually culminating in financial disaster. Ultimately, the curiosity-narrating tendency is shown to be the master discourse, triumphing over the illusions offered by the curiosity-collecting tendency. Being comedies, some of these plays end calamitously only for the *curieux*, not for other protagonists. Like the 'curious impertinent' of theatrical comedy, these *curieux* are integrated into the comic plot by serving as obstacles to a union of lovers, their *curiosité* being the blind, weak point which enables them to be outwitted. Let me summarize the plots of three such plays.

Le Curieux (date unknown) was the first play written by Dampierre de La Sale (1722–93).[127] Polydore, a collector ('Curieux ou Amateur de curiosités', 81), wishes to marry Lucile, an orphan whom he has brought up. She agrees out of a sense of duty. Brocantin, a dealer in *curiosités*, wants to get Lucile on his side, since he is worried that she will persuade his client Polydore to stop buying over-priced objects from him. So Brocantin decides to help Lucile's lover Clitandre in his efforts to prevent the wedding. Brocantin used to be Clitandre's valet but then learned his current trade (*brocanteur*) from his next master, a *curieux*. Brocantin now teaches Clitandre the jargon and introduces him to Polydore as a fellow *curieux*. Criton, a real *curieux*, arrives and execrates Polydore for beating him to a *curiosité* which Criton has been coveting for thirty-five years. Clitandre offers Polydore a life-sized Japanese statue, for which Polydore agrees to barter Lucile. The two lovers proclaim the secret of their relationship, then the statue is revealed to be a hoax: it is Clitandre's valet, in disguise.

Les Curieux de Compiégne, a *comédie-vaudeville* by Florent Carton Dancourt—the second most prolific playwright of seventeenth-century France after Alexandre Hardy[128]—was first performed at the Comédie-Française on 4 October 1698 and then an impressive further twenty-four times before the end of the year.[129] It was set in the military camp which Louis XIV had established in 1698 near Compiègne, after the first phase of the Palatine War had

[127] [Dampierre de la Sale] 1787, i. 78–114 (10).

[128] Lancaster 1929–42, vi. 136.

[129] Dancourt 1729, iv. [259]–314. See Lancaster 1929–42, IV.ii. 804–6 (806). Charles Shadwell wrote an English adaptation (1713).

ended with the Treaty of Rijswijk (1697). Eventually closed on 22 September 1698, the camp had staged war games for the instruction of the King's grandson, the Duc de Bourgogne, and had also been visited by numerous Parisians. In the play, two nobles, Clitandre and a Gascon Chevalier de Fourbignac, both officers at the camp, are broke. Their finances are worsened by the hospitality that they are lavishing on a band of bourgeois camp followers, who include Le Chevalier's suppliers, profiteers to whom he owes money. The hospitality is his way of paying interest on the money he owes them. The cowardly bourgeois, who have brought along their wives, mistresses, and daughters, are _curieux_ to see army life and experience it vicariously. The two nobles scheme to solve their financial problems by marrying the daughter (Angélique) of one of the bourgeois and the mistress of another. To obtain the necessary consent they exploit the anti-bourgeois feeling in the camp. (Angélique's father, who had been dressing up as a soldier with his friends, has just had his uniform ripped off by real soldiers.) The two nobles pretend that twenty _curieux_ are being rounded up as suspected spies. This forces the terrified, duped bourgeois to hand over their women for marriage, along with the wealth that comes with them.

Finally, _Le Curieux_ by François Antoine Eugène de Planard was first performed in 1807. The _curieux_ is Forlange, a guest in the house of his relative Mme Dorval. Her daughter has just married Gerville, who is hiding in the house under the name of Favière, since he has killed his colonel in a duel. His identity has been kept from the untrustworthily _curieux_ Forlange, whose _curiosité_ now wreaks havoc. Although Forlange loves Émilie—another daughter of Mme Dorval—and is loved by her, each is ignorant of the other's feelings; by eavesdropping on and misinterpreting a conversation, he sows confusion about who loves whom in the household. Also, after he has cheerfully informed a disguised spy that 'Favière' is in the house, the latter is arrested. Everyone curses Forlange. But he obtains a pardon for Gerville ('Favière') by making a repentant appeal to the minister. Everyone forgives Forlange, including Émilie, who agrees to marry him on condition that he gives up _curiosité_.

In this third example, _curiosité_ is not the weak point which enables the obstacle to the final marriage to be overcome but rather the obstacle itself, which lies within the male lover and is eventually excised: it is the one fault—in an otherwise admirable man—which makes Émilie hesitate to marry him (Planard 1807, 13).

Two of these comedies, those by Dancourt and Planard, reassuringly oppose love to curiosity, just as Destouches does in his soothing 1706 dramatization of the 'curious impertinent' story. Dancourt grafts the culture of curiosities onto stock comic plots—reminiscent of those adapted by Molière in *L'École des femmes* and *L'Avare*—in order to criticize men for making women equivalent to curiosities, that is, precious objects to be bartered and exchanged. The play attacks the culture of curiosities both for objectifying women and for displacing male sexuality onto inanimate objects:[130] when Polydore skulks off to console himself in his cabinet after his final humiliation (113–14), this recalls contemporary satirical prints of elderly collectors surrounded by erotic statues of women. More unusually, even men are represented by Dancourt as being commodified objects of curiosity. One of the curious *bourgeoises* gazes at the soldiers, exclaiming three times in a row 'I'm dying of pleasure', encouraged sarcastically by Clitandre's valet: 'Quite a selection of merchandise—a fine fair, don't you think, Madame?'[131]

However, although the objectification of women in particular as curiosities is satirized by some of these plays, that does not prevent the plays from turning women into objects: that objectification is merely displaced onto other terms. Jokey references to 'enjoying' and 'possessing' curiosities reinforce the assumption that animate women, not inanimate objects, really ought to be the grammatical objects of these verbs.[132] Even Planard's forgiven *curieux*, Forlange, says to Émilie, when he promises to renounce trying to possess secrets, 'So, do I really possess you?' And even this renunciation of *curiosité* jokily turns her into another, now erotic object of his knowledge: the play ends with his aside 'I hope at least to learn the secret of my wife'.[133]

Moreover, although most of the *curieux* in these plays are men, it is sometimes stated that their *curiosité* makes them rather feminine. Just as Polydore's *curiosité* prevents him from marrying, so it is only by renouncing *curiosité* that Forlange can become truly masculine and get married. The maidservant tells a valet that people are right to

---

[130] e.g. 103, 110.

[131] 'je me meurs de plaisir'; 'Il y a là de la marchandise à choisir, c'est une belle Foire, n'est-ce pas, Madame?' (279–80).

[132] [Dampierre de la Sale] 1787, i. 108 ('jouïr'), 111 ('jouisse'), 112 ('possède').

[133] 'Eh quoi; je vous possède? . . . J'espère au moins savoir le secret de ma femme' (35).

say of Forlange that 'a more curious [*sc.* inquisitive] man has never been seen'. The valet agrees: 'deep down, I believe that when Nature formed him she thought she was making a woman'.[134]

Curiosity is not only gendered; it is also a function of social rank, just as it was for Du Souhait (1600) and for numerous German university academics. Like Du Souhait, Dancourt makes curiosity the opposite of nobility: he gives a monopoly of it to the bourgeoisie— always one of Dancourt's favourite butts. The satirical target of the play is not this stereotyping but any questioning of it: 'Oh! il y a Bourgeois et Bourgeois, Madame', a valet sarcastically reassures a *bourgeoise*, the joke being that in fact they really are all the same. Equally ridiculous are provincials, including noble ones. Their *curiosité* is that of the fashion victim: they gawk in ignorant, uncritical delight at all that Paris has to offer—from opera to automatons—in contrast to the discerning taste of the sophisticated Parisian *connoisseur*.[135]

Certainly, the main point of representing curiosity in these plays is to satirize the culture of curiosities, whether its activities (such as collecting, travel,[136] tourism, watching royal spectacles),[137] its assumptions (curiosity costs money;[138] objects give one something to talk about),[139] or its characteristic recourse to certain lavish rhetorical figures (such as enumeration).[140] But these plays also lump ancient species of curiosity—that had been condemned for centuries— together with the relatively recent species found in the upstart culture of curiosities. For instance, Forlange's curiosity consists not only of tourism but also of *polypragmosyne*—eavesdropping and spilling

---

[134] 'l'on ne vit jamais d'homme si curieux. | . . . je crois au fond de l'âme | Qu'en le formant Nature a cru faire une femme' (Planard 1807, 6)

[135] Forlange's *curiosité* is explained as 'le défaut de sa petite ville'; he is visiting from the provinces (Planard 1807, 4; see also p. 11). See esp. *Les Curieux de province* by Petit (1702, 3–24), a one-act prologue which ridicules provincial nobles; for the *connoistre* family of terms, see pp. 10, 13, 19, 23.

[136] The camp followers are represented as travellers as well as sightseers: 'la curiosité a rendu la Bourgeoisie de Paris très voyageuse' (Dancourt 1729, iv. 266).

[137] See the one-act comedy *Les Democrates et les aristocrates ou Les Curieux du Champ de Mars* ([1789]).

[138] The ruinous expense not only of collecting (Dampierre de la Sale) but also of camp-following (Dancourt) is emphasized .

[139] e.g. Dancourt 1729, iv. 272.

[140] e.g. Forlange's valet lists all the places he had been dragged to that day by his sightseeing master: 'Places, palais, hôtels, jardins, ponts, quais, fontaines, | Eglises, monumens, artistes, porcelaines' (Planard 1807, 5).

secrets. The curiosity of the bourgeois of Compiègne is similarly laced with indecorous *polypragmosyne*, since they have no business to be at the army camp, no role to fulfil there.[141] As for many church writers, so for these playwrights the curiosity that underlies the relatively recent culture of curiosities is really just the same thing as the destructive passion that ancient and patristic writers condemned.

4.4.5   Morality and beyond

Although stories of curiosity continued to be used as a source of moral lessons in some genres throughout the early modern period, in the second half of the seventeenth century in France such exemplarity was undermined by some fictional novellas, such as *Célinte* (1661) by Madeleine de Scudéry and *La Princesse de Clèves* (1678) by Madame de Lafayette. Whereas in *Célinte* the scope of application of curiosity is still extremely wide, in *La Princesse de Clèves* it has been mainly reduced to the context of love. But in both cases, curiosity now exceeds moral or indeed discursive control: it cannot be definitively categorized, defined, or shaped. Certainly, that is also true of countless other texts, as I have tried to show, but in these two works that uncontrollability of curiosity is overt: they do not even try to control it; instead, they represent any attempt to do so as impossible. That makes curiosity extraordinarily rich and open-ended— perhaps more so in Scudéry's novella than in any other early modern text that I have read.[142] It also makes curiosity deeply troubling, especially in *La Princesse de Clèves*. The question of the morality of curiosity is here either irrelevant (Lafayette) or else subject to unresolved contestation (Scudéry). Curiosity has shifted partly or wholly from ethics to aesthetics, as in Corneille. It is used above all not to turn readers into better people but to motivate and propel their reading. Especially for Scudéry, curiosity is what generates endless discourse, in the form either of conversations or of stories.

---

[141] Dancourt 1729, iv. 300.
[142] *Célinte* did not achieve the enormous fame of Scudéry's romances. Its main, narrative section is part romance (in its plot structure), part novella (in its relative brevity and its recent setting), written at a time of transition from the former genre to the latter. See Niderst in Scudéry 1979, 7–9.

4.4.5.1   Scudéry, Célinte

Both forms of discourse—conversation and narrative—were dear to Scudéry. *Célinte* consists of both: it begins with a long conversation about curiosity (the Prologue) and then continues with the narrative about Célinte. The opening conversation is itself a frame narrative, extradiegetic in relation to the Célinte story. The Prologue opens with a group of friends walking in the bois de Vincennes a few days after the 1660 triumphal entry into Paris of Louis XIV and Maria Theresa of Spain. The friends' discussion of the royal entry leads to a much lengthier discussion of curiosity, after one interlocutor evokes a recent work on this passion. The work remains unnamed: in fact it is a short treatise by La Mothe Le Vayer; together with Plutarch, it provides the major source for Scudéry's prologue[143] which, however, goes well beyond its sources. The group conversation ends when one of the interlocutors proposes reading aloud a recently acquired novella, which the company then goes to a house to listen to.

What is the point of the conversation? Ostensibly, it is to define curiosity. Yet the friends fail to agree on any definition. This also occurs in Poissenot's analogous frame narrative of 1583, but there it is strongly implied that some of the friends are right—those who think that curiosity is all bad. By contrast, none of Scudéry's interlocutors are represented as having the final, definitive word. Moreover, whereas all of Poissenot's interlocutors are male, Scudéry's are both female and male: each has an equal right to say what they think curiosity is. Scudéry has avoided simply reversing the pattern of countless male-authored conversations: she has not handed over the power of definitive definition from men to women. Certainly, there are authoritative female voices, such as the *je*—who is perhaps a representation of the author—or else Artelice, who chairs the debate (Denis 1997, 84) and ends it by calling for a general resolution to be agreed.[144] But none is agreed.

The interlocutors shape and reshape curiosity using techniques that we have encountered elsewhere, not least in early modern universities. In trying to decide what counts as curiosity, they sometimes divide it into what they call 'species' or 'sorts', such as tourism, col-

---

[143] See Maître-Dufour 1998, 341; Niderst in Scudéry 1979, 13–14.

[144] 'Mais enfin en general que resoudra la Compagnie de la Curiosité?' (Scudéry 1979, 54). My reading of the prologue thus differs from the more univocal ones by Maître-Dufour (1998, 341) and Niderst (Scudéry 1979, 15). For plurivocal readings of conversations in Scudéry's works, see Denis 1997.

lecting, divination, gossip, reading other people's letters.[145] Or again, one interlocutor, Meriante, resorts to the technique of dismissing some of the current meanings of 'curiosity' as misnomers, as words that have come to be applied to the wrong thing: 'I renounce a thing [*sc. curiosité*] which produces more evil than good. For even when this word *curiosité* is abused and certain people are spoken of as *Curieux*, many ungrounded *curiositez* are still often found among them.'[146] In other words, curiosity is all bad: collectors can be guilty of bad curiosity too, so it is wrong to call them 'curious' as if that were a good quality. Another interlocutor, who agrees that curiosity is all bad, argues that 'the desire to learn', which is good and leads to astronomy and the like, should not be called 'curiosity'.[147] So, for him, what we might think of as nowadays as curiosity—and what Blumenberg calls 'theoretical curiosity'—are, precisely, *not* curiosity.

In this conversation Scudéry does not merely provide a kind of anthology of definitions of curiosity that were possible in 1661; she is also overtly dramatizing the process by which definitions are proposed and undone—a process which is the focus of the present study and yet which is usually only obviously visible in the polemical clashes between different works, since each more usually seeks to enforce at all costs its own definition, in order to further the kind of aim, pragmatic or moral, that Scudéry's text is eschewing. She represents curiosity as being something that is especially highly charged and open to contestation. The mere sound of the word seems to attract to the debate one interlocutor who happens to be passing:

since we were speaking quite loudly, [Cleandre] heard the word 'curiosity' several times and so, after climbing down from his carriage so that he could go by foot, he called over to Clearque and asked him whether there could really be a disagreement [*contestation*] between people who had (he well knew) long been united by respect and friendship.[148]

---

[145] 'espece' (51), 'sorte' (49, 50).

[146] 'je renonce à une chose qui produit plus de mal que [d]e bien. Car lors mesme que l'on abuse du mot de curiosité, et que l'on parle de certaines Gens que l'on appelle Curieux, on trouve bien souvent encore un grand nombre de curiositez mal fondées' (55).

[147] 'Le desir d'apprendre' (46).

[148] 'mais comme nous parlions assez haut, il entendit plusieurs fois le mot de Curiosité, si bien qu'estant descendu de son Carrosse, afin de se promener à pied, il demanda à Clearque, qu'il appella, s'il pouvoit y avoir quelque contestation entre des Personnes qu'il sçavoit bien que l'estime et l'amitié unissoient depuis long-temps' (37).

The interlocutors give categorical definitions, but only to see them immediately challenged. For instance, Meriante, who thinks that he is against all curiosity, is forced to admit that he himself was 'curieux' about the royal entry, yet he still claims that 'that does not prevent me from condemning excessive curiosity in general'.[149] Even this rephrased version shows that his definition cannot be watertight: 'in general' allows for particular exceptions,[150] while 'excessive' now allows for the existence of non-excessive curiosity. Similarly, certain effects of curiosity are carefully described as occurring 'very often', rather than 'always' as in the rhetoric of exemplarity.[151]

Since the debate about curiosity in the Prologue is unresolved, the Célinte story that follows cannot function as an *exemplum*, since it would be unclear exactly *what* universal moral truth it is supposed to illustrate. Certainly, in the Epilogue there is a vestigial claim about the text's capacity to improve readers morally, but this is made about the opening conversation, not about the Célinte story: in the Epilogue the *je* narrator claims that her transcription of the conversation will 'correct' or 'cure' the curiosity of some readers.[152] This parting shot momentarily implies that curiosity is all bad after all, but that reflects neither the conversation nor for that matter the Célinte story. It also conflicts with the curiosity that Scudéry ascribes to, and flagrantly stimulates in, her own readers. This aesthetic use of curiosity in fact turns out to the dominant one in *Célinte*, sitting uneasily alongside the unresolved moral uses.

Scudéry revels wittily in that unease, spelling out more clearly perhaps than any other writer the view that aesthetic and moral, extra- and intradiegetic curiosity are one and the same thing. In the Prologue, the interlocutors indulge their curiosity about the effects that curiosity caused at the recent royal entry: erotic and jealous curiosity was rife among the spectators, causing breakups and reunions galore among lovers. One man jumped from a viewing balcony down to the street to save a woman he loved who was endangered by a falling balcony, while beneath that falling balcony another lover was punishing his rival. At this point one of the interlocutors comments: 'All those disturbances were caused by curiosity . . . but

---

[149] 'cela n'empesche pas qu'en general, je ne blasme l'excessive curiosité' (41).

[150] Scudéry's defenders of curiosity also use 'en general' in this defensive, hedging way (36, 37).

[151] 'bien souvent' (36, 46, 55).

[152] 'corrigeront' (170), 'guerir' (172). See also pp. 169–70.

since they serve to entertain this gathering, we should not yet repent altogether of being curious.'[153] The débris of balconies at this royal event, to which thousands flocked out of 'universal curiosity',[154] almost serves as an emblem for the threat posed to the social fabric by curiosity. And yet the same curiosity is also directed *at* those calamities by the gossipy group of friends. It is sometimes unadvisable, but always irresistible.

This curiosity involves not just listening to stories but also reading them, as is made even more explicit when Artelice responds defiantly to some damning comments on curiosity by announcing that she is burning with curiosity to read the recently acquired novella about Célinte. She is certainly not anticipating that it will cure her of curiosity in the way that an exemplary tale might try to:

> whatever you might say about curiosity, I won't be cured of it easily . . . Since I've been assured that this is a story which contains many true events and that the fictitious names are covers for real people, I have the greatest curiosity possible to see whether I'll be able to guess who they are. And I want to read it all the more (she added) because I've been told that curiosity plays some role in the story's dénouement.[155]

Artelice here identifies two ways in which reading involves curiosity. First, curiosity is the process of trying to decipher the names of the story's protagonists, discovering which real-life people they secretly represent. This model of reading turns the text into a kind of riddle. Later, Artelice claims triumphantly to have found the key: after the Célinte story has been read aloud, Artelice says that she has guessed the real identities of Célinte and Ariston. A recent editor has continued in this vein, taking up where Artelice leaves off, arguing that Célinte begins as Madame de Châtillon and ends up becoming Madeleine de Scudéry herself.[156] However, although Scudéry flagrantly encourages this curiosity of her immediate readers and of her

---

[153] 'Voila bien des desordres causez par la Curiosité . . . mais puis qu'ils servent à divertir la Compagnie, il ne faut pas encore se repentir tout à fait d'estre Curieux' (43)
[154] 'la Curiosité universelle' (35).
[155] 'quoy qu'on puisse dire de la Curiosité, je ne m'en gueriray pas aisément . . . comme on m'a assuré, que c'est une avanture qui a plusieurs evenements veritables, et qu'on a escrite sous des noms suposez, j'ay la plus grande curiosité qu'on puisse avoir, de voir si je pourray deviner qui c'est; et j'en ay d'autant plus d'envie, adjousta t'elle, que la curiosité, à ce qu'on m'a dit, a quelque part au dernier evenement de cette Histoire' (57).
[156] Niderst in Scudéry 1979 (16–18).

future literary historians, she also frustrates it. Lysimene tells Artelice not to 'have this curiosity in [her] head', not to seek the same kind of truth in 'Romans' as one seeks in history-writing.[157] The identity-tease relates not just to the protagonists within the Célinte story, but also to the interlocutors in the Prologue—who are explicitly presented as real people hidden under pseudonyms (35)[158]—and also to the unnamed author herself, into whose identity the *libraire* tells readers not to 'inquire too curiously'.[159] The future obsessions of literary criticism—with the 'real' identities of characters and authors—are ironically foreshadowed within the text through the representation of the reading process as curiosity that is at once futile and irresistible.

Secondly, Artelice, in the quotation above, is also looking forward to finding curiosity playing some role in the dénouement of the Célinte story. Inevitably, her statement acts as an instruction to Scudéry's own readers, prompting them to scour the Célinte story's ending in search of this promised role of curiosity, reading *for* curiosity in the same way that, for instance, readers of Montaigne's *Essais* are prompted to read for the self-portrait that he claims to have written (Cave 1982, 153–4). Scudéry's contemporary readers were perhaps led by Artelice to expect to find curiosity in the Célinte story in the form of a theme, such as a passion experienced by a main protagonist and which led to his or her downfall, as in so many exemplary tales. However, such a reading bears as little tangible fruit as the search for the real identities of the protagonists. The Célinte story contains no single, explicitly signalled chain of events and actions that is triggered by curiosity. Instead, curiosity is disseminated across multiple subplots and protagonists. Was Artelice pointing towards just one of these? If so, nothing in the story itself suggests which. So, what did she mean? The second reading method evoked by her turns out to be a riddle too.

Its answer perhaps lies where we did not expect it. Consideration of the dissemination of curiosity across the various plots and protagonists suggests that it is primarily neither moral nor immoral: the curiosity of the non-virtuous protagonists is not itself what makes them immoral. Curiosity is simply that which always brings lovers to

---

[157] 'ne vous mettez point cette curiosité dans la teste' (169).
[158] For suggestions, see Niderst in Scudéry 1979, 9, 12.
[159] 'Ne t'informe point trop curieusement' (33).

their love object. It is the guiding line that the writer uses to construct her story, to tie up the various ends of her plot. Here is what happens in the Célinte story.

Célinte is a young woman at a European court. Two friends, Meliandre and Ariston, fall in love with her and so fall out with each other, although she loves neither. One of their fights is stopped by a stranger, Poliante, a friend of Célinte's absent brother. Poliante is on his way to deliver a letter from brother to sister. When Poliante arrives, Célinte falls in love with him, and he eventually reciprocates. They marry, and the enraged Meliandre uses the fact that Poliante had previously been exiled from the court to have him imprisoned, telling Célinte that he will spare him only if she annuls her marriage and weds him, Meliandre, instead. In desperation, she feigns her own death; Poliante, thinking that she is dead, escapes from prison, and Célinte mistakenly thinks him dead too. Each spends six years mourning the other. Meliandre is now a top military commander and, visiting a celebrated mourner in the area, is amazed to find that she is Célinte. Meanwhile, the state has been saved by a battle,[160] won almost single-handedly by an unknown soldier. Meliandre orders both his hero and Poliante—suspected of supporting the state's enemies—to be sought. The unknown soldier is found and happens to be brought first to the chamber of Célinte, who recognizes him as Poliante. Each is amazed to find the other alive. Poliante is then taken to the King and Meliandre, who also recognize Poliante and are amazed when he is proved to be also the unknown hero. Meliandre is so appalled that a battle wound reopens and kills him. The King pardons Poliante because he saved the state. The two lovers are reunited.

As Myriam Maître-Dufour has pointed out in brief but incisive remarks on this novella, curiosity appears to lead its protagonists nowhere but then eventually leads them to either virtuous or vicious love, but in either case to the love object (1998, 341–2). In this diegetic world, curiosity is not instrinsically good or bad. Rather, it is the unwitting attraction which one can feel even before seeing someone: Ariston has curiosity to know Célinte, although he has never met her (66).[161] Or one can feel it when hearing about someone

---

[160] According to Niderst (Scudéry 1979, 20), probably an allusion to Rocroi (1643), where the French defeated the Spanish.

[161] See also p. 88 (Poliante).

without knowing that that person is in fact one's lover: Célinte, long 'indifferent' about everything in her bereavement, has her curiosity awakened by hearing of the unknown soldier, without knowing that he is in fact her 'dead' husband (137).[162] Even curiosity that is explicitly cultivated as a diversion from love in fact leads back to it: Ariston and Meliandre are taken on a tour of the 'curiosities of Rome' in order to get over their unrequited passion, only to find in a workshop there a portrait of Célinte which reignites their passion and feud.[163] As in theatrical satires of *curieux*, the curiosity-collecting tendency is thus subordinated to the curiosity-narrating tendency, but not in the same moralizing way: the search to accumulate discrete gratifications turns out to lead not necessarily to calamity but rather to the single telos that one really desires. In this respect, the narrative role of curiosity is here clearer than in, say, the quasi-allegories of Verville, where it was often unclear whether it was a diversion from the main telos or not. In *Célinte* even the curiosity of a third party, that is, of those who are not in love, always turns out to facilitate unwittingly the eventual reunion of the two lovers. The dénouement is explicitly brought closer by the curiosity not only of Meliandre, who wants to visit the mysterious mourning woman (130), but also of the King (150–1) and of Meliandre's officer Arinante, who hunts down Poliante and the unknown soldier like a modern crime detective (137, 148).

The narrative culminates in two recognition scenes, both focusing on the 'unknown man' who had been 'everyone's object of curiosity'.[164] This shows that the two kinds of reading that Artelice called curiosity in the Prologue are in fact one and the same. The curiosity of readers, as of protagonists, is the desire to find out who someone is, to discover the diegetic identity of the 'unknown soldier' or of the person that one loves without ever having met them, or else to discover the extradiegetic identity of Célinte, Artelice, or indeed the very author of *Célinte*. Protagonists are led unwittingly, quasi-

---

[162] 'Indifference' is explicitly the opposite of curiosity in the prologue and novella (54, 90–1; cf. also pp. 128, 136).

[163] 'ces curiositez de Rome' (81). The culture of curiosities, whether collecting or tourism, long continued to function as a displacement of love in narratives, e.g. Schwan's *Suédois exilé ou Lettres curieuses et amusantes* (1768), a cross between an epistolary novel and a travelogue in which the exiled hero is charged by his beloved to prove his love to her by directing his 'curiosité' at Holland and describing it to her in detail in his letters (51).

[164] 'Inconnu'; 'l'object de la curiosité de tout le monde' (136).

magically by their curiosity to their beloved; the name-hunting curiosity of readers who are trying to guess the identity of, say, the 'unknown man' before it is revealed is given proleptic clues in the shape of the curiosity of protagonists, since it always leads to the beloved; and this curiosity of readers and protagonists is what gives the writer the interweaving lines of her narrative structure.

In *Célinte*, as in the exactly contemporary texts by Pierre Corneille which we considered, the uses of curiosity are aesthetic as well as ethical: curiosity is to a considerable extent the cognitive process of writing, reading, and hearing stories; moral distinctions between good and bad curiosity are no longer all-encompassing.[165] In these respects, *Célinte* points forward to the narratives of Marivaux, Prévost, Diderot, and Fielding.[166] And yet, unlike those later fictions, *Célinte* also grapples with a dazzling range of conflicting understandings of curiosity, some of them going back centuries. It dramatizes the very process of attempting to define, once and for all, curiosity; it shows that attempt to be impossible. Precisely because *Célinte* is incomplete—incorporating open-endedly so many semi-integrated strands of discourse on curiosity—it is perhaps the complete early modern text on curiosity.

4.4.5.2 *Lafayette,* La Princesse de Clèves

Seventeen years later, there appeared another anonymous[167] contribution to the newly fashionable genre of the historical novella—*La Princesse de Clèves* (1678) by Marie-Madeleine Pioche de La

---

[165] Cf. Rosellini's pertinent argument that curiosity became above all an aesthetic building block in the poetics of French prose narrative from the 1660s onwards (1998, esp. 138, 146–7, 149–54), associated more with the unravelling of a plot than with 'la curiosité anecdotique, celle du collectionneur ou du touriste' (147) (which I have been labelling the curiosity-collecting tendency).

[166] e.g. Diderot's *Jacques le Fataliste* (1951, 492, 513, 567, 620) as well as his *Bijoux indiscrets*; Marivaux 1978, 87; Prévost 1995, 79 (where 'un reste de curiosité' is given as one possible motive for Manon's return to see Des Grieux, an event which triggers the rest of the narrative). For a Freudian reading of the impulse towards knowledge in Prévost's novels—largely not focusing, however, on the 'curiosity' family of terms—see Leborgne 1998. Henry Fielding's *Tom Jones* (1749) is full of amoral, narrative-generating occurrences of 'curiosity'. For an earlier example, cf. the argument by Giavarini (1998) that erotic 'curiosité' is the motor of the plot of Honoré d'Urfé's major pastoral romance *L'Astrée* (1607–27), though Giavarini's approach again differs from mine in that it is not limited to actual occurrences of this family of terms.

[167] On the reasons for attributing it solely or largely to Lafayette, see Duchêne in Lafayette 1990, 262–4.

Vergne, who from her marriage in 1655 was known as Madame de Lafayette. This novella quickly became much more famous than *Célinte*. It detaches curiosity from morality even more. There are no moral lessons to be given to readers about curiosity since none can provide formulas for avoiding it or for predicting its consequences. This representation of curiosity is designed not so much to improve readers as to move them, to make them sad: curiosity can here be disturbingly tragic, not because protagonists could have avoided it if only they had been better people, but rather because it is sometimes both unavoidable and unbearable.

Whereas in *Célinte* the scope of application of curiosity is still very wide, in La *Princesse de Clèves*, as in *El curioso impertinente* and much eighteenth-century fiction, curiosity is always more or less erotic. 'More or less' because the distance apparently separating curiosity from love is merely a symptom of the lengths to which curiosity will go to conceal its true object. Since in the diegetic world of the court the maintenance of one's social position depends on keeping one's amorous desires secret, curiosity necessarily becomes duplicitous and elusive.[168] Like Scudéry, this woman author attributes erotic curiosity to women as well as to men. On the one hand, it is directed in secret at the love object and is often laced with jealousy, as in the case of the 'curious impertinent': one wants to know who else might be loved by the beloved.[169] On the other hand, this curiosity is carefully hidden by the pretence of a more innocuous curiosity[170] and displaced onto objects which, so one claims, have nothing to do with one's erotic desire. The object in question is a 'pretty letter' in the case of the Queen, who is in fact suspicious that the letter reveals that the Vidame de Chartres has betrayed her quasi-erotic trust in him. Or the object of displaced curiosity can be a summer-house, such as the one in which Nemours shows great interest, in fact because he voyeuristically spied on the princess from there.[171] This

---

[168] The tension—characteristic of French writing under absolutism—between private secrets and a monarch's right to know them shapes curiosity in both *Célinte* (as Maître-Dufour has shown: 1998, 342–3) and La *Princesse de Clèves* (e.g. the subplot involving the Queen and the Vidame de Chartres).

[169] e.g. Lafayette 1970, 333, 339.

[170] e.g. 276, 343.

[171] 'une jolie lettre qui donnait de la curiosité à la reine' (326; see also p. 312); 'une extrême curiosité d'aller voir le pavillon de la forêt' (371). Through this displacement of eroticism onto objects of curiosity, La *Princesse de Clèves* is partly exploiting the culture of curiosities, though to equate this novella wholly with that culture (as effec-

concealment of dark curiosity beneath an apparently innocuous kind resonates with St Augustine's analysis of the duplicitous nature of curiosity. It also has a famous antecedent in narrative fiction, in *El curioso impertinente*, where curiosity was alternately brooding and trifling. Indeed, it is arguable that it still survives in current usage ('I'm just curious, that's all'). So in *La Princesse de Clèves* curiosity is often either claimed to be innocuous or else is denied and hidden (296): the manner in which the Queen asks the Vidame de Chartres whether he has any lovers is designed to make him think that she is not asking 'by curiosity or design'—a sure sign, in this novella's terms, of the presence of both.[172] 'Curiosity' thus becomes one of the novella's many slippery terms: its powerful connotations ('love', 'jealousy') lurk under more innocuous denotations ('inquisitiveness'), just as they did increasingly in much other writing of the period (where 'curiosity' often denoted 'inquisitiveness' but in fact connoted 'sex' or 'satire'). Whereas many an exemplary narrative—such as that of Du Souhait—trained readers how to spot and recognize curiosity, in oneself and in others, *La Princesse de Clèves* shows just why it is so difficult to do that.

The novella also shows why it is impossible to foresee, or else to reconstruct retrospectively and forensically, the chain of events which curiosity—or any other passion—unleashes. Lafayette thematizes the inadequacies of exemplarity by demonstrating the unpredictability of such chains of events (Lyons 1989, ch. 5). She gives a new twist to the curiosity-narrating tendency, showing that the familiar sequences of events repeated by exemplary narratives are not reassuringly repeatable. The princess can only guess—incorrectly, as it turns out—what actions her husband's jealous curiosity about the identity of her lover has led him to take. She wrongly accuses her husband of being the person who made public her excruciating confession to him that she loves another man: 'Only this curiosity could have induced this cruel imprudence of yours, the *consequences* of which could not be more painful.'[173] This three-link chain—curiosity–imprudence–painful consequence—is the most

---

tively does Jaymes 1995) overlooks the predominance in it of the curiosity-narrating tendency (which is also stressed, albeit in different terms, by Rosellini 1998, 146–7).

[172] 'par curiosité ou par dessein' (315).

[173] 'Ce ne peut être que cette seule curiosité qui vous ait fait faire une si cruelle imprudence, les suites en sont aussi fâcheuses qu'elles pouvaient l'être' (348).

plausible that she can imagine. It probably also seems plausible to the reader. But *vraisemblance* is never neutral in this novella: in this case her perception of it has been manipulated by Nemours, who is in love with the princess and intent on covering up the fact that it was *he* who made public her confession:

> Monsieur de Nemours's statement that curiosity could make a husband act imprudently struck her as fitting the state of Monsieur de Clèves so aptly that she could not believe that it had been uttered by chance; and this plausibility resolved her to believe that Monsieur de Clèves had abused the trust she had placed in him.[174]

Notwithstanding talk of 'cruel impudence', curiosity is not, primarily, virtuous or vicious in itself: the main concern of protagonists is to analyse it forensically rather than morally.

Curiosity figures within the diegesis not just as a duplicitous link in uncertain, unpredictable chains of passions and events, but also as the fallible attempt made by some protagonists to predict the course of such unpredictable chains. The King declares that he used to have 'much curiosity' ('beaucoup de curiosité') about the future but that he has now renounced it due to the implausibility ('peu vraisemblables') of one astrological prediction, according to which he would die in a duel (296). Is the reader being given an exemplary message here, enjoining him or her not to indulge in astrological curiosity about the future? That may be so, but Lafayette's contemporary readers were well aware that, ironically, the real Henri II did indeed die in something close to a duel—a tournament. Should the fictional Henri II actually have heeded his astrologer's advice and been more careful? The question is left open. But it is then also applied to the novella's main protagonists too. Upon hearing the King, Nemours whispers to the princess that he too has lost such faith in predictions, because it was predicted to him that his great passion (for her) would be happily requited—a prediction which again later turns out be fulfilled partially but not fully, in that the passion is requited but not happily. As in the Oedipus story, curiosity about love and death is inseparable from divination.

---

[174] 'Ce qu'avait dit M. de Nemours que la curiosité pouvait faire faire des imprudences à un mari lui paraissait se rapporter si juste à l'état de M. de Clèves qu'elle ne pouvait croire que ce fût une chose que le hasard eût fait dire; et cette vraisemblance la déterminait à croire que M. de Clèves avait abusé de la confiance qu'elle avait en lui' (350).

It is also inseparable from the reader's curiosity about what happens next. How will the love between the princess and Nemours work out? The outcome is far less predictable than that of many an exemplary narrative. But who is to say if this readerly desire is curiosity? After all, Lafayette simply does not refer to it. However, it is very likely that she and her circle did think of it as curiosity, just as Corneille and Scudéry did in 1660 and 1661 respectively. A 1683 treatise that defended the controversial new genre—the historical novella—of which Lafayette was the most celebrated exponent, did explicitly call the readerly desire it excited 'curiosity': the treatise justified the relative brevity of the genre by claiming that readers want to find out quickly what happens at the end of a story since, after all, the French in particular 'detest anything that resists [their] curiosity'.[175]

However, the curiosity of Lafayette's readers, to the extent that it locks onto that of her protagonists, does not lead to any satisfying goal: the various chains of events involving curiosity—those surrounding Nemours, the princess, her husband, the Queen, the King, the *reine dauphine*—are not just uncertain and unpredictable but also disparate. They are not obviously harmonized within a single plot-line that leads to a telos which resolves them all (though the relation between this novella's 'digressions' and its main plot has been much debated in the voluminous scholarship on the work). By contrast, even *Célinte*, which eschewed the predictable, morality-based chains of curiosity found in exemplary fictions, nonetheless funnelled the apparently disparate and diversionary chains of various protagonists' curiosity all into a single integrated dénouement.

Lafayette dispels not only the moral certainties that continued to surround curiosity in certain genres of writing, but even the narrative certainties that surrounded it in *Célinte*. Curiosity is left in a kind of moral and aesthetic no man's land: we are uncertain where it comes from and to where it leads. Although it is less morally condemned than in *El curioso impertinente*, in *La Princesse de Clèves* it is just as troubling and frightening, perhaps even more so, since, now that it is beyond the control even of wisdom, there is nothing that protagonists should have done to avoid it or to cope with it better. The

---

[175] 'Nous haïssons tout ce qui s'oppose à nostre curiosité' (Du Plaisir, quoted in Rosellini 1998, 155 n. 20).

princess's husband—caught like Anselmo in a triangle of desire that leads to his death—has 'curiosity that I just cannot live with'.[176]

4.5   CONCLUSIONS

So much for any notion that the culture of curiosities reigned supreme in the early modern period. Not only some university and much church discourse, but a wide range of other genres—from novellas to plays, from ballets for élite boys to fair-shows for anyone—used curiosity in order to prod their audiences *away* from many kinds of knowledge and activity that the culture of curiosities glamorized and commodified. And they sought to do this by telling stories. In an age when people were often urged to accumulate knowledge or material objects, as a process of collecting curiosities, on the other hand the dangers of such accumulation were often impressed upon readers through the narrating of what happens to people who indulge in it. Certainly, there were some attempts, especially in the eighteenth century, to forge stories about the happy progress of human curiosity through history. But on the whole, story-telling was the refuge of the many who instilled and expressed anxiety about curiosity.

Stories about curiosity were not just adjuncts to theoretical definitions of it. They went beyond the limits imposed by the language-game of definition, shaping curiosity in ways that only they could. They represented curiosity as not having any separate existence but as being always part of a chain of passions and actions and as being intrinsically embedded in time. Whereas the culture of curiosities often made knowledge into a metaphorical space, crammed with objects, on the other hand many stories presented that model as an illusion that is undone by the revenge of time: as the days go by, the collecting of curiosities turns out to lead to unhappiness after all. Only stories, by showing that curiosity is always coming from somewhere and going somewhere else, can really teach readers how to recognize its duplicitous, incipient signs for what they are and so avoid it before it is too late.

It might be thought that the curiosity that was condemned in *exempla*, fables, emblems, novellas, comedies, and ballets was

---

[176] 'une curiosité avec laquelle je ne saurais vivre' (339).

simply different from the curiosity that was celebrated so much within the culture of curiosities. Were they not two distinct phenomena which merely happened to share the same name? My point is that this very question was a burning, controversial one at the time, and that answers to it were often conflictual. Whereas many collectors, readers of periodicals, dabblers in divination, gossips, travellers, and naturalists saw nothing in common between their curiosity and that of Icarus, many storytellers disagreed. Many stories were therefore aggressive reshapings of curiosity. They did not encapsulate or typify what one can now call 'the early modern concept of curiosity' any more than did the culture of curiosities. Rather, they too were involved in constant contestation. For example, some stories extended the scope of bad curiosity to include many practices that were defended by their actual practitioners as involving either good curiosity or else none at all. Curiosity's shapes, in stories as in other language-games, depended on what it was being used to promote or condemn.

Certainly, those shapes also partly depended on the date of writing. In some genres, especially from the second half of the seventeenth century, the question of the morality or immorality of curiosity faded somewhat from view. In this respect, some stories anticipate what occurred later in academic discourse, especially in about the mid-eighteenth century (1.2.1 above). In various narrative genres, the uses of curiosity gradually became as much aesthetic as moral. Curiosity, even if was being condemned within the diegesis, became the extradiegetic force that drove writers, readers, and theatre audiences. Here too there is a parallel with some university dissertations which condemned curiosity while also joking uneasily about the role that it had played in the composition of the dissertation itself. The rise of good extradiegetic curiosity was one sign that stories did not remain entirely impervious to the effects of the culture of curiosities: even stories that condemned curiosity sometimes became presented as objects of curiosity themselves, like so many texts that were more straightforwardly flaunted as such within the culture of curiosities. In some stories curiosity came to be both the pain of living and yet also the pleasure of reading. This was one of many ways in which, even in narrative fiction, cracks gradually opened in what, before the seventeenth century, had usually been a largely united front against curiosity. Some writers continued to urge readers to apply a story of curiosity to a range of practices that lay beyond those that were explicitly represented within the story itself, and yet that range gradually reduced.

These historical shifts gave rise to uncertainties that were writ increasingly large in some seventeenth-century fictions. Where does curiosity come from? Where does it lead—are its outcomes really predictable? Is it best avoided? Can we live with it? Can we even say exactly what it is? These questions are explored, but not answered, in stories ranging from *El curioso impertinente* by Cervantes, in which Anselmo's disturbingly gratuitous curiosity lacks comprehensible origins, to Scudéry's *Célinte* and Lafayette's *Princesse de Clèves*. While some writers were busy trying to defuse the anxiety inherent in Cervantes's tale by rewriting it, Scudéry and Lafayette were taking uncertainty surrounding curiosity to new levels. One factor that enabled them to do so was their reluctance to put their fictions to overtly instrumental uses. Unlike the vast majority of early modern texts considered in the present study, *Célinte* and *La Princesse de Clèves* do not primarily use curiosity to try and teach moral lessons or else to ban or promote certain activities or kinds of knowledge. Rather, if their representation of curiosity can be described as having a 'use' at all, it is perhaps to try and make readers recognize that curiosity, like other passions, cannot be pre-judged: it is too complex and opaque to be subject to moral, intellectual, or emotional control. I have tried to show that numerous other early modern texts also reveal that point, whether through their own effective lack of such control or by dint of being contested by counter-texts. But, in France, only by about 1661 was it possible for that discursive uncontrollability of curiosity to become the prime point of a text, as it is of *Célinte*.

Whether or not they called that pleasure 'curiosity', stories of curiosity were designed to be pleasure-giving narratives about a distinctly unpleasurable state of anxiety. Even when, in eighteenth-century erotic fiction, diegetic curiosity was claimed to be pleasurable rather than anxious, anxiety was not far away, as the example of Diderot's *Bijoux indiscrets* suggests. The stories considered so far mainly attribute the anxieties of curiosity to men, whom they also often advise how best to avoid such anxieties. Although by the early nineteenth century one play, by Planard, shows that male curiosity can be cured, in most early modern stories if a man becomes curious he gives away for good his masculine autonomy—to the devil in the case of Faust and Du Souhait, to sloth in the case of Jesuit schoolboys, to women in the case of the 'curious impertinent'. In many stories, such anxiety is caused to men by women, or just by the evocation of women. For masculinity to be salvaged, it might be necessary to take extraordinary measures to avoid curiosity about women, as does Alidor in Corneille's *Place Royale*. Some satirists who ridicule the culture of curiosities present collectors as giving up on real women and taking pleasure instead in their possession and mastery of the feminized, curious objects of their collection. Diderot's *Bijoux indiscrets* is complicit with an even more extreme variation on this male fantasy: the Sultan's ring gives him total knowledge of the sexual secrets of the women who are the objects of his curiosity.

So male anxieties were acute enough when women were objects of curiosity. However, when women were imagined as being—or imagined themselves as being—subjects of curiosity, experiencing it themselves rather than just being objects of men's curiosity, then male anxiety reached fever pitch.

5

Discursive Tendencies: Narrating Sexes: Female

Besides, not for nothing is *curiositas* a feminine noun.[1]

Curiosity was also widely used in narratives to discourage women from trying to know certain things, to try and make them behave in certain ways, or simply to force them to accept a humbling image of themselves. One aim of such stories was to make it more difficult for women to have access to certain kinds of male knowledge: the stories did this by claiming to demonstrate that women harbour illegitimate desires to obtain that knowledge. Those desires were often represented, overtly or covertly, as erotic. In other words, many of the stories attributing bad curiosity to women seem to express male anxiety about female sexuality, this time by making women into subjects who experience curiosity themselves, rather than by making female sexuality the object of anxious male curiosity, as did plots like that of the 'curious impertinent'. The purpose of making women into curious subjects was not, on the whole, to empower them, but on the contrary to show what disasters ensue when women are given leeway to act on the curiosity that storytellers attribute to them.

In the seventeenth century curiosity was often celebrated as well as condemned: having previously been almost always bad, it was now either good or bad or morally indifferent. It may therefore seem surprising that female curiosity, bar a few exceptions, was still usually condemned. Did not women benefit from the new celebration of some curiosity? On the whole, no: while the partial rehabilitation of curiosity was good news for many men, it was to men that it was

[1] 'Curiositas ist ohne das generis fœminini' (Happel 1683–9, i. 295).

largely confined. Indeed, although the near-blanket condemnation of female curiosity went back centuries, in relative terms it was even harsher in the early modern period than before. Whereas previously both men and women had borne the brunt of condemnations of curiosity fairly equally, now women bore it much more than men: because much male curiosity had become good, a much larger proportion of bad curiosity was now female. It is as if women were, even more than before, repositories for the bad kinds of curiosity from which men wished to dissociate themselves. On the whole, women's access to knowledge, far from getting better according to some supposed principle of progress, in fact got worse, at least insofar as one can judge by the case of curiosity.[2] One might expect that the emergence of the Enlightenment would have gradually dispelled this inequality, allowing the two sexes the same right to be curious. However, on the contrary, the eighteenth-century celebration of certain good kinds of curiosity was dependent on the continuing existence of bad kinds (often female or feminized) against which the good kind (often male or masculinized) could stand out by contrast.

Before studying narrative in particular, I will begin by surveying what was commonly written about female curiosity in a wide range of texts, French and German, whether narratives or not (5.1). The aim will be to identify the main topoi that tended to recur in discussions of women's curiosity. I will then investigate what happened to female curiosity when it was embedded in narratives, especially in French ones (5.2). As we have seen, stories used curiosity in ways that were unavailable to more discursive, abstract treatments of it. In the case of female curiosity, an extra specificity of stories is that they had the potential to enjoin even greater misogyny. Whereas in any systematic, discursive analysis of curiosity, its female species could not be mentioned without being situated in a typology that also included male curiosity,[3] on the other hand stories were free to create diegetic worlds in which the only perniciously curious protagonists were women and the question of male curiosity could simply be sidestepped altogether. Moreover, although male discourse on female

---

[2] On the ways in which women were excluded from one area of early modern knowledge—science—see Schiebinger 1997.

[3] e.g. as soon as one 1652 German dissertation has cited an authority in order to prove that women are specifically curious, it then hastens to point out that 'this vice does not cling only to women but doubtless roves across every sex and age-group' ('non tantum mulieribus hoc vitium adhaeret, verùm per omnem Sexum ac aetatem vagatur', Watson/Rose 1690, 796).

curiosity was full of inconsistencies and aporias, stories were free to allow them to go unchecked, unchallenged by systematic thought. For instance, some plays presented female curiosity as reprehensible in principle and yet excusable in practice (5.2.5)—such ambivalence would have been more difficult to sustain in a treatise or dissertation.

5.1   TOPOI

Between the sixteenth and the eighteenth century, a recurring set of topoi characterized much discourse on female curiosity. It was commonly claimed that 'Women in particular are excessively curious'.[4] The fact that this claim was widespread should not prevent us from noticing that it was extraordinary, indeed perhaps incoherent, when measured against the context of the totality of early modern discourse on curiosity: for, although countless texts continued to condemn male curiosity, that did not make it any the less acceptable to argue that women in particular are excessively curious. It is as if the claim that excessive curiosity is especially characteristic of women was so deeply rooted that no amount of counter-evidence—in the form of examples of excessive male curiosity—could dislodge it. The claim about women was made on two grounds: nature and decorum. First, female nature is intrinsically prone to the vice of curiosity. Secondly, the vice arises especially because of an indecorous mismatch between the vocations to which women are called in life, as wives and mothers, and the knowledge that they actually desire, that often exceeds what they require for those vocations.

Let me survey first the arguments based on female nature. Curiosity was sometimes even claimed to be *the* defining feature of women's nature, 'the fault of the sex'.[5] In relation to humankind, this claim was asymmetrical: it was never made with specific reference to men as opposed to women. Rather, when men were being discussed, curiosity was considered to be either just one of numerous passions or, at most, the dominant passion in certain men only. In 1783, a French play continued to promote the argument that 'the most

---

[4] 'les femmes, en particulier, sont excessivement curieuses' (Scudéry 1979, 54). This verdict on women, which one interlocutor expresses in the prologue to *Célinte*, is not necessarily that of Scudéry herself and is not borne out by the ensuing novella. On the relation of curiosity to femininity in Britain, see Benedict 2001, ch. 3.

[5] 'le défaut du sexe' (La Fontaine 1991, 116).

curious animal created by nature is a woman. A feminine being is by definition a curious one, and there's no such thing as a woman without curiosity: she's a chimera.'[6]

However, in most accounts, curiosity was not *the* defining defect of women but rather one of a nexus of defects that, taken together, were specifically female. The curiosity of women was closely connected to their garrulousness, disobedience, strong imagination, weak reason and judgment. As the jurisconsult André Tiraqueau put it in a 1513 commentary which was intended to enshrine the prerogatives of husbands in law and became an enduring anthology of commonplaces about female weakness: 'Thus anyone will think that the curiosity of women has been sufficiently proven if he understands that vices of this kind—that is, garrulousness and curiosity—are joined as if by family ties.'[7] This passage was still being cited as authoritative almost 140 years later, in a 1652 German university dissertation on curiosity (Watson/Rose 1690, 796). The connection with garrulousness is that women—like effeminate men—are curious to discover other people's shameful secrets in order to have the pleasure of gossiping garrulously about them. Plutarch connected the two vices graphically in his description of *polypragmosyne*, later translated as *curiositas*. Female curiosity almost automatically involved such garrulous nosiness: one French-English dictionary of 1688 defined 'Un Curieux' as 'a Vertuoso'—an impressive collector—but 'Une Curieuse' as 'a busy body' (N. Kenny 1998, 73 n.) Similarly, even a treatise that sought to legitimize the participation of the *honnête femme* in gatherings outside the domestic sphere nonetheless equated female curiosity with calumny and defamation, pausing briefly to distinguish it from its implicitly male counterpart: 'I am not condemning that divine curiosity of philosophers and fine minds which has discovered nature's secrets and given us the means to govern the passions of the soul.'[8] The sexing of curiosity was so

---

[6] 'l'animal le plus curieux qu'ait produit la Nature, C'est une femme; Qui dit un être féminin, dit un être Curieux, et une femme sans curiosité est une chimère introuvable' (*Triomphe* 1787, 116[r]).

[7] 'Ex quo et curiositatem mulierum satis probatam putabit, qui intelliget huiusmodi vitia, videlicet loquacitatem, et curiositatem inter se quoque germanas esse, ac veluti quadam cognatione coniunctas' (Tiraqueau 1576, 97[v]). On this work, see Berriot-Salvadore 1990, 30.

[8] 'Je ne blâme pas cette divine curiosité des Philosophes, et des bons esprit[s] qui nous a découvert les secrets de la nature, et qui nous a donné les moyens de regler les passions de l'ame.' (Du Bosc 1665, 133).

asymmetrical that, especially in French *mondain* writing of the second half of the seventeenth century, if a woman wanted to avoid bad curiosity she had to aspire not to good curiosity, which was largely the preserve of the male virtuoso or philosopher, but rather to the feminine virtue of 'discretion', which involved renouncing curiosity and instead being silent or else uninquisitive about secrets.[9] This 'discretion' was certainly not incompatible with conversation, but it was still a variation on the old female virtue of silence. Garrulous female curiosity was abhorred, especially by male writers, because it involved not only discovering and revealing secrets but also talking back, that is, questioning or disobeying male figures, whether husbands or, in the case of Eve, God.[10] 'Me curious? Me disobedient?' a wife protests unconvincingly to her husband in a 1754 play.[11]

Curiosity was thought to exert a particular hold on women's nature because the relative weakness of their reason and judgment enabled erroneous opinions to gain a firmer foot-hold in them. 'Women usually have even weaker and more curious minds than men', wrote the archbishop Fénelon.[12] That is why all heretical sects have thrived through the 'curiosité' and 'présomption' of women, he later explained—in about 1712—probably thinking especially of Jansenism, towards which many female communities had inclined.[13] For the same reason, women were often ridiculed as being especially gullible and superstitious, as allowing their curiosity about the future and the supernatural to be exploited financially by men and spiritually by the Devil.[14]

Finally, the perceived fact that women in particular are excessively curious was widely attributed to women's natural inclination towards excessiveness in general. It is, paradoxically, in women's nature to want to cover itself up by adding unnatural, extraneous layers to itself. Women supplement their nature with art and artifice,

---

[9] See Maître-Dufour 1998, esp. 333–4.

[10] See Tiraqueau 1576, 97ᵛ; Watson/Rose 1690, 796.

[11] 'Moi curieuse! moi désobéissante!' (Framery 1754, 16).

[12] 'Les femmes ont d'ordinaire l'esprit encore plus foible et plus curieux que les hommes' (Fénelon 1983–97, i. 91).

[13] Fénelon 1983–97, ii. 1130. See Rapley 1990, 251 n.54. For other warnings against specifically female curiosity about religion, see Maimbourg 1682, 16; Vives [1558?], Qiʳ. For a more indulgent and unusual attitude, emanating from the milieu of the French court, see Ceriziers 1643, e[i]ʳ.

[14] e.g. *Curieuser Raritäten-Kasten* 1733, 201; Happel 1683–9, i. 295 (quoted n.1 above).

through adornments not just of the body but also of the mind. In this view, female learning has the same supplementary status as clothes, jewellery, perfume, and make-up.[15] To adopt the terminology of Jacques Derrida: these supplements were superfluous on the one hand and yet indispensable to being a woman on the other. Knowledge or practices that were judged supplementary, apparently gratuitous, or unnecessary were often called 'curious', and in particular women's desire for extra layers—whether of clothes or of knowledge—was often called 'curiosity'.[16] Contemporary dictionaries made clear that women's concern with fashion—their collecting of adornments for their bodies—was their equivalent of men's collecting of objects for their cabinets (N. Kenny 1998, 68). But male collecting, whether of material objects or of knowledge, was *not* routinely described as the accretion of supplementary layers in the way that the female equivalent was.

This female curiosity, in the sense of 'supplementary adornment', was widely condemned. The cream of the French episcopate lambasted elaborate female dress and adornment as curiosity: Bossuet called such curiosity 'covetousness' which 'pushes nature beyond its limit'.[17] François de Sales made such 'affected curiosity' one vicious extreme—the opposite being 'dirtiness'—while 'modesty' was the virtuous median between them.[18] For Fénelon, this was the same curiosity as that which also made some women want to acquire too much learning. Like many denigrators of female curiosity *qua* 'adornment' he called it 'vain'—meaning both 'narcissistic', 'ostentatious', and 'futile'—thereby giving a specifically feminine twist to the patristic collocation *vana curiositas*.[19]

On the other hand, within the culture of curiosities, women's alleged curious desire to add extra layers to their bodies and minds was sometimes celebrated. The superfluousness of the extra layers was what made some women seem sophisticated and elegant, far removed from basic needs. For example, among the numerous

---

[15] See Guild (forthcoming); N. Kenny 1995*b*, 216–18.

[16] Ceriziers (1643, a ii^{r-v}), seeking as ever to reverse conventional representations of curiosity, personifies it as an innocent virgin who is *not* laden with pearls and coiffure. But even his representation does not escape from the metaphor of layers: it simply imagines removing instead of adding them.

[17] 'curiosité . . . la convoitise raffine sur la nature' (Bossuet 1890–7, iii. 297).

[18] 'modestie . . . saleté . . . curiosité affectée' (Sales 1892–1964, vi, no. 9).

[19] Fénelon 1983–97, ii. 1129–30 ('curiosité vaine . . . vanités'). See also i. 94–5, 918.

curious manuals printed in late seventeenth- and early eighteenth-century Germany for urban readers who emulated courtly fashion, many were specifically addressed to women. One was the *Useful, Gallant, and Curious Lexicon for Women* (1715). Its compiler, Corvinus, claims to be catering for 'three categories of woman'. Whereas one category ('domestic and conscientious') will find kitchen recipes or advice on rearing children and another kind ('learned') can look up, for example, famous learned women, whose minds were more 'manly' than feminine, the third kind of woman ('curious and gallant') can glean information on foreign fashion, oils and silks, games, fancy turns of phrase, or goddesses who might crop up in a poem at a wedding (Illustration 5).[20] This feminine, curious knowledge was being sold as a mark of distinction precisely because it was not 'useful' in the way that recipes were.[21]

Although such celebrations of female curiosity seem to have countered the more usual denigrations of it, in fact both shared the same assumption, that women, unlike men, are naturally inclined to seek out artificial supplements to their nature.

The second kind of argument deployed to prove that women in particular are excessively curious was based more on decorum. These arguments focused not just on women's nature but on their role in society. Women want to know and acquire things that go beyond the limits of what they need, given their vocation in life. The knowledge that they seek is not necessarily bad in itself, but it is simply inappropriate for them since they have no proper use for it. It is in women's nature to be curious, but there is precious little that it is proper for them to be curious about. As ever, it is Scudéry who, in her open-ended exploration of curiosity, formulates this problem the most lucidly: 'But as for women . . . for whom the secrets you mention are rather inappropriate, what do you expect them to do with *their* curiosity?' The question receives only the playful answer that they should study how a virtuous woman of the interlocutors'

---

[20] [Corvinus] 1715: 'dreyerley Classen Frauenzimmer . . . das haushältige und sorgfältige, das curiöse und galante, und endlich das gelehrte Frauenzimmer' ():(3ʳ); 'männlichen' ():(5ᵛ); see sigs.):(3ʳ–[):(6ʳ]. On this work, see Powell 1988, 63–4.

[21] As ever, the distinction between 'curious' and 'useful' was unstable: how-to-do-it books for women, that included self-adornment and much else, could also be presented as 'curious' (e.g. *Die den Frauenzimmer-Schmuck liebende und auserlesne Künste übende Cammer-Jungfer. Das ist: Curieuses und höchstnützliches Werklein* 1703).

acquaintance came to be so esteemed.[22] Indeed, given the laws of decorum that weigh on women, that is almost the only possible answer: women's curiosity, if it is not to be eradicated, has to be rechannelled towards learning about morals. That was sometimes said of men too (Section 2 above), but much more of women.

Other legitimate channels for women's curiosity were rare indeed, which is what makes non-judgemental, fictional representations of female curiosity by women writers such as Scudéry, Lafayette, and others so unusual and bold.[23] The few male concessions to female curiosity usually had a sting in the tail. For example, German jurisconsults did state that women need to be curious about the man whom they intend to marry, investigating his financial and marital status, but one jurisconsult added defensively that most would think that women barely need any such encouragement, since they generally have too much curiosity anyway.[24] Or again: Archbishop Fénelon argued, in his 1687 treatise on the education of girls, in favour of some relaxation of the decorum that prohibited girls from learning very much. But that was not because he actually wanted them to learn more, but simply because prohibitions could be self-defeating: 'the more they are prohibited from learning about branches of knowledge, the more their curiosity is inflamed by the prohibition; that passion then turns wholly towards the most vain and dangerous objects.'[25] However, this passage was excised from the subsequent 1696 version. Fénelon gradually became straight-forwardly hardline on female curiosity. Whereas this treatise, even in 1696, advocated 'awakening the curiosity' of children, thereby anticipating Locke and Pluche and fostering the erroneous and anachronistic impression up until the twentieth century that Fénelon was an educational liberal, even a feminist,[26] in fact it also severely

[22] 'Mais pour les Dames, reprit Artelice, à qui les secrets dont vous parlez ne sieroient pas trop bien, que voulez vous qu'elles fassent de leur curiosité?' (Scudéry 1979, 53).
[23] See also Benedict 1998. Praise of curious women was relatively rare but, it did occur sometimes within the culture of curiosities, e.g. Du Soucy 1650 (*Triomphe des Dames*, 108); Morvan de Bellegarde 1707, 69.
[24] Cocceji/Lettow 1710, 13. See also Stryk/Lüedecke 1743, 302.
[25] 'plus on leur interdit les sciences, plus leur curiosité s'irrite par cette défense; cette passion se tourne toute du côté des objets les plus vains et les plus dangereux' (Fénelon 1983–97, i. 1203).
[26] See Lougee 1976, 174. As Lougee demonstrates (ch. 11), even by the standards of the time Fénelon's proposed curriculum was relatively narrow and his treatise was an unusually full statement of the anti-feminist position on women's learning.

restricted the reading allowed to girls, lest it stimulate dangerously their 'imagination' and curiosity;[27] moreover, by about 1712, when he penned advice to an aristocratic woman on how to educate her daughter, the girl was now to avoid *all* curiosity (ii. 1129–30).

Does this hardening of Fénelon's prohibitions against female curiosity typify a more general hardening of such prohibitions in the period, contrary to what a progress-based view of history might lead us to expect? Or was Fénelon a reactionary exception to a gradual loosening of such prohibitions that was taking place? Although my own overall narrative is that, on the whole, the early modern period saw a relative hardening of attitudes towards female curiosity, nonetheless the case of Fénelon can serve as a reminder that the position of particular writers and texts in history is always too complex for them to be straightforward illustrations of a single overall historical shift.

According to Fénelon, 'For women as for men, what they learn must be restricted in accordance with their functions.'[28] The rhetorical symmetry with which he here applies this decorum principle to men and women belies the actual asymmetry between their functions. For Fénelon the proper function of aristocratic women consists not in residing at court, where they participate in entertainments, conversation, and intrigue, but rather in running their provincial estates, for which they need to be given specific technical, economic, and even legal expertise (Lougee 1976, 183–4). From a modern point of view, while this makes Fénelon a villain in the history of female curiosity, his ulterior illocutionary aim perhaps makes him a hero in another history, that of pre-Enlightenment resistance to absolutism. As Carolyn Lougee has shown, his frugal, dutiful, hard-working, estate-bound women were to be *the* key players in the reform of the French aristocracy and the implementation of agrarian—as opposed to mercantilist—policies which were to prevent the gigantic court, its luxuries, and Louis XIV's foreign policies from draining the countryside's resources and exacerbating abject rural poverty. Especially after the great famine of 1693–4, Fénelon was developing the agrarian ideas of his friend Fleury, whose treatise on education had similarly been of utilitarian bent, including in its

---

[27] 'réveiller la curiosité des enfants' (i. 120); 'imagination . . . curiosité' (i. 95).
[28] 'La science des femmes, comme celle des hommes, doit se borner à s'instruire par rapport à leurs fonctions' (i. 154).

discussion of women,[29] especially after the great famine of 1693–4. Indeed Fénelon's 1687 treatise was composed for the daughters of the Duc de Beauvillier, leader of the conspiratorial, anti-government group which coalesced around the Duc de Bourgogne.[30]

To what extent Fénelon's pedagogical anti-feminism was really necessary, in his own terms, for his project of political resistance is an open question.[31] Moreover, the attack on the court, salons, and urban polite society was certainly a misogynist backlash against the cultural prominence achieved by some women in the preceding decades: women were now being virtually blamed for luxury as a whole. But the case of Fénelon reminds us that the history of female curiosity—or, for that matter, of curiosity in general—intersects with numerous other histories which have their own, different, and sometimes conflicting trajectories.

While decorum restricted women's curiosity far more than men's, it also circumscribed good male curiosity, which could become bad and effeminate if men sought knowledge from women. For instance, this was a sensitive issue in medicine, which was informally practised within households by many women who had no formal training. For the famous Stahl of Halle, medicine breaches its own proper boundaries and becomes perniciously curious when it incorporates not only other branches—such as chemistry—but also this realm of practical female knowledge. When choosing a remedy, the medical practitioner should not heed the opinions of garrulous women. Such malpractice is doubly curious, both because it breaches decorum and also because it involves consulting a sex notorious for its vice of curiosity, which is inseparable from its fickleness and garrulousness:

various [medical practioners] are greatly inclined towards this curiosity, thereby truly dishonouring their art rather than upholding it, for we honour the art by saying and doing things which are in accordance with healthy reason, rational and prudent experience, not things which satisfy the desires of women, since women, being commonly of curious, doubting, and vacillating mind, advocate now one kind of remedy, now another, which might be congruous only with the symptoms of the illness, neglecting its true root . . . ; the prudent medical practitioner does not approve of these curiosities,

[29] Fleury 1686, 264–70. For Fleury on male curiosity, see 3.4.4.1 above. On Fleury's general influence on Fénelon, see Goré 1957, 252–6.
[30] Lougee 1976, ch. 11. See also Rothkrug 1965, ch. 5.
[31] Following Lougee (1976), I am understanding 'feminism' as the argument that women should have a role beyond the domestic sphere.

which are effeminate and hungry for novelty; rather, he tries patiently and prudently to correct these female polymaths, thereby striving to satisfy truth and its Leader and Author rather than such curious little women.[32]

In some eighteenth-century writing, the notion that decorum should delimit curiosity faded away. One might expect this development to have liberated female curiosity from its constraints. However, it did not necessarily do so, since those constraints could still be justified by the argument from nature, albeit now more surreptitiously. For example, the Enlightenment-style rhetoric of the 1739 aerostatics prospectus *La Curiosité fructueuse* (3.4.2 above) seems at first to make male and female curiosity equal: historians and poets have been wrong to argue that this passion is more natural in women, due to the weakness of their temperament; rather, it is a fault common to every sex, age, and rank. However, the one difference is that men make their 'curiosity' fruitful by seasoning it with 'interest'—that is, with the utilitarian good of society—whereas women seek only to gratify their own imagination, not just through trivia, such as reading poetry and novels, following clothes fashions, gossiping about neighbours, but even through erudition which, however impressive in itself, is in fact motivated by vanity (9–11). On the other hand, '[the curiosity] of men is much more noble and elevated'.[33] The misogyny of this prospectus is in fact even stronger than that which it purports to counter: its message is that women, despite being generously defended here as *not* naturally more prone to this vice than men and despite being released from the shackles of decorum, still manage to waste this graciously granted opportunity, rendering all their curiosity fruitless. Or, if one reads this prospectus against the grain, one can argue that female curiosity is here shackled all the more powerfully by rules of decorum because they have become invisible, tacit, unacknowledged. The early modern period

---

[32] 'varii vero huic curiositati strenue incumbunt, eo ipso vero artem suam magis dehonestant quam defendunt: cum artis honestatem magis promoveat dicere & agere, quae rationi sanae, & experientiae rationabili & prudenti conveniunt, non quae desideriis femellarum respondent, quae, uti communiter curiosi, dubitantis & titubantis animi sunt, ita modo hoc, modo aliud remedii genus, urgent, quod non nisi symptomatibus morbi congruum esse potest, neglecta vero radice morbi . . . ; hisce novitatis avidis & effeminatis curiositatibus nullus prudens medicus annuat, quin patienter & prudenter has feminarum πολῠμαθείας emendare, & sic veritati & duci atque auctori veritatis magis placere laboret, quam eiusmodi curiosis mulierculis.' (Stahl/Donzelina 1714, 59). On this dissertation, see 1.3.2 above.

[33] 'Celle des homes est bien plus noble et bien plus relevée' (11).

certainly did not witness any progressive liberation of female curiosity but rather, if anything, at least in some quarters, a relative increase of harshness in the discourses that purported to identify it.

5.2   NARRATIVES

These topoi about female curiosity were commonly found in a wide range of texts, whether discursive or narrative. Let me now consider more specifically how curiosity was used in narrative. Stories about female curiosity appeared in numerous genres, in theatre, opera, comic opera, fairytales, prose fiction, as well as in brief *exempla* cited in discursive texts. After an initial survey of female exemplarity (5.2.1), I will examine a couple of cautionary, injunctive works aimed at women in the late seventeenth and late eighteenth centuries (5.2.2). By contrast, in his 1669 version of Psyche's story, La Fontaine largely refrains from using her example to enjoin against curiosity. However, that is not because he shares Scudéry's and Lafayette's misgivings about universals, but rather because women are hopeless cases, too mired in this vice to be successfully enjoined to avoid it: the injunctive kind of exemplarity may have been abandoned here, but the illustrative kind thrives (5.2.3). Illustrative exemplarity also thrived from the late seventeenth to the late eighteenth century in numerous stories that were variations on a basic plot in which a woman opens a forbidden receptacle and is thereby proved to be curious. The point was less to urge women not to be curious than to make them eat humble pie, to accept the unpalatable fact that they are curious (5.2.4). However, what happened to these misogynist uses of curiosity when curiosity began to have aesthetic as well as moral force in some story-telling, that is, when it became emphatically the thread that led protagonists, audiences, and writers to the dénouement? Awkwardly enough, in some eighteenth- and early nineteenth-century plays, the morally reprehensible curiosity of female protagonists was what led to the unravelling of the plot's knots and so was deemed to be perhaps not an entirely bad thing after all (5.2.5).

5.2.1   Exempla

The number of female names that circulated in early modern discourse as shorthands for exemplary plots of calamitous curiosity was small—indeed smaller than the equivalent list of male names. Yet these few female exemplars established even more of a monopoly over what it meant to be curious than did their male counterparts. Some were taken from ancient myth (Pandora, Psyche, Io, Procris, Aglauros), some from the Bible (Eve, Lot's wife, Dinah), one or two from more recent sources such as Ariosto (Alcina).[34] The dominant figures were Eve, Dinah, Psyche, and Pandora. The immutability of their stories made all female curiosity seem to be a given and to have inevitable, calamitous consequences. Many newly written stories of female curiosity—most famously the Bluebeard myth—were modelled on them.

The fact that most exemplars of female curiosity were derived from antiquity may seem to suggest that early modern writers simply repeated a ready-made discourse, rather than making it more misogynist. However, they actively participated in transforming those ancient stories into ones about curiosity, by interpreting them as such, thereby tightening rather than loosening strictures against female curiosity. In almost all cases—Psyche being the most striking exception—the 'curiosity' family of terms did not figure in the original source texts or their Latin translations but was injected into the story by early modern commentators or their medieval forebears, in the same way that numerous biblical passages from which curiosity was absent were interpreted as *loci* concerning that vice (2.1 above). Indeed, so far as quotable *loci*—as distinct from narrative *exempla*— are concerned, the sole biblical passage which did describe women explicitly as curious was seized upon enthusiastically: it was St Paul's description of young widows—notoriously rapacious—as 'not only idle, but garrulous and curious ['busybodies', in the King James version], saying what they should not say'.[35] Regularly cited, it too was distorted, becoming a standard proof that women in general,

---

[34] e.g. Camus 1613, vii. 431, 434, 436, 450 (Adam and Eve, Dinah, Psyche, Pandora); *Curiosité fructueuse* 1739, 9–10 (Eve, Lot's wife, Pandora); Faber 1643, iii. 154 (Lot's wife); Garzoni 1586, 69ʳ–70ʳ (Dinah, Procris, Aglauros, Alcina); Granada 1586, 400 (Dinah); [Harcouet de Longeville] 1722, 7 (Eve); Stryk/Lüedecke 1743, 295 (Eve); Tiraqueau 1576, 97ᵛ (Io, Dinah), repeated by Watson/Rose 1690, 796. For Psyche and Pandora, see 5.2.3–4 below. L'Espine (1588, 491), following Plutarch (1971, [63ᵛ]), also mentions Lamia, the fairy who wore her eyes— out of curiosity—whenever she went out but took them off, like glasses, in her own home.

[35] 'non solum otiosae, sed et verbosae, et curiosae, loquentes quae non oportet' (1 Timothy 5.13; Vulgate).

rather than these young widows in particular, were perniciously curious.[36]

Still more radical reinterpretation occurred when the theme of female curiosity was *injected* into old stories that had not originally mentioned it. Female victims of male aggression, who were certainly not described in the source text as having brought the aggression upon themselves, let alone as having done so through their own curiosity, *were* blamed on these counts by subsequent male commentators. Dinah, whose father Jacob was encamped opposite the town of Shechem, 'went out to see the women of that land' and was raped by Schechem (Genesis 34.1–2).[37] In the twelfth century, St Bernard of Clairvaux gave Dinah a motive: comparing her to Eve, he blamed the rape on Dinah's scopic 'idle curiosity' which, he claimed, had made her go out in the first place;[38] in the early modern period this was the standard interpretation. Similarly, Io, who according to Herodotus had come to the sea shore at Argos where some Phoenicians were selling their wares and was then snatched away by them to Egypt, was interpreted in the early modern period as having been motivated by typically female curiosity to see the spectacle of the Phoenician ships.[39]

Real events from the recent past that involved male violence could also be transformed into stories of female curiosity. Bluebeard is one example.[40] Another is the murder of a Flemish girl or young woman that seems to have taken place in Antwerp on 27 May 1582. The event was written up, in the same or the following year, in an anonymous French *canard* which made her 'serve as an example' of the 'punishment' that awaits girls who have 'vanity and excessive curiosity' for the latest clothes fashions.[41] About to attend a wedding, she is described as being so furious at her starcher for failing to prepare her ruffs and head-dress properly that she swears blasphemously

[36] e.g. Fénelon 1983–97, i. 1203; Tiraqueau 1576, 97ᵛ, repeated by Watson/Rose 1690, 796.

[37] 'ut videret mulieres regionis illius' (Vulgate).

[38] 'otiosam curiositatem' (Bernard of Clairvaux 1854, 958).

[39] Tiraqueau 1576, 97ᵛ, repeated by Watson/Rose 1690, 796. See Herodotus 1966, i, 1.1–2.

[40] § 5.2.4 below. The Breton childkiller Gilles de Rais, executed in 1440, was known as Bluebeard, though he in turn is likely to have got that name from the protagonist of a previously existing story (Rouger in Perrault 1967, 120).

[41] Appendix in Habanc 1989, 301–4: 'servir d'exemple' (303), 'Vanité, et trop grande curiosité . . . punition' (301). The episode was later further fictionalized, being switched to 27 February 1604 when it was retold in a 1604 printing.

that she would rather be taken away by the Devil than attend the wedding in that unfashionable state. The Devil obliges: he appears to her disguised as one of her lovers and strangles her. The graphic description of her violent end makes her a female counterpart of her near-contemporary, Faust: whether directed at clothes (female) or occult sciences (male), curiosity is fatal. The title crudely condenses the narrative in typical exemplifying fashion, omitting the mention of blasphemy and so making the chain of events lead, even more terrifyingly, straight from fashion to strangulation.

This retrospective reinterpretation of events and stories, new and old, as being about the consequences of female curiosity occurred through the construction of narrative chains of cause and effect. Surely Dinah, Io, the Flemish woman, and Bluebeard's wives must have been curious, given what happened to them subsequently. With Eve—and Pandora, insofar as she was associated with Eve—that chain encompassed the rest of human history. The punishment of the curiosity of Lot's wife 'was not passed on to anyone else but her, whereas that of Eve had far more calamitous consequences, since it extended to all her descendants'.[42] The wretched human condition 'owes its origin to the curiosity of the first mother'.[43] Even a woman from just a few generations back could be inserted into a sequential chain of curiosity which similarly stretched forward into the present: according to a 1682 Catholic history of Calvinism, Marguerite de Navarre had, alongside her admirable qualities,

> that dangerous fault to which the most intelligent women are usually the most prone . . . : great curiosity to know the secrets of new doctrines, especially religious ones. This leads imperceptibly to presumption, which makes them want to judge those doctrines, and then to error and obstinacy, which make them cling to them.[44]

---

[42] 'la punition de sa faute ne passa point à d'autres qu'elle: au lieu que celle d'Eve eut des suites bien plus funestes, puisqu'elle s'étendit à toute sa postérité' (*Curiosité fructueuse* 1739, 8). Lot's wife was turned into a pillar of salt for turning round to look back at the burning city of Sodom (Genesis 19.26).

[43] 'primae matris Curiositati suam debet originem' (Stryk/Lüedecke 1743, 295).

[44] 'ce dangereux defaut, auquel les Dames les plus spirituelles sont ordinairement le plus sujettes . . . je veux dire, une grande curiosité pour sçavoir les secrets des nouvelles Doctrines, sur tout en matiere de Religion, d'où vient insensiblement la présomption, pour en vouloir juger, et ensuite l'erreur et l'opiniastreté, pour s'y attacher' (Maimbourg 1682, 16). Quoted by Stolle/Schlosser (1724, 25) as evidence for the role of specifically female curiosity in the spread of heresy. Montaigne too uses Marguerite de Navarre as proof that women are ill-fitted to discuss theology (Montaigne 1962, I. 56, p. 310).

The writer then goes on to describe how Protestants exploited this fault of the King's sister in order to give Calvinism a toe-hold in France in the 1520s and 1530s. So the sequential chain instigated by her curiosity had not only consecutive links—presumption, error, obstinacy—that were calamitous for her personally and spiritually but also subsequent links that have brought political and social calamity to France right up to 1682. Whether in historiography or in moral discourse, the construction of narrative chains of curiosity was a powerful tool for blaming women, both for their own misfortunes and for men's.

In stories new and old, the curiosity of women was usually distinctively female, rather than being a sex-neutral vice that was the same in women and men. In particular, it was often accompanied by the related vices of disobedience, lack of chastity, and loose speech (whether 'indiscretion' or defamation).[45] These were far less prominent in stories of male curiosity; if they did occur there, they were often feminized.[46] The anxiety of authors about female chastity manifested itself either overtly[47] or more on the semi-acknowledged level of connotation, unsurprisingly given the delicacy involved in writing cautionary tales about it for young girls (5.2.2 below).

On the other hand, there was scarcely any female equivalent of the anxious sexual jealousy that haunted curious men in numerous stories. Whereas Cervantes's 'curious impertinent' is tortured by the thought that his virtuous wife's chastity might falter under extreme temptation, La Fontaine's Psiché cheerfully wonders whether the reason why her husband hid his identity was to placate some other lover of his—for surely such a beautiful man must have many—but this fleeting thought is far from being what causes *her* curiosity, indeed it only makes her proud of his manliness (1991, 116–17): the male author La Fontaine was as uninterested in exploring anxious female curiosity about a husband's infidelity as he was interested in exploring female curiosity as disobedience to a husband.

---

[45] For a late instance of an English exemplary narrative warning women of the sequential chain that leads from curiosity to defamation and then to downfall, see Luce's novel *Curiosity* (1822): 'owing to her incurable curiosity, [Sophia] has been suspected of defamation, and is prosecuted for this misdemeanour' (iii. 235); 'as you would shun the disgraceful fate of Sophia, beware of—CURIOSITY' (iii. 237; the novel's closing words).

[46] e.g. 4.4.1 above.

[47] The curiosity of the strangled Flemish girl was allegedly motivated by her 'desirs charnelz' and by her wish to please her numerous male admirers (Habanc 1989, 301).

Moreover, whereas the most unlikely men (such as Œdipus) were forced into the mould of the 'curious impertinent', conversely a woman (Procris) who, from a modern perspective, seems a much more likely candidate to be a 'curious impertinent' was instead reinterpreted in the early modern period as an *exemplum* illustrating the proximity of female curiosity not to sexual jealousy but to lack of chastity. According to Ovid (*Metamorphoses* 7.6) and others, Procris is married to Cephalus, with whom Aurora falls in love, carrying him away. Since Cephalus wishes to return to Procris, Aurora sends him to test his wife Procris's fidelity in disguise: she fails the test. Procris subsequently turns the tables on her husband, disguising herself in a test which he in turn fails, and so they are reconciled. But Procris, wrongly suspecting that Cephalus still loves Aurora, spies on him while he is hunting and is accidentally killed by one of his darts. The 'curiosity' family of terms did not figure in the source texts of this tale of a double triangle of desire, but if Procris had been a man then she would surely have been seized upon in the early modern period as a 'curious impertinent'.[48] Instead, in Du Bosc's discussion of female curiosity, Procris's jealousy is made to rebound on her. It becomes a sign of her own lack of chastity, a reminder that a woman's obsession with others' infidelity suggests that she herself is not 'une Dame chaste': being guilty herself, she cannot believe that her husband is innocent (1665, 135). (Her husband's own previous transgression is not even mentioned by Du Bosc.) It was women, not men, who were often thought to be led into curiosity and calamity by their lack of chastity. The 'curious impertinent' was always male. Unlike female curiosity, his never rebounded on him as an interrogation of his own chastity, which, whatever its state, was simply not an issue.

5.2.2   *The corrigible curiosity of daughters*

Some stories of female curiosity were used to instil certain kinds of behaviour not just in women but also in girls, to encourage them to be discreet and obedient and to discourage them from trying to obtain sexual and other knowledge. These stories presupposed that

---

[48] Garzoni comes close (1586, 69ᵛ): in his enumeration of *exempla* of curiosity he attributes Procris's death to a 'trop grande anxieté' to see if Aurora had snatched Cephalus (again).

curiosity was corrigible; and it was often to mothers that they entrusted the responsibility of correcting the curiosity of daughters. Whether or not the stories were explicitly couched in terms of exemplarity, they were firmly injunctive and cautionary. But that is not to say that they made curiosity simple. On the contrary, they made it complex and elusive, especially when sexuality was involved.

For instance, a 1698 novella, *La Curiosité dangereuse*, by Roberday, both shows how a mother manages to cure her daughter's curiosity by reciting to her numerous *exempla* and yet also itself serves as such an *exemplum* for its own readers. In other words, this novella is an *exemplum* that incorporates a representation of the effectiveness of *exempla*. Its plot is simple: the mother (Araminte) welcomes approved suitors of her daughter (Lisette) into the home, but Lisette prefers Lisias—partly because her mother has not chosen him—although neither has even ever met him. Araminte intercepts a letter in which Lisias invites Lisette to go with him to watch a procession of penitents that evening. After lengthy maternal remonstration about the dangers involved, the daughter eventually agrees to refuse the invitation and ends up accepting one of the suitors approved by her mother.

There is a simple injunctive message: this novella seems worlds away from *La Princesse de Clèves*. Yet curiosity is slippery in both works because it involves sexuality that is necessarily veiled, semi-acknowledged. In one sense, Lisette is not actually curious at all, since she is merely following Lisias's advice to pretend to her mother that she is curious to see the religious procession. The plan is that she will therefore be able to go there 'on this feigned pretext of curiosity', 'under the cover of the general curiosity that has taken hold of everyone in Paris'.[49] But if the daughter's curiosity does not really exist, how can it be 'dangerous'? The title can only denote, or rather connote indirectly, the daughter's erotic curiosity, unacknowledged, disobedient, and directed at her unseen lover, perhaps in an echo of Psyche's story. As so often with sex, this connotation never becomes an outright denotation. It has special shock potential when, as here, a female is a subject of sexual curiosity rather than an object of it. Although the mother initially concentrates her attack on the 'belles curiositez' (12) of ostentatious Counter-Reformation devotional

---

[49] [Roberday] 1698: 'ce feint prétexte de Curiosité' (13), 'sous les auspices d'une curiosité assez generale, puis qu'il n'a personne à Paris qui ne l'ait euë' (9).

processions, on the other hand when she subsequently discusses with her daughter whether curiosity is a vice or not the conversation would be nonsensical if the term signified only the desire to see the procession—which is how the daughter still defines it—since the mother knows perfectly well that that desire is a cover for erotic desire anyway. As so often, narrative is especially useful for teaching readers—in this case both mothers and daughters—how to recognize curiosity. When the mother warns of 'the ills and misery which this curiosity causes', she mainly means sex rather than religious spectacle and is hoping to persuade her daughter by evoking this chain of calamitous events without having to say exactly what it consists of.[50] The mother is using the ambiguity of curiosity to push the daughter in a certain direction without yet telling her in graphic—and possibly alluring—detail exactly what she is being pushed away from.[51] And the writer is probably doing the same in relation to young female readers: cautionary tales could backfire and become incitements if they described dangers too explicitly.

However, although many cautionary tales about female curiosity were designed especially to influence sexual behaviour, not all were. The aim was sometimes to train young girls how not to investigate the secrets of adults—whether concerning love or anything else—or, if they did happen to learn those secrets, how not to divulge them. For instance, almost a century after Roberday's novella, Stéphanie Félicité Ducrest de Saint Aubin, who from her marriage in 1763 was known as Madame de Genlis, attempted this in her play *La Curieuse*.[52] Genlis's 'pedagogical theatre' (*théâtre d'éducation*) was no longer so steeped in the terminology of exemplarity, but it still aimed to train girls morally through cautionary narrative.

Let me summarize the plot of the five-act version (first published in 1781), which grew out of the initial two-act play (first published in 1779). The *curieuse* is Pauline, who is convinced that her mother (the Marquise de Valcour), cousin (Constance) and elder sister (Sophie) are keeping a secret from her. The secret, which emerges progressively, is that the Baron de Senanges, who is visiting the Valcour château, is griefstricken at the apparent death of his son in a duel with one Chevalier de Mirville, who in reality is none other than

---

[50] 'des maux et des chagrins que cette Curiosité cause' (15).

[51] She does subsequently become a little more explicit, citing an example of a young woman losing her honour to a fake penitent (27–37).

[52] [Genlis] 1783, ii. [5]–105. On Genlis, see Plagnol-Diéval 1996 and 1997.

Pauline's brother, the Chevalier de Valcour, who is now being hidden in the Valcour château. Unaware of this, Pauline schemes to unravel the secret with the similarly *curieuse* Rose (the gardener's daughter), not realizing its gravity. Pauline inadvertently reveals to the Baron de Senanges that 'Mirville' is in the château. The Baron storms off, intent on killing his son's murderer. Only now does Pauline learn the full secret and the identity of 'Mirville' from her distraught mother, who accuses Pauline of causing her own brother's death. Pauline bitterly regrets her curiosity. However, calamity is averted when the young Senanges turns up, alive after all. The secret romances between him and Sophie and between the Chevalier de Valcour and Constance can now culminate in marriage.

Like the Jesuits of Louis-le-Grand (4.4.2 above), Genlis was aiming to train morally not only those who watched the play but also those who acted in it and for whom she herself had responsibility. She described the first performance in her memoirs. Pauline was played by one of her own daughters, Pulchérie, who was then aged eleven years or less. Whereas this performance took place before an audience of 500—including many friends of Genlis and, a fortnight later, Enlightenment figures such as Jean-François Marmontel and Jean le Rond d'Alembert—on the other hand the play was probably also performed at the convent of Bellechasse, where, from 1777, Genlis brought up her own children and those of the Duchesse d'Orléans, staging (she claimed) all of her pedagogical theatre there.[53]

Unlike the Jesuit boys, however, the girls who saw or acted in *La Curieuse*—or who were educated by an adult who had seen and admired it—were not being encouraged to distinguish between good and bad curiosity, cultivating the good kind in preparation for later civic life. Rather, girls were being taught to flee all curiosity (desire to discover secrets) and 'indiscretion' (desire to divulge them).[54] As in earlier exemplary narratives, they were being taught to do this by recognizing sequential chains of events. But whereas curiosity could sometimes lead boys to good as well as bad chains of events, the options for girls were more limited. Recalling another instance in which her curiosity led to calamity, Pauline protests her innocence:

---

[53] See Genlis 1825–8, ii. 336–9; Plagnol-Diéval 1997, 94–5. Pulchérie was 8 years old when Genlis had just returned from Spa (Genlis 1825–8, ii. 336), that is, in about 1776. It is unclear whether the performance of *La Curieuse* described by Genlis was the 1779 one cited by Brenner (1947, 74) or an earlier one.

[54] These 2 families of terms are constantly connected in the play (e.g. 11).

'but I did not foresee what would happen'. This prompts her wise sister to point out: 'Certainly, you never intend to do something malevolent, of that I'm convinced, but, sister, excessive curiosity always brings with it the most dangerous indiscretions.'[55] The language of *prévoyance* is still being applied to sequential chains of curiosity in the same way as in Du Souhait's exemplary narratives two centuries earlier.

However, unlike Du Souhait, Genlis makes curiosity into an entirely female problem. Only her women protagonists are emphatically moral or immoral, 'discreet' or 'curious'. Unlike many male authors, Genlis is not representing all women as curious and all men—except the odd effeminate one[56]—as not curious.[57] Rather, the ideal woman—the mother, emulated by the aptly named Sophie and Constance—is neither 'curious' nor 'indiscreet'; only certain women (immature or serving-class) are curious,[58] while for men curiosity is simply not an issue either way. They are too busy undertaking or planning direct action—a duel, a revenge killing.[59] The role of the women is to influence events (whether by design or accident) more indirectly, but nonetheless crucially, by withholding or disclosing information about men: what men have done, where they are, who they are. The play seeks to train girls in the management of such information. Such management is considered vital: to feign ignorance of a secret 'is to fulfil an honour-imposed duty which alone ensures the security of society'.[60]

---

[55] 'mais je ne prévoyois pas ce qui est arrivé. SOPH. Assurément vous n'avez jamais l'intention de faire une méchanceté, j'en suis bien certaine: mais, ma sœur, une curiosité excessive entraîne toujours avec elle les indiscrétions les plus dangereuses.' (9). The mother's climactic condemnation of her wayward daughter also emphasizes a chain of cause and effect: 'voilà, voilà le fatal ouvrage de ta coupable curiosité' (96).

[56] e.g. Forlange, the eponymous hero of Planard's play *Le Curieux* (1807) (4.4.4 above), which may well be an imitation of Genlis's *Curieuse*, given the similarities of plot.

[57] Whereas scholarship on Genlis's prolific writings has sometimes interpreted them as conservatively upholding aristocratic and patriarchal values, a recent study has argued that she also protested subtly against them: for a brief survey, see Still 2000, esp. 331–4.

[58] The wayward aristocratic daughter makes the gardener's daughter 'curieuse' (43) by her 'mauvais exemples' (89). This motif of the contagious spread of curiosity from upper to lower class was common in plays about male curiosity too.

[59] Cf. Plagnol-Diéval 1997, 283: 'Le baron se définit comme un homme d'action'.

[60] 'c'est remplir un devoir que l'honneur impose, et qui fait seul la sûreté de la société' (8).

The gulf between the roles of the two sexes is also one between two of the numerous dramatic genres in which Genlis operated. As Marie-Emmanuelle Plagnol-Diéval has shown, whereas the two-act version was characteristic of those plays which Genlis addressed primarily to under-14-year-olds—it appeared in her *Théâtre à l'usage des jeunes personnes* (1779)—on the other hand the five-act version belonged to the mainstream genre of 'society theatre' for adults and so was printed in her *Théâtre de société* (1781); it had much in common with tragedy—despite being labelled a 'comedy'—and with the *drame*. Those early performances of *La Curieuse* seem to have been of the two-act version, in which the only roles were female. The Baron's preparations for revenge were only mentioned, not shown directly onstage. The subsequent five-act version added the love intrigues and all the male roles (the Chevalier de Valcour, the Baron, his son, and the gardener).[61] This version now represented not only the 'discreet' female management of information—and its curious opposite—but also the broader social context which was deemed to make that management crucial.

5.2.3   The 'incorrigible curiosity'[62] of a wife: La Fontaine's Psiché

Like his contemporaries Scudéry and Lafayette, Jean de La Fontaine explored curiosity in a narrative (*Les Amours de Psiché et de Cupidon*, 1669) which was *not* exemplary in the injunctive sense, that is, which did not claim to offer clear models or counter-models that might improve its readers' conduct. Yet whereas those two woman authors were suspicious of ascribing universal applicability to examples, preferring to problematize the conventional gendering of curiosity, by contrast La Fontaine's narrative reasserts exemplarity, but of the illustrative rather than the injunctive kind: because Psiché's curiosity is an 'incorrigible', typically female fault, no hope is held out that other women can avoid it.

The unchangeability of human nature is not an inherently misogynist theme: it was amplified in relation to both sexes in La Fontaine's *Fables* and in various other French works of the 1660s to 1690s within the so-called *moraliste* tradition, to which indeed *La Princesse de Clèves* can be argued to belong loosely. However, in *Les*

---

[61] Plagnol-Diéval 1997, 100–1, 280–4.
[62] 'curiosité incorrigible' (La Fontaine 1991, 207).

Amours de Psiché, La Fontaine goes out of his way to make curiosity a specifically female fault, using an assortment of centuries-old anti-women topoi in order to do so.

Moreover, in keeping with the general tendency of early modern discourse to tighten rather than loosen strictures against female curiosity, La Fontaine makes the centuries-old Psyche story more misogynist than did his source-text, Apuleius's *Metamorphoses* (4.28–6.24). For one thing, in the *Metamorphoses* any misogyny was mitigated by the broader context within which the Psyche story was intercalated: it was overheard by the male hero Lucius, who had been changed into a donkey as a punishment for *his* curiosity. By contrast, La Fontaine removes the Psyche story from that context, thereby clearing the ground for his imputation of the vice to women alone. Secondly, by largely emptying the myth of the allegorical, Platonic meanings which it had for Apuleius,[63] La Fontaine discourages interpretations of Psiché as representing, like Lucius, the human soul, that is, both sexes. His Psiché emphatically represents women, not humanity as a whole.

Thirdly, and most significantly of all, the detailed psychological analysis which La Fontaine adds to Apuleius's version includes female curiosity.[64] La Fontaine is trying to describe a distinctively female psychology which has curiosity at or near its centre, intricately interconnected with its other elements: at the central moment of the plot, half a dozen combining passions are carefully identified as motivating Psiché's forbidden gaze at the husband whom she suspects of being a monster, with curiosity explicitly being the dominant one.[65] Indeed, this theme may have been what drew La Fontaine to Apuleius: the *Metamorphoses* was not any old ancient text in the history of curiosity but arguably the most important. It includes twelve

---

[63] See Jeanneret in La Fontaine 1991, 19–20. Jeanneret's Introduction (5–42) is excellent. On the relation between Platonism and *curiositas* in the *Metamorphoses*, see DeFilippo 1990.

[64] Cf. Jeanneret in La Fontaine 1991, 21: 'Autant les considérations sur la curiosité et la coquetterie des femmes peuvent paraître sommaires, inspirées par une misogynie ou un sexisme qu'on ne cherchera pas à défendre, autant la gamme du désir et la déclinaison du pathétique fournissent l'occasion d'analyses subtiles.' My reading is slightly different, exploring the connections between the theme of female curiosity and the other psychological themes rather than treating the former as brief and distinct. I differ more strongly from Beugnot (1988, 17–20, esp. 18), who reads the work as concerning more the curiosity of humans in general than that of women in particular.

[65] 'L'appréhension, le dépit, la pitié, la colère, et le désespoir, la curiosité principalement' (113). See also pp. 111, 114.

occurrences of *curiositas* and twelve of *curiosus*, which is astonishing given that there is only one prior extant occurrence of the noun in Latin and that even the adjective had previously been rare.[66] Yet even this was not enough for La Fontaine: his version of the Psyche story includes far more occurrences of this family of terms than does Apuleius's.

Whereas Apuleius's Psyche only experiences *curiositas* from the moment when she is tempted by her wicked sisters to look at her unseen husband and she is only described as *curiosa* when she actually does look,[67] La Fontaine's Psiché has a firmly established wish to see him which long predates her sisters' arrival. This wish, called 'curiosité' (97), originates in her alone; it is not planted in her by others. Moreover, to make this particular wish more *vraisemblable*, La Fontaine makes it just one manifestation of Psiché's more general curiosity: finding in Cupidon's palace some representations of herself as an Amazon, huntress, Greek, Persian, and so on, she 'had curiosity to try these out', that is, to dress up in the various costumes.[68] And this curiosity has two feminine dimensions: the preoccupation with adornment—one of the forms of female 'vanity'[69]—and the delight in change. Both dimensions, along with Psiché's overall curiosity, are emphatically applied to women in general: 'To change outfit every day! . . . I can't imagine more of a paradise for our ladies', exclaims one of the men listening to the story.[70] In more tragic tones, this feminine mutability is related to the central plot: '[Fortune] is a woman, and so was Psiché, which means that she was incapable of remaining in the same state, as our heroine certainly demonstrated later on.'[71] Thus, one of the most enduring misogynist topoi of all is grafted on to curiosity: Psiché is curious partly because of the universal fickleness of women. Gallingly, she wants to get a glimpse of her currently invisible husband simply in order to have some change in her present situation, although that situation is blissful. And that fickleness manifests itself in her deceitfulness (which echoes that of her sisters):

---

[66] DeFilippo 1990, 471; Labhardt 1960, 206, 209–10, 215–16; Lancel 1961, 26.

[67] *Metamorphoses*, 5.6, 5.19, 5.23.

[68] 'eut la curiosité de les éprouver' (85). See also p. 156.

[69] It is curiosity in the 'bodily adornment' sense that makes Psiché open Proserpine's box, wanting to try out the cosmetics inside (206–7). Cf. also p. 101.

[70] 'Changer d'ajustement tous les jours! . . . je ne voudrois point d'autre Paradis pour nos Dames' (86).

[71] 'Elle est femme, et Psiché l'estoit aussi, c'est à dire incapable de demeurer en un mesme état. Nostre Héroïne le fit bien voir pas la suite' (95–6).

'This Beauty used all the tricks customarily deployed by wives when they wish to deceive their husbands'.[72]

Such generalizing from particular female protagonists to wives[73] or to female 'nature' in general doggedly accompanies not only curiosity itself—'the fault of the sex', shared by Psiché's sisters too[74]—but all the defects which La Fontaine attributes to Psiché.[75] Only on one occasion is her desire for knowledge implicitly linked to human nature in general, via a universalizing 'we'.[76] Even female faults that are explicitly *not* attributed to the female protagonists of this story are still mentioned by the narrator, for good measure.[77] It is not only the decrees of 'fate' ('destin', 101) but also the fixity of female nature that makes Psiché's curious transgression inevitable, just as female nature made male curiosity inevitably calamitous in the story of the 'curious impertinent'. Moreover, proleptic knowledge of the inevitable chain of events—in which women stumble along obliviously—is the province not so much of gods as of husbands (and male narrators): 'Her husband, who could feel the fatal moment approaching . . .'[78] To know female nature is to know what will happen in a story.

It could be argued that La Fontaine's playful, witty tone—surely more indulgent than vituperative—makes such a reading seem sour and humourless. Yet that is exactly what it is designed to do, forestalling resistance to its representation of female nature in *Les Amours de Psiché* as of human nature in the *Fables*. It could also be argued that La Fontaine is not really condemning curiosity outright, since the narrator and reader become complicit with Psiché's curiosity to see what is forbidden (Beugnot 1988, 19). However, even if this is the case, La Fontaine keeps the 'curiosity' family of terms almost entirely pejorative, choosing not to use it in the positive or

---

[72] 'Tous les artifices dont les femmes ont coustume de se servir quand elles veulent tromper leurs maris, furent employez par la Belle' (112).

[73] Esp. in Book 1, by insistently calling Cupidon an *époux* or *mary* rather than a god, La Fontaine emphasizes the husband/wife rather than the divine/human dynamic between Cupidon and Psiché. Her curiosity is disobedience to the authority primarily of a husband and secondarily of a god (e.g. 'le mary déclamoit toûjours contre les femmes trop curieuses', 97).

[74] 'le défaut du sexe' (116). For the sisters' curiosity, see pp. 106, 108.

[75] In addition to the examples already quoted, see pp. 99, 206 (for curiosity) and 70 (for another defect of 'le naturel et l'esprit des femmes').

[76] 'comme nous voulons tout sçavoir jusqu'aux choses qui nous déplaisent' (96).

[77] e.g. 75, 103.

[78] 'Son mary qui sentoit approcher ce moment fatal . . .' (96).

ambivalent extradiegetic senses that had become common among his contemporaries, such as Scudéry.[79] Moreover, nothing explicitly suggests that Psiché's final triumph is an 'absolution de la curiosité' (*pace* Beugnot 1988, 20): the ending leaves curiosity hanging in the air, neither resolved nor absolved, although Psiché herself is now accepted by Cupidon, out of love. Indeed, if anything, La Fontaine punishes Psiché much more than did Apuleius for her second major transgression—opening Proserpine's box out of curiosity—since the French author turns her temporarily into a black 'Moor'.

In late seventeenth-century France, the conclusions about female curiosity that La Fontaine drew from the Psyche story were not the only ones that it was possible to draw. In one wittily intertextual rewriting of La Fontaine's version—'The Green Serpent' (1697–8)—female curiosity is still wholly bad, but it is *not* incorrigible. Significantly, the author was a woman, Marie-Catherine d'Aulnoy. As Anne L. Birberick has pointed out, the heroine (Laidronnette) of this fairytale, having been punished for the curiosity that led her to look at her husband, then manages to avoid further curiosity by *not* opening Proserpine's phial: her restraint is rewarded with the return of her beauty and the acquisition of 'discretion', the female virtue opposed to curiosity.[80] Female curiosity is not only corrigible, but it is also shared by 'us'—says the narrator, who is not specifically marked as female—by 'most mortals: deranged and curious people'.[81] As Birberick notes, d'Aulnoy engrains curiosity less indelibly in female nature than does La Fontaine. Laidronnette reads the Psyche story in the version written by a recent, fashionable author (clearly La Fontaine) and it is Laidronnette's desire to test her situation against Psyche's—goaded by her mother—that leads Laidronnette to look at her husband to see whether he is Cupid or else the monster that he turns out to be. Curiosity is not so much 'the fault of the sex' as the desire to check a text against reality (Birberick

---

[79] Only on one occasion does La Fontaine echo the positive evaluation of curiosity that had become so common by his time: it is suggested (by a shepherdess) that Psiché's 'curiosité . . . méritoit d'estre loüée, comme ne pouvant provenir d'excès d'amour' (161). Although the claim does echo the earlier hint that Psiché still felt a vestige of love at the moment of transgression (114), it is outweighed by the interpretation (eventually shared by Psiché herself) of her transgression as a failure of love.

[80] Birberick 1999. 'Le serpentin vert' was one of 3 fairytales narrated within a novella (*Don Fernand de Tolède*: D'Aulnoy 1997, 525–61). D'Aulnoy's fairytales were even more popular than those of Perrault in the 18th century (Seifert 1996, 229).

[81] 'nous' (543); 'la plupart des mortels, curieux insensés' (561).

1999, 286). Reading generates curiosity: La Fontaine's text is also what makes Laidronnette want to be visited in her palace by her sisters, just as Psiché was visited by hers. As in other French narratives of this period, curiosity is becoming partly an aesthetic effect of reading.

Yet curiosity still retains its pejorative force for d'Aulnoy. However much she modifies the male tradition of condemnation of female curiosity, she does not escape it entirely. Compared with La Fontaine's more unruly Psiché, who initially questions her husband's discourse of curiosity—'How strange you are to go on about curiosity!'[82]—Laidronnette's transgression is not accompanied by any such questioning: she duly promises 'her husband to have no curiosity contrary to his desires'.[83] Moreover, elements within the text indicate that her curiosity might inhere in her nature after all. Although her eventual renunciation of curiosity suggests that this narrative—unlike La Fontaine's and Apuleius's—involves injunctive exemplarity, since female curiosity can be corrected, on the other hand the text sometimes joins those which undermine such exemplarity in this period: in particular, the closing verse moral ignores Laidronnette's conversion to 'discretion' and focuses only on her transgression, presenting her as incorrigible: 'The example of Psiché cannot make her wise', nor indeed can those of Pandora or Eve.[84] Moreover, in keeping with those exemplars, the moral also argues that the calamitous 'curious desire' to know secrets is found 'especially' in the 'fair sex'.[85] Such discrepancies between tales or fables and their closing morals were rife, but this one points to continuing anxieties surrounding curiosity: was it specific to women? could it be corrected?

5.2.4   Opening the box, bowl, pie, jar, or closet: Pandora, Bluebeard, and others

I only did what he knew I would.[86]

La Fontaine was one of numerous early modern writers who were keener to illustrate female curiosity by example—to prove that

---

[82] 'Que vous estes estrange avec vostre curiosité!' (1991, 97).
[83] 'à son époux de n'avoir aucune curiosité contraire à ses désirs' (541).
[84] 'L'exemple de Psyché ne peut la rendre sage' (560; see also p. 561). See also p. 543: 'Ah! curiosité fatale dont mille affreux exemples ne peuvent nous corriger'.
[85] 'désir curieux . . . I Le beau sexe a surtout cette audace cruelle' (560).
[86] Carter 1981, 37.

pernicious curiosity was almost exclusively the preserve of women—than to enjoin ways of correcting it. These story-proofs often had ferocious force. The point was to humble or humiliate women into accepting what they were really like. Many of these stories were variations on one simple basic plot. A woman opens some kind of receptacle, having been expressly forbidden from doing so by a male authority figure. The woman thereby falls into a trap set by him: although she opens the receptacle in secret, hoping that no one will find out, in fact once it is opened it cannot be closed again, or else its contents cannot be replaced. The trap proves her curiosity, which she has hitherto usually denied. The male always knows in advance that the woman will disobey him. She thus becomes an unwitting protagonist in a plot devised by him, as Angela Carter makes explicit in her modern feminist rewriting of the Bluebeard story: 'I only did what he knew I would,' says her heroine.

These stories were designed to make it legitimate for men and illegitimate for women to possess certain kinds of knowledge. Whereas the male knows both the receptacle's contents and also female nature, which is irremediably curious, the woman is ignorant of both and is often punished for opening the receptacle and thereby aspiring to male knowledge. The illicitness of curiosity is entirely relational and decorum-based, residing not in the knowledge itself but in who tries to know it. There is no question of the authoritative male himself being curious, since he is allowed to have the knowledge: there is no critique of his possession of it. Curiosity is the domain of women, who always try to trespass onto that of male knowledge. From a modern perspective it can be argued that the obsession with female curiosity served to conceal the fact that men prohibited women from this knowledge by projecting responsibility for the prohibition back onto women: if women are too curious, then surely that is hardly the fault of men. The emphasis on female curiosity and its perniciousness allowed men to keep their own prohibitions against women surreptitious and to avoid acknowledging responsibility for them. They were someone else's fault, whether women's or a higher power's. If—in one of the stories to be considered—Merlin refuses to show a document containing magical secrets to his curious wife, it is not by his own vindictive choosing but because, as a magus, 'I was not allowed to show it to her'.[87]

---

[87] 'il ne m'étoit pas permis de le lui montrer' (*Triomphe* 1787, 117ʳ).

These early modern stories were variations on those of Pandora, Psyche, and Eve, which were often conflated. Receptacles figured in the former two. Pandora, according to Hesiod, was sent by Zeus to punish Prometheus; rashly accepted in marriage by Prometheus's brother Epimetheus, she opened her jar, from which poured forth the troubles that have beset humans ever since. As Dora and Erwin Panofsky have shown, from the sixteenth century onwards, the myth was often known through the *Adagia* of the great humanist Erasmus of Rotterdam. His version produced two influential errors. First, he made the large jar (*pithos*) into a small box or casket (*pyxis*), perhaps through association with the *pyxis* containing some of Proserpina's beauty which Psyche opened out of curiosity on her way back from Hades. Especially in the seventeenth century, this box of Pandora then seems sometimes to have symbolized more or less overtly the womb or female genitals: women's sexuality was blamed for the woes of the world. Secondly, Erasmus's Latin left it ambiguous whether Pandora or indeed Epimetheus opened the box.[88] Whoever did open it, Erasmus did not make curiosity their motive, whereas many subsequent early modern interpreters did. If they attributed box-opening curiosity to Epimetheus, then he was just one unfortunate man, representative of a dangerous possibility but not of male nature as a whole ([La Santé] 1737, 2). But if they attributed it to Pandora, then the passage from the particular to the universal was suddenly more straightforward; she was, like La Fontaine's Psiché, representative of female nature as a whole.[89] Moreover, when writers made the myth into a shorthand *exemplum* of curiosity and condensed it into a single proper name, without giving any of the narrative, they mentioned Pandora, not Epimetheus, skirting around the question of who opened the box but nonetheless blaming Pandora's curiosity, along with Eve's, for subsequent human misery.[90]

---

[88] Panofsky and Panofsky 1962, ch. 2. On the myth's transformations, see also Hays 1966, ch. 7. Hays (85–6) persuasively emphasizes more than Panofsky and Panofsky the sexual dimension of the 17th-century evidence that they themselves provide (75–7).

[89] e.g. La Motte's fable 'Pandore': 'Elle étoit femme et partant curieuse'. Although the fable ends with a rollcall of other vices, the only overtly feminized one is 'La Curiosité qui fut mere de tous' (1719, 227–31).

[90] e.g. *Curiosité fructueuse* 1739, 8–9. The Pandora/Eve association goes back to the Church Fathers.

Whereas the authority figures in such ancient stories were divine—God, Zeus/Jupiter, Venus—the early modern period added many human ones. And whereas those ancient authority figures were occasionally female (Venus), their updated early modern human equivalents were always male—princes, lords, magicians, husbands. To the ancient *pithos* or *pyxis* were now added bowls, pies, and closets, all sealed by men in order to give women a test that they were bound to fail. This unauthorized seal-breaking by women had powerful but usually covert sexual connotations, which it would take a psychoanalytic reading—which I am not attempting—to explore. Male concern with unruly female sexuality was a persistent undercurrent.

These stories of tests were designed not only to affirm the dominant male discourse of female curiosity but also to anticipate and destroy any female opposition to it. The pleasure that they offered to male readers or audience members seems to have derived not only from representation of women as curious but also from the spectacle of humiliated female protagonists being forced to accept that they are indeed curious after all, having previously resisted that label. The aim was to allow only one reading position to female readers: enforced acquiescence. Such acquiescence is enacted in the diegetic discussions of exemplarity which are contained, *en abysme*, within some such stories, such as two of the *exempla* of pernicious *curiositas* contained in a German moral treatise of 1673: both include discussion of Adam and Eve. The first concerns a Saxon prince who, pitying the poverty of one of his elderly subjects, employs him and his wife to cut wood and bring it to the court kitchen. Overhearing the wife grumble that they would not have to do such work had Adam and Eve not fallen, the prince then provides the couple with a nice home and meals consisting of six dishes, forbidding them, however, to eat the sixth. *Curiositas* gets the better of the wife, who persuades her husband to open the sixth bowl (*scutella*), only to see a mouse run out of it. The prince returns them to their previous job, comparing them to Adam and Eve, stating that the wife's fault lay in *curiositas* and the husband's in obedience to his wife. The second story is of a prince's banquet at which a nobleman claims that the *curiositas* of today's women is such that they would have eaten every single one of the apples in Eden. The women at the banquet protest—as he knew they would—and he orders a special pie to be brought from the kitchen: itching to know what is inside, the women eventually insist that it be opened and a live bird flies out. Their *curiositas* is proved.[91] The pie seems to be an edible compromise between Eve's apple and Psyche's and Pandora's boxes.

Receptacle-induced acquiescence with the male discourse of female curiosity was also forced upon women protagonists by playwrights and opera librettists. In these instances the woman's curiosity and/or her denial of it becomes both the obstacle which prevents the happy marriage between young lovers and also the weak point which enables the obstacle to be finally overcome, just as the curiosity of the ridiculous male collector or indeed of the 'curious impertinent' is exploited in some comedies in order to allow a happy marriage to occur. This transformation of the curious woman into an obstacle also maximizes the animosity of audiences and other protagonists towards her.

Let me summarize two French instances of such plots. In an *opéra-bouffon* by Nicolas-Étienne Framery, *Nanette and Lucas, or The Curious Peasant Woman* (1754), the peasant Nanette wants her daughter Babet to marry Lubin, but Babet prefers Valere, the son of the village *seigneur*. The benevolent *seigneur* guesses that his son loves Babet and, having heard of Nanette's reputation for curiosity, he gives her a box, telling her that if she does not open it, then he himself will pay for the wedding between Babet and Lubin but that, should she open it, then he, the *seigneur*, will acquire the right to determine whom Babet should marry. Nanette, having assured the *seigneur* that she is not curious but obedient, then secretly opens the box, but she is dismayed to find that it will not shut again: she is rumbled. The *seigneur* then decrees, to everyone's amazement and delight, that Babet shall marry his son Valere.

Secondly, in an unprinted and anonymous play first performed in 1783 as *Women's Curiosity, or Merlin's Triumph*,[92] Merlin the magician explains that he has offended his wife by calling her 'curious' because she demanded to see a piece of paper, covered with magical secrets, which had dropped out of his pocket. 'At this word "curious",

---

[91] Weber 1673, 462–6. In common with most treatises—as opposed to many plays, for example—this one does not make curiosity only female. Indeed, the previous story (461–2) is of male *curiositas* and also involves a small box, but it lacks the plot pattern shared by so many stories of female curiosity that is directed at receptacles.

[92] *La Curiosité des femmes ou le triomphe de Merlin* (Brenner 1947, 8).

goodness did she get incensed; she told me that nothing could be falser and that no-one had less curiosity than her.'[93] So, when Merlin then broaches with his wife the proposed wedding between his pupil Zinzolin and hers, Florine, Madame Merlin spitefully refuses to consent to the marriage unless Merlin can prove that she is indeed curious. So Merlin now offers a mystery prize, hidden inside a box, to any unmarried female aged between 15 and 20 who is still a virgin. Numerous applicants arrive but when they sit upon Merlin's magic throne it plays a tune, indicating that they have already lost their virginity. Madame Merlin's curiosity about the prize makes her open the box, releasing a white bird which flies away. Merlin triumphantly asserts that, since he has proved her curiosity, she 'will not put any further obstacle before the union of our two pupils'.[94] She acquiesces.

In both plays, curiosity is presented as a characteristic of all women and of no men. Although Merlin is engaged in activities— testing female chastity, magic—which, in other discourses, would be called 'curiosity', in this diegetic world they do not count as curiosity. On the other hand, what *is* implicitly associated with curiosity is the universal lack of female chastity revealed by the virginity test: the 15 to 20-year-olds are, in their own way, as uncontrolled as Madame Merlin. By contrast, the male protagonists are all control: not only the authority figures who possess all knowledge, power, and money, but also even the lesser men—Zinzolin and Nanette's husband Lucas—have not the slightest 'curiosité indiscrette' about the box's contents (1787, 120[r]). Whereas in exemplary narratives mothers are supposed to correct curiosity in their daughters, here they *transmit* it to them:

BABET. Mother! what's 'love', and what's a 'lover'?
NANETTE. Goodness! . . . Aren't you curious!
LUCAS. Takes after her mother.[95]

The curiosity of these two wives, Nanette and Madame Merlin, takes the form of disobedience to their husband, like that of La Fontaine's

---

[93] 'A ce mot de curieuse, oh Dame, elle s'est emporté au dernier point, elle m'a soutenu que rien n'était plus faux et que personne n'avoit moins de curiosité qu'elle' (*Triomphe* 1787, 117[r-v]).

[94] 'vous ne mettrez plus d'obstacle a l'union de nos deux éléves' (128[v]).

[95] 'BABET. Ma mere! qu'est-ce donc que l'amour et un Amoureux? NANETTE. Oh! Dame! . . . Mais t'es bian curieuse. LUCAS. Alle tiant de sa mere.' (Framery 1754, 6). Cf. p. 16: 'NANETTE. Moi curieuse! . . . LUCAS. Oui; et t'es en ça comme toutes les autres.'

Psiché. Merlin, by agreeing to his humiliated wife's closing request not to publicize these events—'for the sake of the honour of your sex'[96]—in effect undermines the basis of that honour, implying that it is a sham generously kept up by men to hide the reality of women's dishonourable curiosity. Women are all the same—curious and unchaste.

Not all male writers agreed. Some conceded that some women are chaste, but this did not necessarily prevent them from still asserting that all women, even chaste ones, *are* curious. For example, that was one message of the Bluebeard myth, launched into the world of print in 1697 when Charles Perrault's 1695 fairytale was published (1967, 123–9). Despite his off-putting appearance, the wealthy Bluebeard persuades a young woman to marry him. Telling his new wife that he must go away for six weeks, he gives her all the keys to his castle, including that of a closet which he forbids her to open. She disobeys and finds the corpses of his previous wives hanging in the closet. Some of their blood stains the key, which is under a magic spell and so cannot be cleaned. She is thus obliged to confess her disobedience when her husband returns after only a day. He resolves to kill her but grants her a quarter of an hour to say her prayers, during which she climbs to the top of the tower and alerts her sister who in turn alerts their brothers, who arrive and kill Bluebeard just as he is about to decapitate his wife.

The closet full of dead wives is yet another receptacle to reveal the disobedient curiosity of its opener. What differentiates this receptacle story from many others is that the male figure who sets the woman up to be curious is malevolent, not benevolent like Merlin or the village *seigneur*. The extraordinary interpretation propounded in the early modern period is that, even when a man who forbids a woman from knowing something is himself wicked, she should nonetheless still obey him and not be curious. That is the implication of the first moral stated at the end of Perrault's version: 'Curiosity, however alluring, often brings remorse, as a thousand daily examples show. No disrespect to women, but it is a very slight pleasure, ceasing to exist as soon as it is grasped and always costing too dear.'[97]

---

[96] 'pour l'honneur de votre séxe' (128ᵛ).

[97] 'La curiosité malgré tous ses attraits, | Coûte souvent bien des regrets; | On en voit tous les jours mille exemples paraître. | C'est, n'en déplaise au sexe, un plaisir bien léger; | Dès qu'on le prend il cesse d'être, | Et toujours il coûte trop cher' (128). My reading of Perrault therefore differs from that proposed by Benedict (2001, 133):

This sets the tone for interpretations for centuries to come: the moral, rather than stating that, say, 'Husbands should not kill wives', perhaps 'lest they in turn be killed', instead addresses women and ignores the final wife's happy rescue, preferring to focus on the previous wives' deaths, which are presented as the outcome of a sequential chain of curiosity.

Moreover, Perrault's second moral, which is equally sex-specific, creates a characteristically arch, ironic distance between this story from bygone times and the present, when husbands are neither unreasonable nor in control of their wives anyway (128). This moral seems to undermine any readerly protest that the first moral, blaming women, is too harsh, since it fails to take account of the brutality of Bluebeard: given that husbands have nowadays become so reasonable, the implication is that disobedient female curiosity is now all the more unreasonable.[98]

Subsequent versions imitated Perrault in making Bluebeard's wives culpable, if not always in the same elegant and urbane way.[99] The criminality of Bluebeard could even be lost entirely from view as insignificant when compared with that of female curiosity. Early in Framery's *Nanette and Lucas*, the peasant Lucas recounts a garbled version of the story to his wife Nanette without mentioning Bluebeard by name, just calling him a King. The closet full of corpses may seem very different from the box which the village *seigneur* will later give Nanette, but it anticipates it proleptically and has the same role as it. Moreover, Nanette is as impatient as the King's wife to learn what is in his closet: 'See! you're already as curious as her', taunts her husband Lucas.[100] Nanette asks what the Bluebeard figure did when he realized that his present wife had disobeyed him. Lucas replies: 'first he was really angry, but in the end he pardoned her, realizing that if he killed all the curious women then he'd depopulate his whole kingdom.'[101]

'Thus, the story traditionally connects women's curiosity with the overthrow of a tyranny at once domestic, political, and economic.'

[98] Although Perrault attacked anti-feminists such as Nicolas Boileau who denied that women were important to civility and taste, elsewhere he stressed female subservience and domesticity (Seifert 1996, 92, 94).

[99] e.g. *The History of Blue Beard, or, The Fatal Effects of Curiosity and Disobedience* [1810], a penny chap-book.

[100] 'V'là déja que t'es aussi curieuse qu'elle' (Framery 1754, 16).

[101] 'il fit d'abord bian le méchant, et pis il li pardonnit à la fin, parce qu'il vit bian que s'il tuait toutes les femmes curieuses, il depeuplerait tout son Royaume' (17–18).

On the other hand, other versions played up both of the strands which were present, if not in Perrault's closing moral, then certainly in his narrative: not just culpable female curiosity but also the eventual destruction of male evil. These two themes did not interlock morally in a chain of events: the killing of Bluebeard—by his wife's brothers or, in some versions, by her lover—was not a consequence of female curiosity in the way that the deaths of the previous wives was. Indeed, the strange coexistence of these two tangential themes, whereby the last wife somehow avoids the fate which she should really meet, may have been one source of the fascination exerted by the story. In George Colman's immensely popular gothic extravaganza *Blue Beard, or Female Curiosity!* (first performed in 1798), the title theme of female curiosity, having initially been emphasized, simply fades from view towards the end of the spectacle, when the destruction of evil becomes paramount.[102] And the two moral themes are simply juxtaposed, without being harmonized, in the title of Francis Egerton Ellesmere's tragedy *Bluebeard, or, Dangerous Curiosity and Justifiable Homicide* (1841). Adaptors of Bluebeard's story were anxious to show that the escape of his last wife does not make her curiosity any the less 'dangerous' or 'fatal' a 'weakness' or 'failing'.[103] She is just plain lucky.

In comparison with other stories of female curiosity that were based on the opening of forbidden receptacles, the Bluebeard myth is idiosyncratic, both because the man is evil and because the woman escapes. This idiosyncrasy perhaps implies, on one level, that female curiosity is justifiable and survivable after all. Indeed, that shocking implication may account for the fascination exerted by Bluebeard; yet male authors were also keen to play it down.

5.2.5   The 'excusable curiosity' of serving-class women

It's for the sake of serving others that I'm curious.[104]

Bluebeard's last wife was not the only woman to get off lightly in early modern stories of female curiosity. One group of women whose curiosity was sometimes excused, or at least forgiven rather than

---

[102] Colman and Morton 1983, 181–210, esp. 199, 203. On this play, see pp. 38–43 (Sutcliffe's Introduction). On curiosity in it, see Benedict 2001, 132–4.

[103] For the last 2 terms, see Colman and Morton 1983, 199.

[104] 'C'est pour rendre service que je suis curieuse' ([Carreau] 1813, 1).

punished, were servants, especially in opera and drama from the eighteenth century onwards. Their curiosity, while morally bad, was aesthetically necessary, since on the level of the plot it was what cleared away obstacles and so permitted a happy dénouement. As in some prose fiction from the second half of the seventeenth century onwards, curiosity therefore became integral to the author's plot-construction and so to the audience's following of the plot, whether or not this aesthetic function of curiosity was explicitly pointed out on an extradiegetic level of commentary. In other words, the growing aesthetic function of curiosity sometimes forced a reappraisal of its moral status, even in relation to women.

Some writers tried to resolve this new tension by attributing plot-unravelling curiosity to protagonists of whom one did not expect high moral standards in any case: women in general, and female servants in particular rather than, say, noblewomen. This was a paradoxical strategy, since curiosity was often likely to be least excusable of all in lower-class women, who had no decorum-based justification for trying to know this or that. The lower one went down the female social scale, the more vehement the prohibition against curiosity tended to be. For instance, in the aristocratic Dancourt's *Curieux de Compiégne* (1698), an innkeeper and her cousin Guillaume discuss the relative demerits of the men and the women among the curious bourgeois camp followers. Whereas the innkeeper initially argues that curiosity is more forgivable in women, her mind is changed by Guillaume, who argues that 'curiosity is permissible in certain women, but as for tradeswomen, women who run taverns, and attorneys' wives, is it their job to quit their household and come to the army?'[105] They should stay 'at home' ('cheux elles', 274), their movements restricted even more by decorum than are those of aristocratic women or of men.

Yet in Dancourt's comedy the curiosity of these women does not itself remove obstacles blocking the pathway to the dénouement, for example by uncovering key information. Entirely bad, their curiosity serves rather as the weakness which other protagonists exploit in order to remove obstacles that impede marriage. The same is true of the curiosity of the peasant woman in Framery's *opéra-bouffon*

---

[105] 'la curiosité est permise à de certaines femmes: mais à des Marchandes, à des Cabaretieres, à des Procureuses: est-ce que c'est leur besogne de quitter leur ménage, et de s'en venir à l'armée?' (Dancourt 1729, iv. 274).

(1754). By contrast, when the curiosity of low-ranking female protagonists is itself what removes such obstacles, by bringing crucial
secrets to light, then the condemnation of it is far more ambivalent
and indulgent, sometimes even perfunctory. An early example
is Pierre Corneille's comedy *Mélite*,[106] in which the nurse—along
with another female protagonist, Chloris—has to defend her
dénouement-hastening curiosity.[107] When viewed from the seventeenth-century auditorium, her curiosity therefore ran along the
same plot-lines as the curiosity about the dénouement that Corneille
sometimes explicitly attributed to his audiences. But it was later that
the theme of the excusable curiosity of serving-class women became
especially prominent. Let me briefly describe two instances.

Valville and Clarence—or—The 'Curieuse' is an eighteenth-
century comic opera with an unprinted libretto by C. Sourdon de la
Coretterie. Clarence, a young widow, who is engaged in a potentially
ruinous lawsuit, loves Floricœur, a mercenary philanderer. She is
herself loved by the virtuous Valville, although only he knows
this. Valville secretly pays off Clarence's adversary in the lawsuit.
Clarence's *curieuse* maid Lisette finds out about this secret payment.
She also learns that Valville mysteriously spends hours alone in a
garden summer-house. Floricœur tells Valville that he will now
marry Clarence but that he would not have done so had she lost her
lawsuit. Lisette, who overhears the conversation, tells Clarence.
Lisette then gets her chance to have a look inside the summer-house,
which Valville, distracted by his misery, has forgotten to lock up.
There she finds a statue of Clarence which Valville has been contem-
plating. Clarence now learns about this from Lisette and about
Valville's secret lawsuit settlement from her (Clarence's) sister.
Clarence switches her affections from Floricœur to Valville.

The second example is relatively late—1813—but has a similar
plot. *Felicitous Lies, or Excusable Curiosity* is a one-act comedy by a
writer known as Mademoiselle de Carreau. Delval (aged about 30) is
staying in the house of a widow, Madame de Verneuil (just under 30),
and her daughter Adèle (15), to whom he has been promised since
her birth. The *femme de chambre*, Marthe, 'curieuse' to know why
the wedding is being delayed, obtains from the gardener an unsent
letter in which Delval declares to Madame de Verneuil that he loves

---

[106] First performed 1629–30; first published 1633.
[107] Corneille 1971, i, ll.355, 361, 1152, 1453. By contrast, there is only one mention of male 'curiosité' (l.1040).

her, not her daughter. Marthe shows the letter to Adèle, who condemns the servant's 'esprit curieux' but herself has 'curiosité' to read
it.[108] Adèle then secretly pursues her own benevolent strategy, testing
Delval by urging him to marry her immediately and then, when he is
evasive, revealing to him and her mother that they love each other.
When it emerges that Marthe stole the letter, the servant is severely
reprimanded but not sacked.

In each case, were it not for the servant woman's curiosity, the
happy dénouement would not have been reached, since the crucial
secrets would not have been revealed: two in *Valville and Clarence*—
the payment and the statue—and one in *Felicitous Lies*. Marthe
claims to Madame de Verneuil that she has managed to achieve in ten
minutes what the lovers could not achieve in six months ([Carreau]
1813, 53). Thus the desire to skip time is still part of curiosity, as in
anti-occult stories like those of Faust or Du Souhait, but it is now for
the sake of a virtuous end. But the means to that end are still not virtuous: however essential to the upper-class characters' happiness, the
curiosity of their women servants is still, if not a big vice, then at least
a 'small fault'.[109] Carreau's play ends with the gardener proposing
marriage to Marthe:

JULIEN. If you like, Mademoiselle, I'll overlook your curiosity and
   many other little matters, and I'll marry you despite your faults.
MARTHE. I accept that I've been more curious than is permissible, but
   people should accept that my curiosity was at least excusable.[110]

As the play's oxymoronic title suggests, this notion that 'curiosity'
can be 'excusable' could be, even in 1813, as surprising in moral
discourse as the notion that 'lies' can be 'felicitous'. Although
Marthe hypocritically claims that, whatever 'the most severe moralist might say', her curiosity is 'praiseworthy' because it is intended to
help others,[111] in fact it is made clear that both the servant women are

---

[108] [Carreau] 1813, 1, 32, 29.

[109] 'C'est un petit défaut qu'elle emploie à merveille!' (La Coretterie (n.d.), 40).

[110] 'JULIEN. Si vous voulez, mam'zelle, j'passerons su la curiosité, su ben d'autres
petites choses encore; et je vous épouserons *nonobstant* vos défauts. MARTHE. Je con-
viens que je me suis montrée plus curieuse qu'il n'est permis de l'être; mais on con-
viendra bien aussi que ma curiosité fut du moins excusable.' (53).

[111] 'Ma curiosité est louable, et le moraliste le plus sévère ne pourrait pas m'en faire
un crime. C'est pour rendre service que je suis curieuse' (1). See also p. 6.

curious in order to gratify themselves at least as much as to help others.[112]

As in so many other stories, here curiosity (desire to know secrets) is wholly female.[113] It joins forces either with the 'indiscretion' (desire to reveal secrets)[114] of the woman or else with the 'indiscretion' of a man who, however, is not the slightest bit 'curious' himself: 'il est indiscret, je suis curieuse', says Marthe of the gardener Julien ([Carreau] 1813, 7). Moreover, Julien's 'indiscretion', unlike Marthe's curiosity, is not something that needs to be excused at the end.

Curiosity is here almost entirely the province of lower-class women, with the fleeting exception of Adèle's 'peu de curiosité' (29). Male anxiety, evident in many early modern stories, as to what curious women might discover is here doubled by classic upper-class anxiety, whether male or female, as to what the servants might discover. As Madame de Verneuil puts it: 'I do believe that Marthe is loyal to me, but her curiosity terrifies me! . . . She reads my eyes!'[115]

And yet the upper classes are parasitically dependent on the very curiosity that they so fear and condemn. What makes Valville so virtuous and lovable is the heroic discretion with which he keeps secret not only his love for Clarence and his financial aid to her but even the duplicity of his rival Floricœur. 'Does a more discreet lover exist?', swoons Clarence when she learns of all this.[116] But his pining in secret would have been to no avail if Lisette had not revealed everything. On the level of the plot, the 'small fault' of her curiosity enables his 'discretion' to receive its just reward; on a moral level, it provides the necessary counterpoint through which his 'discretion' can be measured and admired.

These two narratives make curiosity more ambivalent and contradictory than do most discursive treatments of it. It would be difficult to draw a clear injunctive lesson from them. Here curiosity is not 'either good or bad', as it is in many treatises and dissertations, but rather 'both good and bad'. Perhaps the closest discursive equivalent is the startling statement in Fleury's pedagogical treatise that a few people have to be perniciously curious for the benefit of society as a

---

[112] e.g. La Coretterie (n.d.), 1, 22, 37–8.

[113] See [Carreau] 1813, 18; La Coretterie (n.d.), 1.

[114] La Coretterie (n.d.), 17, 28.

[115] 'Marthe m'est attachée, je le crois; mais sa curiosité m'effraye! . . . Elle lit dans mes yeux!' ([Carreau] 1813, 10).

[116] 'Est-il un Amant plus discret?' (La Coretterie (n.d.), 39).

whole, unwittingly sacrificing their own personal morality for the greater good. In the same way, the curiosity attributed to serving-class women is simultaneously disowned and exploited by play-wrights and upper-class protagonists. Whereas for writers like Genlis 'discretion' alone is what makes society tick, for others a little illicit curiosity is also necessary, but the upper classes had better ensure that it is not their own.

5.3 CONCLUSIONS

In contrast to the good curiosity that was often attributed to men in early modern discourse, for the most part only bad curiosity was attributed to women. Female curiosity was occasionally tolerated, but then only ambivalently, with a sting in the tail, or in a way that reinforced rather than undermined the view that women were natu-rally prone to supplementary excessiveness. While it was often fine for male curiosity to be directed at curious objects that were femi-nized or even female, it was usually unacceptable for women to be subjects who had curiosity of their own to direct at objects of any kind. Male writers viewed this prospect with consistent alarm. Since the only curiosity that they sought to legitimize was usually male, it seems that the early modern period saw overall relative regress rather than progress in the legitimation of female curiosity. It is true that the fascination of the Bluebeard myth may have derived from aporias within the prohibition against female curiosity, and that the new aesthetic uses of curiosity led to its being semi-excused in servant-women in some dramatic representations from the eighteenth century onwards, but all this hardly amounts to emancipation. Rather, the case of female curiosity provides yet another reason for viewing with suspicion any claim that the early modern period wit-nessed a general legitimation of curiosity. Such a grand narrative can only be maintained if women—and many men—are excluded from it.

In comparison with stories about male curiosity, stories that attributed curiosity to women had uses that were quite distinct. They were variously designed to discourage women from trying to usurp knowledge that only men should possess, to encourage them to han-dle such knowledge discreetly should they happen upon it, to make them obedient to husbands, and to help them control their or their daughters' sexuality. Or else the point was simply to enforce in female readers humble acquiescence to the inescapable fact that they all had appalling curiosity. Male and female curiosity were asymmetrical, not least because some writers held women to be responsible for both: women's lack of chastity entailed their curious desire for men, and yet men's own curiosity about women's fidelity often arose from well-founded anxiety about women's lack of chastity, as in the 'curious impertinent' story and its variations.

Does the distinctiveness of male and female curiosity mean that the two were entirely separate, different passions or things? Once again, no single answer to that kind of question is possible, precisely because it was much contested in the early modern period. Numerous stories sought to present curiosity as an entirely female problem: they stated or implied that men had no curiosity. These stories naturalize this 'fact' so confidently, presenting it as so self-evident and uncontestable within their diegetic world, that when they are read on their own, in a vacuum, they seem to be expressing what must surely be a 'typical', consensual, early modern view. However, this view was not ubiquitous: it was contradicted by other texts that attributed to men too the kinds of curiosity to which women were allegedly prone, such as gossip, indiscretion, nosiness, *polypragmosyne*. Texts that were more discursively systematic than stories—treatises, dissertations, and so on—related curiosity to humanity as a whole, distinguishing at times between its male and female, masculine and feminine species but nonetheless presenting them as being essentially one and the same passion. Moreover, even a few stories of female curiosity attributed the same passion to men too: perhaps the storyteller who does so the most boldly is a woman, d'Aulnoy; but even the relatively misogynist La Fontaine does so at one point, if only in passing.

Thus, when considered within the broader context of early modern discourse as a whole, stories of female curiosity, however serenely confident they may seem, reveal themselves to be in fact aggressive contestations, reliant upon aporias that narrative can sweep under the carpet more easily than can discursive texts, which lay claim to argumentative coherence. In some genres and contexts, curiosity was entirely bad and female; in others, it was good and largely male; in others still, it was ambivalent and shared, however unequally and asymmetrically, by both sexes. None of these views constitutes the 'typical' early modern 'concept' of curiosity. Instead, each is an ongoing contestation of the others.

Conclusion

Imagine a moderately educated, Latinate man or woman in the 1680s who, in conversation and in reading, had encountered many allusions to curiosity but was still not quite sure exactly what it was. He or she might have turned for help to a bibliographical manual such as the brand new one by Martin Lipen, *The Universal Library of Things* (Frankfurt a. Main). Our inquirer, having often heard curiosity being denounced from the pulpit, might have thought that Lipen's Volume 1, on theology, would be the most promising place to start. There he or she would indeed have found an entry for 'Curiositas', listing two items: the 65-year-old *Treatise on the Pestilence of Curiosity* by the famous pastor Andreae and the more recent dissertation on unhealthy curiosity in theology by the professor Rechenberg. But that entry in Lipen also contained a cross-reference advising the reader to look up curiosity in the law and philosophy volumes of the same bibliographical manual. Sure enough, in the law volume the inquirer would have found mentioned under 'Curiositas' the Frankfurt a.d. Oder dissertation on the topic by the celebrated jurisconsult Stryk, while in the philosophy volume under 'Curiosa: curiositates' he or she would have found the longest entry of all, listing some twenty-seven works, ranging from treatises on nature and art that were presented as collections of curiosities (Schott's *Physica curiosa* and *Technica curiosa*; Gaffarel's *Unheard-of Curiosities*) to discussions of curiosity as a virtue, vice, or passion (the Plutarch treatise known as *De curiositate*; Seger's *Gymnasium* oration on curiosity about nature), ranging from natural and moral philosophy to theology, from the publications of universities and learned societies to a vernacular compilation that was a popular bestseller (Francisci's *Jolly Theatre of All Kinds of Curiosities*).[1]

What would the inquirer have made of all this? He or she might have formed the impression that there was some kind of link between good and bad curiosity, between curious objects and the passion of curiosity, between the versions of that passion discussed in different

---

[1] Lipen 1679–85, i. 482; iii. 122; v. 361–2. See also iv. 3, 151; v. 498.

disciplines, between curiosity as described by high- and by low-brow books. But the bibliographical manual would not have been of much help in clarifying the exact nature of such links. When Lipen wrote in his theology entry 'cf. the law and philosophy volumes',[2] did he imply that the same curiosity operated in these disciplines as in theology, or that these were all different species of curiosity, or else that they were unrelated things that happened to share the same name? Similarly, exactly what links between disparate works were implied by lumping them together as 'Curiosa: curiositates'?

To find answers, our inquirer might have read some of the works listed by Lipen. But he or she would have found in those works an array of differing answers, a network of continually contested links between different things or species or meanings, all denoted by the same 'curiosity' family of terms. He or she would have found not a concept, in any usual modern sense of the term, but instead what Wittgenstein describes as a rope strengthened by numerous intertwined fibres, none of which, however, run through its entire length. To amplify another Wittgensteinian metaphor: works like Lipen's, that lumped together several of the numerous versions of curiosity that were available at the time, can be thought of as family albums containing various snapshots. Such albums did not record family resemblances 'as they were': rather, they were starting-points for arguments about them, since such resemblances are always prone to contestation. 'Don't you think she looks like her father?'—'No, nothing like him; more like her aunt.' By the middle of the eighteenth century, the family gathering of curiosity tended to look a little depleted when compared with 50 or 100 years earlier: it now often included a narrower, less mainstream range of knowledge and behaviour. For example, in German the 'curiosity' family of terms was now used much less to denote desires for knowledge: native Germanic terms such as *Vorwitz* increasingly displaced *Curiosität* and *curieus* and did not create links between good and bad knowledge, between objects and subjects, between the collecting and narrating tendency of discourse, or between different European languages.

In France and the Germanic territories it was roughly between the mid-seventeenth and the mid-eighteenth centuries that the uses of curiosity were at their most central and prominent across an extra-

---

[2] 'c. Bibl. Jurid. & Phil.' (i. 482).

ordinary range of institutions, discourses, and practices. These uses can be provisionally moulded into broad narratives: German Lutheran universities used curiosity to promote themselves and local ideologies, to grant themselves a monopoly over some kinds of knowledge, and to help establish their authority and role after the Thirty Years' War; churches used it to discredit each other or to try to reassert control over secular culture in the post-Reformation world; institutions and social groups within the culture of curiosities used it to cement their collective identity, to widen or limit access to certain kinds of knowledge, and to make money; men used it to try to restrict women's knowledge and to control their behaviour. But battles over curiosity were not fought simply between those who wanted knowledge and those who wished to deny it to them. Curiosity was sometimes used not just to prohibit or justify knowledge or activity but actually to oblige people to try to know or do this or that.

However, such broad narratives distort the specificity of the individual speech-acts in which curiosity was used. They also conceal the process whereby curiosity was endlessly reshaped for those uses. The process involved inventive strategies for including some possible meanings and decontesting others. Curiosity was sometimes made into diverse species or sorts; it was sometimes considered to operate in different spheres of life, which could be linked through allegory or else through the application of a single *exemplum* of curiosity to them all; bad curiosity was sometime given a good double, the status of which was unclear (was it a thing or a textual chimera?) or else, occasionally, curiosity was judged to be merely polysemic, a family of meanings rather than of things.

There was almost always an illocutionary point to the way in which these families of species or of meanings were shaped. In the attempt to achieve some kind of impact on people's views or behaviour, these families were made hierarchical: some of their species or meanings dominated over others, and so the relations between the species or meanings were antagonistic, conflictual, or even ironic. For instance, in his attacks on *libertins* the Jesuit Garasse used the 'curiosity' family of terms in two ways, both in apparently positive, secular, *mondain* senses and also in pejorative, religious senses. But this polysemy was not neutral: the negative meaning had a meta-status, engulfing the positive meaning. Similarly, in some political satires that made parodic use of the language of the culture of curiosities, the apparent denotation of 'curious'—'collectable'—was engulfed by the underlying meta-meaning 'satirical'.

As these two examples show, it was not a question of there being one version of curiosity per discourse. Even with a single discourse—such as Jesuit polemic or political satire—different versions of it clashed. Even discourses which tended to celebrate curiosity and curious objects—such as travel-writing, historiography, occult sciences, periodicals—also revealed qualms that curiosity was in fact driven by avarice and anxiety, that it was superfluous, superficial, and disorganized. It was often less a case of writers wielding curiosity than of it visibly wielding them, exceeding the control that they sought to establish over it.

Whereas Garasse, at least on the face of it, seemed to have his two meanings under control, others did not hide that curiosity was a kind of semantic swamp from which they had to try to extricate themselves in order to make it mean what they wanted it to mean. It was so polysemic that elaborate, explicit decontestation of unwanted meanings was required in order to make it usable for immediate pragmatic purposes: the Hungarian Jesuit college professor Szentivanyi explained that the physical and mathematical facts that he had compiled were 'curious because' they were rare, uncommon, select, collected with great labour from many sources, but not because they were new, unheard-of, or collected all at one go. Szentivanyi's extraordinary semantic care suggests that he was anxious lest readers misinterpret the label 'curious' that he was attaching to his book. The theology student Rechenberg had even greater reason for such anxiety when boldly claiming that there really was such a thing as a good theologian who was 'curious'; he attempted to control interpretation of his language by repeatedly appending the qualifying adverb 'healthily', calling the objects of such a theologian's inquiry 'healthily-curious' (*sanè-curiosum*) rather than just plain 'curious'.

It was not only readers who threatened writers' control of what curiosity was. The book-producing industry could also undermine that control. Although the famous abbot Trithemius went to his grave in the secure knowledge that he had always denounced curiosity in his printed works, his fellow Benedictines subsequently glamorized curiosity in order to market one of those works, relaunching it with the new, eye-grabbing title *A Ruler's Curiosity*. Conversely, although the notorious, occultist, bestselling *Unheard-of Curiosities* by Gaffarel had dismissed centuries of patristic qualms about *curiositas* so that the author could use *curiositas* instead to glamorize the talismans that he was describing, on the other hand forty-seven years later an editor of this same treatise reinstated those qualms with a vengeance in a preface which sat very uneasily alongside Gaffarel's actual text. Writers' attempts to make curiosity this or that determinate thing were always vulnerable to being contested by the very processes that disseminated their work.

However, it would be wrong to represent all writers as resisting the indeterminacy of curiosity: some openly embraced it. For instance, a few flaunted rather than played down the uneasy relationship between ethical and aesthetic uses of curiosity. By 1661 it was possible for Scudéry, in her *Célinte*, to emphasize that although curiosity was often a vice, it was also what led people to read. In the second case was it a different thing, or else a different species of the same thing? Scudéry leaves that question unresolved. The same unease was exploited to generate humour by university disputants who condemned curiosity while also referring with indulgent admiration to their own and their audience's curiosity in discussing this very topic. Or again, a certain renunciation—whether voluntary or not—of determinacy was often evident in church discourse that tenuously evoked a potential good species of curiosity, either through indirect grammatical structures (conditionals, questions, *ne . . . que*) as opposed to straightforward propositions, or else at points of transition between a secular and a spiritual context: 'When will we find men who make, instead of a trip around the world, the slightest effort of curiosity in order to unravel the mystery of their condition?' (Fénelon). Fénelon would not have contemplated describing spirituality as curiosity in this way if had been discussing spirituality alone, without comparing it to travel. The existence of good curiosity is here so tenuous and uncertain that it can emerge neither in a secular nor a religious context, but only at the point of transition between the two.

This brings us back to a question raised in the Introduction: did the degree of determinacy attributed to curiosity correlate closely to the degree of instrumentality that it offered? Is it true that the more definitive was the shape that people tried to give to curiosity, the more forcefully they were using curiosity to try to affect other people's views and behaviour? Was overt cultivation of indeterminacy a luxury which only less precisely instrumental texts could afford?

To a limited extent, the answer is yes. For example, the moral and/or discursive indeterminacy of curiosity is openly explored in certain French novellas which, from the second half of the seventeenth century onwards, eschewed or problematized the ethical instrumentality characteristic of exemplarity (Lafayette, Scudéry, Diderot). These writers used narrative as a way of disrupting any attempt to define curiosity definitively. Narrative did not necessarily have this disruptive effect; it could also be used for opposite purposes, to promote determinacy, often by bypassing definition altogether. For instance, the understanding of curiosity as distinctively—and dangerously—female was easier to sustain in moralizing narratives than in, say, discursive treatises or dissertations, since narrators could simply avoid addressing awkward questions such as 'What about bad male curiosity?', whereas the rules of more discursive genres meant that such questions had to be asked. Would-be clarity about what was and what was not curiosity characterized not just moralizing narratives but also many other precisely instrumental genres, ranging from the polemical treatise (Garasse) to the sermon (Bossuet).

However, even in texts that were designed to be instrumental in precise ways, such clarity was almost always fragile, sometimes spectacularly so. In the Huguenot L'Espine's pastoral treatise, designed to teach people how to live ethically, curiosity was so use-driven, so profoundly shaped by the specific groups (*bandes*) of allegedly curious people whom he wished to condemn, that some of his examples of the vice exceeded his own declared definition of it as 'transgression of one's proper vocation in life'. Moreover, other texts that had precise pragmatic aims did not even gesture towards making curiosity into something determinate. For example, the botanist Boccone tried to drum up business in Paris by calling his plants, his knowledge, and his potential clients all 'curious', thereby exploiting a cluster of contradictory connotations of the term—'popularizing' and yet 'exclusive'; 'expensive' and yet 'gratis'—which would have been impossible to integrate into any definition and which were made compatible not by logic but by the habits of ordinary language. So, although instrumentality did often foster the drive towards determinacy, it could also mitigate against it: indeterminacy too could provide ways of using curiosity to try to get things done. The question whether writers cultivated determinacy or not is perhaps less telling than the question whether they did so surreptitiously (Boccone in his handbill) or overtly (Scudéry in *Célinte*). Drawing explicit attention to the indeterminacy that he ascribed to curiosity would not have won Boccone any more clients, whereas Scudéry was freer to highlight the very processes—such as conversational interaction—by which this thing called curiosity always escapes definition. But, amidst the welter of early modern discourse, texts like *Célinte* were squarely in the minority.

Many of the purposes for which curiosity was used were not themselves verbal, at least not entirely so—Boccone was hoping both to enter communicative networks of exchange in Paris and yet also to earn money. Indeed, this survey of uses of curiosity shows that the verbal and the non-verbal dimensions of their projected outcomes were often, if not coextensive, then at least inseparable. For example, discourse on curiosity did not only represent such hoped-for outcomes but was also itself sometimes incorporated into the very voices or bodies of their outcomes' intended beneficiaries: Genlis's play warning against female curiosity was performed by her daughters, who were among those whom the play was intended to train morally. Similarly, in 1737 the annual prize-giving ceremony of Louis-le-Grand was the culminating scene in the college's ballet on curiosity, with that year's prize-winners embodying virtuous curiosity. In both cases the text became, in a sense, part of its own projected outcome. This also happened, in other ways, with texts that were designed to be the printed raw material for subsequent oral speech-acts, since readers were supposed to memorize them and then introduce them into real-life situations. For example, Bary's curious fragments of physics were designed to be recycled in conversation, where they would ensure social success; Camus's commonplaces on curiosity were designed to be re-applied elsewhere, say in sermons; and even printed sermons on curiosity were designed to be spoken on numerous specific occasions, probably in modified, localized form. In many cases, the immediate projected outcomes were both oral and written: the jurisprudential discussions of curiosity in Brandenburg-Prussian universities probably fed into the framing of state policies, princely counsel, and even—occasionally—positive laws.

Although many other terms were also enlisted for similar purposes, the singularity of the 'curiosity' family of terms gave it a unique role in regulating knowledge and behaviour. And it was often so emotive, so highly charged, so explicitly and lengthily contested, so self-consciously wielded, and in German so visually distinct (like other exotic terms) from the surrounding Gothic text thanks to its roman type that it developed a partial 'lexical membrane',[3] making it less unobtrusively immersed in the flow of printed texts than were many other terms. On the other hand, the approach that I have applied to curiosity could be extended to numerous other terms.

If the case of early modern curiosity is anything to go by, then 'concepts', in the usual senses of the term, do not exist within the flow of history. What did exist in the early modern period were innumerable attempts to intervene in the world by constantly contesting the meanings of words and thereby the shapes of the things, such as curiosity, to which those words were believed to refer. And who is to say that they did not somehow refer to them, even if dimly and imperfectly, in ways that eluded human understanding then and continue to do so now?

However, concepts (in the usual senses) are perhaps fictions that are indispensable to the study *of* history, heuristic tools for probing the past. Indeed, the present study has applied many to the early modern period, some openly anachronistic (such as 'early modern' itself), others less so (such as 'accommodation'). Only in relation to the 'curiosity' family of terms have I tried throughout to follow the contours of the period's ordinary language, rather than reorganizing the contours myself into those of a concept. Once one stops trying to discover concepts and their 'empty coherence' in the past, then the inventiveness, dynamism, and irreducible particularism of early modern uses of curiosity become more visible.[4] The endless reshaping of curiosity was a process in which every single writer who used this family of terms participated—albeit to enormously varying extents—but over which no writer had full control. Since this process was unresolvable, it seems only fitting to give the last word to a philosopher who stresses the impossibility of last words:

it is clear that every sentence in our language 'is in order as it is'. That is to say, we are not *striving after* an ideal, as if our ordinary vague sentences had not yet got a quite unexceptionable sense, and a perfect language awaited construction by us. (Wittgenstein 1968, § 98, p. 45)

---

[3] The phrase is coined in Hobson 1998, 3.
[4] The quotation is from the poet Yves Bonnefoy: 'ces concepts . . . tout cela ne m'est plus qu'une cohérence vide' (1967, 96).

Bibliography

Primary sources
1. German university dissertations and orations devoted to *curiositas, curiosa, polypragmosyne, periergia*
2. General

Secondary sources

Note: Library shelfmarks are given for manuscripts or especially rare books. Unless stated otherwise, the place of publication given is the one indicated on the title-page, which does not always necessarily mean that the work really was published there.

Abbreviations

ADB	*Allgemeine deutsche Biographie* (56 vols.; 1967–71; repr.)
BL	British Library
BNFr	Bibliothèque Nationale de France
Bod.	Bodleian Library, Oxford
BSB	Bayerische Staats-Bibliothek, Munich
CUL	Cambridge University Library
DBE	*Deutsche biographische Enzyklopädie*, ed. W. Killy (Munich, 1995–)
HAB	Herzog August Bibliothek, Wolfenbüttel
NDB	*Neue deutsche Biographie* (Berlin, 1953–)
Curiosité et 'libido sciendi'	*Curiosité et 'libido sciendi' de la Renaissance aux Lumières*, ed. N. Jacques-Chaquin and S. Houdard (2 vols.; Fontenay-aux-Roses, 1998)

PRIMARY SOURCES

1. German university dissertations and orations devoted to curiositas, curiosa, polypragmosyne, periergia

BIERLING, KONRAD FRIEDRICH ERNST (*praeses*)/PESTEL, FRIEDRICH WILHELM (*resp.*) (1740). *Dissertatio de curiositate circa veritatis scrutinium moderanda*, Philosophy Faculty, Univ. of Rinteln, held 1740 (Rinteln). Bod.: Diss.K.180(6).

BRÜCKNER, GEORG HEINRICH (*praeses*)/BRANDIS, JOHANN AUGUST (*resp.*) (1687). *Dissertatio academica continens curiosa juris feudalis*, Law Faculty, Univ. of Erfurt, held 1687 (Erfurt). Bod.: Diss.P 34(19).

BRÜCKNER, GEORG HEINRICH (*praeses*)/SCHULTZ, JACOB (*resp.*) (1688). *Curiosa juris publici*, Law Faculty, Univ. of Erfurt, held 1688 (Erfurt). Bod.: Diss.DD 7(15).

[BRUNNEMANN, JOHANN (*praeses*)]/HENEL, CHRISTIAN (*resp.*) (1691). *Dissertationum juridicarum de πολυπραγμοσυνη, germ: Einmischung in mancherley Haendel, et de partu ancillae furtivae . . . editio tertia*, Law Faculty, Univ. of Frankfurt a.d. Oder, held 1670 (Frankfurt a.d. Oder). HAB: Xb 637. The *polypragmosyne* dissertation was also printed in 1670 (twice) and in 1672 (all Frankfurt a.d. Oder).

COCCEJI, HEINRICH VON (*praeses*)/LETTOW, JOHANN ERNST VON (*resp.*) (1710). *Disputatio solennis juridica, occasione L. 3.§ 9. vers. Curiosus esse debet creditor quo vertatur pecunia. ff. à. in rem verso. De curiositate legali proficua*, Law Faculty, Univ. of Frankfurt a.d. Oder, held 1696 (Frankfurt a.d. Oder). HAB: Li 1453. Also printed in 1696 (presumably) and in 1702.

FICHTNER, JOHANN GEORG (*praeses*)/PUCHELBERGER, JOHANN FRIEDRICH (*resp.*) (1725). *Dissertatio iuridica de periergia*, Law Faculty, Univ. of Altdorf, held 1725 (Altdorf). HAB: Li 2488.

FRIESE, FRIEDRICH (*praeses*)/RITTER, JOHANN CARL (*resp.*) (1691). *Dissertationem physicam de curiosa et superstitiosa rusticorum physica . . . submittit . . . Johann Carl Ritter*, Philosophy Faculty, Leipzig, 1691 (Leipzig). BNFr: S.6399.

HENRICI, HEINRICH (*praeses*)/FRANTZ, GOTTFRIED ELIAS (*resp.*) (1709). *Dissertationem inauguralem medicam, qua in curiositatis physico-medicae nimiae originem et naturam inquiritur . . . exponet autor et respondens*, Medical Faculty, Univ. of Halle, held 1709 (Halle). BL: T.512(20).

HILSCHER PAUL CHRISTIAN (*praeses*)/CRAMER CHRISTIAN (*resp.*) (1693). *De περιεργια, seu inani studio eruditorum αποσπασματια*, Philosophy Faculty, Univ. of Leipzig, held 1693 (Leipzig). HAB: Li 1580.

JOCH, JOHANN GEORG (*praeses*)/SEYFART, ACHAZ (*resp.*) (1708). *Περι τες πολυπραγμοσυνες dissertatio*, Philosophy Faculty, Univ. of Jena, held 1708 (Jena). Dresden: Sächsische Landesbibliothek: Philos.C.211,10.

KRAUSE, RUDOLF WILHELM (1709). *Propempticon inaugurale de curiositate in medicina laudanda*, Medical Faculty, Univ. of Jena, held 1709 (Jena). HAB: Mx 113(67).

KROMAYER, HIERONYMUS (*praeses*)/SCHERZER, JOHANN ADAM (*praeses*)/ RECHENBERG, ADAM (*resp.*) (1675). *Biga dissertationum de malesana et sana in theologia curiositate*, both Theology Faculty, Univ. of Leipzig, held 1668 (*De insana in theologia curiositate*, under Kromayer) and 1672 (*Sana in theologia curiositas*, under Scherzer) (Jena). BL: 491.b.16(9). First printed in 1668 (*De insana...*) and 1672 (*Sana...*).

MITTERNACHT, JOHANN SEBASTIAN (*praeses?*) (1667). *Dissertatiuncula de curiositate quorumdam interpretum S. Scripturae, Judaeorum praecipue*, Gymnasium Rutheneum, Gera, 1667 (Gera). BSB: 4 Diss.518(32).

OLEARIUS, JOHANN FRIEDRICH (*praeses*)/SCHLEGEL, CHRISTIAN BENJAMIN (*resp.*) (1725). *Dissertationem juridicam de culpa ex πολϑπραγμοσϑνη occas. L.XXXVI. Digest. de r. j.... submittit a. et r.*, Law Faculty, Univ. of Leipzig, 1725 (Leipzig). HAB: Li 7924.

ORTLOB, JOHANN CHRISTOPH (*praeses*)/FUCHS THEODOSIUS GOTTFRIED (*resp.*) (1708). Περιεργα Εφεσιων, *sive Dissertatio philologica, de Ephesiorum libris curiosis combustis, ad Act. Apost. XIX, 19*, Philosophy Faculty, Leipzig, held 1708 (Leipzig). HAB: Td Kapsel 3(1).

RINDER, ANDREAS (*praeses*)/LASIUS, LORENZ OTTO (*resp.*) (1699). *Exercitatio academica de moderatione curiositatis in inquirenda veritate*, Philosophy Faculty, Univ. of Helmstedt, held 1699 (Helmstedt). HAB: Xb 3357.

ROSTEUSCHER, JOHANN CHRISTOPH (*praeses*)/SCHELGWIG, JOHANN (*resp.*) (1692). *De immoderata philosophi curiositate*, Philosophy Faculty, Gymnasium Academicum, Danzig, held 1692 (Danzig). Dresden, Sächsische Landesbibliothek: Philos.A.202,40.

SCHALLER, JAKOB (*praeses*)/HUBER, JOHANN (*resp.*) (1670). Πολϑπραγμοσϑνη *in medium producta, ex Plutarcho potissimum*, Philosophy Faculty, Univ. of Strasbourg, held 1670 (Strasbourg). BNFr: RZ-269(43).

SCHAPER, JOHANN ERNST (*praeses*)/BARNSTORFF, JOHANN GEORG (*resp.*) (1711). *Dissertatio circularis medica, sistens medicinae curiosae specimen, duabus quaestionibus enodatum*, Medical Faculty, Univ. of Rostock, held 1711 (Rostock). BL: 1179.d.18(1).

SCHAPER, JOHANN ERNST (*praeses*)/EGGEBRECHT, KARL NIKOLAUS (*resp.*) (1713). *Dissertatio circularis medica, exhibens medicinae curiosae specimen, duabus quaestionibus enodatum*, Medical Faculty, Univ. of Rostock, held 1713 (Rostock). BL: 1179.d.18(5).

SCHAPER, JOHANN ERNST (*praeses*)/GERMANN, JOHANN GOTTFRIED (*resp.*) (1705). *Dissertatio circularis medica, exhibens medicinae curiosae specimen, duabus quaestionibus*, Medical Faculty, Univ. of Rostock, held 1705 (Rostock). BL: 1179.d.16(4).

SCHAPER, JOHANN ERNST (*praeses*)/NEUCRANTZ, PAUL BERNHARD (*resp.*) (1703). *Dissertatio circularis medica, exhibens medicinae curiosae specimen, duabus quaestionibus enodatum*, Medical Faculty, Univ. of Rostock, held 1703 (Rostock). BL: 1179.d.16(3).

SCHAPER, JOHANN ERNST (*praeses*)/SCHAPER, JOHANN LUDWIG (*resp.*) (1712). *Dissertatio circularis medica, sistens medicinae curiosae specimen, duabus quaestionibus enodatum,* Medical Faculty, Univ. of Rostock, held 1712 (Rostock). BL: 1179.d.18(2).

SCHERZER, JOHANN ADAM (jurist) (1730). *Procancellarius . . . disputationem inauguralem . . . a . . . Carolo Rudolpho Graefe . . . habendam . . . indicit simulque de περιεργια jctorum nonnulla disserit,* Law Faculty, Univ. of Leipzig, held 1730 (Leipzig). HAB: Li 3050(2).

SCHERZER, JOHANN ADAM (theologian): see above, under 'Kromayer'.

SCHERZER, JOHANN GEORG (*praeses*)/SALTZMANN, BALTHASAR FRIEDRICH (*resp.*) (1705). *Disputatio moralis de πολυπραγμοσυνη,* Philosophy Faculty, Univ. of Strasbourg, held 1705 (Strasbourg). BNFr: RZ-269(30).

SCHRADER, FRIEDRICH (1701). *De curiositate medica. Programma praelectionibus publicis de methodo medendi praemissum,* Medical Faculty, Univ. of Helmstedt, held 1701 (Helmstedt). BL: 1179.b.12(16).

SCHULZE, JOHANN HEINRICH (1720). *De περιεργια in anatomes studio vitanda pauca praefatus ad orationem inauguralem de anatomici studii iusta aestimatione,* Medical Faculty, Univ. of Altdorf, held 1720 (Altdorf). HAB: Mx 357(3).

SEGER, GEORG (1676). *Oratio inauguralis, de curiositate physica,* Medical Faculty, Gymnasium Academicum, Danzig, held 1675 (Danzig). BL: 1185.b.13(2).

SIBER, CHRISTIAN ANDREAS (*praeses*)/JACOBI, GEORG GOTTLIEB (*resp.*) (1685). *Ex philologia graeca de περιεργια Ephesiorum disputabit . . . respondens,* Philosophy Faculty, Univ. of Wittenberg, held 1685 (Wittenberg). HAB: Gf 118.

SILBERRAD, ELIAS (*praeses*)/CHRISTANN, JOHANN GEORG (*resp.*) (1714). *Meletema morale de curiositate,* Philosophy Faculty, Univ. of Strasbourg, held 1714 (Strasbourg). BNFr: RZ-244.

SIMON, JOHANN GEORG (*praeses*)/RÜHLE, JOHANN ESAIAS (*resp.*) (1674). *Curiosa Justinianea thesibus c. comprehensa* (in fact 50 *theses*), Law Faculty, Univ. of Jena, held 1674 (Jena). Bod.: Diss.DD 53(22). The next 50 *theses* seem to have been defended in 1675 (*Curiosa Justininanea per V. decades ostensa,* Jena, 1675), and all 100 were reprinted together in 1683.

STAHL, GEORG ERNST (*praeses*)/DONZELINA, GIOVANNI FRANCESCO (*resp.*) (1714). *Dissertatio inauguralis medica de medicina medicinae curiosae,* Medical Faculty, Univ. of Halle, held 1714 (Halle). BL: 1179.e.11(15).

STOLLE, GOTTLIEB (*praeses*)/SCHLOSSER, FRIEDRICH PHILIPP (*resp.*) (1724). *Tentamen philosophicum de curiositate,* Philosophy Faculty, Univ. of Jena, held 1724 (Jena). Erlangen, Universitätsbibliothek: Diss.A.S.17 (26).

STREIT, JOHANN PHILIPP (*praeses*)/KALCKHOFF, JOHANN CHRISTOPH (*resp.*) (1706). *Dissertatio inauguralis juridica de viro curioso*, Law Faculty, Univ. of Erfurt, held 1706 (Erfurt). Bod.: Diss.C 100(14).

STRYK, SAMUEL (*praeses*)/LÜEDECKE, URBAN DIETRICH (*resp.*) (1743). *De curiositate*, Law Faculty, Univ. of Frankfurt a.d. Oder, held 1677, in Stryk, *Dissertationum juridicarum Francofortensium volumen III* (Frankfurt a.d. Oder), 289–310. CUL: XXIII.1.15. Also printed in 1677 and 1690.

SUCCOV, SIMON GABRIEL (*praeses?*)/HAAG, JOHANN KARL AUGUST (*resp.*) (1744). *Dissertationis de moralitate curiositatis et epoches prima initia*, Philosophy Faculty, Univ. of Erlangen, held 1744 (Erlangen). BSB: 40Diss.960(1).

WALDSCHMIDT, JOHANN JAKOB (*praeses*)/KESSLER, JOHANN HERMANN (*resp.*) (1685). *Physicae curiosae et utilis specimen, exhibens miscellanea*, Philosophy Faculty, Univ. of Marburg, held 1685 (Marburg). BL: 1185.c.13(3).

WALDSCHMIDT, JOHANN JAKOB (*praeses*)/STIRNN, JAKOB (*resp.*) (1686). *Physicae curiosae et utilis specimen, de sensibus*, Philosophy Faculty, Univ. of Marburg, held 1686 (Marburg). BL: 1185.c.13(6).

WATSON, MICHAEL (*praeses*)/ROSE, ANDREAS (*resp.*) (1690). *Exercitatio academica de curiositate, ut est affectus, virtus, vitium*, Philosophy Faculty, Univ. of Frankfurt a.d. Oder, held 1652, in Daniel Hartnack (ed.), *Curiosa theologica* (Wedel), 745–98. BL: 1351.c.22. Also printed in 1652 (presumably), 1713, and 1735.

WESTPHAL, JOACHIM CHRISTIAN (*praeses*)/PIPPING, HEINRICH (*resp.*) (1708). *De curioso novitatis studio*, Philosophy Faculty, Univ. of Leipzig, held 1687 (in Pipping, *Exercitationes academicae juveniles*, Leipzig). CUL: 7240.d.115(1). Also printed in 1687.

ZEIBLICH, CHRISTOPH HEINRICH (*praeses*)/FEIND, BARTHOLD (*resp.*) (1700). *Ex prudentia morali de πολυπραγμοσύνῃ*, Philosophy Faculty, Univ. of Wittenberg, held 1700 [Wittenberg]. BSB: 40Diss.75(32).

2. General

AMES, WILLIAM (1630). *De conscientia, et eius iure, vel casibus* (Amsterdam).

——(1975). *Conscience with the Power and Cases Thereof* (Amsterdam). 1st edn. 1639.

ANDREAE, JOHANN VALENTIN (1621). *De curiositatis pernicie syntagma* (Strasbourg). 1st edn. 1620.

ANROUX, NAZARE (1662). *Sacree Apologie pour la bien-heureuse Ste Anne, et le bien-heureux Saint Joseph, mere et espoux de la Sainte Vierge Marie. Contre les trigamie et bigamie qui leurs sont imposées. Ou Responses aux questions curieuses meuës sur ce sujet* (Paris). BL: 862.d.29.

ARISTOTLE (1692). *La Poëtique*, tr. and commentary by André Dacier (Paris).

AUGUSTINE, SAINT (1659). *Les Confessions*, tr. René de Ceriziers (Paris). 1st edn. 1638.

——(1671). *Les Confessions*, tr. Robert Arnaud d'Andilly (Paris). 1st edn. 1649.

——(1968). *Confessions* (2 vols.; London and Cambridge, Mass.).

BACON, FRANCIS (1626). *Sylva sylvarum: or A Natural Historie* (London).

BAILLY, PIERRE (1628). *Questions naturelles et curieuses* (Paris).

BARKER, LAURENCE (1599). *Christs Checke to S. Peter for his Curious Question, Out of Those Words in Saint John: Quid ad te?* (London). BL: 4452.a.10.

BARY, RENÉ (1671). *La Physique* (3 vols.; Paris).

BAUDRAND, BARTHÉLEMY (1815). *Histoires édifiantes et curieuses, tirées des meilleurs auteurs* (Lyons). First published in the 1770s.

BEAUMARCHAIS, PIERRE-AUGUSTIN CARON DE (1957). *Théâtre. Lettres relatives à son théâtre*, ed. M. Allem and P. Courant (Paris).

BECMANN, JOHANN CHRISTOPH (1679). *Lineae doctrinae moralis de natura moralium variisque eorum casibus* (Frankfurt a.d. Oder and Berlin).

BEHRENS, GEORG HENNING ([1703]). *Hercynia curiosa oder curieuser Hartz-Wald, das ist Beschreibung der curieusen an und auf dem Hartz gelegenen Hölen, Seen, Bergen u. andern daselbst anzutreffenden Curiositäten* (Nordhausen).

BELEMNON (1728). *Curiöses Bauern-Lexicon, worinnen die meisten in unserer Teutschen Sprache vorkommende fremde Wörter erkläret* ([Frankfurt a. Main?]).

BERNARD OF CLAIRVAUX, SAINT (1854). *De gradibus humilitatis et superbiae tractatus*, in *Patrologiae cursus completus . . . Series secunda*, ed. J.-P. Migne, clxxxii (Paris), cols. 941–71.

BERNON, LÉONARD, SIEUR DE BERNONVILLE (1670). *Recueil des pieces curieuses apportées des Indes, d'Egypte et d'Ethiopie, qui se trouvent dans le cabinet de Leonard Bernon* (Paris).

BIRON, CLAUDE (1703). *Curiositez de la nature et de l'art, aportées dans deux voyages des Indes . . . Avec une relation abregée de ces deux voyages* (Paris).

BOCCONE, PAOLO (1671). *Recherches et observations curieuses sur la nature du corail blanc et rouge* (Paris).

BÖCLER GEORG ANDREAS [1664]. *Architectura curiosa nova* (Nuremberg).

[BOHSE, AUGUST] (1700). *Curieuses Hand-Buch allerhand auserlesener Send-Schreiben und mündlicher Complimenten vom allerneuesten Stylo in hohe Stands-Personen, Patronen, Frauenzimmer, und an seines Gleichen . . . zu gebrauchen* (Leipzig).

Boissard, Jean Jacques (1588). *Emblematum liber . . . Emblemes latins* (Metz). 1st edn. 1584.

'Bon-temps, Gerard' (1671). *La Gallerie des curieux; contenant en divers tableaux, les chef-d'aeuvres des plus excellens railleurs de ce siecle* (Lyons). Arsenal: 80B.20245. 1st edn. 1646.

Bordelon, Laurent (1710a). *De l'astrologie judiciaire. Entretien curieux* (Brussels). 1st edn. 1689.

[——] (1710b). *L'Histoire des imaginations extravagantes de Monsieur Oufle* (2 vols.; Amsterdam).

Bossuet, Jacques Bénigne (1709). *Politique tirée des propres paroles de l'écriture sainte à Monseigneur le Dauphin* (Paris).

——(1890–7). *Œuvres oratoires*, ed. J. Lebarq (7 vols.; Lille and Paris).

——(1930a). *Traité de la concupiscence*, ed. C. Urbain and E. Levesque (Paris).

——(1930b). *Maximes et réflexions sur la comédie*, ed. C. Urbain and E. Levesque (Paris).

Bouchel, Laurent (1616). *La Saincte Curiosité. Où sont contenuës les resolutions de plusieurs belles questions, tant sur ce qui s'est passé dez la creation du monde, que de ce qui adviendra lors du grand et dernier jugement* (Paris).

[Bougeant, Guillaume-Hyacinthe] (1730–7). *Observations curieuses sur toutes les parties de la physique, extraites et recueillies des meilleurs Mémoires* (3 vols.; Paris). Appeared from 1719 onwards. Probably continued by Nicolas Grozelier.

Bouteroue, Claude (1666). *Recherches curieuses des monoyes de France* (Paris).

Böving, Johann Georg (1712). *Curieuse Beschreibung und Nachricht von den Hottentotten* (n.p.).

Boyle, Robert (1744). *Works* (5 vols.; London).

Bräuner, Johann Jakob (1737). *Physicalisch- und historisch-erörterte Curiositaeten* (Frankfurt a. Main). 1st edn. 1735.

Brosse (1645). *Le Curieux impertinent ou Le Jaloux. Comedie* (Paris).

Brunfels, Otto (1520). *Confutatio sophistices et quaestionum curiosarum* (Schlettstadt).

Brunnemann, Johann (1663). *Commentarius in duodecim libros Codicis Justinianei* (Leipzig).

——(1672). *Tractatus juridicus de inquisitionis processu* (Wittenberg). 1st edn. 1647.

Buc'hoz, Pierre Joseph ([1790?]). *Collection precieuse et enluminée des fleurs, les plus belles et les plus curieuses* (2 vols.; Paris).

Buddeus, Johann Franz (1719a). *Institutiones theologiae moralis* (Leipzig). 1st edn. 1711.

BUDDEUS, JOHANN FRANZ (1719*b*). *Einleitung in die Moral-Theologie* (Leipzig). Translation of *Institutiones theologiae moralis.*

BUYS, JEAN (BUSAEUS, JOANNES) (1608). *Panarion, hoc est, arca medica variis divinae scripturae priscorumque patrum antidotis adversus animi morbos instructa* (Mainz).

CALVIN, JEAN (1985). *Advertissement contre l'astrologie judiciaire,* ed. O. Millet (Geneva). 1st edn. 1549.

CAMUS, JEAN-PIERRE (1609). *Les Diversitez,* ii (Paris).

——(1610). *Les Diversitez,* vi (Lyons).

——(1613). *Les Diversitez,* vii–viii (Paris).

——(1620). *Les Diversitez,* iii (Douai). 1st edn. 1610.

[——] (1635). *Les Esclaircissemens de Meliton sur les Entretiens curieux d'Hermodore, à la justification du Directeur desinteressé. Par le sieur de Saint Agatange* (2 vols.; n.p.).

——(1637). *Le Renoncement de soi-mesme. Esclaircissement spirituel* (Paris).

——(1640). *Le Voyageur inconnu. Histoire curieuse, et apologetique pour les religieux* (Paris). 1st edn. 1630.

CARLI, GIUSEPPE FLAMINIO (DIONIGI DA PIACENZA) (1692). *Der nach Venedig überbrachte Mohr, oder: Curiose und warhaffte Erzehlung und Beschreibung aller Curiositäten und Denckwürdigkeiten, welche dem . . . P. Dionysio Carli . . . in seiner etlich-jährigen Mission in allen vier Welt-Theilen, Africa, America, Asia, und Europa . . . aufgestossen* (Augsburg). (*Il moro trasportato nell'inclita città di Venetia,* 1687).

[CARREAU, MADEMOISELLE] (1813). *Les Heureux Mensonges, ou La Curiosité excusable* (Paris).

CARTER, ANGELA (1981). *The Bloody Chamber and Other Stories* (London). 1st edn. 1979.

CASTRO, GUILLÉN DE (1991). *El curioso impertinente,* eds. C. Faliu-Lacourt and M. L. Lobato (Kassel).

Catalogue of Curious but Prohibited Books, etc. Chiefly Modern ([1745?]; London).

CERIZIERS, RENÉ DE (1643). *La Sainte Curiosité, ou Questions curieuses, sur les principaux articles de la foy, mysteres de la religion et ceremonies de l'Eglise* (Paris). BNFR: D-11747.

CERVANTES, MIGUEL DE (1614). *L'Ingenieux Don Quixote de la Manche* (Paris), tr. Cesar Oudin. (*Don Quixote,* Part 1, 1605).

[CHEVANES, JACQUES DE (D'AUTUN, JACQUES)] (1634). *Les Entretiens curieux d'Hermodore et du voyageur inconnu . . . par le sieur de Sainct Agran* (Lyons).

COLLETET, FRANÇOIS (1663). *Le Palais des jeux, de l'amour et de la fortune* (Paris).

COLMAN, GEORGE, and MORTON, THOMAS (1983). *Plays* (Cambridge).

COLMENERO DE LEDESMA, ANTONIO (1643). *Du chocolate. Discours curieux* (Paris). (*Curioso tratado*, 1631).

[COLONNA, FRANCESCO] (1600). *Le Tableau des riches inventions couvertes du voile des feintes amoureuses, qui sont representees dans le Songe de Poliphile* (Paris). (*Hypnerotomachia Poliphili*, 1499).

COLONNA, FRANCESCO (1734). *Histoire naturelle de l'univers* (4 vols.; Paris).

COMIERS, CLAUDE (1694). *Pratique curieuse, ou Les Oracles des sibylles* (The Hague).

CONTANT, PAUL (1609). *Le Jardin, et cabinet poetique* (Poitiers). 1st edn. probably 1600.

[CONTI, NATALE] (1627). *Mythologie ou Explication des fables* (Paris). (*Mythologiae*, 1551).

CORBETTA, FRANCISCO (1639). *Degli scherzi armonici trovati, e facilitati in alcune curiosissime suonate sopra la chitarra spagnyola* (Bologna).

CORNEILLE, PIERRE (1971). *Théâtre complet*, ed. G. Couton (3 vols.; Paris).

[CORVINUS, GOTTLIEB SIGMUND] (1715). *Nutzbares, galantes und curiöses Frauenzimmer-Lexicon* (Leipzig). BL: 1037.i.i.

[COUSTOS, JOHN] ([1756]). *Procedures curieuses de l'inquisition de Portugal contre les francs-maçons* (n.p.) First appeared in English in 1746.

CRESPEL EMMANUEL (1742). *Voyages du R. P. Emmanuel Crespel, dans le Canada et son naufrage* (Frankfurt a. Main).

[CROUCH, NATHANIEL] (1682). *Admirable Curiosities[,] Rarities, and Wonders in England, Scotland, and Ireland* (London).

CROUSAZ, JEAN-PIERRE DE (1720). *La Logique, ou Systeme de reflexions, qui peuvent contribuer à la netteté et à l'étendue de nos connoissances . . . Seconde edition* (3 vols.; Amsterdam).

Curieuse Gedancken, von der wahren Alchymia (1702; n.p.)

La Curieuse impertinente, traduite de l'anglois (1789; 2 vols.; n.p.)

Der curieuse Kayserliche Staats-Courier (1741; Frankfurt a. Main).

Curieuse Nachricht von den schon vor vielen Jahren, auch in diesem 1747. Jahre zum Vorschein gekommenen Weyden-Rosen ([1747]; Erfurt).

Curieuse Unterredungen im Reiche der Todten, zwischen . . . Christian Gerbern, und . . . David Schwerd[t]nern (1732; Frankfurt and Leipzig). BNFR: M10572–10573.

Der curieusen Kunst- und Werck-Schül erster [anderer] Theil (1759–60; Nuremberg).

Curieuser Bericht, mit was vor Solennitäten Ihr. Röm. Käyserl. Maj. Josephus I. die . . . Chur-Fürsten von Kölln und Bayern . . . in die Kayserliche und des Heil. Röm. Reichs Acht und Ober-Acht öffentlich erklären lassen (1706; n.p.).

Curieuser Geschichts-Calender, darinnen die vornehmsten Thaten und Geschichte der großmächtige Könige in Schweden . . . zusammen getragen und in beliebter Kürtze vorgestellet werden (1698; Leipzig).

Curieuser Raritäten-Kasten, in welchen vorgestellet wird die Wind-Macherey (1733; Leipzig). BL: 12316.ee.12.

Le Curieux satisfait contenans soit epigramme et epitaphe[,] enigme et autre chose pour pass[er] le temps ([18th-century]; manuscript). Arsenal: MS 2784.

Der curiose Chymicus, oder Curioses Laboratorium Medico Chymicum, etc. Der curiose Medicus, oder sonderbahre curiose Anleitung zur Medicin, etc. Der curiose Chirurgus, oder Curioser Begriff der Wund-Artzney (1706; Dresden and Leipzig).

La Curiosité fructueuse (1739; Paris). Bibliothèque universitaire de médecine, Paris: 90958, t.513, no.6.

La Curiosité; or, The Gallanté Show (1797; London).

Curiosités de l'église de Notre-Dame de Paris (1753; Paris).

Curiosités des maeurs et coutumes des peuples (n.d.; n.p.).

Curiosités historiques, ou Recueil de pieces utiles à l'histoire de France, et qui n'ont jamais paru (1759; 2 vols.; Amsterdam).

Curious and Authentic Memoirs Concerning a Late Peace, Concluded Between the Rooks and the Jackdaws (1763; London).

DADRÉ, JEAN (1603). *Loci communes similium et dissimilium* (Cologne). 1st edn. 1577.

[DAMPIERRE DE LA SALE] (1787). *Théâtre d'un amateur* (2 vols.; Paris).

DANCOURT, FLORENT CARTON (1729). *Les Œuvres. Troisiéme edition* (9 vols.; Rouen and Paris).

DANNHAUER, JOHANN KONRAD (1642). *Idea boni interpretis et malitiosi calumniatoris* (Strasbourg). Dedication dated 1630.

——(1654). *Hermeneutica sacra sive methodus exponendarum S. Literarum proposita & vindicata* (Strasbourg).

DANNHAUER JOHANN KONRAD (*praeses*)/PICHLER WOLFGANG (*resp.*) (1664). *Gallionismus ex Actor. cap. XIIX, vers. 12. 13. 14. 15. 16. illustratus & profligatus*, Theology Faculty, Univ. of Strasbourg, held 1664 (Strasbourg).

D'ASSONLEVILLE, HUBERT (1625). *Alphabeticum curiositatis promtuarium* (Douai).

DAULIER DESLANDES, ANDRÉ (1673). *Les Beautez de la Perse, ou La Description de ce qu'il y a de plus curieux dans ce royaume* (Paris).

D'AULNOY, MARIE-CATHERINE (1997). *Contes I*, ed. P. Hourcadé (Paris).

DEBURE, GUILLAUME-FRANÇOIS (1763–82). *Bibliographie instructive: ou Traité de la connoissance des livres rares et singuliers* (10 vols.; Paris).

DESCARTES, RENÉ (1963–73). *Œuvres philosophiques* (3 vols.; Paris; 1963–73).

——(1990). *Les Passions de l'âme*, ed. M. Meyer and B. Timmermans (Paris).

DESTOUCHES, PHILIPPE NÉRICAULT (1757). *Œuvres dramatiques* (4 vols.; Paris).

DEXELIUS, GOTTFRIED (1699). *Colloquia historica curiosa das ist Neu-historische curiöse Gesprächs-Lust* (Dresden and Leipzig).

DIDEROT, DENIS (1951). *Œuvres*, ed. A. Billy (Paris).

Die den Frauenzimmer-Schmuck liebende und auserlesne Künste übende Cammer-Jungfer. Das ist: Curieuses und höchstnützliches Werklein (1703; Nuremberg).

DU BOSC, JACQUES (1665). *L'Honneste Femme* (Lyons). 1st edn. 1632.

DU CHESNE, ANDRÉ (1609). *Les Antiquitez et recherches des villes, chasteaux, et places plus remarquables de toute la France* (Paris).

DU HEAULME, PIERRE (1641). *Methode nouvelle et infallible pour faire toutes sortes de quadrans* (Paris).

DU PLEIX, SCIPION (1635). *La Curiosité naturelle* (Rouen). 1st edn. 1606.

DU SOUCY, FRANÇOIS, SIEUR DE GERZAN (1650). *Les Profitables Curiositez inouyes* (Paris). 1st edn. 1649.

DU SOUHAIT, FRANÇOIS (1600). *Le Bonheur des sages/Le Malheur des curieux* (Lyons).

Entretiens curieux touchant les plus secrete[s] affaires de plusieurs cours de l'Europe (1674; Cologne).

ERNST, JAKOB DANIEL (1694). *Lectiones historico-morales curiosae oder Curiöse historische Blumen-Lese* (Leipzig).

L'Esprit curieux, ou Melange divertissant de tours subtils et de secrets naturels (1712; Paris).

ESTIENNE, CHARLES (1603). *Dictionarium historicum, geographicum, poeticum* ([Geneva]). 1st edn. 1553.

ESTIENNE, ROBERT (1546). *Dictionarium latinogallicum* (Paris). 1st edn. 1538.

Every Lady's own Fortune-Teller (1793; London).

FABER, MATTHIAS (1643). *Opus concionum* (3 vols.; Antwerp). 1st edn. 1631.

FABRICIUS, JOHANN (1707). *Curieuse Frage bey dem Heyrahten, ob man in der catholischen Religion könne seelig werden?* (Cologne). HAB: Gn Sammelbd 21(2).

[FASSMANN, DAVID] (1718). *Curieuse Nachricht von denen zweyen in England einander hefftig zuwider seyenden Partheyen derer Whigs und Torys* (Leipzig).

FÉNELON, FRANÇOIS DE SALIGNAC DE LA MOTHE (1983–97). *Œuvres*, ed. J. Le Brun (2 vols.; Paris).

FERRAND, JACQUES (1623). *De la maladie d'amour* (Paris). 1st edn. 1612.

FLEURY, CLAUDE (1686). *Traité du choix et de la méthode des études* (Paris).

FONTENELLE, BERNARD LE BOVIER, SIEUR DE (1989–). *Œuvres complètes*, ed. A. Niderst (Paris).

[FOUILLOU, JACQUES] (1735). *Reflexions sur la requeste de la nommée Charlote, et la consultation des avocats qui y est jointe. Où l'on examine cette curieuse question: S'il est vraisemblable que Dieu ait donné à cette convulsionnaire le don miraculeux des guérisons, comme elle le prétend dans sa requeste* ([Paris]). BL: 697.i.14(4).

FRAMERY, NICOLAS-ÉTIENNE (1754). *Nanette et Lucas, ou La Paysanne curieuse* (Paris).

FRANCISCI, ERASMUS (1673–4). *Die lustige Schau-Bühne von allerhand Curiositäten* (3 vols.; Nuremberg). 1st edn. 1663–73.

[FUZELIER, LOUIS] [1711]. *Le Curieux impertinent[.] Divertissement representé [à] la foire de St Germain* (manuscript). BNFR: Fonds français 25476 (sigs. 36ʳ–43ᵛ).

GAFFAREL, JACQUES (1637). *Curiositez inouyes* (Paris). 1st edn. 1629.

——(1676). *Curiositez inouyes, hoc est: Curiositates inauditae*, tr. and ed. Gregor Michael (Hamburg).

——(1706). *Curiositates inauditae*, tr. and ed. Michael, with preface by Johann Albert Fabricius (Hamburg).

GARASSE, FRANÇOIS (1971). *La Doctrine curieuse des beaux esprits de ce temps.* (2 vols.; Farnborough). 1st edn. 1623.

GARMANN, CHRISTIAN FRIEDRICH ([1691]). *Oologia curiosa* (Zwickau).

GARZONI, TOMMASO (1586). *Le Theatre des divers cerveaux du monde* (Paris). (*Il theatro de vari, e diversi cervelli mondani*, 1583).

GEDNER, CHRISTOPH ELIAS (1762). 'Of the Use of Curiosity', in Benjamin Stillingfleet (ed.), *Miscellaneous Tracts Relating to Natural History, Husbandry, and Physick* (London), 161–200. Gedner piece dated 1752.

[GENLIS, MADAME DE] (1783). *Théatre de société* (2 vols.; Dublin). 1st edn. 1781.

——(1825–8). *Mémoires inédits* (8 vols.; Paris).

GRANADA, LUIS DE (1586). *Sylva locorum communium* (Lyons). 1st edn. 1585.

[GREGORII, JOHANN GOTTFRIED] (1712). *Der curieuse und gelehrte Historicus* (Frankfurt a. Main and Leipzig).

——(1713). *Curieuse Gedancken von den vornehmsten und accuratesten Alt- und Neuen Land-Charten* (Frankfurt a. Main and Leipzig).

——(1715). *Die curieuse Orographia, oder Accurate Beschreibung derer berühmtesten Berge* (Frankfurt a. Main and Leipzig).

GRIFFITH, THOMAS (1760). *The Evils Arising From Misapply'd Curiosity. A Sermon Preached Before the University of Oxford, at St Mary's, on Sunday March 9. 1760* (Oxford).

HABANC, VÉRITÉ (1989). *Nouvelles Histoires tant tragiques que comiques* (Geneva), ed. J.-C. Arnould and R. Carr. 1st edn. 1585.

HALCKE, PAUL ([1718]). *Verbesserter Hamburgischer Curiositäten-Calender, auff das 1719. Jahr Christi* (Hamburg).

HALLEY, EDMOND (ed.) (1705–7). *Miscellanea curiosa. Being a Collection of Some of the Principal Phaenomena in Nature* (3 vols.; London).

HAPPEL, EBERHARD WERNER (1683–9). *Gröste Denkwürdigkeiten der Welt oder so genannte Relationes curiosae* (Hamburg). It continued to appear until 1691.

[HARCOUET DE LONGEVILLE] (1722). *Long Livers: A Curious History of Such Persons of Both Sexes who have Liv'd Several Ages, and Grown Young Again* (London). (*Histoire des personnes*, 1715).

HARTNACK, DANIEL (1685). *Curiosa naturae seu Admiranda physica* (Frankfurt a. Main and Leipzig).

——(ed.) (1690). *Curiosa theologica . . . Theologische Curiositäten* (Wedel).

[HAYWOOD, ELIZA] (1724). *The Masqueraders; or Fatal Curiosity: being the Secret History of a Late Amour* (London).

HELLWIG, CHRISTOPH VON (1702). *Auf hundert Jahr gestellter curiöser Calender* (Erfurt).

——(1704). *Curiöse Beschreibung unterschiedlicher rarer und schöner physic. medicinischer, chymischer und aeconomischer Dinge* (Frankfurt a. Main and Leipzig).

——(1711). *Exotica curiosa, oder: Curiöse und nützliche Beschreibung derer ausländischen Dinge* (Erfurt).

——(1710–11). *Casus et observationes medicinales, anatomicae, chymicae, chirurgicae, physicae, etc. rariores, selectae et curiosae* (Frankfurt a. Main and Leipzig).

——(1718). *Neue und curieuse Schatz-kammer aeconomischer Wißenschafften* (Frankfurt a. Main and Leipzig).

——(1738). *Der curieuse und wohl-erfahrne Chymist* (Leipzig and Arnstadt). 1st edn. 1729.

HERODOTUS (1966). *Herodotus*, with a translation by A. D. Godley (4 vols.; London and Cambridge, Mass.). 1st edn. 1920.

HIETLING, CONRAD (1713). *Peregrinus affectuose per terram sanctam et Jerusalem a Devotione et Curiositate conductus* (Augsburg). BL: 985.h.14.

The History of Blue Beard, or, The Fatal Effects of Curiosity and Disobedience ([1810]; London).

HOHBERG, WOLFGANG HELMARD VON (1715–16). *Georgica curiosa aucta* (3 vols.; Nuremberg). 1st edn. 1682.

HÖPFNER, HEINRICH (1674). *Idea veri theologi* (1st edn. 1628), in *Memoriae theologorum nostri seculi clarissimorum renovatae*, ed. Henning Witte (Frankfurt a. Main).

[HORTENSIUS LAMBERTUS] (1695). *Histoire des Anabatistes ou Relation curieuse de leur doctrine, regne et revolutions* (Paris). Translation of *Tumultuum Anabaptistarum* (1548).

[HUGUETAN, JEAN, and SPON, JACOB] (1681). *Voyage d'Italie curieux et nouveau, enrichi de deux listes* (Lyons).

[HUHOLD, MARCUS PAUL] (1716). *Curieuse Nachricht von denen heute zu Tage grand mode gewordenen J[ou]rnal- Quartal- und Annual-Schrifften* ([Jena]). 1st edn. 1715 or earlier.

HUNOLD, CHRISTIAN FRIEDRICH (1978). *Der Europaeischen Höfe, Liebes- und Helden-Geschichte*, ed. H. Wagener (2 vols.; Bern; repr.). 1st edn. 1705.

HUTTER, LEONHARD (1614). *Calvinista aulico-politicus alter* (Wittenberg).

JANSEN, CORNELIUS (1641). *Augustinus* (3 vols. in one; Paris). 1st edn. 1640.

——(1659). *Traduction d'un discours de la reformation de l'homme interieur* [tr. Robert Arnaud d'Andilly] (Paris). *Privilège* dated 1642.

JAUGEON, LE SIEUR (1684). *Le Jeu du monde ou L'Intelligence des plus curieuses choses qui se trouvent dans tous les estats, les terres, et les mers du monde* (Paris).

[JOB, JOHANN GEORG] (1717). *Anleitung zu denen curiösen Wißenschafften* (Frankfurt a. Main and Leipzig).

JONSON, BEN (1998). *Every Man in his Humour*, ed. R. Watson, A. and C. Black (London and New York). First performed 1598.

[JURIEU, PIERRE] (1682). *La Politique du clergé en France, ou Entretiens curieux de deux catholiques romains, l'un parisien et l'autre provincial, sur les moyens dont on se sert aujourd'huy, pour destruire la religion protestante dans ce royaume* (The Hague). 1st edn. 1681.

JUVENAL D'ANAGNI (1680). *Manuductio neophyti, seu Clara et simplex instructio novelli religiosi* (Augsburg).

JUVENEL DE CARLENCAS, FÉLIX (1749). *Essais sur l'histoire des belles lettres, des s[c]iences et des arts* (4 vols.; Lyons). 1st edn. 1740–4.

KANOLD, JOHANN (ed.) (1718). *Sammlung von Natur- und Medicin- wie auch hierzu gehörigen Kunst- und Literatur-Geschichten* (Breslau). Appeared 1718–36.

——(ed.) (1728–9). *Supplementum II. Curieuser und nutzbarer Anmerckungen von Natur- und Kunst-Geschichten . . . gesammlet* (n.p.).

KELLNER, DAVID (1701). *Praxis metallica curiosa oder Curieus-angestellt, und experimentirte Schmeltz Proben* (Nordhausen).

K[ELLNER], D[AVID] (1715). *Collectanea chymico-metallurgica curiosa* (Leipzig).

LA BARRE, ANTOINE DE (1644). *Les Leçons publiques . . . Prises sur les questions curieuses et problematiques des plus beaux esprits de ce temps* (Leiden).

LA BRUYÈRE, JEAN DE (1962). *Les Caractères*, ed. R. Garapon (Paris). 1st edn. 1688.

LA CORETTERIE, C. SOURDON DE (n.d.). *Valville et Clarence—ou—La Curieuse* (manuscript). Arsenal: Rondel MS 552.

LAFAYETTE, MADAME DE (1970). *Romans et nouvelles*, ed. É. Magne and A. Niderst (Paris).

——(1990). *Œuvres complètes*, ed. R. Duchêne (Paris).

LA FONTAINE, JEAN DE (1966). *Fables*, ed. A. Adam (Paris). First published from 1668 onwards.

——(1991). *Les Amours de Psyché et de Cupidon*, ed. M. Jeanneret, in collaboration with S. Schoettke (Paris). 1st edn. 1669.

LAMBERT, JACQUES (1661–2). *La Morale des saints* (3 vols.; Paris). Appeared from 1756 onwards, under various titles, including *Les Reflexions du sage* (1662; 4 vols.; Lyons).

LA MOTHE LE VAYER, FRANÇOIS DE (1662). *Œuvres* (rev. edn.; 2 vols. in 3; Paris).

LA MOTTE, ANTOINE HOUDART DE (1719). *Fables nouvelles* (Paris).

LA PRIMAUDAYE, PIERRE DE (1581–90). *Academie françoise* (3 vols.; Paris). 1st edn. 1577.

LA ROCHEFOUCAULD, FRANÇOIS, DUC DE (1714). *Curious Amusements* (London). Partly a translation of La Rochefoucauld's *Maximes*.

[LA SANTÉ, GILLES ANNE XAVIER DE] (1737). *La Curiosité, ballet moral* (Paris).

LA TAILLE, JEAN DE (1972). *Dramatic Works*, ed. K. M. Hall and C. N. Smith (London).

LAURENBERG, HANS VILLUMSEN (1677). *Description exacte et curieuse de l'ancienne et nouvelle Grèce* (Amsterdam). (*Graecia antiqua*, 1660).

LEFEBVRE, JACQUES (1689). *Les Plus Curieux Endroits de l'histoire* (Paris).

LEIBNIZ, GOTTFRIED WILHELM (1923–). *Sämtliche Schriften und Briefe* (Darmstadt).

LE LORRAIN DE VALMONT, PIERRE (1692). *Description de l'aimant, qui s'est formé à la pointe du clocher neuf de N. Dame de Chartres* (Paris).

——(1693). *La Physique occulte, ou Traité de la baguette divinatoire* (Paris).

——(1708). *Curiositez de la nature et de l'art sur la vegetation* (Paris). 1st edn. 1705.

LEMERY, NICOLAS (1684). *Recueil des curiositez rares et nouvelles des plus admirables effets de la nature et de l'art* (Leiden).

——(1685). *Le Nouveau Recueil de curiositez rares et nouvelles des plus admirables effets de la nature et de l'art* (Leiden).

——(1692). *Recueil de secrets* (Toulouse).

——(1694). *Nouveau Recueil des plus beaux secrets de medecine* (Paris).

LEMERY, NICOLAS (1709). *Nouveau Recueil de secrets et curiositez* and *Recueil des plus beaux secrets de medecine* (2 vols.; Amsterdam).

——(1737). *Nouveau Recueil des plus beaux secrets de medecine* (4 vols.; Paris).

[LENGLET-DUFRESNOY, NICOLAS] (1734). *De l'usage des romans . . . Avec une bibliotheque des romans* (2 vols.; [Rouen]).

L'ESPINE, JEAN DE (1588). *Excellens Discours . . . touchant le repos et contentement de l'esprit* (La Rochelle). 1st edn. 1587. Latin translation 1591.

LESSIUS, LEONARDUS (LEYS, LÉONARD) (1605). *De iustitia et iure caeterisque virtutibus cardinalibus* (Louvain).

L'ESTOILE, PIERRE DE (1880). *Mémoires-journaux*, ed. G. Brunet et al., viii (Paris).

A Letter on the Nature and State of Curiosity as at Present with Us (1736; London).

Lettre curieuse à un ami, dans laquelle on fait l'analise de la nouvelle théologie mystique du docteur Molinos . . . Nouvellement revûe, corrigée et augmentée (Dijon). BL: RB.23.a.215.

Lettre curieuse sur ce qui s'est passé de plus remarquable à Paris depuis le jour des roys (1649; Paris).

Lettres du Cardinal Mazarin (1690; Amsterdam).

LILLO, GEORGE (1737). *Fatal Curiosity: A True Tragedy of Three Acts* (London).

LINNAEUS (LINNÉ, CARL VON) (1972). *L'Équilibre de la nature*, tr. B. Jasmin, ed. C. Limoges (Paris).

LIPEN, MARTIN (1679–85). *Bibliotheca realis universalis* (Frankfurt a. Main). 1st edn. 1675–82.

LIPSIUS, JUSTUS (1615). *Oratio in calumniam* (London). 1st edn. 1607.

LOCKE, JOHN (1989). *Some Thoughts Concerning Education*, ed. J. W. and J. S. Yolton (Oxford).

Lotterie à la mode composée de cent lots tres-curieux ([1620–30?]; 'Brinda', = Brindas?).

LUCE, JOAN DE (1822). *Curiosity* (3 vols. in 1; London).

MAIMBOURG, LOUIS (1682). *Histoire du calvinisme* (Paris). 1st edn. also 1682.

MÄNNLING, JOHANN CHRISTOPH (1713). *Denckwürdige Curiositäten derer, so wohl inn- als ausländischer abergläubischen Albertäten* (Frankfurt a. Main and Leipzig).

——(1738). *Angenehme Schau-Bühne historischer Ergetzlichkeiten* (3 vols.; Breslau and Leipzig). 1st edn. 1720–1.

MARANDÉ, LÉONARD DE (1649). *Abbregé curieux et familier de toute la philosophie, logique, morale, physique et metaphysique: et des matieres plus importantes du theologien françois* (Lyons). 1st edn. 1647.

MARIVAUX, PIERRE CARLET DE CHAMBLAIN DE (1978). *La Vie de Marianne* (Paris). 1st edn. 1731–42.

[MARPERGER, PAUL JAKOB] (1727). *Curieuses und reales Natur- Kunst-Gewerck- und Handlungs-Lexicon* (Leipzig). 1st edn. 1712.

——([1730?]). *Anleitung zum rechten Verstand und nutzbarer Lesung allerhand so wohl gedruckter als geschriebener . . . Zeitungen oder Avisen, wie auch der so genannten Journalen* (n.p.).

MASEN, JAKOB (1672). *Utilis Curiositas de humanae vitae felicitate* (Cologne).

MAUPERTUIS, PIERRE LOUIS MOREAU DE (1752). *Œuvres* (Dresden).

MAURER, FELIX (1713). *Observationes curioso-physicae* (Nuremberg).

[MAYOLAS, SIEUR DE] (1699–71). *Lettre en vers et en prose, dediée et presentée au roy, contenant ce qui se passe de plus curieux dans l'Europe* (Paris).

MEDRANO, JULIANO DE (1583). *La silva curiosa* (Paris).

MÉNESTRIER, CLAUDE-FRANÇOIS (1704). *Bibliotheque curieuse et instructive de divers ouvrages anciens et modernes* (2 vols.; Trévoux).

MERCIER DE SAINT-LÉGER, BARTHÉLEMY (1763). *Lettre aux auteurs de ces Mémoires sur la 'Bibliographie instructive' de M. Debure*, in *Mémoires pour l'histoire des sciences et beaux-arts* (the *Journal de Trévoux*) (Trévoux; July), pp. 1617–82.

——(1783). *Lettres . . . sur différentes éditions rares du XVe. siècle* (Paris).

Mercure de France (1968; xxxiii, repr. of July–December 1737; Geneva).

Le Mercure voyageur, et le Politique curieux (1693; Cologne).

MERSENNE, MARIN (1985). *Questions inouyes* and other works, ed. A. Pessel (Paris).

Miscellanea curiosa medico-physica academiae naturae curiosorum sive Ephemeridum medico-physicarum germanicarum curiosarum annus primus (1670; Leipzig).

MOELLENBROCK, VALENTIN ANDREAS (1674). *Cochlearia curiosa* (Leipzig).

——(1676). *Cochlearia curiosa: or the Curiosities of Scurvygrass*, tr. Thomas Sherley (London).

MONTAIGNE, MICHEL DE (1962). *Essais*, in *Œuvres complètes*, ed. A. Thibaudet and M. Rat (Paris), [1]-1097.

MONTESQUIEU, CHARLES DE SECONDAT, BARON DE (1964). *Œuvres complètes*, ed. R. Caillois (2 vols.; [Paris]).

MORVAN DE BELLEGARDE, JEAN BAPTISTE (1707). *Lettres curieuses de litterature et de morale* (Amsterdam). 1st edn. 1702.

NEINER, JOHANN VALENTIN (1734). *Neu ausgelegter curioser Tändl-Marckt der jetzigen Welt* (Vienna and Brno).

Das neugierige und veränderte Teutschland (1988; n.p.; repr.). 1st edn. 1684.

NEWTON, WILLIAM ([1725]). *An Essay Against Unnecessary Curiosity in Matters of Religion. Apply'd Particularly to the Doctrine of the Blessed Trinity* (London).

NICERON, JEAN FRANÇOIS (1638). *La Perspective curieuse* (Paris).

NICOLE, PIERRE (1670). *De l'Education d'un prince* (Paris).

NICQUET, HONORAT (1648). *Physiognomia humana* (Lyons).

Die Niederländische Amazone oder Curieuse Lebens-Beschreibung und Helden-Thaten einer gewissen Weibs-Person (1717; Augsburg).

Nouveau Meslange de pieces curieuses (1664; Paris).

[OGIER, FRANÇOIS] (1623). *Jugement et censure du livre de la Doctrine curieuse* (Paris).

OLEARIUS, ADAM (1727). *Voyages très-curieux et très-renommez faits en Moscovie, Tartarie et Perse . . . Nouvelle edition* (Amsterdam). Tr. from German.

OSORIO DA FONSECA, JERONYMO (1666). *Theologie curieuse. Contenant la naissance du monde. Avec douze questions belles et curieuses sur ce sujet. Traduittes . . . par le Chevalier de Jant* (Dijon). BNFR: R13678.

PALMA-CAYET, PIERRE-VICTOR (1982). *L'Histoire prodigieuse du Docteur Fauste*, ed. Y. Cazaux (Geneva). 1st edn. 1598 or earlier. (*Faustbuch*, 1587.)

PASCAL, BLAISE (1727). *Thoughts on Religion, and Other Curious Subjects*, tr. Basil Kennet (London). 1st edn. 1704.

——(1963). *Œuvres complètes*, ed. L. Lafuma (Paris).

PASCH, GEORG (1695). *Schediasma de curiosis hujus seculi inventis* (Kiel).

PAULLINI, ANTON (1717–18). *Curieuses Cabinet ausländischer und anderer Merckwürdigkeiten* (Frankfurt a. Main and Leipzig).

PAULLINI, CHRISTIAN FRANZ (1685). *Cynographia curiosa seu Canis descriptio* (Nuremberg).

——(1686). *Bufo . . . descriptus* (Nuremberg).

——([1688]). *Sacra herba, seu Nobilis salvia* (Augsburg).

——(1691). *Lagographia curiosa, seu Leporis descriptio* (Augsburg).

——(1695). *De asino liber historico-physico-medicus* (Frankfurt a. Main).

——(1698). *Flagellum salutis, das ist: Curieuse Erzählung, wie mit Schlägen allerhand . . . Krnnckheiten . . . curiret worden* (Frankfurt a. Main).

——(1699). *Gaeographia curiosa, seu De pagis antiquae praesertim Germaniae commentarius* (Frankfurt a. Main).

——(1703a). *Anmuhtige lange Weile oder Allerhand feine, außerlesene, seltene und curieuse Discursen, Fragen und Begebenheiten* (Frankfurt a. Main).

——(1703b). *De candore* (Frankfurt a. Main and Leipzig).

——(1703c). *Disquisitio curiosa an mors naturalis plerumque sit substantia verminosa?* (Frankfurt a. Main and Leipzig).

——(1705*a*). *Kleine, doch curieuse Bauren-Physic* (Frankfurt a. Main and Leipzig).

——(1705*b*). *Historischer Wunder-Baum merckwürdiger Curiositäten* (Frankfurt a. Main and Leipzig).

——(1706). *Philosophische Lust-Stunden, oder, Allerhand schöne, anmutige, rare, so nützlich- als erbauliche, politische, physicalische, historische, u. d. geist- und weltliche Curiositäten* (2 vols.; Frankfurt a. Main and Leipzig).

PEIGNOT, ÉTIENNE GABRIEL (1804). *Curiosités bibliographiques* (Paris).

PERNETY, ANTOINE JOSEPH (1758). *Dictionnaire mytho-hermétique* (Paris).

PERRAULT, CHARLES (1967). *Contes*, ed. G. Rouger (Paris). 1st edn. 1697.

PERUCHIO, SIEUR DE (1657). *La Chiromance, la physionomie, et la geomance* (Paris).

PETIT, LE SIEUR (1702). *Les Curieux de province, ou L'Oncle dupé* (The Hague).

Pieces echapees du feu ou La Curiosité, la rar[e]té ([1750?]; n.p.).

PITHOYS, CLAUDE (1641). *Traitté curieux de l'astrologie judiciaire* (Sedan).

PLANARD, FRANÇOIS ANTOINE EUGÈNE DE (1807). *Le Curieux, comédie* (Paris).

[PLUCHE, NOËL ANTOINE] (1732–51). *Le Spectacle de la nature, ou Entretiens sur les particularités de l'histoire naturelle, qui ont paru les plus propres à rendre les jeunes-gens curieux, et à leur former l'esprit* (8 vols.; Paris). 1st edn. 1732–42.

'Plusieurs Curiositez trouvees dans le cabinet du Chevalier de Fourilles' ([1682?]; manuscript). Arsenal: MS 6543 (fo. 43r–v).

PLUTARCH (1971). *Les Œuvres morales et meslees* (2 vols.; Paris and The Hague; repr.), tr. Jacques Amyot. 1st edn. 1572.

POISSENOT, BÉNIGNE (1987). *L'Esté*, ed. G.-A. Pérouse and M. Simonin (Geneva).

PRAETORIUS, JOHANN [= SCHULTZE, HANS] (1713). *Collegium curiosum privatissimum physiognom-chiromant-metoposcop-anthropologicum* (Frankfurt and Leipzig). 1st edn. 1704.

PRÉVOST, ANTOINE-FRANÇOIS (1995). *Histoire du chevalier Des Grieux et de Manon Lescaut* (Paris). 1st edn. 1731.

PURLING, ERASMUS (1657). *Le Cabinet de la nature* (Paris).

Recueil de quelques pieces curieuses, servant à l'esclaircissment de l'histoire de la vie de la reyne Christine (1668; [Utrecht]).

Recueil des gazettes de l'année 1631 (1632; Paris).

Recueil des gazettes . . . de toute l'annee 1632 (1633; Paris).

REGNAULT, NOËL (1745–50). *Les Entretiens physiques d'Ariste et d'Eudoxe, ou Physique nouvelle en dialogues, qui renferme précisément ce qui s'est découvert de plus curieux et de plus utile dans la Nature* (5 vols.; Paris). 1st edn. 1729.

Relation curieuse de differens pays nouvellement decouverts (1741; Paris).

REUTER, CHRISTIAN (1964). *Schelmuffskys warhafftige curiöse und sehr gefährliche Reisebeschreibung zu Wasser und Lande*, ed. I.-M. Barth (Stuttgart). 1st edn. 1696.

RIVET, ANDREAS (1634). *Commentarii, in librum secundum Mosis, qui exodus apud Graecos inscribitur* (Leiden).

RIVET DE LA GRANGE, ANDRÉ, et al. (eds.) (1733–). *Histoire literaire de la France* (Paris).

[ROBERDAY] (1698). *La Curiosité dangereuse* (Paris).

ROUSSEAU, JEAN-JACQUES (1964). *Discours sur les sciences et les arts*, ed. F. Bouchardy, in *Œuvres complètes*, iii, ed. B. Gagnebin and M. Raymond (Paris), 1–107.

[RUNCKEL, ANDREAS WOLFGANG VON] (1727). *Curiose Erwegung der Worte Mosis Gen. VI*, 2 (Amsterdam). 2nd edn.?

Sächsiches Curiositäten-Cabinet, darinnen ... merckwürdige Begebenheiten aus der historia politica, ecclesiastica, artificiali, literaria und mixta, ingleichen aus der Genealogie, physica, oeconomia, mechanica, natura etc. anzutreffen (1731; 2 vols.; Dresden).

SALES, SAINT FRANÇOIS DE (1892–1964). *Œuvres* (27 vols.; Annecy).

SCHÄFFER, JOHANN BALTHASAR (1748). *Zwey gelehrte Robinson, oder Wahrhaffte und sehr curieuse Geschichte* (Frankfurt a. Main and Leipzig).

Schatzkammer rarer und neuer Curiositäten, in den aller-wunderbahresten Würckungen der Natur und der Kunst (1686; Hamburg). 1st edn. 1684.

SCHERZER, JOHANN ADAM (theologian) (1672). *Collegium anti-Socinianum CLIV disputationibus publicis absolutum* (Leipzig).

[SCHMIDT JOHANN GEORG] (1707). *Curiöse Speculationes bey schlaf-losen Nächten* (Chemnitz and Leipzig).

Schola curiositatis sive Antidotum melancholiae joco-serium ([after 1670]; n.p.). 1st edn. 1667.

SCHOTT, KASPAR (1664). *Technica curiosa, sive Mirabilia artis* (Würzburg).

——(1667). *Physica curiosa, sive Mirabilia naturae et artis* (Würzburg). 1st edn. 1662.

SCHULTZE, HANS: see PRAETORIUS, JOHANN (above).

SCHWIMMER, JOHANN MICHAEL (1672). *Ex physica secretiori curiositates* (Jena).

SCUDÉRY, MADELEINE DE (1979). *Célinte: Nouvelle première*, ed. A. Niderst (Paris). 1st edn. 1661.

Sehr curiose und denckwürdige Nachricht von den Solennitäten, Ceremonien und andern notablen Sachen, so bey dem Czarowitzischen-Beylager (1711; n.p.).

[SINOLD VON SCHÜTZ, PHILIPP BALTHASAR] (1698). *Das curieuse Caffe-Hauß zu Venedig* ('Freyburg').

SPIZEL, GOTTLIEB (1676). *Felix literatus* (Augsburg).

——(1680). *Infelix literatus* (Augsburg).

SPON, JACOB (1683). *Recherches curieuses d'antiquité* (Lyons). BL: G.2635.

[——] (1685). *Traitez nouveaux et curieux du café, du thé et du chocolate* (Lyons).

——see also HUGUETAN, JEAN (above).

SPRAT, T. (1959). *History of the Royal Society*, ed. J. I. Cope and H. W. Jones (St Louis and London). 1st edn. 1667.

[STERNE, LAURENCE] ([1759]–67). *The Life and Opinions of Tristram Shandy, Gentleman* (9 vols.; [York and London]).

STIELER, KASPAR (1969). *Zeitungs Lust und Nutz*, ed. G. Hagelweide (Bremen). 1st edn. 1695.

STURM, JOHANN CHRISTOPH (1676). *Collegium experimentale, sive curiosum* (Nuremberg).

SYDRAC (1531). *Mil IIII. vingtz et quatre demandes avec les solutions et responses a tous propoz, oeuvre curieux et moult recreatif* (Paris).

SZENTIVANYI, MARTON (1689–1709). *Curiosiora et selectiora variarum scientiarum miscellanea* (4 vols.; Tirnau).

TAHUREAU, JACQUES (1981). *Les Dialogues*, ed. M. Gauna (Geneva). 1st edn. 1565.

TENTZEL, WILHELM ERNST (1706). *Curieuse Bibliothec* (Frankfurt and Leipzig). Appeared 1704–6.

THÉVENOT, MELCHISEDECH (ed.) (1696). *Relations de divers voyages curieux* (2 vols.; Paris). 1st edn. 1663.

THOMASIUS, CHRISTIAN (1706). *Specimen jurisprudentiae judicialis ex jure naturae et gentium* (Halle and Leipzig).

——(1713). *Hoechstnoethige Cautelen welche ein studiosus juris, der sich zu Erlernung der Rechts-Gelahrheit auff eine kluge und geschickte Weise vorbereiten will, zu beobachten hat* (Halle). Dedication signed 1710.

THOMASIUS, JAKOB (1702). *Curiöse Gedancken, vom Dreßdnischen Peter* (Dresden and Leipzig). Tr. from Latin.

TILING, MATTHIAS ([1679]). *Rhabarbarologia seu Curiosa rhabarbari disquisitio* (Frankfurt a. Main).

——(1683). *Lilium curiosum, seu Accurata lilii albi descriptio* (Frankfurt a. Main).

TIPPER, JOHN (ed.) (1711). *Delights for the Ingenious: or, A Monthly Entertainment for the Curious of Both Sexes* (London).

TIRAQUEAU, ANDRÉ (1576). *De legibus connubialibus, et iure maritali* (Venice). 1st edn. 1513.

'TRANQUILLUS' (1705). *Rare auserlesene Historien und Curiositäten dieser Zeit* (2 vols.; Cologne).

Le Triomphe de Merlin ou La Rareté et la Curiosité (1787; manuscript). BNFR: Nouvelles acquisitions françaises 3003 (sigs. 115–29). First performed in 1783.

TRISMOSIN, SALOMON (1613). *La Toyson d'or* (Paris). 1st edn. 1612. (*Aureum vellus*, 1598).

TRITHEMIUS JOHANNES (1621). *Curiositas regia* (Douai).

TYLKOWSKI, WOJCIECH (1669a). *Philosophia curiosa. Seu Quaestiones et Conclusiones curiosae, ex universa Aristotelis philosophia, ad genium & ingenium huius saeculi formatae & propositae* (Cracow).

—— (1669b). *Meteorologia curiosa* (Cracow).

Unschuldige Nachrichten von alten und neuen theologischen Sachen (1702–19). Ed. Valentin Ernst Löscher (18 vols.; Leipzig).

'VALENTINE, BASIL' (1624). *Les Douze Clefs de philosophie* (Paris). Tr. from Latin.

VALLE, PIETRO DELLA (1665–70). *Les Fameux Voyages* (4 vols.; Paris). 1st edn. 1661–2. (*Viaggi*, 1650).

'VALLON, MONSIEUR DE' (1743). *Neu-eröffnete Lust- und Lehr-reiche Schau-Bühne* (Altdorf).

Véritable Origine des biens ecclésiastiques. Fragmens historiques et curieux (1790; Paris).

VERVILLE, FRANÇOIS BÉROALDE DE (1592). *Les Avantures de Floride* (Tours). Part 1.

—— (1597). *Le Restablissement de Troye* (Tours).

La Vie de la duchesse de La Valiere (1695; Cologne).

VILLAVICENCIO, LORENZO DE (1566). *Conciones in evangelia et epistolas, quae festis totius anni diebus populo in ecclesia proponi solent*, ed. Aegidius Dominicus Topiarius (Antwerp).

VIVES, JUAN LUIS ([1558?]). *The Office and Duetie of an Husband* (London). (*De officio mariti*, 1529).

VOIGT, GOTTFRIED (1668). *Curiositates physicae* (Güstrow).

Le Voyageur curieux qui fait le tour du monde. Avec ses matieres d'entretien qui composent l'histoire curieuse. Par le Sr le B. (1664; 2 vols.; Paris).

[VULSON DE LA COLOMBIÈRE, MARC, SIEUR DE] (1655). *Le Palais des curieux* (Troyes). 1st edn. 1646.

WEBER, JOHANN ADAM (1673). *Discursus curiosi et fructuosi* (Salzburg).

WEIDLING, CHRISTIAN (1701). *Curieuse und gründliche Moralite* (Leipzig).

WEISE, CHRISTIAN (1693). *Curiöse Gedancken von deutschen Versen* [Leipzig].

—— (1698). *Curiöse Gedancken von der Imitation* (Leipzig).

—— (1700). *Curieuse Fragen über die Logica* (Leipzig). 1st edn. 1696.

—— (1701). *Curiöse Gedancken von Wolcken-Brüchen* (Dresden and Leipzig). Tr. from Latin.

—— (1702). *Curiöse Gedancken von deutschen Briefen* (Leipzig and Dresden). 1st edn. 1691.

——(1703). *Curieuse Gedancken von den Nouvellen oder Zeitungen* (Frankfurt a. Main and Leipzig). (*Schediasma curiosum de lectione novellarum*, 1685). Tr. Christian Juncker.

WESTPHAL, JOACHIM (1573). *De vitanda curiositate oratio . . . in consessu ministrorum ecclesiae recitata* (Hamburg). HAB: Yv 625 Helmst.80(4).

WOHLHAUSEN JOHANN CHRISTOPH (1677). *Neu-erfundene mathematische und optische Curiositäten* (Leipzig).

[WOHLRAB, J.] (1733). *Curieuser Mischmasch* (n.p.).

[WOLCOT, JOHN] (1787). *Instructions to a Celebrated Laureat; alias The Progress of Curiosity* (London).

WOLLEY, HANNAH (1674). *Frauen-Zimmers Zeit-Vertreib, oder Reiches Gemach von außerlesenen Experimenten und Curiositäten betreffend die rechte Praeservir- und Candier-Kunst* (Hamburg). (*The Ladies Directory*, 1661.)

ZEDLER, JOHANN HEINRICH (1961–4). *Grosses vollständiges Universal-Lexikon* (62 vols.; Graz; repr.). 1st edn. 1732–51.

ZENNER, GOTTFRIED (1695). *Frühlings- [Sommer-, etc.]Parnaß, oder Abhandlung von viertzig galant-gelehrten Curiositäten* (Frankfurt a. Main and Leipzig). Appeared 1694–5.

SECONDARY SOURCES

ADAM, A. (1969). *Du Mysticisme à la révolte: Les Jansénistes au XVIIe siècle* (Paris).

ADELUNG, J. C. (1784–1897). *Fortsetzung und Ergänzungen zu Christian Gottlieb Jöchers allgemeinem Gelehrten-Lexicon* (7 vols.; Leipzig).

ÅKERMAN, S. (1998). *Rose Cross over the Baltic: The Spread of Rosicrucianism in Northern Europe* (Leiden, Boston, Cologne).

ALAND, K. (ed.) (1974). *Lutherlexikon* (3rd edn.; Vandenhoeck and Göttingen).

ALLWEISS, W. (1979). 'Von der Disputation zur Dissertation. Das Promotionswesen in Deutschland vom Mittelalter bis zum 19. Jahrhundert', in R. Jung and P. Kaegbein (eds.), *Dissertationen in Wissenschaft und Bibliotheken* (Munich), 13–28.

ALTHAUS, P. (1967). *Die Prinzipien der deutschen reformierten Dogmatik im Zeitalter der aristotelischen Scholastik* (Darmstadt; repr.). 1st edn. 1914.

AUSTIN, J. L. (1962). *How to do Things with Words* (Oxford).

BAL, M. (1994). 'Telling Objects: A Narrative on Collecting', in J. Elsner and R. Cardinal (eds.), *The Cultures of Collecting* (London), 96–115.

BALSIGER, B. (1970). 'The *Kunst- und Wunderkammern*: A Catalogue Raisonné of Collecting in Germany, France, and England, 1565–1750' (Ph.D. dissertation, Univ. of Pittsburgh).

BARNER, W. (1970). *Barockrhetorik: Untersuchungen zu ihren geschichtlichen Grundlagen* (Tübingen).

BATAILLON, M. (1947). 'Cervantès et le "mariage chrétien"', *Bulletin hispanique*, 49: 129–44.

BAUSINGER, H. (1963). 'Aufklärung und Aberglaube', *Deutsche Vierteljahrsschrift für Literaturwissenchaft und Geistesgeschichte*, 37: 345–62.

BAYLEY, P. (1980). *French Pulpit Oratory 1598–1650: A Study in Themes and Styles, with a Descriptive Catalogue of Printed Texts* (Cambridge).

——(ed.) (1983). *Selected Sermons of the French Baroque (1600–1650)* (New York and London).

——(1999). 'What was Quietism subversive of?', *Seventeenth-Century French Studies*, 21: 195–204.

BEELER, S. (1996). 'Johann Valentin Andreae', in J. Hardin (ed.), *Dictionary of Literary Biography*, clxiv: *German Baroque Writers, 1580–1660* (Detroit), 13–19.

BELLANGER, C., *et al.* (eds.) (1969–76). *Histoire générale de la presse française* (5 vols.; Paris).

BENEDICT, B. (1990). 'The "Curious Attitude" in Eighteenth-Century Britain: Observing and Owning', *Eighteenth Century Life*, 14: 59–98.

——(2001). *Curiosity: A Cultural History of Early Modern Inquiry* (Chicago and London).

BENHAMOU, R. (1987). 'From *Curiosité* to *Utilité*: The Automaton in Eighteenth-Century France', *Studies in Eighteenth-Century Culture*, 17: 91–105.

BEPLER, J. (1988). *Ferdinand Albrecht Duke of Braunschweig-Lüneburg (1636–1687): A Traveller and his Travelogue* (Wiesbaden).

BERRIOT-SALVADORE, E. (1990). *Les Femmes dans la société française de la Renaissance* (Geneva).

BERRY, C. J. (1994). *The Idea of Luxury: A Conceptual and Historical Investigation* (Cambridge).

BEUGNOT, B. (1988). 'La Curiosité dans l'anthropologie classique', in U. Döring, A. Lyroudias, and R. Zaiser (eds.), *Ouverture et dialogue: Mélanges offerts à Wolfgang Leiner* (Tübingen), 17–30.

BIRBERICK, A. L. (1999). 'Fatal Curiosity: D'Aulnoy's "Le Serpentin vert"', *Papers on French Seventeenth Century Literature*, 36: 282–8.

BLAIR, A. (2003). 'Curieux, curieusement, curiosité', *Littératures classiques*, 47: 101–7.

BLAUFUß, D. (1977). *Reichsstadt und Pietismus: Philipp Jacob Spener und Gottlieb Spizel aus Augsburg* (Neustadt a.d. Aisch).

BLÉCHET, F. (1991). *Les Ventes publiques de livres en France, 1630–1750: Répertoire des catalogues conservés à la Bibliothèque Nationale* (Oxford).

BLUM, W. (1969). *Curiosi und regendarii: Untersuchungen zur geheimen Staatspolizei der Spätantike* (Munich).

BLUMENBERG, H. (1988). *Der Prozeß der theoretischen Neugierde* (4th edn.; Frankfurt a. Main).

BOEHM, L., and MÜLLER, R. A. (eds.) (1983). *Universitäten und Hochschulen in Deutschland, Österreich und der Schweiz: Eine Universitätsgeschichte in Einzeldarstellungen* (Düsseldorf and Vienna).

BOGEL, E., and BLÜHM, E. (1971–85). *Die deutschen Zeitungen des 17. Jahrhunderts: Ein Bestandsverzeichnis mit historischen und bibliographischen Angaben* (2 vols.; Bremen).

BONNEFOY, Y. (1967). *Un Rêve fait à Mantoue* (Paris).

BOYSSE, E. (1880). *Le Théâtre des Jésuites* (Paris).

BRENNER, C. (1947). *A Bibliographical List of Plays in the French Language 1700–1789* (Berkeley).

BROCKLISS, L. (1987). *French Higher Education in the Seventeenth and Eighteenth Centuries: A Cultural History* (Oxford).

BROWN, H. (1934). *Scientific Organizations in Seventeenth Century France (1620–1680)* (Baltimore).

BRUMBLE, H. (1998). *Classical Myths and Legends in the Middle Ages and the Renaissance: A Dictionary of Allegorical Meanings* (London and Chicago).

BURKE, P. (1987). 'Introduction', in P. Burke and R. Porter (eds.), *The Social History of Language* (Cambridge), 1–20.

——(2000). *A Social History of Knowledge: From Gutenberg to Diderot* (Cambridge).

BUSSON, H. (1948). *La Religion des classiques (1660–1685)* (Paris).

BUTTERWORTH, E. (2002). 'Representations of Calumny in Late Renaissance French Writing' (Ph.D. thesis, University of Cambridge).

CABASSUT, A. (1953). 'Curiosité', in *Dictionnaire de spiritualité: Ascétique et mystique, doctrine et histoire*, ii.2 (Paris), cols. 2654–61.

CALVET, J. (1956). *La Littérature religieuse de François de Sales à Fénelon* (Paris).

CARRIER, H. (1996). *Les Muses guerrières* (Paris).

CARRUTHERS, M. (1998). *The Craft of Thought: Meditation, Rhetoric, and the Making of Images, 400–1200* (Cambridge).

CAVE, T. (1982). 'Problems of Reading in the *Essais*', in I. D. McFarlane and I. Maclean (eds.), *Montaigne: Essays in Memory of Richard Sayce* (Oxford), 133–66.

——(1988). *Recognitions: A Study in Poetics* (Oxford).

——(1999). *Pré-histoires: Textes troublés au seuil de la modernité* (Geneva).

CENSER, J. (1994). *The French Press in the Age of the Enlightenment* (London and New York).

CHARPENTER, F. (1986). 'Les *Essais* de Montaigne: curiosité/incuriosité', in
J. Céard (ed.), *La Curiosité à la Renaissance* (Paris), 111–21.

CHESNEAU, C. (1946). *Le Père Yves de Paris en son temps (1590–1678)*, i: *La
Querelle des évêques et des réguliers (1630–1638)* (Meaux).

CHÉZODEAU, B. (1997). 'Situation de l'histoire en France au XVIIe siècle',
Chroniques de Port-Royal, 46: 7–14.

CLARK, W. (1992). 'The Scientific Revolution in the German Nations', in
R. Porter and M. Teich (eds.), *The Scientific Revolution in National
Context* (Cambridge), 90–114.

COGNET, L. (1964). *Le Jansénisme* (Paris).

COHEN, R. (1986). 'History and Genre', *New Literary History*, 17/2: 203–19.

COURCELLE, P. (1963). *Les Confessions de Saint Augustin dans la tradition
littéraire: Antécédents et postérité* (Paris).

CROOKS, E. (1931). *The Influence of Cervantes in France in the Seventeenth
Century* (Baltimore).

CUNNINGHAM, A., and FRENCH, R. (eds.) (1990). *The Medical Enlightenment of the Eighteenth Century* (Cambridge).

CZIESLA, W. (1989). *Aktaion polyprágmon: Variationen eines antiken
Themas in der europäischen Renaissance* (Frankfurt a. Main).

DACOSTA KAUFMANN, T. (1993). *The Mastery of Nature: Aspects of Art,
Science, and Humanism in the Renaissance* (Princeton).

DAHM, G. (1972). 'On the Reception of Roman and Italian Law in
Germany', in G. Strauss (ed.), *Pre-Reformation Germany* (London and
Basingstoke), 282–315.

DAINVILLE, F. DE (1940). *Les Jésuites et l'éducation de la société française*
(2 vols.; Paris).

——(1978). *L'Éducation des Jésuites (XVIe–XVIIIe siècles)* (Paris).

DASTON, L. (1994). 'Neugierde als Empfindung und Epistemologie in
der frühmodernen Wissenschaft', in A. Grote (ed.), *Macrocosmos in
Microcosmo: Die Welt in der Stube. Zur Geschichte des Sammelns 1450
bis 1800* (Opladen), 35–59.

——(1995). 'The Moral Economy of Science', *Osiris*, 10: 2–24.

DASTON, L., and PARK, K. (1998). *Wonders and the Order of Nature
1150–1750* (New York).

DAXELMÜLLER, C. (1979). *Disputationes curiosae: Zum 'volkskundlichen'
Polyhistorismus an den Universitäten des 17. und 18. Jahrhunderts*
(Würzburg).

DEAR, P. (1988). *Mersenne and the Learning of the Schools* (Ithaca, NY, and
London).

——(1995). *Discipline and Experience: The Mathematical Way in the
Scientific Revolution* (Chicago and London).

DEBUS, A. (1991). *The French Paracelsians: The Chemical Challenge to
Medical and Scientific Tradition in Early Modern France* (Cambridge).

DEFAUX, G. (1982). *Le Curieux, le glorieux et la sagesse du monde dans la première moitié du XVIe siècle: L'exemple de Panurge (Ulysse, Démosthène, Empédocle)* (Lexington, Ky).

DEFILIPPO, J. (1990). 'Curiositas and the Platonism of Apuleius's *Golden Ass*', *American Journal of Philology*, 111: 471–92.

DEITZ, L. (1995). 'Ioannes Wower of Hamburg, Philologist and Polymath. A Preliminary Sketch of his Life and Works', *Journal of the Warburg and Courtauld Institutes*, 58: 132–51.

DELON, M. (1998). 'De la curiosité des maux d'autrui', in *Curiosité et 'libido sciendi'*, i. 183–206.

DENIS, D. (1997). *La Muse galante: Poétique de la conversation dans l'oeuvre de Madeleine de Scudéry* (Paris).

DESCRAINS, J. (1985). *Jean-Pierre Camus (1584–1652) et ses 'Diversités' (1609–1618) ou la culture d'un évêque humaniste* (Lille).

——(1992). *Essais sur Jean-Pierre Camus* (Paris).

DÉSIRAT, D. (1998). 'La Peinture de la curiosité ou les statuts de l'image', in *Curiosité et 'libido sciendi'*, ii. 517–41.

DEW, N. (1999). 'The Pursuit of Oriental Learning in Louis XIV's France' (D.Phil. thesis, University of Oxford).

DIAZ Y DIAZ, M. C. (1974). 'Juvénal d'Anagni', in *Dictionnaire de spiritualité: Ascétique et mystique, doctrine et histoire*, viii.2 (Paris), cols. 1649–52.

Dictionnaire de biographie française (1933–), ed. J. Balteau, M. Barroux, and M. Prevost (Paris).

DIERSE, U. (1977). *Enzyklopädie: Zur Geschichte eines philosophischen und wissenschaftstheoretischen Begriffs* (Bonn).

DIPIERO, T. (1992). *Dangerous Truths and Criminal Passions: The Evolution of the French Novel, 1569–1791* (Stanford, Calif.).

DITCHFIELD, S. (1998). ' "In Search of Local Knowledge": Rewriting Early Modern Italian Religious History', *Cristianesimo nella storia*, 19: 255–96.

DORWART, R. A. (1938). 'Church Organization in Brandenburg-Prussia from the Reformation to 1740', *Harvard Theological Review*, 31: 275–90.

DUBU, J. (1970). 'L'Église catholique et la condamnation du théâtre en France au XVIIe siècle', *Quaderni francesi*, 1: 319–49.

DUHR, B. (1907–28). *Geschichte der Jesuiten in den Ländern deutscher Zunge* (4 vols.; Munich and Regensburg).

DUNN, J. (1985). *Rethinking Political Theory: Essays 1979–83* (Cambridge).

DÜNNHAUPT, G. (1990–3). *Personalbibliographien zu den Drucken des Barock* (6 vols.; Stuttgart).

DUPÈBE, J. (1986). 'Curiosité et magie chez Johannes Trithemius', in J. Céard (ed.), *La Curiosité à la Renaissance* (Paris), 71–97.

DUPONT-FERRIER, G. (1921–5). *Du Collège de Clermont au Lycée Louis-le-Grand (1563–1920)* (3 vols.; Paris).

DYCK, J. (1976). 'Zum Funktionswandel der Universitäten vom 17. zum 18. Jahrhundert. Am Beispiel Halle', in A. Schöne (ed.), *Stadt-Schule-Universität-Buchwesen und die deutsche Literatur im 17. Jahrhundert* (Munich), 371–82.

EAMON, W. (1994). *Science and the Secrets of Nature: Books of Secrets in Medieval and Early Modern Culture* (Princeton).

ECK, E. (1893). 'Römisches Recht', in W. Lexis (ed.), *Die deutschen Universitäten* (2 vols.; Berlin), i. 298–318.

ENGELSING, R. (1973). *Analphabetentum und Lektüre: zur Sozialgeschichte des Lesens in Deutschland zwischen feudaler und industrieller Gesellschaft* (Stuttgart).

——(1974). *Der Bürger als Leser: Lesergeschichte in Deutschland 1500–1800* (Stuttgart).

ERLER, G. (ed.) (1909). *Die jüngere Matrikel der Universität Leipzig 1559–1809* (3 vols.; Leipzig).

ÉTIENNE, R., and MOSSIÈRE, J.-C. (eds.) (1993). *Jacob Spon: Un humaniste lyonnais du XVIIème siècle* (Lyons).

EVANS, R. (1973). *Rudolf II and his World: A Study in Intellectual History, 1576–1612* (Oxford).

——(1977). 'Learned Societies in Germany in the Seventeenth Century', *European Studies Review*, 7: 129–51.

——(1981). 'German Universities after the Thirty Years War', *History of Universities*, 1: 169–90.

FABER DU FAUR, C. VON (1958–69). *German Baroque Literature: A Catalogue of the Collection in the Yale University Library* (2 vols.; New Haven and London).

FEYEL, G. (1987). 'Richelieu et la *Gazette*: aux origines de la presse de propagande', in R. Mousnier (ed.), *Richelieu et la culture* (Paris), 103–23.

FINDLEN, P. (1994). *Possessing Nature: Museums, Collecting, and Scientific Culture in Early Modern Italy* (Berkeley).

FODOR, J. (2003). 'Is it a bird? Problems with Old and New Approaches to the Theory of Concepts', *Times Literary Supplement* (17 Jan.), 3–4.

FOUCAULT, M. (1966). *Les Mots et les choses* (Paris).

FOUQUERAY, H. (1910–25). *Histoire de la Compagnie de Jésus en France des origines à la suppression (1528–1762)* (5 vols.; Paris).

FREEDEN, M. (1996). *Ideologies and Political Theory: A Conceptual Approach* (Oxford).

FREEDMAN, J. (1999). *Philosophy and the Arts in Central Europe, 1500–1700: Teaching and Texts at Schools and Universities* (Aldershot).

FRENCH, R. (1990). 'Sickness and the Soul: Stahl, Hoffmann and Sauvages on Pathology', in A. Cunningham and R. French (eds.), *The Medical Enlightenment of the Eighteenth Century* (Cambridge), 88–110.

—— and WEAR, A. (eds.) (1989). *The Medical Revolution of the Seventeenth Century* (Cambridge).

FRIEDLAENDER, E. (ed.) (1887–91). *Ältere Universitäts-Matrikeln. I. Universität Frankfurt a. O.* (3 vols.; Leipzig).

FRÜHSORGE, G. (1974). *Der politische Körper: Zum Begriff des Politischen im 17. Jahrhundert und in den Romanen Christian Weisens* (Stuttgart).

FULBROOK, M. (1983). *Piety and Politics: Religion and the Rise of Absolutism in England, Württemberg and Prussia* (Cambridge).

FUMAROLI, M. (1980). *L'Âge de l'éloquence: Rhétorique et 'res literaria' de la Renaissance au seuil de l'époque classique* (Geneva).

—— (1984). ' "Nous serons guéris, si nous le voulons': Classicisme français et maladie de l'âme', *Le Débat*, 29: 92–114.

GAGLIARDO, J. G. (1991). *Germany under the Old Regime, 1600–1790* (London and New York).

GALLIANI, R. (1989). *Rousseau, le luxe et l'idéologie nobiliaire-étude socio-historique* (Oxford).

GALLIE, W. B. (1966). 'Essentially Contested Concepts', *Proceedings of the Aristotelian Society*, 56: 167–98.

GASCOIGNE, J. (1990). 'A Reappraisal of the Role of the Universities in the Scientific Revolution', in D. C. Lindberg and R. S. Westman (eds.), *Reappraisals of the Scientific Revolution* (Cambridge), 208–60.

GEYER-KORDESCH, J. (1989). 'Passions and the Ghost in the Machine: or What not to Ask about Science in Seventeenth- and Eighteenth-Century Germany', in R. French and A. Wear (eds.), *The Medical Revolution of the Seventeenth Century* (Cambridge), 144–63.

—— (1990). 'Georg Ernst Stahl's radical Pietist medicine and its influence on the German Enlightenment', in A. Cunningham and R. French (eds.), *The Medical Enlightenment of the Eighteenth Century* (Cambridge), 67–87.

GIAVARINI, L. (1998). ' "Le sentiment ordinaire de ceux qui aiment": *locus amaenus*, curiosité, *ethos* endeuillé dans l'*Astrée* d'Honoré d'Urfé (1607–1628)', in *Curiosité et 'libido sciendi'*, ii. 282–303.

GILBERT, N. (1960). *Renaissance Concepts of Method* (New York).

GILMAN, E. (1978). *The Curious Perspective: Literary and Pictorial Wit in the Seventeenth Century* (New Haven and London).

GINZBURG, C. (1976). 'High and Low: The Theme of Forbidden Knowledge in the Sixteenth and Seventeenth Centuries', *Past and Present*, 83: 28–41.

—— (1990). 'Clues: Roots of an Evidential Paradigm', in *Myths, Emblems, Clues*, tr. J. and A. C. Tedeschi (London), 96–125. First published in Italian, 1979.

GIRARD, R. (1973). *Mensonge romantique et vérité romanesque* (Paris). 1st edn. 1961.

GODARD DE DONVILLE, L. (1989). *Le Libertin des origines à 1665: Un produit des apologètes* (Paris, Seattle, Tübingen).

GOLDBERG, R. (1984). *Sex and Enlightenment: Women in Richardson and Diderot* (Cambridge).

GOLDGAR, A. (1995). *Impolite Learning: Conduct and Community in the Republic of Letters 1680–1750* (New Haven and London).

GOLDMANN, K. (1967). *Verzeichnis der Hochschulen* (Neustadt a.d. Aisch).

GOLINSKI, J. (1998). *Making Natural Knowledge: Constructivism and the History of Science* (Cambridge).

GORÉ, J.-L. (1957). *L'Itinéraire de Fénelon: Humanisme et spiritualité* (Paris).

GOUHIER, H. (1977). *Fénelon philosophe* (Paris).

GRAFTON, A. (1985). 'The World of the Polyhistors: Humanism and Encyclopedism', *Central European History*, 18: 31–47.

——(1997). *The Footnote: A Curious History* (London).

GREENBLATT, S. (1992). *Marvelous Possessions: The Wonder of the New World* (Oxford).

GUILD, E. (forthcoming). 'Montaigne's *commerce* with Women: "Jusques où va la possibilité"?', in M. Tudeau-Clayton and P. Berry (eds.), *The Texture of Renaissance Knowledge* (Manchester).

GUNN, J. (1995). *Queen of the World: Opinion in the Public Life of France from the Renaissance to the Revolution* (Oxford).

HAFFEMAYER, S. (2002). *L'Information dans la France du XVIIe siècle: La Gazette de Renaudot de 1647 à 1663* (Paris).

HAHN, R. (1971). *The Anatomy of a Scientific Institution: The Paris Academy of Sciences, 1666–1803* (Berkeley).

HAMMERSTEIN, N. (1970). 'Zur Geschichte der deutschen Universität im Zeitalter der Aufklärung', in H. Rössler and G. Franz (eds.), *Universität und Gelehrtenstand 1400–1800* (Limburg a.d. Lahn), 145–82.

——(1972). *Jus und Historie: Ein Beitrag zur Geschichte des historischen Denkens an deutschen Universitäten im späten 17. und im 18. Jahrhundert* (Göttingen, 1972).

——(1981). 'Universitäten des Heiligen Römischen Reiches deutscher Nation als Ort der Philosophie des Barock', *Studia Leibnitiana*, 13: 242–66.

HAMMOND, N. (1994). *Playing With Truth: Language and the Human Condition in Pascal's 'Pensées'* (Oxford).

HAMPSHER-MONK, I. (1998). 'Speech Acts, Languages or Conceptual History?', in I. Hampsher-Monk, K. Tilmans, and F. van Vree (eds.), *History of Concepts: Comparative Perspectives* (Amsterdam), 37–50.

HAMPSON, N. (1987). *The Enlightenment* (London). 1st edn. 1968.

HAMPTON, T. (1990). *Writing from History: The Rhetoric of Exemplarity in Renaissance Literature* (Ithaca).

HARRIS, B. (1996). *Politics and the Rise of the Press: Britain and France, 1620–1800* (London and New York).

HARRISON, P. (2001). 'Curiosity, Forbidden Knowledge, and the Reformation of Natural Philosophy in Early Modern England', *Isis*, 92: 265–91.

HAYS, H. R. (1966). *The Dangerous Sex: The Myth of Feminine Evil* (London). 1st edn. 1964.

HERZOG, U. (1991). *Geistliche Wohlredenheit: Die katholische Barockpredigt* (Munich).

HIRSCH, A. (ed.) (1884–8). *Biographisches Lexikon der hervorragenden Ärzte aller Zeiten und Völker* (6 vols.; Vienna and Leipzig).

HIRSCH, T. (1858). 'Geschichte des Danziger Gymnasium seit 1814', in *Gymnasii Gedanensis sacra saecularia tertia* (Danzig). 1st edn. 1837.

HIRSCHMAN, A. (1977). *The Passions and the Interests: Political Arguments for Capitalism Before its Triumph* (Princeton).

HOBSON, M. (1998). *Jacques Derrida: Opening Lines* (London and New York).

HOFFBAUER, J. C. (1805). *Geschichte der Universität zu Halle bis zum Jahre 1805* (Halle).

HOFFMEISTER, G. (ed.) (1983). *European Baroque Literature: The European Perspective* (New York).

HOGU, L. (1913). *Jean de l'Espine, moraliste et théologien (1505?-1597): Sa vie, son oeuvre, ses idées* (Paris).

HORN, E. (1893). *Die Disputationen und Promotionen an den deutschen Universitäten vornehmlich seit dem 16. Jahrhundert* (Leipzig).

HOTSON, H. (2000). *Johann Heinrich Alsted 1588–1638: Between Renaissance, Reformation, and Universal Reform* (Oxford).

——(forthcoming). *Between Ramus and Comenius: Encyclopedic Learning in Reformed Central Europe, c.1569–1630* (Oxford).

HSIA, R. PO-CHIA (1989). *Social Discipline in the Reformation: Central Europe 1550–1750* (London and New York).

HUGHES, M. (1992). *Early Modern Germany, 1477–1806* (Basingstoke and London).

HÜLLEN, W. (1994). 'Die Darstellung der Welt in Kirchen, Wunderkammern und naturkundlichen Museen', in H. Wenzel in collaboration with F. Kittler and M. Schneider (eds.), *Gutenberg und die Neue Welt* (Munich), 121–34.

HUOT-BOKDAM, S. (1986). 'La Figure du Curieux dans les *Discours philosophiques* de Pontus de Tyard', in J. Céard (ed.), *La Curiosité à la Renaissance* (Paris), 99–110.

HUPPERT, G. (1984). *Public Schools in Renaissance France* (Urbana, Ill.).

IMPEY, O., and MACGREGOR, A. (eds.) (1985). *The Origins of Museums: The Cabinet of Curiosities in Sixteenth- and Seventeenth-Century Europe* (Oxford).

JACQUES-CHAQUIN, N. (1998a). 'La Curiosité, ou les espaces du savoir', in *Curiosité et 'libido sciendi'*, i. 13–32.

——(1998b). 'La Passion des sciences interdites: curiosité et démonologie (xve–xviie siècles)', in *Curiosité et 'libido sciendi'*, i. 73–107.

——and HOUDARD, S. (eds.) (1998). *Curiosité et 'libido sciendi' de la Renaissance aux Lumières* (2 vols.; Fontenay-aux-Roses).

JAMES, S. (1997). *Passion and Action: The Emotions in Seventeenth-Century Philosophy* (Oxford).

——(1998a). 'Reasons, the Passions, and the Good Life', in M. Ayers and D. Garber (eds.), *The Cambridge History of Seventeenth-Century Philosophy* (2 vols.; Cambridge), ii. 1358–96.

——(1998b). 'The Passions in Metaphysics and the Theory of Action', in M. Ayers and D. Garber (eds.), *The Cambridge History of Seventeenth-Century Philosophy* (2 vols.; Cambridge), i. 913–49.

JANTZ, H. (1974). *German Baroque Literature: A Descriptive Catalogue* (2 vols.; New Haven).

JAYMES, D. (1995). 'The Princesse de Clèves through a Microscope Darkly', *Papers on French Seventeenth Century Literature*, 22: 611–19.

JEANNERET, M. (1994). *Le Défi des signes: Rabelais et la crise de l'interprétation à la Renaissance* (Orléans).

JÖCHER, C. G. (1750–1). *Allgemeines Gelehrten-Lexicon* (4 vols.; Leipzig).

JOLLEY, N. (1998). 'The Relation between Theology and Philosophy', in M. Ayers and D. Garber (eds.), *The Cambridge History of Seventeenth-Century Philosophy* (2 vols.; Cambridge), i. 363–92.

JONES, A. H. M. (ed.) (1970). *A History of Rome Through the Fifth Century*, ii: *The Empire* (London and Melbourne).

JOUHAUD, C. (1996). 'La Méthode de François Garasse', in L. Giard and L. de Vaucelles (eds.), *Les Jésuites à l'âge baroque (1540–1640)* (Grenoble), 243–60.

JUBERT, G. (1981). 'La Légende dorée de Théophraste Renaudot', *Bulletin de la Société des Antiquaires de l'Ouest et des Musées de Poitiers*, 16: 141–62.

JULIEN-EYMARD D'ANGERS (1952). *Du Stoïcisme chrétien à l'humanisme chrétien: Les 'Diversités' de J. P. Camus (1609–1618)* (Meaux).

JUNCKE, F. (ed.) (1960). *Matrikel der Martin-Luther-Universität Halle-Wittenberg*, i: *1690–1730* (Halle).

KAISER, W. (ed.) (1985). *Georg Ernst Stahl (1659–1734): Hallesches Symposium 1984* (Halle).

——and VÖLKER, A. (1980). *Johann Heinrich Schulze (1687–1744)* (Halle).

KAUFMANN, G. (1898). *Die Geschichte der deutschen Universitäten*, ii (Stuttgart).

KELLY, W. (1996). 'Johann Sebastian Mitternacht (30 March 1613–25 July 1679)', in J. Hardin (ed.), *Dictionary of Literary Biography*, clxviii: *German Baroque Writers, 1661–1730* (Detroit, Washington, DC, and London), 286–91.

KENNY, A. (1973). *Wittgenstein* (London).

KENNY, N. (1991*a*). *The Palace of Secrets: Béroalde de Verville and Renaissance Conceptions of Knowledge* (Oxford).

——(1991*b*). 'Curiosité and Philosophical Poetry in the French Renaissance', *Renaissance Studies*, 5: 263–76.

——(1995*a*). 'Interpreting Concepts after the Linguistic Turn: The Example of *curiosité* in *Le Bonheur des sages/Le Malheur des curieux* by Du Souhait (1600)', *Michigan Romance Studies*, 15 (J. O'Brien (ed.), *[Ré]interprétations: études sur le seizième siècle*), 241–70.

——(1995*b*). 'Montaigne et "les bien-nées [. . .] attachées à la rhétorique": autour d'un passage de l'essai "De trois commerces"', in J. O'Brien, M. Quainton, and J. Supple (eds.), *Montaigne et la rhétorique* (Paris), 203–19.

——(1998). *Curiosity in Early Modern Europe: Word Histories* (Wiesbaden).

——(2000*a*). 'Books in Space and Time: Bibliomania and Early Modern Histories of Learning and "Literature" in France', *Modern Language Quarterly*, 61: 253–86.

——(2000*b*). '"La France, si curieuse de nouveautez": le concept composite de "curiosité" aux débuts de la presse périodique en France (1631–1633)', in J.-R. Fanlo (ed.), *'D'une fantastique bigarrure': Le Texte composite à la Renaissance. Études offertes à André Tournon* (Paris), 289–302.

——(2003). 'Plautus, Panurge, and "les aventures des gens curieux"', in G. Ferguson and C. Hampton (eds.), *(Re)inventing the Past: Essays in Honour of Ann Moss* (Durham), 51–71.

——(forthcoming). 'The Metaphorical Collecting of Curiosities in Early Modern France and Germany', in R. Evans and A. Marr (eds.), *Curiosity and Wonder from the Renaissance to the Enlightenment* (Aldershot).

KESTNER, C. W. (1971). *Medicinisches Gelehrten-Lexicon* (Hildesheim and New York; repr.). 1st edn. 1740.

KING, K. (1998). 'Spying upon the Conjurer: Haywood, Curiosity, and "the Novel" in the 1720s', *Studies in the Novel*, 30: 178–93.

KING, L. (1964). 'Stahl and Hoffmann: A Study in Eighteenth Century Animism', *Journal of the History of Medicine and Allied Sciences*, 19: 118–30.

KING, L. (1970). *The Road to Medical Enlightenment 1650–1695* (London and New York).

——(1978). *The Philosophy of Medicine: The Early Eighteenth Century* (Cambridge, Mass.).

KIRCHNER, J. (1958–62). *Die deutsche Zeitschriftenwesen: Seine Geschichte und seine Probleme* (2 vols.; Wiesbaden).

KITCHEN, M. (1996). *The Cambridge Illustrated History of Germany* (Cambridge).

KLAITS, J. (1976). *Printed Propaganda under Louis XIV: Absolute Monarchy and Public Opinion* (Princeton).

KLEINEIDAM, E. (1981). *Universitas studii Erffordensis: Überblick über die Geschichte der Universität Erfurt*, iv: *Die Universität Erfurt und ihre theologische Fakultät von 1633 biz zum Untergang 1816* (Leipzig).

KOMORSKI, M. (1995). 'Research on Early Modern German Dissertations: A Report on Work in Progress', in *The German Book 1450–1750: Studies Presented to David L. Paisey* (London), 259–68.

KOPPITZ, H.-J. (1979). 'Ungehobene Schätze in unseren Bibliotheken', in R. Jung and P. Kaegbein (eds.), *Dissertationen in Wissenschaft und Bibliotheken* (Munich), 29–39.

KOSCHAKER, P. (1966). *Europa und das römische Recht* (Munich and Berlin; 4th edn.).

KOSELLECK, R. (1985). *Futures Past: On the Semantics of Historical Time*, tr. K. Tribe (Cambridge, Mass., and London).

KÜHLMANN, W. (1982). *Gelehrten-Republik und Fürstenstaat: Entwicklung und Kritik deutschen Späthumanismus in der Literatur des Barockzeitalters* (Tübingen).

KUNDERT, W. (1984). *Katalog der Helmstedter juristischen Disputationen, Programme und Reden 1574–1810* (Wiesbaden).

LABHARDT, A. (1960). 'Curiositas: Notes sur l'histoire d'un mot et d'une notion', *Museum Helveticum*, 206–24.

LABROUSSE, É. (1968). 'Le Paradoxe de l'érudit cartésien Pierre Bayle', in *Religion, érudition et critique à la fin du XVIIe siècle et au début du XVIIIe* (Paris), 53–70.

LaCAPRA, D. (1983). *Rethinking Intellectual History: Texts, Contexts, Language* (Ithaca, NY, and London).

LANCASTER, H. C. (1929–42). *French Dramatic Literature in the Seventeenth Century* (9 vols. in 5 parts; Baltimore).

LANCEL, S. (1961). '*Curiositas* et préoccupations spirituelles chez Apulée', *Revue de l'histoire des religions*, 160: 25–46.

LEASK, N. (2002). *Curiosity and the Aesthetics of Travel Writing, 1770–1840: 'From an Antique Land'* (Oxford).

LEBORGNE, E. (1998). 'Destins de la pulsion de savoir dans les romans "philosophiques" de Prévost', in *Curiosité et 'libido sciendi'*, ii. 447–74.

LEBRUN, F. (ed.) (1988). *Du Christianisme flamboyant à l'aube des Lumières (XIVe–XVIIIe siècle)* (Paris). (Vol. ii of J.-P. Lapie and M. Winock (eds.), *Histoire de la France religieuse*).

LE BRUN, J. (1986). 'Quiétisme en France', in *Dictionnnaire de spiritualité: Ascétique et mystique, doctrine et histoire*, xii.2 (Paris), cols. 2805–42.

LECLERCQ, J. (1957). *L'Amour des lettres et le désir de Dieu: Initiation aux auteurs monastiques du moyen âge* (Paris).

LEPLATRE, O. (1998). 'La Bruyère ou le livre de curiosités', *Papers on French Seventeenth Century Literature*, 25/48: 55–67.

LEVER, M. (1981). *Le Roman français au XVIIe siècle* (Paris).

LICOPPE, C. (1996). *La Formation de la pratique scientifique: Le Discours de l'expérience en France et en Angleterre (1630–1820)* (Paris).

LINDEMANN, M. (1969). *Deutsche Presse bis 1815* (Berlin).

——(1996). *Health and Healing in Eighteenth-Century Germany* (Baltimore and London).

LOCHER, E. (1989). ' "Ein Weiser hat Augen unnd ein Haupt und die Augen im Kopff / aber ein Narr hat den discurs deß Kopffs im anschawen der Augen/ [. . .]." ' Zur Curiositas-Problematik bei Aegidius Albertinus', *Simpliciana: Schriften der Grimmelshausen-Gesellschaft*, 11: 71–98.

——(1990). *'Curiositas' und 'memoria' im deutschen Barock* (Vienna and Lana).

LOEMKER, L. (1972). *Struggle for Synthesis: The Seventeenth Century Background of Leibniz's Synthesis of Order and Freedom* (Cambridge, Mass.).

LOUGEE, C. (1976). *'Le Paradis des femmes': Women, Salons, and Social Stratification in Seventeenth-Century France* (Princeton).

LUGLI, A. (1983). *Naturalia et mirabilia: Il collezionismo enciclopedico nelle Wunderkammern d'Europa* (Milan).

LYONS, J. D. (1989). *Exemplum: The Rhetoric of Example in Early Modern France and Italy* (Princeton).

MCCLELLAN III, J. E. (1985). *Science Reorganized: Scientific Societies in the Eighteenth Century* (New York).

MCCLELLAND, C. (1980). *State, Society, and University in Germany* (Cambridge).

MCGRATH, A. E. (1986). 'Reformation to Enlightenment', in *The History of Christian Theology*, i: *The Science of Theology*, ed. G. Evans, A. McGrath, and A. Galloway (Basingstoke and Grand Rapids), 105–229.

MACLEAN, I. (1991). 'The Market for Scholarly Books and Conceptions of Genre in Northern Europe, 1570–1630', in G. Kauffmann (ed.), *Die Renaissance im Blick der Nationen Europas* (Wiesbaden).

MCNAY, L. (1994). *Foucault: A Critical Introduction* (Cambridge).

Maître-Dufour, M. (1998). 'Une anti-curiosité: la discrétion chez Mlle de Scudéry et dans la littérature mondaine (1648–1696)', in *Curiosité et 'libido sciendi'*, ii. 333–58.

Marchand, J. (1980). 'Apologie du Père Garasse (1585–1631): le Jésuite et les libertins', *Cahiers laïques*, 173: 92–106.

Martens, W. (1968). *Die Botschaft der Tugend: Die Aufklärung im Spiegel der deutschen Moralischen Wochenschriften* (Stuttgart).

Marti, H. (1981). 'Der wissenschaftsgeschichtliche Dokumentationswert alter Dissertationen', *Nouvelles de la république des lettres*, 1: 117–32.

——(1982). *Philosophische Dissertationen deutscher Universitäten 1660–1750: Eine Auswahlbibliographie* (Munich).

Matthias, M. (1995). 'Orthodoxie I', in G. Müller (ed.), *Theologische Realenzyklopädie* (Berlin and New York), xxv. 464–85.

Mauri, D. (1992). 'Il *Tableau* di Beroalde de Verville: un viaggio attraverso i testi, alla ricerca della perfezione', *Studi di letteratura francese*, 19: 367–81.

——(1996). '*Le Voyage des princes fortunez* di Beroalde de Verville: un'avventura tra amore, alchimia e scrittura', in *Il romanzo nella Francia del Rinascimento: dall'eredità medievale all' 'Astraea'* (Fasano), 129–41.

Mazaheri, H. (1991). 'A propos de tulipes et de prunes: le fétichisme de la marchandise dans les *Caractères* de La Bruyère', *Europe*, 748–9: 144–9.

Meijering, E. P. (1980). *Calvin wider die Neugierde: Ein Beitrag zum Vergleich zwischen reformatorischem und patristischem Denken* (Nieuwkoop).

Mellot, J.-D. (1998). *L'Édition rouennaise et ses marchés (vers 1600–vers 1730)* (Paris).

Merlin, H. (1998). 'Curiosité et espace particulier au xviie siècle', in *Curiosité et 'libido sciendi'*, i. 109–35.

Mette, H. J. (1956). 'Curiositas', in *Festschrift Bruno Snell* (Munich), 227–35.

Michaud (1843–). *Biographie universelle, ancienne et moderne. Nouvelle édition* (45 vols.; Paris).

Mitchell, O. C. (1980). *A Concise History of Brandenburg-Prussia to 1786* (Washington, DC).

Mittenzwei, I., and Herzfeld, E. (1987). *Brandenburg-Preußen 1648 bis 1789: Das Zeitalter des Absolutismus in Text und Bild* (Berlin).

Moisan, C. (1990). *L'Histoire littéraire* (Paris).

Moller, J. (1744). *Cimbria literata, sive Scriptorum ducatus utriusque Slesvicensis et Holsatici . . . historia literaria* (3 vols.; Copenhagen).

Momigliano, A. (1990). *The Classical Foundations of Modern Historiography* (Berkeley).

Montgomery, J. W. (1973). *Cross and Crucible: Johann Valentin Andreae (1586–1654), Phoenix of the Theologians* (2 vols.; The Hague).

MORIARTY, M. (1988). *Taste and Ideology in Seventeenth-Century France* (Cambridge).

MORNET, D. (1910). 'Les Enseignements des bibliothèques privées (1750–1780)', *Revue d'histoire littéraire de la France*, 17: 449–96.

MORTGAT, E. (forthcoming). *Clio au Parnasse* (Paris).

MOSS, A. (1996). *Printed Commonplace-Books and the Structuring of Renaissance Thought* (Oxford).

MÜLLER, J.-D. (1984). '*Curiositas* und *erfarung* der Welt im frühen deutschen Prosaroman', in L. Grenzmann and K. Stackmann (eds.), *Literatur und Laienbildung im Spätmittelalter und in der Reformationszeit* (Stuttgart), 252–72.

MÜLLER, K. (1970). 'Zur Entstehung und Wirkung der Wissenschaftlichen Akademien und Gelehrten Gesellschaften des 17. Jahrhunderts', in H. Rössler and G. Franz (eds.), *Universität und Gelehrtenstand 1400–1800* (Limburg a.d. Lahn), 127–44.

MÜLLER, W. (1990). *Die Drucke des 17. Jahrhunderts im deutschen Sprachraum: Untersuchungen zu ihrer Verzeichnung in einem VD17* (Wiesbaden).

NELLES, P. (1997). 'The Library as an Instrument of Discovery: Gabriel Naudé and the Uses of History', in D. R. Kelley (ed.), *History and the Disciplines: The Reclassification of Knowledge in Early Modern Europe* (Rochester), 41–57.

——(1999). '*Historia magistra antiquitatis*: Cicero and Jesuit History Teaching', *Renaissance Studies*, 13: 130–72.

——(2000). 'Private Teaching and Professorial Collections at the University of Kiel: Morhof and *historia litteraria*', in F. Waquet (ed.), *Mapping the World of Learning: The 'Polyhistor' of Daniel Georg Morhof* (Wiesbaden), 31–56.

——(2001). '*Historia litteraria* at Helmstedt: Books, Professors and Students in the Early Enlightenment University', in H. Zedelmaier and M. Mulsow (eds.), *Die Pratiken der Gelehrsamkeit in der Frühen Neuzeit* (Tübingen), 147–76.

NEUBER, W. (1991). *Fremde Welt: Zur Topik der deutschen Amerika-Reiseberichte der Frühen Neuzeit* (Berlin).

NEUSCHÄFER, H.-J. (1990). '*El curioso impertinente* y la tradición de la novelistica europea', *Nueva revista de filología hispánica*, 38: 605–20.

New Catholic Encyclopedia (1967–79; 17 vols.; New York).

NEWHAUSER, R. (1982). 'Towards a History of Human Curiosity: A Prolegomenon to its Medieval Phase', *Deutsche Vierteljahrsschrift für Literaturwissenschaft und Geistesgeschichte*, 56: 559–75.

NISCHAN, B. (1994). *Prince, People, and Confession: The Second Reformation in Brandenburg* (Philadelphia).

OBERMAN, H. A. (1974). *Contra vanam curiositatem: Ein Kapitel der Theologie zwischen Seelenwinkel und Weltall* (Zürich).

OESTREICH, G. (1980). *Strukturprobleme der frühen Neuzeit* (Berlin).

——(1982). *Neostoicism and the Early Modern State*, tr. D. McLintock (Cambridge).

OLMI, G. (1992). *L'inventario del mondo: Catalogazione della natura e luoghi del sapere nella prima età moderna* (Bologna).

O'MALLEY, J. W. (1993). *The First Jesuits* (Cambridge, Mass., and London).

ORNSTEIN, M. (1963). *The Rôle of Scientific Societies in the Seventeenth Century* (Hamden and London). 1st edn. 1913.

The Oxford Encyclopaedia of the Reformation (1996), ed. H. J. Hillerbrand (4 vols.; New York and Oxford).

PAISEY, D. (1988). *Deutsche Buchdrucker, Buchhändler und Verleger 1701–1750* (Wiesbaden).

PANOFSKY, D., and PANOFSKY, E. (1978). *Pandora's Box: The Changing Aspects of a Mythical Symbol* (Princeton). 1st edn. 1956.

PANTIN, I. (1995). *La Poésie du ciel en France dans la seconde moitié du seizième siècle* (Geneva).

——(1998). 'L'Astronomie sur la roue de la curiosité: des représentations emblématiques à la crise de la cosmologie', in *Curiosité et 'libido sciendi'*, i. 51–71.

PARKER, G. (ed.) (1997). *The Thirty Years' War* (London and New York). 2nd edn.

PÉREZ, M.-F., in collaboration with GUILLEMAIN, J. (1993). 'Curieux et collectionneurs à Lyon d'après le texte de Spon (1673)', in Étienne and Mossière (eds.), *Jacob Spon* (see above), 39–50.

PETERS, E. (1985). '*Libertas inquirendi* and the *vitium curiositatis* in Medieval Thought', in G. Makdisi, D. Sourdel, and J. Sourdel-Thomine (eds.), *La Notion de liberté au Moyen Âge: Islam, Byzance, Occident* (Paris), 89–98.

PETERSEN, P. (1964). *Geschichte der aristotelischen Philosophie im protestantischen Deutschland* (Stuttgart and Bad Cannstatt). 1st edn. 1921.

PHILLIPS, H. (1997). *Church and Culture in Seventeenth-Century France* (Cambridge).

PLAGNOL-DIÉVAL, M.-E. (1996). *Bibliographie des écrivains français, 6: Madame de Genlis* (Paris).

——(1997). *Madame de Genlis et le théâtre d'éducation au XVIIIe siècle* (Oxford).

POCOCK, J. (1987). 'The Concept of a Language and the *métier d'historien*: Some Considerations on Practice', in A. Pagden (ed.), *The Languages of Political Theory in Early-Modern Europe* (Cambridge).

——(1996). 'Concepts and Discourses: A Difference in Culture? Comment on a Paper by Melvin Richter', in H. Lehmann and M. Richter (eds.), *The*

Meaning of Historical Terms and Concepts: New Studies on Begriffsgeschichte (Washington, DC), 47–58.

POMIAN, K. (1987). *Collectionneurs, amateurs et curieux. Paris, Venise: XVIe–XVIIIe siècle* ([Paris]).

POPKIN, J. (1991). 'Periodical Publication and the Nature of Knowledge in Eighteenth-Century Europe', in *The Shapes of Knowledge from the Renaissance to the Enlightenment*, ed. D. R. Kelley and R. H. Popkin (Dordrecht), 203–13.

POWELL, H. (1988). *Trammels of Tradition: Aspects of German Life and Culture in the Seventeenth Century and their Impact on Contemporary Literature* (Tübingen).

PRANGE, C. (1978). *Die Zeitungen und Zeitschriften des 17. Jahrhunderts in Hamburg und Altona* (Hamburg).

PRESS, V. (1991). *Kriege und Krisen: Deutschland 1600–1715* (Munich).

PREUS, R. (1955). *The Inspiration of Scripture: A Study of the Theology of the Seventeenth Century Lutheran Dogmaticians* (Edinburgh and London).

PUTNAM, H. (1981). *Reason, Truth, and History* (Cambridge).

QUINN, D. (1995). '*Polypragmosyne* in the Renaissance: Ben Jonson', *Ben Jonson Journal*, 2: 157–69.

RAEFF, M. (1983). *The Well-Ordered Police State: Social and Institutional Change through Law in the Germanies and Russia, 1600–1800* (New Haven and London).

RAPLEY, E. (1990). *The Dévotes: Women and Church in Seventeenth-Century France* (Montreal and Kingston).

RATHMANN, L. (ed.) (1984). *Alma mater Lipsiensis: Geschichte der Karl-Marx Universität* (Leipzig).

RAWLS, J. (1973). *A Theory of Justice* (Oxford).

RENOUARD, P. (1995). *Le Répertoire des imprimeurs parisiens, libraires et fondeurs de caractères en exercice à Paris au XVIIe siècle* (Nogent Le Roi).

REY, G. (1998). 'Concepts', in E. Craig (ed.), *Routledge Encyclopedia of Philosophy* (10 vols.; London and New York), ii. 505–17.

RICHTER, M. (1996). 'Appreciating a Contemporary Classic: the *Geschichtiche Grundbegriffe* and Future Scholarship', in *The Meaning of Historical Terms and Concepts: New Studies on Begriffsgeschichte*, ed. H. Lehmann and M. Richter (Washington, DC), 7–19.

RIDDER-SYMOENS, H. DE (ed.) (1996). *A History of the University in Europe*, ii: *Universities in Early Modern Europe (1500–1600)* (Cambridge).

RITTER, J., and GRÜNDER, K. (eds.) (1984). *Historisches Wörterbuch der Philosophie*, vi (Basel and Stuttgart).

RIZZA, C. (1996). *Libertinage et littérature* (Paris).

ROBIC-DE BAECQUE, S. (1999). *Le Salut par l'excès: Jean-Pierre Camus (1584–1652), la poétique d'un évêque romancier* (Paris).

ROSELLINI, M. (1998). 'Curiosité et théorie du roman dans le dernier tiers du XVIIe siècle: entre éthique et esthétique', in *Curiosité et 'libido sciendi'*, i. 137–56.

ROSSI, P. (1970). *Philosophy, Technology, and the Arts in the Early Modern Era* (New York). (*I filosofi e le macchine*, 1962.)

ROTHKRUG, L. (1965). *Opposition to Louis XIV: The Political and Social Origins of the French Enlightenment* (Princeton).

RUTLEDGE, J. (1974). *The Dialogue of the Dead in Eighteenth-Century Germany* (Berne and Frankfurt a. Main).

SAISSELIN, R. (1970). *The Rule of Reason and the Ruses of the Heart: A Philosophical Dictionary of Classical French Criticism, Critics and Aesthetic Issues* (Cleveland and London).

SCAGLIONE, A. (1986). *The Liberal Arts and the Jesuit College System* (Amsterdam and Philadelphia).

SCHENDA, R. (1963). 'Die deutschen Prodigiensammlungen des 16. und 17. Jahrhunderts', *Archiv für Geschichte des Buchwesens*, 4: 637–710.

SCHIEBINGER, L. (1997). 'Gender in Early Modern Science', in D. R. Kelley (ed.), *History and the Disciplines: The Reclassification of Knowledge in Early Modern Europe* (Rochester, NY), 319–34.

SCHILLING, H. (1989). *Höfe und Allianzen: Deutschland 1648–1763* (Berlin).

——(ed.) (1994). *Kirchenzucht und Sozialdisziplinierung im frühneuzeitlichen Europa* (Berlin).

SCHLOSSER, J. von (1908). *Die Kunst- und Wunderkammern der Spätrenaissance* (Leipzig).

SCHMIDT-BIGGEMANN, W. (1983). *Topica universalis: Eine Modellgeschichte humanistischer und barocker Wissenschaft* (Hamburg).

SCHNAPPER, A. (1988). 'The King of France as collector in the seventeenth century', in R. Rotberg and T. Rabb (eds.), *Art and History: Images and their Meaning* (Cambridge), 185–202.

——(1988–94), *Collections et collectionneurs dans la France du XVIIe siècle* (2 vols.; Paris).

SEGUIN, J.-P. (1964). *L'Information en France avant le périodique: 517 canards imprimés entre 1529 et 1631* (Paris).

SEIFERT, L. (1996). *Fairy Tales, Sexuality, and Gender in France, 1690–1715: Nostalgic Utopias* (Cambridge).

SELLIER, P. (1970). *Pascal et Saint Augustin* (Paris).

SGARD, J. (1984). 'La Multiplication des périodiques', in H.-J. Martin and R. Chartier (eds.), *Histoire de l'édition française*, i: *Le Livre triomphant, 1660–1830* (Paris), 198–205.

——(ed.) (1991). *Dictionnaire des journaux 1600–1789* (2 vols.; Paris and Oxford).

SHAPIN, S. (1994). *A Social History of Truth: Civility and Science in Seventeenth-Century England* (Chicago and London).

——(1996). *The Scientific Revolution* (Chicago and London).

SHATTUCK, R. (1996). *Forbidden Knowledge: From Prometheus to Pornography* (New York).

SHELTON, A. (1994). 'Cabinets of Transgression: Renaissance Collections and the Incorporation of the New World', in J. Elsner and R. Cardinal (eds.), *The Cultures of Collecting* (London), 177–203.

SIMON, A. (1998). *Sigmund Feyerabend's 'Das Reyßbuch deß heyligen Lands': A Study in Printing and Literary History* (Wiesbaden).

SKINNER, Q. (1988). 'A Reply to my Critics', in J. Tully (ed.), *Meaning and Context: Quentin Skinner and his Critics* (Cambridge), 68–78.

——(1991). 'Thomas Hobbes: Rhetoric and the Construction of Morality', *Proceedings of the British Academy*, 76: 1–91.

——(1996). *Reason and Rhetoric in the Philosophy of Hobbes* (Cambridge).

SMITH, P. H. (1994). *The Business of Alchemy: Science and Culture in the Holy Roman Empire* (Princeton).

SOLOMON, H. (1972). *Public Welfare, Science, and Propaganda in Seventeenth Century France: The Innovations of Théophraste Renaudot* (Princeton).

SOMMERVOGEL, C. (ed.) (1890–1911). *Bibliothèque de la Compagnie de Jésus . . . nouvelle édition* (12 vols.; Brussels and Paris).

STAFFORD, B. M. (1994). *Artful Science: Enlightenment Entertainment and the Eclipse of Visual Education* (Cambridge, Mass., and London).

STAGL, J. (1995). *A History of Curiosity: The Theory of Travel 1550–1800* (Chur).

STEFANOVSKA, M. (1999). 'Un *voyeux* à la cour de Louis XIV: curiosité et écriture dans les *Mémoires* de Saint-Simon', *Papers on French Seventeenth Century Literature*, 26/51: 289–98.

STEINHAUSEN, G. (1895). 'Galant, Curiös und Politisch: drei Schlag- und Modeworte des Perrücken-Zeitalters', *Zeitschrift für den deutschen Unterricht*, 9: 22–37.

STEINMETZ, M., et al. (eds.) (1958). *Geschichte der Universität Jena 1548/58–1958* (2 vols.; Jena).

STERN, L. (1952). *Zur Geschichte und wissenschaftlichen Leistung der deutschen Akademie der Naturforscher* (Halle).

STILL, J. (2000). 'Genlis's *Mademoiselle de Clermont*: A Textual and Intertextual Reading', *Australian Journal of French Studies*, 37: 331–47.

STINTZING, R., and LANDSBERG, E. (1880–1910). *Geschichte der deutschen Rechtswissenschaft* (5 vols.; Munich, Leipzig, Berlin).

STRAUSS, G. (1986). *Law, Resistance, and the State: The Opposition to Roman Law in Reformation Germany* (Princeton).

SULEIMAN, S. (1977). 'Le Récit exemplaire: parabole fable, roman à thèse', *Poétique* 32: 468–89.

THIROUIN, L. (1997). *L'Aveuglement salutaire: Le Réquisitoire contre le théâtre dans la France classique* (Paris).

THOMAS, N. (1994). 'Licensed Curiosity: Cook's Pacific Voyages', in J. Elsner and R. Cardinal (eds.), *The Cultures of Collecting* (London), 116–36.

TOEWS, J. (1987). 'Intellectual History after the Linguistic Turn: The Autonomy of Meaning and the Irreducibility of Experience', *American Historical Review*, 92: 879–907.

Trésor de la langue française (1971–94). (16 vols.; Paris).

TREVISANI, F. (1992). *Descartes in Germania: La ricezione del cartesianesimo nella facoltà filosofica e medica di Duisberg (1652–1703)* (Milan).

TROOZ, C. de (1947). 'Le Père Garasse et *La Doctrine curieuse*', *Lettres romanes*, 1: 113–34.

TULLY, J. (1988a). 'The Pen is a Mighty Sword: Quentin Skinner's Analysis of Politics', in *Meaning and Context: Quentin Skinner and his Critics*, ed. J. Tully (Cambridge), 7–25.

——(ed.) (1988b). *Meaning and Context: Quentin Skinner and his Critics* (Cambridge).

TWOREK, Paul (1938). *Leben und Werke des Johann Christoph Männling* (Breslau).

VALENTIN, J.-M. (1978). *Le Théâtre des Jésuites dans les pays de langue allemande* (3 vols.; Berne, Frankfurt a. Main, Las Vegas).

VAN DER CRUYSSE, D. (1986). 'L'Exotisme pluriel de Raynal: le discours exotique dans l'*Histoire des deux Indes*', *French Literature Series*, 13: 13–27.

VASOLI, C. (1978). *L'enciclopedismo del seicento* (1978).

VERBEECK-VERHELST, M. (1988). 'Magie et curiosité au XVIIe siècle', *Revue d'histoire ecclésiastique*, 83: 349–68.

VEYNE, P. (1979). *Comment on écrit l'histoire: suivi de Foucault révolutionne l'histoire* (Paris).

VIARDOT, J. (1984). 'Livres rares et pratiques bibliophiliques', in H.-J. Martin and R. Chartier (eds.), *Histoire de l'édition française*, i: *Le Livre triomphant, 1660–1830* (Paris), 447–67.

——(1988). 'Naissance de la bibliophilie: les cabinets de livres rares', in C. Jolly (ed.), *Histoire des bibliothèques françaises*, ii: *Les Bibliothèques sous l'Ancien Régime, 1530–1789* (Paris), 269–89.

VIERHAUS, R. (1988). *Germany in the Age of Absolutism*, tr. J. B. Knudsen (Cambridge).

VITTU J.-P. (1994). ' "Le Peuple est fort curieux de nouvelles": l'information périodique dans la France des années 1690', *Studies on Voltaire and the Eighteenth Century*, 320: 105–44.

VOSS, J. (1980). 'Die Akademie als Organisationsträger der Wissenschaften im 18. Jahrhundert', *Historische Zeitschrift*, 231: 43–74.

WAGENER, H. (1968). 'Eberhard Werner Happel: Vernunft und Aberglaube im Spätbarock', *Hessische Blätter für Volkskunde*, 59: 45–55.

WAGMAN, F. (1942). *Magic and Natural Science in German Baroque Literature* (New York).

WALKER, D. P. (1958). *Spiritual and Demonic Magic from Ficino to Campanella* (London).

WALLMANN, J. (1985). *Kirchengeschichte Deutschlands seit der Reformation* (2nd edn.; Tübingen).

——(1992). 'Erfurt und der Pietismus im 17. Jahrhundert', in U. Weiss (ed.), *Erfurt 742–1992: Stadtgeschichte, Universitätsgeschichte* (Weimar), 403–22.

WAQUET, F. (ed.) (2000). *Mapping the World of Learning: The 'Polyhistor' of Daniel Georg Morhof* (Wiesbaden).

WEIGER, J. G. (1983). 'Cervantes's Curious Curate', *Kentucky Romance Quarterly*, 30: 87–106.

WEITZ, M. (1977). *The Opening Mind: A Philosophical Study of Humanistic Concepts* (Chicago and London).

——(1988). *Theories of Concepts: A History of the Major Philosophical Tradition* (London and New York).

WHALEY, J. (1985). *Religious Toleration and Social Change in Hamburg 1529–1819* (Cambridge).

WHITAKER, K. (1996). 'The Culture of Curiosity', in N. Jardine, J. A. Secord, and E. C. Spary (eds.), *Cultures of Natural History* (Cambridge), 75–90.

WHITE, H. (1991). 'The Metaphysics of Narrativity: Time and Symbol in Ricoeur's Philosophy of History', in D. Wood (ed.), *On Paul Ricoeur: Narrative and Interpretation* (London and New York), 140–59.

WILLIAMS, G. (1962). *The Radical Reformation* (London).

WILLIAMS, W. (1998). *Pilgrimage and Narrative in the French Renaissance: 'The Undiscovered Country'* (Oxford).

WINAU, R. (1968). 'Christian Mentzels wissenschaftliche Interessen im Spiegel seiner Beiträge in den *Miscellanea curiosa*', in G. Keil et al. (eds.), *Fachliteratur des Mittelalters: Festschrift für Gerhard Eis* (Stuttgart), 101–11.

——(1977). 'Zur Frühgeschichte der Academia Naturae Curiosorum', in F. Hartmann and R. Vierhaus (eds.), *Der Akademiegedanke im 17. und 18. Jahrhundert* (Bremen and Wolfenbüttel), 117–37.

WITTGENSTEIN, L. (1968). *Philosophical Investigations*, tr. G. E. M. Anscombe (Oxford). (*Philosophische Untersuchungen*, 1953.)

ZACHER, C. (1976). *Curiosity and Pilgrimage: The Literature of Discovery in Fourteenth-Century England* (Baltimore and London).

ZARKA, Y.-C. (1998). 'La Curiosité chez Hobbes', in *Curiosité et 'libido sciendi'*, i. 157–66.

ZEDELMAIER, H. (1992). *Bibliotheca universalis und bibliotheca selecta: Das Problem der Ordnung des gelehrten Wissens in der frühen Neuzeit* (Cologne, Weimar, Vienna).

ZEEDEN, E. W. (1965). *Die Entstehung der Konfessionen: Grundlagen und Formen der Konfessionsbildung im Zeitalter der Glaubenskämpfe* (Munich and Vienna).

Index

Note: page references in *italics* indicate illustrations, tables, and figures.